D0887546

VENDEL

VALSGARDE

UPPSALA

BORRE

SKÅNE

BORNHOLM

BALTIC SEA

RIBE

GUDME
LUNDEBORG

HAITHABU

Elbe

Weser

Rhine

THURINGIA

COLOGNE

METZ

0   100   200   300 miles

0   100   200   300   400 kms

The Age of Sutton Hoo

THE SEVENTH CENTURY IN NORTH-WESTERN EUROPE

Excavations at Sutton Hoo, 1987. The Mound 2 burial chamber and the trenches of earlier excavations (of 1860 and 1938) being disentangled by archaeologists of the Sutton Hoo Research Trust, including its director, Martin Carver (centre). Photo: N. Macbeth.

The Age of Sutton Hoo

THE SEVENTH CENTURY IN NORTH-WESTERN EUROPE

EDITED BY

M. O. H. CARVER

THE BOYDELL PRESS

First published 1992 by The Boydell Press, Woodbridge
Reprinted in hardback and paperback 1994

The Boydell Press is an imprint of Boydell & Brewer Ltd
PO Box 9, Woodbridge, Suffolk IP12 3DF, UK
and of Boydell & Brewer Inc.
PO Box 41026, Rochester, NY 14604-4126, USA

ISBN 0 85115 330 5 hardback
ISBN 0 85115 361 5 paperback

British Library Cataloguing-in-Publication Data
Age of Sutton Hoo: Seventh Century in
North-western Europe
I. Carver, Martin
940.1
ISBN 0–85115–330–5
ISBN 0–85115–361–5 pbk

Library of Congress Cataloging-in-Publication Data
The Age of Sutton Hoo : the seventh century in north-western Europe /
edited by M.O.H. Carver.
    p.   cm.
Includes bibliographical references and index.
ISBN 0–85115–330–5
1. Sutton Hoo Ship Burial (England) 2. Anglo-Saxons – Kings and
rulers – Death and burial. 3. Excavations (Archaeology) – Europe,
Northern. 4. Excavations (Archaeology) – England – Suffolk.
5. Suffolk (England) – Antiquities. 6. England – Civilization – To
1066. 7. Anglo-Saxons – England – Suffolk. 8. Ship burial – Europe,
Northern. 9. Europe, Northern – Antiquities. 10. Ship burial –
England – Suffolk. 11. Civilization, Anglo-Saxon. 12. Seventh
century. I. Carver, M. O. H.
DA155.A5   1992
942.6′4–dc20   92–32558

This publication is printed on acid-free paper

Printed in Great Britain by
St Edmundsbury Press Ltd, Bury St Edmunds, Suffolk

CONTENTS

PREFACE

The archaeological site at Sutton Hoo, famous for its treasure, its buried ships and its early English warrior-kings, occupies a special place in the public affection – a place at once brave and murky. As our book goes to press, British prime-time television is showing Andrew Davies' highly entertaining adaptation of *Anglo-Saxon Attitudes*, Angus Wilson's splendid piece of scholastic myth-making (and a beautiful novel), which features mysterious discoveries in a royal tomb at 'Melpham' – discoveries which mingle Christian and pagan, secular and sacred, and of course phallic, imagery and provide the point of departure for that human and academic scheming and dreaming which is exposed in the *attitudes* of Wilson's title. How well those of us involved in Dark Age burials, particularly rich ones, know this twilight world so beloved of the public, so full of sensuous allusions and so meagre in its supply of hard evidence. In practice of course, it is the very darkness of the Dark Ages which draws public and academic alike; but the hard evidence, while meagre, is glittering and richly varied: – myths, king-lists, place-names, sagas, settlements, runic inscriptions, palaces, belt-buckles, post-holes, middens and graves are all grist to our mill. Varied expertise and varied approaches greet each other in the gloom. The quarry of our researches, moreover, is not in the least marginal; it consists of real people in real communities at the very moment they were forming 'kingdoms', a moment in which political decisions were taken, the consequences of which are still being worked out in the Europe of 1992. We are therefore engaged in an important hunt, relevant to the world we live in, and in good company.

When the Sutton Hoo Research Project began in 1983, it followed more than forty years of research by the British Museum under Dr R.L.S. Bruce-Mitford. That research was principally on the ship-burial discovered in 1939 – but not exclusively. The site of the cemetery, its surroundings and its historical context were also explored, and Bruce-Mitford's conclusions were published in his great three-volume descriptive synthesis *The Sutton Hoo Ship Burial* (1975, 1978, 1983). A great many of Dr Bruce-Mitford's ideas and speculations, which he wished to see tested, were indeed tested by the new campaign; and in most cases they were vindicated or endorsed by its findings. This needs saying right at the beginning of this book, to profit from an opportunity to salute a very great student of Anglo-Saxon culture. However, testing the questions raised by the 1938–39 excavations was not the only, or even the principal purpose of the current project. This needs saying too, to warn the reader that with the new campaign, the agenda, inevitably, changed. The new targets did not consist of digging up more things, or more kings, or even of digging up Sutton Hoo, or even, more discursively, of finding a context for the cemetery. The purpose of the new campaign was to explore the formation of early historic kingdoms, using the kingdom of East Anglia as an example, and East Anglia's strangest cemetery as a beacon for the times. The main item on the agenda was therefore to throw light on the way people behaved, and thought, at that cardinal moment in the formation of European consciousness, the seventh century.

Whether any of these targets has been dealt even a glancing blow through work on the site itself must be judged by others (see *Postscript*, Ch. 24). But it was clear from the start of the project that such an ambitious objective would need to address not only the corrosive soil of the sandlings, but the culture of the whole region in which Sutton Hoo lay. Furthermore, it could be seen that East Anglia was only one of many North Sea regions, that had experienced some major transformation in the mid-first millennium A.D. Professional co-operation would therefore be of the greatest importance: in the first place with the highly respected field Units of East Anglia, and in the second with those scholars already engaged, often with great prominence, in the problem of the origins of the North Sea kingdoms. The fruits of this collaboration have been rich, and the Sutton Hoo project itself has surely gained the most. To ensure that the results of the campaign would be expeditiously available to all, the *Bulletin of the Sutton Hoo Research Committee* was published (more or less) annually. And to ensure that the project could benefit from the reactions of the community of experts, a series of *Sutton Hoo seminars* was held at intervals: first at Cambridge, where the subject was 'Princely Burials', second at Ipswich, where we studied the evolution of Anglo-Saxon society in East Anglia; then to Oxford where the relevance of Sutton Hoo's topography and prehistoric site were explored. And finally to York in 1989, 50 years on, to examine the forma-tion of early kingdoms in north-west Europe. This last conference, the only one of the series to be published, is the subject of this book.

The theme of the book, as of the seminar, is the formation of early states, known to us in this period in this region (without, however, knowing exactly what the word means) as 'kingdoms'; our quarry is that community which had, or believed it had, or believed it ought to have had, a territorial identity recognised by others. The premise is that, before about A.D.400 in north west Europe such kingdoms were unknown, or unacknowledged; but that after about A.D.700, they were ubiquitous and constituted the basic building blocks of modern countries. Something had therefore happened which was of the greatest interest for European history, during that era, the 'age of Sutton Hoo', for which this book provides new materials and new ideas.

The organisation of the book reflects the centrality of this theme, leading the reader from the Sutton Hoo site to ever wider theatres of action in East Anglia, England and north-west Europe. In each section, contributions come from archaeologists, historians, and philologists. Part 1 is concerned with the East Anglian kingdom itself, beginning with a thoroughly documented discussion of the state formation process, while the papers which follow each sketch some

facet of the emerging character of the kingdom, as seen in the changing settlement pattern, in the cemeteries, in place-names, in Old English literature, and
in history. Part 2 relates to England, and includes a re-assessment of the remarkable pyre-barrow at Asthall, seen as giving out foreign signals in Wessex
and provoking thoughts pursued in other papers in this section: on the changing burial practices of seventh century England, and their significance for the
changing ideology of a society whose mood and motivation can also, perhaps
can only, be examined through symbol and language. Part 3 takes us on a tour
of the early kingdoms: the Celtic west, Pictland, France, Denmark and
Norway, a group of papers as valuable for their presentation of the evidence as
for their generation of ideas. If Sweden is not represented, the reader can still
find solace in the excellent *Vendel Studies* (1983), of which *The Age of Sutton Hoo*
is to some degree an imitation. And similar disappointment at our apparent
lack of attention to Ireland, may be partly assuaged by the recent appearance
of Harold Mytum's study of the changing social formations in that island in
the early Christian period (Mytum 1992).

This book therefore explores the sources which exist, or may yet exist, for the
seventh century in north-west Europe, and what they may be made to mean.
But the reader will not expect to hear orthodox questions posed, or answered,
in unison. The theoretical perspectives of our contributors vary a great deal;
there is a difference of approach between historians, linguists and archaeologists, and between scholars separated by the seas as well as by discipline. If we
can agree that sacred sites existed on fifth century Funen, chiefdoms in sixth
century Norway, and ship-graves in seventh century Sweden, we are much
less united in why such things occured: why then, why there? For some, we
are just observing the track of a small mobile group of heroic if slightly psycho-
pathic aristocrats, responsible in their day for forming taste and making history. For others, we are seeing the tangible results of internal social change,
stimulated by a predatory probing between imperial centre and barbarian
periphery, between the Franks and the rest. For others again, the mere existence of one's neighbours is a sufficient provocation for change (all the more so
if they are claiming to be equal to oneself!). The interaction of such 'peer
polities', whether through competition, defiance or admiration, can be seen as
the motor which changes both parties. But here we find yet more differences in
perception, between those for whom the peer polities are small territorial
parcels, landlocked and contiguous, and those for whom the relevant protagonists are already proto-states, confronted across the thoroughfares of the
North Sea, the Channel or the Irish Sea. A message of this book is its persua-
sion that the Dark Ages, the early medieval period, cannot be treated as an
isolated 'Anglo-Saxon', 'late Celtic', 'Germanic' or 'Frankish' study: the action
is on a European stage, and its true theatre of operations is the sea.

Another message emanates particularly from the archaeologists, who have
increased the quantity of their data in the last century, and will do so still more
in the next. But as the amount of evidence increases, so, paradoxically, our

confidence in our interpretations declines. Even while reading about the new discoveries at Borre, Gudme, Snape or Sutton Hoo, we can experience here those doubts about meaning which come from knowing so much more. If we think we can observe a change in the relative wealth of burials at a given moment in a given place, are we obliged to interpret that as a change in the distribution of wealth and power among the living? Supposing instead that historical circumstances obliged a people to celebrate a hierarchy they already had, in a new way, or in an old way with a new insistence. On this construction, a ship-burial might be a sign of weakness, while a land with no rich burials (such as seventh century Denmark) can be read as an area of self-confident affluence. Perhaps especially with burials, then, we are not dealing so much with the documents of social advance as with the signals of the damned, signals which pre-echo or yearn for change, rather than record it. For some, social change must have its basis in reality, and ideology is merely a psychological weapon wielded by the human agents of power. For others – unreformed processualists – ideology is merely another of society's sub-systems, able on occasion to act on its own. However it is also possible that social change, while internally primed, occured not in response to reality, but to desires and fears whose connection with reality is, and possibly was, undemonstrable; and possible too that while the apprehension was cast in bronze, the reality never arrived. The material culture of the graves is thus used, as a common language, to signal political affiliation and allegiance rather than events. In this wordless debate, which was perhaps without an outcome, the men of Kent could brandish Frankish culture, the early Irish and the Northumbrians could use what could then be gathered from Greece and Rome, mixing it with a resurrected Celtic heritage, and the East Angles could re-enact and replicate what they imagined to be the culture of pagan Scandinavia, and the regalia of Byzantium, without necessarily having seen either.

This then is the language of the seventh century – difficult enough even when the language is in words. When it is in the language of things, the trajectory from encounter to understanding will be a long one, and digging is only the beginning. The field work of the Sutton Hoo research campaign was concluded this year, and the results will, in the next five years, be presented for publication by the Society of Antiquaries of London and the British Museum. The present volume is intended to be the many-sided companion to that forthcoming report. On site and in the lecture-theatre over the last nine years, our project has made many friends in many countries. On behalf of the Sutton Hoo Research Trust I would like to thank them for their help, their thoughts and their interest – none more so than the colleagues who have written here: they have done Sutton Hoo and British archaeology a great honour, by sharing their discoveries and ideas with us.

Martin Carver
Department of Archaeology, University of York
1 June 1992

PLATES

FIGURES

PART I

East Anglia in
the Age of Sutton Hoo

1

Before Sutton Hoo:
Structures of Power and Society
in Early East Anglia

CHRISTOPHER SCULL

This paper considers some aspects of the fifth- and sixth-century background to the historically-attested East Anglian kingdom. It is not intended as a detailed discussion of the regional archaeology. Rather it aims to address some broader questions and issues arising from, and affecting, archaeological approaches to the study of social and political development in migration-period England and, from this, to define some of the processes and trajectories of development which may have contributed to the emergence and consolidation of the seventh-century kingdom.

The *provincia Orientalium Anglorum* is poorly documented in comparison with other major Anglo-Saxon kingdoms. The principal source for the East Anglian dynasty and church before the eighth century is Bede's *Historia Ecclesiastica*. However Bede's account of the East Angles, subordinate as it is to the wider demands of his history, is by no means comprehensive, and although it can be supplemented from other sources, these are scanty. The lack of records from the pre-Viking period in East Anglia, attributed to the disruption and destruction of the ninth century (Davis 1955; Hart 1966, 10–11; Yorke 1990, 58) is compounded by the frequently selective nature of other sources which include material relating to the East Anglian kingdom. There is no body of early history nor of origin-myth equivalent to those surviving for Kent, for instance (Brooks 1989; Yorke 1990), and in the Anglo-Saxon Chronicle the East Angles merit just seven brief mentions in contexts of A.D. 655 or earlier against thirty for the West Saxons or their leaders. The *Tribal Hidage*, almost certainly a seventh-century compilation (Davies and Vierck 1974; Dumville 1989a, 132–33), is the earliest surviving record of the East Angles as a contemporary political unit. A royal genealogy is known from British Library manuscript Cotton Vespasian Bvi and Chapter 59 of the *Historia Britonnum* (Stenton 1959; Dumville 1976), and a Life of Foillan, brother of St Fursa, written at Nivelles before A.D. 656, has some details of seventh-century East Anglian dynastic

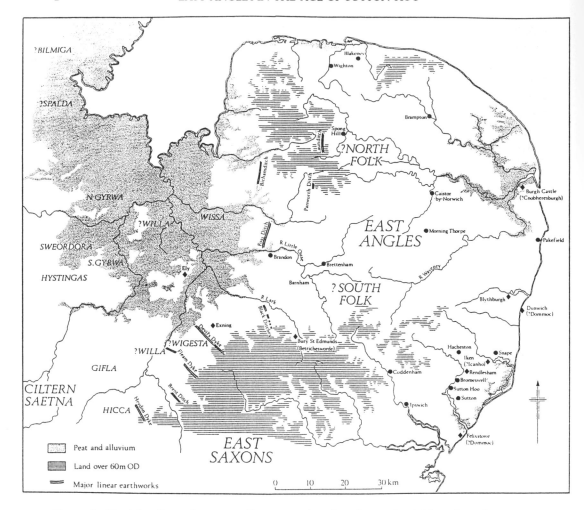

Figure 1. East Anglia and surrounding areas showing the territorial location of groups recorded in Tribal Hidage and other early sources. Diamonds indicate East Anglian places mentioned in major sources in contexts of the seventh and eigth centuries. Dots indicate other sites mentioned in the text. The early Medieval coastline and drainage of the fenland is shown

history (Whitelock 1972). The picture can be fleshed-out further from post-conquest documents, notably *Liber Eliensis*, Florence of Worcester's Chronicle, and the *Historia Anglorum* of Henry of Huntingdon and *Flores Historiarum* of Roger of Wendover and Matthew Paris, but much of what can be culled from these is contradictory and of doubtful historical validity (Stenton 1959; Blake 1962; Davies 1977; Yorke 1990, 58).

The documentary sources are almost silent about the period before Redwald's kingship. Bede records the continental origin of *Orientales Angli*, among others, in his account of the English invasion of Britain (H.E. i, 15) which he sets, on the authority of Gildas' *De Excidio* (Miller 1975), in the middle of the fifth century. The only other known reference to the East Angles in a context before A.D. 570 is in annals for A.D. 527 in the *Historia Anglorum* and *Flores Historiarum* which record a migration, from Germany, of pagans who occupied East Anglia and invaded Mercia. Professor Davies (1977) has argued that these derive from a Victorian Easter Table, that A.D. 515, not A.D. 527, was the date intended, and that the suggestion of a migration leading to settlement in East Anglia and Mercia, or the settlement of Mercia from East Anglia, in the early sixth century is, though retrospective, of seventh-century origin. Annals for A.D. 571 in *Flores Historiarum* and *Historia Anglorum* may also come from this same Easter Table, and so too have seventh-century origins: these read 'Wuffa in East Anglia' and 'Beginning of East Anglia with Wuffa'. Wuffa appears in the genealogy as the son of Wehha and the father of Tytil, and so as the grandfather of Redwald. Bede (H.E. ii, 15) records that the East Anglian kings took their family name, the Wuffings, from him, suggesting that he was regarded as the founder of the royal lineage. There is, however, a gloss against Wehha's name in the *Historia Britonnum* genealogy stating that he, rather than Wuffa, was first to rule over the East Angles in Britain. There does not seem to be any conclusive reason to reject the A.D. 571 annal in favour of the *Historia Britonnum* gloss, or vice-versa, or even to take either at face value. In the absence of any other evidence it seems reasonable to accept that Wuffa was a genuine historical figure and that the Wuffings were established as a dominant or paramount lineage by or during his lifetime. That he began to rule *c.* A.D. 570 cannot be corroborated, but is consistent with what little else is known of the East Anglian succession, and with the wider pattern of evidence which suggests that the major Anglo-Saxon kingdoms had been established by the later sixth century (Davies and Vierck 1974; Yorke 1990, 13). It would be unsafe, however, to draw any firmer or more detailed inferences about the origins of the East Anglian *provincia* from this material. The Wuffings need not have been the first or the only lineage to exercise or to claim some regional authority. It must be remembered too that the late sixth-century threshold which in the documentary sources appears to mark the emergence of kingdoms and ruling dynasties may be as much a reflection of the limits of memory in societies dependent upon oral tradition as of historical reality (Davies and Vierck 1974; Davies 1977).

The approximate territorial extent of the seventh-century kingdom can be estimated from a variety of sources (Fig. 1). It was bordered to the south by the East Saxon kingdom, and to the west by the Middle Angles. The traditional equation of Dioceses and Shires of the tenth century or later with earlier political units would suggest that the East Anglian *provincia* was fossilized in the medieval Diocese of Norwich (Stenton 1971, 53; Hart 1971, 136; 1977, 47–9). To the west it has been stated as axiomatic that the eastern fen edge or fen margins marked the western edge of the East Anglian kingdom (Darby 1934), but Bede's unequivocal statement that Ely was a *regio* of 600 hides within the

East Anglian *provincia* (H.E. iv, 19) would argue otherwise. Davies' location of the territorial interests of the Middle Anglian groups assessed in Tribal Hidage places these smaller independent entities in the western and southern fenland (Davies and Vierck 1974), and it could be argued that East Anglian overlordship of Ely and, possibly, other groups in the eastern and central fens must have been well-established by the time of Sigeberht in order to survive the dynastic reverses which culminated in the deaths of Anna and Aethelhere. The linear earthworks of Cambridgeshire have been claimed as East Anglian border works (Fox 1923, 292–4; Thackray 1980, 406) but none can be closely dated and most are too far west to be interpreted convincingly as boundaries to the seventh-century or later kingdom. The Devil's Dyke, which formed part of the boundary of the medieval Diocese of Norwich, is perhaps the most convincing candidate, but on current evidence its construction can be dated no more precisely than to some time between the later fourth century and the earlier tenth century (Hope-Taylor 1976; Thackray 1980, 232–5); it could thus be attributed equally well to the sub-Roman or Viking period as to the middle Saxon kingdom. The linear earthworks of west Norfolk and Suffolk are well within the suggested territory of the seventh-century kingdom, and may therefore reflect earlier political configurations (cf. Wade-Martins 1974). When considering the extent of the kingdom, however, it must be stressed that we need not necessarily expect rigid or precise territorial boundaries at a time when political authority appears to have been primarily invested in people rather than territory (Davies and Vierck, 1974, 228–9); nor, given the dynastic vicissitudes of the East Anglian rulers during the first half of the seventh century, need we expect the area they controlled to have remained constant.

The fact of Wuffing kingship, and the likelihood that their authority was established in the later sixth century, appears to find archaeological support in the princely burials at Snape and Sutton Hoo, but this beguiling relationship between archaeology and a sketchy historical record can disguise our ignorance both of contemporary structures of authority and power, and society and economy, and of the conditions from which they developed.

Further detailed information about the seventh-century kingdom is at a premium, and what there is is not always unambiguous. Bede's mention of a *vicus regius* at Rendlesham in a context of the 650s or 660s (H.E. iii, 22) may imply that at this time the countryside was organized into estates and administered through royal vills. His statement that Sigeberht's kinsman Ecgric had had some ruling power or authority prior to his sole rule (H.E. iii, 18) has been interpreted as evidence for joint or shared kingship among the East Angles (Fisher 1988, 130; Yorke 1990, 69), but can be interpreted equally plausibly as evidence for administrative subdivisions, or for smaller constituent groupings under East Anglian hegemony, perhaps ruled by *principes* or *subreguli*. The *regio* of Ely may have been one such, and the division between Norfolk and Suffolk, although not recorded until the eleventh century, may also reflect such arrangements (Hart 1971, 153–4; Yorke 1990, 69). This interpretation would also be supported by the suggestion that the Wissa, a people mentioned in the eighth-century Life of Guthlac and usually located in the central fenland or its eastern margins, are omitted from Tribal Hidage because they had lost political autonomy, if not social identity, to the East Anglian kings by the second half of the seventh century (Davies and Vierck 1974, 240). The possibility arises, then, that the seventh-century kingdom of the Wuffings was a hegemony over a number of regional groups, some of which may have been subsumed in a common identity or integrated into a single polity for some time, others of which, like the Wissa, may have retained some independent identity (cf. Sawyer 1978, 47–9).

There is no evidence to suggest that the East Anglian *provincia*, as it can be defined in the seventh century, was a long-standing entity which had been established in the immediate aftermath of the fifth-century migrations, and so it is best explained as the outcome of longer-term developments in the fifth and sixth centuries. Identifiable constituents or subdivisions of the seventh-century kingdom might be explained as relics of earlier autonomous groupings, hinting at a process of conflict or competition between regional elites which eventually culminated in the establishment of a wider supremacy: the process of competitive exclusion proposed by Bassett to explain the development of middle Saxon kingdoms (Bassett 1989, cf. Carneiro 1978). The available documentary evidence can be interpreted to suggest that such political consolidation coincided with the establishment of a Wuffing supremacy in the later sixth century, but, however this may have been attained, dynastic kingship as reflected in the sources for the seventh century could not have developed or been imposed, and sustained, without a pre-existing capacity for political integration in the social and economic configurations of the fifth and sixth centuries. To this extent the origins of the East Anglian *provincia* can be explored independently of its dynastic history.

Any detailed understanding of this prehistory of the kingdom will depend on the archaeological record and on generalizing approaches to the emergence of social and political complexity derived from the social sciences, which have been applied and developed in the study of prehistory (cf. Haselgrove 1979; Hodges 1982a; Austin 1990). Nonetheless, the historical framework, however limited, defines basic points of reference and avenues of enquiry, and may provide a context which forces revision or refining of general archaeological models before they can be applied satisfactorily. In particular, the detailed application to this period of some archaeological models, such as the Early State Module (Renfrew 1974; 1975), which rather simply assume a fairly precise coincidence of group identity, territorial interest and central political control can be questioned.

Despite some recent scepticism (Hodges 1989b, 28–30) the fact of settlement in East Anglia, as in the rest of south-east Britain, by people from north Germany and south Scandinavia in the fifth century is established beyond reasonable doubt. In the archaeological record this is particularly evident in mortuary practice and material culture. Material culture similarities, especially in ceramics and female dress accessories, satisfactorily establish the continental affinities and antecedents of the new groups (Böhme 1974; 1986; Evison 1981; Hines 1984; 1990; Myres 1969; 1972), although we should be cautious about assigning them over-precise ethnic identities on this basis (Hills 1979, 313–18; Richards 1987, 203–4). The date, duration and processes of settlement are less certain, however, and different theories embody different assumptions about the circumstances of migration and settlement, the sophistication and political cohesion of the incomers, and their relationships with the indigenous population, any of which has implications for how subsequent social and political developments might be explained. However, the traditional model of an *adventus Saxonum*, implying a short period of migration and settlement – if not a single event – in the mid fifth century, must now be abandoned in favour of a scenario which allows settlement over a longer period, varying in intensity and velocity with time and place. There is strong archaeological evidence for some otherwise unrecorded migration from west Scandinavia to eastern England in the second half of the fifth century (Hines 1984), and it is clear that an extensive network of relationships across the North Sea was established and maintained by the Anglo-Saxon settlers of Britain (Hawkes and Pollard 1981; Vierck 1970; Welch 1991). It may not be too fanciful to argue that every region or locality would have seen its own *adventus Saxonum*: either the first arrival, or a watershed that in later perception came to stand for a longer or more gradual process of settlement or colonization.

The early dating of cremation pottery proposed by Myres is not supported by the associated metalwork (Hawkes 1982, 65) and the earliest Anglo-Saxon material from East Anglia would, on current dating, be consistent with settlement from the second quarter or middle of the fifth century (cf. Böhme 1986; Hines 1990, 21–5). Myres' specific model of controlled settlements of *foederati* or *laeti* (Myres 1956; 1969, 67–83) during the late Roman period cannot therefore be sustained, but the hypothesis that Germanic mercenaries, or contingents of troops not drafted to the continent by Constantine III, may have formed the nuclei of later free settlement remains influential, if difficult to demonstrate convincingly from the archaeological record (Hawkes and Dunning 1961; Böhme 1986). Distinctions have been drawn between federate settlement and revolt in Britain south of the Thames, according to the framework derived from Gildas' *De Excidio*, and a different process of free settlement elsewhere (Böhme 1986). An explicit contrast has also been suggested between takeover by aristocratic warleaders in the south, and more gradual settlement by humbler groups of refugees from environmental deterioration on the continental North Sea coast in, for instance, East Anglia (Hawkes 1982). Each of these views has important implications. The 'military settlement' model, whether in a late Roman or sub-Roman context, anticipates the problems of explaining later English dominance by introducing a fifth column of well-organized barbarian groups, who may have had some trappings of official authority, and who would be well placed to establish themselves at the expense of indigenous authority and population. As with conventional invasion hypotheses, this gives priority to 'top-down' or 'elite-dominance' processes, one corollary of which is that some degree of continuity in administrative structures, or the existence of well-established Anglo-Saxon polities from some time in the fifth century, or both, might be expected. Refugee settlement, on the other hand, would fall into Renfrew's category of population replacement models (Renfrew 1987, 120–44), and might imply more gradual processes of conflict and consolidation before the emergence or establishment of any widespread political authority.

In reality, it is unlikely that either of these over-simple alternatives would have operated exclusively. At a time of political and demographic instability almost unlimited opportunities might be open to anyone with a claim to authority and the means to impose it. Conversely, the opportunities afforded by such a figure, and the protection offered by a warleader and warband, might be powerfully attractive to the ambitious and vulnerable alike. It is important to stress, too, that folk movement rather than professional military adventure need not imply, as sometimes seems to have been assumed (cf. Arnold 1988, 163–88), that the earliest Germanic settlements in Britain were simple egalitarian peasant communities requiring a couple of generations of social evolution before they developed sufficient complexity and cohesion to form even the most rudimentary political structures. The Germanic settlers of eastern Britain were from continental societies with complex hierarchical structures which in some cases demonstrably had the capacity to impose and maintain some authority, however impermanent, over considerable areas (Hedeager 1980; 1987; Ilkjaer and Lønstrup 1982; Myhre 1987b). Some Roman Iron Age and migration-period settlements on the North Sea littoral show evidence for ranking and a diversity of social and economic roles within individual communities (Schmid 1974; Zimmerman 1974; 1978), and the migration-period weapon deposits of south Scandinavia appear to confirm military leadership and social ranking on a regional scale (Hines 1989; Ilkjaer and Lønstrup 1982). These structures are unlikely to have been forgotten especially if, as seems most plausible, migration was more often a group than an individual undertaking. It is possible, in fact, that strengthened adherence to distinctive practices and institutions, reinforcing group or cultural identity, may have been one response to the stresses and uncertainties of migration. The archaeological evidence for fifth-century Germanic groups settled north of the Thames suggests rural agrarian communities practising unostentatious cremation burial, but this cannot necessarily be equated with an egalitarian peasant society, nor should an initial political subordination to indigenous authority or groups (if such an inference is justified) be confused with an absence of internal structures of authority. The extensive polities identified in south Scandinavia, for instance, at this time, appear to be the result of fairly long-term economic and social dynamics (Hedeager 1978b; Myhre 1987b; Parker-Pearson

1984); one would not, therefore, expect to find evidence for hegemony or political integration on this scale in the fifth-century archaeology of eastern England. Nonetheless, it would be legitimate to expect in the earliest Germanic communities in England the basic social units and institutions on which the more complex polities of the continent were built, and so to expect the potential for comparable social and political developments.

Other important questions concern the structures of indigenous societies; the relationship between incomers and indigenous population; and the fate of indigenous elites. Archaeology cannot answer such questions directly, but some general conclusions can be drawn from the comparison of Romano-British and early Anglo-Saxon archaeology at both regional and local levels. Any such exercise is bedeviled by familiar problems of differential survival and retrieval of material, differential recognition of site-types, and chronological imprecision. Nonetheless, if fifth- to seventh-century settlement or activity was in any way significantly affected or constrained by patterns similar to those of the Roman period it should be detectable.

With the exception of the Fenland, where the dramatic decrease in settlement density can be attributed to environmental deterioration (Phillips 1970), the regional distribution of early Anglo-Saxon sites and finds is very similar to that of the Romano-British period (Figs 2–3; cf. Newman, this vol.). The settlement pattern is riverine, with the densest concentrations of sites and finds on the lighter soils of the east Norfolk and south-east Suffolk, and west Norfolk and north-west Suffolk. There are fewer sites of the fifth to seventh centuries, but without being able to calibrate better for differential survival and retrieval, and given the possibility that we can identify in distinctive Anglo-Saxon material culture only one element of the population, it would be rash to conclude too cataclysmic a decline in levels of population from the archaeological evidence. A comparison of the Romano-British and early Anglo-Saxon cemetery evidence alone, for instance, would suggest a dramatic increase rather than a decline in population in the immediate post-Roman period. The scarcity of early Anglo-Saxon sites and finds on the Suffolk claylands is marked, but the view that this reflects a large-scale post-Roman abandonment may have to be modified in view of Williamson's work in north-west Essex, his identification of possible early Medieval co-axial field systems on the claylands of south Norfolk and north Suffolk, and the long-standing recognition of this as an area of 'ancient landscape' (Williamson 1984; 1987; Dymond 1968). However, against this conclusion stand the dangers of arguing from negative evidence, and the failure of Warner's work in Blything Hundred to identity early or middle Saxon material on the claylands (Warner 1987).

The archaeological evidence for the first recognizably Germanic elements in the population, or the earliest established Germanic communities, although sparse, reflects the regional pattern of Romano-British settlement. There is no suggestion from the distribution of early sites and finds that there are demarcated 'core areas' of settlement, as has been suggested for Sussex (Welch 1971;

TF TG

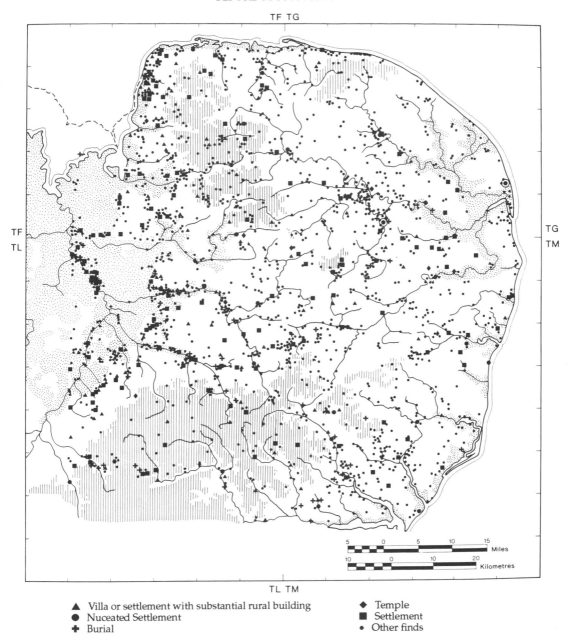

TF
TL

TG
TM

TL TM

▲ Villa or settlement with substantial rural building   ◆ Temple
● Nuceated Settlement   ■ Settlement
✚ Burial   • Other finds

Figure 2. Distribution map of Romano-British sites and finds in East Anglia

1983), which one might expect to develop as the centres of early polities and from which an expansion of settlement might be postulated. Moreover, there is a faint but persistent pattern of early Anglo-Saxon occupation on, or activity immediately adjacent to, the sites of Romano-British towns or nucleated settlements: this has been recognised at Coddenham, Hacheston, Brettenham, Brampton, Wighton and the cantonal capital of the Iceni, *Venta Icenorum*, at Caistor-by-Norwich. Of these, there is some evidence that Caistor-by-Norwich, or the communities in or around it, retained a central importance from the fifth century until at least the seventh century (cf. Atkin 1985, 30). Surface finds, which include an early fifth-century cruciform brooch, high-quality sixth-century metalwork, *sceattas*, and the coptic bowl discovered in the nineteenth century, suggest at least one more cemetery adjacent to the town in addition to that known from excavation (Myres and Green 1973). As yet, however, there are no indications of continued importance or activity into the seventh century, or in some cases into the sixth, at any of the other town sites. The poor sample and chronological imprecision of material from rural sites obscures the picture, but it is possible to make some observations. There is very little direct evidence that many villas or other higher-status Romano-British sites retained their importance through the fifth century. A quantity of early Anglo-Saxon pottery is known from the villa at Stanton Chare, but there is no evidence here for continuous occupation or activity (Russel 1983, 289–95). Where archaeological evidence for lower-status Romano-British rural settlements and early Anglo-Saxon activity does coincide exactly, there is rarely evidence for precise site-type continuity. At Spong Hill, for instance, the cemetery was established on the site of a Romano-British farmstead and enclosures, with a new settlement adjacent. In south-east Suffolk fieldwalking has defined concentrations of early Anglo-Saxon material adjacent to late Romano-British sites (Newman 1988; this vol.). This might be explained, as has been suggested for the Lark valley, by postulating incomers settled in the gaps in the agricultural landscape (West 1978); equally, however, the juxtaposition might reflect a situation similar to that at Spong Hill. Either way, the discontinuity or disruption apparent at the level of the individual site occurs within a more stable general pattern of location.

The broad regional pattern of coincidence between the distribution of Romano-British and early Anglo-Saxon sites and finds suggests that the former structured the latter. The occurrence of early Anglo-Saxon material on or adjacent to the sites of Roman-British towns and nucleated settlements further suggests that the earliest Germanic settlement took place within a British society in which elements of the settlement hierarchy most closely associated with the cantonal administration and Romano-British economic structures still exercised some pull. This would imply that the major re-alignments in political geography, and so presumably in the regional infrastructures of power and authority, evident by the seventh century are probably not a simple direct result of Anglo-Saxon settlement or invasion, which in the first instance may

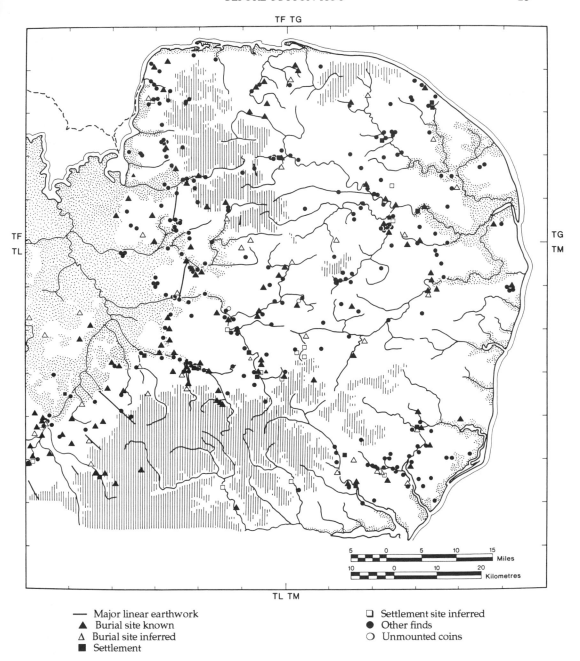

Figure 3. Distribution map of Anglo-Saxon sites and finds of the fifth to mid-seventh centuries in East Anglia

have involved only a relatively small number of people, but of more complex and longer-term processes in which the incomers are only one factor, albeit an important one (cf. Esmond-Cleary 1989).

The crucial imponderable remains the nature of post-Roman British society in the region. We can infer a devolution of authority to cantonal aristocracies in the wake of the disintegration or withdrawal of the diocesan or provincial administrations, and a subsequent fissioning of power between local magnates with sufficient lands to attract the clients to back them up. It is impossible to say how rapid such a process may have been, nor whether any groups or individuals may have claimed, or even exercised, power at the cantonal or provincial level; but in general the model of fragmentation of political structures to a more local and personal level is supported by the apparent failure of most if not all the physical correlates of central or cantonal administration to survive the sixth century, and by the subsequent emergence of new patterns of settlement hierarchy and political configuration by the seventh century. This offers a plausible context in which relatively small incoming groups might establish themselves, and would allow us to break-away from the constraints of a Briton:Saxon dichotomy to postulate a more complex and fluctuating network of relationships and competition between local groups and leaders, some British, some Germanic. The apparent continuing importance of Caistor-by-Norwich may argue for some continuity of a central authority, or a claim to central authority, if not of the groups or individuals who claimed or exercised it. The potential value of claims to Roman legitimacy or sanction in regional power games must also be considered. The presence of Caesar as well as Woden in the East Anglian genealogy (Campbell 1982, 67) may suggest that at some time a member of the Wuffing lineage felt it necessary to attempt to legitimize a claim to authority over Britons and, possibly, that such a claim may have required an element of consent. By the late fifth century characteristic Anglo-Saxon material culture and burial practices dominate the archaeological record, but the probability must be that they disguise a substantial proportion of the population which was Romano-British by descent, their adoption of new material culture types and cultural practices expressing new affinities and identities, and rooted in the reality of new social and political configurations. The use of red enamel on Anglo-Saxon metalwork of the late fifth and sixth centuries may represent the transference of a surviving British craft skill under such circumstances (Scull 1985).

Unfortunately, fifth-century potentates, however probable their existence, have left little directly-recognisable impact on the archaeology of the region. There is no evidence that villas, the strongest expression of a rural landowning class in late Roman Britain, long survived the collapse of the Roman economic system that sustained them and, unlike western Britain in the post-Roman period, there is no new class of higher-status or princely sites whose existence reflects the survival or re-emergence of native elites. The probability that native dynasties in eastern England faced too much competition too soon for them to be able to establish stable or widespread authority may explain this. Nonetheless, it may be possible to point to a post-Roman British presence at two sites at least. At Wighton, Norfolk, an 8 ha. defended enclosure was established within the area of the nucleated settlement in the late Roman or early post-Roman period (Gregory 1986, 15). The glass hoard at Burgh Castle, which may have been buried as late as the third decade of the fifth century (Harden 1983), might suggest early post-Roman occupation or activity within the defended circuit. In both cases one possible explanation might be that secure or defensible sites were being established or re-used by local leaders or elites.

The territorial identification of any fifth- or sixth-century polities, British or Anglo-Saxon, within the region must remain speculative. The distribution of sites and finds, both Romano-British and early Anglo-Saxon, suggests concentrations of population in east Norfolk, south-east Suffolk, and west Norfolk and Suffolk, and the linear earthworks of Norfolk and Suffolk can be used to support the possibility that these broadly coincided with independent political groupings at some time during the fifth and sixth centuries. The Black Ditches might relate to a local grouping in the Lark Valley. It has been argued, too, that the paired dykes of west Norfolk may have demarcated the territorial interests of groups in central and eastern Norfolk from those of the north-east fenland and fen edge (Wade-Martins 1974), but this hypothesis has to be modified in the light of recent excavation which has demonstrated that the Launditch is an Iron-Age earthwork (K. Penn, pers. comm.). There is, moreover, no convincing way of corroborating the social and political integrity of these suggested divisions, nor any guarantee that they represent contemporary configurations. Nonetheless both the Foss Ditch and Bichamditch in west Norfolk cordon-off areas of intensive and relatively rich late-Roman settlement on the fen-edge, where it would be legitimate to expect a landowning class capable of establishing and maintaining political autonomy in the fifth century (Gregory 1982; Gurney 1986). This coincidence might suggest a group with its origins in the political fragmentation of the immediate post-Roman period, but how long it might have retained an independent identity cannot be assessed. Interestingly, though, this is an area where the Wissa might be located (Courtney 1981). A differentiation between groups in east and central Norfolk on the one hand and west Norfolk and the Lark Valley on the other in the sixth century may be reflected in some aspects of material culture and, possibly, in burial practice (Green et al. 1981; Fisher 1988; Russel 1983) but the social realities which underlie such distinctions are unclear, and need not correlate with political autonomy. Similar considerations also militate against the use of the Early State Module as a predictive spatial model. It is unsafe to assume either the existence of permanent central places, or that they are centres of an authority exercised over a formally-administered territory which is ultimately defined by energy-expenditure constraints. Instead one might be dealing with central persons whose direct control over territory is very limited but whose personal authority over other key individuals is such that they exercise a wide hegemony, however impermanent, over groups whose own territories need not be contiguous or together form a spatially-discrete unit. Some general comparisons might be drawn here with political developments during and after the Mfecane in nineteenth-century southern Africa, in particular the establishment of the confederacies of Dingiswayo and Zwide, and the formation of the Zulu, Ndebele and Sotho nations (Brown 1969; Owen-Cooper 1966; 1969; Thompson 1975; Ritter 1955). Power is not necessarily directly reflected in the formal administration of territory; neither is widespread power an exclusive attribute of state societies. Moreover, although one might expect the establishment of a more permanent hegemony to involve formalized structures of central territorial control and administration, this might be achieved by the translation of a widespread authority over people into a more direct and formal authority over territory rather than by the integration into a larger whole of small, autonomous, centrally-organized territories. The devolved lordship of middle Saxon England, apparent in the hierarchy of *reges, subreguli* and *principes* and their corresponding territorial interests (Davies and Vierck 1974; Campbell 1979; Dumville 1989; Blair 1989), and in the administration of complex or multiple estates, might be represented convincingly as the outcome of just such processes. Another possible element in such a transformation might be the conversion of tribute-taking to more formal exactions or even taxation.

Processual orthodoxy has sought to explain the development of Anglo-Saxon kingdoms within a framework of social evolution, with middle Saxon kingdoms defined as state societies and general models of state formation adduced to elucidate or explain some of the processes or interactions which may have governed their emergence (Arnold 1980; 1988; Hodges 1978; 1982b). Although there is no doubt about the general value of such approaches there is a danger that their over-simple or uncritical application may mask complexities and diversity in a way that is misleading. One major problem is taxonomic (cf. Cherry 1978, 415; Cohen 1978, 4): what exactly defines a state, and what constitutes the threshold between pre-state chiefdom societies and state societies? This is crucial to the period in question, and remains to be resolved. For instance the inchoate state, evolutionary precursor of the early state as defined by Claessen (1978) and Claessen and Skalník (1978a; 1978b), has more in common with chiefdoms than states as defined, for example, by Service (1971; 1975). There are different assumptions here about the character and complexity of pre-state societies, and about processes and likely trajectories of development, which require rigorous appraisal before any such model is applied in detail; nonetheless the position adopted by Claessen and Skalnick has been used unmodified as the theoretical base for a recent study of Anglo-Saxon kingdom origins (Arnold 1988, 163). Although the taxonomic schemes commonly appealed to propose complex criteria of sophistication in economic, political and social structures, discussions of sixth and seventh century

England from such perspectives have not examined these complexities rigorously, nor attempted to predict in detail their potential range of archaeological correlates. It is legitimate to talk of a late Saxon state, and England at the time of Offa can in some ways be considered an emerging state society, but the diversity of political groupings apparent in seventh and early eighth century England, the transience of any inter-regional supremacy, and what is known or can be inferred about the structures of leadership and authority suggest that these polities are better characterized as complex chiefdoms. It seems unlikely, too, that all middle Saxon kingdoms and small groupings reached the same level of socio-political complexity or cohesion at precisely the same time, or that – whatever the general similarities – the specific circumstances which governed the emergence of each were identical. To be useful, any general evolutionary model needs to allow different pathways of development (cf. Carneiro 1970; Wright 1978).

There are clear implications here for the application of social evolutionary perspectives to the early Anglo-Saxon period. The fifth to seventh centuries in Britain have been characterized as a period of 'post-collapse resurgence' (Renfrew 1982; Arnold 1984; 1988), when after the collapse of the Roman state structure increasing social stratification culminated in the emergence of paramount socio-political elites and the concomitant kingdom structure. The stimulus underlying this process has most frequently been identified as competition for resources: differential access can then be used to explain both increasing inequalities within societies and competition between regional elites leading, through success in acquisition or control of resources, frequently involving armed conflict, to the establishment of larger political entities (Arnold 1980; 1988; Hodges 1978; 1982b; 1986). In many ways this is plausible: similar explanations are widely accepted for the emergence of hierarchical and stratified societies in prehistoric Europe. However, it cannot be accepted wholly uncritically. The concept of 'post-collapse resurgence' is unsatisfactory: it substitutes labelling for explanation and it invites a mechanistic unilinear view of social and political development. It is particularly inappropriate to Anglo-Saxon England in that it makes no allowance for groups whose own societies had not collapsed catastrophically: the Anglo-Saxons. The way in which resurgence is modelled assumes that, post-collapse, one is dealing with pristine societies: insufficient account is taken of the possibility that power structures other than those of the Roman state survived, nor is it sufficiently recognized that if a social evolutionary perspective is to be adopted the presence of incomers from sophisticated (if pre-state) societies on the continent has to be taken into account. It is here that the approach is deeply flawed. The assumption is made that increasing social stratification is the natural and necessary precondition and generator for the development of larger and more stable political units through the fifth and into the seventh century. However, these are societies which are already sufficiently complex for individuals or groups to wield considerable power, and it is the attempts to consolidate these configurations, and to reproduce or perpetuate them, and the strategies adopted to achieve this, that need to be understood. We are not dealing with the long-term evolution of sophisticated hierarchical societies, but with a much shorter-term transformation and subsequent consolidation of power configurations within such societies, and it is misleading to equate the two.

Military, economic and social competition – in dynastic warfare, or for the fruits of trade, or in prestige exchange – can therefore be viewed as actively-chosen elements in dominance strategies rather than simply as adaptive responses to changes in the socio-political habitat. In the case of long-distance exchange this perspective also goes some way towards resolving the chicken-and-egg conundrum which arises when the emergence of elites and control of trade are linked in a simple cause-and-effect relationship (Scull 1990). It is interesting, however, that concern with differential access to resources so often focuses on long-distance exchange (cf. Hodges 1978; Arnold 1980). The importance of access to, and control of, foreign contacts and trade cannot be dismissed, and was particularly important to the development of permanent institutions of administration and the consolidation of royal power in middle Saxon England, but it can be over-emphasized. If there is any single physical resource which can be identified as fundamental to the maintenance and reproduction of internal structures of status and power in Anglo-Saxon society it is land, and the surplus that it generated. Charles-Edwards (1972) has discussed the links between the territorialization of authority and changes in the relationship between status and landholding in middle Saxon England. If he is correct in his initial assumptions, and given even a relatively small increase in the number of individuals who might expect to hold the land necessary to maintain their status by birth (which might be explained by natural population growth within elite or privileged groups), it is plausible that in some areas the sixth century saw pressure on land as a social rather than as an economic resource. One outcome of this might have been external conflict between local groups or chiefdoms. Another, internal, result may have been to increase the number of higher-status individuals dependent on a local potentate in a client: lord relationship, a process which would concentrate political power and, indirectly, control of land in fewer and fewer hands. Either would enhance or accelerate the social and political dynamics whereby a group or individual might eventually establish a wider regional hegemony.

It has been argued that evidence for social differentiation and, by extension, political and social leadership from the earliest years of the Anglo-Saxon settlement can be seen in the distinction between cremation and inhumation in the cemetery at Spong Hill, North Elmham, Norfolk (Böhme 1986, 542; Carver 1989, 149). However, the interpretation of grave 40 as that of an early fifth-century leader, upon which this hypothesis depends, is based upon the earliest item in the burial assemblage. This is the Sjörup-style scabbard mouthpiece, which is, however, unlikely to be earlier than the middle of the fifth century (Haselof 1981, 74–5, Abb. 51–2). The form of the shield boss from this grave suggests that it is unlikely to be earlier than the sixth century (Dickinson 1976, 273–90), and the other inhumations, where datable, belong to the later fifth and sixth centuries, whereas the earliest cremations could date to the second quarter of the fifth century. At Spong Hill, therefore, inhumation appears to be a secondary development in the life of the cemetery (Hills *et al.* 1984a, 41), and if its adoption genuinely reflects social or political differentiation, or a concern to emphasize this, then it must be seen as a later development rather than a direct reflection of society at the time of the initial settlement. However, if the scabbard mouthpiece, and the sword it was buried with, was an heirloom interred two or three generations after it was brought to England, then its presence in grave 40 might indirectly reflect the earlier existence of a dominant individual or group among the community buried at Spong Hill. Another individual with a special identity who died in the middle or second half of the fifth century might also be identifiable in cremation 2376, which contained an equal-arm brooch of Nesse type (Hills *et al.* 1987). On the continent equal-arm brooches are considered a high-status type, and a Nesse type equal-arm was the principal brooch in the grave of the so-called 'princess' at Zweelo (van Es and Ypey 1977). The example from Spong Hill is copper-alloy rather than silver, but it stands out by virtue of the relative scarcity of the type in England. Another Nesse type equal-arm brooch is known from Westgarth Gardens, Bury St. Edmunds, Suffolk grave 55 (Evison 1977; West 1988). There is no stronger evidence in the archaeological record for ranking in the region before the end of the fifth century than the occurrence in a few burials of items which might be identified as high-status types, and in some cases these may have been buried a generation or more after the lifetime of their first owner.

Assessing ranking from burial practice is complicated by the differences between cremation and inhumation. It is clear at Spong Hill, for instance, that the superficially unimpressive fragments from some cremations include fragments from grave goods such as glass beakers which would be considered indicators of wealth or status in contemporary inhumations. But although no simple status distinction can be drawn between cremation and inhumation, it is plausible that at Spong Hill the inhumations represent a group concerned to differentiate themselves from the rest of burial community and, given the chamber grave and the ring ditches which imply barrows, both prominent features of the repertoire of elite burial practice defined at Sutton Hoo, it is not unreasonable to presume that this is a local elite lineage. If so it is possible that they were incomers of the later fifth century, but a concern to differentiate or to emphasize a new identity may reflect the emergence of a prominent lineage from within existing communities. Ranking is also more widely discernible in the region's sixth-century inhumations, either in the differential provision of grave goods or, less frequently, in the construction of barrows or grave structures. However, there appears to be a greater degree of social differentiation within sixth-century cemeteries (and so, presumably, within the communities using them) than between them. This may well reflect the existence of more-or-less equal, internally-ranked communities or groups with a local focus, perhaps based on ranked lineages. There is no archaeological evidence which might correlate with a permanent wider regional power before the late sixth century, but it is not impossible that an intermittent authority might have been imposed by some groups or individuals. The high proportion of place-names in -*ingas* in Norfolk would also support this model of local groupings (Dodgson, pers. comm.). The obstacles to identifying such chiefdom territories have already been discussed. The suggestion that Norfolk and Suffolk may have their origins in a pre-kingdom division (Yorke 1990, 69) would cut across the proposed division between east and central Norfolk and west Norfolk and the Lark Valley, but there is no archaeological evidence for a cultural or political boundary along the Waveney and Ouse valleys at this time; the Sandlings province proposed by Carver (1986a, 47; 1989) also awaits firm archaeological corroboration.

The region's outstanding graves, at Snape and Sutton Hoo, belong to the later sixth century and the first half of the seventh century (Bruce-Mitford 1974, 114–40; 1975–83; Filmer-Sankey 1984). Outstandingly wealthy burials and barrow cemeteries are new and apparently short-lived phenomena, most plausibly linked to the success of a few groups or a single dynasty in establishing and perpetuating a wider supremacy and eventually a regional hegemony, and to their concern to legitimize and reproduce a new status, authority and political identity. Competition between local elites might stimulate the development or consciousness of a new status or identity (cf. Renfrew 1986) and if, as suggested above, the early kingdom depended upon authority over local chiefs rather than the direct administration of territory, the new relationship with an overlord might accelerate such changes. One way of expressing this would be to adopt a burial practice which emphasized affinity with peer groups or new overlords and social distance from the subordinate population. These princely graves may therefore be interpreted as expressing the uncertainties and concerns surrounding the shift from a cyclical or intermittent to a permanent paramount authority. It seems most probable that this new political power and paramount status was achieved as a result of conflict or competition between regional elites, and evidence of the ranking apparent at a more local level from the later fifth century can still be seen in the later sixth and earlier seventh centuries in burials such as Morning Thorpe, Norfolk, Grave 218 and the barrow burials at Barnham, Suffolk, and Blakeney, Norfolk, and in the later seventh century in wealthier graves like those recently excavated at Harford Farm, Caistor-by-Norwich. The Snape barrow cemetery appears to have been established on a pre-existing flat cemetery (Filmer-Sankey 1988), and this may suggest that the forebears of the elite group buried under large barrows are represented in the earlier graves which do not exhibit such dramatic social demarcation.

At Sutton Hoo, however, there is no such evidence for an antecedent flat cemetery, suggesting that the barrow cemetery may have been established from the first as an elite burial ground. The relationship between Snape and Sutton Hoo has yet to be resolved. If these cemeteries are attributed to the Wuffings, Snape could be interpreted either as the burial ground of another segment of the royal kindred, or as an earlier cemetery later abandoned in favour of a new dynastic burial ground at Sutton Hoo (Filmer-Sankey 1984). There is, however, no compelling reason to assign Snape to the Wuffing dynasty, nor any certainty – whatever the circumstantial evidence – in the case of Sutton Hoo (cf. Wallace-Hadrill 1975). Another probable princely burial site at Pakefield, Suffolk, where a barrow burial with high-class grave goods was discovered in 1758 (Douglas 1793, 3, 8, 82–3, 88, Pls. 20–1; Rigold 1975, 663, 667), must also be considered. Recent surface finds (Martin *et al.* 1983), if from the same site as the eighteenth-century discoveries, would be consistent with a sequence of development similar to that at Snape, with later sixth- or seventh-century elite graves in a pre-existing flat cemetery. In the absence of any conclusive evidence for a link between Sutton Hoo and the East Anglian kings it could be argued that all three sites should be seen simply as reflecting the local elites from whose ranks the Wuffings emerged, and who subsequently constituted the highest level of society below the paramount – Wuffing – apex of the East Anglian kingdom structure. The location of these three cemeteries in river valleys along the Suffolk coast may therefore indicate some constituent units of the kingdom, or even hint at some earlier chiefdom territories. However, it would be perverse to deny that there is a strong case for Sutton Hoo as a royal burial ground. If the sequence of development is indeed similar at Snape and Pakefield, and if its establishment from the first as an elite cemetery is genuinely an integral aspect of Sutton Hoo's unique character and status, then this alone would distinguish Sutton Hoo on the one hand from Snape and Pakefield on the other.

The first clear evidence of a settlement hierarchy is also apparent in the seventh century. Sites like that excavated at Brandon, Suffolk (Carr *et al.* 1988), or known from surface finds at Bromeswell and Sutton (Carver 1986a, 33, Figs 4, 22; Mango *et al.* 1989), are more extensive than the few known examples of the fifth and sixth centuries, and have yielded material culture items of a different order. The implication of an established authority, and the beginnings of territorial control on a large scale, reflected also in the development of Ipswich during the seventh century (Wade 1988), accords with the social changes inferred from the burial record. The role of external contracts or alliances in establishing a permanent regional power is impossible to assess, but there can be little doubt that, once established, they were important to its maintenance (cf. Hodges 1986; Hodges and Moreland 1988). Although the degree to which the Mound 1 ship burial at Sutton Hoo might reflect direct dynastic links with Scandinavia can be questioned seriously (Wilson 1983), there is no doubt about the more general ideological and cultural affinities reflected in the practice of boat burial and in some of the material culture (Carver 1986b; 1989). There is no doubt, either, about the importance of contacts between East Anglia and the Frankish continent in the early seventh century; they too are reflected in the burial assemblage from the Mound 1 ship burial, and were maintained at the highest level of East Anglian society (Wood 1991). Control of continental trade through the *emporium* at Ipswich, a focus of cross-channel exchange, directly or via Kent, from the first half of the seventh century, must also have been important to the later seventh and eighth century East Anglian kings. However, a significant relationship between trade as reflected at Ipswich and the rise of the Wuffing dynasty as reflected in the burials at Sutton Hoo cannot simply be assumed. Even though there is a strong presumption that Sutton Hoo is an East Anglian royal cemetery, the geographical proximity need not, in itself, be significant; more importantly, the development of Ipswich as a major *emporium* post-dates the climax of princely barrow burial at Sutton Hoo.

To conclude: a case can be made for the existence of a number of local groupings in fifth-century East Anglia, sustained by societies which were more sophisticated, and had a greater capacity for political integration, however impermanent, than is often assumed. The development of a regional hegemony by the end of the sixth century can be explained plausibly as a result of competition and conflict between progressively more powerful local potentates or elites. It is possible to identify a number of factors, economic and social, which may have caused conflict; in particular, the unstable internal political dynamics of some migration-period Germanic societies may have helped precipitate migration to Britain in the first place, and subsequently acted to promote dynastic conflicts (cf. Hedeager 1978a, 1987). Exactly how and why the Wuffings in particular eventually established a regional supremacy is difficult to explain. If the heartland of their power was in south-east Suffolk, proximity to and control of foreign contacts and overseas exchange may have given them a crucial edge over less well-situated rivals; and the school of thought which would see them initially as maritime adventurers from the highest levels of Scandinavian society would provide them with the necessary status and contacts from the outset (O'Loughlin 1964; cf. Carver 1989, 152, 158). As has already been argued, however, the development of the East Anglian *provincia* and the specific dynastic history of its first recorded rulers may be considered as separate issues. It could be argued that the principle of contingency (cf. Gould 1989) is as applicable to social as to biological evolution; and that if the Wuffings had failed, another lineage – given the social and political circumstances of the sixth and seventh centuries – would very probably have succeeded.

ACKNOWLEDGEMENTS

This paper is based on my aspects of my postgraduate research, and my thanks are due to the many individuals who have helped me with this. I am especially grateful to Barbara Green, Norwich Castle Museum; Kenneth Penn, Andrew Rogerson and Robert Rickett, Norfolk Archaeological Unit; and Dr S.E. West and John Newman, Suffolk County Council Archaeological Section, for their generosity in allowing me access to records and excavated material; and to my academic supervisor, Mrs S.E. Hawkes. Earlier versions of this paper were presented to seminars in London and Cardiff, as well at the York conference, and I am grateful too to all who discussed them or offered comments, in particular Dr J. Hines, Dr M. Welch, and the late Prof. J. Dodgson to whom I am indebted for information on Norfolk place-names. Responsibility for the opinions expressed here, however, remains mine alone.

2

The Late Roman and Anglo-Saxon Settlement Pattern in the Sandlings of Suffolk

JOHN NEWMAN

East Anglia has always been recognised as having a key role to play in any study of the development of England in the Anglo-Saxon period and since its formation in 1974 the Suffolk Archaeological Unit has taken every opportunity to examine areas or sites which might throw more light on one of the major kingdoms of this era. The work has included major projects, such as the study of Anglo-Saxon urban development in Ipswich (Wade 1988, 93) and the extensive excavation of a wealthy Middle Saxon rural settlement at Brandon, (Carr and Tester 1988, 371) as well as support for the recent work on the Snape cemetery site (Filmer-Sankey, this vol.). Smaller projects have included the fabric analysis and small scale excavation at Iken church which confirmed that this was the site of St Botolph's monastery in the seventh century (West et al. 1984, 279). In many ways this range of activities carrying on a fieldwork tradition in Suffolk which Basil Brown's work did so much to enhance. For it was his discoveries at Sutton Hoo in 1939 which triggered off such a great range of research over the last fifty years into every aspect of Anglo-Saxon society. Now we can take the opportunity to review the present state of knowledge and suggest profitable avenues for organised and systematic research in the future.

Even in an area such as East Anglia where the current state of knowledge for the Anglo-Saxon period can legitimately be judged to be fairly good, the data base is really very patchy. For the early Anglo-Saxon period between the fifth and mid seventh centuries much of the evidence still consists of cemetery material, both from recent, well excavated sites and from older excavations where much of the finer detail is often missing. The remaining archaeological evidence largely being made up of stray metalwork finds, these isolated discoveries often being taken as indicators of more burials and cemeteries. However, there is still very little settlement-evidence for the period, the continued dominance in any discussion of early Anglo-Saxon settlement in East Anglia by the results from West Stow indicating how thin the material is elsewhere in the region (West 1985). Whether the proto-village type settlement at West Stow is typical of East Anglia is far from certain. One other area where relatively good settlement evidence has been collected and studied being Witton, in north east Norfolk, where the settlement picture is, instead, one of dispersed farmsteads (Lawson 1983).

In the following Middle Saxon period, between the mid-seventh and the mid-ninth centuries, the archaeological evidence becomes even thinner. During this conversion period earlier, pagan, cemeteries gradually go out of use and with the adoption of Christian burial rites our ability to recognise and closely date graves is lost. As many of these Middle Saxon cemeteries are also likely to be under the present parish churches and graveyards they are usually inaccessible and often badly damaged by later activity. The discovery and excavation of a well-preserved Middle Saxon settlement and cemetery at Brandon in north west Suffolk being a rare occurrence, as it is reliant on a major settlement shift in the early Late Saxon period (Carr & Tester 1988, 371). Our evidence for settlement in the Middle Saxon period is also fairly poor with the majority of the excavated material coming from the early trading port and urban centre of Ipswich (Wade 1988, 93), the wealthy, high status settlement at Brandon and from North Elmham in Norfolk (Wade-Martins 1980). The latter site, at least in its later phases, was of high ecclesiastical status. Other sites which have produced evidence of Middle and Late Saxon occupation on a smaller scale include Burrow Hill in Suffolk (Fenwick 1984, 35), which with its isolated, almost island-type location and male dominated cemetery must be far from the norm of rural settlement, and Middle Harling in Norfolk (Youngs et al. 1984, 234), excavation on the latter site being stimulated by the discovery of a coin hoard of mid-eighth century date. As this background indicates, the study of Anglo-Saxon archaeology lacks a consistent and systematic approach, this being a problem held in common with other periods in this country. The common tendency in archaeology to concentrate on particularly wealthy or productive sites without a context study should be seen as a step sideways rather than forwards. For the Anglo-Saxon period it may be tempting to rely on the documentary and historical sources as well as placename evidence for indicators of where to look. However, this type of evidence should be used with extreme caution in the initial stages of an archaeological fieldwork programme. It is in the later stages of synthesis that information from all of the available sources can be gathered together. In the initial phases of project design it is better in many ways to treat the Anglo-Saxon period as a pre-historic era, using all the rigour and discipline that pre-historians would use in assembling a body of archaeological data (Wilson 1976, 4).

Much of the theoretical basis for an understanding of the development of Anglo-Saxon social and economic structures and state formation through the crucial phases of the sixth and seventh centuries may now be in place. This has been shown by recent publications that have attempted to bring together and analyze the archaeological data known at present (Bassett 1989). However, as much of this data-base has been assembled in an unsystematic way, consisting as it does of chance reports and lucky finds, it is impossible to use it as a reliable testing ground for sophisticated theories. Some areas are better known through the efforts of individual fieldworkers, but it is difficult to see how these fit into the very patchy background picture. To move on from this archaeological data-base, which can only be used in very general terms to support complex models and theories, to a stage where a body of systematically collected information is available will take considerable effort. But if we are to move forwards from the base laid over the last fifty years, then at least one region needs to be systematically studied in order to gain a better understanding of the social and economic processes that were taking place between the early fifth and the tenth centuries. That is the period which saw the development and emergence of a unified Anglo-Saxon state.

Preferably such a study should take place in a region that meets various crucial criteria, not just an area that is now a convenient part of the present local government structure. Of importance among these criteria are that the area under study should be a historically recognisable entity and it should have a good archaeological potential for the Anglo-Saxon period. The area should also have major flagship projects under way, as much of the necessary fieldwork will be at the unglamorous end of archaeology where public and media interests will generally be at a low level. Finally, the present land use pattern in the area must be largely arable so that effective fieldwork can take place. For the Anglo-Saxon period, East Anglia meets all of these criteria. The region still maintains a distinct identity with the counties of Norfolk and Suffolk making up most of the historically known kingdom of East Anglia. It has a very good Anglo-Saxon archaeological potential with a strong ceramic tradition and a large corpus of metal finds to build on. For the Middle Saxon period, settlement sites can be identified by the presence of Ipswich ware, produced between the mid seventh and the mid ninth centuries and the first mass-produced pottery tradition in the post-Roman period. Late Saxon settlement sites can be identified by the presence of the Thetford-type wares which were produced between the mid ninth and the mid twelfth centuries. The corpus of older Anglo-Saxon metalwork finds is large and has grown considerably over the last ten to fifteen years through the positive attitude taken in both counties to local, responsible metal-detector users. The region is also mainly under arable cultivation which is vital for large scale fieldwork projects. Finally, as a region, East Anglia has major archaeological excavations which a fieldwork project can be integrated with. These include not only the recent work at Sutton Hoo but also the major projects undertaken by the strong county units in Norfolk and Suffolk.

When the feasibility of a renewed Sutton Hoo research programme was discussed at the Oxford Anglo-Saxon symposium in 1979, an area survey was considered essential for a fuller understanding of the cemetery site (Rahtz

1980). Therefore, in 1983 when the Sutton Hoo Project started, a serious attempt was made to launch an East Anglian Kingdom research programme in order to redress some of the problems outlined above. The research design for the fieldwork project was unashamedly ambitious, as its ultimate goal was an understanding of the development of one of the major kingdoms of Anglo-Saxon England (Wade & West 1983, 18). Prior knowledge, both archaeological and documentary, was to be assessed and a fieldwork project would be undertaken in various areas of the region to locate and characterise Early, Middle and Late Saxon sites. Areas for fieldwork would be chosen so that all of the major sub-regions and soil types were represented and they would be examined in a systematic and consistent manner so that the results could be confidently compared and contrasted (Wade 1986). In the field it has only proved possible to examine one area so far and this work has been funded by the Sutton Hoo Research Trust. However, this pilot survey does show the potential for fieldwork in the region and it may confidently be argued that the results achieved between 1983 and 1988 confirm that a systematic study of East Anglia offers the greatest hope we have for an understanding of the development of a major Anglo-Saxon kingdom (Newman 1989, 17).

The area chosen for this survey was initially a box in the landscape of 216 square kilometres centred on Sutton Hoo in south east Suffolk. The Deben valley bisects the survey area and it was deliberately positioned to include both the light sand and gravel-derived soils of the Sandlings, which run along the Suffolk coast, and a portion of the heavier boulder-clay soils which cover the centre of the country. It must be admitted that the historically important area of Rendlesham was deliberately included in the survey area, otherwise the limits of the box have been taken along convenient National Grid lines. In the five winters of field survey an area of 134 square kilometres was comprehensively covered and this area is shown on Fig. 4. The figure also shows a simplified version of the basic drift geology for the area of south-east Suffolk which will be considered in this paper. While the settlement patterns in the survey area can be studied with greater confidence, since the material it is based on has been systematically collected, such an arbitrary box in the landscape cannot be divorced from its local setting. The Sandlings area of south-east Suffolk, with its very light soils, is a very distinct sub-region of East Anglia and is worthy of special consideration. It is also worthwhile to compare the development of the Sandlings with the heavier soils of the adjacent boulder clay plateau to the north west. Over the 134 square-kilometres of the survey area, a total of 5,500 hectares of arable land was systematically fieldwalked in 20 metre transects. Nearly all of the Anglo-Saxon sites located in this initial stage of the survey were then intensively searched on a gridded pattern so that a hierarchy of settlement size, based on ceramic evidence, could be constructed. Of the 134 square kilometres that was covered, just over 90 square kilometres was on light Sandling type soils with the remainder on the heavier boulder clay soils. The 5,500 hectares covered representing nearly all of the

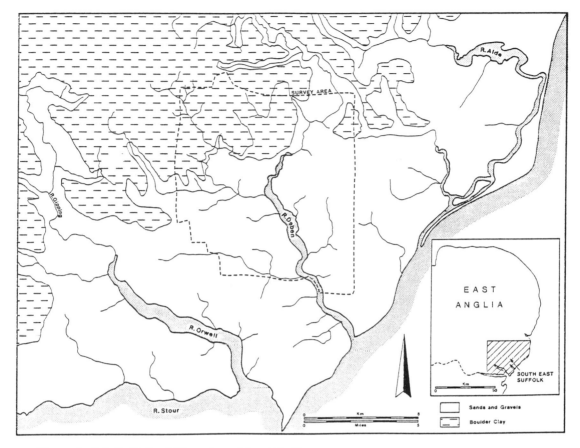

Figure 4. S.E. Suffolk: drift geology (simplified)

arable land in the survey area and the project is indebted to the numerous
landowners and tenants who allowed the fieldwork to take place.

     After covering such an area it is now possible to talk with some confidence
about the settlement pattern for each period. In the Romano-British period,
south-east Suffolk was extensively cleared and settled, only some of the
heaviest areas of boulder clay apparently not being intensively exploited, as
can be seen on Fig. 5. No new villa-type settlements were located and the
previously known sites at Burgh-by-Woodbridge, Farnham, Stonham Aspal
and Whitton (Ipswich), remain the high status sites for the area in the Roman
period (Moore 1988, 47). The site at Castle Hill, Whitton, being especially
noteworthy as it appears to be the largest villa-type settlement in Suffolk. The
area as a whole was served by larger settlement-sites which can confidently be
termed small towns. These were at Coddenham, in the Gipping valley, and
Hacheston, near Wickham Market, in the Deben valley (see Fig. 5). A large
settlement also existed around the Saxon Shore Fort of Walton Castle, Felix-

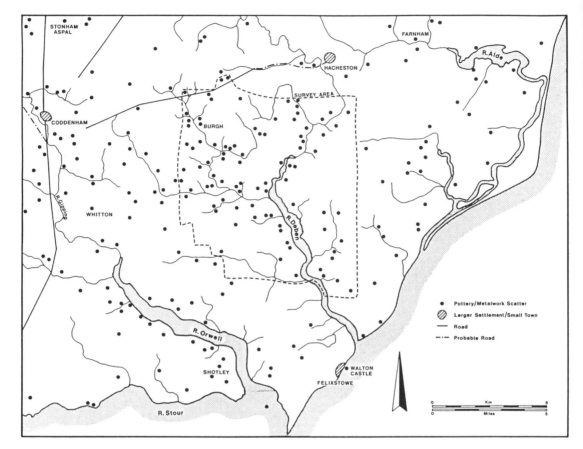

Figure 5. S.E. Suffolk: Romano-British sites

stowe. However, the site has largely been eroded away and information on it is mainly based on stray finds. Over the rest of south-east Suffolk, the Roman settlement pattern is represented by numerous scatters of greyware pottery sherds which probably indicate the locations of small farm sites. As with other periods in the area the settlement pattern is a very dispersed one which is strongly riverine in character. Within the survey area the site density is nearly one per square kilometre on the boulder-clay-derived soils and one every two square kilometres on the Sandling areas. Such site densities compare well with data from elsewhere in lowland England (Ford 1987, 94) and demonstrate the greater carrying capacity of the heavier, boulder-clay-derived soils.

The collection of ceramic evidence through fieldwork can locate settlement sites for the Romano-British period easily enough, but it can do little to date closely their use and decline when the bulk of the finds are the common, greyware pottery types. However, through the positive policy in the county towards responsible metal-detector users, it has been possible to gain far more

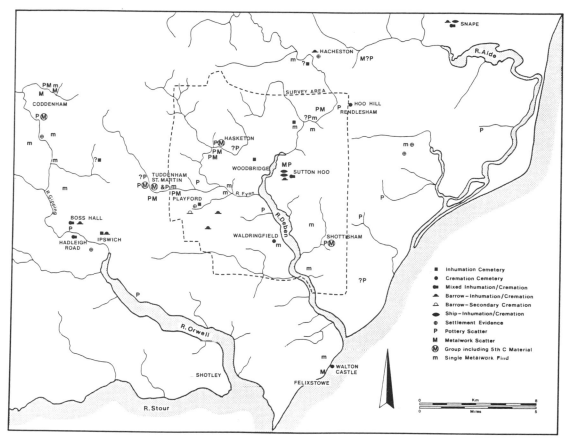

Figure 6. S.E. Suffolk: early Anglo-Saxon sites

evidence about a good number of these sites. Examination of the coin-finds from many of the Romano-British sites in the area shows that a decline had set in by the third or fourth quarter of the fourth century (J. Plouviez, personal comment). Definite evidence of late fourth century occupation is very rare in south-east Suffolk. If not a drop in population, at least a marked economic decline, had set in towards the end of the Roman period. The severe social and economic dislocation associated with the fifth century in the Roman province of Britain may already have started in the mid to late fourth century in south-east Suffolk. This potentially vulnerable coastal area perhaps suffered at an earlier stage in the complex process that eventually saw the complete collapse of the Roman province by the early to mid fifth century.

In the following fifth and sixth centuries we are again dependent on metal-work finds to give some secure dating. Traditional forms of field-work can locate early Anglo-Saxon pottery scatters but cannot differentiate fifth from sixth or early seventh century activity. Fortunately we can again turn to recent metalwork finds. These finds indicate a higher level of fifth century activity in south-east Suffolk than was thought to be the case just a few years ago. Apart from the known, early cremation urn from Waldringfield (Page 1911, 329), there are now fifth century brooch finds from Coddenham, Hasketon, Shottisham and Tuddenham St Martin. These sites are shown on Fig. 6. However, the level of settlement activity in south east Suffolk in the fifth and sixth centuries is much lower than it was in the preceding Romano-British period. All of the Early Anglo-Saxon sites are on the light soils of the Sandlings and it appears that the boulder clay areas were abandoned through this period. The marked difference in settlement activity between the two periods can clearly be seen by comparing Figs 5 and 6. While a case for continued use may be made for some former Roman sites, the majority of the settlement sites from the preceding period appear to have been abandoned. Perhaps significantly, early Anglo-Saxon material is known from all of the larger sites, that is Coddenham, Hacheston and the area around Walton Castle, Felixstowe. It is surprising, however, that the area of light soils behind Felixstowe has produced very little evidence for this period and the Shotley peninsula is a complete blank between the fourth and eighth centuries. The Felixstowe and Shotley peninsulas are predominantly made up of a relatively light brickearth type deposit over sands and gravels. Whether this difference in drift geology to the true Sandling areas just to the north is the significant factor explaining the lack of Early Anglo-Saxon settlement evidence is difficult to judge at present. The Shotley peninsula has seen a large amount of metal-detector activity over the last fifteen years and if fifth or sixth century material was present in any quantity it should have been located by now.

The fifth century therefore appears as a period when there was little pressure on land and other resources. It is only towards the end of the fifth and into the sixth century that the landscape began to fill up. As can be seen from Fig. 6, many more metalwork finds are known from the second half of the early Anglo-Saxon period indicating a rise in population on the Sandlings through the time when the kingdom of East Anglia was emerging as a recognisable entity under its royal family, the Wuffingas. That south-east Suffolk is likely to have been the power base for the emergent kingdom has already been suggested by other authors (e.g. Carver 1986, 47), and more recent evidence supports this theory. Not only are the major cemetery sites of Snape and Sutton Hoo in south-east Suffolk, but significant sites have recently been located in the Gipping valley on the south-western edge of the Sandlings area (see Fig. 6). At Boss Hall, part of an early Anglo-Saxon cemetery has been excavated close to a pottery scatter which indicates settlement evidence nearby (Newman forthcoming in *Bull.* 8). Of the five cremations and twenty-two inhumations excavated, one was of a male in a chamber-grave under a small barrow and another was a high-status female with a very wealthy grave assemblage (Webster 1991, 51). The latter, female grave dated to c A.D.700 while the bulk of the cemetery falls into the sixth and early seventh centuries. The evidence

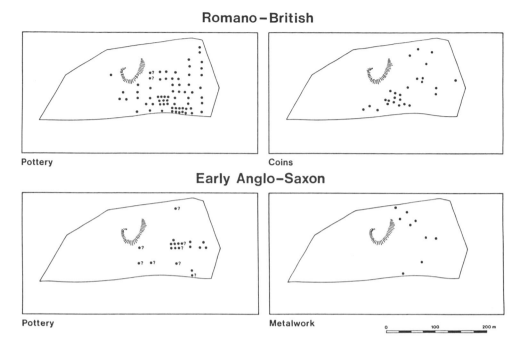

Figure 7. Playford, Suffolk: ceramic and metalwork scatter

recovered so far indicates that the Boss Hall cemetery is to be associated with a high status settlement in an area which, on evidence from later records, contained large royal estates. Further up the Gipping valley an impressive and varied metalwork assemblage has been recovered from a new site at Coddenham. All the material has been recovered by local, responsible metal-detector users from the ploughsoil and consists of some sixth century objects and a very rich group of seventh-century coins and metalwork. Whether this represents material from badly disturbed graves is, at present, impossible to say. However, it must be a site of significant regional importance and it illustrates the benefits of constructive co-operation with metal-detector users. Finally, the importance of the early trading port and town of Ipswich has been re-emphasised by the discovery and excavation of a major seventh and eighth century cemetery on The Buttermarket site (Gaimster et al. 1989, 209). The presence of various foreign objects amongst the grave goods on The Buttermarket indicates strong and important links between south-east Suffolk and the Merovingian kingdom on the Continent at this time.

In many cases it may be possible to identify early Anglo-Saxon settlements, through scatters of pottery sherds, and adjacent cemeteries, through metalwork scatters. This is a close association that is often commented on (Vierck 1980), and Fig. 6 shows various pairings of ceramic and metalwork finds. One of the best examples located to date is in Playford parish in the Fynn valley to

the north-east of Ipswich. The results from extensive metal-detector searching
and a gridded fieldwalking survey are shown on Fig. 7. Some of the Early
Anglo-Saxon metalwork finds are in a small, discrete, scatter that appears to be
separate from the pottery scatter and these objects may be from plough-
damaged burials. Fieldwork has now reached the stage on this site where trial
excavation is needed to test the theories put forward for the patterning of finds
in the ploughsoil. The date range for the finds from Playford is between the
late fifth and the early seventh century. The size of the pottery-scatter at
Playford is typical for many of the Early Anglo-Saxon sites located in south-
east Suffolk which suggests that the settlement pattern in the area has more in
common with the type of dispersed farmstead proposed for Witton, in Norfolk
(Lawson 1983), than the larger proto-village type seen at West Stow (West
1985).

The steady growth in settlement through the sixth century can be seen to
have increased in the Middle and Late Saxon periods as the population increased and more pressure was put on available resources. For the study of
these later periods, more emphasis can be put on ceramic evidence collected
during fieldwork: the region's distinctive pottery traditions of Ipswich ware
and the Thetford-type wares define the Middle and Late Saxon periods respectively. In south-east Suffolk, very few of the Early Anglo-Saxon sites show a
continuity of use into the Middle Saxon period. With the presence of a few
sherds of Ipswich ware on these earlier sites, the shift in location probably
came in the seventh century, as it did at West Stow (West 1985, 161). The
seventh century is also the period from which the claylands of Suffolk were
re-colonised, again indicating an increased pressure on the available resources.
The majority of the known Middle Saxon sites in south-east Suffolk have either
been located within the survey area or have been found during other fieldwork projects in the Sandlings area, as can be seen on Fig. 8. All of these major
Ipswich ware scatters are near parish churches, emphasising the importance of
these nuclei around which the parish system and Later Saxon and Medieval
settlement patterns grew. In the survey area, where no Middle Saxon sites
were known before 1980, there are now 12 seventh or eighth century sites close
to parish churches. A further 6 churches do not have any areas close by that are
suitable for fieldwork. The re-settlement of the boulder clay areas in the
Middle Saxon period can be seen on Fig. 8 with Ipswich ware scatters in
Clopton, Culpho and Grundisburgh parishes. A special mention should also
be made of the recently located Middle to Late Saxon settlement at Foxhall.
The site was discovered during the excavation of a large Iron Age enclosure
and cropmark complex. The Saxon phase of activity in the area of the site
examined consisting of various field ditches and evidence for two, rectangular,
hall-type buildings. The Foxhall site is close to the known location of the parish
church, which is now demolished, but as an uncertain proportion of the settlement was examined, it is difficult to gauge its potential size and importance. In
the Gipping valley Middle Saxon sites are relatively rare. The extensive

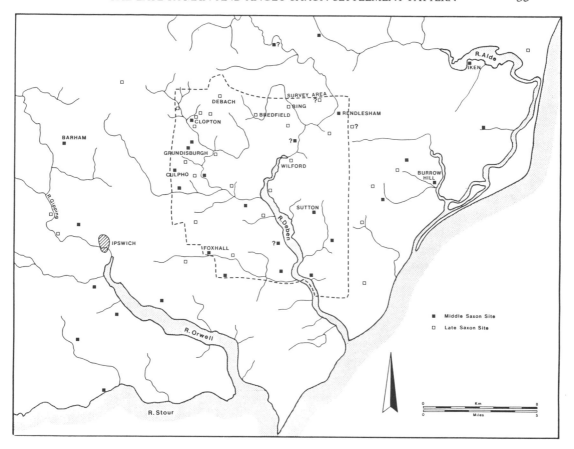

Figure 8. S.E. Suffolk: middle and late Saxon sites

ceramic and metalwork scatter at Barham stands out as an extremely prolific site which may have been a rural market or meeting place in the seventh to ninth centuries, as well as a settlement site (Newman, forthcoming).

The remaining sites close to parish churches that have been located fall into the next recognisable phase of settlement expansion in the ninth and tenth centuries and are shown on Fig. 8 by the open squares. These sites are dated by the presence of small quantities of Ipswich ware as well as Thetford-type wares. This group of sites includes those settlements which were re-colonising the heavier boulder-clay areas in Bredfield and Debach parishes as well as the lost vills of the Domesday Book. The lost vills never achieved parish status and are usually situated close to parish boundaries, that is halfway between the (earlier) Middle Saxon settlements from which they must have originated. Good examples of these lost vills in south-east Suffolk are Bing, in Pettistree parish and Wilford, in Bromeswell parish. The Middle and Late Saxon settlement pattern, shown on Fig. 8, within the survey area clearly demonstrates the advantages of a good blanket cover of a large block of land with a clearly defined ceramic tradition in order to come to grips with growth and change over time. From the well established seventh and eighth century sites close to churches in the larger parishes a phase of population growth and pressure on resources can be clearly seen in the ninth and tenth centuries. In the latter period a phase of settlement expansion, noted above, occurred and this growth saw the first, obvious, use of particularly dry heathland and heavy boulder-clay areas in the post-Roman period; that is, expansion into areas which were not first-choice settlement zones in the Early to Middle Saxon period and areas which often came to be seen as marginal by the period of rural depopulation in the thirteenth and fourteenth centuries.

The broad framework of settlement change and growth for south-east Suffolk outlined above clearly shows that East Anglia has the archaeological potential for an understanding of the development of an Anglo-Saxon king-dom. However, the project cannot end satisfactorily at this survey stage. Now that numerous Early, Middle and Late Saxon sites have been located and characterised, the model of settlement change and growth needs to be tested and refined through more detailed survey and sample excavation. Within the research design for the project this stage of the survey was treated separately as it should follow on from the initial fieldwork; but in practice it has been necessary to examine some sites in more detail as the opportunity arose.

The parish of Rendlesham, which is 6 kilometres to the north of Sutton Hoo, has always been of particular interest to Anglo-Saxon archaeologists since it is mentioned as a royal site by Bede. Other factors which have reinforced this interest include the dedication of the parish church to St Gregory and the early nineteenth century discovery of a cremation cemetery at Hoo Hill, within the parish. After the discoveries at Sutton Hoo in 1939, attention was re-focused on Rendlesham as a royal site but it was not until the winter of 1981/82 that any of the parish was systematically fieldwalked (by Tom Loader). All the available arable fields close to the River Deben and near the parish church were exam-ined in detail and an extensive pottery-scatter was located in one of the areas predicted in 1948 by Bruce-Mitford as a possible settlement site (1948, 246). This area is just to the north of St Gregory's church on a spur of land that has commanding views of the Deben valley. The site is of considerable size and is multi-period with evidence of prehistoric, Romano-British, Anglo-Saxon and later activity. For the Early Anglo-Saxon period the pottery-scatter covers 3 to 4 hectares, while the spread of Middle Saxon Ipswich ware covers nearly 15 hectares. While the pottery-scatter is not dense, its sheer size does put Rendle-sham into a special category within the survey area. Of the other Ipswich ware scatters located, the next largest is in Sutton parish and is 5 to 6 hectares in extent while the majority are in the 1 to 3 hectare size-range. These compari-sons are made between sites which have all been fieldwalked using the same methods, highlighting the value of a systematic and consistent approach to the

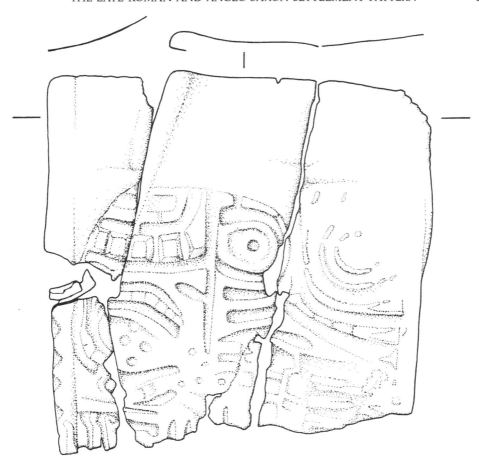

Figure 9. Fragment of repoussé decorated copper-alloy sheet metal from Rendlesham. The site is County SMR No. RLM 011

material in the field. Therefore Rendlesham would stand out in the hierarchy of Anglo-Saxon sites on size alone even if there were no other indicators of its importance. The site would also stand out because it goes against the trend for a settlement shift in the seventh century which is seen on the majority of Anglo-Saxon settlement sites. Continuity through the seventh century is naturally of particular interest given Rendlesham's close royal connections over this period.

An opportunity arose in 1982 to examine a small part of the area within the large pottery-scatter at Rendlesham prior to the erection of a barn. The small-scale excavation covered an area of 300 square metres and it revealed two small ditches of Middle Saxon date, with Ipswich ware, and a few later Medieval features (Martin et al. 1982, 235). The excavation, therefore, confirmed the Middle Saxon settlement evidence shown by the pottery-scatter located during fieldwalking. The excavated area probably being peripheral to the main Anglo-Saxon activity areas. Of particular interest was the recovery of a piece of scrap copper alloy sheet metal from one of the Middle Saxon ditches. When found, the fragment of sheet metal was folded over and it has been opened up for study. As Fig. 9 shows, the find is a fragment of repoussé decorated sheet metal, possibly part of the decorative binding from a bucket or similar vessel. The great interest in this small fragment of sixth or early seventh century metalwork is its similarity to another fragment of repoussé decorated sheet metal found at Sutton Hoo in the 1960s (Webster 1980, 30). Not only does the fragment from Rendlesham confirm late sixth or early seventh century activity on the site, it also provides yet another link between the royal cemetery at Sutton Hoo and the probable royal settlement at Rendlesham.

As this brief outline of Roman and Anglo-Saxon settlement patterns in south-east Suffolk demonstrates, the survey in the Deben valley has achieved its initial goal of locating and characterising Early, Middle and Late Saxon sites. The next stage of creating a settlement hierarchy within a coherent chronology is also well under way. The fieldwork results from the survey area form a solid data-base in which the sub-region of south-east Suffolk can be seen as one of the major stepping-stones towards an understanding of the growth and development of the kingdom of East Anglia. Apart from the information gained from work at Rendlesham, which is potentially of the very highest status, the survey appears to have located evidence from various levels of the Anglo-Saxon settlement hierarchy. It is only through further, systematic work on sites representing all of these levels of Anglo-Saxon society that a fuller understanding of the social and economic changes that occurred between the fifth and tenth centuries is going to be achieved. The south-east Suffolk survey also demonstrates how East Anglia is one of the few regions in the country which has the archaeological potential to answer these questions. To take Anglo-Saxon archaeology forward over the next fifty years from the basis laid over the last half-century almost certainly means a major commitment to systematic survey, excavation and research in at least one area. The results from south-east Suffolk clearly indicate that East Anglia has a very strong case in favour of being this selected research area.

ACKNOWLEDGEMENTS

I would like to thank the following who have assisted in the production of this paper: Leslie Webster and Stanley West for commenting on the copper alloy find from Rendlesham, Donna Wreathall for drawing the copper alloy find, Henry Skinner for drawing the other figures, Jude Plouviez for examining Roman pottery from the survey area, Kath Simpson for typing this and Keith Wade for doing so much to initiate this project and for examining large quantities of fieldwalked pottery.

3

Snape Anglo-Saxon Cemetery: The Current State of Knowledge

WILLIAM FILMER-SANKEY

Introduction

In 1984 I published a paper entitled 'The Snape Anglo-Saxon cemetery and ship burial: the current state of knowledge' (Filmer-Sankey 1984) containing a number of confident statements on the character and state of preservation of the site which subsequent excavation proved to be wholly incorrect! In this present paper I have attempted not only to put right these previous errors, but also to avoid similar pitfalls by separating knowledge of the site from the wider deductions that may be based on that knowledge. Accordingly, I shall begin by describing what has been found in the excavations that have taken place on the site between 1827 and 1990. This will be followed by a section of interpretation, in which more general deductions will be put forward, not only about the overall character of the cemetery, but also about its relationship to Sutton Hoo. These interpretative sections may well need revision, particularly if the anticipated further excavation at Snape takes place, but are nevertheless worth including.

Location

The Snape Anglo-Saxon cemetery lies 17 kilometres north-east of Sutton Hoo, in the extreme north-east corner of the modern parish of Snape (TM 4059). The river Alde flows 2.5 kilometres to the south and the North Sea at Aldeburgh is 7 kilometres to the east (Fig. 10).

The site today lies beneath arable fields, a house and rough garden, and a road. Until this century, however, it was part of a substantial block of acid Sandlings Heathland which stretched from Snape to Aldeburgh.

Before the planting of woodland it is probable that both the river Alde and the sea would have been visible from the cemetery, as would Iken, thought to be the site of St Botolph's monastery of *Icanho* (West, Scarfe and Cramp 1984).

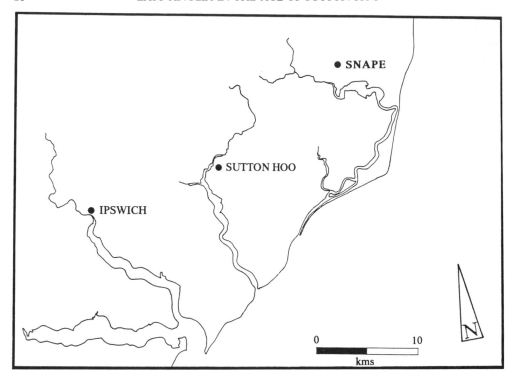

Figure 10. The location of the Snape Anglo-Saxon cemetery

Excavations 1827–1972

The first recorded excavation at the site took place in 1827. In this year, according to a letter in *The Field* of March 1863, seven or eight gentlemen, reported to be Londoners, opened several barrows and found 'quantities of gold rings, brooches, chains, etc.'. From Snape, they moved on to a tumulus on Blaxhall common and subsequently they and their activities disappear from the records.

In 1862 a more systematic and better recorded excavation was carried out by the then landowner, Septimus Davidson (Davidson 1863; Francis 1863a, b; Hele 1870, 24–29). According to Davidson and his colleagues, the site (which was then heathland) consisted of a group of nine or ten mounds. Of these, five or six were described as 'large' and lay in two lines on either side of the main Aldeburgh road (A1094). The largest was approximately 25.5 metres in diameter and stood approximately 2 metres tall (Francis 1863a, 61), though it was clear to the excavators that all the mounds had originally been much taller. The remaining four or five mounds were smaller, 'some no more than 6–7 feet in diameter' (Davidson 1863, 177).

Septimus Davidson excavated the three large mounds owned by him to the north of the road which were being damaged by passing traffic. In the first two he found no traces of a grave, despite digging deep into the natural sand. In the third and largest mound, which had a diameter of 22 metres and a height of 1.7 metres, he came upon 'a complete layer of pieces of iron, encased with wood' (Hele 1870, 26), which he recognized as the remains of a boat. Septimus Davidson's engraving of the ship was the first plan of a boat-burial to have been published (Müller-Wille 1970, 9) and his skill in both excavating and recording the ship is in marked contrast to the activities of the anonymous diggers at Sutton Hoo just two years earlier (Hoppit 1985).

Our knowledge of the Snape ship derives from Septimus Davidson's plan, from the three accounts of the excavation and from the surviving rivets and other ironwork in Aldeburgh Museum. The most reliable version of the plan is a watercolour in the library of the Society of Antiquaries, which must have been done either during or very shortly after the excavation, and which forms the basis for the published engraving, to which extra (not always correct) details have been added.

The ship was of clinker-built and riveted construction, at least 14 metres in length and with a beam of 3 metres. The watercolour plan shows a transom stern, but the accounts refer to each row of rivets 'terminating with two bolts lying parallel with each other, one at the stem, the other at the stern' (Davidson 1863, 181). This implies that the ship was (as one would expect) 'double-ended'. The rivets were spaced at approximately 140 millimetre intervals and, if the watercolour is accurate, there were nine strakes a side. The surviving rivets in Aldeburgh Museum are of the usual type, with domed heads and diamond roves. In addition, there are fragments of a metal strip, at least 300 millimetres in length, which appears to have been riveted vertically to the outside of the hull. This could be interpreted as a chain plate to hold the shrouds of a mast, though metal fittings of this type are not known until later (McGrail 1987, 229).

The ship lay east-west (Hele 1870, 26) and the grave contained within it had probably been robbed, as the 1862 excavators noted that the mound showed clear signs of earlier digging. Some gravegoods nevertheless remained and allow some deductions about the grave's character. Two iron spearheads (recently relocated among the ironwork in Aldeburgh Museum) were found within the mound above the level of the boat and if, as seems likely, they derive from the robbed grave, a male burial is suggested (Bruce-Mitford 1974, 126). The remaining finds apparently lay either in the centre or towards one end of the floor of the ship. High status is indicated principally by a magnificent gold finger-ring, which was found while shovelling out sand from the base of the ship.

The Snape ring (now in the British Museum) is a superb example of Germanic craftsmanship. A Roman onyx gemstone, portraying the standing figure of Bonus Eventus (Happy Outcome) has been set in a massive hoop, its wide shoulders decorated with granules and beaded and twisted wire (Bruce-

Mitford 1974, 123–4). The combination of granules and hook-and-eye on the shoulders gives a zoomorphic effect (Müller-Wille 1968/9, 45).

Despite Bruce-Mitford's arguments to the contrary, there is little doubt that the Snape ring is of Continental, probably Frankish, workmanship and of early-mid sixth century date. This is indicated not only by the closest parallels of form and decoration (the rings from Krefeld-Gellep gr. 1782 and Lorsch) but also by the fact that Germanic settings of Roman intaglios are reasonably common on the continent but unknown in Anglo-Saxon England (Filmer-Sankey 1990b; Pirling 1974, 61–8; Roth & Wamers 1984, 137).

The evidence from the Continent suggests that such rings were used as signets for sealing documents. Gold rings occur only in graves of Christlein's highest status groups, *Qualitatsgruppen* C and D (Christlein 1973, Abb. 11).

Another indication of high status is the glass claw-beaker from the grave. It belongs to Evison's type 3c, which she dates to the mid-sixth century (Evison 1982a, 48).

The ring and the claw-beaker enable no more than a very tentative *terminus post quem* of c.550 to be given to the burial of the ship.

Further finds were made by the 1862 excavators, but these have since disappeared. They included 'a mass of human hair, about the covering of one head [. . .] dark dirty red [. . .] wrapped in a cloth of some kind' (Francis 1863a, 62). This has been identified not as human hair but as a shaggy cloak, similar to those from Sutton Hoo and Broomfield (Bruce-Mitford 1974, 117). There were also some fragments described as 'jasper' and a solitary fragment of blue glass, said to have been thicker and more opaque than the claw beaker (Francis 1863a, 75).

While digging the three mounds, the 1862 excavators also encountered a number of intact urned cremation-burials and further urns were found when, after digging the mounds, the area around them was 'double dug' (Francis 1863b). More than 40 urns, all but one of them Anglo-Saxon, were found in this way and some survive in Aldeburgh Museum. The exception is a Bronze Age collared urn which was found, upside down and containing burnt bone, during the excavation of the ship burial mound.

The 1862 excavation caused a flurry of excitement. Two of the three accounts of the find were published within a year and produced a flood of comment. Links were made with the last stand of Boadicea, with Druidical sacrifices and with the Vikings. Thereafter, however, serious consideration ceased and by the 1920s the owner was telling visiting schoolgirls that the ship contained a 7 foot Viking in full armour! A house was built on the site in the 1920s, when more urns were found, and the heathland was ploughed up in the 1940s and 50s so that, by 1960, only one of the barrows was still visible.

Despite the general neglect and lack of interest, the site was still remembered. Basil Brown visited Aldeburgh Museum while excavating mound 2 at Sutton Hoo in 1938 and seems to have been influenced by the transom stern of the Snape boat in his interpretation of the mound 2 boat (Bruce-Mitford 1974,

149–51). In 1952, Rupert Bruce-Mitford, having found the missing ring, published an important paper on the site (reprinted and up-dated in Bruce-Mitford 1974, 114–40).

In 1970 a dowser proved his skill by finding a single urn (Owles 1970, 103). Two years later, a service trench was put down the main road which traverses the site, cutting through the segment of a ring-ditch and producing nine intact cremation burials. Of these, seven were urned, one was in a thin-walled bronze dish and one was unurned (West and Owles 1973).

Excavations 1985–90

If the excavation of the Sutton Hoo ship burial had done much to eclipse the Snape ship, it was clear, nevertheless, that Snape continued to have an important role, if only as a point of comparison. It was clear also that much remained unknown about the site, in particular its size, the location of most of the barrows and its state of preservation. Knowledge of the site to date had been derived from a series of scattered excavations of differing scale and skill, so that there was a need for a coherently planned programme to provide more reliable data (Fig. 11).

The imperfect nature of information about the site was only emphasised by the failure of an attempt in 1985 to answer all the outstanding questions with a series of fourteen 3 x 3 metre trenches (Martin et al. 1986, 154–5). The strategy was based on the assumption that the site was principally a Spong-Hill-type cremation cemetery, with densely-packed urns which would be easily located in small trenches (Filmer-Sankey 1984). The discovery of a flat inhumation grave immediately threw doubt on this assumption. The problem was further compounded by the failure of field-walking to locate any surface traces. Magnetometer and Resistivity surveys were also tried, but proved unable to locate grave cuts.

It was therefore decided that a two stage process of excavation was needed. The first stage (1986–8) was to gain a clear understanding of the character of the cemetery and this was achieved by the total excavation of an area of 17 x 20 metres in the field adjacent to the assumed site of the 1862 ship burial. This area produced some seventeen cremation and twenty-one inhumation burials, with a density of one per 21.45 metres^2 and one per 16.3 metres^2 respectively (Fig. 12). One of the inhumation-burials was in a small boat (Filmer-Sankey 1990a) but in other respects the graves were all, at first sight, typically pagan Anglo-Saxon with an affluent, though hardly outstanding, selection of grave-goods.

The second stage (1989–90) was to use the information on character and density gained from the 17 x 20 metres area to devise a strategy to fix the limits of the cemetery. A total of eighteen 2 metre wide trenches, oriented N-S, were positioned around the assumed edges of the cemetery and excavated to the top of the natural sand. An empty trench was to be assumed to lie outside the site.

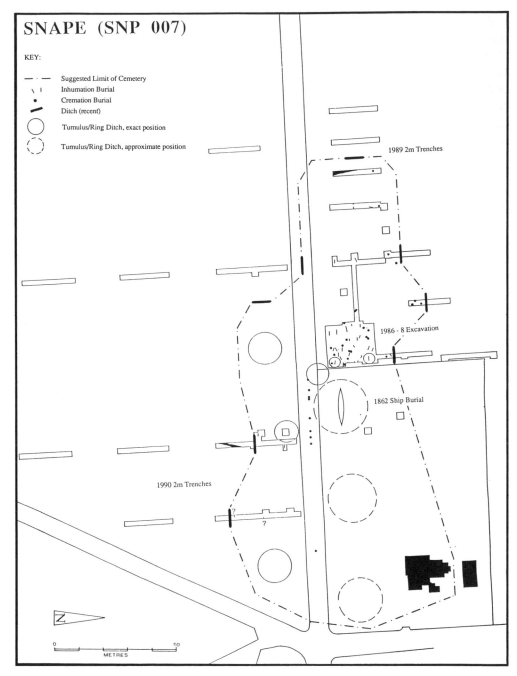

Figure 11. Site plan, showing the locations of the 1985–90 excavations and the suggested limits of the cemetery

Both stages of the 'Evaluation' of the cemetery provided information on its state of preservation, which was found to vary widely from perfect to very seriously damaged, depending on current landuse. The crucial factor in the survival of the cremation burials is a layer of pale grey sand sandwiched between the base of the ploughsoil and the underlying natural sand. The cremation burials are found within this layer, while the inhumation graves have been cut through it; from this it is assumed that the layer represents the remains of the Anglo-Saxon topsoil, which has been truncated by ploughing. Its thickness varies from 300–0 millimetres, corresponding to undulations in the underlying natural sand. These undulations would previously have been matched by humps and hollows on the surface of the heathland, but these have been completely erased by 40–50 years of ploughing.

The evaluation also showed that plough and subsoiler damage to the site is continuing, exacerbated by soil erosion of the light land. In some areas, ploughing is threatening the bases of the inhumation graves. Yet a further problem of modern agriculture is the neutralisation of the natural acidity of the soil through the repeated application of lime-based fertilizers. It is feared that these chemicals, which reach down to 0.9 metres beneath the surface, may be damaging the sand-silhouettes and other organic remains which have so far been preserved through the natural acidity of the soil.

The Snape Historical Trust, in co-operation with English Heritage and the Suffolk County Council, is currently devising a management plan which, with a mixture of excavation and preservation, will ensure the future of the site.

Extrapolations and Discussion

The 1985–90 evaluation of the cemetery was carefully designed to answer the outstanding problems of size, character and preservation. It is estimated that a sample of approximately 6.5% of the site has been examined. This work is therefore a far more reliable basis for wider deductions about the site than that which was available in 1985 (Fig. 11).

The Snape Anglo-Saxon cemetery appears to have had an east-west dimension of approximately 200 metres and a north-south dimension of approximately 70 metres. This compares with 90 x 70 metres at Spong Hill and 140 x 70 metres at Mucking Cemetery II (Selkirk 1975, 75). The main axis of the cemetery lies at an angle to the modern road, which may originally have followed its southern edge.

The ratio of cremation to inhumation burials is approximately 1:1 and, if the grave density remains constant throughout the site, there would have been approximately 1200 graves. This compares with more than 3,000 at Spong Hill and nearly 800 at Mucking Cemetery II.

The exact or approximate position of nine tumuli is now known, two of which (both small) were excavated in 1986–8 (Fig. 12). It is not known to what

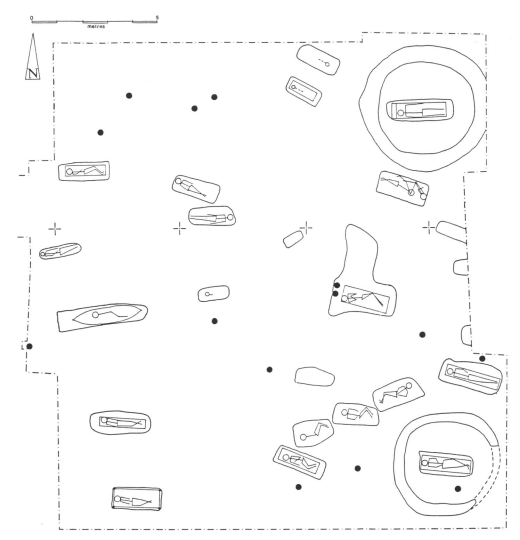

Figure 12. Plan of the 1986–8 excavated area. The black dots are cremation burials

extent these nine correspond with the nine – ten tumuli said to have been visible in 1862, so that further tumuli may remain to be rediscovered. The known mounds group along the southern and eastern edge of the cemetery with the 'flat' inhumation and cremation graves spreading out to the north and west.

The excavated areas have produced no evidence to suggest a spatial division between the inhumations and cremations, such as occurs at Spong Hill. The two rites seem to have been completely intermixed, as at Mucking Cemetery II and there is stratigraphic evidence for inhumation and cremation being in contemporary use for at least part of the time.

The area excavated has not been large enough for any horizontal stratigraphy to be observed, while there are no cases of vertical stratigraphy caused by intercutting graves. Indeed, great care seems to have been taken to avoid disturbing earlier graves (Fig. 12). Dating of the excavated graves is therefore dependent on typology-based dating of the gravegoods. The problems of this approach have been emphasised by Hills (Hills et al. 1984, 13–15). Nevertheless, in the opinion of Dr Stanley West, a number of the cremation-urns date to the fifth century whilst others are of sixth and even seventh century date. The excavated inhumation graves all appear to date to the second half of the sixth or early seventh century.

It is possible to see the ship-burial, with its *terminus post quem* of approximately 550, as the 'founder grave' of a phase of inhumation burials in a pre-existing cremation cemetery. This would parallel, albeit at a later date, the situation at Spong Hill as interpreted by Böhme (Böhme 1986, 542 & Abb. 59).

The original focus for the cemetery may have been provided by a Bronze Age barrow, the possible source of the collared urn found in 1862. It is of course also possible that others of the known tumuli are Bronze Age in date. The 1862 ship burial appears to have swamped the existing Bronze Age barrow and this may have been done deliberately (Bradley 1987). It is likely that the choice of a barrow visible from both the river and the sea was also deliberate, recalling the desire of the dying Beowulf to be buried where his mound could be seen by passing ships. The use of Medieval church towers as navigational marks on an otherwise featureless Suffolk coast (Arnott 1955, 25) may be no more than the continuation of a pre-Christian tradition.

In addition to wider deductions about the nature of the Snape Anglo-Saxon cemetery, the 1985–90 excavations have also given new insights into the detail of pagan Anglo-Saxon burial rite. A remarkable feature has been the variety of burial rite that has been observed in both the cremation and the inhumation graves.

In the inhumation graves this variety manifests itself mainly in the containers which have been used to bury the body. Traces of these containers, in every case of wood or another organic substance, have been preserved by soil conditions which are very similar to those at Sutton Hoo. Sand silhouettes, for example, occur at both sites. The containers usually survive as dark stains within the pale grey backfill of the grave and are often visible from a high level. At the same time, the sandy stone-free nature of the soil enables highly detailed recording so that complete reconstruction in three dimensions is often possible.

Of the twenty-one inhumation graves excavated in the 17 x 20 metre area, six were placed directly into the earth. There were six coffins, one of which had been completely charred before burial. There is no evidence for any of the coffins having lids and, in one case, positive evidence that there had been no lid as a shield had been propped up against the inner face of the coffin. Two of the coffins had small compartments above the head.

Three bodies had been placed on full-length biers and there were several cases where the bier appears to have been only half-length.

The boat grave excavated in 1988 contained a 3 metre logboat, with a beam of 0.7 metres, and distinctive 'fins' at bow and stern. The sand silhouette within the boat was very poorly preserved but may have been that of an adolescent, buried with a pair of drinking(?) horns (remarkably preserved despite the absence of metal fittings), a small knife and an iron buckle and stud (Filmer-Sankey 1990a).

In one larger than normal grave, four posts were visible at the corners. Dark brown stains around the edge of the grave cut were initially interpreted as the wooden walls of a chamber. However, approximately 200 millimetres above the base of the grave, they suddenly curved in and seem best interpreted as organic hangings of some sort (bark, skin or textile) which had been draped down the sides and over the base of the grave. The body had either been laid on a bier or wrapped in a similar organic 'blanket'.

Soil-stains occasionally indicate other objects that have been placed into the grave, the most intriguing of which was a stain bearing a striking resemblance to the 'fin' on the bow/stern of the logboat in the boat grave. This was observed about half way down the fill of an inhumation grave which, at the bottom, contained a female in a coffin. It is suggested that this may have been either part of a boat or a model boat, which had been placed into the grave during backfilling. If this is correct, then it is an example in miniature of the practice of burial underneath a boat, better known from Sutton Hoo mound 2 and from Hedeby (Carver and Evans 1989, 7–11; Müller-Wille 1976).

A further variation in burial rite was the placing of pieces of charred wood in four graves. This could be done either before the body was put in or during the process of backfilling. Normally, only one or two pieces, small 'planks' of approximately 400 millimetres in length, were used but in one grave whole branches up to 1.2 metres in length were placed throughout the backfill. In no case was there any trace of burning having taken place within the grave.

There appear to be three basic body positions: extended, feet parallel; extended, feet crossed; and flexed. In one grave a normally laid-out female was overlain by a body which appears to have been thrown carelessly into the grave. Although there was no evidence for 'human sacrifice', the relationship between a correctly buried body and casually disposed of body is reminiscent of Sewerby grave G41/49 (Hirst 1985, 38–40) and, on a larger scale, of the relationship between the burial in Sutton Hoo mound 5 and the flat graves around it (Carver 1990, fig. 2).

The rite of cremation burial is often assumed to be boringly uniform. However, a similar variety can be glimpsed. In addition to the usual urned and unurned cremations, the 1972 sewer trench produced a cremation which had been placed in a bronze bowl, wrapped in a cloth. Remains of similar burials have, of course, been found in mounds 4, 5, 6 and 18 at Sutton Hoo.

Work is currently in progress on a Snape feature which consists of a spread of burnt bone, fragmentary pottery vessels and burnt gravegoods; it may represent the remains of a cremation pyre, similar to those identified in the Roman Iron Age and Early Medieval Saxon cemetery of Liebenau (Carnegie and Filmer-Sankey forthcoming; Häβler 1990).

Although the excavated sample at Snape is too small for any patterns to emerge, there can be little doubt that this variation in inhumation and cremation burial is not random. Rather, it reflects a series of clearly defined choices (cremation or inhumation, type of container, position of body, inclusion of charred wood, etc.) which had to be made as part of the burial ritual. These choices must reflect first and foremost the religious beliefs of the buriers and the buried. Since the little available written evidence for pagan Anglo-Saxon belief points to numerous deities worshipped in numerous ways (Mayr-Harting 1972, 22–30), the variety is hardly surprising.

Variations in religious belief can be accounted for in several ways. They could result from changes over time or reflect individual or family preference for a specific family of gods, as has been suggested by Crumlin-Pedersen to account for the boat graves of Slusegård, which are strikingly similar to that from Snape (Riek and Crumlin-Pedersen 1988, 151–2). Religious belief could be a signal of ethnic origin. It has been suggested that the cremation pyres of Liebenau, which have parallels in the Iron Age, are an exclusively Saxon phenomenon (Genrich 1981, 18). Boat graves and wrist clasps have been seen as a sign of Scandinavian origin (Hines 1984). Finally, religious belief might reflect current political concerns, in the way that Carver has suggested that Sutton Hoo represents a reaction to Merovingian Christianity by an emphasis on Scandinavian pagan practices (Carver 1989, 152).

The evidence from the restricted area of excavation at Snape does not favour any of these explanations over the others, although chronological change seems unlikely, in view of the restricted date range of the inhumations. What cannot be denied, however, is that the most striking differences between graves are caused by factors that have nothing to do with status. This is not to deny that status may be signalled by the contents or layout of a pagan Anglo-Saxon grave. However, any attempt to 'rank' individual graves will fail unless it has first taken full account of the more powerful signals of religious belief. The dangers of concentrating on status in Anglo-Saxon graves have been emphasised by several authors (Pader 1982; Fisher 1988). Their arguments, however, have had to depend mainly on the gravegoods. By providing the extra dimension of information on the containers and on other hitherto unnoticed variations, Snape emphatically confirms the need for a new approach to Anglo-Saxon cemeteries.

This discussion of the significance of the variety of burial ritual leads naturally into a consideration of the relationship between Snape and Sutton Hoo, where the variety of burial rite has also been commented on (Carver 1990a, 19).

That there must be a link between the two sites has been apparent ever since Basil Brown visited Aldeburgh Museum to view the finds in 1938. In addition to the shared rite of (rich) ship burial, there are some obvious similarities. They are similarly positioned on marginal heathland, in close proximity to a major East Suffolk estuary. Both survived as visible barrow cemeteries.

The recent excavations at both sites have done much to clarify this picture, both by emphasising the similarities and by drawing attention to hitherto unsuspected differences.

The most striking of the similarities is the parallel variety of burial rite. Carver has listed the principal rites found at Sutton Hoo as inhumation(?) burial in ship (mound 1), inhumation burial in (?) tray or dugout (mound 3), inhumation burial under ship (mound 2), cremation burial in bronze bowl (mounds 4, 5, 6, 18) and secondary, 'deviant' burials, including human sacrifice (mound 5) (Carver 1990a, table 2).

Carver sees this variety as one of the remarkable features of Sutton Hoo, yet all the variations just listed have also been recorded at Snape, albeit on a smaller scale.

A further similarity relates to the attitude of the Anglo-Saxon mound builders to existing Prehistoric earthworks. At Sutton Hoo, every effort seems to have been made to place the mounds astride the linear banks and ditches which criss-cross the site (Carver 1990, fig. 5). At Snape, as already discussed, the 1862 ship burial was probably positioned so as to swamp an existing Bronze Age mound.

The most striking difference is one of date. Whereas all the cremation graves at Snape belong to the fifth – early seventh centuries and the inhumations (including the ship burial) to the mid-sixth – early seventh century, those at Sutton Hoo appear all to be seventh century or later (Carver 1989, 150). Despite the difficulties of dating at both sites, Snape is clearly earlier.

The second difference concerns the nature of the excavated graves. Carver has suggested that Sutton Hoo contains only the graves of the elite or of those bound to them and that this fact distinguishes Sutton Hoo from the long-lived 'folk cemeteries' of the fifth and sixth centuries (such as Spong Hill) where graves of all ranks are intermingled (Carver 1990a, 19). Snape belongs clearly to the latter group.

Snape therefore shares characteristics with both the long-lived 'folk cemeteries' and the short-lived elitist burial ground of Sutton Hoo and may be seen as a link between the two (Carver 1989, 150). If Sutton Hoo is indeed a royal cemetery, then the 1862 ship burial (and the other mounds?) from Snape must belong to an intermediate stage in the establishment of the kingdom of East Anglia. They may, for example, mark the graves of a ruling group who had not yet broken free of dependence on a local tribal base.

As for the 'folk cemetery' element of the site, it is notable that its closest parallel of character and size is to be found not among the East Anglian cemeteries of Spong Hill and Morning Thorpe, but with East Saxon cemetery II at Mucking. This is not necessarily a coincidence, but may reflect the continuation of a long-lived link between south-east Suffolk and Essex. In the late Iron

Age, south-east Suffolk looked south to the Catuvellauni rather than north to the Iceni (Martin 1988, 68–72). If anything, the geographical element of this link would have been strengthened in the early Medieval period by the relative ease of sea communications between the deeply-penetrating estuaries of the south-east Suffolk and Essex coasts, in contrast both to the lack of such estuaries to the north and to the slow and cumbersome nature of land communication (Carver 1990b, 122 & fig. 15.3).

On account of Sutton Hoo, it is often assumed that the Sandlings of south-east Suffolk formed the core of the seventh century East Anglian kingdom. If Snape's similarity to Mucking does indicate a continuation of the link between south-east Suffolk and Essex, this assumption may well be incorrect. Instead it becomes necessary to explain why, by the time of the baptism of the East Saxon king Swidhelm at Rendlesham in the mid seventh century, the Sandlings belonged to the East Anglian rather than to the East Saxon kingdom.

In 1984 I suggested that the primary importance of Snape was as a point of comparison for Sutton Hoo (Filmer-Sankey 1984, 14). The excavations on the site since then have shown that, both through the general knowledge of its size and nature and through the detailed reconstruction of the complexities of Anglo-Saxon burial rite, Snape has a wider role as a site crucial to our understanding of early medieval East Anglia.

ACKNOWLEDGEMENTS

The excavations at Snape could not have taken place without the support of the landowner, Mrs Vernon-Wentworth, grant-aid from English Heritage and the Society of Antiquaries, the generosity of the Moncrieff and Scarfe Trusts and the efforts of the trustees of the Snape Historical Trust, in particular Mary Harrison. I am most grateful to Stanley West for his encouragement and inspiration and to Shirley Carnegie for providing much of the information upon which this paper is based. Sam Newton first raised the question of the visibility of the site from river and sea and Edward Martin that of the Essex connection.

4

A Chronology for Suffolk Place-Names

MARGARET GELLING

The chronology of English place-names has been the subject of much study since 1966, when John McNeal Dodgson published his famous article attacking the ancient belief that names of the Reading/Hastings type denoted the earliest Anglo-Saxon settlements. There had already been a challenge to the similarly venerable view which held that names referring to pagan gods or temples were evidence of a particularly early Anglo-Saxon presence (Gelling 1961), and from these challenges there followed a fundamental revision. The aim of this paper is to enquire into the chronology of Suffolk place-names in the light of this rethinking, and to offer some hypotheses concerning the types of settlement-name which are likely to have been established by the time of King Redwald.

The study is based on an analysis of the parish-names of Suffolk. With the exception of the first two groups discussed, the names have been arranged in sections according to their main component, which is technically known as the generic.

Wickham and associated names

John Dodgson's paper of 1966, which appeared in *Medieval Archaeology X*, was followed in the next issue of that journal by a paper (Gelling 1967) which presented evidence of close association between Romano-British settlements and names derived from the Old English compound *wīchām*, which has as its first element a derivative of the Latin word *vicus*. This paper was followed by a wider study of English place-names which contain words borrowed from Latin (Gelling 1977). One of the words considered was *camp*, which is a borrowing of Latin *campus*. Since Old English *feld* has exactly the same significance as *campus* this borrowing was not made for the purpose of filling a gap in the Old English vocabulary; and it is therefore suggested that when *camp* appears in English names it is echoing district-names which were once used by Latin speakers.

A marked characteristic of all the names discussed in Gelling 1977 is a tendency to cluster, and there are several instances of names containing *camp* which adjoin places called *wīchām*, one of these being in the part of Suffolk with which we are particularly concerned. Here we have not only the conjunction of the parishes of Wickham Market and Campsey Ash, but also the close proximity of the Roman town in Hacheston parish, which adjoins both of them. The Hacheston site is one of several Roman-British settlements lying in close proximity to *wīchām* names which have been discovered since the *wīchām* paper was published: these are listed in Gelling 1988: 245–7.

In addition to Wickham Market and Campsey Ash, Suffolk has Wickhambrook, Wickham Skeith and Bulcamp. These five names may fairly be considered to date from the earliest years of the English settlement.

There are two Suffolk names, Dunwich and Ipswich, in which *wīc* has its middle-Saxon sense of 'trading centre'.

Names in -*ingas*

If John Dodgson's chronology be accepted, place-names like Gipping ('followers of Gyppa') and Creeting ('followers of Crǣta') are more likely to have crystallised at the end than at the beginning of the Anglo-Saxon pagan period. There is, however, no objection to the hypothesis that groups of people calling themselves the *Crǣtingas* and the *Gyppingas* were flourishing in East Anglia from the very beginning of the English settlement. It is likely that some such groups adopted these names on the Continent or in the course of migration. But there is no need to assume that the transfer of the tribal names to the settlements of Gipping and Creeting took place at a very early date, or that these were the central settlements in the tribal territory. In many areas of southern and eastern England the archaeological evidence accords better with the hypothesis that tribal names were felt to be appropriate as names of relatively late settlements near the border of the tribal territory, where they would serve to distinguish the inhabitants from an immediately-adjacent different social group.

Until there is a detailed survey of Suffolk place-names it will not be possible to say with any conviction how many -*ingas* names the county has. The plural suffix -*ingas* is notoriously difficult to distinguish from the singular suffix -*ing*, which could be added to a man's name or to a word (noun or adjective) to give place-names meaning 'place associated with a man named x' or 'place characterised by x'. The distinction is clear if there are pre-Norman-Conquest spellinngs, but if documentation starts with Domesday Book or later it is desirable to have a considerable number of early spellings before assigning the name to one category rather than the other. The only documentation easily available for Suffolk names is that provided in Ekwall 1960. There is no doubt that Nedging (*Hnyddinge* c.995) is singular and that Barking (*Berchinges* c.1050) is plural. As regards other examples, the sparse documentation available suggests that Cowlinge, Exning, Gedding and Shimpling are singular, while Bealings, Creeting, Gipping and Swefling are plural.

Another complication in estimating the historical significance of -*ingas* names is that the plural suffix, like the singular -*ing*, is not exclusively used with personal names. It was also used as a way of designating the inhabitants of a place or district, and this usage continued throughout the Anglo-Saxon period. The people of the Danelaw, for instance, were called *Fifburgingas* 'men of the Five Boroughs', and the monks of Berkeley, Gloucestershire, were the *Berclingas*. Some instances of this usage in place-names are easy to detect. Nazeing, Essex, means 'promontory people', and Twyning, Gloucestershire, is 'people who live between the rivers'. In other examples it is more difficult to decide between a personal name and a word. One Suffolk -*ingas* name which may be based on a significant word is Bealings, close to Sutton. This could mean 'people of the funeral pyre' (as suggested in Copley 1988: 40), perhaps referring to a community which practised cremation in a predominantly inhumation culture.

In spite of the uncertainties surrounding -ing names in Suffolk, those which are clearly plural probably do relate to social units, and these groups were probably also administrative units. A wider picture of such an organisation in early Suffolk is provided by the much more numerous names in which a habitative or topographical generic is qualified by the genitive of one of these group names. The number and distribution of these suggest that in the time of Redwald the whole of his kingdom was partitioned among groups known as 'followers of x' or 'dwellers at x'. Sixteen of these -*inga*- names have *hām* as generic, and this is the next place-name element to require discussion.

Names in -*hām*

There are good reasons for regarding *hām* as the habitative term which was most favoured in the earliest years of English name-giving in some parts of the country. It is the commonest habitative element in names which were recorded by A.D.730 (Cox 1976). Place-names containing *hām* in the Midlands and East Anglia were the subject of a detailed study by Barrie Cox in 1973. They are very much more numerous in East Anglia than in the Midlands, and in Suffolk there appears to be a spatial relationship between -*hām* names and the pagan cemeteries of the north-west and the south-east of the county.

The number of -*hām* names in Suffolk is at least eighty, and in this county there is little reason to suspect that some of the apparent examples may contain the topographical term *hamm*, confusion with which presents problems in some other counties. Sixteen of the -*hām* names contain -*inga*-, and all but one of these are believed to have a personal name as first element. The exception, Cretingham, is one of the examples which lie in the south-east of the county.

Cretingham is considered to mean 'homestead of the dwellers in a gravelly place'. The other south-eastern *-ingahām* names, Aldringham, Framlingham and Letheringham, are 'homestead of the people of Aldhere/Framela/Leodhere'. According to the chronology proposed by Cox, these *-ingahām* names would be slightly later formations than compounds of *hām* without *-inga-*. Of the considerable number of Suffolk names in this last category half, at least, have personal names as first element, and with very few exceptions these are monothematic, as in Shottisham, 'Scēot's homestead'. Single-theme personal names like *Scēot* are considered to have been favoured in the earliest years of the Anglo-Saxon period, whereas dithematic names like *Aldhere* and *Lēodhere* were commoner at a later date. A third type of personal name is the hypocoristic one, formed by the addition of suffixes like *-el* and *-uc* to monothemes. *Framela* is of this kind, and so is *Rendel*, conjectured to be present in Rendlesham. Diminutive endings are, however, added to nouns as well as to personal names, and Rendlesham could be 'homestead of the little shore' rather than 'homestead of a man named Little Shield'.

The distinction between personal names and significant terms in qualifying elements is fraught with difficulty. We are on firmer ground, however, in considering the administrative status of the Suffolk places with *-ingahām* and *-hām* names. It is a noteworthy fact that with very few exceptions (such as Benningham in Occold and Loudham in Pettistree) they are names of parishes, and this constitutes a strong argument for considering them to belong to a primary stratum of English name-giving. It seems likely that most of the *-hām* names of East Anglia were in use in Redwald's time. They are widely distributed over the area, and well-represented in south-east Suffolk.

Names in *-tūn*

The only generic which outnumbers *hām* in Suffolk parish-names is *tūn*, which also means 'settlement'. This is overwhelmingly the commonest English place-name element, but there is good evidence that it did not become popular as a place-name-forming term until the middle of the eighth century. In Barrie Cox's analysis of the 224 place-names recorded by A.D.730, there are only six which contain *tūn*. This indicates that while any particular example of a *tūn* name may legitimately be suspected of having equal antiquity with names in *-hām*, the great majority of them must be of later origin.

Postulation of a post-750 date for most *-tūn* names does not carry with it any suggestion that the settlements came into existence as late as that. There is evidence that when *-tūn* names became fashionable they replaced earlier names for ancient settlements. This evidence is only available for regions which have abundant pre-Conquest documentation, however, and the process cannot be observed in East Anglia. The problem of what was replaced by *-tūn* names in Suffolk cannot be explored here, but it can fairly be asserted that in King Redwald's time most of the settlements were known by other names.

There are documented instances in Berkshire and Wiltshire of -*tūn* names which have as first element the personal name of an identifiable landowner (Gelling 1978: 180ff). A possible association of a Suffolk -*tūn* name with a recorded individual occurs in Euston. The place-name means 'Efe's estate', and it is very likely to refer to the moneyer with the rare name *Efe* who was striking coins for King Beonna of East Anglia in the mid-eighth century (Archibald 1985). It is more likely that the other 'x's *tūn*' names, such as Hacheston, Brandeston, Hasketon, Levington, were formed in this 'manorial' context than that the eponymous Hæcci, Brant, Haseca and Leofa were among the earliest English settlers.

The-*tūn* names of south-east Suffolk include three which are 'directional', i.e. referring to a spatial relationship with another settlement. These are Easton, Sutton and Middleton. There is no direct evidence bearing on the date at which such names arose. Easton and Sutton, however, probably imply a subordinate status to a more important place, and Middleton suggests a stable settlement pattern, so these are probably not among the earliest English names. A -*tūn* name in south-east Suffolk which must be of relatively late origin is Kirton, which is a Scandinavianised form of *cyrice-tūn* 'church settlement'. Kirton cannot have had a Christian church in Redwald's time.

Other habitative terms

Parish-names ending in -*hām* and -*tūn* are so numerous in Suffolk that they leave little scope for other habitative terms to be well represented at this administrative level. There are, however, nine parish-names in -*worth*, and to these may be added *Beadriceswyrth*, the old name of Bury St Edmunds. There has not yet been a thorough study of Old English *worth* and its variants, but such evidence as is available suggests that its use in place-names belongs to the period after A.D.750.

Unlike *worth*, the generic *burh* 'fortified place' is well evidenced in names recorded by A.D.730. The word had various applications ranging from 'prehistoric fort' to 'manor house' and, in the late Anglo-Saxon period, 'town'. Burgh Castle near Yarmouth is one of the rare instances in which it refers to a Roman site, and Bury St Edmunds exemplifies the late sense 'town'. There are seven Suffolk parish-names with *burh* as generic. The meaning is open to discussion in Aldeburgh, Blythburgh, Burgh, Grundisburgh, Rumburgh and Sudbury. There is no apparent 'archaeological' reference to pre-English sites, and it would be reasonable to consider these names to refer to fortified sites of the early Anglo-Saxon period. Burgh and Grundisburgh adjoin.

The generic *stōw* occurs in Felixstowe, West Stow, Stowlangtoft and Stowmarket. Three of these were originally simplex names to which West-, -langtoft and -market were added. Felixstowe is a compound name with an obscure first element: it appears as *Filchestou* in thirteenth-century records and association with St Felix is probably a later development. Study of the whole corpus of names containing *stōw* (Gelling 1982) suggests that there is always something special about a settlement described by this term. The word means 'venue for a particular activity'. It is used for sites associated with saints, for secular meeting-places, and for markets. Unlike the related term *stoc* (which also appears in four Suffolk parish-names), *stōw* is very rarely used in minor place-names, and there is reason to believe that it always denotes a place of special importance.

The generics *stōw* and *stoc* belong to a group of words which are capable of being translated 'place'. Another member of this group is *stede*, which occurs in twelve parish-names in Suffolk. There is a comprehensive study of *stede* (Sandred 1963), which establishes that when used freely in compound place-names (as opposed to being part of a compound appellative like *cēapstede* 'market') it is likely to be of considerable antiquity. Names in -*stede* are concentrated in south-east England, and they are very frequently parish-names. In Suffolk, this last characteristic applies to twelve out of fifteen examples. These Suffolk parishes (Belstead, Boxted, Harkstead, Hawstead, Henstead, Linstead, Nettlestead, Polstead, Saxtead, Stanstead, Whepstead and Wherstead) are widely distributed in the county. Belstead, like Bealings, may refer to the practice of cremation.

Topographical names

Since the major revision of the 1960s and 1970s it has become an accepted hypothesis that many, perhaps most, of the earliest names coined by English speakers were of the type which defines a settlement by describing its situation without making any reference to the habitation. There is no question of such names being exclusively early; they were still being applied to new settlements at the very end of the Anglo-Saxon era. Recent studies have, however, made it possible to distinguish some topographical words which were particularly favoured at the beginning of the period.

Names containing ēg

In Barrie Cox's analysis of names recorded by A.D.730 the generic which occurs most frequently is Old English *ēg* 'island'. The ecclesiastical bias of the sources is partly responsible for this. Since they are concerned with saints and monasteries, these sources reflect the liking of early evangelists for island sites. Nevertheless, since *ēg* is not one of the commoner generics in the corpus of English place-names, its high score in early-recorded names must mean that it was used much more frequently before A.D.730 than after.

The characteristic use of *ēg* in place-names is for a sub-circular patch of slightly raised ground in a very wet area. The greatest concentration is to be found on the River Thames in the area centring on Oxford, Dorchester and Abingdon, where there is also a major concentration of very early Saxon burials. The term is not as frequent as this in Suffolk, but it occurs in six parish-names, and these may fairly be assumed to date from the earliest decades of the English settlement.

In the large parish of Eye, the central settlement has a classic *ēg* site on a round island made by the 100′ contour, with minor names like Moor Hall and Alder Carr indicating the nature of the surrounding land. Eye is the largest parish in its area, and ten surrounding parishes abut on its circumference. Bungay (probably an *-inga-* name) occupies the neck of a great loop of the River Waveney, presumably placed on a strip of firm ground in the narrow corridor available there. Bawdsey, one of two *ēg* names near Sutton, is surrounded by coastal marshes. The exact site of Campsey is uncertain. The village is now called Campsey Ash, but Ash was originally a separate settlement. Local knowledge would be needed for an evaluation of settlement topography, but the conjunction of Wickham Market, Campsey Ash and the Roman town in Hacheston has already been remarked on as suggesting that English place-names here were established at a very early date in the post-Roman period. Lindsey and Kersey, which adjoin each other west of Ipswich, are in territory which may have been much wetter in post-Roman times than it is now. Kersey has a high promontory site, and this use of *ēg*, though not common, can be paralleled elsewhere.

Names in *-ford*

There are twenty three parish-names in Suffolk which end in *-ford*, and the word is probably found in other names of lesser administrative status. This is the second commonest topographical generic in English place-names. The river-crossings referred to by *ford* fall into two distinct classes. There is a clear distinction between the majority, which are on small streams, and a smaller group which are on major rivers. In Suffolk, Stratford St Mary, Bramford, Blyford and Ufford refer to major river-crossings, and Orford may refer to a causeway across the marshes by the estuary of the River Alde. In Suffolk, as elsewhere, most ancient settlement-names in *-ford* refer, however, to crossings of very small streams, not associated with long-distance travel routes. It is a reasonable hypothesis that stream-crossings such as those at Marlesford, Cransford, Yoxford, Stratford and Chillesford (to take the south-eastern examples) would only be of interest to people in the immediate neighbourhood, and that they are likely to have given name to settlements at an early stage of the English take-over, before there were organised kingdoms in which larger considerations applied.

Names in *-field*, *-land* and *-æcer*

Suffolk has twenty nine parish-names in which the generic is Old English *feld* 'open land'. These are mostly to be found in a wide belt running north-east to south-west through the eastern part of the county, from Homersfield and Ringsfield near the Norfolk border to Westerfield and Waldringfield north and east of Ipswich. There are three adjacent parishes, Bradfield, Cockfield and Stanningfield, lying to the west of this belt, and other examples are scattered over the county. In the south east are Charsfield, Bredfield and Waldringfield, the last being adjacent to Sutton.

feld is a place-name generic which should be of particular interest to the landscape historian. It has been suggested that when it occurs in ancient settlement-names it denotes areas which were pasture land at the beginning of the Anglo-Saxon period but which were broken into by the plough as part of an early expansion of settlement (Gelling 1984: 238–9). In the country as a whole such names frequently occur on the outskirts of forest or at the junction of plain and hills. In some parts of Suffolk, however, it seems likely that heath or marsh was reclaimed to provide resources for these settlements.

At least six of the Suffolk parish-names in *-feld* have as their first component the genitive of a group-name in *-ingas*. The hypothesis that the use of *-ingas* in place-names belongs to a secondary stage of the English take-over fits with the hypothesis that *-feld* names indicate expansion of arable land in the sixth and seventh centuries.

Incursion of plough on pasture has also been postulated to explain settlement-names in *-land* and *-æcer*. The sense of both generics is likely to be 'newly-cultivated land' (Gelling 1984: 231). Suffolk has three parish-names in the first category - Kessingland, Shelland and Swilland – and one in the second – Benacre, which adjoins Kessingland, south of Lowestoft. Study of *land* and *æcer* in the whole country has led to the conclusion that both refer to arable land broken in at a relatively late date in the Anglo-Saxon period, perhaps mostly as late as the ninth or tenth centuries, though Kessingland ('newly-cultivated land of Cyssi's people') is likely to be earlier. Old English *erth* 'ploughland', a rare generic which occurs in the Suffolk names Cornard and Horringer, probably has the same significance as *æcer*.

Hills and Valleys

Hill-terms are not frequent in Suffolk settlement-names. The most desirable type of hill-site was designated by the Old English word *dūn*, but the sort of low hill shaped like an inverted bowl to which this word regularly applies in many parts of the country is not a common landscape feature in East Anglia.

The word *dūn* is more frequently used here of large areas of raised ground which provide the hinterland for a settlement. The clearest instance in Suffolk is Brandon ('broom down'), and Raydon and Thorndon also refer to extensive areas of ground above the 150' contour. Hawkedon occupies a promontory between streams, again not the typical *dūn* of other counties. Smaller hills were called *beorg* (if rounded) or *hyll* (if spiky), and these also are rare terms in Suffolk parish-names occurring only in Chedburgh, Finborough, Kettleburgh and Haverhill.

Promontories and hill-spurs have a distinctive place-name vocabulary. This does not figure largely in Suffolk, but mention should obviously be made of the word *hōh*, which is the origin of Hoo in Sutton Hoo. This term occurs in four parish-names, three of which – Hoo, Culpho and Dallinghoo – are in south-east Suffolk. The fourth, Wixoe, is in the south west. The spurs referred to in these Suffolk names are probably too slightly elevated to present the typical *hōh* shape visually, though a person walking along them could no doubt discern it through the feet. The typical shape is seen in more dramatic landscapes such as that along the north scarp of the Chilterns. Ivinghoe Beacon is a fine specimen. In profile a *hōh* rises to a peak and then falls sharply with a slightly concave curve. The word means 'heel', and the outline is that of the heel and instep of a person lying face down. The hill-spur at Sutton Hoo has been subjected to a great deal of surface disturbance and its original outline would be difficult to establish.

In Suffolk, valley-sites are probably more common than hill-sites for the positioning of villages. The usual Old English term for a long, curving valley was *denu*, and this is the generic of nine Suffolk parish-names. Wantisden, adjacent to Rendlesham, is a good example. A commoner term in this county, however, is Old English *halh*, which occurs in thirteen parish-names. These have the modern endings -hall, -all or -ale (but it should be noted that in Stradishall, Lawshall, Foxhall and possibly Ringshall the modern form -hall has developed from different generics, and Tunstall is Old English *tūnstall* 'farmstead').

The prevalence of *halh* in East Anglia is due to the low relief of the area. The Anglo-Saxons used the term to describe hollows which were not sufficiently well-defined to qualify for more specific valley terms. The characteristic use in Norfolk and Suffolk is for shallow recesses in the 50', 100' or 150' contours. Peasenhall, Kelsale, Benhall, Knodishall and Blaxhall lie fairly close together in east-central Suffolk, and in all these the reference is to slightly recessed sites. This is typical *halh* country. Ancient settlement-names which make simple statements of this kind about the physical setting of the habitation are likely to date from the earliest years of English speech in any area. There are a number of parish-names in south-east Suffolk to which this consideration applies but which do not fall into categories discussed here – Brightwell, Bromeswell and Debach, for example.

Woodland

The place-name term which is the soundest guide to ancient woodland is Old English *lēah*. This word has a range of meanings, from 'forest' to 'clearing in woodland' and, at the end of the Anglo-Saxon period, 'pasture'. Names in which *lēah* has this latest sense are not common, and they are fairly easily detected. In the vast majority of instances, whether the word means 'wood' or 'clearing' its occurrence in a place-name is an indication of woodland which the Anglo-Saxons recognised as ancient.

lēah is by far the commonest topographical term in English place-names, but (like *tūn*) it makes a very poor showing in the names recorded in the earliest records. It cannot have become fashionable in place-name formation until about A.D.750. There would be very few place-names in -*lēah* in King Redwald's time, but although such names are almost certainly of later origin they are probably a safe guide to areas which had been continuously wooded since the first coming of the English.

lēah is much less common in Norfolk and Suffolk than in counties to the west. There are twenty one Suffolk parish-names in which it is the generic. The sense 'clearing' may not always be the relevant one here. Where *lēah* names occur in large groups (as in north Warwickshire, for instance) the obvious translation is 'clearing', but where they are more widely distributed the word is more likely to have its earlier sense of 'wood'. In areas which were not well-provided with woodland, stands of trees would be preserved and exploited with care. It seems likely that -*ley* names in some parts of Suffolk refer to such ancient woods. The relevant parish-names in the south east of the county are Butley, Hemley, Hollesley, Otley, Shotley and Trimley. These are settlements now, but it is a reasonable hypothesis that in Redwald's time they were carefully preserved woods. Gedgrave, an adjacent parish to Butley, contains *grāf(a)* 'grove', which is likely to have been the Old English term for an area of coppiced woodland (Gelling 1984: 192–4). Kesgrave is another 'grove' in this part of the county.

Scandinavian and French names

Names in the Old Norse and French languages have an obvious *terminus post quem*: they must have originated long after the reign of King Redwald. The presence of some such names in south-east Suffolk supports other indications that expansion of settlement continued here up to and after the Norman Conquest.

There are at least twenty parishes in Suffolk with names which are wholly or partly Scandinavian. One of these, Eyke, lies between Sutton and Rendlesham. Eyke is from Old Scandinavian *eik* 'oak tree', and the fact that a single oak tree could serve as a marker for a settlement could be added to evidence noted above for scarcity of woodland. Other wholly or partly Scandinavian names occur along the east coast. Thorpe is the Old Norse term for a secondary settlement. Westleton has an Old Norse personal name as first element. Lowestoft ('Hlothver's dwelling') is a wholly Norse compound, and Barnby, Ashby and Lound are additional Norse names in the north-east corner of the county. Closer to Sutton are Nacton, south-east of Ipswich, and Kettleburgh, some twelve miles north, both of which contain Old Norse personal names.

Snape may well be an Old Norse name. The likeliest explanation of some north-country examples of this name is that they derive from a Scandinavian word *snap*, only recorded in Icelandic, where it means 'poor pasturage'. Since there were Scandinavian speakers in Suffolk this explanation is reasonable for the Suffolk name. In discussions of this place-name element the issue has been clouded by reluctance to associate some minor names in southern England with the northern ones. This has led to a belief in an Old English word *snæp* of unknown meaning: but it is possible that the Norse word became a loan-word in late Old English, and is ultimately responsible for southern as well as northern examples of Snape. The Norse word is probably the immediate origin of the Suffolk name, and here again we have evidence for late expansion of settlement.

In relation to Sutton Hoo studies the most important Scandinavian name in south-east Suffolk is *Stockerland*. This is a Domesday Book manor, and it is shown as a hamlet on a map of c.1630. The Domesday manor is believed to have comprised most of the north-western portion of Sutton parish (Warner 1984, 1985). As noted above, *land* can be either an Old English or a Scandinavian term for newly-broken-in arable. The first element of this name, which is a word meaning 'tree-stump', also exists in both languages, but in this case it is identified as Old Norse by the *-er-*, which is a reflex of Old Norse *-ar-*, a genitive singular or nominative plural ending. 'Newly-cultivated land where there are tree-stumps' is the etymology.

Evidence for even later expansion of settlement in south-east Suffolk is provided by the parish-name Boulge. This is a French topographical name, a rare phenomenon in England. It is Old French *bouge*, 'uncultivated land covered with heather'. The manor is described in Domesday Book, so the reclamation of this land must have happened soon after 1066. The shape of the parish is appropriate to an infill settlement. Capel St Andrew, also in Domesday Book, is from Norman French *capele* 'chapel'.

Conclusion

When the parish-names of south-east Suffolk are analyzed in the light of current assumptions about place-name chronology, the results suggest that some of the settlements – Bredfield, Charsfield, Waldringfield, Swilland and the six with names in -*ley* – are likely to have been established after Redwald's time. This is probably true also for the settlements with Scandinavian and French names. The use of the habitative term *tūn* in place-names dates for the most part from after Redwald's time, but -*ton* names probably replaced earlier ones belonging to settlements established much earlier than this naming fashion.

This part of Suffolk was well-populated and quite heavily cultivated in 1086, as can be seen from the mapping of Domesday statistics in Darby 1952. Professor Darby's discussion of the Domesday evidence for The Sandlings (p. 206) suggests a certain amount of surprise at the results of his analysis. Of the hundred of *Colneis*, which comprised the area south-west of Sutton, across the River Deben, he notes that 'its prosperity is a striking feature, as we have seen, the soil is locally very fertile.' The area of Wilford hundred, in which Sutton lies, had fewer plough teams but only a slightly lower density of population. Professor Darby points, however, to the fact that many of the Domesday settlements in The Sandlings declined in importance or disappeared in later times. This observation fits well enough with the hypothesis that there was an expansion of settlement in the eighth-eleventh centuries, perhaps taking exploitation of the land to a point from which decline was to be expected.

5

Beowulf and the East Anglian Royal Pedigree

SAM NEWTON

My purpose here is to reconsider the question of the origin of the Old English epic of *Beowulf* in relation to a reappraisal of the pedigree of Ælfwald, king of East Anglia during the first half of the eighth century.[1]

The unique manuscript of *Beowulf*, the British Library, Cotton Vitellius A.xv, was copied at an unknown English location between the last few years of the tenth and the end of the first decade of the eleventh centuries (Dumville 1988). The poem itself has been regarded by some scholars as a tenth-century work reflecting the interaction of English and Scandinavian culture in the aftermath of the Viking settlements of the late ninth century. I maintain, however, that independent linguistic points, together with comparative literary, historical, and archaeological considerations, collectively imply that *Beowulf* may have been composed in an Anglian kingdom during the eighth century (Newton, in press).

Its rich strands of Northern heroic legend, moreover, seem *not* to have been acquired from Scandinavian sources of the Viking period. This point is indicated initially by two related linguistic observations. First, as scholars have noted (Klaeber 1950, cxvii; Frank 1981, 123), the language of the poem lacks any demonstrable Norse loan-words such as we find in some of the Old English poetry which is datable to the tenth century. This seems curious in a tale which is set in the Northlands and which largely involves Danes, Geats, and Swedes. Second, the forms of the names of several of its Scandinavian heroes are not what we might expect if *Beowulf* was derived from ninth- or tenth-century Northern sources. For example, as they stand, the names borne by members of the Danish royal family, such as *Hrōðgār, Hrōþulf, Hrēðrīc* and *Hrōðmund*, appear to contain no evidence of any Norse sound-changes, yet runic evidence suggests that the forms of such names were contracting in

---

[1] Almost all of the points outlined herein are set out in more detail in my book, *The Origins of Beowulf and the pre-Viking Kingdom of East Anglia* (in press).

Scandinavia as early as the ninth century (de Vries 1962, *s.v. Hróarr, Hrólfr, Hroerekr* and *Hrómundr*). Other *Beowulf* examples include the names used for the Danish kingdom, *Scedeland* and *Scedenīg* (de Vries 1962, *s.v. Skáney*; Frank 1981, 124–125, n.8; and Fulk 1982, 343–344). Unless we are prepared to accept Professor Eric Stanley's assertion that they were transposed by a poet 'who was unusually good at comparative Germanic philology' (Stanley 1981, 207), the archaic accuracy of the spellings of these names implies that they are unlikely to have been transpositions from Viking Age Norse. A more reasonable explanation is that they stem from an ancestral English source and were committed to writing at an early date (Fulk 1982, 344–345).

If certain proper names in *Beowulf* are of early English origin, then some of the narrative material to which those names are bound might be of a similar antiquity. The epic is concerned with three early sixth-century Scandinavian dynasties: the Danish Scyldings, the Geatish Hreðlings and the Swedish Scylfings.[2] Although the hero of *Beowulf* is a Geatish Hreðling, at least on his mother's side (lines 373–375a), the poem shows the greatest interest in the Danish Scyldings. Their importance is apparent from the very beginning.

> Hwæt! wē Gār-Dena   in gēardagum,
> þēodcyninga   þrym gefrūnon,
> hū ðā æþelingas   ellen fremedon!
>
> '*Hwæt!* We have heard of the renown of the spear-
> Danes' folk-kings in days of yore, and of how those
> nobles achieved deeds of courage.' (lines 1–3)

As these lines state, the original audience of *Beowulf* is assumed to know already of the renown of the Danish *þēodcyningas*. As if to remind them, the legend of the eponymous founding-father of the dynasty, Scyld Scefing, is related (lines 4–52). We then hear how Scyld's son succeeded him (lines 53–55a), and how he in turn was succeeded by his grandson, *hēah Healfdene*, 'high Healfdene' (lines 56b–57a), who himself had *fēower bearn*, 'four bairns' – Heorogar, Hroðgar, Halga, and a daughter (lines 59–63). In this way, we are introduced to one of the poem's principal characters, the venerable King Hroðgar. The opening movement of *Beowulf* thus is structured on a genealogy of the Danish Scyldings (O.N. *Skjǫldungar*). Because the variously stated relationships between Scylding family-members throughout the poem are nowhere contradictory, we can reconstruct this genealogy as follows:

---

[2] This early sixth-century dating may be inferred from the poem's single externally verifiable event, the death in battle of the Geatish king Hygelac Hreðling. This was clearly an important event in the background of the poem as it is referred to five times (lines 1202–1214a; 2201b; 2354b–2366; 2493b–2508a; and 2910b–2921). If we may accept the authority of the sixth-century Frankish historian Gregory of Tours, Hygelac's fall may be dated to around the year 523 (Klaeber 1950, xxxix–xl; Magoun 1953; Magoun 1954; Storms 1970).

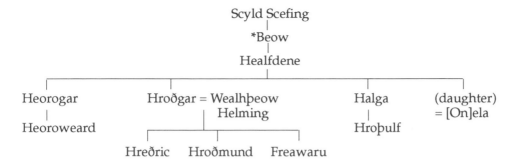

Genealogy also appears to have underpinned the later Northern account of the family, *Skjǫldunga saga*, as far as may be discerned from our only record of it, Arngrímur Joónsson's sixteenth-century Latin abstract of a lost, probably twelfth-century, Icelandic work (Benediktsson 1957–1959, 59–62; Guðnasson 1963, 314–317). *Skjǫldunga saga* appears to have been originally compiled by someone well-versed in the genealogical traditions of an Icelandic family which considered itself to be descended from the *Skjǫldungar* (Benediktsson 1957–1959, 63–65; Guðnasson 1963, 323–325). Similarly, *Beowulf* may have been composed by someone connected with an Old English family which numbered the *Scyldingas* among its forebears. In other words, the genealogical context of the poem may have been assumed rather than stated explicitly.

In order to try to explain the marked attention to Northern, especially Danish, dynastic affairs in *Beowulf*, Klaeber advanced the hypothesis that there may have been 'close relations, perhaps through marriage, between an Anglian court and the kingdom of Denmark, whereby a special interest in Scandinavian traditions was fostered among the English nobility' (Klaeber 1950, cxv). I have already pointed out that the archaic forms of several Scylding names in the poem imply that its Danish material may be of early English origin. There are also significant differences between the genealogical traditions of the Scyldings underpinning *Beowulf*, where the emphasis is on Hroðgar's branch of the family, and those of the *Skjǫldungar* in surviving Scandinavian sources, where the emphasis is on Halga and his son, Hroþulf (O.N. *Hrólfr*).[3] These differences imply that the former developed inde-

---

3 The principal Scandinavian sources in question are:

   (1) Arngrímur Jónssón's late sixteenth-century abstract of the lost, probably twelfth-century, *Skjǫldunga saga* (Benediktsson 1950–1957);

   (2) the early thirteenth-century *Gesta Danorum* of Saxo Grammaticus (Olrik and Raeder 1931), the second book of which contains its author's Latin version the *Bjarka-mál*, an Old Danish poem which may have originated in the tenth century, if not earlier; and

   (3) the probably fourteenth-century *Hrólfs saga kraka* (Slay 1960). For a conveniently translated edition of these and other Northern sources relevant to the study of *Beowulf*, see Garmonsway and Simpson 1960.

pendently of the latter; so if *Beowulf* was derived from, or influenced by, Northern sources during the Vịking period, we would expect its picture of the *Scyldingas* to be more in keeping with that of the *Skjǫldungar*. In that case, as Kemp Malone pointed out, 'Hroþulf, not Hroðgar, would have been the Danish king served by the hero' (Malone 1931, 149–150).

The suggestion is then that *Beowulf* was composed by someone well-versed in the genealogical traditions of a pre-Viking Anglo-Saxon nobility which considered itself to be descended from the Scyldings. As some of the poem's Danish names also occur in some surviving Old English royal genealogies, it might be possible to establish a clue as to the identity of that family. Scholars have often noted the possible relation of *Beowulf* to pedigrees pertaining to the dynasties of Mercia and Wessex, but its potential connection with East Anglian royal genealogy has yet to be closely considered.

The pedigree of King Ælfwald of East Anglia is preserved in the Anglian Collection of royal genealogies (Dumville 1976), the earliest surviving manuscript of which, the British Library, Cotton Vespasian B.vi, was probably copied in Mercia in the early ninth century (Dumville 1976, 24–25). Within the Anglian Collection, Ælfwald's pedigree can be seen to be grouped with those of Ine of Wessex (688–726) and Æþelberht II of Kent (725–762), the relative regnal dates of whom suggest that this group may have been originally compiled in 725 or 726 (Dumville 1976, 40, n. 2). If so, as Ælfwald appears to have ruled from around 713 until his death in 749 (Stenton 1959, 46), his pedigree can be seen to have been put into writing during his own reign. His interest in literacy is shown by the *Vita Sancti Guthlaci*, 'The Life of St Guthlac', which, as its author, Felix, tells us, was written at Ælfwald's behest (Colgrave 1956). Felix seems to make an implicit reference to his lord's pedigree when he states in his prologue that King Ælfwald 'rules by right over the realm of the East Angles'. That East Anglian royal genealogy had been committed to writing by around the end of the first quarter of the eighth century is also indicated by Bede's statement that Rædwald (Ælfwald's great-grandfather's brother) was 'the son of Tytil, whose father was Uuffa' (*Historia Ecclesiastica*, II, 15). These two ancestral names appear in the same order in Ælfwald's pedigree, which suggests that both were compiled using the same royal genealogical sources.

King Ælfwald's pedigree, as listed in the Anglian Collection, is reckoned as follows:

(1)	Ælfwald	Alduulfing
(2)	Alduulf	Eðilricing
(3)	Eðilric	Ening
(4)	Eni	Tyttling
(5)	Tyttla	Wuffing
(6)	Wuffa	Wehhing
(7)	Wehha	Wilhelming

(8)	Wilhelm	Hryping
(9)	Hryp	Hroðmunding
(10)	Hroðmund	Trygling
(11)	Trygil	Tyttmaning
(12)	Tyttman	Casering
(13)	Caser	Uodning
(14)	Uoden	(frealafing).

Ælfwald's lineage is presented in ascending order with patronymics (fathers' names) for each generation given in the right-hand column. The ascending lineage is a vernacular form distinct from the biblical 'X begat Y' model, where ancestors are listed in descending order (Dumville 1977, 89). Like others in the Anglian Collection, Ælfwald's pedigree appears to have been constructed originally with fourteen generations from subject to royal progenitor, Woden, inclusive (Sisam 1953, 326–328; Dumville 1977, 89–90). This fourteen-generation structure probably follows a biblical model: the first book of the Gospel of St Matthew lists a descending pedigree of Jesus in three fourteen-name sections, running from Abraham to David, from David until the exile in Babylon, and from thence to Jesus (verses 1–17). A fourteen-generation descending version of King Ælfwald's pedigree is preserved in a section of the Cambro-Latin *Historia Brittonum* (ch. 59). This version does not show the beginnings of a growing tendency for retrospective genealogical accretion beyond Woden which is evident in the Anglian Collection, a tendency which reaches an extreme form in the late ninth-century West Saxon royal pedigree listed in the *Anglo-Saxon Chronicle* (e.g., ms *A*, *s.a.* 855).

Although the format of Ælfwald's pedigree may have followed a literary model, much of its content was almost certainly drawn from vernacular genealogical tradition. This was probably maintained in verse, as is implied by its use of groups of alliterating names as well as its use of symbolic filiation, the listing of ancestral conventions in stereotypical father-to-son succession (Henige 1971), e.g. the filiation of *Caser*, 'Caesar', to Woden. That genealogical verse was maintained by the royal families of early England is also suggested by the aforementioned *Vita Sancti Guthlaci*, which refers to the pedigree of St Guthlac's father, Penwalh, a Mercian aristocrat, as being 'traced in set order through the most noble and ancient names of illustrious kings, back to Icel in whom it began in days of old' (ch. 2). Icel is also listed in the version of the Mercian royal pedigree preserved in the Anglian Collection; but that Icel is named as a founding-father of the line and that others enjoy noble and illustrious reputations implies that the form of Penwalh's pedigree was more than a simple list of names such as we have in the Anglian Collection. Another indication that this was the case arises from a later reference to St Guthlac's Icling lineage. Following the account of his successful nine-year career as leader of a war-band, we hear how the young saint became increasingly anxious over the transitory nature of mortal life when 'he contemplated the wretched deaths and the shameful ends of the ancient kings of his line' (ch. 18). That Guthlac knew of the circumstances of the deaths of his ancestors again implies that the form of his family's genealogy was not just a name-list. The overall suggestion, as Hermann Moisl has argued, is that this version of the Mercian royal pedigree was maintained in the medium of verse (Moisl 1981, 232). An explicit indication that East Anglian royal genealogy may have been maintained in verse is contained in the *Passio Sancti Athelberhti*, the twelfth-century Latin account of the martyrdom of one of the kingdom's late eighth-century rulers (James 1917). The *Passio*, which appears to draw on earlier sources, refers to the performance of 'royal songs' concerning King Æþelberht's own line by 'two skilled in the art of song' (James 1917, 218–219, 238; Moisl 1981, 231–232).

An example of royal genealogical verse seems actually to have survived in Old Norse, namely, *Ynglingatal*, the 'Tally of the Ynglings', attributed to the late ninth-century poet Þjóðólfr of Hvin.[4] Writing in Iceland in the thirteenth century, Snorri Sturluson used *Ynglingatal* as one of the main sources for *Ynglinga saga*, the opening section of his great saga of the Norse kings, *Heimskringla* (Aðalbjarnason 1941). Þjóðólfr's poem is essentially an ancestral verse-tally concerned with the Yngling dynasty of the late ninth-century Norse kingdom of Vestfold. Snorri quotes twenty-seven verses of *Ynglingatal*, with a verse for each generation. Like the ancestral traditions of the Mercian Iclings to which young St Guthlac is said to have listened, *Ynglingatal* refers regularly to the circumstances of the deaths and burials of many kings of the Yngling line. This kind of information appears to be a distinctive feature of the genre of royal genealogical poetry. As Joan Turville-Petre has put it, 'the social correlative of this literary genre is a grave-cult' (Turville-Petre 1978–1979, 51).

If then most of the names listed in King Ælfwald's fourteen-generation pedigree were drawn from a pre-literary genre of dynastic verse, we should hesitate to accept their order and relation at face-value. References in Bede's *Historia Ecclesiastica*, permit us to infer that the names of Ælfwald's father, grandfather and great-grandfather may represent historically consecutive generations, but there is no evidence which warrants extending the pedigree's horizon of historical credibility any earlier. The bearer of the name *Wuffa*, for example, was probably a figure of ancestral legend, for according to Bede, *Wuffa* was the East Anglian dynastic eponym (*Historia Ecclesiastica*, II, 15). Like the Kentish dynastic eponym *Oisc* (Bede, *Historia Ecclesiastica*, II, 5; Chadwick 1907, 44–48; Redin 1919, 33; Ström 1939, 73–74; Sims-Williams 1983, 22–23; and Brooks 1989, 58–59), *Wuffa* seems more likely to have been the East Anglian

---

4 I am grateful to Professor Bjørn Myhre for a copy of the English summary of recent research by Claus Krag (1991). Krag contends that *Ynglingatal* may be a twelfth-century work, but provides no argument which compels us to doubt Snorri Sturluson's attribution to the late ninth-century poet Þjóðólfr of Hvin. The classic study of *Ynglingatal* remains that by Akerland (1939).

royal *cognomen*, the distinguishing family-name, rather than the historical father of *Tyttla*. Genealogically, therefore, he may be best regarded as an emblematic figure personified from royal origin-myth.

The bearer of the name *Wehha* may also be a figure derived from royal origin-myth. In the descending version of Ælfwald's pedigree preserved in the *Historia Brittonum*, *Guecha*, 'Wehha', appears to be referred to as the 'first to rule in Britain over the East Anglian folk' (ch. 59). This version, however, which seems to survive only in late eleventh- or early twelfth-century manuscripts, shows evidence of considerable scribal confusion. The spellings of several of the names appear corrupt and the formulaic *genuit*, 'begat' seems to have been omitted between *Guecha*, 'Wehha', and his predecessor, *Guillem*, 'Wilhelm'. As it stands, therefore, the *Historia Brittonum* appears to state that it was *Guillem Guechan* who was the 'first to rule' the East Anglian kingdom. Because of this apparent ambiguity, the historical significance of the reference will remain uncertain, at least perhaps until the completion of Dr David Dumville's forthcoming edition of the *Historia Brittonum*. Yet even if we could accept it at face-value, Wehha's status may have been determined more by genealogical convention than by any concern with historical accuracy, for his name occupies the pivotal seventh position of Ælfwald's fourteen-generation pedigree. Seventh position seems to have been popular with founding-figures in the ancestral lists of the Anglian Collection: in the pedigree of Edwin of Deira this position is occupied by the name *Soemel*, said to be the 'first' to separate Deira from Bernicia (*Historia Brittonum*, ch. 61); in that of Ecgfrið of Bernicia it is *Oesa*, said to be the 'first' to come to Britain (Dumville 1973); and in that of Æþelræd of Mercia it is *Icel*, in whom the Mercian royal line 'began in days of old' (*Vita Sancti Guthlaci*, ch. 2).

All of this suggests that, beyond its first few generations, the pedigree of King Ælfwald is perhaps best regarded as a tally of ancestral names selected largely from a pre-literary genre of genealogical verse.

Now, in relation to the matter of the origin of *Beowulf*, what we seek are indications of Scandinavian, especially Danish, dynastic elements in King Ælfwald's pedigree. Immediately apparent in its upper reaches is the name *Hrōðmund*, which is exactly the same form as that borne by one of the sons of King Hroðgar in *Beowulf*. Within the pedigree, *Hrōðmund* is listed as a 'son' of *Trygil*, a filiation likely to be symbolic. It is also alliteratively paired with *Hryp*, a characteristic form which suggests that its bearer was regarded as a figure associated with a dynastic myth of origins (Turville-Petre 1958).

In *Beowulf*, Hroðmund and his brother Hreðric appear to be the foci of a special sympathy. During the victory-feast held in Heorot to celebrate the defeat of Grendel (lines 991–1250) these two princes can be seen to be, in Kemp Malone's words, 'central and unifying figures in an episode so fraught with pity and terror that even now, after twelve centuries, we read and are deeply moved' (Malone 1927, 268). The bright picture of the victory-feast in this episode is counterpointed by a grim irony which reveals within the Scylding dynasty a latent rivalry between cousins contesting the question of Hroðgar's successor. Tragically, as the princes' mother, Queen Wealhþeow, seems to forebode, and as Saxo's twelfth-century Latin paraphrase of the Old Danish *Bjarkamál* also implies, this rivalry leads to bloodshed when Hreðric is later killed by his cousin Hroþulf (O.N. *Hrólfr*).

The fate of Hroðmund in all of this is not mentioned in any of the Northern sources, but the presence of his rare compound name in the upper reaches of King Ælfwald's pedigree could suggest that this prince of Denmark avoided his brother's fate and somehow came to be associated with the legendary roots of East Anglia. Yet there is no reason why we should suppose that these two instances of the name *Hroðmund* should refer to the same figure. If, however, we return to the East Anglian dynastic eponym, *Wuffa*, we shall see that there are independent indications that Queen Wealhþeow of *Beowulf* may have been regarded as a Wuffing forebear. As was suggested above, *Wuffa* himself may be an emblematic figure personified from royal origin-myth. Etymologically, *Wuffa* seems best explained as a diminutive variant of *Wulf* (Redin 1919, 10, 73; Ström 1939, 79). The patronymic *Wuffingas* itself seems to be a variant of *Wulfingas* or *Wylfingas*. As O'Loughlin observed, 'the forms are etymologically identical, and the phonological variations irrelevant' (O'Loughlin 1964, 4). *Wulfingas* (or *Wylfingas*) is a theriomorphic folk-name meaning 'the children of the wolf', a name which may denote an ultimately totemic affinity with the wolf (Smithers 1971, 90–93).

The *Wylfingas* are referred to in *Beowulf* as a formidable folk (lines 459–471). Hroðgar relates how Beowulf's father, Ecgþeow, had once incurred a feud through the killing of one Heaðolaf *'mid Wilfingum'*, ' "among the Wulfings" ' (lines 460–461[a]). We hear how Ecgþeow sought help from *'sūð-Dena folc'* (line 463[b]), a compound which appears not to refer to a regional sub-division of the Danes, but to the Danes from a *northern* point of view (Bryan 1929, 125; Storms 1957, 12–13). *Beowulf* thus suggests that the Danes were deemed to live to the south of the Wulfings, in the same way that the only other usage of this compound in the poem (line 1996[a]) suggests that they live to the south of the Geats. Moreover, just as the latter are separated from the Danes by sea (lines 210–224[a]; 1903[b]–1913), so too are the Wulfings, for Hroðgar is able to settle Ecgþeow's feud by sending them treasure, presumably Heaþolaf's *wergild*, across the sea: *'sende ic Wylfingum ofer wæteres hrycg / ealde mādmas'*, ' "I sent ancient treasures over the waters to the Wulfings" ' (lines 471–472[a]). As the Geats themselves appear to have been based in the vicinity of what is now the Swedish province of Västergötland (Klaeber 1950, xlvi–xlviii; Farrell 1972, 34–36, 38), the implication is that the Wulfings were thought to dwell in what is now south-eastern Norway or south-western Sweden during the period to which the poem seems to refer, that is, around the early sixth century. If, as Professor Martin Carver has argued in recent papers, the East Anglian dynasty sought to 'signal allegiance' with one or more of the aristocracies of southern

Scandinavia (Carver 1989, 1990b, and in press), then such allegiance may well have been secured through marriage, and hence kinship, at some stage. It is not, therefore, unreasonable to suppose that there may be more than an etymological connection between *Wuffingas* of East Anglia and *Wylfingas* of *Beowulf*. The Wuffings, in other words, may have been descended from the Wulfings.

Ecgþeow's feud *mid Wilfingum* in *Beowulf* also shows that the Wulfings had relations with – and were mutually respected by – the Danish Scyldings. Indeed, that King Hroðgar had the authority to settle the feud peacefully implies that there may have been an unstated special relationship between Scyldings and Wulfings. This point is also suggested by the indications that Hroðgar's queen may have been of Wulfing blood.

Apart perhaps from Grendel's mother, Queen Wealhþeow can be said to be *Beowulf*'s leading lady. She is introduced in the poem as *ides Helminga*, 'the lady of the Helmings' (line 620[b]). The Old English catalogue-poem *Widsith* implies that *Helming* is synonymous with *Wulfing*, for '*Helm (wēold) Wulfingum*', ' "Helm (ruled) the Wulfings" ' (line 29[b]). Wealhþeow would thus have been a Wulfing princess prior to her marriage to the Scylding king, as several scholars have noted (Sarrazin 1897, 228–229; Arnold 1898, 43; Gordon 1935, 169; Malone 1940, 40; Malone 1962, 169; O'Loughlin 1964, 5; Farrell 1972, 19). If so, given the possibility that the East Anglian Wuffings may have been descended from the Wulfings, *Beowulf*'s Queen Wealhþeow may have been regarded as a Wuffing ancestor. Her name is not listed, of course, in the tally of King Ælfwald's forefathers, although it does alliterate with the triad *Wilhelm*, *Wehha*, and *Wuffa*. The East Anglian place-name *Helmingham*, moreover, may preserve the name of her family, for it appears to be based on the personal name *Helming*. As far as I am able to establish, there are only two instances of the place-name *Helmingham* in England and both are in East Anglia. One is the name of a lost village on the upper reaches of the River Wensum in Norfolk (Sarrazin 1897, 229; Allison 1955, 149); the other is on a tributary of the upper River Deben in Suffolk. Although there is no necessary connection with the Helmings of *Beowulf*, the geographical location of the Suffolk *Helmingham* may be significant in relation to the East Anglian royal sites downstream at Rendlesham and Sutton Hoo.[5]

As a Wulfing princess and possible Wuffing ancestor, Wealhþeow's marriage to the Scylding king would establish a genealogical connection pointing to East Anglia as the source of the poem's Danish dynastic interests. The royal kinship constituted by her conjugal union with Hroðgar would have also realised a political allegiance between Wulfings and Scyldings. In this sense, Wealhþeow's formal title, *friðusibb folca*, 'the kindred pledge of peace between peoples' (line 2017[a]), can be seen to be especially appropriate, for it would

---

[5] Also worth noting here is the place-name *Hemley*, if it is based on the personal name *Helm* (Arnott 1946, 30). It is sited on the western side of the Deben estuary some four miles south of Sutton Hoo.

denote succinctly her matrimonial function (Malone 1959, 140; Sklute 1971, 538–540). Any children born of the marriage, moreover, would greatly strengthen the suggested kindred allegiance of Danes and Wulfings, for in their veins would be mingled the blood of their parents' two peoples. In the episode of the victory-feast (lines 991–1250), therefore, Wealhþeow can be seen to have been seeking to secure not only the future well-being of her two boys, Hreðric and Hroðmund, but also the continuity of the kindred allegiance between Danes and Wylfings which they can be seen to embody. As we have seen, one of these boys could have been associated with the legendary roots of the East Anglian kingdom, for the name *Hroðmund* is listed in King Ælfwald's pedigree. In the light of his mother's suggested status as a Wuffing forebear, this point can now be seen to be a real possibility.

On the basis of two arguably complementary names in King Ælfwald's ancestral tally, therefore, the pre-Viking kingdom of East Anglia is identifiable as a possible source of some of the poem's ubiquitous Northern, especially Danish, dynastic concerns. Positive evidence for the origin of *Beowulf* is still lacking, however, and Mercian or Middle Anglian composition cannot be ruled out, especially if any of the ruling families in these regions considered themselves to be descended from some of the same ancestors as the East Anglian Wuffings.[6] Nevertheless, we may have grounds, independent of any suppositions concerning the relation of the poem's account of royal ship-funeral (lines 26–52) to the events entailed by the contents of Mound 1 at Sutton Hoo, for a claim that *Beowulf* may have been composed using Danish dynastic legend which had been fostered in the Wuffing kingdom of East Anglia.

[6] Hroðmund's alliterative counterpart in Ælfwald's pedigree, *Hryp*, although etymologically problematic as it stands (Redin 1919, 31), may be related to the first element of the Yorkshire place-name *Ripon* (Smith 1961–1963, vol. 5, 165), as well as to that of the early Derbyshire place-name *Repton* (Cameron 1959, vol. 3, 653). As Repton was a Mercian royal burial place in the eighth and ninth centuries, if not earlier, the possibility arises that the name *Hryp* in Ælfwald's pedigree could signal East Anglian solidarity with Mercia. At least by 731, all the kingdoms south of the Humber were subject to King Æþelbald of Mercia, as we know from Bede (*Historia Ecclesiastica*, V, 23). At about the same time, the *Vita Sancti Guthlaci* also implies that Ælfwald of East Anglia was subject to Æþelbald, but that the relationship between them was friendly (Colgrave 1956, 16, 176). Perhaps the cult of St Guthlac helped to provide a unifying focus for the continuity of friendship between East Anglia and Mercia. As there is nothing to suggest that relations were radically different in 725 or 726, the possible date of compilation for Ælfwald's pedigree, the presence of the name *Hryp* therein could relate to some aspect of the shared background of the two kingdoms (the possibility that the two had common roots has been noted by Martin 1976; Davies 1977, 22–24; and Rumble 1977, 170–171).

6

Kings, Gesiths and Thegns

H.R. LOYN

It is sometimes useful to reconsider old certainties in the light of new thought, and it was with some such purpose in mind that I suggested this particular theme as appropriate for a meeting summoned to celebrate the anniversary of the discovery of the great ship burial at Sutton Hoo. Linguistic and legal evidence was held clearly in the middle years of this century to point to a change in the nature of the English nobility in the course of the conversion of the English to Christianity in the seventh century. Commonsense supported this view, sustained by our general awareness that the Christian missionaries brought with them in language and thought more than a vestige of truly Roman ideas concerning stability of government and the social order. Terminological usage pointed significantly in favour of such a change, notably that present in the text of Bede's *Historia Ecclesiastica,* and preserved to some degree in fossilized form in the Anglo-Saxon translation of the *Historia* prepared in its final literary form under strong Mercian influence late in the ninth century. Bede himself used a rich vocabulary to indicate men of rank (Loyn 1953, 1955). To take a relatively simple example, the Anglo-Saxon translator found himself compelled to use the term *ealdorman* to render no fewer than eleven of Bede's terms of rank and prestige, ranging from *dux, maior domus regiae, patricius, princeps, satrap, subregulus* and *tribunus,* to the more generalized *maior, maior natu, optimas* and *primas.* Not that the Anglo-Saxon usage was all that simple and unthinking. Some of Bede's *duces,* well-known in other contexts, were called kings by the translator, and others again, of a significantly independent turn of mind were referred to as *heretogan,* or as *heretogan* and *latteowas.* These distinctions tell us much of the developed structures of rank in Alfredian England where Christian kingship had reached the point of development at which an *ealdorman* was expected to be a royal servant and subordinate. They also hint, in their anxiety to express a degree of independence and in the use of *heretoga,* war-leader, at the more fluid form of society we suspect we are dealing with in the seventh century and in Sutton Hoo.

Heretoga had a relatively undistinguished future as a term in English context, certainly when contrasted with its continental German cognate, *Herzog.* The *duces* were important men, operating on a political level and as such have a direct relevance to the Sutton Hoo scene. The most interesting passage in the Ecclesiastical History from this point of view, terminological as well as substantial, is the 24th chapter of the Third book in which Bede describes the downfall of the pagan Penda and its aftermath (Bede H.E., III, 24; Colgrave 288–95). No fewer than 30 *duces regii* were on Penda's side, leading his legions to defeat at the hands of King Oswy in the battle of Winwaed. It is highly likely that the 30 contained a mixture of Christian and pagan, some leading troops from the small folk later described in the Tribal Hidage, some from the western parts, the Hwicce and the Magonsætan, war-leaders, dependent provincial governors, some subordinated in rank as Penda took over, others legitimized and upgraded in rank as Penda stabilized their military authority. There were British princes among their number, but most prominent of all was Ethelhere, the East Anglian king, described in a somewhat gnomic phrase as the 'originator of the war', who himself perished after losing his soldiers and auxiliaries (*auctor ipse belli*, or *ordfruma* in the Anglo-Saxon). When numismatic evidence permitted it, and when it seemed likely that our great Mound 1 at Sutton Hoo was a cenotaph not a burial, it was tempting to associate Ethelhere with the prince commemorated in true royal style in the ship burial. In these harsher times when the numismatists take us back firmly to the 620s this is no longer possible, but the example of Ethelhere, more *heretoga* than *ealdorman*, is there as a reminder of the still fluid world of rank and authority that confronts us when we consider the world of Sutton Hoo.

Nor is the wealth of insight provided by Bede's chapter exhausted by the death of Penda. We are told that for three years after his death the Mercian kingdom passed under Northumbrian control until three *duces gentis Merciorum*, Immin, Eafa and Eadberht, rebelled against King Oswy, overthrew the *principes* of the alien king (*regis non proprii*), and set up, as freemen, Wulfhere, Penda's son, whom they had concealed, as their lawful king (*sicque cum suo rege liberi*; Bede H.E., III, 24; Colgrave, 294). The Anglo-Saxon translator had no difficulty in making a subtle distinction here. The *duces* who deserted were described as *heretogan* and *ealdormen*: the unlawful Northumbrian *principes* were dismissed merely as *ealdormen*.

Now what has such apparent niceness in terminological usage to do with Sutton Hoo? The main interest of the burial ground as such, as we all recognize, lies not solely in the splendour of the ship-burial itself with all its treasure, but rather in the apparent integrity of the group of barrows, as indicator of a special social group, set apart from the hoi polloi, an aristocratic burial ground. This presents problems, easier to state than to solve, which are much in our minds as recent careful excavation yields increasing evidence of the complexity of the site. In rough, raw terms two principal solutions are beginning to emerge. The first, and the more likely is that the inner heart of Sutton Hoo represents the sacred and special burial place of the *cynecynn* of the East Angles, anxious in pagan days and in a pagan setting to demonstrate their difference in life and in death from the folk over whom they exercised their authority. We remember how in Christian days Sigeberht, who had elected to become a monk, was dragged from his monastic retirement because as king, he had proved himself a great leader of men in battle, and how, refusing to take up weapons, he had perished at the hands of his pagan opponent (Bede H.E., III 18, Colgrave, 268). The symbolic value and strength of kingship was deeply rooted in the East Anglian experience. It is by no means implausible that the aristocratic graveyard at Sutton Hoo was reserved for kings, and princes close to the throne, powerful men capable from their own resources of providing the means by which this expensive and spectacular set of burials could be effected. If not kings they, of the royal kin, were potential rulers.

But there is, of course, another possibility, and that is that Sutton Hoo was reserved for kings over a relatively limited period, perhaps fifty to seventy years, who would share their special resting place with the greatest of their supporters, who might or might not possess the royal blood. The royal genealogies suggest that there were only two kings of the East Angles who exercised their royal rule between Wehha and Redwald. Who then should we expect to find in person, or commemorated, in the other mounds and what rank should we expect their contemporaries to afford them? From the bits and pieces we can assemble from the legal codes, the lives of saints and from Bede, it seems likely that two terms are worthy of serious consideration: *eorl* (or *eorlcundman*) and *gesith* (or *gesithcund*). *Eorl* or *eorlcund* were the only terms denoting superior rank to appear in the earliest Kentish laws. Special compensation had to be paid for killing a man on an *eorl*'s estate, and even more for lying with his serving-woman (Ethelbert 13 and 14: Liebermann 1903, 4; EHD 1, 392;). Late in the seventh century an important line of social division was drawn between the *eorl* and the *ceorl*, and in what became a useful jingle, *eorl and ceorl*, noble and simple freeman, the term survived in complicated fashion as a living part of the language in poetry and prose. But in law and in everyday social life *eorl* fell into disuse, to be replaced in the Alfredian period by the ubiquitous *ealdorman* and *thegn* (*dux et minister*). It needed the Scandinavian invasions and settlement to give a new lease of life to *eorl* which emerged then into the Anglo-Norman world as a special rank of distinction, evolving into the English earl. But we can be sure that at the time of the ship-burial at Sutton Hoo a great man could be known as an *eorl* or as one of *eorlcund* stock.

And yet there is another possibility. In times of turbulence – migration is a supreme example of such times – principles of lordship, often intertwined with ties of blood and kindred, became powerful, and legal evidence suggests that the common word for companion, *comes* in Latin, *gesith* in Anglo-Saxon, grew increasingly important, coming to replace *eorl* in the vocabulary of Anglo-Saxon law. Rather like *heretoga*, *gesith* had no long-term future in its simple form in Anglo-Saxon, though in poetry and in the more generalised notion of a *gesithcund* man it survived late, even into Anglo-Norman days (Loyn 1955). In the late seventh and early eighth centuries it was used as a common term for nobleman in two special senses, that of a tried retainer, a fully-fledged warrior, one of the *duguð*, the *probati ac robusti*, as opposed to the *geoguð*, at this stage still the *thegn*, and also that of an estate-holder, one who had already received a reward for service in the shape of a landed estate. In the first of these meanings *gesith* came to be replaced by thegn or king's thegn, the true maid-of-all work in Anglo-Saxon terminology at this level. In the second sense it probably survived quite late though appearing in the records only in its Latin guise *comes*. For the seventh century situation there are passages in Bede's Ecclesiastical History which again prove helpful. We are told that Oswin of Deira quarrelled with Oswy, his partner in the royal dignity, and finding that his army was inferior to Oswy's he disbanded it, seeking refuge himself with one faithful retainer *in domum comitis Hunualdi* (translated later as *gesith*) who betrayed him (Bede H.E., III, 14; Colgrave, 256).

Nevertheless a *gesith/comes* was a substantial nobleman, well set up and capable of protecting a fugitive even against King Oswy if he had chosen to do so. Even more significant, and nearer home from our point of view, was Bede's account of the murder of Sigeberht, King of the East Saxons, which he interpreted as just retribution for the king's failure to take notice of the sentence of excommunication placed on two *comites* (again later translated *gesiths*) who eventually slew him (Bede H.E. III, 22; Colgrave, 284). These *gesiths* were kinsmen of the king, they possessed an estate, and one of them was unlawfully married. Too much must not be read into a ninth-century translator's choice of *gesith* to translate Bede's *comes*, but, taken with a shift in contemporary legal terminology it seems reasonable to suggest that some of the men commemorated in the barrows at Sutton Hoo could indeed have been known to their contemporaries as *gesiths*, the dear companions of war-leaders who already in heathen times were making their kingship a reality, based on the ownership of land. A *gesith* would be expected to own an estate from the resources of which could be found the wherewithal to enable a powerful man's heirs to sustain the cost of burial and ceremony and feasting at such a privileged site.

Most historians of the early Middle Ages, the sub-Roman period as it was once fashionable to call it, agree that in kingship, pagan as well as Christian, rested the best hope of bringing rational order into society. All are agreed that there were kings and kings, a wide variety both in name and fact, with the intensity of royal control and its hope of permanence dependent on a delicate balance of military and religious prestige and the ability to exact permanent tribute and food rents. Sutton Hoo stands alone and exposed on the English scene, offering a tantalizing glimpse of a social order at a moment of crisis, a movement from pagan to Christian. We hesitate to press parallels too far even with the great Scandinavian burial grounds, to say nothing of possible analogies with discoveries more remote in time and space. We rightly ponder what the corresponding graveyards must have been for the royal kin of Kent or of Wessex or of Northumbria, if East Anglia did so well. But the thought that the main site at Sutton Hoo may have been reserved over a limited period of time for the royal kin and the *swæse gesiðas* whose heirs could afford to see their lord duly honoured is at least worthy of passing consideration, even if only to be proved devastatingly wrong as modern archaeological techniques home in onto the crucial questions of dating and sequence.

PART II

England in
the Age of Sutton Hoo

7

Burial Practice in
Seventh- and Eighth-Century England

HELEN GEAKE

The purpose of this paper is to examine, and briefly to review, burial practice in England in the middle Anglo-Saxon period (c. A.D.600–800). Burial sites from this period are generally less well understood than those from the period immediately preceding, with their wealth of artifacts and variety of burial rites, or from the period succeeding, which are, by convention, uniform and unfurnished. The relationship between earlier and later practice is likely to be complex, and the seventh-century 'watershed' can therefore seem hard to characterise. Many books and courses cover the themes of either early (pagan) Anglo-Saxon burial or later (christian) churchyard burial, but few treat the transitions from the one to the other. A publication in point is *Anglo-Saxon Cemeteries 1979* (Rahtz, Dickinson and Watts 1980) which contains no paper that fills the gap between Sutton Hoo and the ninth century.

The seventh century saw many innovations, both in the form of ideological and political experiments documented from texts, and in the form of new material investments: in churches, sculpture and manuscripts. But, however the lives of people alter, they still have basic necessities, and one of these is to bury their dead. Seventh-century burial grounds did exist and develop, sometimes recognised and sometimes not, and they have the potential to reflect important aspects of the life of the community which created and changed them.

Definitions

The first person to recognise a seventh- or eighth-century Anglo-Saxon cemetery was James Douglas, a late eighteenth-century surveyor in the Royal Corps of Engineers. His hobby was exploring the barrow cemeteries of Kent, which until then had been classified as Romano-British (Hawkes 1990, 4). He concluded, from the presence of Christian motifs on some of the artifacts, that the burials must be those of very early Christians, who died in the seventh or early eighth centuries, before churchyard burial was widely introduced (Douglas 1793, 122–131; quoted in Hawkes 1990, 4). The nineteenth century saw many small-scale excavations of middle Anglo-Saxon burials, but Douglas's work had gone unnoticed and these were usually simply recorded as 'Roman', 'Anglo-Saxon' or 'Saxon'.

It was not until the twentieth century that interest in these graves as a group began. Thomas Lethbridge recognised two seventh-century cemeteries during his series of cemetery explorations in Cambridgeshire during the 1920s and 1930s. Although he initially saw these burials as merely poor, the late date of the cemeteries and the lack of 'pagan' objects such as weapons convinced him that these were the burial sites of the earliest Anglo-Saxon Christians (Lethbridge 1931 and 1936).

E.T. Leeds excavated two middle Anglo-Saxon cemeteries in Oxfordshire, at North Leigh in 1928, and at Chadlington in 1930. He studied material from these sites, Lethbridge's cemeteries and the Kentish barrow cemeteries in the concluding chapter of his book *Anglo-Saxon Art and Archaeology* (1936). This chapter was entitled 'The Final Phase', as Leeds did not see these cemeteries as a separate, possibly Christian group, but as the last manifestation of a pagan way of life. This argument was based on the richness and quantity of the grave-goods, which Leeds recognised as differing from the later Saxon practice of unfurnished burial.

The 'final phase' cemetery has received much attention since Leeds defined it. Notable articles are those by Evison (1956), Hyslop (1963), Meaney and Hawkes (1970), and Hawkes (1973). These are all excavation reports, and although they include some comparative material, there has only been one purely synthetic work (Boddington 1990). Some directions for further work on the 'final phase' cemetery have been suggested by Morris (1983, 55) who gives a list, seemingly comprehensive at the time, of 37 such burial sites. There is broad agreement on what constitutes a 'final phase' or furnished middle Anglo-Saxon burial (Boddington 1990, 181), but it is not the only type of burial used in this period. At least four types of mortuary practice can now be defined, and it might be useful to review these briefly.

Type 1: 'Final Phase' Burials

The 'final phase' furnished burial is generally regarded as typical of a seventh- and early eighth-century cemetery site. On first acquaintance it looks like a neat transition between the pagan rite of inhumation or cremation in clothes, furnished with jewellery or weapons and other personal accoutrements, and the Christian rite of unfurnished inhumation, unclothed except for a shroud. Although most burials in the furnished middle Anglo-Saxon cemetery have some grave-goods, these are usually very few compared to the previous two centuries. Up to a third or even half of these burials may have no grave-goods at all (Lethbridge 1931; Hyslop 1963), but a very few have comparatively rich burials with gold and silver necklaces (Meaney 1964, 188) or inlaid seaxes. It seems that we are seeing an increasing polarity of grave wealth in these burial sites (Arnold 1982, and figs 15.1 and 15.2).

It is not only the comparative distribution of grave-good wealth that changes. The repertoire of the grave-goods alters, with brooches and long strings of beads (for women) and weapons (for men) becoming less common. The women's assemblages now consist of pins, necklaces of small monochrome beads, gold pendants and silver or bronze slip-rings, and chatelaines with accessories such as purse-mounts and workboxes. Bags or boxes, sometimes containing objects, are also found. Men's graves are less easily recognised, but they commonly have small buckles, knives often with angled backs, and perhaps the occasional shoelace tag. The regional distribution of the grave-good types also alters. The sixth-century 'Anglian' or 'Saxon' cultural groupings become less marked, with the new assemblages being found right across the country, from Somerset to Northumbria.

Some other attributes of seventh- and eighth-century cemeteries with furnished graves have been recognised. The graves seem to be almost all inhumations; only a very few cremations dating to the seventh century have been found, at the large cemeteries of Apple Down (Down and Welch 1990, 213) and Loveden Hill (Meaney 1964, 159). The inhumations tend to be oriented west-east, although whether this represents a significant change from earlier practice remains to be seen. The bodies are generally supine, extended or slightly flexed, with the arms at the sides or folded at an angle across the body. Within this regularity, though, there can be quite a large range of variation in burial rite; structures found in or around graves, for example, include beds, chambers, ring-ditches, mounds, postholes and parts of boats (Hogarth 1973).

Type 2: 'Princely' Burials

A second type of middle Anglo-Saxon burial that has been recognised and studied is the rich or 'princely' burial. This is usually found underneath a mound, and is characterised by the large number and high quality of its grave-goods. It can be difficult to determine the other characteristics of the princely burial site, since many of them have been disturbed or poorly excavated, but it seems that they often stand alone, and may contain either an inhumation or a cremation. In some ways they bear a resemblance to less monumental furnished burials, such as in the orientation and position of the body, and the great variety of structures to be found in or around the grave.

Rich burials such as those at Sutton Hoo, Taplow, Broomfield, Cuddesdon, Asthall, Caenby and Coombe, have been, or are currently, the subject of much detailed study (e.g. Ellis Davidson and Webster 1967, Dickinson 1974, Bruce-Mitford 1975, 1978, 1983, Webster and East (this volume), Dickinson and

Speake (this volume)). Although it seems that there are few problems in recognising the rich isolated burial, there is little precise definition of the criteria for inclusion in this class (Dickinson 1974, 1 and note 7). Shephard has categorised Sutton Hoo, Taplow and Broomfield as class Aa, at the top of a range of burial types A to E based on grave-good wealth. His definition of the class, however, is not easy to use (1979a, 62). Many of the explanations given (Yorke 1990, 9; Dickinson 1976, 443) link the rise of the 'princely' burial to the historical emergence of royal dynasties. Carver has examined this hypothesis for East Anglia and found it theoretically defensible (1989, 143, 147–152).

Type 3: Unfurnished

A third type of middle Anglo-Saxon burial site is the hardest to define. There have recently been a number of excavations, both in rural and in urban contexts, of probable seventh- and eighth-century cemeteries in which the great majority of burials are unfurnished. These can be extremely difficult to date accurately, but it seems that Staple Gardens, Winchester (G. Scobie pers comm) and Castle Green, Hereford (Shoesmith 1980) are two urban examples, and that Burrow Hill (Fenwick 1984), Burgh Castle (Johnson 1983) and Nazeingbury (Huggins 1978), are rural ones. These unfurnished burials are characterised by supine extended inhumations, absent or sparse grave-goods (generally a few knives or pins are the only artefactual dating evidence), and usually a roughly west-east alignment.

The dating of unfurnished burials is usually accomplished by a combination of radiometric and stratigraphic methods. Neither of these provide the precision of artefactual dating, and so the chronological relationship between furnished cemeteries and the types above is not known exactly. However, groups of west-east unfurnished burials are known from as early as the mid-seventh century, while furnished burial continues at least until the early eighth century (Speake 1989; Evison 1987). The use of grave-goods is therefore not likely to be a simple matter of chronologically evolving preferences.

The seventh century is the period of the documented conversion of the English kingdoms to Christianity, and the date ascribed to the earliest churches (Taylor and Taylor 1965). In this period we might, therefore, expect to find the first churchyard burials. However, the general relationship of early groups of unfurnished burials to churches is unclear. Some churchyard excavations, such as Castle Green, Hereford, have burials which appear to date from the seventh century (Shoesmith 1980). On the other hand, a number of excavations of contemporary unfurnished cemeteries, such as Bromfield, Shropshire, or Burrow Hill, Suffolk, have not as yet located any structure which could be a church (Stanford 1980, 178–9; Fenwick 1984). This may be due in some cases to the relevant structure escaping identification. It must be likely, though, given the probable number of churches in seventh- and eighth-century England

(Morris 1989; Blair 1988), that many unfurnished cemeteries were not sited around a church. Some later churches may have been built on the site of an unfurnished cemetery; although Morris thinks this is theoretically unlikely (1989, 153), he does list a number of churches which appear from excavation to be preceded by burials (Morris 1989, table 1).

Because of the problems involved in recognising these burials, they have hardly ever been compared as a group. Morris presented a resumé of the evidence, such as it was, nearly ten years ago (1983, 49–62), but this did not consider the use of features within the grave, such as stone, charcoal or coffins, which might distinguish a middle Anglo-Saxon unfurnished burial from that of a later period.

Type 4: 'Deviant' Burials

A fourth type of middle Anglo-Saxon cemetery has, unlike the other three, not been defined before. Excavated examples have variously been interpreted as 'execution cemeteries' (Dickinson 1974, 23 and note 78) or 'battlefield cemeteries' (Meaney 1964, 272). They are characterised by a scarcity or complete lack of grave-goods, and by an unusual way of positioning both the grave and the body within the grave. Individual grave-cuts may be absent, with all the bodies placed within one enormous trench, as at Ocklynge Hill (Meaney 1964, 252). The graves may be disposed around a barrow as at Sutton Hoo, there called 'satellite burials' (Carver 1990) and Cuddesdon (Dickinson 1974). Bodies may be found decapitated or with the neck broken, buried prone, with the feet and hands apparently bound, or in a variety of other positions indicating that some sort of ritual abuse or mutilation was carried out just before or just after death.

The phenomenon of the 'ritual abuse' or 'deviant' burials seems to be more common in the middle Anglo-Saxon period than in the earlier period, but these burials are again hard to date with any precision, due to the absence of grave-goods. They are perhaps even harder to date than the more normal unfurnished graves, as the examples so far discovered lack clear stratigraphic dating evidence, as well as artefacts, apart from residual material. As a result of this, the dates that have been suggested for these sites vary from early Anglo-Saxon to post-Conquest. It is hoped that some light will be thrown on this question by a programme of radiocarbon dating to be carried out at York. So far, the best documented example of this type is the collection of flat graves at Sutton Hoo. Three of these have already been radiocarbon dated, to A.D. 620±90, 746±79 and 750±70 (Carver 1989, 150).

Some comparative work has been done on individual aspects of graves, which are applicable to the entire range of seventh- and eighth-century Anglo-Saxon burials. Most has concentrated on artefacts as dating tools (Meaney and Hawkes 1970; Hawkes 1973; Speake 1989) but there have also been contribu-

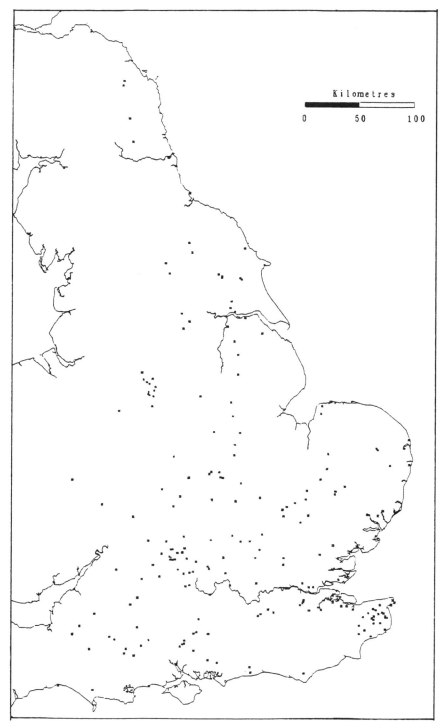

Figure 13. Preliminary location map of identified Middle Saxon burial sites

tions on the origins of the new sorts of grave-goods (Hyslop 1963), a catalogue of structures associated with graves (Hogarth 1973) and a useful typology and explanation of barrows (Shephard 1979b).

Examination of the work previously carried out on seventh- and eighth-century cemeteries therefore appears to divide them into four groups, depending on the predominance of *furnished, unfurnished, rich,* and *deviant* burials. Some sites only contain one type, but some contain more. Three types are present at Sutton Hoo. Taking burial type (rather than cemetery type) as the basis of classification is likely to be more diagnostic of social and ideological trends, if an acceptable sampling strategy can be devised. The work of gathering and classifying all English burials of the seventh and eighth centuries has begun at York.[1] The corpus, contrary to expectation, appears to be large; preliminary reconnaissance has located 7,000 or so individual graves within 300 burial sites (Fig. 13). The remainder of this paper is concerned with the archaeological and historical potential of this material.

A Choice of Explanations

Richards has presented a summary of theoretical approaches to cemetery archaeology, and how these have been used by scholars working in the Anglo-Saxon period. He distinguishes four broad theoretical phases, resulting in interpretations based on religious belief, culture-histories, functionalism and structuralism (1987, 2–15). Culture-history and functionalism often feature in early Anglo-Saxon studies but, perhaps because of their emphasis on grave-goods, have not been so popular for the middle Anglo-Saxon period. The variety of mortuary practices at this time has tended to favour a structuralist approach, in which material culture is seen to communicate actively rather than passively in order to reflect social interactions.

Many traditional explanations have been built around the framework of the documented conversion of the Anglo-Saxons to Christianity. Christian ideology, encompassing as it does a system of beliefs in an afterlife, has in the past been seen as somehow responsible for the character of many of the new types of seventh-century grave-goods, for the overall decline in grave-goods, and for the west-east orientation (Hyslop 1963; Meaney and Hawkes 1970, 53). More recently, though, attention has been drawn to the lack of specific regulations for the mode or location of the burial of the faithful at this time (Morris 1983, 49–50; James 1988, 139). But although there is little evidence that burial practices simply reflect religious belief, explanations involving a change in religious practice may still have something to offer.

Although there are no statutes specifically banning the inclusion of objects in

[1] The preliminary survey and interpretation of middle Saxon burial rites is the subject of a doctoral programme by the author.

graves, there are church laws from the seventh and eighth centuries which prohibit practices such as divinations, fortune-telling and the carrying of amulets (Meaney 1981, 255–67; Morris 1989, 60). Contrary to these laws, amulets and curing stones actually occur proportionately more often in furnished graves of the seventh century than in those of previous centuries (Meaney 1981, 168). Although the presence of these objects does not necessarily make the burials pagan, and perhaps does not even preclude those buried in them having been nominal Christians, it does suggest that the church did not have an strong influence over their mode of burial. There have been, on the other hand, a number of excavations of cemeteries which are unequivocally linked to historically known seventh- and eighth-century Christian institutions, such as the monasteries of Monkwearmouth and Jarrow, which provide a basis of data to work from. As a result, it ought to be possible to at least recognise those people who were using mortuary practices to actively signal a greater allegiance to Christianity.

This is not to say that the differences in the burial customs of the middle Anglo-Saxon period must be equated with simple religious differences (Boddington 1990, 196). As has been seen, there is little evidence that west-east oriented, unfurnished burials were required by mainstream Christian orthodoxy. The aspects of these burials that are familiar to us from later Christian practice may have been selected from the earlier repertoire, perhaps partly in order to project a possibly Christian ideal of egalitarianism (Carver 1989, 143). The behaviour adopted towards this end might have been influenced by Celtic burial practices, as seen in Ireland or in some parts of Northumbria. Support for this comes from the earliest cemeteries at Monkwearmouth and Jarrow; they apparently pre-date the monastic buildings and may be pre-Saxon (Rahtz 1977, 56).

Similarly, there is no evidence that the behaviour that resulted in the 'ritual abuse' grave was part of ordinary paganism. This type of burial forms a set with other elaborate burials of the period, such as those including a boat, a bed or a mound, and also with the increased incidence of votive offerings (Bradley and Gordon 1988). These burials are different in character from earlier 'pagan' burials, and may be a manifestation of a new activity, in essence political rather than religious. The same phenomenon, aggressive or 'defiant' paganism, can also be seen during the period of missionary activity in Scandinavia, where the arrival of the missionaries, it has been suggested, spurred the pagan Scandinavians to create new and competitively extreme aspects of their religion, such as temples and human sacrifice (Carver 1989, note 52; Carver in press).

There has been much debate in recent years over state formation and the origins of kingship in Anglo-Saxon England (e.g. Arnold 1988; Bassett 1989; Yorke 1990). These processes are intimately bound up with the arrival of the church (Wallace-Hadrill 1975, 181–2) and must be the end result of a process of increased stratification on one level or another of society. There is, however, disagreement about when and how this came about, and whether it can be observed in burial remains (Carver 1989, 151). An altered stratification in grave-goods may, of course, imply not so much a change in social complexity, as a change in the use of burial as a social signal (Hodder 1980, 166–7). But such a change of use may well have been provoked by a revised ideology which included kingship (Carver 1989, 158). It has also been noted that states, whether Christian or not, tend to use more elaborate external surroundings for the body (such as chapels, pyramids and mausolea) than pre-state societies (Randsborg 1981, 106); this also implies an adjustment in the way that burial is used for social signalling.

Morris has examined the political implications of conversion for inter-kingdom relationships in England (1983, 46–8). The decisions of the English kings to convert to the Roman church, or to remain pagan, must be seen in the light of the influence of Catholic Merovingian Francia, the kings of which had claimed overlordship beyond the Channel since the days of Theudebert (534–548) (Campbell 1971, 16). To convert to Catholicism was to throw in one's lot with Francia as much as with Rome. To remain pagan (or to become defiantly pagan) was to assert independence (Carver 1989, 155), and many aristocratic Anglo-Saxon families hedged their bets by doing both (HE II, 5; Angenendt 1986, 749–754).

The style of burial was one way of indicating these allegiances. The largely unfurnished cemetery could signal allegiance to the Christian world of western and southern Europe, while the 'ritual abuse' and rich burials (which can occur together, as at Cuddesdon and Sutton Hoo) announce a more independent stance, or perhaps a tie to northern Europe (Carver in press). This leaves the 'final phase' burials, whose social context, on this analysis, remains to be established.

Other models have been put forward which take into account the secondary changes that accompany the political and religious shifts. The arrival of the church had immense economic implications. The needs of the church were enormous; communities could be up to six hundred strong, and their requirements for the production of a single manuscript could run to hundreds of calves (Bruce-Mitford 1969, 2). Both monastic and secular churches expected grants of land to be made for their upkeep (Blair 1988), which may have led to the introduction of a new system of landholding, from temporary personal tenure to grants in perpetuity (John 1960).

John's hypothesis has been used by Shephard in a functionalist analysis of why one category of burials, those under mounds, rose in popularity, as they are a highly visible way of staking a long-term claim to an area of land or a similar resource, such as mineral deposits. The notion of family property may later have developed further, perhaps leading to personal possessions becoming heritable and thus not forming part of a burial deposit (Shephard 1979b, 8.7).

The church was not the only influence over economic structures at this time. It has been suggested that the appearance of kings can be equated with the return of taxation, and that this new way of extracting a surplus led to a decline in grave-goods (Carver 1989, 157). Another profitable line of research in this area may be the examination of alternative forms of investment to grave-goods, such as the building and furnishing of churches, the production of manuscripts and stone sculptures, or the construction and manning of town defences.

Halsall has recently argued that the decline of the furnished burial custom in Merovingian France reflects the decline of social differences based on gender and age, in favour of those based on class, wealth and rank. In general, the Frankish grave assemblages become less varied, and therefore less significant, and the items which retain an importance as grave-goods longest are those which are least gender-specific, such as pins, knives and buckles. Halsall has postulated that this phenomenon could be related to a rise in power of the Frankish aristocracy in the decades around 600, leading to an increased rigid-ity in society. The death of a member of the family became less of a threat, and so the funeral became less important (Halsall 1990). To what extent these changes also occur in contemporary Anglo-Saxon England is debatable. Al-though both settlement and cemetery sites appear to show increasing social stratification in the later sixth and early seventh centuries, the rigidity or stability of these social classes is less clear.

The fact that the sixth-century regionalisation of grave-good types and burial rite is replaced by a range of types found across the whole of Anglo-Saxon England suggests an additional interpretation. The regionally distinct assemblages in England seem not to be present from the earliest period of Anglo-Saxon settlement and influence, but are rather a phenomenon of the sixth century (Hills 1979, 316). This argues that the sixth-century regional trends should be seen as markers of newly perceived identities rather than ethnic realities (Hines 1984, 27–5; Hills 1979, 317).

The early seventh-century change in the spatial patterning of grave-good types, from smaller regional distributions to larger ones, can be interpreted in a similar way. This might be used to show that the Anglo-Saxon peoples now began to perceive a new identity as a larger cultural group – the English. The same mechanism as was used in the sixth century to show regional allegiance can be used to emit a different range of signals, indicating a different group identity, in the seventh century.

The hypothesis of a re-alignment of cultural identity in this period has also been put forward by scholars in other fields. John Hines has used philological evidence to suggest that differences in the regional dialects of Old English were already in decline by A.D.600 (1990, 33). Patrick Wormald has suggested that the idea of a unified *gens Anglorum* can be seen only from the time of Bede, promoted for the purposes of the church and out of respect for the memory of Gregory the Great. The church always regarded the various tribes as a single identity and, moreover, equated this with the Angles. He suggests, however, that such an ideal of national unity only later became a reality (1983, 103). The archaeological evidence from seventh-century cemeteries may provide some corroboration for the ideals expressed in the literature, but at the rather earlier date suggested by the dialectal evidence.

A composite model, that would reconcile these different explanations, might be as follows. The formation process of proto-states of the English regions culminates in kings and an aristocracy, who indicate their superior status with rich burials in mounds, towards the end of the sixth century. As these classes become more stable and powerful, the need to insist on their status with rich burials lessens. At the same time, under diplomatic pressure from the church in Rome and Francia, parts of some communities convert to Christianity, accepting all its revised allegiances. They signal these allegiances through the medium of the unfurnished burial, provoking those with different allegiances to maintain or invent quite different signals.

The new political and religious authorities, wishing to exert their control over the general population, promote the concept of a unified Christian country reflected in a less geographically varied repertoire of burial practice. The new economic organisation brought in by the church and the state, however, together with the more rigid class structure, eventually mean that grave-goods lose their ability to signal personal status in the grave. Sometimes the artifacts are buried in bags or boxes where they are not visible, and therefore not capable of making these statements, but increasingly they are not buried at all. The unfurnished grave becomes the most popular type, and needs virtually no adjustment to pass into Christian orthodoxy.

It could be countered, however, that if it suited the church to emphasise the community of the Christian English rather than the individualism of the pagan Saxon or Anglian, then those who wished to assert their independence from the church would also tend to show their regional individualism in some way. They would not all be using the same mechanism of defiant paganism such as the 'ritual abuse' cemetery. This remains to be investigated, and it may be that sites showing this form of ritual are more common in certain parts of southern England than elsewhere. However, since it also seems possible that the phenomenon of defiant paganism occurred in various manifestations in later Scandinavia (e.g. Roesdahl 1982, 171–6), it was perhaps a common reaction to a common stress.

It might be expected, too, that even without the influence of the church, the early kings would wish to foster a sense of territorial identity different to other, competing kingdoms. The analysis of seventh- and eighth-century graves should discover whether the historically known kingdoms are visible in the archaeological record at this time; and, if not, suggest a reason why. There are perhaps differences in emphasis between public identity, on the level of the kingdom, and private identity, on the level of the grave, which are not reconciled until the time of Alfred.

ACKNOWLEDGEMENTS

I would like to thank Guy Halsall and John Shephard for allowing me to use their unpublished theses. I am also grateful to Tania Dickinson, Martin Carver and Neil Price for commenting on earlier drafts of this paper, and Jeff Chartrand for helping with the production of the map.

8

The Seventh-Century Cremation Burial in Asthall Barrow, Oxfordshire: A Reassessment

TANIA M. DICKINSON AND GEORGE SPEAKE

Introduction

The demonstration by Martin Carver and his team that the most frequent mode of burial under the barrows at Sutton Hoo was not inhumation (in a ship) but cremation (usually in a metal vessel) provides an important new perspective on that cemetery and turns the spotlight on to other evidence for the use of cremation in high-status contexts at this period. Evidence from England is restricted, however, because of the circumstances and nature of recovery and publication, and its interpretation is often dependent, in turn, on the far higher quality information from Sutton Hoo, both from the recent excavations and Rupert Bruce-Mitford's publications of the earlier finds. This applies even to the most unequivocal other case of a rich and total cremation under a primary Anglo-Saxon barrow, that at Asthall in Oxfordshire. Although work over the past twenty-five years (particularly by David Brown, Vera Evison and ourselves) shows that more can be teased out about Asthall than was known to E.T. Leeds when he originally published the burial (Leeds 1924), we are still far from being able to offer a definitive publication. But, with the reassessment of Sutton Hoo and its context, the time is ripe to present our current knowledge and opinions about Asthall; by its nature this paper is interim and contentious (cf. Dickinson 1976, vol. I, 253–4, 360, 364–7, 440–2, vol. II, 35–7; Speake 1980, 39; our arguments were summarized and endorsed by Hawkes 1986, 91).

We shall begin our discussion with mainly factual accounts of the available evidence, the excavation and its results and the nature of the grave assemblage; an outline catalogue of the finds is provided in the Appendix. The thrust of the paper is directed, however, to interpretation: it revolves round three issues – dating, the social identity of the dead person and the cultural context of the burial ritual, which together may suggest a historical context for the burial.

The Archaeological Record

Asthall barrow (Pl. 2.1; figs 14–15) was excavated in August 1923 and again in 1924 by George S. Bowles, the brother-in-law of the second Baron Redesdale, on whose land it lay. Bowles, as described by his daughter (Julia Budworth, pers. comm.), was a 'gentleman amateur', but he benefited from advice from E.T. Leeds, then Assistant Keeper at the Ashmolean Museum, Oxford, who visited the site and undertook publication of the main 1923 discoveries (Leeds 1924) and more briefly the 1924 work (Leeds 1939b, 365). These published accounts can be supplemented by some hitherto unpublished material. The Ashmolean Museum possesses a plan on blue linen showing the 1923 *and* 1924 trenches (cf. Leeds 1924, fig. 2), probably by Leeds, and a typescript of a report on the cremated bone by H. Carter of Reading Museum (dated 1968). The Institute of Archaeology in Oxford owns a set of three-and-a-quarter-inch slides, copied from Bowles' plates but including four not published: one shows Lord Redesdale's daughter, Nancy Mitford, beside the barrow, two show excavation in progress (one reproduced here, Pl. 2.2) and the fourth is a close-up of pit or posthole Y (see Pl. 2.3). More recently, the land immediately south of the barrow has been extensively disturbed during the building of the Witney (A40) bypass, though without archaeological consequences (Chambers 1976, 19), and R.A. Chambers and ourselves have re-inspected the barrow and drawn a contour section (Fig. 15.A). Nonetheless, many ambiguities and uncertainties in the primary published record remain and these constrain understanding of the burial, pending any re-excavation.

Greater advances can be made with the material recovered from the excavation and deposited in the Ashmolean Museum (Accession Register 1923.769–782 and 1949.297). It is, however, all in fragments, mostly very small fragments (testimony to the efficacious use of a garden sieve, Pl. 2.2; Leeds 1924, 117), and nearly all of it has been burnt resulting in distortion and obscurity. A little conservation work has been carried out (between 1966 and 1976, at the instigation of David Brown, though without a full record being kept), which has resulted in the recognition of at least one entirely new item and the cleaning of others. But most of the material remains covered with, or even consists of, concretions of soil, charcoal, organic materials and metal corrosion products. Identification, let alone reconstruction, of the original grave goods is therefore highly problematic, and we would stress that the interpretations offered here are mostly based on simple visual observation. Moreover, while we have been able to add more pieces to the objects recognised by Leeds, both to those to which he gave individual accession numbers and to those to which he did not, and have isolated items which he does not seem to have noticed, our examinations have not been exhaustive. Knowledge would undoubtedly be increased were a systematic and comprehensive programme of sorting, conservation and metallurgical and organic analyses undertaken, for which this paper may now provide both the stimulus and agenda.

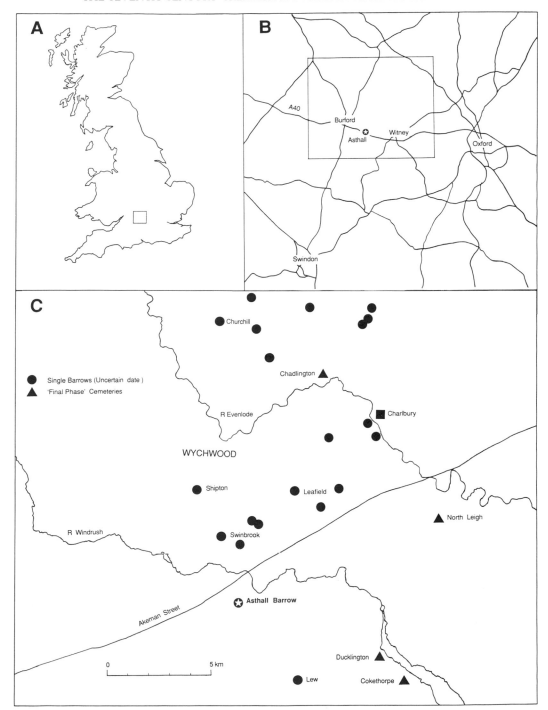

Figure 14. Location maps: A. National location; B: Regional location, showing major modern roads and towns; C. Local archaeological context, showing other seventh-century cemeteries and round barrows (of uncertain date) [GS].

The Barrow Excavation and its Results

Asthall barrow stands now to a height of 2.4 metres (approximately 7 feet 10 inches). Its height was recorded as 8 feet 6 inches (2.6 metres) at the beginning of the century (Potts 1907, 345) but as 12 feet (3.66 metres) in 1923 (Leeds 1924, 114). It is still covered with the remnants of a planting of trees, probably made in the nineteenth century, and surrounded by a circular dry-stone retaining wall, 55 feet (16.76 m.) in diameter at its top (Pl. 2.1; Fig. 15). It is likely that the barrow was originally larger: Bowles recorded an elliptical raised area, 4 inches (102 millimetres) high, skirting the retaining wall to the south-west (Leeds 1924, 114, 116), which could imply a basal diameter nearer 68 feet (20.73 metres). If so, and applying the trigonometric principle used by Lance Vatcher at Swallowcliffe Down (Speake 1989, 5), the original centre would have been not at point X but just south of point T on Leeds' plan (points X1 and X2 on Fig. 15.B; Leeds 1924, fig. 2). Indeed the centre may have been further south yet (and the barrow therefore even bigger) if, as is likely, the grave finds and a layer of clay, which underlay the barrow (see below), were located centrally (cf. Leeds 1939b, 365). Alternatively the 'skirt' may have resulted partly from pre-wall soil-slippage off the mound: certainly post-1923 slippage is evident and would help to account for the recorded reduction in height.

Bowles' excavation consisted of an irregular polygonal trench, its corners designated A–H (dug in 1923), and a rectangular trench, K–P (dug in 1924): Leeds' unpublished sketch plan also marks four additional trenches, barely 18 inches square and all lettered S, round the raised area beyond the stone wall (Fig. 15.B: the corner points have been labelled in lower case to reduce confusion with the lettered find-spots within the excavated area and are so referred to hereafter). Leeds (1924, 114) says that the trenches were dug to a depth of 12 feet, to and below the level of the field. Since the clay layer (see below) was also said to be at 12 feet deep (ibid., 115) and the trench went into the underlying rubbly limestone, it must actually have been deeper. It also casts doubt over Leeds' figure for the barrow height, which may not have been arrived at independently.

The mound was composed of homogeneous soil and stones, and included a quantity of Romano-British grey wares. This might suggest that the mound had been scraped up from the surrounding topsoil. Certainly the current ground surface falls away from the perimeter of the barrow by about 0.3 metres, leaving the limestone brash exposed (cf. Pl. 2.1 and Fig. 15.A), while no differential growth can be observed in the barley crops which might indicate a quarry ditch. However, there is little other evidence for a Romano-British site in the immediate vicinity apart from the finding of a brooch recorded in the Ashmolean Museum archives. Chamber's watching brief on the Witney by-pass yielded no archaeological material here and the crop marks observed in this area may be periglacial (Chambers 1976, 19; R.A. Chambers, pers. comm.).

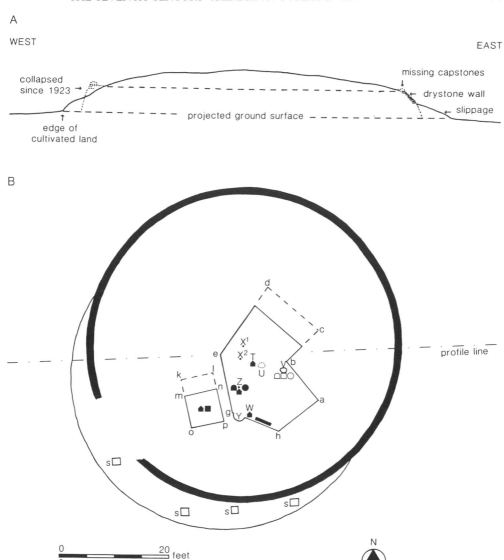

Figure 15. A. Contour profile in 1991 [TMD after R.A. Chambers]; B. Excavation plan 1923–24. Key: a–p and s = excavated areas; U and Y = postholes; X1 = centre of walled barrow; X2 = estimated centre of original barrow; T,V,W and Z = specific find-spots (exact location of finds within mnop not known). The top of the wall round the barrow is shown in solid black; the four-inch-high raised area to the south-west is delineated by a thin line. [TMD after Bowles in Leeds 1924, fig. 2 and unpublished plan in Ashmolean Museum]. Sc. 1:180.

An old ground surface was not explicitly noticed in excavation; instead, overlying the limestone substratum was a layer of yellowish clay, which appeared to fade away beyond corner b. On this was a layer, up to 6 inches (152 millimetres) thick (as at point V, which is close to corner b and so towards the presumed edge of the deposit), composed of the remains of a cremation – ashes, charcoal, largish 'charred' timber (in the area between corners g and h), bones and artefacts. Only a few of the find-spots of artefacts are recorded, but they exhibit no rationale, and sherds of the pottery bottle were found in at least four separate places over 10 feet apart in the centre of the barrow (at T,W, and Z and within m,n,o,p).

A number of pits or postholes were also observed, but their interpretation is unclear, not least because those found in the 1924 trench were neither described nor plotted (Leeds 1939b, 365). The two observed in 1923 were labelled U and Y. The former was 2 feet (0.61 metres) deep, 18 inches (0.46 metres) in diameter and filled with loose earth (that is apparently no different from the barrow make-up). In his text Leeds (1924, 116) describes U as penetrating the limestone substratum, but in his annotation to the plan he says that it was lined with pitched stones which *rested on* the ashy layer (*ibid.*, fig. 2). The stratigraphic position of U (later or possibly earlier than the ashy layer) and its structure (cut into the limestone or packed with limestones, or both) is thus obscure. So too is the larger pit, Y, which measured 2 feet 6 inches (0.76 metres) in diameter and 2 feet (0.61 metres) in depth. It was not covered by the clay layer and was filled with 'a loose blackish soil' (clearly evident in one of the hitherto unpublished slides, Pl. 2.3). Interpretation is complicated, however, by the appearance immediately above Y of a hollow, post-like, cavity, 4 feet (1.22 metres) high and 1 foot 6 inches (0.46 metres) in diameter (Leeds 1924, fig. 3). Leeds preferred to explain this as the ghost of a post, set into pit Y after the deposition of the cremation layer and as a central marker for the future barrow, though he could not account for the loss of its substance: this could not be equated with the black soil in pit Y, since if the post had thus collapsed its base must originally have been unsupported in its hole (Leeds 1924, 116–17; 1939b, 365). We would also point out that it is at some distance from the apparent centre of the barrow, either as Leeds marked it or as we have now reconstructed it, and even from a putative centre located in relation to the clay layer and the distribution of finds. Further, if the post had been inserted through the cremation layer, we might expect posthole Y to have contained calcined bone and charcoal. Its fill is more consistent with a decayed and/or burnt post stump, which stratigraphically was erected before the cremation deposit. Possibly the superimposition of Y and the cavity, both coincidentally at corner g of the excavation trench, was fortuitous. Indeed, given the manner of the excavation (Pl. 2.2), the cavity might have been merely an unobserved collapse of loose mound soil. Similar vertical cavities have been recorded, however, in a barrow from Staby, Uppland, Sweden, where they were thought to represent birch stems placed on the cairn as guides for the construction of the overlying earthen mound (Ekholm 1931; Lindqvist 1936, 30–33, fig. 23). It is also worth noting that point V was represented on Bowles' plan (Leeds 1924, fig. 2; cf. Fig. 15.B) as an oval of the same dimension as U; it might have been the base of another posthole into which cremation debris had sunk.

A final problem is whether the burial had been preserved intact. Leeds reports that the excavated sections showed no evidence of earlier interference (Leeds 1924, 114); no cremated material was noticed in the barrow make-up, and if the cavity above posthole Y was real, it is unlikely to have survived disturbance. However, in view of the less than professional manner of excavation and the fact that the finds were spread about widely and randomly (though this may have other explanations), the possibility of a previous, but undetected, intrusion cannot be completely discounted.

In view of the many uncertainties highlighted in the excavation record, there can be no straightforward reading of the burial sequence at Asthall. Any interpretation involves weighing a series of alternatives, in which comparison with other sites is essential. It is deferred, therefore, to the section on the cultural context of the burial ritual.

The Grave Assemblage

Discussion of the grave assemblage is no more straightforward than that of the burial sequence. We shall introduce the artefacts here (see also Appendix) but reserve most comment, where appropriate, until later. The assemblage consists of three main materials: ceramics, animal products (bone and antler) and metals, primarily copper alloys and silver (which cannot always be distinguished reliably by eye) but with a minimal amount of iron (four 'nails') and lead (a disc, Pl. 4.18). In functional terms the two largest identifiable groups are vessels and strap fittings.

There is a minimum of seven vessels, if, on the grounds of economy of hypothesis, all comparable fragments are interpreted as deriving from a single vessel. But some of the vessel-types can occur in multiple sets, and had this been so at Asthall the total number of vessels could have been higher. There are three pottery vessels, two plain hand-made jars (Fig. 16.A–B) and a Merovingian wheel-made and roulette-decorated bottle (Fig. 16.C). A small silver vessel, probably a bowl or cup, is represented by many fragments, in colour a distinctive pinkish-purple grey (Pl. 3.1–2).

There are at least two vessels made entirely of copper alloy. One is a cast Byzantine bowl of Werner's Type B1, of which several fragments can now be recognized (Fig. 17; Werner 1957; Richards 1980, esp. 51–3 and 265–7). Its single beaded rim is unusual, though this occurs on some Continental finds, for example one from Aschheim in southern Germany. Richard's drawing of the latter also helps to identify another Asthall fragment, distinctively faceted in profile, as part of the openwork foot-ring (Richards 1980, fig. 18). The

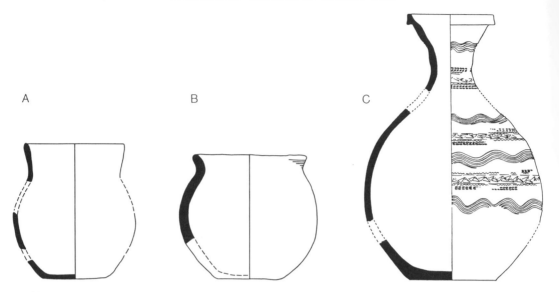

Figure 16. Pottery: A. Hand-made pot 1; B. Hand-made pot 2; C. Merovingian pottery bottle (A–B after Myres 1977; C after Evison 1979). Sc. 1:3.

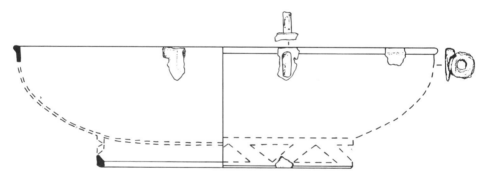

Figure 17. Byzantine cast metal bowl: hypothetical reconstruction, incorporating extant fragments on the basis of analogies with Richards 1980, figs 6 (Wickhambreux) for approximate size and 18 (Aschheim) for openwork foot-ring. [TMD/GS]. Sc. 1:3.

Asthall bowl would seem to be larger, however, than that from Aschheim, approximating to the larger-sized bowls more often found in England.

The other certain copper-alloy vessel is made of sheet metal and is represented by a piece of body which has escaped the burning; it is marked on both surfaces by fine parallel (lathe-turned polishing?) lines (Pl. 3.3). Arguably from this vessel or a similar one may be a very small fragment which exhibits a hammered and slightly thickened top (Fig 18.A). It might be compared with hanging bowl rims of Kendrick's Type A (Kendrick 1932, 164, fig. 1A; cf. Sutton Hoo large hanging bowl, Bruce-Mitford 1983, fig. 58b and 156, though this is much larger and more angular). Similar hammered and thickened rims can

A

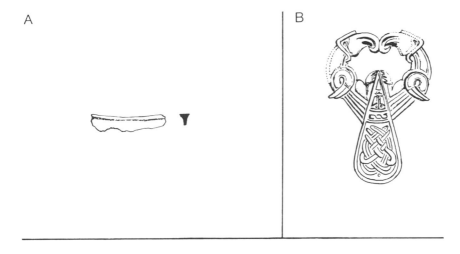

B

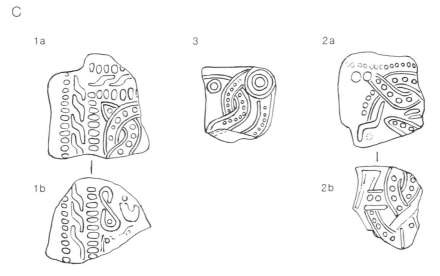

Figure 18. A. Sheet-metal copper-alloy rim fragment. Sc. 1:1; B. Style II mount. C. Reconstruction of decoration on copper-alloy repoussé foils. [GS]. Sc. 2:1.

occur too on sheet-metal (not cast; Richards 1980, 19–20) tripod-ring bowls found in rich Continental graves mainly of the sixth century and also more rarely in Kent (e.g. Coombe, though this is also larger than the Asthall vessel; Ellis Davidson and Webster 1967, 32–3, fig. 5). The fluted bowl from Broomfield (recently restored by the British Museum) and the much larger Taplow cauldron also have such a rim (Katherine East, pers. comm.), but lug-eared cauldrons of Vestland and Gotland type seem generally not to have thickened rims. It does not seem possible to determine the kind of vessel represented, though a lathe-finished bowl or pan of insular or west European manufacture is likely.

The remainder of the sheet copper-alloy fragments are very small, corroded and/or burnt and how many of them belong to the preceding vessel is uncertain, but among them are pieces which might suggest further vessels. First, there are some very tightly rolled tubular fragments, some with evidence of an unrolled portion (Pl. 3.4). They are far too small to come from the rolled rim of a late hanging bowl, examples of which have an iron core (Fowler 1968, fig. 70.9); equally, the curled-over rim-edges of some sheet-metal vessels from Anglo-Saxon graves are not so tubular and are larger (e.g. copper-alloy dish from Ash, Kent or tripod-ring bowl from Kingston grave 205, Kent, Richards 1980, figs 60 and 63). Yet the Asthall fragments look like vessel rim.

Second, there are pieces of repoussé foil with billeted borders (Pl. 3.7), five of which bear elements of zoomorphic interlace (Fig. 18.C) with two forming the corner of a rectangular mount with 'guilloche' border (Fig. 18.C, 1a–b). In addition there are at least six pieces of four-ribbed fluted binding strip with dome-headed rivets, one of which clamps a further fragment of repoussé foil with (?) triple-strand ornament (Pl. 3.5), and many pieces of distorted U-sectioned edge-binding (Pl. 3.6). Now while the decorated foils have been published as possible analogies to the foils from the Sutton Hoo helmet (Bruce-Mitford 1978, 207 and fig. 154), and the fluted and U-sectioned bindings might indeed be compared with those on helmets (*ibid.*, 146, fig. 142 and for reconstruction, fig. 136), the apparent absence of iron backing to the Asthall foils ought to preclude their derivation from a helmet. Equally compelling parallels may be found among the remains of drinking horns, wooden bottles, and cups (Bruce-Mitford 1983, 316–95). The scale of the fragments compares at Sutton Hoo with the maplewood bottles (and even perhaps with the tiny burr-wood cups) rather than with the large drinking horns. The style of the ribbed fluting and the complex intertwining, spotted bands of Salin's Style II on the foils points more specifically to the smaller pair of drinking horns from Taplow (Speake 1980, pl. 14i), though spotted and triple-strand bands in general are not uncommon on cups (e.g. from Taplow, Faversham and Farthingdown: *ibid.*, 74–6, pl. 14k, j, m; Bruce-Mitford 1983, 387–90, figs 281a, d and 282a). There was then at least one vessel of organic material with copper-alloy mounts, and, given the occurrence of these in multiple sets in other seventh-century barrow burials, possibly more than one.

The next largest functional group consists of copper-alloy strap fittings, all characterized by relief-cast decoration involving fine parallel lines, which may imply they belong to a single suite. The decorative similarities between the hinged strap attachment (Pl. 4.8–9) and buckle-like looped mount with cast-in-one plate (Pl. 4.10), on the one hand, and between the strap end (Pl. 4.11) and looped strap tab (Pl. 4.12), on the other hand, may even indicate that each pair functioned in some way together. To these may be added the openwork swivel suspension fitting (Pl. 4.13), some small rivets with concentric rings on their disc-heads (Pl. 4.15) and, arguably, the best-known object of all from the Asthall assemblage – the 'pear-shaped' mount with Style II ornament (Fig. 18.B) – for it too is characterized by narrow parallel lines and interlace. Fine gilding survives on the mount, so that although it does not appear on the other items its former existence might be suspected.

There are several other miscellaneous studs, rivets and mounts, which might derive from related strapwork or from other organic-based (wood, bone or leather?) items, but which cannot yet be securely attributed. Among these is a rectangular mount (Pl. 4.14), said to be silver but almost certainly copper alloy, with notched and fine line decoration comparable with the strap end and looped strap tab. Mention should also be made of a stud with sunken field (Pl. 4.17), perhaps for an inlay of shell or similar white substance and through which a dome-headed rivet passes, which might be compared with garnet-inlaid studs such as ornamented the Sutton Hoo lyre escutcheons (Bruce-Mitford 1983, 630, fig. 469a), and part of a relief-cast disc or ring which seems to bear Style I animal ornament (Pl. 4.19).

Finally, there are three groups made from animal products, some of which might have borne some of the metal mounts. Most identifiable are the pieces from a gaming set, seven large and nineteen small fragments from low plano-convex counters (Pl. 5.20), probably of bone, estimated to represent at least fourteen originally (Bruce-Mitford 1983, 874, no. 37), and an antler die with an anomalous arrangement of its numbered faces (Pl. 5.21; Brown 1990, 692–4; Arthur MacGregor, pers. comm.). Second, there are at least fifty-five fragments of inlay (Pl. 5.22), cut from major limbs of cattle or horse (Leeds 1924, 118, was misled into thinking these were ivory because of their highly compacted white condition, indicative of heating to 700–800° C or more; Terry O'Connor, pers. comm.). These are variously grooved and/or cross-hatched especially on their inner (medullary) surface, but also on their edges and sometimes even outer surfaces (in the last case possibly implying that they in turn bore some superior covering, though no trace of this survives). Leeds (1924, 118) suggested that they belonged to a casket, but a comb case or even the edging of a gaming board might be other possibilities. However, none of the fragments exhibits the incised and/or ring-and-dot decoration so typical of such fittings and their identification remains a problem. Also of unknown purpose are eleven fragments of 'pin-like' form (Pl. 5.23), likewise made from major limbs of a large mammal (*not* the branchiostegal rays of a large Telesotean fish, *contra* Leeds 1924, 115, 125; Andrew Jones and Terry O'Connor, pers. comm.). They have been shaved to form roughly circular-section tapering rods and some of them show close-set marks transversely across the worked surfaces, which may be caused by the 'chattering' of the knife-blade. These rods are far too thick to have come from Anglo-Saxon combs, while their curvature and number should rule out pins, whether for hair or dress.

Dating

While some of the grave goods point to a date of deposition at any time between the late sixth century and third quarter of the seventh century, others suggest a dating as narrow as the second to fourth decades of the seventh century. So the hand-made pot with tall flaring neck (Fig. 16.A) can be paralleled by finds from several seventh-century graves (Myres 1977, 5). Coin-dated contexts in western Europe show that the date of deposition for Byzantine cast vessels falls within the first three-quarters of the seventh century, whatever their actual date of manufacture in the eastern Mediterranean (Richards 1980, 102–113), the Anglo-Saxon examples being no exception (Mundell Mango et al. 1989). The date-range for Merovingian wheel-made pottery bottles extends from perhaps the mid-sixth to the mid-seventh century, or even later (Evison 1979, 26), but the Asthall example is linked through form (Evison's Group 1) and fabric (Evison's Type II) with one high-quality workshop, whose other products occur in English burials of the late sixth to early seventh century (*ibid.*, 12–13, 23–25, 55–56).

The closest dates are suggested by the decorated metalwork, in particular the Style II mount (Leeds 1924, 123; 1936, 35). Leeds' reconstruction of the pear-shaped plaque with paired rampant (or pendent?) birds of prey, their beaks abutting (Leeds 1924, fig. 6) is confirmed (as against the more tentative drawing of Speake 1980, fig. 6r) by David Brown's recognition of the major part of the left-hand bird-head and the attached beak of its pair (Fig. 18.B). The birds' necks are bounded by double contours, their wings are swept back with triple pinions above a five-feathered grooved fantail and their legs consist of a pear-shaped hip and braceleted triple-clawed foot. The ornament within the pear-shaped plaque consists of two creatures, whose jaws and limbless, triple-stranded, bodies interlink; a small human mask topped by a simple interlaced strand fits in the apex.

Iconographically, the motif of paired pendent birds either side of a human mask is widespread in the Germanic world, but the Asthall-type of crouching predatory bird belongs in the sixth- and seventh-century Scandinavian tradition and compares with a series of Anglo-Saxon examples (Speake 1980, 81–5, fig. 17; Hicks 1986). Although different in scale and material, the cloisonné examples from the Sutton Hoo purse and the silver belt mount from Gilton grave 23, Kent (Speake 1980, fig. 17d and h), share its angled eye-surround, folded wing and squared-off tail. A pair of gilt-bronze and silver-plated mounts from Shelford Farm, Hackington, Kent, and a debased mount from Gilton are probably from shields (*ibid.*, fig. 17c and 17a), echoing the magnificent bird-mount from the Sutton Hoo shield and in turn the mount from Vallstenarum, Gotland (*ibid.*, fig. 17g). Other examples occur among mounts probably from an elaborate belt suite or purse from Buttsole, Eastry, Kent and on a fragmentary pin from Gilton (*ibid.*, fig. 17j, k, i). Paired arrangements of predatory bird heads, executed in gold filigree, surround the pin-fixture of the Kingston Down grave 205 composite brooch, for which a date-range perhaps as narrow as c.610–630 has been proposed (Avent 1975, 63, pl. 69; Speake 1980, pl. 11d). Twinned pairs of opposed bird heads appear also in gold filigree on buckles from Faversham, Kent, which must be close in date to the Kingston brooch (Leeds 1924, 124; Speake 1980, pl. 2h).

The animals within the mount are less distinctive but compare with other Anglo-Saxon Style II creatures (Speake 1980, fig. 6). Their lack of eyes and limbs is a result of the exigencies of space rather than stylistic devolution, and they are clearly more distinct than the triple-strand zoomorphic interlace on the two gilt-bronze discs from Caenby, Lincolnshire, for example, which can be argued to be later (Speake 1980, 64–5). In general the Asthall mount is distinguished by ornament which in the clarity of its design and organisation is matched by the best of Anglo-Saxon Style II, for which the date of Sutton Hoo mound 1 provides a focal point within the earlier seventh century.

The same horizon is indicated by parallels between Asthall and Taplow barrow for the zoomorphic ornament on the copper-alloy foils from putative drinking vessels (see above, p. 104). Also the face mask on the Asthall mount is an abbreviated version of the masks decorating eighteen surviving vandykes on the Taplow drinking cups (Speake 1980, 75, fig. 7m). Parallels might be extended even further with the recognition at Asthall of a fragmentary disc or ring with Style I decoration (Pl. 4.19), reminiscent of the combination of fittings in both styles on the large drinking horns at Taplow (cf. Speake 1980, 94). Whether at Asthall this coexistence also resulted from the longevity and repair of heirlooms or is evidence for the persistence of Style I in the Upper Thames region into the seventh century (cf. Hawkes 1986, 83 and 94) cannot, in the circumstances, be decided.

In sum, although a wider date-range cannot be excluded altogether, we would agree with Leeds' mature judgement (Leeds 1936, 35) that Asthall barrow belongs in the first half of the seventh century.

Social Identity

What kind of person was buried under Asthall barrow? In practice, only three aspects of 'social identity' are accessible, and those not easily. Little human bone has been identified and the anatomical facts of age and sex have yet to be established accurately; their resolution currently depends, just like assessment of status or rank, on archaeological arguments.

Age
Carter's re-examination of the bone identified phalanges with fused epipheses and closed roots from two teeth, which indicated to him a person over 15 years of age.

Sex

Leeds believed that the cremation was that of a female, though he cited no evidence (Leeds 1924, 125 and 126). Carter observed that the finger bones were not very robust and the teeth were relatively small for a male, so that they might have come from a female. Certainly, no male-specific grave goods can be identified. There are no weapons, for example, though this is not a strong argument given the state of the evidence and the fact that weapon burial is infrequent both in cremations and during the seventh century (Härke 1989, esp. 49–52; 1990, 25 and 28–33).

But neither is there any typically female jewellery. At one time we considered the openwork swivel fitting (Pl. 4.13) might be relevant, for it compares closely with the openwork spheres and dodecahedrons, sometimes with swivel mechanisms, which ornament complex châtelaines from seventh-century Alamannic graves in south-west Germany (Koch 1967, 42, 217 Liste 15, Taf. 92; Neuffer-Müller 1983, Taf. 115). A related openwork pendant, but in two-D, was found in the late seventh-century grave F2 at Marina Drive, Dunstable, Bedfordshire, and is assumed to be an import from southern Germany (Matthews 1962, 32, 39, fig. 5.6). However, not only do these parallels lack the doubled-over strap attachment of the Asthall piece, but not all come from female graves: graves 1883/3 and 9 at Pfahlheim are cited as males (the former had prick-spurs: Veeck 1931, 58–9, 165, Taf. 43A1–2).

Alternatively, given the decorative similarity of the openwork swivel fitting with the other identifiable strap fittings, it might have been part of a complex and flexible *system* of straps. Swivel attachments, composed of wire wrapped in a loop round itself or a nail, which passes through the head of a looped strap fitting, do occur in Vendel and Viking graves in Sweden, where they are part of either horse bridles or dog leashes (e.g. Valsgärde 6 Bridle I, Arwidsson 1942, 63, Taf. 26.513; Vendel VII, Arne and Stolpe 1926, pl. XXI, 5 and 10; Ihre grave 108, Gotland, Stenberger 1961, Abb. 92; Sund barrow A54, Säffle, Värmland, Lundborg 1961, 166–7, fig. 5). These are, however, all of iron and much bigger than the delicate Asthall piece, though the newly-discovered looped strap tab from Asthall (Pl. 4.12) adds force to the parallel: its solid loop seems designed to bear a metal ring in the way that the larger fittings on the bridles from Valsgärde 6 and 7 link cheek-straps to snaffle-bit (Arwidsson 1942, 59, Taf. 22.311, 328, 329 and 344; Arwidsson 1977, 58–9, Taf. 23.233 and 251, Taf. 24.230). If the straps did come from an animal leash, a bird of prey would be more in proportion, but though these birds are found occasionally in Vendel graves (e.g. Rickeby, Vallentuna, Sjösvard et al. 1983, 140–2; Sten and Vretemark 1988) we know of none with metal fittings for their leashes, and modern swivels used to link the varvels on jesse straps to the leash are far simpler in design than our Asthall piece.

Analogies for the other Asthall strap fittings can also be drawn with complex belt suites associated with swords and purses or satchels. The hinged strap attachment and buckle-like looped mount compare formally with the, admittedly larger and resplendent, T-shaped strap distributor and plain gold looped mount from the harness in Sutton Hoo mound 1, even to the thicknesses of the straps which they bore (2 millimetres for the looped mounts, 2 millimetres and c.1.5 millimetres for the hinged mounts; Bruce-Mitford 1978, 465–9, 485–6, 564–81). The hinged strap attachment compares even more closely to the hinge fittings from the Sutton Hoo purse (*ibid.*, fig. 362): its thicker strap was fastened on the back by a washer of the same shape as that which held the double-thickness of the Sutton Hoo bag and purse lid (*ibid.*, fig. 363e, 499–500); its thinner strap, as noted, is close to the 1 millimetre of the Sutton Hoo purse hinges, indicative of cloth rather than leather; and the rivets of the Sutton Hoo purse hinges have been stamped or drilled to look like bull's-eyes (*ibid.*, 494), echoing the stamps on the Asthall hinged attachment and exactly like the disc-head rivets with concentric rings (Pl. 4.15) which we have associated with the belt fittings. Whether the Style II mount also ornamented a purse lid cannot be known, but its stylistic links with the belt fittings and with mounts from purses, as at Sutton Hoo and probably Buttsole (see above, p. 106), make the interpretation tempting.

The openwork swivel fitting may have been for a shoulder strap or to support some item hung below the waist, but it cannot indicate the sex of its owner. Indeed, if our later arguments are nearer the truth, this was male rather than female. This is also the conclusion if the sex-associations of other aspects of the burial are considered.

First, there is the gaming set (Pl. 5.20–21). Gaming counters and, more rarely, dice occur in many of the large cremation sites of fifth- and sixth-century eastern England, though their incidence per site is low. Richards records only twelve cases where the sex of the skeleton is also known, seven male and five female (Richards 1987, 108–110, 130–1). Hills notes, however, that all of the urns with gaming pieces from the 1968 season at Spong Hill proved to contain males (Hills 1974, 89 note 5). There are obvious problems in evaluating this evidence in terms of poor sample size, possibly false data and the fact that, with cremations in urns, sex seems to be expressed less through grave goods and more through the urn itself (Richards 1987). It contrasts certainly with the pattern for gaming pieces found in inhumations and/or barrows, which date primarily from the later sixth and seventh centuries and whose distribution extends into southern England (Youngs in Bruce-Mitford 1983, 861). Using Youngs' list of thirty-nine English sites which have yielded gaming pieces (*ibid.*, 873–4), but excluding Asthall and the sixteen urn-cemeteries and adding in Sutton Hoo itself (giving twenty-five burials from twenty-three sites), the following figures result: ten burials are definitely male, including the barrow burials at Sutton Hoo mound 1, Taplow, Oxton, Bishopsbourne barrow 3 and Bishop's Canning barrow 3 (=Roundway Down I); three are definitely female and one is a multiple burial including a female (Brightwell Heath), though these contain only one or two gaming pieces which are, variously, a Roman survival, used as a pendant or unusual in some other way; Sutton Hoo mound

4 may be a double burial of a male and female or a female alone (N.-G. Gejvall in Bruce-Mitford 1975, 135–6). This leaves ten graves for which sex is not known. The pattern is even more strongly displayed in Shephard's analysis of 341 grave assemblages drawn from a comparable constituency of inhumation cemeteries in southern England and seventh-century barrows: gaming pieces fall squarely within a cluster of apparently male-linked grave-good types (Shephard 1979a, 51–2, fig. 3).

Second, the number of vessels can be considered. Asthall had at least seven vessels, possibly eight or even more. In the Upper Thames region, graves with more than two vessels are rare: the late fifth-/early sixth-century Long Witten-ham I, grave 26 ('bronze'-bound bucket, 'bronze' dish and cauldron) and the early seventh-century Cuddesdon (two glass bowls and Byzantine bucket) are male and high status, contrasting apparently with Abingdon I, grave B14, a female with three hand-made pots and a wooden vessel (Dickinson 1976, 362–72). Large numbers of vessels are a hallmark of the highest-status burials among the Germanic peoples from the Roman Iron Age onwards and in England characterize the early seventh-century phase of rich, adult male, pri-mary barrows: Sutton Hoo mound 1 with forty-four (Bruce-Mitford 1975, 440–4) far outstrips the others (Taplow: about nineteen, Leslie Webster, pers. comm.; Broomfield: eleven, Read 1894; Sutton Hoo mound 2: six or seven or more, Evans 1989; Carver 1990a, table 2). The later seventh-century phase of barrow burial, which includes female graves, is still marked by fine vessels but fewer: Swallowcliffe Down, for example, mustered five (Speake 1989).

Third, the types of vessel convey the same message (cf. also Shephard 1979a, fig. 3). Drinking horns, bottles and cups are nearly all from male graves, the few exceptions also being atypical in form and possibly incorrectly identified (East in Bruce-Mitford 1983, 390). Merovingian pottery bottles (in comparison with other wheel-made imports) occur nearly three times as often in male as in female graves (Evison 1979, 25–6). Data for Byzantine vessels are available for fewer than half the known corpus and the picture is less conclusive: the Euro-pean figures give thirty-nine males:sixteen females according to Richards (1980, table 6), whereas his figures for English finds are six males:four females, which differs perplexingly from a male:female ratio of three:one cited by Mundell Mango et al. (1989, 307). We may note in passing, however, that these ratios contrast with those for sheet-metal vessels in Anglo-Saxon graves (lug-eared cauldrons: seven males:fourteen females (twenty-one not known); other sheet metal vessels: thirteen males:seventeen females (twenty-eight not known); Richards 1980, 13, table 14).

Fourth, there is the presence of animal bone, which is thought to constitute the bulk of the cremated bone (Leeds 1924, 117–18). Carter was able to identify four pieces from a horse and one, possibly three, from a sheep. Richards' study of Anglo-Saxon cremations in urns recorded animal bones from only five sites (144 out of 706 urns *in toto*) giving an incidence per site of between 15% and 30% (Richards 1987, 125, table 21; see also Richards this volume), though more recent work on Spong Hill indicates that up to 43% of urns contained animal bones (Julie Bond, pers. comm.). Skeletal sexing of the human bone and species identification of the animals respectively was available from four of Richards' sites, but in combination from only three (cf. Richards 1987, 114 and 125). Animals in general proved to be linked at a *statistically significant level* with human males, but this could not be extended to individual species. Sheep emerged as the most frequent species and were more likely to occur with males than with females, but were also appropriate to children. Horses were far more likely to be with males than females and they did *not* occur with children (*ibid.*, 125, 128–9, 132–33, tables 21, 24, 28). Given our comments above about problems with data quality and about the possible differences in symbolising sex in cremations in urns, these observations are instructive. The correlation may be yet more marked, for the Spong Hill study showed that there horse was by far the most frequent animal; in the cremation record, horses may be underestimated while sheep are overestimated (Julie Bond, pers. comm.). Certainly, a strong correlation has been observed between males and horse burial in general. In a sample of 287 sites drawn from across Continental Europe, horses were definitely or possibly associated with male burials at one hundred sites compared with just twenty sites where they were linked with female graves, of which six were double (male and female) graves; in the south Baltic region horse burials are again said to be overwhelmingly linked with male graves (Müller-Wille 1970–71, 141–6, 160–2) and horses are, of course, a notable component of the primarily adult male and rich Vendel period graves of the Mälar region (Sten and Vretemark 1988). Vierck listed examples for Müller-Wille's study from twenty-eight English sites (1970–71, 218–20), though at least one was Viking period (Reading) and another a false reference (Kemp Town; cf. Welch 1983, 431–2). Excluding those two, nine were associated with males (this includes Sutton Hoo mound 3 and two urns rather than one from Illington, cf. Richards 1987, table 21), three were linked with double graves (one of which was definitely a male plus female, another a female plus another adult, and the third is Sutton Hoo mound 4) and a fourth was situated close to a female and a male grave, though nearer the former (Marston St Lawrence). To these may be added Roundway Down II, a rich late seventh-century female barrow, in which 'the bones of four animals, *said to be* (our italics) of a dog and a cat, a horse and boar' were reportedly found; if true, and recovery and recording was far from reliable (Merewether 1849, 111–12), this would be the only unequivocal association of horse and female (of the remaining burials listed by Vierck, thirteen are not certainly related to or even contemporaneous with human graves, while in the other eight cases the sex of the human burials is unknown).

Finally, Shephard's work allows the very size and nature of the Asthall barrow to be invoked. Female burials in *primary* barrows are rare (just seven instances), the great majority (78.5%) dating from the *late* seventh century, and the barrows in which women were buried, whether primary or secondary, were small (<12 metres; Shephard 1979b, chapters 2 and 7.5). The primary barrow at Asthall, datable to the first half of the seventh century and with a diameter of at least 16.76 metres and possibly as much as 20.73 metres or more, ought to belong to a man.

In sum, the possibility that Asthall was the burial of a woman cannot be excluded, but the cumulative balance of probability weighs strongly in favour of a man. It is just possible that Asthall was a double grave of a man and woman, for which Sutton Hoo mound 4 offers an apt, albeit also ambiguous, parallel.

Status

Leeds had no doubt that Asthall was the grave of someone of high rank (Leeds 1924, 125). Since Leeds' day, the premises, methods *and* problems involved in making such an inference have been more extensively explored and scrutinized (for the early medieval period, see now especially James 1989), although few archaeologists, faced with positive evidence of exceptional complexity, monumentality and buried wealth, would dissent from Leeds' conclusion. Attempting a finer definition is controversial, however: Vierck, for example, characterized Asthall as a 'princely grave', to be mapped alongside Sutton Hoo, Snape, Taplow, Broomfield and Benty Grange (Davies and Vierck 1974, 277 and fig. 5), whereas Mundell Mango et al. (1989, 307) classed it as 'exceptionally rich' but below the royal or princely ranking of Sutton Hoo and Taplow. These arguments resurrect the wider theoretical issues, for they depend necessarily on functionalist assumptions, as well as raising more methodological points. Shephard's ranking of barrow burials isolated a premier male group (Aa: Sutton Hoo mound 1, Taplow and Broomfield), which, he emphasized, not only outstripped by far the very rich burials of his contemporaneous male Group A2 but was not itself a homogeneous group (Shephard 1979b). Indeed, a paradoxical identifier of Group A as a whole was its *diversity* of grave goods. Likewise Carver (1990a, 19) has noted that Sutton Hoo, *the* Anglo-Saxon paradigm for a dynastic cemetery, is marked by diversity of burial styles, albeit all ones which involve exclusiveness. Sutton Hoo cautions us too not to be misled by incomplete assemblages, whether caused by robbing and/or cremation (*ibid.*, table 2; cf. Evans 1989).

In the context of these arguments, we would propose that Asthall belongs with the most impressive of the barrow burials of the late sixth/earlier seventh century. Some of the parallels have already been mentioned and they must stand. Perhaps the most compelling analogy is the presence of large numbers of vessels: this at once links Asthall with Shephard's Group Aa. The combination of vessel-types, especially of Byzantine bowl, sheet-metal bowl, metal-bound organic vessel(s) and pottery, is also comparable, though of course any one or two of these might be found in less spectacular graves. It is also true, as far as we can tell, that Asthall lacks large cauldrons suitable for supplying the needs of many followers, such as characterize Sutton Hoo mounds 1 and 2, Taplow and Broomfield.

But two of the Asthall vessels may be diagnostic in their own right. While the fine pottery bottle (Fig. 16.C) clearly fits into the corpus of wheel-made pottery imported from France into England, it is unique in form, decoration and context (Evison 1979, 12; cf. Evison 1974). Bottles, even more than other types of wheel-made pot, were a monopoly of Kent, where they seem to have fulfilled a special role in the burial rites of some families (*ibid.*, 25–7). The only other bottle found *outside* Kent is the much clumsier example from Sutton Hoo mound 1 (*ibid.*, 12, 24, 55). If the monopoly imports of Kent imply privileged trading links with the Merovingian world and internal controlled redistribution (Huggett 1988), the rare occurrence of outliers in high-status burials might betoken more personal and exclusive gifts between those who controlled the trade and their peers in other regions.

The other vessel which may link Asthall uniquely with Sutton Hoo mound 1 is the silver bowl or cup. The difficulty here is establishing quite what type of vessel is represented. The metal itself is so corroded that accurate metallurgical assays are not possible. Catherine Mortimer (at the instigation of Marlia Mundell Mango) has been able to achieve at best 'semi-quantitative' readings of between approximatly 2.8% and 7% copper, with the silver represented as silver bromide; she estimates that 'the silver was originally *more than* 90% pure' (C. Mortimer *in litt.*; our italics). It may well then have fallen within the normal range for Roman and Early Byzantine silver which is 92%–99% pure, with the majority between 94% and 98% pure (Hughes et al. in Baratte and Painter 1989, 22), though there is just a possibility that it did not.

The proportions of the rim fragment (Pl. 3.1) suggest a fairly small bowl or cup with uprightish rim which had been finished on a lathe. Four fragments bear embossed decoration, of which potentially the most diagnostic are two with parts of almost abutting grooved circles enclosing low bosses (as seen from one side; from the other they appear as raised rings around a plane disc: Pl. 3.2). Within the known corpus of Antique silver the most striking parallels are on a series of second-/third-century small bowls and beakers decorated with round or oval facets or dimples (Strong 1966, 174–5). The majority comes from within the Empire, especially from Gaul (viz. Chaourse: Baratte and Painter 1989, 119–21; Notre-Dame d'Allençon: Baratte 1981, 49–53; Taragnat: *ibid.*; and Saint-Pabu, (found close to a fourth-century coin hoard: du Châtelier 1889), but there is one find from Switzerland (Wettingen: Simonett 1946, Taf. 3.10) and two from Britain (Walbrook Mithraeum, London: Bird 1986; and the 'hanging' bowl from the probably early fourth-century hoard from Water Newton: Painter 1977, 11–12, pl. 4). Examples are also known, however, from 'princely' Germanic burials north of the *Limes* (viz. Leuna grave 1917/2, Germany: Schulz 1953, 11, Taf. V,1; Hagerup, Denmark: Broholm 1960, 224–6, figs 111–112; cf. Lund Hansen 1987, 426). Of these the closest parallel to Asthall is one of the Chaourse bowls (British Museum GR 1890, 9–23, 8) because it is almost the only example on which the facets are not separated by a vegetative motif (Baratte and Painter 1989, 120, no. 59).

Dimples and bosses were popular in general, however, on Later Roman glass, from which they may have been copied on to silver, and on pottery, and the basic motif seems to have persisted on silver beyond the third century. A simplified version in *pointillé* appears on the bowl from Coleraine, a presumptively fifth-century deposit (Mattingley and Pearce 1937, 45, pl. III) and it recurs, executed in deeper relief, in the form of 'egg-and-palmette' on friezes and borders of Early Byzantine silver. The best analogies known to us here are the 'Stuma' paten from the reconstructed Kaper Koraon treasure and the two chalices from the Beth Misona treasure, both in Syria (Mundell Mango 1986, 159–64, 229–30, nos 34, 58–59). Interestingly, the 'trifoliate' motif separating the 'eggs' on the Beth Misona chalices looks identical in form to that separating the facets on the Walbrook Mithraeum bowl. Abutting circles also occur on the Sutton Hoo Byzantine silver bowls, but here they are also part of complex intersecting circles (Bruce-Mitford 1983, 69–125, cf. esp. figs 66, 83 and 84).

Although the Middle/Late Roman parallels seem formally closer than the Early Byzantine, such an identification for the Asthall vessel would be remarkable. On the whole, vessels in Late Antique hoards do not seem to have survived in circulation for more than about eighty five years (Kenneth Painter, pers. comm.), though there are some archaeological and historical analogies for greater longevity (Mundell Mango 1990; cf. Painter 1990; whether the fourth-century silver of the 'Sevso' hoard was buried as late as the late sixth or early seventh century is still contentious, Hedges 1991, 294). It might, of course, be argued that the Asthall vessel was recovered by chance from a Roman hoard, or even from a grave within or beyond the Empire (the silver vessels from northern Germania seem also to have been deposited fairly soon after importation: Hedeager 1988, 150–2; a grave-find within Britain is unlikely, however, for metal vessels are scarce in Late Romano-British burials: White 1988, 134). But had such lucky opportunities existed we might expect more evidence: metal vessels of any kind datable before the late fourth century are rare in Anglo-Saxon burials (White 1988, 119–21, 134–6).

Alternatively, the Asthall vessel dates from nearer to its time of deposition, especially given the analogy of Byzantine silver in Sutton Hoo mound 1. Our inability to point to any good parallels may then be attributed to the inadequate condition of the material, or perhaps to limited knowledge of fifth-century, as against sixth- and seventh-century, silver (cf. Mundell Mango 1990, 11), or even to the possibility, given the uncertain metal analysis, that the vessel is not authentic Roman or Byzantine silver, but a contemporaneous west European (Merovingian) product (cf. the Valdonne plates: Bruce-Mitford 1983, 164; Baratte and Painter 1989, 280–1).

Whatever the origin of the Asthall vessel, it cannot detract from its basic identification as a piece of Late Antique silver, which is likely to have reached its destination through privileged contacts of 'gift-giving' and/or descent. As Bruce-Mitford (1983, 163) has emphasized, such material (spoons apart) is exceptionally rare in Migration and Merovingian period graves. If Asthall is overshadowed by the sixteen pieces of silver (fourteen vessels) from Sutton Hoo, it nonetheless ranks with it by being the only other Anglo-Saxon burial to have yielded a solid silver vessel (*pace* Bruce-Mitford).

Finally, the barrow size (see above) is commensurate with the richest, eastern English, barrows from the early seventh century (Shephard 1979b, chapter 2), while the barrow itself occupies a classic position for isolated barrows: it stands (at about 430 feet (131 metres) O.D.) near the summit of a limestone spur at the edge of the southern Cotswolds whence it commands stupendous views, southwards across the entire length of the Upper Thames valley to the scarps of the Berkshire Downs and Chilterns, and northwards across the tributary valley of the Windrush (Fig. 14.B–C). It was designed to 'see' and be seen. All these arguments link Asthall to the topmost echelon of Early Anglo-Saxon 'princely' burials.

Cultural Context of the Burial Ritual

The evidence from Asthall for a total cremation of a rich grave assemblage under a barrow is remarkable. It would appear to differ from most other excavated Anglo-Saxon burial sites both in the Upper Thames region and further afield. Thus within the Upper Thames other assuredly Anglo-Saxon and individual barrow burials are all inhumations (probably Cuddesdon, of the early seventh century, just north of the Thames, and certainly East Ilsley mound 3 and Lowbury Hill of the later seventh century to the south on the Berkshire Downs, Hawkes 1986, 90–91). Only one other cremation can be dated for certain to the seventh century, though admittedly dating the end of cremation in general is not easy: interestingly, this one – Bledlow Cop grave D, Buckinghamshire – is one of seven burials secondary to a Bronze Age barrow (Dickinson 1976, vol. I 218, vol. II 44).

Consideration must also be given to a remarkable series of large round barrows in the very neighbourhood of Asthall, to which Leeds himself drew attention (Fig. 14.C; Leeds 1939a, 243–4; 1939b, 365, 367): one – at Leafield – is visible on the skyline to the north of Asthall. Some of these barrows are probably Bronze Age, but the discovery of Late Roman coins in one at Swinbrook and the comparison in size with Asthall and Taplow might indicate that others were built or used in the Anglo-Saxon period (*ibid.*; Potts 1907, 345–7; cf. Hawkes 1986, 91). Further, some of them seem to have contained cremations: at Chalford, north of Chadlington, two barrows, contained 'an enormous mass of black and red ashes and charred earth' and one remains of 'charred metal'; another at Spelsbury Down Farm revealed a layer of burnt earth, 30 feet (9.1 metres) in diameter, as well as very large stones, thought to be the remains of a cist; the Swinbrook barrow too was composed of stones and contained charcoal and bones (Leeds 1939a, 243). Unfortunately, the quality of this evidence, however tantalizing, severely limits its contribution to evaluating Asthall, just as the ambiguity of the excavation record at Asthall itself impedes reconstruction of the burial sequence and thence the wider cultural context. Nonetheless, it is with the burial sequence which we must start; we shall treat it stratigraphically and draw on likely parallels to further the interpretation.

The burial appears to have been on the surface of the land, not in a grave or pit, for the ashes, covering an area about 20 feet (6.1 metres) in diameter, lay over a layer of yellowish clay, which in turn lay over the natural limestone. However, the discrepancies in the given height of the barrow and description of the depth of the excavation trench (above, p. 98) raise the possibility that the burial area had been sunken below the level of the land.

The nature of the clay layer is also problematic: was it a deliberate deposit, part of the burial ritual, or natural? Leeds asserted that it had been 'brought up from the valley of the Windrush, three-quarters of a mile away' (Leeds 1924, 115). The association of clay layers with burials has been discussed more recently in connection with the equally problematic finds, including a crema- tion in a metal bowl, from Coombe, Kent (see further below): here, a grave pit lay 6 feet *below* a clay spread, 20 yards (approximatly 18 metres) in diameter (Ellis Davidson and Webster 1967, 1, 9–10, esp. note 34). In fact, in England the most common use of clay would seem to be *inside* a grave, whether as a complete fill or as a layer under or over the skeleton, sometimes at sites where there is, apparently, no naturally occurring clay (e.g. Kingston Down grave 103, Kent: *ibid.*; Swarkeston, Derbyshire; Prittlewell, Essex; Bower Chalke, Wiltshire: Meaney 1964, 78, 87, 266; Swallowcliffe Down, Wiltshire: Speake 1989, 14). The hard-stamped chalk over graves at Chessell Down, Isle of Wight, is probably natural, for the site was situated on heavy marl (Arnold 1982b, 18). Likewise the 'clay pans' in both Sutton Hoo mound 1 and 3 have now been identified as natural sedimentation from the mound after the collapse of wooden grave structures (Bruce-Mitford 1975, 108–9, fig. 57, 173–6). In turn, this invites comparison with the clay layer which covered the *in situ* cremation in the Vendel period barrow at Rickeby; it was created by soil filtering through a stone cairn from the superincumbent earth mound (Sjösvard et al. 1983, 135). These last examples may strengthen the hypothesis that Coombe once had a barrow (Ellis Davidson and Webster 1967, 4–9), but none of them is helpful to Asthall.

But the use of a clay layer, as the base for a funeral pyre, has been attested in several Swedish cremation barrows, for example in both the western and eastern mounds of Old Uppsala excavated by Hagdahl and Hildebrand. In the former the clay was 3 metres in diameter and 0.60 millimetres thick and had been spread over the previously levelled gravel ridge (Lindqvist 1936, 146–7); in the latter it was considerably larger in size, approximatly 300 millimetres thick and enclosed by the walled edge of the cairn (*ibid.*, 152). If Asthall too had been treated in this way, it might also explain the apparent failure to identify an old ground surface: it would have been swept away at a preparatory stage, to be reused later for the mound (wasteful of energy though this might seem to us) along with the topsoil scraped up from a wider area.

A more prosaic explanation, however, is that the Asthall clay layer was a natural deposit. At Asthall undisturbed subsoil can be sticky, orange-yellow in colour, and includes small decaying lumps of limestone brash: possibly this was what the excavators uncovered. The limestone at Asthall belongs to the Forest Marble series, which consists of highly variable seams of clays and limestones; where the clay lies beneath topsoil it weathers to a brown or yellow colour as the iron salts oxidize (R.A. Chambers, pers. comm., quoting information from J. Hazelden of the Soil Survey and Land Research Centre; Richardson et al. 1946, 34–80). The local farmer, George Walker, reports that clay patches do exist in the vicinity of the barrow. So even if the clay layer had been deliberately deposited, it need not have been brought up from the Windrush valley.

Whatever its source, the clay layer was the scene of two subsequent stratigraphic events, though their relationship cannot be established for certain. First there is the broad spread of cremation debris up to 6 inches (152 millimetres) thick (Fig. 15.B), from which approximately 2 litres of bone survive. Nowhere near this quantity has been recovered, for example, from the cremation barrows at Sutton Hoo. Much larger quantities of material, however, come from the total, *in situ*, cremations of Vendel period Sweden. At Rickeby the cremation covered an area comparable with that at Asthall – 4 metres x 6 metres – but had a central rectangular core 3 metres x 1.8 metres in area and up to 300 millimetres thick, which represented the actual pyre on which the deceased had been laid surrounded by his animals, just like contemporary inhumations; it yielded 32 litres of bone (Sjösvard et al. 1983, 136–7), though this is dwarfed by the 100 litres of bone from another rich male grave at Spelvik, Södermanland (Lamm 1962, 278).

Second there are the various postholes reported from Asthall as well as 'charred remains of what must have been timber of considerable size' (Leeds 1924, 116). Given the spread of cremation debris and the various Swedish parallels cited so far, it would be attractive to conclude with Leeds that the Asthall barrow covered the site of the funeral pyre which was 'evidently held together by a series of posts, some of the holes for which were observed in the extension of 1924' (Leeds 1939b, 365). Unfortunately, this interpretation is beset with difficulties.

We have already discussed the problems of interpreting the postholes (above, p. 100). The location and stratigraphy of those found in 1924 cannot be verified. It seems more likely that posthole Y cut through the clay, predating the cremation deposit, and contained a post which burnt and/or rotted *in situ*; it could have belonged to the pyre, though we might then have expected cremation debris to have filtered into its socket (cf. Liebenau, Germany: Cosack 1982, 15), just as seems to be the case at point V, which may *be* the base of a pyre posthole. Posthole U might also have belonged to a pyre, if it had penetrated the clay layer. But if it had rested on the cremation debris, it would have to be explained as part of the mound construction, along with the cavity above posthole Y, assuming the latter was genuine.

The largish charred timber, found near to posthole Y, might also be good evidence for a pyre: the description seems sufficiently clear to believe that that was what was found and not simply decayed wood, although there is no guarantee that it represented structural members rather than some substantial wooden object. But a major objection remains: the underlying clay is described as 'yellowish'. In the western mound at Old Uppsala, the clay bed as well as possible wattle-wall caulking had been burnt to brick; the clay floor in the eastern mound, pierced by eight perpendicular timbers, had been similarly burnt (Lindqvist 1936, 146–7, 152). Had Asthall also been the site of a timber-framed pyre structure, the clay ought to have become red and hard – unless, of course, the accumulating wood ash acted as an insulating layer. If there had not been a pyre under the mound, we must explain any postholes predating the deposition of the cremation debris in another way: possibly they represented some kind of mortuary structure. We must also speculate on where the pyre had been: pyres have not certainly been recorded in association with Anglo-Saxon cremation cemeteries and may be assumed to be elsewhere, yet the large charred timber at Asthall is unlikely to have been brought from any distance.

Finally, there is the point that the cremated remains were spread over such a large area. If this was not the result of later grave-robbery (see above, p. 101), it could be consistent with the collapse of a raised funeral pyre and/or subsequent raking of the ashes (cf. Liebenau again: Cosack 1982, 18–20). The wide distribution of the pottery bottle sherds could also have resulted from containers being ritually broken during the firing. Asthall thus differs in this respect from other known English examples of cremations in barrows (see below, p. 119): in these the ashes have been selectively placed in a container, most frequently a metal vessel, but in Sutton Hoo mound 3 at opposite ends of a wooden 'plank', or, as at Cold Eaton, Derbyshire, in a small pit 'as compactly as if they had first been deposited within a shallow basket or similar perishable vessel' (Bateman 1861, 179). Admittedly, some of the cremated bones from Asthall are stained green from prolonged contact with copper alloy, but this could have resulted from proximity to other grave goods as much as from their original deposition in a metal vessel, and the single unburnt fragment of a sheet-metal vessel may simply have escaped burning (because the vessel was placed on the edge of the pyre) rather than be the sole survivor of a cinerary receptacle.

So we might speculate that Asthall was the scene of an *in situ* funeral pyre, built on a series of wooden supports, which was subsequently covered by a large earth mound, paralleling (but for the absence of an intermediary stone cairn) the ritual of total cremation under a barrow found in Sweden. The evidence from other barrows near Asthall, especially that from Spelsbury

Down Farm, might even suggest that the ritual – possibly including a stone make-up – was locally established. But we must admit that at nearly every point in the argument there are reservations.

If, however, we consider the burial ritual at Asthall in terms of its more secure attributes – the components of the grave assemblage and as a cremation-barrow – then its cultural context comes more into focus. In Early Saxon England barrows are associated with about 20% of sites with cremation burials (Sales 1991, 22, map 10 and database). The vast majority is not easily related to our enquiry, for it consists of either 'mixed rite' or, in some half-dozen cases, cremation-only *cemeteries* in and/or adjacent to *pre-Saxon* barrows (these barrow-associated sites tending to be in regions peripheral to the main eastern English core of cremation cemeteries). Because of inexpert or incomplete excavation it is not always possible to discriminate between barrow-usage which is 'communal', and even coincidental, and the deliberate location of an individual cremation within a barrow: records of a single urn (as at Mepal Fen, Cambridgeshire, or Risby Heath, Suffolk, Meaney 1964, 68, 232) may mask a larger site, while rarely is it known assuredly that urns are from primary Saxon barrows rather than being secondary insertions (e.g. Pitsford, Northamptonshire, is questionable as a primary barrow, cf. Meaney 1964, 195; Snape, Suffolk, is a particularly nice conundrum, Bruce-Mitford 1974, 133–6; Filmer-Sankey, this volume). At just a few cemeteries, small primary mounds or ring-ditches are associated with individual cremations: interestingly these are often unurned and southern English (e.g. Bowcombe Down, Isle of Wight, Arnold 1982b, 89–94; Apple Down 1, Sussex, Down and Welch 1990, 25; possibly also, therefore, six barrows on Whitmoor Common, Surrey, which Pitt Rivers supposed were primary, Meaney 1964, 245). These are, however, very different from the Asthall-type of cremation barrow in both their context and poverty of assemblage.

Quite distinct is a select group of cremations in individual primary barrows, to which reference has already been made (cf. Table 1). These are six of the barrows investigated so far at Sutton Hoo (mounds 3, 4, 5, 6, 7 and 18, all but the first robbed), Brightwell Heath mound 3, also in south-east Suffolk and sited within a prehistoric barrow-cemetery (Reid Moir 1921, 11–13; Vierck 1972, 33–4, Abb.7), and Cold Eaton, Derbyshire (Bateman 1861, 179; Ozanne 1962–3, 37). Coombe, Kent, with its cremation in a bronze bowl, was arguably also under a barrow (see above, p. 116), though there are problems concerning the integrity of this find (Ellis Davidson and Webster 1967; see below). *Like* Asthall, all are datable from the late sixth or seventh century, all but one are in large mounds (>15 metres diameter), five contain gaming pieces (a set of twenty-eight counters in the case of Cold Eaton) and four include animals (horse twice, dog thrice, ox once). *Unlike* Asthall, six contained combs and four, possibly more, included unburnt as well as burnt grave goods. As we have already remarked, six had their cremated bone deposited in a bronze vessel, covered or wrapped with cloth, and at the others the ashes were deliberately deposited in a confined space.

With only three certain sites other than Asthall in this group, it might seem unwise to make much of its distribution falling within the normally accepted 'Anglian-cultural' area of Early Saxon England, especially if the less secure site at Coombe is admitted, extending the distribution to Kent. But the contents of their assemblages – singly and together – also point to an Anglian context, and behind that to Scandinavia, a heritage to which Kent also laid claim. Of course, these components may be found with cremations of any type (cf. Richards 1987), and cremation *per se* is not geographically (and hence culturally) segregated in England (cf. Down and Welch 1990, 25), but there is no doubt that it was practised most intensively and consistently in the Scandinavian-influenced Anglian areas of eastern England, from Suffolk to Humberside (Sales 1990, maps 4 and 5; cf. Hines 1984). Gaming pieces seem to occur in cremations, Asthall apart, only in Anglian districts. Early Saxon horse-burials, whether inhumed or in cremations, as well as finds of bridles, are predominantly though not exclusively found in Anglian areas plus Kent (Vierck 1970–71, 197–8). Gaming pieces, animal bones, sometimes in spectacular quantities, and combs are regular components of total cremations under barrows in Scandinavia, both in Norway and Sweden (e.g. Arne 1919; Lindqvist 1936; Vierck 1970–71, 197–8; 1972; Sjösvärd et al. 1983, 138–9).

The use of metal bowls as cinerary containers and the association of burnt with unburnt grave goods, characteristic of the English cremation barrows except probably Asthall, have also been singled out by Ellis Davidson and Webster (1967, 9–16), with reference to Coombe, and by Vierck (1972), in the course of proposing that Sutton Hoo mound 1 contained a cremation. Vierck argued that both were Anglian rites derived from Norway. Unfortunately, their lists of examples require some critical editing (cf. Table 1). In arguing for a rite in which a cremated body is accompanied by unburnt, inhumation-style, rich grave goods, they underestimated the inadequate and ambiguous nature of the available record, in particular for Loveden Hill, Lincolnshire, and arguably also for Coombe itself, which are the principal candidates for such a rite (cf. Evison 1976, 306–7). In all other cases unburnt items are few, small and, where known, from within the cinerary receptacle: they compare with ordinary urned cremations in which unburnt items, especially combs, are not uncommon elements. In the case of cremations in metal vessels, they include instances for which there is *no* positive evidence for cremation (that is no bones at all were found). Indeed, it is interesting to note that, excepting again Coombe and Loveden Hill, cases of cremation in a copper-alloy bowl *not* under a barrow share few of the attributes which mark out the assemblages of cremations *under* barrows, apart from their dating (later sixth and seventh centuries) and presumptively higher status (if only by virtue of the metal vessel). The distribution of cremations in copper-alloy vessels in England is, however, markedly Anglian, with a concentration in East Anglia, an outlying enclave at Baginton, Warwickshire, and Coombe the sole certain representative from Kent.

The idea that Asthall was the burial of a man with a sacrificed female – a hypothesis ventured in 1976 (Dickinson 1976, 441) in the wake of discussion of Coombe (where the unburnt grave goods included male and female items: Ellis Davidson and Webster 1967, esp. 11) and Cuddesdon (Dickinson 1974, 19–24), and repeated by Hawkes (1986, 91) – now seems intemperate and should not be used in support of any Anglian/Scandinavian cultural affinities. The evidence for human sacrifice as part of burial ritual at this period has been well reviewed by Hirst (1985, 40–43) in the context of the far from conclusive case at Sewerby, East Yorkshire. Although it is attested historically, especially for northern Europe and the Viking Age, identification of instances in the archaeological record is fraught with problems. The satellite burials around mound 5 at Sutton Hoo are perhaps the most plausible Early Saxon case to date. But where identification depends simply on the presence of more than one individual in the same grave or cremation (as possibly at Asthall) or, worse, on the apparent concurrence of male and female 'kits' in a single context (as at Coombe), we should be wary of piling hypothesis upon hypothesis (though the case has been made again for high-status Vendel period cremations, which may contain a man with up to four other individuals, Sten and Vretemark 1988, 148–9).

Historical Context

The existence of an early seventh-century burial at Asthall not only of very high status but also Anglian in its cultural background invites finally some consideration of its historical context. But first we must take the archaeological explanation a stage further, for modern theoretical approaches offer some useful glosses on the significance of both aspects. Burial rites should be seen as cultural artifices: they can express notions about personal and social relationships and so serve as arenas for acting out ideology, reflecting or manipulating accepted norms according to current needs. The use of monumental, extravagant and exclusive burial may indicate therefore not simply 'high status' but also the need to justify (legitimize) that status, and is more likely to occur when the nature of power and/or the individuals holding it are changing rapidly. There is every reason to link the appearance of the grandest of Early Saxon burials in the late sixth and early seventh century with the emergence of regional kingship. Likewise the forms which these burials take may embody both widely understood metaphors and individual expressions of them: they may symbolize allegiance to a common culture, or defiance. Thus Carver explains the 'Nordic associations' at Sutton Hoo in terms of their role in establishing political allegiance among the East Anglian elite (cf. Carver 1990a, 19; Carver forthcoming). Further this use of burials to promote dynastic claims may have been more potent at the edges of territories rather than at their centres. It has often been noticed how 'princely' barrows need not relate to known political centres: Taplow and the Vendel/Valsgärde cemeteries (Ambrosiani 1983) are prime examples, and even Sutton Hoo is eccentric within East Anglia (cf. Wood 1991, 13; Carver forthcoming).

In terms of sixth-century material culture Asthall lies well within the Saxon Upper Thames region (Fig. 14): the boundary with Anglian cultural areas would be put some 40 kilometres to the north-east (Davies and Vierck 1974, 277; Vierck 1978). In the late sixth/early seventh century this area was the core of an emergent and expansionist Saxon regional kingdom, centred around Dorchester-on-Thames. In the course of the seventh century, however, political competition with other (Anglian) regional kingdoms, initially Northumbria but subsequently and primarily Mercia, turned the Thames valley into disputed border territory (Yorke 1990, passim). Detail about political conditions and institutions becomes available only with the later seventh century and it is an obvious problem whether these can be extrapolated backwards to the time of Asthall. So while the few notices in Bede's *Historia Ecclesiastica* and in the *Anglo-Saxon Chronicle* for the first half of the seventh century suggest intermittent conflict and Anglian involvement (Edwin's retaliation *s.a.* 626 for a West Saxon murderous (and pre-emptive?) attempt upon him; Oswald's godfathership to Cynegils *s.a.* 635 and later marriage to his daughter; Penda's fight at Cirencester *s.a.* 628 and expulsion of Cenwalh *s.a.* 645), it is not until the 660s that a real watershed seems to have been reached with the withdrawal of the West Saxon bishopric from Dorchester-on-Thames to Winchester and subsequent rivalry between Mercia and Wessex for control of southern England.

Asthall's situation may have been marginal also in terms of the smaller provinces or subkingdoms by which the overkingdoms were constituted and through which they consolidated their powers. Asthall lies just south of Wychwood, outside the south-eastern boundary of the kingdom of the Hwicce. By the 670s this had emerged as an important Mercian satellite but with its own dynasty, benefiting probably from enlarged local control (Davies and Vierck 1974, 225–6, 237; Hooke 1985, 3–23; Bassett 1989, 6–17; Sims-Williams 1990, esp. 33, 70). Asthall could have been within a neighbouring province, perhaps one of the ill-known (garbled) units named in *Tribal Hidage* which may belong in the Thames valley (Davies and Vierck 1974; Yorke 1990, 106) or in Middle Anglia, a province placed in 653 under the direct control of the *princeps* Peada, Penda's son (Bede, *Historia Ecclesiastica*, III.21; Dumville 1989a). There is some evidence that Middle Anglia reached to Dorchester-on-Thames, and that it included a minor 'tribe' or district, the *Faerpingas* (thus *Tribal Hidage*) or *Feppingas* (thus Bede), for the first bishop of the Middle Angles, Diuma, died in their territory (Dumville 1989a, 133–4). Later traditions placed his relics at Charlbury in Oxfordshire, just 11 kilometres north-east of Asthall, and the presence of his cult may indicate that Charlbury was a royal administrative centre (Rollason 1989, 120).

As we have seen (above, p. 115), this area, centred on the valleys of the Windrush and Evenlode, might have been marked by other Anglo-Saxon barrow burials, including cremations not unlike Asthall. Without further information, especially about their relationship to Asthall in terms of date and status, any explanation must be speculative: they might indicate a more general need in this locality to express status and power through exceptional burial. In the later seventh century the area is also marked by a series of well-endowed 'Final Phase' graves (Fig. 14.C; Dickinson 1976, 443–7; Sims-Williams 1990, 70), suggesting a continued need to assert social position through burial (Hawkes 1986, 93–4 has a slightly different explanation).

Asthall barrow, with its Anglian attributes, overlooking to the south the core lands of early Wessex in the Thames valley and to the north perhaps the territory of the *Feppingas* could be explained in two ways. If the cultural affiliations of the burial are interpreted in a simple one-to-one manner, then Asthall could be the deliberate burial of a pagan Anglian king or prince, a Mercian or Middle Anglian rather than Hwiccian, who perhaps in life and certainly in death played a forward role in the establishment of the Mercian overkingdom (cf. Dickinson 1976; Hawkes 1986). But if the cultural symbolism is read as an act of 'transculturation', that is the incorporation of elite Anglian burial fashions in order to resist external domination, then we might consider an independent local king, perhaps of the *Feppingas*, threatened on all sides by rival kingdoms seeking his subordination, or even, a member of the West Saxon dynasty in the early days of its resistance to Northumbrian or Mercian aggression.

ACKNOWLEDGEMENTS

We are indebted to Roger Moorey, Keeper of Archaeology at the Ashmolean Museum, for permission to publish the material in his care from Asthall, and to Arthur MacGregor and his sometime deputy, Helena Hamerow, for unstinted encouragement and help. R.A. (Charlie) Chambers has been equally enthusiastic and generous in helping solve some of the problems in the field. Julia Budworth provided information about her father, George Bowles; Kenneth Painter, Catherine Johns and Marlia Mundell Mango have contributed much advice on the identity of the silver vessel; Arthur MacGregor, Andrew Jones and Terry O'Connor have helped to identify the bone and antler artefacts, and Catherine Mortimer and Mark Norman the silver and lead materials respectively; John Shephard and Peter Richards have unhesitatingly allowed us to quote from their unpublished Cambridge Ph.D. theses; and Julie Bond generously informed us of her work on the Spong Hill animal cremations. Finally, Martin Carver has generously given access to data from Sutton

Hoo ahead of his publication, and he, Katherine East, Richard Morris, Leslie Webster and Susan Youngs have read earlier drafts of this paper and offered much useful comment and criticism.

APPENDIX

Outline Catalogue of Grave Goods

I. Vessels

1923.769	**Merovingian wheel-made pottery bottle** (Fig. 16.C) H. 247 mm., max. dia. 168 mm. Leeds 1924, 122, figs 8–9; Evison 1979, 12, 74, pl. VB–C, fig. 10a.
1923.770	**Hand-made pot** (Fig. 16.A) H. 125 mm., max. dia. 110 mm. Leeds 1924, 121–2, fig. 7 left; Myres 1977, fig. 35 **3129**.
1923.771	**Hand-made pot** (Fig. 16.B) H. 115 mm., max. dia. 127 mm. Leeds 1924, 121–2, fig. 7 right; Myres 1977, fig. 46 **3128**.
1923.778	**Silver bowl or cup** (Pl. 3.1–2) At least thirteen fragments of heavily oxidized metal, including rim and body pieces. Leeds 1924, 119, fig. 5A.
1923.776	**Byzantine cast copper-alloy bowl** (Fig. 17) At least four fragments, including rim, hinge-loop and foot-ring. Leeds 1924, 119, fig. 5K; Bruce-Mitford 1983, 756 (metallurgical analysis).
1923.779	**Copper-alloy bowl or cauldron?** (Pl. 3.3) One body fragment in sheet metal, unburnt, th. 0.4 mm.; rim fragment from ? same or similar vessel, W. of rim edge 3 mm. (Fig. 18.A). Leeds 1924, 120, fig. 5H.
1923.779	**Drinking horn(s), bottle(s) or cup(s)** (Pl. 3.5–7; Fig. 18.C) Copper-alloy sheet-metal fittings for vessel(s) of organic material including repoussé foils decorated in Salin's Style II and/or with billeted border, fluted binding strips with dome-headed rivets and U-sectioned rim-edge bindings. Not recognised by Leeds 1924.
1923.779	**? Copper-alloy vessel** (Pl. 3.4) Several fragments of sheet metal with one edge rolled into a narrow tube, dia. 3.0 – 3.5 mm. Not recognised by Leeds 1924.

II. Suite (?) of Strap Fittings

1923.774	**Strap end** (Pl. 4.11) L. 41 mm., W. 19 mm. Cast copper alloy. Mineralized textile on back. Leeds 1924, 120–1, fig. 5D; conserved in 1972.
1923.775	**Looped strap tab** (Pl. 4.12) L. 35 mm., W. 11 mm., ext. dia. loop 13 mm. Cast copper alloy. Discovered by David Brown c. 1966.
1923.777	**Hinged strap attachment** (Pl. 4.8–9) Total L. 22 mm., W. 'horizontal' plate 14.5 mm., W. 'vertical' plate 13 mm. Cast copper alloy with iron hinge-pin. Leeds 1924, 120, fig. 5G.
1923.779	**Looped strap mount** (Pl. 4.10) L. 12.5 mm., max. W. 13 mm. Cast copper alloy. Not recognised by Leeds 1924.
1923.775	**Openwork swivel suspension fitting** (Pl. 4.13) Openwork cuboid, L. 12.5 mm., W. 9 mm.; swivel loop, L. 20 mm.; looped strap tab, L. 19.5 mm., W. 6mm. Cast copper alloy. Leeds 1924, 120, fig. 5B; conserved in 1967.
1923.779	**Disc-headed rivets** (Pl. 4.15) Three fragments. Max. dia. 8mm., int. L. shank 5 mm. Heads decorated with (cast?) concentric rings. Not recognised by Leeds 1924.
1923.773	**'Pear-shaped' mount** (Fig. 18.B) L. reconstructed 47 mm. Cast copper alloy. Gilt. Salin's Style II on front; two cast-in-one disc-ended rivets on back, int. L. shank 2 mm. Leeds 1924, 121, figs 5C and 6; conserved in 1967; one terminal discovered by David Brown.

III. Gaming Set

1923.782	**Counters** (Pl. 5.20) 26 fragments. Dia. 30 mm., H. 4 mm. Plano-convex; bone. Leeds 1924, 118, fig. 4.
1949.297	**Die** (Pl. 5.21) 14 mm. cube. Antler. Faces: $\frac{6:5:4:1}{3}$ 2 Leeds 1939b, 365.

IV. Unassignable Items

Silver:

1923.779

Rectangular-headed rivet
Head L. 6.7 mm., W. 5 mm., shank L. 7 mm.
Leeds 1924, 119.

Lead:

1923.779

Disc (Pl. 4.18)
Dia. 17 mm., th. 4.3 mm. Bevelled edge.
Not recognised by Leeds 1924.

Copper Alloy:

1923.779

'Silver' strap mount (Pl. 4.14)
L. extant 19 mm., W. 6 mm., int. L. shanks c. 4.5 mm. Cast.
Two rivets on back corroded green, front grey.
Leeds 1924, 119, fig. 5F.

1923.779

Two crescentic studs (Pl. 4.16)
Dia. 15 mm. Cast. Decorated with punched triangles. Rivet on back, int. L. c. 6 mm.
Leeds 1924, 120, fig. 5E upper (better preserved one only).

1923.779

Sunken-field stud (Pl. 4.17)
Dia. 10.5 mm., H. 2.5mm., L. shank 8 mm. Cast. Dome-headed rivet passes through centre of sunken field and bent flat on underside.
Leeds 1924, 120, fig. 5E lower.

1923.779

Disc-headed rivet
Dia. 6.5 mm., extant L. shank 5.5 mm. Plain.
Not recognised by Leeds 1924.

1923.779

Dome-headed rivet pin
Dia. head 3.3mm., L. 9.5mm., L. shank 8.5mm.
Not recognised by Leeds 1924.

1923.779

Relief-decorated disc or ring (Pl. 4.19)
Fragment with thickened edge and hint of curvature. L. 15 mm., W. 14 mm. Cast. Notched ridge border and Style I zoomorphic field(?).
Leeds 1924, 121 note 2.

1923.779

Plain disc
Dia. 23 mm. Irregular surface.
Not recognised by Leeds 1924.

1923.779

Unidentifiable copper-alloy fragments
Constitutes the majority of the material registered under 1923.779. Includes sandwiched foil fragments, pieces covered with/incorporating corrosion products, charcoal and soil, generally thicker than the foils, and globules of melted metal. May come from the copper-alloy vessels identified in Section I or from other copper-alloy items.

	Iron:
1923.779	**Four 'nail' fragments** L. extant 22 – 11.5 mm. Not recognised by Leeds 1924.
	Bone:
1923.780	**Inlays (?)** (Pl. 5.22) 55 fragments with flat rectangular or slightly plano-convex section; most with plain outer surface and grooved or cross-grooved inner surface; some with grooved outer surface also, and two with cross-hatched edges. W. 15 mm. and 4 – 5 mm. Leeds 1924, 118, fig. 4.
1923.781	**'Rods'** (Pl. 5.23) 11 fragments, slightly curved and tapered; max. L. 46 mm.; max. dia. 6.5 mm. Leeds 1924, 118–19, fig. 4.

V. Cremated Bone

Total quantity:	Approx. 2 litres.
Identified human bone:	Four finger bones; fragments of jaw; roots of a canine and lower molar. H. Carter *in litt*.
Identified animal bone:	**Horse**: Left tibia; right lateral cuneiform; a sesamoid; probably a metatarsal. **Sheep**: Astragalus; ? tail vertebrae and skull fragments. H. Carter *in litt*.

VI. From Barrow Make-up

1923.772	**Romano-British Pottery Sherds** Worn residual material including thick soft sandy, grey and orange fabric and thin hard sandy grey fabric. Leeds 1924, 114–15.

TABLE 1: ATTRIBUTES OF INDIVIDUAL CREMATION BURIALS

A: In barrows; B: In copper-alloy vessels; C: Rejected examples of cremations in copper-alloy vessels

A. CREMATIONS IN BARROWS

BURIAL	Primary barrow	Approx. dia. (m.)	Burnt objects	Unburnt objects	Animal bones	Gaming pieces	Metal cinerary vessel	Textile	Other vessels	Comb	Multiple bodies	Sex(es)	Age(s)	COMMENTS/REFS.
Asthall	*	>17	*	–	*	*	?	–	*	–	?	?M / ?F	A	
Brightwell Heath 3	*	5	*	*	*	*	*	*	–	2	*	NK / F	A / A	Two neonates doubtful
Cold Eaton	*	18	NK	NK	NK	*	–	?	–	2	NK	NK	NK	? organic container
Coombe	?	18	–	*	NK	–	*	*	*	–	?	?M / ?F	NK / NK	Association of unburnt items uncertain
Sutton Hoo 3	*	26	*	*	*	–	–	*	*	1	–	M	A	On oak 'tray'
Sutton Hoo 4	*	>18	*	–	*	*	*	*	–	–	?	?M / F	A / A	Male bones like those in mound 3: ? bones muddled
Sutton Hoo 5	*	15	*	*	*	*	*	*	*	*	NK	?M	NK	Sword cut in skull should imply male
Sutton Hoo 6	*	17	*	–	–	*	*	*	–	1	NK	?M	NK	Pyramidal sword stud from robber trench
Sutton Hoo 7	*	24	–	*	–	*	*	–	–	–	NK	NK	NK	Glass bead; iron
Sutton Hoo 18	*	15	*	–	–	–	*	*	–	1	NK	NK	NK	

											References
Baginton	–	–	–	–	*	–	–	–	–	–	Edwards 1948, 49–50; Richards 1980, 351, 369; pearl-rimmed bowl
Baginton	–	–	–	–	*	–	–	–	–	–	ibid.; fragments
Baginton	–	–	–	–	*	–	–	–	–	–	ibid.; fragments
Baginton	–	–	–	–	*	*	–	–	–	–	ibid.; cauldron
Baginton	–	–	–	–	*	–	–	–	–	–	ibid.; hanging bowl
Field Dalling	?	?	–	–	*	–	1	–	–	–	Webster & Cherry 1977, 167; Richards 1980, 354; cauldron; shears
Illington	–	–	–	–	*	*	–	–	–	–	Ellis Davidson & Webster 1967, 13; Vierck 1972, 47; Richards 1980, 356
Little Wilbraham 28.x.1852[1]	*	*	*	–	*	–	1	–	–	–	Neville 1852, 23, pls. 16, 23; C7th comb; unburnt horse & ox bones; cauldron
Little Wilbraham 28.x.1851[2]	–	–	–	–	*	–	–	–	–	–	ibid., 23, pl. 40; Richards 1980, 388; handle from ?tripod-ring bowl
Loveden Hill H.B. 1	*	*	*	–	*	*	1	–	–	A	Table lists contents of bowl, not sword and ? bucket bindings found by it nor Bowl 4 assemblage (see below)
Loveden Hill H.B. 2	?	–	–	–	*	*	–	–	?	A	Unburnt firesteel and mount in bowl; ? pot associated; ? fused glass
Snape 1972/1	–	–	–	–	*	*	–	–	?F	–	West & Owles 1976

C. REJECTED CREMATIONS IN COPPER-ALLOY VESSELS

SITE	COMMENTS	REFS.
Badleybridge	Drawing of globular vase, with enamelled Celtic fittings, found during cutting of railway, allegedly with Byzantine bowl and Roman pot containing C2nd denarii. No evidence that vase contained a cremation; association of vessels and veracity of drawing uncertain.	White 1988, 123, 135; cf. Allen 1900; Henry 1936, 229; Meaney 1964, 224
Barlaston	7' long grave with sword, knife and hanging bowl; no bones; probably an inhumation.	Ellis Davidson & Webster 1967, 12
Loveden Hill Bowl 4 [Vierck's grave B.2]	Group of objects including a hemispherical bowl, spearhead, large bucket, fused amber glass, snaffle bit and handle from a ?tripod-ring bowl; found apparently >2m from H.B. 1 (see above) but related variously to it in published accounts. Reports are ambiguous and conflicting; it is unclear if the group constitutes a single assemblage, let alone if it belongs with H.B. 1 or another cremation.	Fennell 1957; 1960; 1964; 1969; Wilson & Hurst 1957, 148; 1959, 297; Meaney 1964, 158–9; Ellis Davidson & Webster, 1967, 13; Vierck 1972, 28; Swanton 1973, 159; Richards 1980, 349, 394
Manton Common	Hanging bowl with cloth on rim. No record of discovery; could be an inhumation or cremation.	Ellis Davidson & Webster 1967, 13
Stodmarch Court	Bronze bowls and many other items in a barrow.	*ibid.*, 11; Evison 1976, 307
Wickhambreux	Rich male grave-assemblage; no reason to suppose it was not an inhumation.	Ellis Davidson & Webster 1967, 12

9

Anglo-Saxon Symbolism

J.D. RICHARDS

In 1939, when the Mound One ship burial was discovered at Sutton Hoo, it was immediately recognised to be rich with symbols of power and prestige. The artifacts from the burial deposit do not 'function' in a twentieth-century practical sense. Even a cursory analysis reveals a ship that no longer floats, utensils for a feast at which none will be dirtied, a whetstone sceptre that has never been used to sharpen a sword, a helmet that is unlikely to have ever protected the head in battle, a bronze bowl containing an enamelled fish, and coins from 39 different mints to pay the imaginary oarsmen. Artifacts are decorated with both real and mythical beasts. If symbols should be read as music, with an audience, a performance, and an underlying score, then here is a veritable cacophony of sound.

In our own age Sutton Hoo continues to take on new meanings. It evokes both the dawn of the English kingdoms, and the scientific pursuit of archaeology. The Sutton Hoo helmet has become a powerful symbol in its own right, of the Dark Ages, and even of Archaeology in general.

The complexity of messages evoked by the burials at Sutton Hoo is too large a subject to tackle safely here. Aspects of the symbolism of Sutton Hoo have, in any case, been discussed at length elsewhere (e.g. Bruce-Mitford 1975; 1978; 1983; Carver 1986b; Storms 1978). The basis of this paper is that we should not just evoke symbolism to explain the unusual, the 'ritual deposits', the 'Sutton Hoos'. Using written sources, Barley (1974) has studied Anglo-Saxon symbolism in naming-systems, colour-systems and kinship terminology. It is proposed here that symbolism also pervades Anglo-Saxon artifacts, and can be observed, even if not yet fully understood, in all aspects of their material culture. Following Shanks and Tilley, 'No social practices exist without signification and without being situated within an overall symbolic field' (1987, 75).

Symbolism

A symbol is an abbreviated form of communication. It is therefore appropriate to use a linguistic analogy for material culture:

> All the various non-verbal dimensions of culture, such as styles in cloth-
> ing, village lay-out, architecture, furniture, food, cooking, music, physi-
> cal gestures, postural attitudes and so on are organised in patterned sets
> so as to incorporate coded information in a manner analogous to the
> sounds and words and sentences of a natural language. (Leach 1976, 10)

Linguistics has had a significant influence on anthropology, particularly
through the impact of structuralism (Levi-Strauss 1977). Verbal communication has been seen as providing a window onto the human mind; it has been
emphasised at the expense of non-verbal communication, although this may
also play an important role in the organisation of human communities (Hall
1959).

Deetz (1967) and Hymes (1970) have each tried to borrow ideas of linguistics
as part of general approaches to artifacts. These ideas were also implicit in
Boas's work on American North-West coastal art (1955), and more recently in
Munn's analysis of Walibiri iconography (1973). The extent of variability
means that ceramics, in particular, provide a rich field for the analysis of style
and symbol. Chomsky's (1957) transformational grammar has been applied to
pottery design and production (Hodder 1982). A growing number of anthropological studies can be used to illustrate the role of pottery decoration to
represent concepts:

> Amongst the Mafa and Bulahay of northern Cameroon, pots are assimi-
> lated to persons and represent human and other spirits.
>   (David et al. 1988, 365)

> Pottery decoration may here be described as a restricted code, charac-
> terised by a small number of motifs arranged in a limited and rigidly
> organised set of designs and affirming the social order. (*ibid.* 378)

Miller (1985) has shown how pottery vessels are used as categories in the
Dalwa area of central India, and Braithwaite (1982), taking an active view of
material symbolism, has shown how decoration may be part of a silent ritual
discourse. Sterner (1989), describing the use of pottery amongst the Sirak
Bulahay, concludes that decoration is used for reflexive signalling, by the users
of pots to themselves, in a form of communication with the spirit world.

In societies with a strong oral tradition, material culture is frequently used to
store and pass on information and, given its relative permanence, it may be
used as an alternative to writing. In order to translate the message one needs to
understand the conventions which apply, although the syntax of non-verbal
communication is simpler than that of written language. Like words, symbols
do not occur in isolation: a symbol is always a member of a set of contrasted
symbols which function within a specific cultural context:

> A symbol only has meaning from its relation to other symbols in a
> pattern. The pattern gives the meaning. Therefore no item in the pattern
> can carry meaning by itself isolated from the rest. (Douglas 1973, 11)

The interpretation of colour symbols, for example, depends upon context, although contexts may be separated in time and place (see Turner 1967). The significance of white in a bride's dress is part of the same symbolic code as the use of black in mourning. Yet both may convey a different message in other contexts. Individual symbols have layers of meaning which depend upon what is being contrasted with what. In the Catholic Church a priest performing secular duties wears black: whilst performing religious duties he wears white.

Material-culture meanings are less logical and more dependent upon context than meanings in language. Symbols may also be appropriated by particular cultural groups. The innocuous safety pin, when used as an item of costume jewellery rather than to secure an infant's nappy, becomes a badge of a sub-tribal grouping. Much material culture is not obviously representational and has little figurative or iconic content (Hodder 1989). Material-culture meanings are often ambiguous; speech and writing are both linear forms of communication; whereas with material culture there is no fixed direction in which to read a message. Thus ambiguity is an important aspect of material culture symbolism. Leigh (1984) has discussed animal-man transformations on Anglo-Saxon brooches. The ability of a symbol to carry several possible meanings at the same time is its power (Richards 1987, 1988). The meaning of symbols can also change through time. Material objects have durability but their meanings are fluid. A Roman object in an Anglo-Saxon grave may be used to evoke stereotyped images of an imperial past. The meanings of symbols are not intrinsic to them. They become established through cultural tradition; one reads meaning into, not out of, a text.

But symbols are not just a means of communication. As Bourdieu (1979) notes, they also function as an instrument for knowledge and construction of the world. In other words, symbolic systems operate to categorise information as an aid to the regulation and direction of appropriate behaviour. Language is just one means by which the world is classified and made understandable and controllable. Artifacts are also tools for thinking about the world.

To this end, we may generate abstract ideas in our heads, such as the opposition between good and bad, and then give these abstractions manifest form by projecting them into the external world, for example by projecting them into the colour difference, black vs white. This is part of thinking. By converting ideas into artifacts we make them concrete and can manipulate them.

For anthropologists the most important area where material symbolism is in evidence is in religious ritual, either in telling stories, or myths, in which metaphysical ideas are represented by the activities of the actors, or in using material objects to represent metaphysical ideas. For Durkheim (1915) mythologies are expressions of classification systems. One of the functions of religion is the creation of a cognitive framework whereby the world can be understood.

The New Testament Story of the Last Supper is an example of a religious myth; in the Communion service the metaphysics become translated into physical acts and associated artifacts. Only when part of a myth is shown in pictorial fashion, such as the scene on the Sutton Hoo purse, does it become accessible to archaeologists. With the help of literary sources, we might interpret this as a scene from the story of Daniel in the lion's den. Artifacts used to represent metaphysical ideas may also only be understood with the help of literary sources.

But, finally, artifacts are not only a passive symbolic reflection of the world. They are used to constitute and change it. Bourdieu (1979) writes that symbolism establishes and legitimates the dominant culture. Post-structuralist analyses acknowledge the symbolic power of artifacts and have raised issues of power and ideology (Miller and Tilley 1984):

> Material culture is thus an active participant in the construction of the social system, and its meaning is internal to that system.
>
> (Barrett 1981, 206)

> Reality is not reflected by language or material culture as much as actively produced by it. (Shanks and Tilley 1987, 98)

Material culture does not provide a mirror to society, or a window through which we can see it. Symbolism may be used in relations of dominance between competing groups. It does not simply express a balanced social order.

To summarise, following Bourdieu, symbols act:

(i)   as a means of communication;
(ii)   as an instrument for knowledge and construction of the world;
(iii)   as an instrument of domination.

Thus we may suppose that the Sutton Hoo ship communicates the idea of a journey, and the ancestral importance of water transport in seventh-century East Anglia. It can be read as a symbol of the gods, of fertility and the new life, and of the sexual act (Storms 1978, 318). It also divides that world into those who are buried in ships, and those who are not. Its burial, as an example of conspicuous consumption of wealth, reaffirms and constructs the power relations of the East Anglians. And, Carver suggests (1986b), it attempts to reassert pagan traditions against the new religion.

So far I have used 'symbol' in a very general sense, as one thing which stands for another. It is now time to distinguish sign from symbol. An object is a sign when there is an intrinsic relationship between it, and what it represents. A crown or a helmet is a sign. It may be part of the uniform of kingship. Similarly a sword is a sign of a warrior; it is part of his armoury.

In the case of a symbol, there is no intrinsic relationship between the symbol and what it stands for. Thus the swastika has meant many different things at different times. Leach (1976), following Saussure (1959), further distinguishes between conventional but wholly arbitrary symbols, and icons, which bear a planned resemblance to what they represent. The use of a hanging arch to represent females is an arbitrary symbol; the use of a *wyrm* motif to represent a serpent is an icon.

The purpose of an analysis of symbols, therefore, must be to examine the pattern, as much as the content. In many cases the content may be purely arbitrary. To note a pattern is simultaneously to give it meaning, as one describes dimensions of variability as being related to age, sex, race and so on.

Approaches to Anglo-Saxon Symbolism

In the space available it is only possible to sketch out some examples of how Anglo-Saxon symbolism might be investigated. Firstly I will suggest that despite the temptation to concentrate on cemeteries as stages for ritual and symbolism, it is important not to isolate them from the settlements which used them. They are linked in the same symbolic system, and the meaning of one cannot be understood without comprehending how it is related to the other, just as the significance of white can only be defined through a knowledge of the meaning of black. Secondly, I will take the occurrence of animal remains, in settlements and cemeteries, as an example of how a symbolic approach might be applied to an area which has traditionally been interpreted in purely functional terms. Thirdly, I shall look at cremation vessels and demonstrate that even aspects of design which have been thought of as simply decorative may have a symbolic role. Finally, I shall suggest that this symbolic code is also transformed into other aspects of material culture, particularly metalworking, which would profit from a similar investigation.

Cemeteries and Settlements: the Sacred and the Profane

An Anglo-Saxon grave contains a complex message. On one level it defines ideas of the afterlife and the needs of the dead. On another level, the grave-goods codify the age, sex and social status of the deceased; they may also denote tribal and sub-tribal groupings. It is important to remember, however, that these are all cultural constructs, rather than natural categories. Mortuary ritual reinforces cultural differences and helps classify Anglo-Saxon society. It provides a means of describing social identity. The symbols are also instruments of domination, asserting one group's view of the world. For example, it is generally accepted that although we can identify an Anglo-Saxon burial rite, there is not an equivalent native British burial rite over much of Anglo-Saxon England although a substantial element of the native population must have survived the Anglo-Saxon settlement and coexisted alongside immigrant groups. We must accept that many of those given a Germanic burial rite were not immigrants from North Germany and Scandinavia. The form of burial is a symbol being used to assert the domination of Germanic culture, not the annihilation of the previous inhabitants.

A widespread tendency has been to invoke the symbolic only in order to explain the unusual. Decapitated bodies, 'double' graves, such as that from Sewerby (Hirst 1985), and other instances of bodies in unusual postures, such as the Sutton Hoo 'ploughman' have been interpreted as examples of ritual killings. This may be so, but such graves must be seen in the context of the whole spectrum of the Anglo-Saxon treatment of the dead body.

Similarly, unusual features of cremation burials have also led to speculative comments about ritual practices. Approximately ten percent of cremation vessels have been deliberately damaged in one way or another. Some are simply punctured with one or more holes; in some cases the hole is blocked with a piece of window glass; in others it is plugged with lead. Evidence from some sites suggest that the molten lead was poured into the hole whilst the urn was already in the ground, as part of some grave-side ritual (Reynolds *pers comm*). None of the proposed explanations are entirely satisfactory; are the holes to 'kill' the pot, or are they to allow the spirit to escape, or see out? In which case, why are some holes sealed, and why are only certain urns treated in this fashion?

In order to understand symbols one must be as aware of what is missing as what is present. Germanic burial takes its meaning from the absence of Romano-British burial. Wherever possible, cemetery assemblages must also be viewed in the context of the objects in associated settlements. It is insufficient to regard cemeteries as being part of sacred practice, and settlements as part of the profane (Durkheim 1915). The ritual and symbolic are just as likely to be found in the house as the grave.

One clear contrast between cemeteries and settlements is in the general absence of tools in cemeteries, and the emphasis upon weapons. Iron tools are found in domestic contexts but almost never in Anglo-Saxon graves. This is in contrast to Viking burials when smithing and farming tools frequently accompany rich male inhumations. At West Stow, for example, needles, pin-beaters and other tools are rarely represented in the neighbouring cemetery, despite being common finds in the settlement (Fig. 19). In the cemetery weapons and brooches are common, although bracelets are not. Clearly some items are appropriate grave-goods, and other are not. Artifacts are selected to symbolise some aspects of social identity, such as the warrior and hunter, and to ignore others, such as the farmer. Ellis Davidson has found evidence of a warrior cult in Viking Scandinavia (1972); this may be an earlier manifestation of a similar system. Heinrich Härke's study of warrior burials has revealed that many of those buried with weapons were not warriors (1990); they include the old and the young, and even those suffering from debilitating physical conditions, including spina bifida.

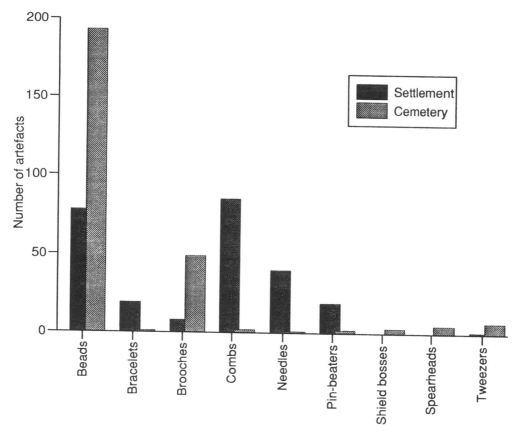

Figure 19. Comparison of numbers of selected artifacts found in the settlement and cemetery sites at West Stow, Suffolk (from West 1985)

Anglo-Saxon Animals

The role of animals in Anglo-Saxon settlements and cemeteries provides a case study of the need to integrate the symbolic in our interpretations. The importance of animal symbolism has been observed throughout the Celtic, Germanic and Scandinavian worlds (cf. Ellis Davidson 1988), although the specific meanings attached to the use of animals apparently varies according to the spatial and temporal context. Control of animals must have been an essential attribute of Anglo-Saxon power. Faunal remains from settlements testify to the importance of animal husbandry (Clutton-Brock 1976), although the use of animal symbolism goes beyond a passive reflection of their economic value. The repeated appearance of animals as grave offerings and as designs on artifacts indicates their symbolic role.

A common pattern is emerging at sites such as Cowdrey's Down, Chalton, Raunds, and Foxley, where at each site a large building straddles an enclosure boundary. These have sometimes been described as controlling access to the

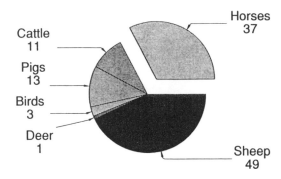

Figure 20. Proportions of animals found in
cremation burials at Elsham, Humberside
(from Richards 1987)

enclosure, despite the fact that in the example from Cowdrey's Down all the
entrances are clearly outside the enclosure to which there is no access from
the building. Rather their position must be seen in terms of the social and
ideological use of space. If these are animal enclosures then the buildings
have a symbolic rather than a practical relationship with them. Individual
buildings, normally seen as having a secular function, may also have symbolic
aspects. At Cowdrey's Down, a circular pit, 1 x 1.5 metres was dug just
outside the west entrance of a rectangular timber building; the bottom metre
was filled with clay in which the body of a cow was curled (Millett with
James 1983, 258).

The deposition of animals in Anglo-Saxon cemeteries formed a significant
part of the mortuary ritual. The cremation cemetery at Elsham (Humberside)
provides a typical example of the relative proportions of animals buried (Fig.
20). In total, traces of 131 animals were recovered from 630 burials, representing
over 20 percent of burials. Recent analyses of skeletal material from Sancton
(Humberside) and Spong Hill (Norfolk) suggest that in some cases, where there
is good preservation, the proportion of burial deposits which include animal
remains may be closer to 4 in 10 (McKinley 1989). There is also evidence for the
sacrifice of animals from inhumation cemeteries, including both joints of meat
and complete animals. At Sutton Hoo, there was provision not only of food, but
also of the means of feasting in the form of the cauldron. The elaborate nature of
the preparation suggests that it was based on more than just the need for food in
the afterlife. Ellis Davidson (1988) suggests that the symbolism of the Other
World Banquet contains an implication of the renewal of life.

Analysis of the animal remains included in cremation deposits indicates that
the animals are not solely the remains of ritual feasting as the species are
correlated with particular groups of burials (Richards 1987). The chief animals
represented were boar, bull/ox, horse and sheep. To the Anglo-Saxons each
category was either age or sex-linked, and some were both. Animals were used
as a form of totemic classification (Levi-Strauss 1964), and were placed with

the dead to differentiate social groupings. It is not that the Anglo-Saxons thought of certain people as being like cows and others as being like horses, but that the relationship between the human groups was perceived as analogous to the relationship between the animal groups, such that Group A is to Group B as cow is to horse. For instance, the categories of animals represented varies between adult and child cremations. Child and adult burials contain equal proportions of sheep. A few child burials include pigs, but cattle and horses are absent (Fig. 21). Similarly, males are more likely to be buried with animals than females, and horses are a particularly male attribute (Fig. 22). Each animal had particular associations, although the proportions of the major species found in the cemeteries largely reflect the relative importance of these animals in settlement assemblages.

Horse-burials are the exception. At Portchester and Bishopstone, horses formed only two percent of the faunal remains (Cunliffe 1976; Bell 1978); at West Stow there were fewer horses than sheep, cattle or pigs (Crabtree 1989). In the cemeteries the horse is more significant, and may itself be given individual inhumation, as at Sutton Hoo where a horse inhumation has been found under Mound 17 (p. 362); and cremated horses were found in Mounds 3 and 4. The grave of Childeric, at Tournai, was probably associated with the burial of about 30 horses in nearby pits (James 1988a, 63).

The horse may have been associated with the war-god, Tiw; chalk white horses are, of course, undated, but Tacitus speaks of white horses kept in sacred groves amongst Germanic tribes. According to Bede, the possession of a good horse was regarded as a status symbol amongst the Angles of the seventh century (HE, 3, 14; trans. Whitelock 1979). Horse-burials, therefore, should not simply be regarded as food offerings. They are status-defining statements. Like the Sutton Hoo ship, the horse symbolised wealth and mobility, in a society which by the seventh century had become largely settled.

The importance of the horse is also signified by its appearance as animal stamps on pottery, and in decorative metalworking. The portrayal is frequently schematic; the decorative role is unimportant; it is the presence of the animal as a symbol that is crucial (Capelle 1987; Hills 1983). The animal representations are not just passive reflections of the fauna; they are derived from images in the mind (Ingram 1989). The way in which animals are represented tells us something about the way they are conceived and understood, such as in the parts selected for depiction:

> When animals are transformed into art they often become reflections on the human condition . . .
> . . . in using animals for certain purposes and encoding them in particular ways people inevitably affect the concept of an animal that they have. (Morphy 1989, 14)

Anglo-Saxon cruciform brooches are decorated with a stylised horse's head, frequently with flaring nostrils. On cremation urns, horses may be depicted in

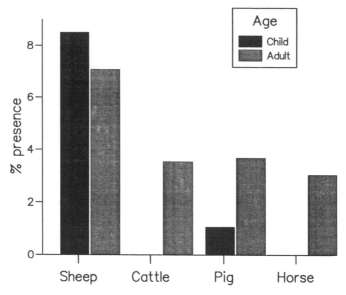

Figure 21. Comparison of proportions of animals found in
Anglo-Saxon child and adult cremation burials
(Richards 1987, 133; n=109)

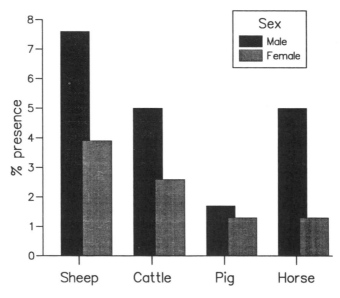

Figure 22. Comparison of proportions of animals found
in Anglo-Saxon male and female cremation burials
(Richards 1987, 129; n=37)

stamped profile, or brooch feet may themselves be utilised as stamps, although the negative imprint may render them barely recognisable as horse's heads (Briscoe 1985). At Sutton Hoo, the horse appears as a motif on the shield boss, and as a purse mount. Life, and death, may also mimic art in the cases of the horses buried in pairs facing each other with intertwined legs at Beckum, Westphalia (Bruce-Mitford 1978, 521). Fabech (1989) has noted the importance of substitution amongst the Scandinavian peoples, with the depiction of animals and use of animal style ornament, first exclusively on gold and silver, and then spreading to base metals, suggesting that the symbols of the gods have been transformed as personal symbols.

Bede's record of a letter from Pope Gregory to Abbot Mellitus tells us that the ox was another important sacrificial animal: 'they are accustomed to slaughter many oxen in sacrifice to devils . . .' (HE, 1, 30; trans. Whitelock 1979, 655). Finds from several excavations apparently back this up. At Yeavering there was a pit filled with ox skulls in the enigmatic D4 building (Hope Taylor 1977); at Sutton Courtenay an ox skull was found in the centre of the floor of House XII (Leeds 1927, 64); an ox head was buried at the cemetery of Soham (Owen 1981, 45). A cremation urn at Caistor apparently rested upon an ox or horse skull (Myres and Green 1973); at Harrow Hill (where to judge from its name, a pagan temple once stood), over 1000 ox skulls are reported to have been found. In the sixteenth century a heap of ox skulls was found on the south side of St Pauls Cathedral, London. At Sutton Hoo the significance of the ox or bull is underlined by the bulls's heads on the 'standard' (Storms 1978). One of the ring of pits around Mound 5 contained ox horns (Carver 1989, 7).

The position as well as the presence of animal offerings may also have been important (see Pader 1982). At Sutton Hoo a tree-trunk burial to the east of the cemetery had a joint of meat at the corpse's feet (Carver 1986c, 146). And of course, the Anastasius dish, with its mysterious phosphate concentration was found at the foot of the body space in Mound 1 (Bruce-Mitford 1975). At Buckland, grave 139 also had ox bones at the foot (Evison 1987). At Garton Station most of the twelve Anglo-Saxon burials had animal remains at their feet (Anon. 1987). At Yeavering a flexed skeleton only occupied half of a grave, whilst an ox tooth was in a central position in the empty half of the burial (Hope-Taylor 1977). A grave from Winnall II had a pig's tooth placed on the corpse's feet (Meaney 1981, 133).

Pots and Cremations

Designs applied to pottery or metalwork are generally seen as being purely decorative. I have argued elsewhere that, in fact, the designs of Anglo-Saxon cremation urns may be read as burial inscriptions, codifying information about age, sex, status and other aspects of social role (Richards 1987). Some aspects of decoration, such as stamped motifs of swastikas, *wyrms* and runes, are overtly

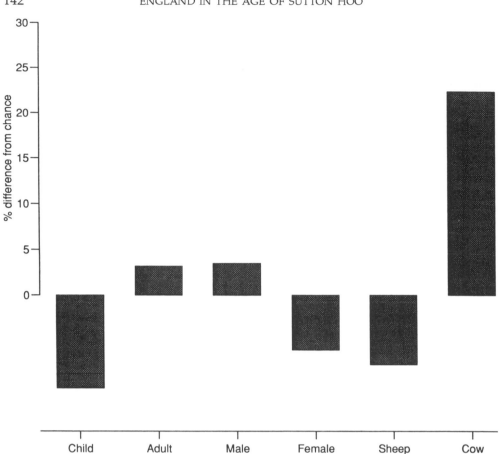

Figure 23. Use of plastic (applied) decoration on Anglo-Saxon cremation vessels. Graph indicates percentage difference from chance for age (n=216), gender (n=70), and sheep vs cow (n=20); for example, there are over 20% more cremations with cow bones in vessels with applied decoration than one would expect under a random distribution

symbolic, often representing powerful evocations to specific gods; with other aspects the meaning is less clear and the analyst has to concentrate on pattern rather than form. There is a striking similarity with many of the designs found on Scandinavian rock carvings although direct parallels are unjustified (see Richards 1987; Ellis Davidson 1967, 50–9). Although we are dealing with the same iconographic tradition the meaning may be completely different. Reynolds (1980) has argued, on the basis of urn A1242 from Sancton, decorated with a swastika and containing a whetstone, that here was evidence for worship of Thor, the god of thunder, and of the forge. Similarly, runic evocations of Tiw (e.g. Spong Hill Stamp Group 3) seem to be clear cases of Pagan symbolism. Chance survivals mean that it is still possible to interpret these symbols. On the other hand, to the Anglo-Saxons, the chevron and the hanging arch

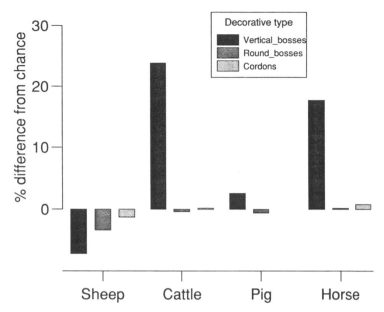

Figure 24. Categories of animals found in Anglo-Saxon cremation vessels with various types of applied decoration (n=37). Graph indicates percentage difference from chance (Richards 1987, 178)

may have been as powerful as the swastika. To us the meaning is obscure, and the symbols must be studied as part of patterned sets. At this stage of analysis we may not be able to say why a particular symbol was chosen, although we can still define the set of oppositions, thereby indicating what the Anglo-Saxons chose to symbolise.

By investigating links between symbols and people it is possible to identify some of the forces structuring Anglo-Saxon society. Rather than being randomly distributed, various aspects of decoration are correlated with particular skeletal groups. The use of plastic decoration, such as applied bosses, for example, is linked with adults rather than children, males rather than females, and cows rather than sheep (Fig. 23). The differences from chance are not huge, but the sample size is large and they are statistically significant. Clear links cannot be expected given the element of 'noise', and the difficulty of defining meaningful categories of decoration. If several different categories of applied decoration are distinguished then it becomes apparent that the positive links are principally with vertical bosses (Fig. 24). Incised hanging arches are associated with children rather than adults, and females rather than males; whilst groups of diagonal lines, sloping to the right, are linked with adults and males (Fig. 25). In each case we have to try to define the vocabulary of the Anglo-Saxons.

In all societies death is a traumatic event which destroys existing relationships and moulds new ones. Symbols were used in Anglo-Saxon mortuary

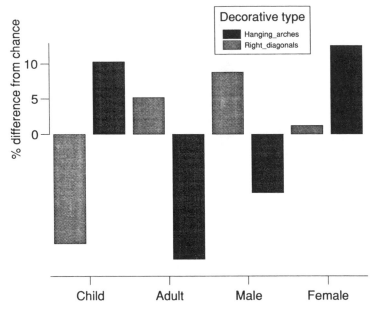

Figure 25. Use of two classes of incised decoration on Anglo-Saxon cremation vessels. Graph indicates percentage difference from chance for age (n=809) and gender (n=272) groups (Richards 1987, 168)

ritual as statements about the identity of the dead, which would have been understood by the Anglo-Saxon audience. They defined and maintained the structuring principles of society, which rested partly upon age and sex.

The symbolic role of many Anglo-Saxon grave-goods is also clear. Miniature tweezers and combs, especially, are generally unburnt and are deliberately deposited in the urns. Frequently only token pieces are included, confirming that it is their symbolic presence that is important, not their functional use. A common motif stamped on cremation vessels takes the form of a stylised comb. At Sutton Hoo the presence of no fewer than three combs tends to confirm their ritual importance (see Taylor 1989). Anthropologists have noted the magical associations of hair amongst many societies (Leach 1958), and in primitive cults such as voodooism, control of hair or nail clippings provides control over the individual. The Anglo-Saxons apparently shared this concern about objects related to those parts of the body which might become separated from the body. Anglo-Saxon amulets have been catalogued and studied by Meaney (1981). So called 'girdle-hangers', for instance, are common finds in female inhumations; they have been variously interpreted as symbolic copies of Roman keys, or as signifying the sexual act. Crystal balls are also found in female graves in Kent and the Isle of Wight, and have also been invested with magical properties.

Those grave-goods found with cremation burials also appear to be linked

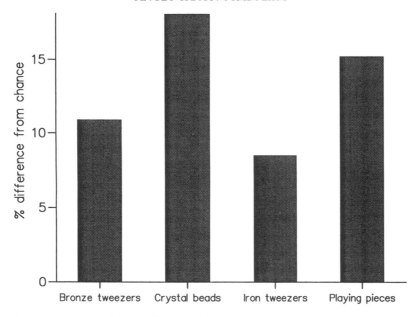

Figure 26. Use of plastic (applied) decoration on Anglo-Saxon cremation vessels (n=738). Graph indicates percentage difference from chance for four categories of grave-good (Richards 1987, 175)

with aspects of the decoration of the urns. Applied decoration is associated with bronze and iron tweezers, crystal beads and playing pieces for instance (Fig. 26). In each case the same social groupings which are symbolised by particular grave-goods are also represented by the use of particular decorative styles.

Metalwork

Finally, I would like to suggest that the same symbolic motifs and grammatical rules used in pottery decoration can also be found in bronze metalworking. Superficially there appears to be little similarity between pots and brooches, and the specialisms have been vigorously defended. This is despite the fact that at a micro-level there are some obvious similarities, for example in the selection of stamped motifs on pots and brooches. Capelle (1987, 94), for instance, considers that there is 'some likeness' between the animal designs stamped on pottery and those on Quoit brooch style metalwork. The problem is principally that of perception. It is conventional that Anglo-Saxon cremation vessels should be drawn in profile, as if they are symmetrical, with one side a repeat of another. However, by representing them in this fashion we make a nonsense of their intended appearance. The vessels were coil-built by a potter working from above; the need to lay out concentric circular fields of decoration demanded that they should also be decorated from above. And most import-

Figure 27. Comparison of decorative schemes on Anglo-Saxon cremation vessels and annular brooches (Left: Spong Hill 1776; Spong Hill 2777; Caister-by-Norwich, Myres 1905; Right: Morningthorpe 397; 262; 114)

antly, when buried in a shallow urn pit as part of the mortuary ritual, they were designed to be viewed from above by the participants in the funerary ceremony. Once perceived as concentric bands of motifs then the parallels between pottery and metalwork become self-evident (Fig. 27). One can see, therefore, a transformation of a coded message from one medium to another, and in some cases a substitution of one medium for another.

Conclusion

In non-literate societies, such as Pagan Anglo-Saxon England, pictorial symbolism can play a particularly important role. The vacuum left by the decline of Roman power was filled by various competing groups. all emphasising their similarities or differences, both from each other, and from the native Romano-British, with the aim of gaining cultural and political domination. The assertion of aspects of ethnic identity using material culture has frequently been documented in contemporary migrant contexts (for example, Cohen 1974). In sub-Roman Britain the surviving native population was swiftly culturally subsumed and became archaeologically invisible. The newcomers were then left to fight it out amongst themselves in asserting their various cultural identities. In a society under stress cultural and social roles were continually redefined and reinforced. One mechanism for asserting identity, whether real or assumed, was through mortuary ritual.

Hodges (1989b) has noted that the heroic manner of Anglo-Saxon mortuary ritual is at odds with egalitarian farming communities. Härke (1990) has demonstrated that many of those buried in weapon graves can never have borne arms in life. The increasing popularity of weapons burial amongst the inhabitants of sixth- and seventh-century England may represent the growth of an 'Anglo-Saxon invasion' origin-myth as much as an increase in warfare. The myth probably emphasised a shared ethnic past, valiant sea journeys and distinguished ancestors rather than post-Roman colonial vestiges. Hodges (1989) suggests that connections with a non-classical heritage were also emphasised; both pottery and metal-work decoration support this. Southern Scandinavian and Germanic symbols abound in rich ornamentation.

Symbols were used to construct a new reality. Objects signified relationships of power between groups. We must be aware, however, that meanings can change. Symbols take on new meanings because they are realised in relation to specific political objectives. Any study of Anglo-Saxon material culture needs to analyze artifacts in terms of political and social strategies. Only in this way can we hope to understand both the symbolism and the society.

ACKNOWLEDGMENTS

Some of these ideas were originally presented in my doctoral thesis (Richards 1987), where the full supporting data and significance tests are presented. They have been extended and developed through discussions with colleagues, particularly Dr Tania Dickinson and Steve Roskams. I am also grateful to Dr Guy Halsall and John Ingram for discussions of animal symbolism, and to Dr Janet Levy for drawing my attention to the significance of colour symbolism amongst the Anglo-Saxons.

10

Changing Symbols in a Changing Society: The Anglo-Saxon Weapon Burial Rite in the Seventh Century

HEINRICH HÄRKE

The ship burial in mound 1 at Sutton Hoo contained the largest and most varied weapon assemblage of the early Anglo-Saxon Period: a sword, an axe-hammer and nine spears (including three *angons*, or barbed throwing-spears), complemented by shield, mailcoat and helmet (Bruce-Mitford 1978). This is all the more remarkable as this grave dates to the early seventh century at which time the custom of depositing weapons in graves was already in decline in England. Thus, Sutton Hoo and contemporary, rich male burials raise questions as to the meaning of the weapon burial rite in the seventh century, and how this may have differed from its meaning in the fifth and sixth centuries when it was far more common.

The decline, and ultimately the end, of the weapon burial rite in the seventh century was part of the overall decline of the grave-goods custom, and this, in turn, was only one of several changes affecting the Pagan Saxon burial rite between the late sixth and early eighth centuries. Other changes include the appearance of isolated barrows (from the late sixth century), the end of the cremation rite (in the seventh century), and the use of separate 'late' cemeteries (early/mid-seventh to mid-eighth centuries). These changes have traditionally been explained as a consequence of Christianisation (Hyslop 1963, 189–193; Lethbridge 1931, 82–84; Meaney and Hawkes 1970, 45–46). Later 'processual' analyses have focused on factors such as increasing social stratification and declining resources (Arnold 1980; *id*. 1982a; Shephard 1979). In recent years, 'symbolism' has been used as an explanation of variability in the Anglo-Saxon burial rite (Pader 1982; Richards 1987), but so far symbolism has been treated as a largely static phenomenon. Thus, a number of important questions have not yet been tackled: how a symbol can change its meaning, how it may be replaced over time by another of identical, or similar, meaning, and how symbols may become redundant because of changed circumstances.

This contribution is an attempt to analyse the dynamic aspects of the Anglo-

Saxon weapon-burial rite. In order to discuss the seventh-century changes, it will be necessary to establish first the symbolism of burial with weapons, and the symbolism attached to particular types of weapons in the burial rite. The analysis is based on a sample of 47 burial sites in England with some 3800 inhumations of the fifth to early eighth centuries.[1] The regional bias of the sample is largely a consequence of the state of excavation and publication, and of differential access to unpublished evidence (Fig. 28). Cremations have been excluded from this study because of the very low incidence of weapons in them (between nil and 1.2% of cremations in any one cemetery), and because they do not provide the range of skeletal data required for the following analysis.

The Symbolism of Burial with Weapons

In Early Anglo-Saxon cemeteries, 47% of male adults and 9% of all juveniles (referring here to children *and* adolescents throughout) were buried with weapons. The proportion of adult weapon burials is much too high to suggest that they all represent a social élite (unless the term is applied very loosely). The usual assumption is that these are 'warrior burials', and this term is used throughout the archaeological and historical literature. However, a systematic comparison of burials with and without weapons, using archaeological and skeletal data, suggests that this assumption is much too simplistic and even misleading.

The obvious starting point for the archaeological analysis is associated finds and grave structures because these might indicate if burial with weapons was linked to superior wealth. To an extent, this appears to have been the case (Table 1): men with weapons have, on average, more grave-goods, more types of finds, and more objects made of, or decorated with, precious metals than men without weapons. This difference remains even if male burials without finds are excluded from the comparison (as already done in Table 1), or if the weapons are subtracted from the number of finds in weapon burials. It is more difficult to compare juveniles in the same way because their skeletons cannot

[1] The sites in the sample are listed in Härke 1989a, 60–61. It may be worth pointing out here that Sutton Hoo is not represented in this sample. A complete catalogue of the 1600 burials analysed in detail (702 weapon burials, 898 comparative juvenile and male adult burials without weapons) will be included in the full publication of the research on which this paper is based (Härke 1992). This study would have been impossible without the assistance of colleagues who kindly gave access to unpublished data and information. Whilst it is impossible to list them all in this footnote, I should like to acknowledge the generosity of those colleagues who gave access to unpublished data of sites referred to specifically in this paper: K. Annable, Devizes; D. Brown, Oxford; W. Ford, Alnwick; Mrs S.C. Hawkes, Oxford; D. Miles, Oxford; Mrs L. Webster, London; S.E. West, Bury St Edmunds.

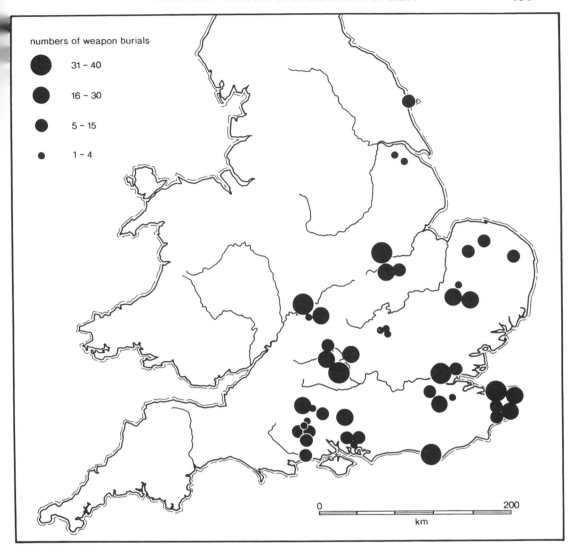

Figure 28. Distribution of the weapon burials in the sample

be sexed, and the inclusion of female juveniles would distort the comparison because their dress ornaments make them appear 'richer' than male juveniles. After excluding juvenile burials with diagnostically female objects, the same wealth differential between weapon burials and others can be seen among juveniles (Table 1). It should be noted, however, that there is no one-to-one correlation between burial wealth and weapons: poorly equipped weapon burials are frequent, and well-furnished male graves without weapons, although rare, have been found.

The difference between the two groups extends beyond mere numbers of objects in the graves: there is also a difference in the frequencies of certain

TABLE 1: BURIAL WEALTH AND WEAPON BURIAL
IN JUVENILE AND MALE ADULT BURIALS
(UNDISTURBED BURIALS ONLY)

	MALE ADULTS		JUVENILES (WITHOUT FEMALES)	
	size of sample	aver. no. of finds	size of sample	aver. no. of finds
with weapons	363	4.05	65	2.48
without weapons (excl. unfurnished burials)	206	2.32	150	1.59

types of grave-goods. Drinking vessels and liquid containers, including glass vessels, bronze-bound wooden vessels and 'buckets', have been found in 13.8% of male adults with weapons, against only 1.8% of those without weapons. The differences are equally marked in the case of box fittings (in 12 of 363 male adult weapon burials, but in only one of 337 without weapons) and bronze vessels (six in the sample of male adults, all of them associated with weapons). The situation is very similar for juvenile burials if those with female grave-goods are, again, excluded from the comparison: juveniles with weapons have more drinking vessels (in 12.3% of cases) than other juveniles (0.3%), and the two bronze vessels from children's burials were found associated with weapons. The types of artefacts which constitute the difference between the two groups relate to leisure, to feasting, and to moveable property (suggested by the presence of boxes).

Labour investment in the graves emphasizes the 'wealth' difference. Males with weapons do not usually have larger grave pits, but they are less often in multiple burials, and they more often have a coffin or a burial chamber (Table 2). This differential does not extend to barrows, probably because barrow burial is a late feature which coincides with the decline of the weapon burial rite in the seventh century, or because barrow burial took over some of the symbolic functions formerly fulfilled by burial with weapons (cf. below). Apart from grave structures, no other features show clear or significant correlations with the absence or presence of weapons. There are no differences between the two groups in the orientation of the graves, in the deposition of the bodies, or in the frequencies of unusual burial practices. Ritual decapitation and prone burial, for example, have also been observed in weapon graves.

Physical anthropology can supply more specific information about the individuals compared here. In fact, only skeletal data can suggest, with some degree of reliability, whether the men buried with weapons (there do not

TABLE 2: GRAVE STRUCTURES AND WEAPON BURIAL
IN JUVENILE AND MALE ADULT BURIALS

	MALE ADULTS				JUVENILES (WITHOUT FEMALES)			
	size of sample	coffin	burial chamber	ditch, barrow	size of sample	coffin	burial chamber	ditch, barrow
with weapons	353 (100%)	62 (18%)	3 (1%)	10 (3%)	52 (100%)	11 (21%)	–	1 (2%)
without weapons	329 (100%)	32 (10%)	1 (0.3%)	8 (2%)	302 (100%)	16 (5%)	–	7 (2%)

appear to be any cases of Anglo-Saxon females interred with functional weapons) are likely to have been warriors, in contrast to the men buried without weapons. The results of the analysis are surprising because of the absence of correlations one would expect if this assumption were true. There is no difference between the two groups in their age ranges: mature individuals too old to be effective fighters were accompanied by weapons, as were children too young to be warriors. No less than 8% of individuals in weapon burials were below the age of puberty (about 12–14 years), the youngest of them being only 12 months old. By way of contrast, a considerable number of male adults in their prime have been found without weapons. Men in weapon burials were exactly as healthy or unhealthy, and as fit or unfit to fight, as men without weapons. Severe osteo-arthritis, malunited fractures and, even more significantly, congenital disabilities were no obstacle to burial with weapons. Finally, there is absolutely no correlation between weapon burial and the incidence of wounds (mainly cut marks on the skull or on long bones). Of the fifth/sixth century cases in the sample, five were buried with weapons, and three without; in the seventh/early eighth centuries, none of the six cases had weapons. These observations suggest that neither the ability to fight, nor the actual experience of fighting were relevant for the decision as to who was buried with, or without, weapons.

The two types of skeletal data which are correlated with weapon burial, stature and epigenetic traits, point to a different meaning of this rite. The stature data had to be analysed separately for each cemetery in order to eliminate local variations, and small samples were omitted in order to obtain meaningful results. The figures for the remaining, early cemeteries indicate that in the fifth/sixth centuries men with weapons were usually between 2 and 5 centimetres taller than their local counterparts without weapons (Table 3). The interpretation of this differential poses a complex problem because stature is determined by a number of factors, including diet and stress in childhood.

TABLE 3: MALE ADULT STATURE AND WEAPON BURIAL

	INDIVIDUALS WITH WEAPONS		INDIVIDUALS WITHOUT WEAPONS		SIZE OF SAMPLE
cemeteries	aver.	var.	aver.	var.	
5th – Early 7th Cent.					
Pewsey	174.1	17	171.9	28	23
Worthy Park	176.1	19	171.4	21	25
Abingdon I	175.7	24	171.9	29	28
Berinsfield	174.1	10	173.9	24	23
Empingham II	173.2	22	170.8	29	31
Late 5th – Late 7th Cent.					
Broadstairs I	170.6	5	165.8	9	10
Finglesham	173.1	16	173.7	21	45
7th – 8th Cent.					
Polhill	172.1	10	175.8	20	22

Legend: aver. –   average stature (in cm)
          var.   –   variation (difference between smallest and
                     and largest value in the sample, in cm)

One of the consequences observable in many societies up to the present day is the higher average stature of members of the élite. However, other skeletal data, most importantly the incidence of hypoplasia (tooth enamel defects), suggest that the risk of famine and illness in childhood was identical for all Anglo-Saxon males. Also, the stature differential appears to break down in the seventh/early eighth centuries (cf. below). Therefore it cannot have been only the reflection of a social hierarchy because that hierarchy did not disappear in the seventh century – on the contrary, it became more pronounced (Arnold 1982a; Shephard 1979).

This makes it necessary to look for an alternative explanation of the stature differential, and the most obvious one is ethnicity. Anglo-Saxon men were an average 4 cm taller than the native Romano-Britons and the pre-Roman Celts in Britain (Harman et al. 1981, 149; Wells 1969, 459–460). However, it may be too simplistic to suggest that all men buried with weapons were of Germanic origin, whilst the men without weapons were native Britons of Celtic stock. There are a few cases in the sample where archaeological and anthropological data suggest that some Britons were buried with weapons, according to the rite of the immigrants. Also, the larger stature variations and standard deviations of the men without weapons (Table 3) suggest that they were a more heterogeneous group, possibly comprising Germani as well as Britons, although it should not be forgotten that the Roman episode in Britain had already led to a substantially mixed population. This modified ethnic interpretation of the stature differential is paralleled by observations in Alamannic cemeteries of south-west Germany.[2] It also provides a useful hint as to where we may have to look for the 'missing' native population in post-Roman Britain, which cannot be identified on the basis of archaeological evidence alone.

The other type of skeletal data correlated with weapon burial is easier to interpret: epigenetic traits are indicative of family relationships. These traits have not always been looked for and are rarely published, so that sufficient data are available for only five cemeteries, all of them as yet unpublished. In two of these (Berinsfield and Finglesham), we find a clear pattern linking weapon burial to certain traits (Härke 1990, 41 table 5). This can only mean that in these communities, the men with weapons belonged to different descent groups from the men without weapons. In the remaining three cemeteries (Broadstairs I, Stretton-on-Fosse II and Worthy Park), the patterns are inconclusive, arguing neither for nor against this interpretation.

Although the sub-samples for stature and epigenetic traits may appear rather small, their results are in agreement with all the other skeletal data. Together with the analysis of other data, such as weapon combinations, technical observations and historically recorded military activity (Härke 1990), they leave only one conclusion concerning the meaning of burial with weapons. An Anglo-Saxon inhumation was furnished with weapons *not* because it was the burial of an individual warrior – it was furnished with weapons in order to display the status of a family which was of Germanic descent and whose status was also linked to greater disposable wealth. Thus, the post-Roman weapon burial rite in England was a symbol of ethnic and social affiliation in a complex and ethnically mixed society. Shephard (1979, 70) has suggested on the evidence from barrow burials that the transition from achieved to ascribed status in Anglo-Saxon society happened in the seventh century. However, the emphasis on descent in the weapon burial rite may indicate that ascribed status was important well before that, possibly as early as the late fifth century.

[2] Straub (1956, using a sample of six Alamannic cemeteries and one Gallo-Roman burial site) and Huber (1967, analysing a large Alamannic cemetery) found that there was a correlation between burial wealth and weapon burial, on the one hand, and stature and cranial indices, on the other hand. They suggested that the taller, wealthier, and better-armed males in Alamannic cemeteries were Germani of North German origin, whereas the shorter and less well-armed, or unarmed, men represented the native Gallo-Roman population of South-West Germany (Huber 1967, 12–15; Straub 1956, 132–134). Even the absolute stature data and the stature differential involved (about 5 centimetres) closely match the Anglo-Saxon data. I am grateful to H. Steuer, Freiburg i.Br., for drawing my attention to these publications.

TABLE 4: AGE GROUPS AND WEAPON TYPES IN 291 WEAPON BURIALS

AGE GROUPS	ARROW	SPEAR	SECOND SPEAR	SHIELD	SWORD	SEAX	AXE	TOTAL OF WEAPON BURIALS
0– 1 years		1						1
2– 7 years	2	5		?1				7
8–14 years	1	22	1	2	1			23
15–20 years		25	1	4	2	?1		29
20–40 years		136	9	87	10	9	2	163
40–60+ years		63	3	33	6	7	3	68

The Symbolism of Weapon Types

In the above discussion, Anglo-Saxon weapon burials have been treated as a single group. Whilst this is useful and necessary for comparing them with male burials without weapons, it must be emphasized that archaeologically they are by no means a homogenous group. There are vast differences in burial wealth and grave construction between, say, Sutton Hoo and a simple inhumation with just a single spear. The most obvious differentiation of this group is by weapon types, and an analysis along these lines provides a basis for identifying the symbolism attached to certain types of weapons and to some of their characteristics, like size and decoration.

Weapon types are clearly related to the age at death of the individuals they were buried with (Table 4). A single spear could accompany any male burial from the age of about 3 (with only one younger case in the sample), but all other types and numbers of weapons have clear age constraints. Arrowheads seem to be limited to children's burials (maximum age about 14 years), although possible cases of bows and archers' bracers have been reported from adult graves (cf. Arnold 1982b, 66–67). Two spears, a shield or a sword could be deposited with individuals from the age of about 12 years, but they are predominantly the grave-goods of adults. Seax and axe were confined to adult burials, and have been found mainly in the graves of older adults (average age of 35–39, compared with 28–31 years for individuals with spear, sword or shield).[3] There are no obvious, practical reasons for these age constraints. On

---

3   The average ages for the various weapon types were computed by using for each individual the median of the age span determined by the anthropologist (e.g. age span 20–30, median age 25). The median values of all individuals with a particular type of weapon (e.g. seax: sample of 16 aged individuals) were then used to work out the average for this type (seax: 35 years). Possible exceptions from the age constraints,

TABLE 5: PHYSIQUE AND WEAPON TYPES (MALE ADULTS ONLY)

	sample *	weak	PHYSIQUE (normal)	strong
spear(s) only	92	9%	(73%)	18%
shield (+ spear)	104	2%	(87%)	11%
sword/seax/axe (+ others)	35	–	(74%)	26%

* No. of aged individuals

the contrary: adolescents' burials were occasionally furnished with the heavy spatha (double-edged sword), but never with the much lighter, single-edged seax nor with the light *francisca* (throwing axe). The absence of functional arguments supports the case for an interpretation in terms of symbolism. The age constraints of weapon burial point to three threshold ages of males in Anglo-Saxon society: about 3 years (related to weaning?), about 12 to 14 years (undoubtedly puberty), and about 18 to 20 years (probably full adulthood).

Two other correlates of weapon types are physique and burial wealth. Physique, like stature, is partly hereditary and partly influenced by environmental factors, like diet and stress in childhood, but muscle development is also determined by physical exercise and diet in adulthood. The scale of muscle development can be inferred from ridges of muscle attachment on the bones, but most anthropologists would remark only on cases of 'weak' or 'strong' muscle development or build (the latter usually referring to size or robustness of the bones). For the purposes of this analysis, we have to assume, therefore, that all skeletons that were aged, but not otherwise remarked upon, were of 'normal' build. The comparison by weapon types (Table 5) shows that swords, seaxes and axes have not been found in the graves of weakly built men, and they were clearly more often associated with strong individuals than is the case with shield or spear.

The analysis of burial wealth by weapon types (Table 6) underlines the particular significance of sword, seax and axe. They are, on average, associated with more grave-goods than are the other types of weapons. This 'wealth' differential is even more marked in the provision of objects made of, or dec-

marked '?' in Table 4, are: a shield in grave 50 at Westgarth Gardens (West 1988, 8: juvenile; *ibid.*, 33: no age given); and a seax that is said to have come from Polhill grave 9 which was disturbed during roadworks (individual aged 15–16; Philp 1973, 174). At Morning Thorpe (which was published too late to be included in the sample), arrowheads have been found with the possibly adult individual in grave 178 (Green et al. 1987, 85).

TABLE 6: BURIAL WEALTH AND WEAPON TYPES
(UNDISTURBED BURIALS ONLY)

	MALE ADULTS		JUVENILES	
	size of sample	aver. no of assoc. finds	size of sample	aver. no. of assoc. finds
arrow	–	–	5	1.80
spear	312	4.19	60	2.53
shield	184	4.55	5	4.80
seax	17	5.12	–	–
sword	34	5.68	1	10.00
axe	10	6.70	–	–

orated with, precious metals where sword and axe score twice as high, or more, than other weapon types, the lower score of the seax probably being due to its late date in the 'impoverished' seventh century. Moreover, sword, seax and axe are almost regularly found together with drinking vessels or liquid containers of some kind or other. Together, these observations suggest that sword, seax and axe were high-status weapons: men buried with them had more time for physical exercise (as professional warriors would), and wealth and feasting were part of their displayed status.

Sizes and decorations of weapons are significant, too, and their correlations are more easily interpretable. Sizes of spearheads are related to age at death: the majority of children had been provided with small spearheads, whilst adults had, on average, longer spearheads in their graves. This may partly be the consequence of practical requirements: small 'toy spears' for children, and real weapons for adults. However, this would not explain why the longest spearheads have regularly been found in the graves of mature and old adults. The correlation between size and age may, therefore, be symbolic, as it seems to be in the case of knives (cf. below). Finally, the presence of decorated weapons in burials is unambiguously related to burial wealth and age at death. This suggests that decoration of weapons was partly display of wealth and partly an age symbol.

Thus, weapon types served as symbolic markers in the burial rite, denoting age groups and élite status within the weapon-burying social group (or groups). The observation of a clear correlation between weapon types and age at death is all the more significant as age is not something which differentiates individuals buried with weapons from those buried without (cf. above). And the identification of sword, seax and axe as burial deposits of a wealthy and physically trained élite puts the Sutton Hoo ship burial in perspective: the inclusion there of a sword and an axe in a rich, high-status burial, probably of an adult individual (if the conventional identification with king Raedwald is correct), conforms to a wider Anglo-Saxon pattern. The helmet, found at Sutton Hoo but not represented in the analysed sample, is another marker of exalted social status, not just in Anglo-Saxon England but elsewhere in Early Medieval Europe (Steuer 1987).

Weapon Burial in the Seventh Century

This static picture of the symbolism of weapons in Anglo-Saxon graves needs to be complemented by an analysis of the dynamic aspects of this rite. The composition of weapon sets, and the relative frequencies of weapon types deposited in graves, remained relatively stable throughout the fifth and sixth centuries, but changed markedly in the seventh century (Fig. 29).[4] Several trends can be identified, the dominant one being the slow, but steady increase in popularity of the seax, accompanied by a decline of all other weapon types. Arrowheads appear to be exclusively early, and as far as can be judged from the few datable cases, have not turned up in seventh-century contexts. The axe disappeared from grave associations by the early seventh century; the iron axe-hammer from Sutton Hoo seems to be the latest axe from a burial in Anglo-Saxon England. The sword had ceased to be a grave deposit by the final phase of the weapon burial rite, the late seventh century.

Whilst these changes in weapon types are likely to reflect, in however a distorted fashion, underlying changes in military equipment, they are also significant in terms of symbolism. Both the axe and the seax are adult grave-goods with the same age correlation, and both are élite symbols with similar 'wealth' correlations. The decline of the one and the rise of the other in the burial rite may, therefore, be a simple case of substitution. By contrast, the disappearance of arrows signals a more fundamental change because it implies the disappearance of a predominantly, or even exclusively, juvenile symbol (cf. below).

The second, main change in outward appearance of the weapon burial rite was a steady decline, throughout the seventh century, in the frequency of graves furnished with weapons, eventually leading to an end of this rite by the early eighth century. The decline in absolute terms is reflected in the sharp fall in the numbers of graves with the various weapon types (Fig. 29). In relative terms, the decline was a more gradual one (Fig. 30). The proportion of weapon burials among all inhumations dropped from 20% in cemetery date group B

---

4   An outline of the system of 'burial date groups' and 'cemetery date groups' used in this
    section and in Figs 29–32 is provided in Härke 1989a, 51. A more detailed explanation
    of this method of grouping burials and cemeteries with similar, absolute date spans for
    chronological comparisons will be included in Härke 1992.

number of burials

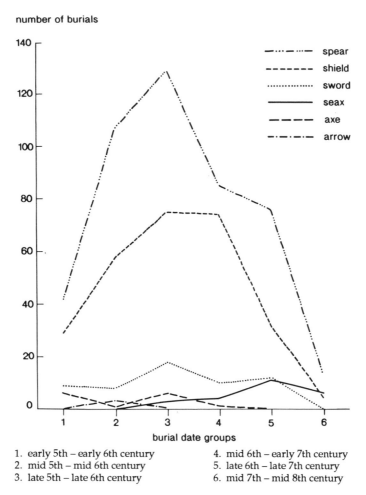

1. early 5th – early 6th century   4. mid 6th – early 7th century
2. mid 5th – mid 6th century   5. late 6th – late 7th century
3. late 5th – late 6th century   6. mid 7th – mid 8th century

Figure 29. Weapon types in Anglo-Saxon inhumations over time

(late fifth to early seventh century, with a median in the sixth century) to 1.5% in group E (early seventh to mid-eighth century, with a median in the late seventh century). Similarly, the proportion of male adults buried with weapons decreased slowly from its peak of about 60%, to less than 10% in the final phase of the grave-goods custom.

Part of the decrease in numbers is accounted for by the exclusion of juveniles from the weapon burial rite. Like all other changes, this did not happen suddenly but progressively (Fig. 31): by the earlier seventh century (beginning of burial date group 5), weapons had ceased to be deposited in children's burials; by the late seventh century (beginning of burial date group 6), they had also disappeared from burials of adolescents.[5] This increasing emphasis on adult

[5] 'Late' cemeteries outside the sample seem to conform to this pattern, with one possible

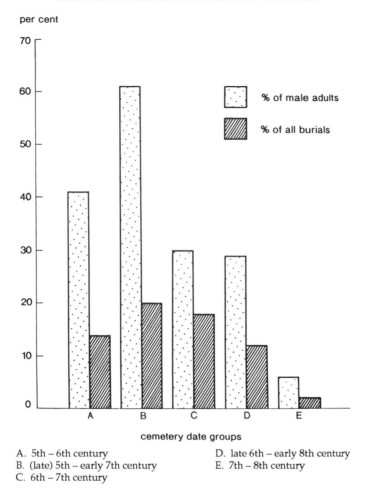

per cent

A. 5th – 6th century
B. (late) 5th – early 7th century
C. 6th – 7th century
D. late 6th – early 8th century
E. 7th – 8th century

cemetery date groups

Figure 30. Relative frequencies of weapon burials over time

status in the weapon burial rite is all the more intriguing as it parallels another seventh-century process which it partly overlapped. Shephard (1979, 67) has suggested that membership of the 'superordinate class' buried in isolated barrows was linked to adulthood, because juveniles have not been found on their own (i.e. without an adult) in barrow burials.

Among adults, the decline of the weapon burial rite involved many 'poorer' burials dropping out from this rite. Weapon burials decreased in numbers during the seventh century, but maintained their average wealth, whilst that of other furnished male burials dropped (Fig. 32). Over the same period, the proportion of male adult burials without grave-goods rose from about 10% in

exception: a 'child's grave' with an iron spearhead has been reported from Shudy Camps (grave 30; Lethbridge 1936, 12). The excavator noted a 'skull with milk teeth', but there was no specialist report on the skeletal material from this site.

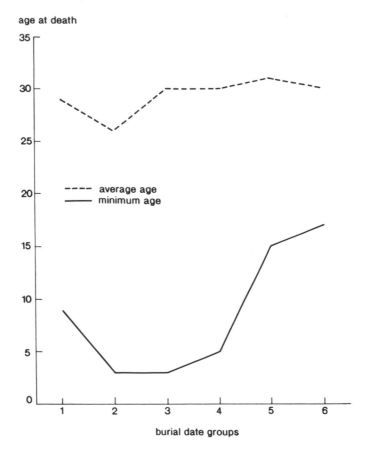

Figure 31. Age at death of individuals buried with weapons
over time (for burial date groups, cf. Fig. 29)

the fifth/sixth centuries to over 30% in the seventh/eighth centuries. In other
words: in the seventh century, the male burial wealth was gradually concentrated in a decreasing number of adult weapon burials.

Knives became an alternative means of displaying male adult status in
poorer burials. Large knives, with a blade length of 130 to 170 millimetres,
began to appear in the late sixth century, but were most numerous and widespread in the seventh century (Härke 1989b). They are really too small to be
called 'seaxes' because they are even shorter than the Continental *Kurzsax* (cf.
Koch 1977, 106). Although they could hardly have been intended as weapons,
they were restricted, without exception, to burials of male adults. But unlike
the seax and other weapons, the large knife is not associated with above-
average burial wealth, suggesting that it is a symbol of male adult status only,
without claim to the social status displayed in weapon burials.

The end of the cremation rite in the seventh century may, in some English
regions, have contributed to the relative decrease in the proportion of weapon

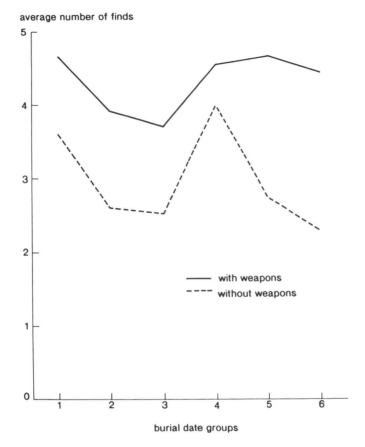

average number of finds

burial date groups

Figure 32. Burial wealth of male adults over time (for burial date groups, cf. Fig. 29)

burials. The regional comparison shows that areas with a high proportion of cremations also had a high proportion of inhumations with weapons, and *vice versa* (Härke 1989a, 50 fig. 4.1). It is not easy to find a convincing explanation for this linkage. It would appear that those social groups or sections which did not practise weapon burial, had a slightly higher tendency to cremate wherever this was an accepted rite. The very low incidence of weapons in cremations may serve to support this explanation. If it is correct, the decline of the cremation rite could have resulted in an increased proportion among inhumations of groups not practising weapon burial. However, this result would not follow automatically if weapon burial and cremation were alternative means of expressing ethnicity.

But another change was perhaps more significant than all other processes and changes apparent in the burial rite. In the seventh century, the stature differential between men with and without weapons, suggested above to be mainly ethnic, appears to have broken down (Table 3). This is accompanied by a general decrease in average stature in the sample (342 male adults), from just under 175 centimetres in the fifth/sixth centuries to 173 centimetres in the seventh/eighth centuries. An obvious cause for this decrease is hard to find: there was no new influx of a different population in the seventh century; and a fundamental shift in the diet from animal protein to plant protein (which could have had this effect, as it did during the High and Late Middle Ages) is highly unlikely at this early date. If this stature decrease is not just a statistical fluke, there seems to be only one possible explanation for it: an increasing assimilation of native Britons into the population buried in recognizably 'Anglo-Saxon' cemeteries. This implies, incidentally, that a large proportion, or even the majority, of the native population had previously buried in unidentified cemeteries, and that it is only their 'Saxonisation' from the seventh century onwards which makes them recognizable in the archaeological record. The suggested assimilation would also imply the lowering of ethnic boundaries in the Anglo-Saxon settlement areas of England, thus obviating the need to express ethnicity in the burial rite, be it by burial with weapons or by cremation.

Conclusions

The Anglo-Saxon weapon burial rite involved a complex ritual symbolism: it was multi-dimensional, displaying ethnic affiliation, descent, wealth, élite status, and age groups. In the seventh century, there were some outward changes in the composition of weapon sets deposited, but more importantly, the symbolic content changed:

— burial with weapons ceased to be an ethnic marker;
— as a 'badge' of family affiliation, it was phased out in juvenile burials;
— as a means of displaying male adult status, weapons were partly replaced by a 'poorer' substitute (large knives);
— as an élite symbol, weapon burial was complemented, and partly superseded, by an alternative (barrow burial).

The deposition of weapons continued as a social symbol, displaying in male adult burials the status and wealth of an ever smaller élite, or section of the élite. Thus, in the seventh century, weapon burial became much more constrained, and it changed from a complex to a more simplex, almost 'mono-dimensional' symbol.[6] It eventually disappeared altogether in the early eighth century, the last weapons being deposited in Anglo-Saxon graves around

---

6 Halsall (1988) has suggested that in the cemeteries around Metz, particularly at Ennery (Moselle), grave furniture was originally symbolic (in relation to socio-economic roles), but in the seventh century this symbolic role declined, and furnishing the graves became just 'une pratique habituelle' (*ibid.*, 51).

A.D.700. This cannot have been due to the spreading influence of Christianity alone, not least because the decline of the grave-goods custom was paralleled in Continental Western Europe where Christianity had taken hold much earlier without affecting the deposition of grave-goods in any noticeable way (cf. e.g. Stein 1967). Looking at the Anglo-Saxon weapon burial rite in isolation, it is probable that it was phased out after its one remaining, symbolic function had become redundant because of the stabilisation of the social and political system, or even more likely, it was replaced by other, archaeologically invisible symbols which accompanied the living, but not the dead.

11

Royal Power and Royal Symbols in *Beowulf*

BARBARA RAW

Royal power in *Beowulf* is based primarily on success in war and the possession of a large warband. The *Beowulf*-poet describes three kings as 'good': Scyld, Hrothgar and Beowulf (*Beowulf* 11, 863, 2390). Scyld, the founder of the Danish royal house, appeared miraculously from over the sea and was returned to the sea in a ship-funeral after a long and successful reign. His virtue consisted in defeating the tribes whose lands surrounded those of the Danes, taking away their mead-benches and reducing them to paying tribute (*Beowulf* 4–11). Hrothgar, Scyld's great-grandson, was successful in war. He acquired a large warband. He celebrated his success by building an enormous hall, imposing the work of decorating it on many tribes (*Beowulf* 63–76). He ruled the Danes for fifty years, protected them in war and was immune from attack until the coming of Grendel (*Beowulf* 1769–73). Beowulf shares some of Hrothgar's qualities. He, too, has ruled for fifty years, has protected his people and has been sufficiently strong to deter attacks by neighbouring tribes; the chief fear of his followers after his death is that their nation will be destroyed by hostile neighbours now that Beowulf's protection has gone (*Beowulf* 2733–6, 2910–13, 2922–3, 2999–3007). His ambitions as king do not seem to include the extension of his territory, however. As he lies dying, he congratulates himself on having awaited his fate in his own land – unlike his uncle, Hygelac, who went out looking for trouble, and died defending his spoils during an apparently unprovoked raid on the Frisians (*Beowulf* 2736–7, 1202–14). His followers praise him for his kindness and gentleness as well as for his military achievements (*Beowulf* 3173–5, 3180–2). Yet he is not passive. When Onela, the Swedish king, kills Hygelac's young son, Heardred, because he has harboured his rebellious nephews, Beowulf not only fulfils his duty of taking vengeance for Heardred; he assists Onela's one surviving nephew to defeat him and gain the Swedish throne (*Beowulf* 2379–96). The action is particularly striking since Beowulf had been placed on the Geatish throne by Onela, after the death of Heardred, and presumably owed him allegiance.

The adjective *god* used to describe these kings, and translated above as 'good', was discussed many years ago by Margery Daunt, who concluded that it implied fitness for a particular purpose (Daunt 1966, 68–70). To describe a man as *god cyning*, then, implies that his actions were appropriate to a king. In Old English gnomic poetry the king's role is defined in terms of power and generosity. His task is to rule (*Maxims II*, 1). He is eager for power and especially for land (*Maxims I*, 58–9). He sits in his hall, sharing out rings (*Maxims II*, 28–9). In *Beowulf* we see what lies behind this image: land is acquired by fighting and rings are the spoils of war. The king is the *drihten*, the leader of the *driht* or warband. He is *guðcyning*, 'a war-king'. He is characterised as *sigerof*, 'victorious', *heaðorof* and *niðheard*, 'brave in battle'. He is not only the friend of his people (*wine*), the lord of his household (*frea*), the giver of rings (*beaga brytta*), the famous ruler (*þeoden mære*), but *se goda*, the hero (*Beowulf* 350–55). Birth and family are important but heroism is the main requirement for an aspiring king. Scyld, who arrived in Denmark destitute, alone in a boat, became king because of his ability in war (*Beowulf* 4–11). Hrothgar and his followers acclaim Beowulf as worthy of a kingdom after his killing of Grendel (*Beowulf* 856–61, 1845–53), and when Hrothgar adopts Beowulf as his son, apparently intending to disinherit his own sons (*Beowulf* 946–55, 1175–80), it is because of his physical strength.

Once power had been acquired, it had to be maintained and displayed. Hrothgar displays his power primarily through his hall and the ceremonies connected with it. The hall is large, because Hrothgar has a large warband (*Beowulf* 64–79). It was built by non-Danish workmen. It is expensively equipped, bright with treasure (*Beowulf* 167, 308), the mead-benches and roof decorated with gold (*Beowulf* 777, 927), the walls hung with golden tapestries (*Beowulf* 994–5). Hrothgar himself does not seem to be distinguished by any special dress or ornaments, though his queen and daughter are decked with gold and his queen appears to wear a crown (*Beowulf* 612–14, 1162–3, 2025). His status is manifested instead by position, ritual and deference. He sits on a raised seat (*on yppan*, 1815) at the centre of the hall, his þyle at his feet and his *gedriht* or warband around him (*Beowulf* 356–7, 500, 1165–6). When Hrothgar's officers approach him to speak, they stand in the correct place because they know the customs of the *duguð* (*Beowulf* 359). When Wealhtheow moves through the hall with the ceremonial drinking cup she goes first to Hrothgar, then to the *duguð*, the tried warriors who sit near the king, and finally to the *geogoð*, the younger warriors who sit at the end of the hall (*Beowulf* 612–24, 1188–91). Sometimes she serves only the more important warriors while the younger ones are served by her daughter, Freawaru (*Beowulf* 2016–24). Everyone and everything has its proper place and order (Enright 1988, 179–80).

Hrothgar's hall is not simply an example of magnificence. It demonstrates his dominance over his neighbours and his control of material and human resources (*Beowulf* 67–79). The hall stands in the border-country, presumably to remind the neighbouring tribes of their subjection. It is exceptionally large, and therefore a visible sign of Hrothgar's power. It shows that his command extends beyond the kingdom he inherited, for it is built and decorated by men from many tribes. It demonstrates Hrothgar's feeling of security – at least, until the arrival of Grendel – for it has no gatehouse or other defence works. A guard watches the coastline and an officer controls entry to the hall itself but, apart from this, Hrothgar's home lies open to all comers. As he himself says when looking back on his fifty-year reign, he did not fear attack (*Beowulf* 1769–73).

The ability to organise men and resources which allows Hrothgar to build his hall is only one example of the way in which royal power works in *Beowulf*. Having acquired land and loot, kings controlled its disposal. The second symbol of royal power, therefore, is the gift-stool from which the king distributed treasure (cf. Chaney 1962, 516–17). Kings were expected to be lavish with gifts and meanness was considered a major crime (*Maxims I* 81–3). Scyld's predecessor on the Danish throne ended his life as an exile from his kingdom because he failed to distribute rings to the Danes, and Hrothgar warns Beowulf against following the same path (*Beowulf* 1709–24, 1748–50). But the giving of treasure is not merely a matter of generosity; it confers prestige on both giver and recipient. The king gives rings to demonstrate his wealth, as a boast or *gylp* (*Beowulf* 1749–50; Leisi 1952–3, 263–4); the retainer expects gifts of which he need not be ashamed before other warriors (*Beowulf* 1025–6). Gifts are an incentive to future performance as well as a reward for services performed. Hrothgar offers Beowulf treasures in exchange for fighting Grendel before he even knows that that is the purpose of his visit (*Beowulf* 384–5). In this case the exchange of gifts and services, which is completed after the death of Grendel, is a matter of equality, because the gifts are offered to someone who is not in Hrothgar's service. The relationship between lord and retainer, on the other hand, is one of subordination. The gifts given by the lord to his retainers are not merely an incentive to serve him; they create an obligation to do so, as Wiglaf reminds Beowulf's followers during the dragon-fight (*Beowulf* 2633–38).

Gifts of land, like gifts of treasure, imposed obligations on a king's followers and bound them to him. T.M. Charles-Edwards has drawn a distinction between the grant of land by the king which enabled a warrior to marry, and which was reciprocated by military service, and inheritance of land on the death of one's father (Charles-Edwards 1976, 183). In *Beowulf*, however, inheritance, like gift, involves a reciprocal relationship with the lord. Wiglaf repays Beowulf for the gift of his father's estate by helping him against the dragon (*Beowulf* 2606–10). Beowulf himself obtains his inheritance only when he hands over the treasures he won by killing Grendel and his mother (*Beowulf* 2155–66, 2190–99; John 1973–4, 409–10).

In addition to ensuring the loyalty of the warband, gift-giving could be used to promote friendship between tribes. Hrothgar had learned of Beowulf's reputation from the seafarers who carried gifts from the Danes to the Geats

(*Beowulf* 377–81) and he anticipates a continuing exchange of gifts after Beowulf's defeat of Grendel and his mother (*Beowulf* 1855–63). These gifts are to be a sign that the former hostility between the tribes is at an end, suggesting that the relationship between the two tribes has not been entirely peaceful, and that the gift-giving has been more than a simple exchange between friends. Further evidence of inter-tribal diplomacy comes from Hrothgar's reminiscences about Beowulf's father, who had killed a member of the tribe of the Wylfings and had consequently become involved in a blood-feud which would have brought war on the Geats (*Beowulf* 457–72). Hrothgar, whose wife probably came from the tribe of the Wylfings (*Beowulf* 620, *Widsith* 29), sent treasures over the sea to settle the feud. By doing so, he imposed an obligation on Beowulf's family which he believes the latter is repaying by coming to help him against Grendel.

The control over the lives of others described so far is the result either of a free exchange of gifts and services or of defeat in war. In places, however, the *Beowulf*-poet hints at a more autocratic kind of kingship, which brought with it absolute control over the lives of family as well as retainers. The first victims are women. Superficially, their status seems high. Wealhtheow is in a position to give advice to Hrothgar; like him, she controls wealth, and offers gifts to Beowulf (*Beowulf* 1169–87, 2172–3). Hygd is honoured during her husband's lifetime and is free to choose who will succeed him on the Geatish throne (*Beowulf* 1926–31, 2369–79). But whereas queens seem to share their husbands' power, princesses can be used in the pursuit of diplomacy, rather as though they were examples of moveable wealth. Hrothgar's daughter is to be married to Ingeld in an unsuccessful attempt to patch up a feud between their two tribes (*Beowulf* 2024–9). The tale of Finnsburg, recited at the feast held to celebrate Beowulf's defeat of Grendel, involves the marriage of another Danish princess to the Frisian king, with equally unhappy results (*Beowulf* 1071–1159). The *Beowulf*-poet expresses sympathy for these women, but he does not criticise the way in which royal power is being used. His attitude to the relationship between king and retainers is different. Eric John claims that the *Beowulf*-poet is writing from the point of view of a retainer who was aware that he was totally at the mercy of an all-powerful lord (John 1973–4, 415, 418–9). It is clear, however, that the poet does not consider such a relationship as either normal or acceptable. He describes how the Danes, faced with a king who was in the habit of killing his table-companions, deposed him and drove him out (*Beowulf* 902–4, 1709–22). In his account of Hrothgar's rise to power he draws attention to the limits within which this power operated. Hrothgar promises to share all the treasure he acquires, but not the common land or men's lives (*folcscare ond feorum gumena*, *Beowulf* 71–3). The reference to the lives of men is puzzling. It is tempting to link it to the passage later in the poem which describes the Danes' reversion to devil-worship after the coming of Grendel (*Beowulf* 175–83) and to interpret it as a reference to ritual killing, condemned by the Christian poet.

The final form of control exercised by kings concerns the succession, and there are several examples in *Beowulf* of kings (and queens) trying to ensure transfer of power to someone other than the direct heir. Heorogar's son was passed over in favour of his uncle, Hrothgar, apparently at Heorogar's instigation (*Beowulf* 2155–62). Hrothgar adopts Beowulf as his son, and Wealhtheow, at least, believes that he intends him as his heir (*Beowulf* 1175–80). Hygd offers Beowulf the throne after the death of Hygelac, because she believes her son is too young to rule successfully (*Beowulf* 2369–72). These attempts by Hrothgar and Hygd to control the succession fail because Beowulf refuses to accept. Onela, on the other hand, does achieve control when he places Beowulf on the Geatish throne after the death of Heardred (*Beowulf* 2389–90), but the kind of power being exercised here is quite different because it derives from his position as military conqueror.

One would expect the transfer of royal power to be accompanied by the transfer of some material object, which would symbolise what was being transferred, and for there to be some special role for the new king at the funeral of his predecessor, but this is not always the case. Scyld's funeral is organised by his followers in accordance with instructions given before his death (*Beowulf* 28–30), and his heir seems to play no part in the ceremonies. Beowulf, too, plans his own funeral, giving detailed instructions about the barrow which is to be raised over his remains (*Beowulf* 2802–8, 3096–3100), though in this case the funeral itself is controlled by Wiglaf, who succeeds him as king. Both funerals are designed to reflect the prestige of the dead man but their implications in terms of power are very different. Scyld's military achievements are symbolised by the armour and weapons placed round his body, and his wide-reaching power is recalled by the treasures brought from distant parts (*Beowulf* 32–42). The choice of a ship-burial is particularly appropriate because Scyld is portrayed as a sea-king: he not only arrived over the waves (*Beowulf* 45–6); he makes his neighbours pay him tribute *ofer hronrade* (*Beowulf* 10). There is no indication that the lavish funeral is intended to show that wealth, generosity and power now rest with Scyld's successor. Beowulf's funeral, on the other hand, indicates that power is now in the hands of his heir. Wiglaf is no longer the young follower fighting with his lord for the first time (*Beowulf* 2625–7). He has received power to command, and his authority extends even to the senior retainers who were closest to the dead king. He assembles a large body of house-holders to fetch wood for the funeral pyre (*Beowulf* 3110–14); he organises the removal of the treasure from the dragon's lair by a group of seven king's thanes (*Beowulf* 3120–36). His command of resources is seen in the building of the barrow, a task which takes ten days to complete (*Beowulf* 3156–62); his generosity and his devotion to his dead lord is seen in the placing of the whole of the dragon's treasure in the grave-mound, even though Beowulf himself had intended that it should go to his people (*Beowulf* 2794–8, 3163–8).

Wiglaf exercises moral authority because he was the only one of Beowulf's retainers to help him against the dragon, but his unchallenged command of Beowulf's retainers must also derive from some formal handover of power. This raises the question of whether the kings described in *Beowulf* possessed status symbols which were inherited rather than being buried. The main such status symbol is, of course, the gift-stool, control over which was essential to the exercise of kingship because of the central role played by gift-giving in maintaining and enhancing royal power. When Hygd offers Beowulf the kingdom of the Geats after the death of Hygelac, she offers him *hord ond rice, beagas ond bregostol*, 'treasure and kingdom, rings and royal seat' (*Beowulf* 2369–70). When Onela allows Beowulf to succeed Hygelac's son, Heardred, dominion is once again expressed in terms of possession of the *bregostol* (*Beowulf* 2389–90). When the dragon attacks the Geats his first act is to destroy the symbols of Beowulf's power, the hall and gift-stool of the Geats (*Beowulf* 2325–7). Other items which may belong to the king in virtue of his office are the ornaments and military equipment given by Hrothgar to Beowulf and by Beowulf to Wiglaf. Hrothgar gives Beowulf four items: a golden standard, a helmet, a coat of mail and a sword (*Beowulf* 1020–4). There is a strong case for believing that this equipment was royal rather than personal property. It had belonged originally to Hrothgar's predecessor, Heorogar, who had chosen to leave it to his brother rather than to his son (*Beowulf* 2158–62). The fact that Hrothgar succeeded his brother as king and that the gift to Beowulf is made shortly after his adoption by Hrothgar suggests that the gift is part of an attempt to designate Beowulf as Hrothgar's successor (*Beowulf* 946–9, 1175–6, Hill 1982, 180–5). The equipment left to Wiglaf by the dying Beowulf consists of a golden neck-ring, a helmet decorated with gold and a coat of mail. These items are not given a pedigree like Hrothgar's gifts, though the reference to Wiglaf as the last member of Beowulf's tribe suggests that they are not merely personal belongings (*Beowulf* 2809–16).

Possession of a helmet and coat of mail seems to have been fairly widespread among the warriors described by the *Beowulf*-poet, though this does not necessarily rule them out as symbols of royal power in a society where the king was also the leader of the warband. The standard and neck-ring are more plausible symbols of rank, however. Anglo-Saxon poets frequently refer to royal standards. In the Old English *Exodus*, Pharoah is described as *segncyning*, a king who owns a standard (*Exodus* 172). The emperor Constantine has a *þuf* or *segn* raised in battle and sleeps beneath his *eofurcumbul*, his boar-standard (*Elene* 76, 123–4). The most interesting example is the standard devised by Satan as a first stage in setting himself up as a rival to God; the possession of *segn and side byrnan* clearly symbolises his move from retainer to *drihten* (*Solomon and Saturn* 454). Three standards are mentioned in *Beowulf*, apart from that given to Beowulf by Hrothgar. Scyld's standard is placed in his funeral ship and must therefore be a personal item (*Beowulf* 47). Hygelac's standard was probably captured, together with his neck-ring, after his death in Frisia (*Beowulf* 1202–14); it is impossible to know whether it was a national symbol or a personal one, since it could not be passed to his successor. The standard in the dragon's cave, on the other hand, is clearly a tribal possession rather than a personal one, for it forms part of the treasure of a whole race, buried by a man who is its sole survivor (*Beowulf* 2232–70, 2767–71). The neck-ring, like the standard, seems sometimes to be a personal item, sometimes a public one. When Beowulf gives his neck-ring to Wiglaf, the gift is clearly connected with his designation of Wiglaf as his successor (*Beowulf* 2809–12). Hygelac's neck-ring, on the other hand, was a gift by Wealhtheow to Beowulf, given by Beowulf to Hygelac's wife, Hygd, and by her to her husband (*Beowulf* 1195–1211, 2172–76). It is highly unlikely that it was a symbol of kingship.

One striking feature of royal power in *Beowulf* is its fragility. Heremod fails as king because he misuses his power, killing his companions, and keeping his treasure to himself (*Beowulf* 1709–22). Hygelac and Heardred fail because they over-reach themselves. Hygelac attacks the Frisians, much as Scyld and Hrothgar attacked their neighbours, but his power is insufficient to carry the expedition off; Heardred tries to influence Swedish politics by harbouring Onela's rebellious nephews but lacks the strength to oppose the Swedish king successfully. Hrothgar and Beowulf fail, partly as a result of external forces which are not under their control, and partly because of character traits which are inherent in their conception of kingship. Hrothgar's kingship is threatened by the activities of Grendel, who behaves in a thoroughly uncivilised way, restricting the king's use of his hall, killing his retainers and refusing to pay wergild; it is possible, however, that Grendel would not have caused trouble if Hrothgar had confined his rule to Danish territory and had not built so ostentatious a hall. The second, and perhaps more serious threat, comes from Hrothgar's ambitious nephew and co-ruler, Hrothulf and from the feud with the Heathobards, which will result in the burning of Hrothgar's hall. Beowulf fails because a runaway slave steals a cup from a dormant dragon, which, once roused, burns the royal hall, forcing Beowulf to engage in a fight in which he loses his life. Behind this fight, however, lies another failure. Beowulf's fifty-year reign has resulted in a band of retainers who are too weak and cowardly to carry out their duty of supporting their king under attack.

The picture of royal power outlined above has been limited deliberately to material drawn from a work of literature, and no attempt has been made to combine the evidence of the poem with documentary evidence. When the Sutton Hoo ship-burial was excavated in 1939 scholars saw clear parallels between it and *Beowulf*. For literary scholars, Sutton Hoo provided confirmation that the allusions to wealth and splendour in *Beowulf* were not the result of poetic exaggeration; for archaeologists, the description of Scyld's funeral at the beginning of *Beowulf* offered a context for the objects excavated at Sutton Hoo. But a poem cannot be used like a historical document. The events described by the *Beowulf*-poet date from the late fifth and early sixth centuries, long before the composition of the poem in its present form. It is doubtful whether even the most conservative scholar would now date the composition of the poem before the eighth century and some would place it as late as the tenth or even the early eleventh. The *Beowulf*-poet himself makes it clear in the opening lines of the poem that he is writing about the distant past. His descriptions of halls, funerals and feasts are his vision of what this pagan past might have been like. But although a poet might well include descriptions of objects which were not of his own period in his main narrative, he is less likely to invent when making casual passing references. The implications of what he says, therefore, the assumptions lurking between the lines, are probably an accurate reflection of the society in which he lived. They may also be an accurate reflection of the society to which the king of Sutton Hoo belonged, but that is something of which it is impossible to be sure.

12

Christianity in Sixth- and Seventh-Century Southumbria

JANE STEVENSON

My intention in this paper is to clarify some aspects of the Christian context which lies behind and around the ship-burial at Sutton Hoo. My focus of concentration, therefore, is on East Anglia itself, Kent, and Mercia; the cultures of the south-east, rather than on the entire area south of the Humber.

Christianity had a long history in southern Britain by the time of the ship-burial at Sutton Hoo. Even without believing that Joseph of Arimathea was exerting himself at Glastonbury in the first century A.D., there is no reason to doubt that Christianity had reached our island considerably before it became the state religion of the Roman Empire, and was well established by the time that Constantine the Great swept down from York to make himself master of the whole Roman world. This is not to say that Southumbria had unanimously accepted the message of the Gospels. For example, the great temple of Nodens at Lydney on the Severn was built around the time of Julian the Apostate, late in the fourth century (Salway 1981, 362, 686). Also in the west, where Romano-British Christianity was later to hold its ground tenaciously against the pagan Saxons, the goddess Sulis Minerva continued to receive lead curse-tablets (*defixiones*) advising her of private vendettas well into the fourth century, by which time the empire was of course officially Christian (Tomlin 1987, 18–19). Some of the people named on tablets bear such obviously British names as Vindocunus (Tomlin 1982), from two Celtic words meaning 'white dog', which confirms that this was not a practice confined to resident aliens. Compounds with *find-* are very frequent in Celtic onomastics, and the cognate *Findchu* is found in early medieval Ireland, though it is not in itself particularly common (O'Brien 1983). A particularly interesting *defixio* curses the person, 'whether Gentile or Christian, male or female, boy or girl, who stole six silver pieces from my purse' (Hassall & Tomlin 1981, 404). As Tomlin has pointed out, the extremely unusual opposition of *gentilis* and *Christianus* beside the more traditional formulae of 'either . . .or' suggests that this particular devotee of Sulis Minerva was acquainted with the letter of St Paul to the Galatians: 'there is neither bond or free, there is neither male nor female, for ye are all one in Christ Jesus' (Gal. iii.28).

There is some evidence, then, for coexistence and indeed overlap between Romano-British Christianity and Romano-British paganism (Frend 1979, 140–1). But when Germanus of Auxerre arrived in southern Britain in the fifth century, the problem confronting him is said to have been heresy rather than paganism as such (Hoare 1945, 297–8, Krusch & Levison 1920, 260–1 [14]). Even the common people are presented as securely Christianised, and the church, on the evidence of his *Vita* and the writings of Gildas, was only too well established, with complacent and worldly bishops, a good deal of money, and heretical tendencies (Winterbottom 1978, 52–4, 118–20 [III.66–8]). This again is confirmed to some extent by archaeological evidence, for instance, the Christian villa at Frampton (Gloucestershire), with its syncretistic mosaics (Toynbee 1968), and the Water Newton silver from East Anglia (near Peterborough), the earliest hoard of Christian silver yet found in the Roman Empire (Painter 1977, 22–24). The silver in particular demonstrates that some syncretistic impulses remained in the British church, evidenced by the unique Christian silver votive tablets. Some names survive from the early British church; most notably St Alban, martyred at Verulamium, Aaron and Julius, and a mysterious Sixtus, still venerated at Canterbury in the days of king Æthelbert (Brooks 1984, 20). The name of Sixtus, and the presence of two *eccles* placenames in Norfolk (Cameron 1968, 87–92), point, however problematically, towards the conclusion that Christianity was never completely eradicated from south-eastern Britain, whatever may have happened to its organizational superstructure. There is additionally an Eccles in Kent, and another in Norfolk, which also has a Beccles (see further Gelling 1988, 96–8). Bede's version of the later name Dunwich, the first see of East Anglia, is *Dommoc*, which might just be a *dominicus* formation, like Old Irish *domnach*, which is in Irish contexts normally held to be an indication of a very ancient site of Christian worship.

The *adventus Saxonum* crushed the earlier inhabitants of Kent and East Anglia into silence and the dark. If Arnold (1984, 133–7) is correct in his interpretation of cemetery evidence, the invaders may have followed the simple and logical plan of murdering the most bellicose of the men, and making use of the women. Evidence from Hampshire cemeteries shows (at Lankhills and Owslebury) a very low ratio of women to men in late Romano-British burialsites, and also physical homogeneity between female skeletons in Romano-British and early Saxon graveyards, beside a considerable difference in stature between the one and the other group of men. This, of course, would point towards a crude continuity in the population on the level of *coloni* (i.e., the servile element of the population) and females in general. But there is a distinction to be drawn between a genetic heritage, and a cultural and linguistic heritage. The invading Angles, Saxons and Jutes imposed their language and culture with great effectiveness. Nick Higham (1986, 273) comments:

the crude picture of genocidal conflict is a highly misleading interpretation of contact between Celt and English, and the mechanisms by which one language group was replaced by another are likely to have been highly complex. That comparatively little true ethnic replacement occurred is at least a defensible opinion.

Patches of the older civilisation remained, such as the British kingdom of Elmet, which survived until the seventh century in the environs of Leeds, nested in the midst of Northumbrian Deira; and further south of the Humber, J.N.L. Myres (1986, 181–2) has suggested that Lincoln might also have survived the *adventus Saxonum* relatively intact, which would help to explain the survival of the name, part of the city's buildings, and the name Caedbaed borne by a sixth-century king of Lindsey, which appears to contain the Celtic element cath- ('battle'). The enigmatic 'Tribal Hidage' corroborates the impression that the Anglo-Saxon kingdoms were anything but monolithic in structure by listing thirty-four separate population-groups recognizable in England at some time before the tenth century (the date at which the 'Tribal Hidage' was composed remains unknown), most of which can be located east of the Severn and south of the Humber (see further Dumville 1989 and Davies & Vierck 1974).

By the end of the sixth century, southern England was once more studded with pagan places of worship as it can hardly have been since the days of Carausius, though instead of temples and groves, there were Harrows, Wensleys and Thunderfields. The numbers of pagan religious sites evidenced by placenames is a much-argued question, but there are forty-three, all in Southumbria, for which the evidence has been judged acceptable (Gelling 1978, 158–61, and see Wilson 1985). Few, if any, of these are likely to have been hallowed later than the seventh century, and most must surely date to the few generations between the Germanic settlements and the arrival of St Augustine. However, we cannot assume, on the basis of the overwhelmingly Anglo-Saxon placenames of the south-eastern quadrant of the country, and the many pagan Anglo-Saxon sites already referred to, that pockets of Christianity and British culture were entirely absent from Kent, Essex and East Anglia. One of the lessons which archaeology has been teaching us in the last half-century is how much more complex and nebulous a business the Anglo-Saxon settlement was in reality from the simple picture of the replacement of one population by another which used once to be offered to us. Guthlac, who flourished in the late seventh and early eighth century and was brought up in the land of the Middle Angles, spent some time in exile among the Britons in his piratical youth, and when he was living as a hermit in the desolate fens of East Anglia at Crowland, he seems to have heard a group of people, identified by his biographer as demons, speaking together in British (Colgrave 1956, 110 [34]). This suggests two things to me: first, that there were still Britons in East Anglia around the year 700; and second, that they were rare enough, and furtive enough in their movements, not to be taken for granted when overheard by an excitable saint.

So much for the British element in Southumbrian Christianity; a subterranean, tenacious, obstinate attachment of a subject people to the God who might be punishing them, as Gildas had warned, for the sins of their fathers. Next, it is desirable to turn to the Irish element. Entirely independent of the well-known influence of Iona on the development of Northumbria, various Irishmen are known to have settled in southern England. By far the best attested of these is Fursa, who lived in East Anglia in the 630s, since he was the subject of a quite lengthy and detailed seventh-century Life, preserved on the continent (Krusch 1902, 434–40), and known to Bede, who gave him a detailed write-up in the *Historia Ecclesiastica* (Colgrave & Mynors 1969, 268 [III.19]). King Sigeberht, himself a Christian, gave Fursa a site called *Cnobheresburg*; possibly the distinctly liminal territory of Burgh Castle, one of the old Saxon Shore forts, across the river from Caistor-on-Sea, for his little settlement, which included at least four other named Irishmen (Krusch 1902, 438 [8]). Other names of Irishmen settled in Southumbria and attested by Bede are Dicuil, settled at Bosham in Sussex (Colgrave & Mynors 1969, 372 [IV.13]) before that kingdom became Christian, Diuma and Cellach, first bishops of the Middle Angles and the Mercians, and Maildub, who Bede tells us gave his name to Malmesbury. These Irishmen were not concerned to proselytise: in any case, Bede tells us specifically, à propos of Dicuil, that he had no language in common with the locals, which would have made it impossible without powerful royal assistance, and the Life of Fursa tells us that the saint was concerned only for eremitic solitude, and left *Cnobheresburg* for Merovingian Gaul once too many (Irish) people knew how to find him (Krusch 1902, 438 [9]). The latter comment is of considerable interest, suggesting that Christian Irishmen could travel with reasonable confidence through (or round) southern Britain to almost the easternmost point of the entire country, without being molested, and therefore that the local population viewed a gradually increasing population of oddly-dressed aliens with phlegmatic solidity, or at least without overtly hostile gestures. However, there is no evidence that Southumbrian Christianity as it developed was influenced by the peculiarities of Irish Christian practice (Whitelock 1972, 5–6).

The next obvious Christian input into the culture of sixth-century Southumbria is contact with the world of Merovingian Gaul, nominally Christian since the conversion of Clovis in 496. The kingdom of Kent, the most contiguous with the Channel, is the place where such contact was most deeply rooted, as is clearly witnessed by the arrival of Clovis's great-granddaughter Bertha, complete with her bishop, as the wife of Æthelbert of Kent towards the end of the sixth century. Merovingian kings were not indifferent to the fate of their womenfolk (as the story of Clotild, for example, bears witness: Thorpe 1974, 170 and Arndt & Krusch, [III.10]), and the marriage is likely to be the visible product of prolonged diplomatic contact (Drewett *et al.* 1988, 258). Franks settled in Kent during the sixth century, and Kentish jewellery is found in the graves of Northern France, implying two-way contacts, trading and probable intermarriage. More generally, Byzantine and Frankish treasures, in Sutton Hoo and elsewhere, are reminders that the leaders of the Anglo-Saxons were aware of a larger world beyond their immediate horizon, and almost certainly, that Christianity was the religion followed by persons of wealth, taste and social position, and a passport to friendlier contact with the rich lands of the South. This point was implicitly made by Bishop Daniel of Winchester in the eighth century, when he said to Boniface:

> whilst the Christians are allowed to possess the countries that are rich in oil and wine and other commodities, why have they left to the heathens the frozen lands of the north? . . . the heathens are frequently to be reminded of the supremacy of the Christian world and of the fact that they who still cling to outworn beliefs are in a very small minority.
> (Talbot 1956, 77, Tangl 1916, 40 [23])

It is also possible that the Merovingians exercised some kind of overlordship in Southern England, or Kent in particular, in the first half of the sixth century. Procopius believed this to be the case (Dewing 1923, 255 [VIII.20]); and Bertha's marriage, with the religious conditions imposed on, and accepted by, Æthelbert, may be an additional pointer to his client status. It is interesting that Gregory I, writing to Theoderic and Theudebert, claimed that the English nation 'eagerly desires to be converted to the Christian faith, but that the priests in the neighbourhood neglect it' (Whitelock 1955, 727–8, Gregory I, 423).

However, it seems to me that the inevitability of the anti-magnetic pull of the south for the inhabitants of lowland Britain may to some extent be simplified by hindsight; the classicising mentality which sees the Mediterranean as 'mare nostrum' by adoption. In an international context, the late antique world is characterised not only by political fragmentation, but also by the slow and relentless expansion of monotheism as a guiding principle of religious and cultural organization from its heartland in the Middle East, to the far West and the far East. The absorption of the pagan Franks by this gradual expansion made the absorption of the English merely a matter of time. Gergory's mission met a people already softened up by the insidious processes of cultural imperialism. All this is obvious, possibly so obvious as to overshadow trends pointing in quite different directions.

Sutton Hoo, it seems to me, encourages us to look again, and more sharply at this process, and the smoothly triumphalist account given by Bede. The Sutton Hoo hoard certainly contains Byzantine silver, and exhibits its owner, or his grieving relatives, as persons of international connections and tastes. But the whole context suggests that this lord of the Sandlings province, up to date though he clearly was in many respects, may have found his main point of orientation to the world not by looking south, but by looking north and east.

The hoard, its ship-burial context, and the bizarre graveyard surrounding it, seems to be some kind of evidence for a *mentality* in the south-east of Anglo-Saxon England at the earliest period remotely accessible to historical investigation, which perceived it as the south-western outpost of the interlocking group of peoples we call the Scandinavians. It may be a reminder that the Celts were not the only people to think of the open sea as a means of communication rather than a barrier; and an early example of the susceptibility of Britain to inclusion in the Scandinavian rather than the Roman world which was tested again in the ninth and tenth centuries. In the fascinatingly varied culture of these islands, it is possible to overlook that the difference between west coast and east coast outlooks has sometimes been as real and distinctive as the difference between the lowland and highland zones, or between north and south. That is to say, just as the west coast of Britain was to some extent part of a Celtic culture-province in the fifth and sixth centuries, as E.G. Bowen (1977), among others, has long since shown, so the east coast was part of a Scandinavian culture-province at the same period.

In the generation after Æthelbert of Kent, it was Rædwald of East Anglia who was the most powerful king in southern England. Æthelbert had been connected with Frankia, married to a Merovingian, and Christian. Rædwald was a very different matter. His wife's name and affiliations are unknown. Bede tells two stories involving her: the first, that she argued against Rædwald's compromising his personal honour by accepting a bribe to kill Edwin when the young Northumbrian was in exile at his court; the second, that after Rædwald had accepted Christianity in Kent (presumably in the days of Æthelbert's ascendancy), she persuaded him out of abandoning the religion of his forefathers (Colgrave & Mynors 1969, 180 [II.12], and 188–9 [II.15]). Put together, these anecdotes suggest a woman of heroic and inflexible temperament. Like many a Scandinavian lord in later centuries, Rædwald went on to add Christ to the pantheon of deities he culted, without accepting his claims to exclusive worship (Jones 1968, 277). Sigeberht, the next East Anglian king but one, was to seek exile in Gaul, staying out of the way of his half-brother while the latter was on the throne, and came back a Christian (Colgrave & Mynors 1969, 190 [II.15]), but the stories told of Rædwald and his wife do not suggest that Gaul would have been their own first thoughts in such circumstances. The family relationships between these people are problematic. Rædwald had a son, Rægnheri, killed in the battle which restored Edwin to the Northumbrian throne. The son later mentioned, Eorpwald, has a name formed from the second, not the first, part of his father's; one possible implication could be that he was not by the same mother. Bede describes Sigeberht as brother of Earpwald, not as son of Rædwald, so they may have been half-brothers sharing a mother that is, Rædwald had two sons by different women, and the second of the women had a second son by a different man. The names of Rædwald's father and grandfather are given by Bede as Tytil and Wuffa: either this family ignored the principles of alliterating given names followed elsewhere in the Anglo-Saxon world, or the genealogical relationships presented here are polite fiction. It is interesting that Rædwald's name alliterates with Rendil, the eponym of the *vicus regius* Rendlesham, near Sutton Hoo (Colgrave & Mynors 1969, 284 [III.22]: see Stenton 1959). It also may be relevant to observe that since Sigeberht was probably not a son of Rædwald, he may have been concerned to define himself as much as possible in opposition to the previous dynasty. It may also be the case that Sigeberht resembles that other princely exile, Oswald of Northumbria, in being impressed by the Irish type of Christianity: Gaul in the 630s, during his period of exile, was strongly influenced by the followers of Columbanus, and his Burgundian bishop could not unreasonably be connected with the new ascetic movement. The Luxeuil daughter-house of Faremoutiers was a place of resort for English women only a generation later (Campbell 1971, 71), notably the East Anglian princesses Saethryth and Æthelburh (not related to Sigeberht).

The Scandinavian connections of East Anglia were particularly strong. Square-headed, gilt-bronze brooches, wrist-clasps, and above all, the practice of ship-burial, are links between the culture which spread out across East Anglia from the Sandlings province, and southern Sweden. Clarke (1961, 138–9) suggests that the Wuffingas came from Sweden, and were an offshoot of the Scylfings, the royal house of Uppsala: 'the practice of boat-burial at this time is known only from the Swedish province of Uppland and the Ipswich Zone of East Anglia, and it would be reasonable to derive the latter from the former. Further intimate links between East Anglia and Sweden are provided by the sword, helmet, and shield in the Sutton Hoo ship-burial, as these were almost certainly made in Sweden.' They were a powerful group (Newton, this vol.): the post-Conquest *Flores Historiarum* suggests that they invaded Mercia in 527 (Davies 1977, 20), and eighty years later, Rædwald the apostate was, according to Bede, the most powerful king in the South, and able to withstand Æthelfrith of Northumbria. Even later in the century, after the power of East Anglia had waned, Cenwealh of the West Saxons was able to stay out of the reach of Penda of Mercia for three years, from 645–8, in East Anglia. Penda had a long arm, and was justifiably angry with Cenwealh who had deserted his sister (Colgrave & Mynors 1969, 232–4 [III.7]). The Christianization of East Anglia must be seen in the light of this Scandinavian orientation, which must surely have had some effect on the acceptability of the new faith, not just in the eyes of Rædwald and his wife.

After the death of Rædwald, Edwin, his one-time protegé and now the most powerful king in England, persuaded his coeval Eorpwald, Rædwald's son, to accept Christianity; that is, he demonstrated his power over a lesser king by forcing him to the font, as Oswald did with Cynegisl of Wessex (Colgrave & Mynors 1969, 232 [III.7]). There is nothing in Bede or elsewhere to suggest that this 'conversion' extended beyond the immediate court circles. No bishop, or monastic settlement, is mentioned, and the rapid murder of Eorpwald by one Ricbert, specifically described by Bede as 'a pagan' (*gentilis*) caused the country immediately to return to its old ways: 'et exinde tribus annis prouincia in errore uersata est' (Colgrave & Mynors 1969, 190 [II.15]). It was only with the accession of Sigebert, apparently of a different lineage, educated in Frankia, equipped with a Burgundian bishop, Felix, and supportive both of the saintly Fursa and his *familia* and of monastic education on Kentish lines (Colgrave & Mynors 1969, 268 [III.18]), that any serious attempt seems to have been made to Christianise the country. It still cannot have been plain sailing, since Rædwald's temple continued to stand at the end of the seventh century, after several decades of rule by Rædwald's nephews, who included Anna, father of four saintly daughters. In Essex, the first Christian king, Sæberht, died *circa* 616, and was succeeded by three sons who remained contumacious pagans. The population at large was more than happy to stay in the old ways (Colgrave & Mynors 1969, 152 [II.5]). The next Christian king of Essex, Sigeberht (a different Sigeberht, acc. around 653, d. between 653 and 664) was murdered for his inappropriate sanctity by two brothers (Colgrave & Mynors 1969, 284 [III.22]), suggesting that the people's absorption of the Christian message was less than wholehearted. Sussex seems to have remained entirely heathen until Bishop Wilfred interested himself in it in the 670s (Colgrave & Mynors 1969, 372 [IV.13]). It is probably also relevant to the question of what we actually *mean* by 'conversion to Christianity' in a sixth- and seventh-century context, that Archbishop Theodore's *Penitential* lists a whole range of heathen practices presumably relevant to Anglo-Saxon England:

> he who sacrifices to demons in trivial matters shall do penance for one year; but he who [does so] in serious matters shall do penance for ten years.   (MacNeill & Gamer, 198 [XV.1])

Centuries later, the compiler of *Lacnunga* (provenance unknown) achieved a fine, rich mixture of Irish Christian, Roman Christian and pagan Germanic medical magic (Grattan & Singer, 1952). Bede's implied view, in the highly public context of the *Ecclesiastical History* is that a country is 'Christian' once its ruler has firmly accepted the faith, prevailed upon his heirs to do likewise, acquired a bishop, and put good money into the formation of an ecclesiastical establishment on his territory. The *Letter to Egbert*, in which Bede was writing as between one cleric and another, shows that he was well aware that there was more to the creation of a Christian kingdom than that, in his frank comment that,

> many villages and hamlets of our people are situated in inaccessible mountains and dense woodlands, where a bishop is never seen for many years at a time to exhibit any ministry or celestial grace; not one man of which, however, is immune from rendering dues to the bishop . . . there is not even a teacher to teach the rules of the faith.   (Whitelock 1955, 738)

This is tantamount to a free admission that for many, or even most, inhabitants of the country, the Christian faith entered their lives as a negative force enforcing a series of inexplicable prohibitions and digging into their pockets. Among the rulers of the south-east before the end of the seventh century, the acceptability of Christianity must often be seen in the light of the current king's relationship to his predecessor, and whether he wished to present himself as a worthy successor to the paternal inheritance, or as a new broom.

13

Anglo-Saxon Vocabulary as a Reflection of Material Culture

JANE ROBERTS

> . . . nis þǣr hearpan swēg,
> gomen in geardum,   swylce ðǣr iū wǣron.
> . . . the music of the lyre is there no more nor the sound of joy
> in the courts, as once they were there.
> (*Beowulf* 2458–59, trans. Bradley 1982, 476)

Archaeology reveals a silent past, and it is notoriously hard to match the words that remain to the artefacts removed from the earth. Yet, just as archaeologists build up from things an interpretation of the past, treating the things as a code or language, so too it is possible to look at a picture put together from the words of a thousand years ago. The objects taken from the ground at Sutton Hoo had already lost their contexts when chosen for the grave. Similarly, the words presented here in a Word List, which serve to reflect some aspects of the everyday world of Anglo-Saxon England, being taken from dictionaries (Bosworth and Toller 1898; Clark Hall 1960), have been removed from the syntax which properly gives them meaning.[1] Such words for things may, however, help in the elucidation of actual broken and fragmentary things, though I think the reverse may more often turn out to be the case. After all, the

---

[1] These dictionaries are being superseded by the work of the Dictionary of Old English Project of the University of Toronto, and the letters D (1986), C (1988) and B (1991) are now available as microfiche publications. For the unlemmatized materials of the dictionary see Antonette diPaolo Healey and Richard L.Venezky *A Microfiche Concordance to Old English*, Publications of the Dictionary of Old English, 1 (Toronto, 1980) and Richard L.Venezky and Sharon Butler, *A Microfiche Concordance to Old English: The High Frequency Words*, PDOE, 2 (Newark and Toronto, 1985). A recent account of the project is: Antonette diPaolo Healey, 'The Corpus of the Dictionary of Old English: Its Delimitation, Compilation and Application', *Dictionaries in the Electronic Age*, Proceedings of the Fifth Annual Conference of the University of Waterloo Centre for the New Oxford English Dictionary (University of Waterloo, 1989).

scrappy bits of wood at first thought to be the remains of a harp transmuted more convincingly on later reconstruction to add up to a lyre – well, the sort of instrument plucked by David with a plectrum (*hearpenægl, sceacol, slegel*), as, for example, in the Vespasian Psalter (Wright and Campbell 1967, frontispiece). I suspect that an early Anglo-Saxon called this instrument a harp (*hearpe*), though given our more elaborated sets of musical instruments we might prefer to label it with a poet's descriptive compound as a wooden plaything, a box of delights (*gamenwudu*). Its noise (*hearpsweg, sang*) can no longer bring joy to a hall, with plectrum plucking (*niomiende*) the strings (*sner, streng*). Its presence in the hoard at Sutton Hoo bears witness to lost happiness (*dream, gomen, gliw*), an abstraction that is not to be found in the soil.

We cannot with certainty identify the man who was buried in Mound 1 at Sutton Hoo, but we know this of him: he was in worldly terms a success. His possessions, where not lost to acidic soils, are tangible, the gear (*geatwe*) of a warrior who looked out to the north of Britain, to Ireland, to Gaul – and knew of a world far beyond. Wonders have been done in reconstructing from fragments bowls and horns, buckets and cauldrons, as well as such eye-catching memorials of past splendour as helmet, sword, purse and shield. We can no longer get behind these things to the thoughts and behaviour of the man commemorated, except by consulting literature assumed to reflect much his context – as Professor Cramp did ably in 1957, when she looked closely at *Beowulf* (Cramp 1957). Then there was general agreement that the poem, although preserved in a manuscript dated c.1000, came from the eighth century, and it was possible to move from her examination of the poem to theorize that some of the items found at Sutton Hoo were known and remembered in the poem (O'Loughlin 1964; Farrell 1972), a view that then made me recall the inventiveness of Thomas Arnold, who argued in 1898 for associating Wealhþeow with 'the Wulfings, or Uffings' of East Anglia (Arnold 1898, 43). Dates for the composition of *Beowulf* range now between the late seventh century and the early eleventh century, a span that would allow its vocabulary to be tied tightly to artefacts from any period within these centuries or to all artefacts extant from Anglo-Saxon England. It must indeed be acknowledged that most of what we call the 'pre-Alfredian' poems of the four codices cannot be proved to come from much before the year 1000, though I for one shall continue to think that they may and that therefore they provide some of the earliest extant English vocabulary. Near them in time is the 'Alfredian' prose dated to the end of the ninth century and the earlier part of the tenth century. Distant and distinct is the prose that remains from England of the Benedictine reform. The words I cite, however, will be drawn not only from these three groups of literature, but from a motley collection of other sources: laws, inscriptions, charters and glosses. The manuscripts are very often late, showing signs of improvement or carelessness. And the words, too often found once only, may not therefore carry much evidence of their meaning. For example, *calc* 'shoe' is a nonceword, yet is pressed into service in more than one chapter of a recent excellent examination of dress in Anglo-Saxon England (Owen-Crocker 1986, 128, 146, 168). In the Old English pilot thesaurus currently nearing completion and from which the Word List is drawn, forms are tagged if thought to be noncewords (preceding superscript o) or if restricted to poetry or to glosses (following superscript p or g), as a warning of the word's being in some way unusual. These tags reflect the information to be found in current standard dictionaries and must be checked against the fuller evidence for Old English vocabulary assembled by the Toronto Dictionary of Old English team.

Mound 1 commemorates a fighting-man, whether pagan or Christian we do not know. I concur that Rædwald is a suitable contender, but do not put out of bounds some one of his immediate successors or their senior colleagues. Conversion did not, after all, affect the practice of laying the dead to rest fully clothed and supplied with weapons, jewellery and utensils in nearby Gaul until maybe the Carolingian period (Bullough 1983, 188):

> Such burials were not statements of religious belief but of social and cultural continuity – solidarity with their ancestors who had been so interred. (Geary 1988, 174)

Admittedly, Bede tells us (II.15) that Rædwald, a leader important outside his own small kingdom, saw no need to set aside older religious practices on embracing Christianity. But the poet of *The Seafarer* indicates that burial with treasure might last well beyond conversion:

> Þeah þe græf wille   golde stregan,
> broþor his geborenum,   byrgan be deadum
> maþmum mislicum,   þæt hine mid wille, [2]
> ne mæg þære sawle   þe biþ synna ful
> gold to geoce   for Godes egsan,
> þonne he hit ær hydeð   þenden he her leofað.
>
> (97–102)

> Although a brother may wish to strew the grave with gold for his kinsman, to heap up by the dead man's side various treasures that he would like to go with him, the gold he hides in advance while he lives here cannot be of help to the soul which is full of sins, in the face of God's awesomeness. (Gordon 1960, trans. Bradley 1982, 334)

Matching a proper name to the inhabitant of Mound 1 (one inhabitant, with four shoes) is, however, an enticing game, and for me looking at the appropriate extant vocabulary of the Anglo-Saxons provides every bit as much

---

[2] The manuscript *wille* is reinstated here for editorial *nille* (line 99), with comma immediately following instead of semicolon.

amusement. Words on their own can bear witness to the interest in and knowledge of particular concepts. So, we can look first at the burial ground.

A glance at the list in the Word List may at first suggest that there is almost an embarrassment of words. There are words for burials, for burial grounds, graves . . . Among them are four for 'a burial mound': *beorg, beorghliþ, hlæw* and *morþcrundel*. The last of these, *morþcrundel*, occurs in a single charter and its meaning is disputed. The base element indicates a pit, quarry or ravine, the first part a corpse. It is unlikely therefore to be a true word for a burial mound. The other compound, *beorghliþ*, should probably be understood as 'hill-slope', despite its reference to the dragon's mound in *Beowulf*. The central term of the group is *hlæw*. Only after considerable hesitation have I included *beorg*, a word used referentially in Old English literature for 'grave, burial mound' but generally with contextual reinforcement. This sense for the word more or less disappeared from literary English by the modern period, except where reinforced in particular localities by being part of a proper name (in the south-west; and in the north, with support from Old Norse *bjarg* 'rockface', as *bargh*). Sixteenth- and seventeenth-century antiquaries are responsible for the modern archaeological use of barrow 'grave-mound' and the ousting of *low* from the general vocabulary (Stjerna 1912, 205ff, 242; Roberts 1979, 132).

The ship had to be got up from the shore to the mound, doubtless by the use of *slidor* 'slides to launch or pull up a ship'. Two of the words for 'boat' we still use: *bat* and *scip*. Some other words in general use relate to the wood used, whether non-specific *beam* and *bord* (*bord* occurs for 'side of a ship' as well) or specific *ac* 'oak' and *æsc* 'ash' (the latter unlikely for this ship, but it is used of the Danish warships built of ashwood in Alfred's day). Both *naca* and *flota* are in the sense 'boat' rather literary words,[3] and *ceol(e)* 'boat' is also found mainly in poetry (compare *ceole* 'prow'). Both *cnearr* and *scegð*, words borrowed from the Danes, are not recorded until late in the Anglo-Saxon period. The words restricted to poetry are for the most part made up of common enough elements, although quite a few of them are found once only. Do the twisted ends of the Mound 1 ship mean it was a *barda*? If so, a poet could have used the words *hornscip, hringedstefna, hringnaca* or *wundenstefna* of it and described it as *brandstæfn, bundenstefna, wundenhals* and, if thrusting through waves, *famigheals*. Rather more everyday descriptions are provided by the adjectives *heahstefn* and *hyrned*. Reading along the Word List, you will find a word for a boat with oars, *rewet*, and another to describe a large rowing vessel, *sixtigære*. The Sutton Hoo ship was oar-propelled (*æren*), and, we can guess from the evidence remaining, **fortigære*. It was a well-made ship (*bunden*), capacious (*sægeap, sidfæþme(d)*) and its sides were riveted (*nægledbord*). If prow and stern

---

3 That *naca* is 'poetic' is generally recognized (it is so marked by a dagger in both the Clark Hall dictionary and in Klaeber's *Beowulf*), but the poetic marker for *flota* is used by Clark Hall only in reference to pirate ships.

were scarcely differentiated, the most likely terms to select here are *bile, ceole, heals* and *stefn(a)*. Rowers would have had their bench (*scipsetl, poft(e)*). Our word oar descends from *ar*; the alternative *ropor* has narrowed in focus to become a rudder to-day. The oars had blades (*blæd, arblæd*). Words remain too for rowlocks (of those in the Word List *arwippe* might seem etymologically appropriate) and pins. As no evidence remains for any use of sail on the Mound 1 boat, vocabulary for mast and tackle is omitted from the Word List.

Sheets of bronze, according to Mr Brown's log, 'gave out a hollow sound' (Evans 1986, 22). His words were in a way prophetic: metals (*ora* 'metal') survived better than bodies at Sutton Hoo. Most of the metal words required for describing Sutton Hoo finds have been with us since Anglo-Saxon times, for example 'gold', 'silver', 'iron', 'lead', 'steel'. They are, oddly enough, largely Germanic, which is why, of course, English youngsters find it hard to match up with these words their chemical symbols. It is curious that 'steel' should lack cognates outside Germanic, that 'lead' and 'iron' should be common to Germanic and Celtic and that 'gold' and 'silver' should be distributed within Germanic and Slavic languages ('tin' by the way is, like 'steel', restricted to Germanic, and its appearance in Irish is considered a loan from Old English). Here it seems in the wordshapes of the past we find evidence of the craftsmen of the northern world. It would be foolish, however, to push the suggestion too far, given the diminution in numbers of words now accepted as common Germanic. What is worth noting is that these words were not ousted either by Scandinavian loans or by French ones and indeed that they were not borrowed from Latin. The word 'copper' had already been borrowed from Latin before the Anglo-Saxons got to Britain, but they also used the native terms *ar* and *bræs* for copper and for copper alloys that yield brass. The first of these, *ar*, is cognate with Latin *aeris* 'metal', but *bræs* is a word not found outside Old English. (Equally 'bronze' is a mysterious word, apparently from Late Latin, but its root must lie in Germanic *brun*.) The metal workers (*smipas*) of the Anglo-Saxon period had a fixed and long known vocabulary for the major metals, words we still retain. Words for 'glass' you will see listed; and *carbunculus*, a borrowing unlikely to have had much currency outside translations from Latin into Old English, may represent the garnet.

When first I drew together the Anglo-Saxon jewel words I was alarmed at how few specific terms there seemed to be. There are words aplenty to describe jewelled objects and adornments, but the value and beauty of these artefacts is a result of the craftsmanship worked upon the small range of components readily available in northern Europe. The specific jewel-words to be found in Old English are there as often as not because they were needed to convey jewels mentioned in biblical and other Latin texts. There may even be a parallel to be drawn with the growth of colour vocabulary in Old English, where the poetry little beholden to Latin sources uses few colour terms by contrast with, for example, *The Phoenix*, whose author has an obviously more developed eye for colour effects.[4]

Mound 1 does not supply non-functional pieces of jewellery. The heroic world glimpsed in, for example, *Beowulf* and *Widsith* brings to the eye great golden torcs and armlets, extravagant rewards for unusual or outstanding service. These are conspicuously absent from the Sutton Hoo hoard. Its lavish clasps (*bul(a)*, *dalc*,[5] *preon*, *sigil*) would have fastened clothing. The decorative belt fittings found in the Sutton Hoo mound, perhaps owing something in their elaboration to the garb of soldiers of the Empire, are intricately-fashioned buckles and strap distributors that work. The purse, secured on the belt, held coins, and suggests a context in which Merovingian currency commanded respect. Did the pyramids serve in some way, maybe on a length of the mysterious tape, to hold the scabbard in position? I find it hard to believe that they are mere toggles. What is often noted is that all these fittings show little sign of wear. Whether or not the armour was similarly little used is impossible to tell: it is made of substances more liable to disintegration within the soil. Overall the ensemble, and indeed certain of its more striking items, indicate an important owner. Better maybe for such things to lie *unnyt* 'useless' in the ground (*Beowulf*, 3168). That way no old campaigner, with a long and bitter memory, could use them to stir up new trouble, needling a spryer youngster into action:

> 'Meaht ðū, mīn wine,   mēce gecnāwan,
> þone þīn fæder   tō gefeohte bær
> under heregrīman   hindeman sīðe,
> dȳre īren,   þær hine Dene slōgon . . .
> Nū hēr þāra banena   byre nāthwylces
> frætwum hrēmig   on flet gǣð,
> morðres gylpeð,   ond þone māðþum byreð,
> þone þe ðū mid rihte   rǣdan sceoldest.'

> 'Can you recognize that blade, my friend, the precious
> iron sword which your father carried into battle on his
> last expedition in vizored war-helmet – where the
> Danes killed him . . . Now the son of one or other of
> those killers walks into the hall taking delight in his

---

[4] C.P. Biggam of Strathclyde University discussed developments within the Anglo-Saxon period in her paper 'The Evolution of Basic Colour Terms in English' at ICEHL 5, Cambridge 1987.

[5] Although this word is glossed 'brooch, clasp, bracelet' in the *Dictionary of Old English*, archaeologists at the conference were strongly convinced that the object named by this word, because it is a loan from Irish, should be understood as having a pin, and it is therefore now taken with the words thought to mean 'clasp' (a meaning indicated in the earlier dictionaries).

> adornments, brags of the murder and wears that treas-
> ure which by right you should possess.'
>> (*Beowulf* 2047–56; Bradley 1982, 465)

Perhaps the most tantalising of these objects is the whetstone, obviously ceremonial because it shows no sign of use as a sharpener. Together in our terms
these possessions may have added up to regalia.

Once the stag was detached, the identity of the iron stand as a symbol of
power became shaky. First thoughts were that it was some kind of a portable
torch, an identification which would square nicely with the compound
leohtisern used in glossing a candlestick, except that there is no decisive evidence for its having been used with flaming materials. The hoard does include
what is undeniably a lamp vessel made of iron, to which alternatively this
word might be attached – as could *cielle, fyrencylle, leohtfæt* or *leohtfætels*.

The most utilitarian of the many containers taken from the mound are
buckets and cauldrons. Two Old English terms remain for 'bucket': *embren*
(also in Old High German) and *stoppa* (more specifically *wæterstoppa*, and
compare *butterstoppa* 'churn'); and vessels made from ashwood (*æscen*) could
be of varied sizes. Among the terms used of cooking vessels and cauldrons
(*alfæt, citel, fyrcruce, gripu* and *lead*) one at least is still familiar: *citel* is likely to
have been the central term then for a large cooking pot.

Chapters 7 and 8 in Angela Evans's *Guide* are labelled respectively
'Mediterranean silver', for the silver bowls, etc., and, for the drinking horns
and vessels, 'Feasting in the great hall'. Now I know only too well that most
Old English words for feasting focus on drink rather than food, but surely in
so well equipped a grave some thought must have been given to the dishing
up of food? More plebian dishes made of wood may well have disappeared,
but the silver could have served. King Oswald, in Ælfric's Life, received food
on anum sylfrenan disce (Skeat 1881–1900, xxvi, 90) – or on a *micel seolfren disc* in
the Alfredian account (Miller 1890–1, I, 164, 31). Admittedly the Sutton Hoo
ladle (*cruce, hlædel, turl*) looks suited to spooning out liquid refreshment from a
large bowl, but the spoons would have been useful for eating from one of the
nest of silver bowls. The image summoned up by the terms *sticca* and *metesticca*
for spoon falls short of these implements, so perhaps the Latin derived *cuclere*
might have been used of them. Overall the vocabulary for containers for food
is a fairly vague bunch of words. The conclusion must be that bowls and
dishes could have doubled as cups and beakers.

It may be possible to differentiate rather more among the words for drinking
vessels. An image of buried treasure in *Beowulf*, in which relevant words
appear, for me encapsulates the Sutton Hoo hoard:

> Him big stōdan   bunan ond orcas,
> discas lāgon   ond dȳre swyrd,
> ōmige þurhetone,   swā hīe wið eorðan fæðm
> þūsend wintra   þær eardodon;

þonne wæs þæt yrfe   ēacencræftig,
iūmonna gold   galdre bewunden,
þæt ðām hringsele   hrīnan ne mōste
gumena ǣnig . . .

Beside him chalices and bowls were standing and
dishes and precious swords were lying, rusty and
eaten through as though they had rested there against
the bosom of the earth for a thousand years. During
that time the enormous legacy, the gold of men long
gone, was wound about with a spell so that nobody
could have touched the ring-filled chamber . . .

(*Beowulf* 3047–54; Bradley 1982, 491)

The Word List is derived from the Old English thesaurus, an experimental
research tool assembled from the standard Old English dictionaries for the
Historical Thesaurus archive at the University of Glasgow (Roberts 1978,
1985). The senses recorded for Anglo-Saxon words were sorted first according
to Roget categories, a broadly semantic arrangement summarised in the 1982
microfiche publication restricted to research use in the Glasgow University
Thesaurus archive and the Toronto Dictionary of Old English project.[6] My
reordering of these materials according to the classification devised by M.L.
Samuels and C.J. Kay for the Historical Thesaurus of English was completed in
1986,[7] and over the last few years Christian Kay and I have been transferring
the materials into a machine-held database from which photoready copy for
wider publication will be generated.[8] Only from a completed thesaurus can a
thesaurus be tested, and with that in mind work has already gone ahead at
King's College London to evaluate the Old English thesaurus materials and to
draw up preliminary guidelines for the construction of a thesaurus specific to
the Anglo-Saxon period.[9] Meanwhile, during the final stages of getting a full
pilot Old English thesaurus into book form, there are plenty of puzzles to
ponder on. For example, I have come to doubt entirely the usual dictionary
meaning for one form in the glossary, *heoru*, and to reconsider the usual understanding of a few more, *wælsteng*, *hlenc*, and *wælhlenc*.[10] But we have still more

---

6 *Skeleton Old English Thesaurus* (1982). Research tool, on 9 microfiches. Prepared with the
   help of C. Brown at the King's College London Computer Centre.
7 I wish to thank the Leverhulme Trust for a Research Grant in 1985–86 to cover teaching
   replacement costs during two terms.
8 See Jane Roberts, 'Old English Thesaurus', *Old English Newsletter* 21:2 (1988), 21–23, for
   some discussion of the conventions adopted.
9 An award from the Academic Development Fund of King's College London was made
   for the development of an annotated thesaurus of Old English, and Dr Lynne Grundy
   is currently helping establish criteria for the Annotated Thesaurus project.
10 As a simplex *heoru* appears only twice: *Beowulf* 1285 and *Maxims I*, 200 (G.P. Krapp and
   E. van K. Dobbie, *The Exeter Book*, Anglo-Saxon Poetic Records, 3 (1936), p. 163); and is

to learn from Sutton Hoo about the material culture of early Anglo-Saxon England, before achieving a better understanding of one context for the words that remain.

WORD LIST

[The vocabulary materials in this Word List are taken from the Old English Thesaurus slips.]

gamen, glīw

Stringed instruments

Harp, lyre, etc.: citere, hearpe, gamenwudu[P], glīwbēam, saltere, sealmfæt
Wooden frame: stālu
String: hearpestreng, sner, streng
—— *with specific number of strings:* twīstrenge, þrīstrenge, fēowerstrenge, tīenstrenge(d)
Plectrum: hearpenægl, hearpslege, nægel, sceacol, slege, °slegel
Fiddle: fiþele

Wind/brass instruments

Pipe or flute: hwistle, pīpe, sangpīpe
Trumpet or horn: bīeme, blǣdhorn, blæshorn, horn, sarga, stocc, sweglhorn[g], trūþhorn[g]
War-trumpet, war-horn: herebȳme, herehorn
Victory-trumpet: °sigebȳme[P]
Heavenly trumpet: °heofonbȳme[P]
Ship's trumpet: °scipbȳme[P]

interpreted as 'sword'. In both places the meaning 'warfare, battle' is appropriate, as it would be also for the compound *heorosweng* (*Beowulf* 1590). Compare the full discussion of these terms in Caroline Brady, ' "Weapons" in "Beowulf" ', *Anglo-Saxon England*, 8 (1979), p. 91 and footnote 2.

The nonceword *wælsteng* is often visualized as a spear. Given that at *Beowulf* 1638 the form is accompanied by the definite article some previous referent might be expected within the text, 'sword' therefore argued and a task found for Hrunting. N.O. Waldorf, *The 'hapax legomena'* . . . lists the word as 'sword'; I have not checked to see if it is so understood anywhere else. Compare Brady, ' "Weapons" in "Beowulf" ', pp. 82–83, 132.

For *hlenc* (*Exodus* 218) and *wælhlenc* (*Exodus* 176, *Elene* 24) I follow the interpretation 'spear' suggested by G. Storms in his review of P.O.E. Gradon's *Elene* (*English Studies*, 46 (1965), p. 54).

Percussion

Drum: °tunnebotm^g
Cymbal: cimbal(a)
Timbrel: timpana, °wīfhearpe^g

Playthings

Plaything, implement for a game: plega
Top: top
Ball: þōþor
Boardgame: tæfl
Gaming board/table: blēobord, tabule, tæfl
Gambling stone, die: cyningstān, tæflstān, teosel

byrging

Burying

A burial, burying: bebyrg(ed)nes, °bebyrgung, °gebyrgednes, byrgen, byrging,
    byrignes
—— *pertaining to – :* °hrāwlic^g, °līclic^g
To bury, lay (to rest): lecgan, onswebban, gesettan
To bury, inter: bebyrgan, bedelfan, befæstan, befēolan, bemyldan^g, (ge)byrgan,
    delfan
Entombment: °niþerlecgung
To place in a tomb: gelōgian
To lie unburied: licgan, (ge)restan
Unburied: unbebyriged, unbyrged
To exhume: gedōn ūp, niman ūp

Burial place

Place of burial: byrgenstōw, legerstōw, līcburg^g, līcrest, °līcstōw, līctūn
Churchyard: cirichege
A grave, burial place, sepulchre: (ge)byrgen, byrignes, dēaþbedd, °dēaþræced^P,
    eorþærn, °eorþbyrgen, °eorþgrāp, eorþscræf, foldærn, foldgræf^P, foldræst^P,
    gærsbedd^P, græf, græfhūs^P, °grype^g, °landrest^P, leger, legerbedd^P,
    moldærn^P, moldgræf, °moldstōw^g, pytt, rest, °sandhof^P, sepulcer, wælrest^P
Concealment: dīegol, °heolstorcofa^P, °hoþma^P
A burial mound: beorg, beorghliþ^P, hlǣw, °morþcrundel

Preparations

Digger of grave: byrgend
A pyre: ād, bæl, bælfȳr^P, °wælfȳr^P
Place of pyre: °bælstede^P
A tomb, coffin: byrgels, byrgennes, līcbeorg^g, līcrest, °līcþrūh, ofer(ge)weorc,
    °þēostorloca^P, þrūh, °ymbfæstnung^g
To put in a coffin: cystian

A bier: bǣr, līcrest
A corpse-bearer: byrgere^g, līcmann
To prepare for burial: behweorfan
Act of preparation for burial: dēaþþēnung, līcþēnung
Laying out: līcþēnung
Grave-clothes: ^odēadhrægl^g, gewǣd(e)
Winding-sheet: līchrægl, scīete
Winding-sheet for head: hēafodclāþ
To attend the dead: bestandan
Watching over dead: hēafodweard
Visit to grave: ^odūstscēawung
A place of mourning: wōpstōw
An epitaph: ^obyrgelslēoþ^g, byrgelssang^g, byrg(en)lēoþ
A dirge, lament: byrgelssang^g, byrgensang^g, fūslēoþ^P, gēomorgidd^P, ^ohēafsang^g,
    līclēoþ^g, līcsang^g
To toll the dead: cnyllan

sǣsīþ, seglung

Sea-voyaging
A place for a ship: scipsteall
Landing-place: lending
Slides to launch or pull up ships: slidor

Boats, ships
A ship, boat: āc, æsc, bāt, bēam, bord, ^obrenting^P, brimhengest^P, brimþyssa^P,
    brimwudu^P, cēol, cnearr, fær, faroþhengest^P, flodwudu^P, flota, hærnflota^P,
    lagumearg^P, lid^P, naca, merebāt^P, merehengest^P, mereþyssa^P, sǣbāt^P,
    sǣflota^P, sǣgenga^P, sǣhengest^P, sǣliþend^P, sǣmearh^P, sǣnaca^P, sǣwudu^P,
    scegþ, scip, sundhengest^P, sundwudu^P, wǣgbord^P, wǣgflota^P,
    wǣghengest^P, wǣgþel^P, wæterþyssa^P, wudubāt^P, ȳþ engest^P, ȳþhof^P,
    ȳþlid^P, ȳþlida^P, ȳþmearh^P
—— *with beaked prow:* barda/bar(þ)a^g, ^ohornscip^P, hringedstefna^P, ^ohringnaca^P,
    ^owundenstefna^P
—— *with flat bottom:* flēote(e), flīete, punt
—— *that is canoe-like:* trog, trogscip^g
—— *rowing-boat:* rewet
—— *that is nail-fastened:* nægledcnearr^P
—— *skiff, small boat:* cuopel^g, flēge, flōtscip, hulc, plegscip, scipincel, þurruc,
    wræc
—— *trading-vessel:* cēapscip, ^ohlæstscip
—— *transport:* sciphlæst
—— *scouting vessel:* ǣrendscip
—— *guardship:* friþscip
—— *enemy ship:* unfriþscip
—— *piratical vessel:* hȳþscip, þēofscip

—— *small vessel, warship:* snacc
—— *warship of some kind:* dulmunus
—— *sixty-oared ship:* sixtigǣre
—— *trireme:* þrīrēþrcēol, þrīrēþre
———— *pertaining to trireme:* þrīrēþre

Pertaining to a ship: sciplic
—— *lashed together:* bunden
—— *seaworthy:* fēre
—— *capacious:* sǣgēap, sīdfæþme(d)[P]
—— *newly-tarred:* nīwtyrwed[P]
—— *dug-out:* ānbȳme
—— *oar-propelled:* ǣren
—— *with nailed sides:* nægledbord[P]
—— *with beak:* brandstæfn[P], bundenstefna[P], hēahstefn, hyrned, [o]wundenhals[P],
—— *foamy-necked:* fāmigheals[P]
—— *equipped for service, ready:* gearo

Parts of boats

Keel: bytme, bytming
Keel, hold: bōsm, heald, lecþa, þurruc, wranga
Deck: [o]cēolþel
Side: bord, [o]bordstæþ[P], bordweall, [o]ȳþbord[P]
Starboard: stēorbord
Larboard: bæcbord
Prow: ancorsetl, bile, ceole, forscip, forþstefn, frumstemn, heals, stefn(a)
Figurehead: hēafod
Stern: stēorsetl, stēorstefn
Helm: helma, sciprōþor, stēor, stēordalc, stēornægl, stēorscofel, stēorrōþor
Gangway: bolca
A ship's ladder: sciphlǣder
Rowers' bench: scipsetl, þoft(e)
Oars: (ge)rēþru
An oar: ār, rōþor
—— *blade:* ǣrblæd, blæd
Pin: þol
Rowlock: ārloc, ārmidl, ārwiþþe, hā, hān, [o]hamele, midl, strop
Hammer: hamor, sciphamor
A cable: mǣrelsrāp, scipmǣrls, sciprāp
A sounding-line: sundlīne, sundrāp
A sounding-rod: sundgyrd
Ship's trumpet: [o]scipbȳme[g]
An anchor: ancor
—— *anchor cable:* ancorbend, ancorrāp, ancorstrenge

The Ark

An ark: cofa, earce, °geofonhūs, °holmærn, °mereciest, merehūs, °sundreced, þellfæsten, wudufæsten

cræft, cræftweorc

Some materials

Amber: eolhsand, smelting
Amber, resin: glær
Crystal: cristalla
Of crystal: cristallisc
Glass: glæs
Made of glass: glæsen
Vitreous, glassy: glæren
What is made of molten glass: °glæsgegot

Gemstones

Jewel: eorclanstān, eorcnanstān, gimm, gimstān, māþþumsigle, searogim, sincgim, sincstān, stān
Kind of jewel: gimcynn
Carbuncle: carbunculus
Jacinth: īacinctus
Jasper: geaspis
Jet: blæcgymm, gagāte(stān), sǣcol
Pearl: meregrot(a), pærl
Topaz: baswa stān, °topazius, topazion

Torches and lamps

A torch, firebrand: blæse, brand, bryne, blysa, cēn, fæcele[g], þæcele
A taper, torch: sceaft, speld, tapor
A wick: tapor, wēoce
Wick made of cloth: °clāþwēoce[g]
Lamp, lantern, candel: candel
Wick for – : °candelbrȳd, candelwēoce
Wax candle: weaxcandel[g]
Candlestick: candelstæf, candelsticca, lēohtīsern[g]
—— *branching – :* candeltrēow
Snuffers: °candelsnȳtels[g], candeltwist, °īsentange[g]
Lamp, lantern: blæcern, þæcele
Lamp vessel: cielle, °fȳrencylle, glæsfæt, lēohtfæt, °lēohtfætels[g], °lēohtstān[g]

Regalia

Crown, diadem: byge, corōna, °corenbēag, °cynebend, cynegold, cynehelm, cynewiþþe[g], °gyldenbēag, °hēafodbēag, hēafodbend, hēafodgold, helm, hrōþgirela[g], °mind[g], sigebēah

Sceptre: cynegyrd
(Pastoral) staff: stæf
Whetstone: hwet(e)stān

Jewellery, etc.

Ornaments, trappings, accoutrements: geatwe/getawe, gerāde
An ornament or jewel that is worn: gegierela, sigil
A clasp, pin, brooch: būl(a), dalc, prēon, sigil
A mantle-pin, brooch: mentelprēon
A button, brooch: cnæpp
A breast-ornament: °brēostweorþung[P]
A band, chaplet, crown, ornament, ribbon: bend
A circlet: clīewen, hoppe
A garland: cynehelm
A ring (for finger, arm, neck): hring
A necklace, collar, ornament, jewel: mene
A moon-shaped ornament: hlif, menescilling, scilling
A torque, collar, necklace: bēag, bol, °halswurþing[P], healsbeag[P], °healsbeorggold[g],
    healsmyne, °healswriþa[P], sāl, sigle, swēorbēag, °swēorracentēh[g]
A bracelet, armlet: bēag, °bēagwriþa[P], earmbēag, °earmgegirela[g], °earmhrēad[P]
A betrothal ring (lit./fig.): hring
An ear-ring: ēarhring, ēarprēon, °ēarspinl[g]
A costly ring, ring given to do honour to receiver: °hringweorþung[P]
A belt: belt, gyrdel(s)
A girdle-buckle: gyrdel(s)hring
A buckle: clofe, °fifele[g]
A buckle, clasp: hringe, oferfeng[g], gespan
A wallet, purse: bigyrdel, bisæc

Armour

Body armour: °eorlgewǣde[P], frætwe, °fyrdhrægl[P], °fyrdsceorp[P], fyrdsearu[P],
    gearwe, geatwe, gūþgeatwe[P], gūþgewǣde[P], °gūþrēaf[P], °gūþsceorp[P],
    °gūþscrūd[P], gūþsearu[P], °heaþurēaf[P], °heaþuwǣd[P], °heresceorp[P],
    °herewǣd[P], hildegeatwe[P], °hildesceorp[P], hrægl, hyrst, gerǣde, searo
—— *twisted (of mail):* °handlocen[P], hringed[P], wriþen
Helmet: °bānhelm[P], °beadugrīma[P], grīma, grīmhelm[P], °gūþhelm[P],
    °hēafodbeorg[P], helm, °heoloþhelm[P], heregrīma[P], °īsenhelm[g], °wīgheafola[P]
Crest of a helmet: camb
—— *having a crest:* cambiht
—— *towering in battle:* heaþustēap[P]
Boar image on helmet: eofor, °eoforlīc[P]
Cheek-piece: °cinberg[P], °hlēorberg[P]
Leather helmet: leþerhelm
Visor: grīma
Helmet ridge: walu
Chainmail guard: °frēawrāsn[P]
Neck armour: healsbeorg[g], °healsbrynige[g]

Coat of mail/corselet: [o]beaduhrægl[P], [o]beaduserce[P], beaduscrūd[P], brēostgewædu[P], brēostnet[P], byrne, byrnham(a)[P], [o]fyrdhama[P], [o]goldhoma[P], [o]gūþbyrne[P], heaþubyrne[P], [o]heoruserce[P], [o]herebyrne[P], [o]herenett[P], herepād[P], [o]heresyrce[P], [o]hildeserce[P], [o]hlence[P], [o]hringloca[P], [o]hringnett[P], īsenbyrne[P], leoþusyrce[P], [o]līcsyrce[P], [o]searonet[P], serc, wælhlenc[P], [o]wælnett[P]

—— *cunningly inlaid:* searofāh

Greaves: bān(ge)beorg[g], bānrift[g], [o]scancgebeorg[g], scinhosu[g]

Shield: [o]bōhscild, bord, bordhrēoþa[P], [o]bordrand[P], bordweall[P], [o]bordwudu[P], campwudu[P], geolorand[P], gūþbilla gripe, gūþbord[P], [o]heaþulind[P], hildebord[P], [o]hilderand[P], lind[P], plegscyld[g], rand[P], randbēag, scield, scildhrēoþa, [o]sīdrand[P], targa, tudenard[g], [o]þrȳþbord[P], wīgbord[P]

Boss of a shield: rand, randbēah

Border (?cover) of a shield: lǣrig

Military clothing: [o]feohtgegyrela[g]

Military equipment: [o]beadusearo[P], [o]ēoredgeatwe[P], [o]fyrdgeatwe[P], [o]gryregeatwe[P], heregeatu, [o]heorusceorp[P], [o]wǣpenþrǣge[P], gewǣpnung, [o]wīggetawe[P], [o]wīghyrst[P]

Arms (left as inheritance): lāf

Store of military equipment: [o]wǣpenhūs[g]

Battle-horn: feohtehorn[g], [o]gūþhorn[P]

Banner, flag, standard: cumbol[P], draca, eoforcumbol[P], [o]eoforhēafodsegn[P], fana, gierela, godweb, gūþfana, herebēacen, [o]heorucumbol[P], [o]herecumbol[P], [o]hiltecumbor[P], hræfn, mearc, segn, þūf

Banner that will lead to victory: [o]sigebēacen[g], [o]sigeþūf[P]

Weapons

A weapon: beaduwǣpen[P], campwǣpen[P], [o]herewǣpen, [o]hildewǣpen[P], tōl, wǣpen, [o]wīgwǣpen, [o]woruldwǣpen

Weapons (collective): bēag, [o]hildefrōfor[P], gewǣpnu

Part of weapon: holt

Tested (of weapon): gecost

Victorious weapon: [o]sigewǣpen[P]

Club/stick: cycgel, repel, sāgol, stæf, steng, þīsl, trēow

Sharp weapon: ecg

Blade of cutting weapon: ecg, ecglāst

Head of cutting/piercing weapon: gār, ord

Spear: æsc, æscholt[P], ætgǣre, ætgār, [o]bangār[P], daroþ, [o]daroþsceaft[P], [o]dēaþspere[P], franca, gār, [o]gārbēam[P], [o]gārholt[P], [o]gārwudu[P], gafeluc, [o]gūþwudu[P], [o]heresceaft[P], hildepīl[P], [o]mægenwudu[P], ord, [o]pǣl[g], sceaft, spere, sprēot, [o]þēox[g], [o]þræcwudu[P], wælgār[P], [o]wælsceaft[P], wælspere, [o]wīgār[g], [o]wīgspere[g]

Armed with spear/lance: [o]daroþhæbbende[P], gesperod

Shaft: sceaft, speresceaft, [o]wælsteng[P]

Having a shaft: [o]getridwet[g]

Having a long shaft: langsceaft

Without head or point: [o]sperelēas[g]

Poisoned spear: [o]ātorspere[P]

A shot, missile, dart, etc.: gescot, [o]scotspere[g], scotung, scyte, wifer

Flying-dart: °flygepīl[P]

Spear-strap: sceaftlōg, °sceafttog[g]

A shower of missiles: scūr

Sword: °beaduleoma[P], °beadumēce[P], bēag, brand, ecg, gūþbill[P], °gūþsweord[P], heoru[P], °heoruwæpen[P], hildebil[P], °hildeleoma[P], °hildemēce[P], °hilting[g], īsen, lāf feole, lāf fȳres, lāf hamera, mēce, secg, sweord, wæpen, °wīgbill[P]

A hilted sword: °hæftmēce[P], °hiltsweord

A costly sword: °māþþumsweord[P]

A sword wielded by a victorious hand: °sigemēce[P]

A flaming sword: byrnsweord

A damascened sword: brogdenmæl[P], hringmæl[P], mālsweord, °sceadenmæl[P], °wægsweord[P]

—— *damascened:* brogden, °grægmæl[P], hringmæl(ed)[P], °scīrmæled[P], °wundenmæl[P], °wyrmfāh[P]

A broad sword: brādsweord[P]

A short sword, dagger: handseax, hypeseax[g], þeohseax, seax, °wælseax[P]

A staff-sword: stæfsweord[g]

Keen/sharp of edge: °beaduscearp[P], ecgheard, heardecg[P], stiþecg, stȳlecg, stȳled

Very sharp: °feolheard[P], °steþeheard[P]

Fire-hardened: °fȳrheard[P]

Strong in battle: °wīgcræftig[P]

One-edged: ānecge

Notched (in war): °heaþusceard[P], sceard

Hilt: (ge)hilte

Pertaining to types of hilt: °fealohilte[P], °fetelhilt[P], °goldhilted[P], gyldenhilt(e), seolforhilt(ed), °wreoþenhilt[P]

?Belted: (ge)fetelsod

Scabbard: cocer, fetel(s), lecg, sceaþ, °sweordfætels

Having no hilt: °hiltleas[g]

Ornamented: bunden, °gescæned[P]

Plate of metal on hilt: °scenn[P]

Pike: pīc

Axe: °ceorfæx, taperæx, wifle

Back of axe: ȳr

Warlike engine: wīgcræft

Battering ram: ramm, °wæhþoll[g]

Sling: liþere, stæfliþere[g]

Bow: boga, flānboga[P], hornboga[P]

End of bow: horn

String: streng

Case for a bow: °bogefōdder[g], cocer

Deceitful bow: °brægdboga[P]

Arrow: anga, arwe, bolt, earh, flā, flān, gār, °gūþflā[P], °herestræl[P], °heorufla[g], hildenædre[P], scutel, stræl, °wæpenstræl[P]

Treacherous arrow: °inwitflān[P]

Shaft (of arrow): sceaft

Feathers: feþergearwe

Volley of arrows: earhfaru, flāngeweorc, °īsenscūrᴾ, scūr, storm
Quiver: cocer
Cross-bow: °arblæst

Pots and pans, etc.

Cooking vessel/pot: bæcelingᵍ, cyll, hwer, panne, °þolleᵍ
Cauldron/kettle: ālfæt, citel, fȳrcrūceᵍ, °gripuᴾ, lēad
Frying pan: brǣdepanneᵍ, brǣdingpanneᵍ, cōcerpanne, hierste, hierstepanne,
    hiersting, īsenpanne
Chafing dish: fȳrpanne, °glǣdfæt
Food receptacle/basket: binn, cawl, fōþor
Provision bag: °metbælgᵍ, °metefætelsᵍ, °nestpohhaᵍ, sceattcod
Containers for specific foodstuffs: °æppelfætᵍ, bearmtēag, ecedfæt, elefæt, elehorn,
    °hunigbin, °lēactrogᵍ, °piporhorn, sealtfæt, sealtlēap
Pot, vessel, crock: crocc, crocca, crocchwer, grēofa, pott, tigel(e)
Vessel/utensil/cup: fæt
Stone vessel: stānfæt
Vessel of particular metal: ārfæt, goldfæt, mæstling, °seolforfæt
Wondrous vessel: °wundorfætᴾ
Dish for food/serving dish: °hlæddiscᵍ, þēningfæt
Tray: °bǣrdiscᵍ, trig
Plate, platter, bowl, dish: bēod, disc, læpeldre, °lempitᵍ, °metefætᵍ, °scutelᵍ
Small dish/side-dish: gaboteᵍ
Bowl/?cream dish: °credicᵍ
Cup, bowl, basin: bledu, bolla, gellet, hnæpp, læfel, mǣle, orc, scealu, °wearr
Table bowl/table vessel: bēodbolle, °bēodfætᵍ
Wine flask/can: wīnbelgᵍ, wīnsesterᵍ
Cup for sops: sopcuppe

Cutlery

Ladle, scoop: crūce, hlǣdel, turl
Spoon: cucler, °metesticcaᵍ, sticca
Knife: °metseax

Cups, jugs, buckets, etc.

Drinking vessel: °bēodfætᵍ, bune, calic, canne, coppᵍ, cuppe, °drenccuppeᵍ,
    drencfæt/dryncfæt, ful, °gropaᵍ, scenc, wǣgeᴾ, °wearr, wriþaᴾ
Horn –: drenchorn/dryncehorn, horn, °wīnhorn
Glass –: glæs, glæsfæt
—— *used in hall:* °selefulᴾ
—— *for specific liquor:* ealuwǣgeᴾ, °liþwǣgeᴾ, medufulᴾ, °meduscencᴾ,
    wætermēleᵍ, °wīntrog
Water pitcher: wæterbuc, °wætercrōgᵍ, °wætercrūceᵍ, wæterfæt, °wæterflaxeᵍ
Lipped vessel, beaker: °ēaseᵍ, °næsterᵍ
Cup/?jug: °scencingcuppe
Vessel, pitcher, jug, etc.: cēac, crōgᵍ, crūce, crusneᵍ, stǣne

Vessel with stem or handle: amber, °stelmēle

Flask, flagon, bottle: ampelle, būc, °būt, butruc, bytt, cyll, flæsce, glæsfæt, °pinne⁸, stēap

A kind of vessel (or winejar): °crōgcynn⁸

Barrel, tun, vat, cask: byden, bydenfæt, cȳf, °cȳfl, sā, trog, tunne

Tub: °tyncen

Cask bottom: °tunnebotme⁸

Butt lid: byttehlid⁸

Wine vat: °wīncole⁸, wīnfæt, °wīnmēre⁸

Wine cask: °wīntunne⁸

Beer/ale barrel: °bēorbyden, °ealufæt

Water cask: °wæterbyden⁸

Bucket, pail: æscen, embren, stoppa

Water bucket: wæterstoppa

Vessel for drawing water: °hlæden⁸, °hlædfæt⁸

Plate 1. Recent finds from Middle Anglo-Saxon East Anglia. (Suffolk Archaeological Unit, Suffolk County Council)

1 Copper alloy Mediterranean bucket from Bromeswell parish, Suffolk. (Photo: R. D. Carr, Suffolk CC) **2** Silver bracelet from the Boss Hall Anglo-Saxon Cemetery, Ipswich, Suffolk. (Photo: D. Nuttall, Suffolk CC) **3** Copper alloy saucer brooch from the Boss Hall Anglo-Saxon Cemetery, Ipswich, Suffolk. (Photo: D. Nuttall, Suffolk CC).

1

2　　　　　　　　　　3

Plate 2. **1** Asthall Barrow in April 1991 viewed from the west; **2** Asthall Barrow under excavation in 1923; **3** Close-up of posthole Y.   Photo: (1) T.M. Dickinson, (2–3) G.S. Bowles.

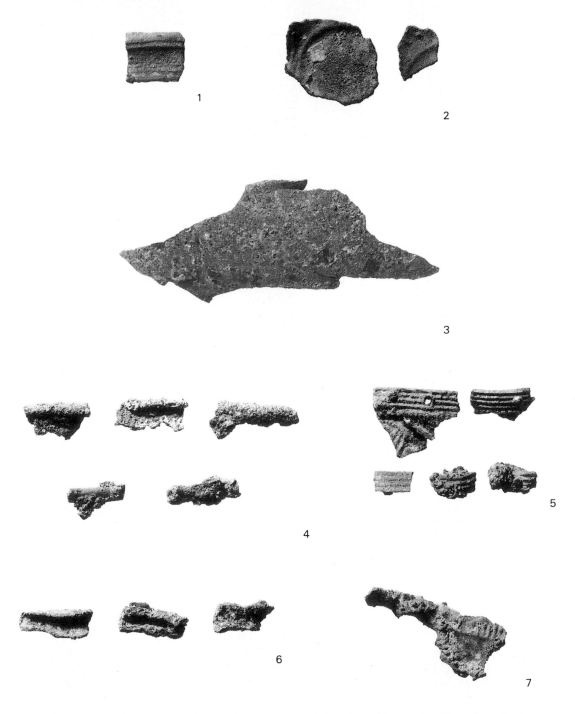

Plate 3. **1–2** Fragments from silver vessel; **3** Fragment of sheet-metal vessel; **4** Tightly rolled tubular rim fragments?; **5** Fluted strips; **6** U-sectioned rim binding; **7** 'Sandwiched' foil fragment with billeted border. Sc. 3:2.   Photo: T.M. Dickinson.

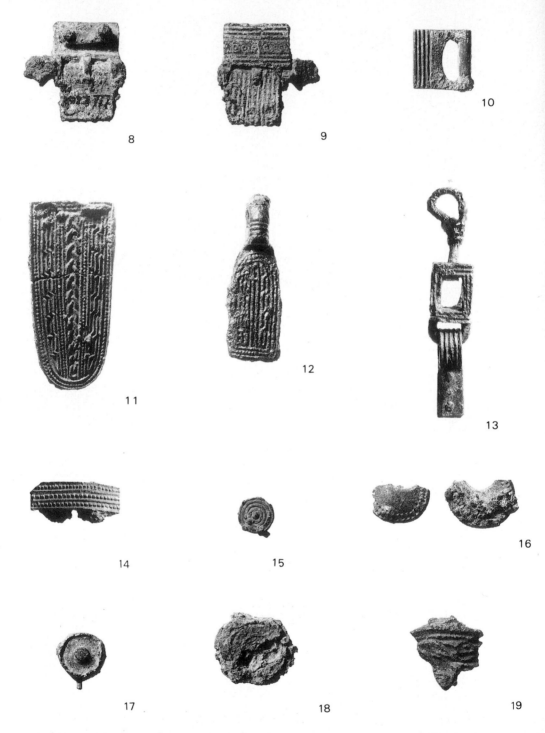

Plate 4. **8–9** Hinged strap attachment, back and front; **10** Looped mount; **11** Strap end; **12** Looped strap tab; **13** Openwork swivel fitting; **14** 'Silver' strap mount; **15** Rivet with concentric rings; **16** Crescentic studs; **17** Sunken-field stud; **18** Lead disc; **19** Style I ring or disc. Sc. 3:2.   Photo: T.M. Dickinson.

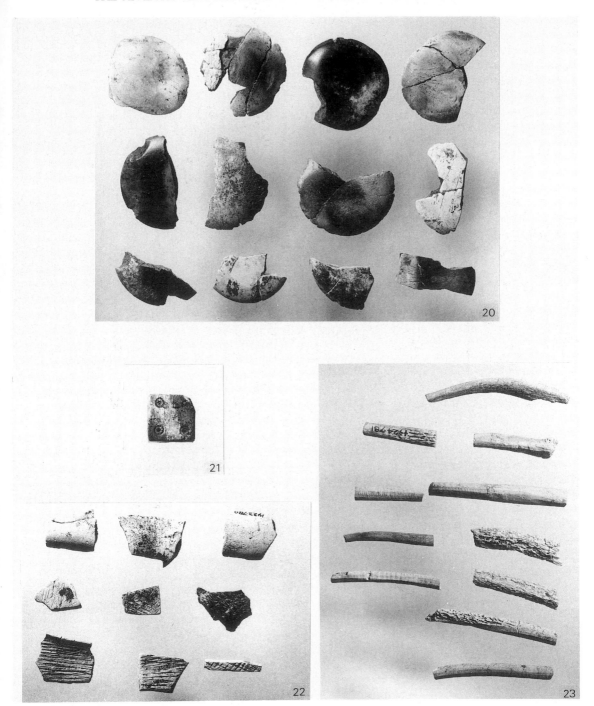

Plate 5. **20** Gaming pieces; **21** Die; **22** Bone inlays: plain outer surface (top row); grooved outer surface (middle row); grooved lower surface and edge (bottom row); **23** Bone rods. Sc. 1:1. Photo: T.M. Dickinson.

Plate 6. Class I stone from Rhynie, Grampian Region.
(Copyright T.E. Gray)

Plate 7. Depiction of a warrior on a pillar from Collessie, Fife.
(Copyright T.E. Gray)

Plate 8. View of the crypt of the old Saint-Geneviève church after the profanation of the graves in 1793. Watercolour by Bourla junior, drawn after the sketches of his father. Bibl. nat. Est. coll. Destailleur, t.2, 63, n° 303. Photo: B.N.

Plate 9. Recumbent statue of Clovis (around 1220–1230). Present state in the Saint-Denis basilica. Photo: Editions Errance.

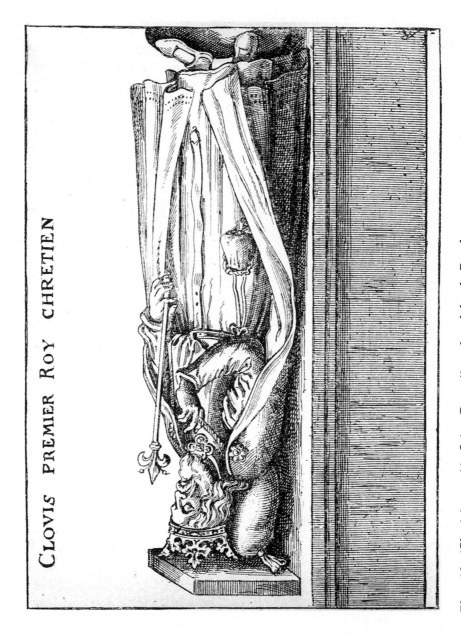

CLOVIS PREMIER ROY CHRETIEN

Plate 10. 'Clovis' grave' in Saint-Geneviève church by du Breul.
(Du Breul, 1639).

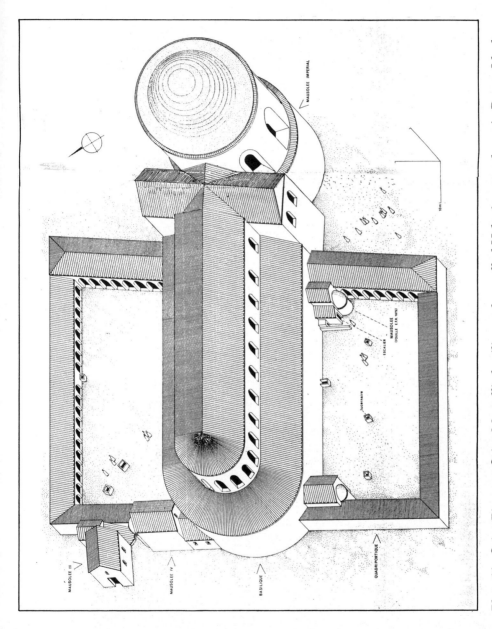

Plate 11. Saint-Pierre-et-Saint-Marcellin basilica and so-called Helen's mausoleum in Rome. Ideal axonometric reconstitution of the monumental whole (by H. Broise, École Française of Rome). From Guyon, 1976.

Plate 12. View of the excavations carried out in the nave of the old Saint-Geneviève church in 1807 (in the direction of the choir). Watercolour by Bourla junior, drawn after the sketches of his father. B.N. Est. coll. Destailleur, t.II, fol 62, n° 302. Fol 63, n° 303 is another example of Bourla's work. Photo: B.N.

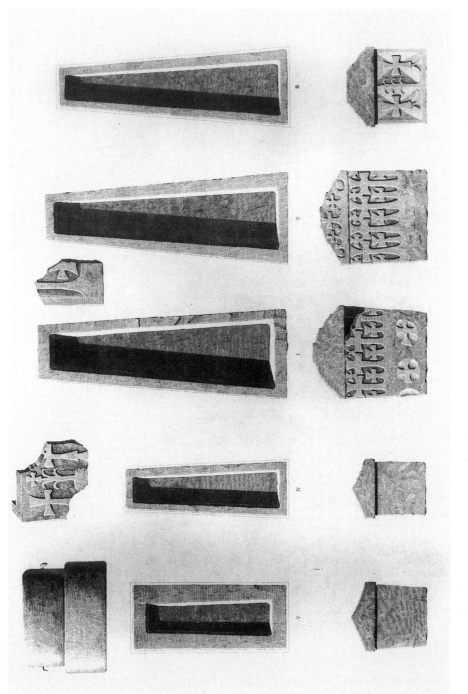

Plate 13. Merovingian sarcophagi discovered in 1807 in Saint-Geneviève's church. Lenoir, 1867, pl. 1. Photo: Musée Carnavalet.

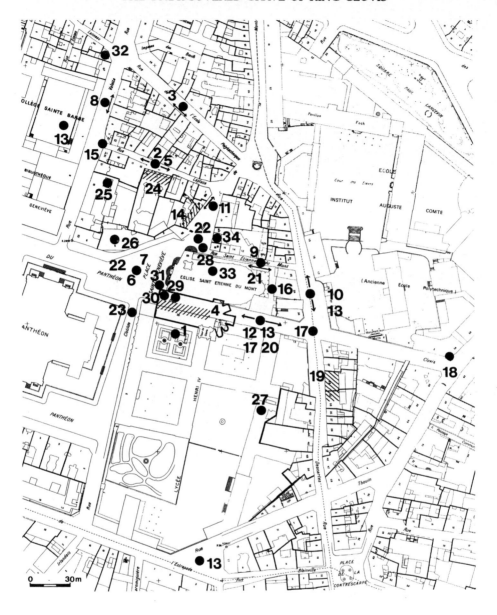

1. 1620. 2. Fin XVIIe-début XVIIIe siècle.
3. Fin XVIIe-début XVIIIe siècle. 4. 1807.
5. Vers 1840. 6. 1850. 7. 1850. 8. 1857.
9. 1873. 10. 1873. 11. 1873. 12. 1877.
13. Vers 1880. 14. 1883. 15. 1893. 16. 1893.

17. 1893. 18. 1896. 19. 1898. 20. 1901.
21. 1901. 22. 1901. 23. 1903. 24. 1909.
25. 1921. 26. 1926. 27. 1933. 28. 1934.
29. 1946. 30. 1963. 31. 1963. 32. 1975.
33. 1973. 34. 1976.

Plate 14. Merovingian necropolis at the Holy Apostles in Paris (with the site of the old Saint-Geneviève church). From Périn *et al.*, 1985, fig. 27, p. 148.

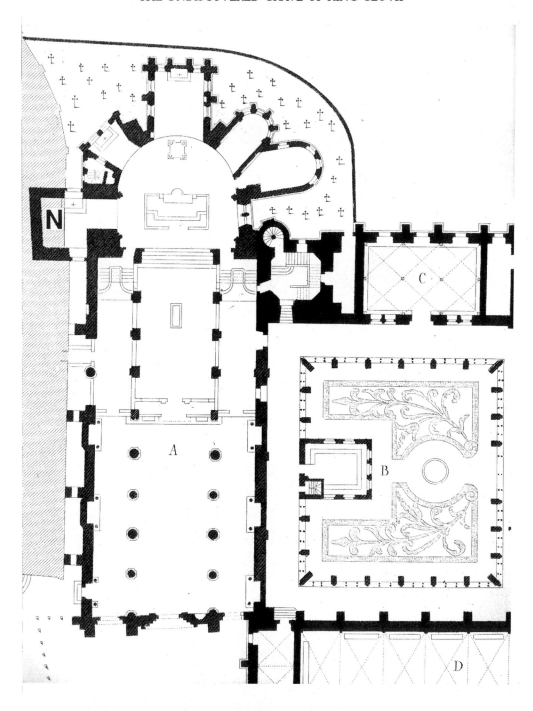

Plate 15. Plan of the crypt and of the excavations carried out in the nave of the old Saint-Geneviève church in 1807 by Lenoir, 1867, v.
Photo: Musée Carnavalet. The letter 'N' marks the position of the northern chapel.

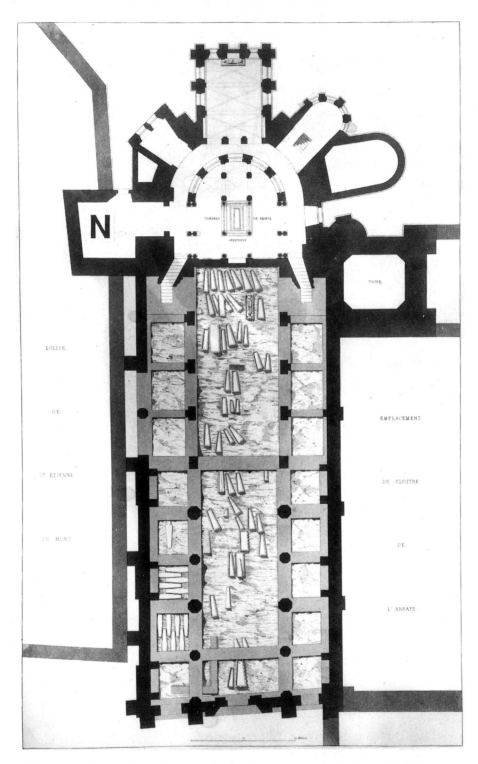

Plate 16. Plan of the old Saint-Geneviève church. By Lenoir, 1867, I.
Photo: Musée Carnavalet. The letter 'N' marks the position of the northern chapel.

Plate 17. Belt appliqué with zoomorphic decoration (silver 3 x 2.6 cm.) discovered in 1656 in Saint-Germain des Prés, in the burial of King Childeric II (+675). Reproduction of the plate published by Dom Montfaucon, 1729, t. i, p. 274.

Plate 18. Clovis Street taken towards the east. Present state. Photo: P. Périn.

Plate 19. Borre, Norway: some of the decorated bronze mounts and horse-trappings from the Viking period grave in Mound 1. (After Müller-Wille 1986, fig. 3.).

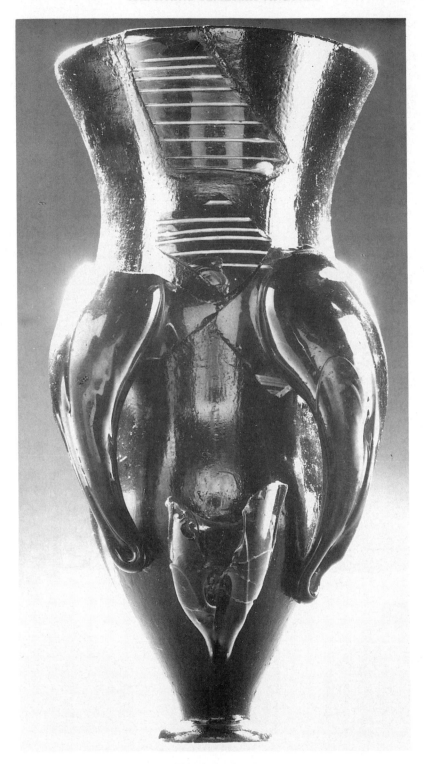

Plate 20. Borre, Norway: The reconstructed claw-beaker based on five fragments found in Mound 1. It may be an antique in a Viking period grave, or, just as possible, an object belonging to earlier activity on the site of Borre itself. (Photo: Oldsaksamlingen, Oslo).

Plate 21. Style II decorated objects from the sixth-century find from Åker, Hedmark.
Fragments of a ring-sword, a shield and belt equipment (Photo: Oldsaksamlingen, Oslo).

Plate 22. Fragments of helmets from By in Hedmark, and Stabu in Oppland, found in cremation graves (Photo: Oldsaksamlingen, Oslo).

Plate 23A. The Sutton Hoo burial mounds (foreground: to the left of the wood) with the River Deben and the North Sea. Photo: C. Hoppitt.

Plate 23B. The Sutton Hoo site in 1983, looking west. The 'zip fasteners' are anti-glider ditches cut during the Second World War. Photo: C. Hoppitt.

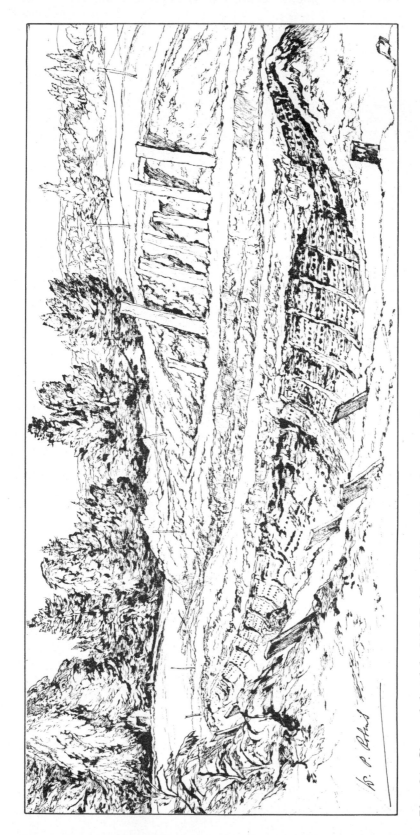

Plate 24. Charcoal sketch by *W. P. Robins* of Mound 1 under excavation.

Plate 25. Sutton Hoo: the excavated sample. (Photo: N. Macbeth).

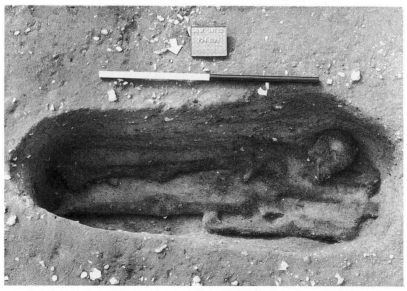

Plate 26. 'Satellite' burials: (top) Mound 5, Group 2, and (bottom) Eastern Cemetery, Group 1. (Photo: N. Macbeth).

Plate 27. Mound 2: the chamber and later trenches. (Photo: N. Macbeth)

Plate 28. Mound 2 and Mound 5 (foreground) under excavation. Mound 20 can be seen at bottom, right of excavated area. (Photo: N. Macbeth).

Plate 29. Mound 14: under excavation. (Photo: N. Macbeth).

Plate 30. Mound 17: the two burials. (Photo: M. Carver).

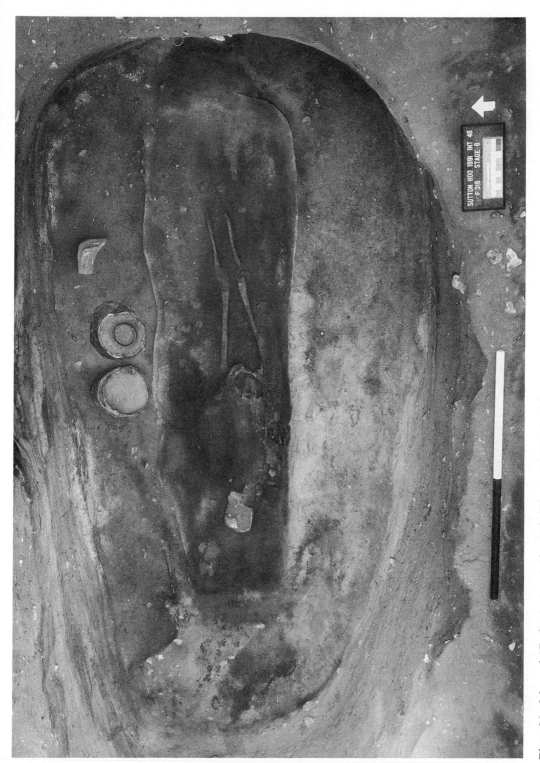

Plate 31. Mound 17: the 'prince's' burial. (Photo: N. Macbeth).

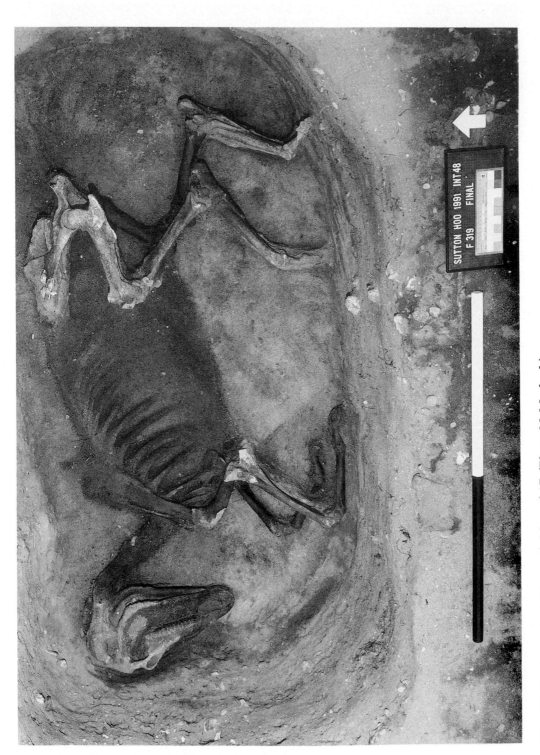

Plate 32. The horse-burial beneath Mound 17. (Photo N. Macbeth).

PART III

North-Western Europe in
the Age of Sutton Hoo

14

Message from the Dark Side of the Moon: Western and Northern Britain in the Age of Sutton Hoo

LESLIE ALCOCK

The Sutton Hoo ship-burial was a celebration of kingship, especially in its modes of militarism and ostentation. Any holistic view of the background to the business of kings in south-east England must take account of evidence not only from the Continent, the Mediterranean, and Scandinavia; but also from the north and west of Britain: the Dark Side of the Moon of my title. As it happens, from the later sixth century to the eighth, an information window opens up in northern Britain in the form of verbal evidence for the military activities of kings. Over the same period, in both the north and the west, there is a burgeoning of archaeological evidence both for the military business of kings, and also for their role as generous providers, especially of wine and rich jewellery. All this has obvious relevance to the warrior king symbolized at Sutton Hoo. The evidence is abundant, but much of it is unpublished in detail; so I can give no more than a sample.

I

We may look first at the early Welsh poetry: partly because its composition may precede any of our other verbal evidence, but more particularly because its heroic theme chimes with the long-established stereotype of Dark Age kings, whether Germanic or Celtic. I have in mind particularly the *Gododdin* poem of the bard Aneirin, and poems attributed to Taliesin in celebration and lamentation for Urien of Rheged.

It would be unwise to look in the poetry for actual historical events, such as a doomed expedition from Edinburgh into the heart of Deira. We cannot use it for a historian's assessment of political realities, nor of strategy, tactics or weapon play. What we do have is the bard's view of the correct attitude of kings and warriors to battle itself. Indeed it is worth recalling here that, while the heroes of the *Tain* are supernatural beings fighting with supernatural weapons, and Beowulf's principal foes are at least superhuman, in the Welsh poems it is normal – if heroic – men who fight against heroes.

The essence of heroic warfare is that it is fought for personal glory. Here, one stanza from *Y Gododdin* must serve for many:

> He slew a great host/ To achieve fame. The son of Nwython slew/ of the gold-torqued/ A hundred princes/ so that he might be praised.
>
> (Jarman 1988, 62)

A lesser motive, relevant to the hospitality of kings, was that:

> He attacked in battle, in the forefront,/ In return for mead in the hall and drinking of wine./ He cast his spears between two armies.
>
> (Jarman 1988, 28)

The outcome of this was that:

> The retinue of Mynyddog, renowned in battle,/ they paid for their mead-feast with their lives.   (Jarman 1988, 24)

Blatant exaggeration is another characteristic of the poetry, so that we are told of several warriors that:

> Five fifties fell before his blades   (e.g. Jarman 1988, 4)

Heroic poetry, however, is not our only source of information about warfare. We must now turn to the contemporary *Annals*, especially those from Iona, and to the narrative of Bede. In the *Annals*, flashing blades and showers of spears are replaced by burning forts. Again, one example must represent many:

> A.D.736. Oengus, son of Fergus, king of the Picts, devastated [*vastavit*] the provinces of Dalriada, and captured Dunadd [a fort in Argyll], and burned Creic [unidentified], and bound in chains the two sons of Selbach [king of Dalriada].

Named forts were built by kings, and then besieged, captured, burned and destroyed by other kings. In all this, the role of the king is plainly paramount.

Some named forts can be firmly identified on the ground. The list can then be extended, especially into Wales and south-west Britain, where the written evidence is absent, by means of comparisons of fort plans and of artifacts, as well as on the basis of radiometric dates. Similar evidence shows that some places were defended by water or swamp rather than by built ramparts. It is convenient to bring all these together into a class of enclosed places. Moreover, since we cannot be certain that all of them were the seats of kings, it is useful to use the term 'potentates'.

At least 107 enclosed places of potentates are now known in northern and western Britain. Here the map discloses a major difference between Anglo-

Saxon England and Celtic Britain. Before the evolution of the Late Saxon *burh*, substantially defended settlements appear to be unknown in the south and east; even the hill-forts of earlier centuries were spurned. This clearly implies differences in the character of warfare, and no less in the role of kings.

The annal for 736 refers to *vastatio*, the ravaging of territory. This is also a favourite theme of Bede, especially about the dealings of Cadwallon and Penda with Northumbria. Bede's account of the confrontation of Cadwallon and Oswald no doubt owes as much to heroic literature as it does to hagiography, especially with Old Testament roots. This in no way lessens the brutality of such ravagings, nor the suffering which they caused.

Sea battles are also recorded in the *Annals* between the kindreds of Dalriada, or between Dalriada and Ireland. They may lead to a 'great slaughter', or to the loss of a number of *comites*. In 729, one hundred and fifty ships of the Picts were wrecked. Our best knowledge of sea-faring in north-western waters comes from the biography of Columba. His island monastery of Iona depended on sea travel, and its people, whether religious or lay, knew about boats, oars and sails. The normal vessel of the time had been developed from that of the 1st century BC, known from the Broighter hoard, which had a single sail and nine benches of oars.

The *Annals* reveal military objectives which are more serious than the quest for glory or the payment for mead. Dynasties rise and fall, royal hostages are taken, forts and territory change hands. The most serious recorded outcome of a single battle is that of Nectansmere in 685: not only the death of Ecgfrith and the slaughter of the army of Northumbria but, as Bede tells us, 'the Picts recovered their own land . . . while the Irish in Britain and some part of the British nation recovered their independence . . . and the hopes and strength of the English Kingdom began to "ebb and fall away" '. In modern political terms, the Northumbrian claim to hegemony in northern Britain was terminated.

What we see here is not the heroic exploits of war-bands, dependent on personal relationships with outstanding war leaders, cemented by mead-feasts, and motivated by glory; but rather the activities of nations or kingdoms organized for war. The provision of resources for the prosecution of such warfare depended on the right of kings (or members of the king's family) to lead hostings, both in defence of their own territory and also into a foreign country; the right to taxes and tribute as well as services; the power to enforce those rights; and the systematic assessment of land for taxes and military musters. It is on the last two points that there is particularly interesting evidence from northern Britain.

In 729, after an internal battle between two Pictish kings, several of the dead were described as *exactores*, 'tax gatherers or enforcers'. Presumably they were on an expedition to enforce the payment of tribute. Since their descent is cited, they may represent a nobility of blood as well as of service.

For an example of a fully worked-out land assessment, we may turn to the

Senchus Fer n'Alban, a pseudo-history and assessment of Dalriada, originally compiled in the late seventh century. This includes a civil survey in terms of a unit known as *tech*, meaning house or household, and akin to the English hide or *familia*. There follows a survey for the military muster, which assesses the three kindreds of Dalriada respectively at 600, 800 and 600 men: a total of 2000. Finally there is a naval survey, in which the *tech*-unit is organized into groups of 20, each responsible for providing two seven-benched ships, probably vessels with a sail as well as oars like the Broighter boat. The manpower required for the navy is similar to the military muster, and suggests that every able-bodied man in Dalriada was required to serve. This is not compatible with a war-band raised on the heroic model; but it reinforces my earlier comment about nations organized for war.

II

From this account of the military activities of kings, based largely on verbal evidence, I turn now to their role in providing the necessary luxuries of noble life through the importation of wine, glass drinking-vessels, and good quality pottery. Here the evidence is largely archaeological.

A characteristic of a majority of potentate-sites is that they yield exotic pottery and glass. Our knowledge of the character, the broad chronology and the site-occurrence of these exotica has grown steadily over the past fifty years; but explanations of the means by which they were introduced and distributed in an insular context are still defective.

Two main phases of importation are distinguishable. In the first, Map 1, beginning late in the fifth century, and continuing until the end of the sixth, the main import was wine and oil in diagnostic pottery amphorae, of which the sherds are well preserved on site (B-ware) (Fig. 33). Their source is the Mediterranean, especially its eastern end, and the north African littoral. They are accompanied by a smaller quantity of red slip wares (A-ware), and by even rarer glass of late Roman and east Mediterranean origin. They contrast markedly in opulence with the east Mediterranean imports at Sutton Hoo.

In the seventh century, (Fig. 34) there is a marked shift from Mediterranean sources to Continental ones, and specifically to largely unidentified sources in western Gaul between the Garonne and the Loire. The leading visible import is now pottery as such: table- and kitchen-ware (E-ware) which doubtless had a higher prestige than local vessels of treen and leather. The pottery was accompanied by glass drinking vessels, often in some quantity; and by a distinctly rare table-ware from Bordeaux (D-ware), which may have come in on the back of a trade in wine in cask, archaeologically undetectable, but reasonably inferred. The dating evidence for this second phase is entirely Insular, but includes radiocarbon dates suggesting a range covering the seventh and eighth centuries.

This second phase invites immediate comparison with J.W. Huggett's study of imported glass vessels from Anglo-Saxon graves. On the accompanying map (Fig. 35), sites with less than five examples are omitted for the sake of clarity and emphasis. For the west and north, three points must be remembered: none of the sites, which are predominantly enclosed places, has been fully excavated; few have been adequately published; and some are still under excavation. The map therefore presents minimum figures, which may ultimately need considerable expansion, but which nonetheless compare favourably with those from the graves. It must also be emphasized that all the western sites, and a *fortiori* those in the north, are farther away from their continental source (wherever exactly that may be) than are the Anglo-Saxon examples. Finally, present opinion has moved away from either an Anglo-Saxon or a Rhineland source for the glass.

The relatively large quantity of E-ware, and its wide distribution around the Irish Sea, has led Ewan Campbell to attempt to distinguish between major import centres and lesser, dependent sites, by compiling 'isobars' of minimum numbers of vessels on individual sites. The results are interesting if we are trying to build models of trade and exchange mechanisms. Empirically, however, they are questionable because of the varied levels and standards of excavation on different sites, and also because of intra-site variability.

To quote examples: Dunadd and Dunollie are contemporary royal sites, and indeed, of the two, Dunollie is mentioned more frequently in the *Annals*. But Dunollie has only 4 E-ware vessels against Dunadd's minimum of 23. On the other hand, Dunadd has been extensively excavated, but, until recently, at a low standard, whereas only 6% of Dunollie has been explored – but to a higher standard. We cannot, however, simply multiply that 6% up to 100%, because of the problem of intra-site variability. There is just no objective basis for numerical comparison, and this obviously undermines the value of Campbell's 'isobar' map.

A striking example of intra-site variability is presented for this area and period by the distribution of red slip ware, and more especially of amphora sherds, at Cadbury. These are not scattered evenly over the interior of the site. Fifty-three per cent of them are concentrated around a large building, identified as a feasting hall. This distribution demonstrates the point that a (metaphorically) highly structured society creates architectural structures related to its activities which in turn (and again metaphorically) structure the use, breakage, dispersal and deposition of artifacts. It also means, of course, that had the area of the feasting hall not been excavated, then the count of Mediterranean imports from Cadbury would have been halved; and by the same token, it is not possible to extrapolate total numbers of finds from any one area of excavation.

What was the political, social and economic status of the major importing sites of both the Mediterranean and the Continental phases? Hodges bestowed the accolade of emporium status on two of them, Bantham and Dalkey, but ignored the most impressive of all, Tintagel.

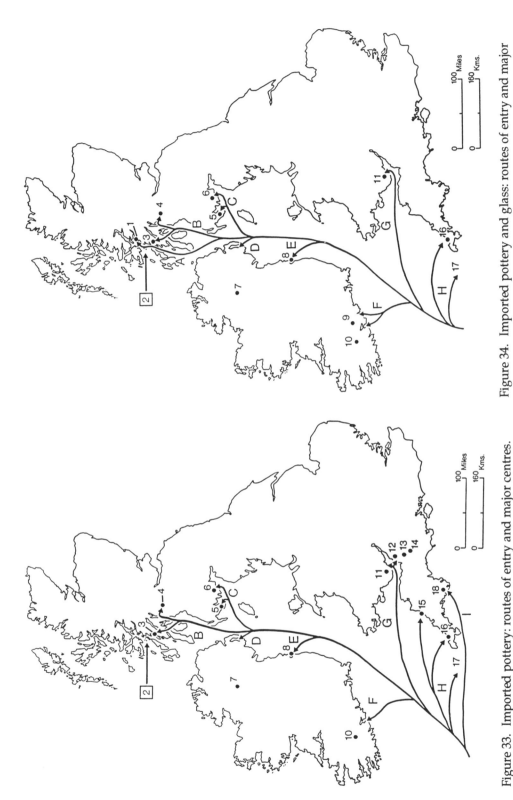

Figure 34. Imported pottery and glass: routes of entry and major centres. Second phase, seventh–eighth centuries A.D. from West Gaul. For sources, see Appendix

Figure 33. Imported pottery: routes of entry and major centres. First phase, late fifth–late sixth centuries A.D. from Mediterranean

It is convenient here to review, briefly, the major sites, starting in the north. On the west coast, Dunollie and Dunadd are fortified craggy hills, both with excellent sea access; both with royal connections, especially military; both producing evidence not merely for imports, but also for the making of jewellery in gold and silver as well as bronze. At an unidentified port in the area, Saint Columba in the late sixth century met sailors who had come from Gaul. His biographer Adomnan does not name the place, but calls it *caput regionis*, a term which readily translates as 'central place'.

The Clyde entry is dominated by the Rock of Clyde, Dumbarton: a formidable site with an excellent harbour, yielding both Mediterranean and Continental imports, and also evidence for fine metalworking. Already a royal seat in the sixth century, and perhaps even in the fifth, it was described by Bede as *civitas Brettonum munitissima*, 'a strongly defended political centre of the Britons'. It survived until the 870s, when Viking kings from Dublin destroyed it as the prelude to a major slave raid throughout northern Britain.

On the Solway estuary, the major site is now the ecclesiastical centre of Whithorn, where Saint Ninian founded his *candida casa*, 'shining house', in the late fifth century, and where Bede records a bishop's seat and *ecclesia insignis* in the early eighth. The imports come from both the Mediterranean and the Continent, with glass vessels especially prominent. In the ninth century, Whithorn lay within the Anglo-Scandinavian monetary economy based on York, and its urban development was continuous thereafter. Already in the Mediterranean phase, buildings and other activity extended up to 100 metres from the church, suggesting an overall occupied area of about 0.8 ha: a small emporium.

South from the Solway there is a gap, unless indeed finds off the Wirral peninsula at Meols betoken a sea-eroded port. In the Mediterranean phase, the Severn entry served the inland sites of Congresbury, Glastonbury Tor and Cadbury, and the near-coastal fortlet of Dinas Powys. At the latter, occupation continued to flourish through the Continental phase, and indeed Dinas Powys has the richest range of pottery, glass and metal-working of any published site of the period. This very richness, combined with the small area of the enclosure, makes it difficult to propose a satisfactory political and economic status for the site.

Further to the south-west, Tintagel is the outstanding site of the Mediterranean phase. A large promontory, massively defended by nature and requiring only a minimum of man-made fortification, it has the further advantage of a reasonable harbour. Given its position on the western approaches to Britain, it is not surprising that its yield of both red slip wares and amphorae outnumbers any other site at least tenfold. What is surprising is its failure to survive into the seventh century.

Finally, round the south coast to Hodges's emporium at Bantham. Originally this was known only as a scatter of amphora sherds, antler combs and other objects from coastal sand dunes: but more recent work suggests that a 10 ha.

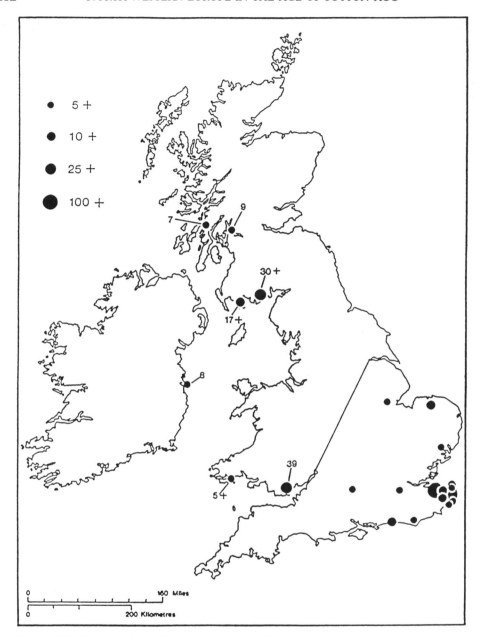

Figure 35. Distribution of 'exotic' glass vessels, mainly sixth–seventh centuries
A.D., in Anglo-Saxon England, and west and north Britain and Ireland.
Sites with fewer than 5 vessels are omitted.

headland beside a natural harbour may have been occupied through the sixth and seventh centuries.

East again, of course we come back to the bright side of the moon, with Hamwih, London, Ipswich and Eoforwic-York.

When we ask about the status of the south-western sites, we lack the written evidence which is so revealing in the north-west. In two cases we have hints. In the crisis of the early eleventh century, the emergency *burh* and mint of *Caddanburh* replaced the low-lying Ilchester. Might Cadbury likewise have replaced the Roman *civitas* of Ilchester in the troubled decades of the late fifth and early sixth centuries? What the term *civitas* might have meant at Cadbury is no more difficult a question than what it meant for Bede when he used it of Dumbarton. As for Tintagel: the speculative suggestion has now been advanced that 'perhaps it was a dwelling of the rulers of Cornwall in the period of the imported pottery'. Only one comment is possible: who else but the kings of Cornwall could have commanded the wealth and power to attract imported wine and fine table-ware on such a massive scale?

In this paper, I have presented some of the evidence, verbal and artefactual, for the activities of kings in northern and western Britain from the late fifth to the eighth century. What I have not attempted is a coherent model, gift-wrapped and tied around with the pale pink ribbon of this month's favourite social theory. What we need at this moment is not more theories, but the full publication of numerous relevant excavations.

TAIL PIECE: February 1991

Circumstances have prevented any substantial revision of this text, which remains largely as it was delivered. Nor has there been any opportunity to provide full bibliographic references. However, the Appendix below gives a state-of-the-art guide to the principal written sources for Part I of the paper. Moreover, the topic is dealt with more extensively in L. Alcock, *An Heroic Age: war and society in northern Britain, A.D.450–850. The Rhind Lectures 1988–89*, forthcoming. A synopsis of the lectures is published in *Proc. Soc. Antiq. Scot.* 118 (1988), 327–334.

The main theme of Part II of this paper is now exhaustively discussed, with a fully referenced gazetteer of 107 sites, in L. & E.A. Alcock, 'Reconnaissance excavations on Early Historic fortifications and other royal sites in Scotland, 1974–84: 4, Excavations at Alt Clut, Clyde Rock, Strathclyde, 1974–75', *Proc. Soc. Antiq. Scot.* 120 (1990), 95–149 plus fiche.

APPENDIX

The Seventh/Eighth-Century Information Window in North Britain: Some Key Texts

Annals

Irish Annals, especially Annals of Ulster, incorporating Iona Annals, contemporary over period c.640–740 A.D. Text and translation, MacAirt, S. & MacNiocaill, G, *The Annals of Ulster (to A.D.1131)*, Dublin 1983.

Commentary: Bannerman, J., *Studies in the history of Dalriada*, Edinburgh 1974; Anderson, M.O., *Kings and kingship in early Scotland*, Edinburgh 1973; 1980.

Survey/Assessment

Senchus Fer n'Alban, late seventh century with later amendments, Text, translation & commentary: Bannerman 1974; further commentary, Anderson 1973, 1980.

Hagiography and Other Narrative

Bede, *Ecclesiastical History*, completed A.D.731, most useful for late seventh-early eighth centuries. Accessible text and translation: Colgrave, B. & Mynors, R.A.B, *Bede's Ecclesiastical History*, Oxford 1969; commentary now by Wallace-Hadrill, J.M., Oxford 1988.

Columba: Text, translation & commentary: Anderson, A.O. & M.O., *Adomnan's Life of Columba*, Edinburgh 1961; revised edition by M.O. Anderson, Oxford 1991.

Cuthbert: text, translation & commentary: Colgrave, B., *Two Lives of Saint Cuthbert*, Cambridge 1940; 1985.

Wilfrid: text, translation & commentary: Colgrave, B., *The Life of Bishop Wilfrid by Eddius Stephanus*, Cambridge 1927; 1985.

Heroic Poetry

Y Gododdin: most accessible text, translation & commentary: Jarman, A.O.H., *Aneirin: Y Gododdin*, Llandysul 1988. See also Roberts, B.F. (ed.), *Early Welsh poetry: studies in the Book of Aneirin*, National Library of Wales, Aberystwyth 1988.

For Taliesin, Llywarch Hen and other early poetry, see translations and commentary in Jarman, A.O.H., *The Cynfeirdd: early Welsh poets and poetry*, University of Wales 1981

Key to Maps (Figs 33, 34): Imported pottery, routes of entry and major centres

Principal source for pottery: C. Thomas, *A provisional list of imported pottery in post-Roman western Britain and Ireland*, Redruth 1981.

Commentary on sites: L. Alcock, 'The activities of potentates in Celtic Britain, A.D.500–800' in S.T. Driscoll & M.R. Nieke (eds), *Power & Politics in Early Medieval Britain & Ireland*, Edinburgh 1988.

Historical references: 1, Dunollie, Irish, i.e. Iona Annals 686, 698, 701, 714, 734; 2, *Caput regionis*, Life of Columba 31a, Columba meets Gallic sailors; 3, Dunadd,

Iona Annals 683, 736; 4, Dumbarton, Bede, HE I, 1 & 12, *civitas Brettonum muni-tissima, urbs*; 5, Whithorn, Bede, HE III, 4, *sedes episcopatus et ecclesia insignis.*

Conventions for list of major centres: 5–9 = fifth to ninth centuries A.D.; f = fort; fr = with contemporary royal associations; e = ecclesiastical site; ? = type of site unknown; m = metalworking.

Routes of Entry	Major Centres	
A FIRTH OF LORN	1 Dunollie	7–8 fr m
	2 Caput regionis	6–7 ?
B CLYDE	3 Dunadd	6–9 fr m
	4 Dumbarton	5–9 fr m
C SOLWAY	5 Whithorn	5 > e m
	6 Mote of Mark	6–8 f m
D STRANGFORD LOUGH	7 Clogher	6–9 fr m
E DUBLIN BAY	8 Dalkey	6–8 f m
F CORK/YOUGHAL	9 Garryduff	7–8 f m
	10 Garranes	6–8 f m
G SEVERN	11 Dinas Powys	5–9 f m
	12 Congresbury	4–6 f m
	13 Glastonbury Tor	5–6 ? m
	14 Cadbury	5–6 f
H SOUTHWESTERN	15 Tintagel	5–6 f
	16 Gwithian	5–8 ? m
	17 Scillies	6–8
I ENGLISH CHANNEL	18 Bantham	6–7 ?

15

The State of Pictland in the Age of Sutton Hoo

SALLY FOSTER

In the seventh century the modern geographical entity known today as Scotland was the home of four different races and cultures: the Picts, Britons, Scots and Angles (Fig. 36). The Picts lived to the east of the mountainous region that separates modern Argyllshire and Perthshire, whilst their southern boundary (which fluctuated throughout the seventh century as a result of Anglian incursions) was the Firth of Forth. Skye may have been part of Pictland during its early seventh century 'zenith' (Thomas 1986, 92), whilst Orkney and even Shetland (Henderson 1967, 24) were incorporated by the early eighth century at the latest. It can therefore come as no surprise to learn that Pictland was by no means a uniform area, and our understanding of it is fractured by differing archaeological attention. But the general consensus now is that, despite their enigmatic symbol stones and putative matrilineal descent, the Picts were 'a typical northwest European barbarian society, with wide connections and parallels' (Alcock 1987, 90), just like the Anglo-Saxons. They shared much common or similar material culture and a closely inter-related political development with all their neighbours.[1]

Since the publication of the first comprehensive survey of Pictish archaeology (*The Problem of the Picts*: Wainwright 1955; reprinted 1980) our evidence for Pictish society has dramatically increased through excavation, field survey and interpretative analyses from a range of differing perspectives. Useful summaries and overviews can now be found in both academic (Friell and Watson (eds) 1984; Small (ed.) 1987) and popular format (e.g. Ritchie 1989), whilst more regional and thematic aspects have been covered in a variety of sources (see bibliography). To move from these published sources to an assessment of

---

[1] The early history of the Picts is well-rehearsed elsewhere; Smyth 1984; Anderson 1987, 31–3; Maxwell 1987. Alcock 1984, for example, suggests a division into 'Heartland' and 'Peripheral' Picts. Anderson (1987) and Smyth (1984) argue for and against matrilineal descent respectively. Smyth (1984) argues that Kings of Dalriada and Strathclyde possibly even had overlordship of Pictland at times.

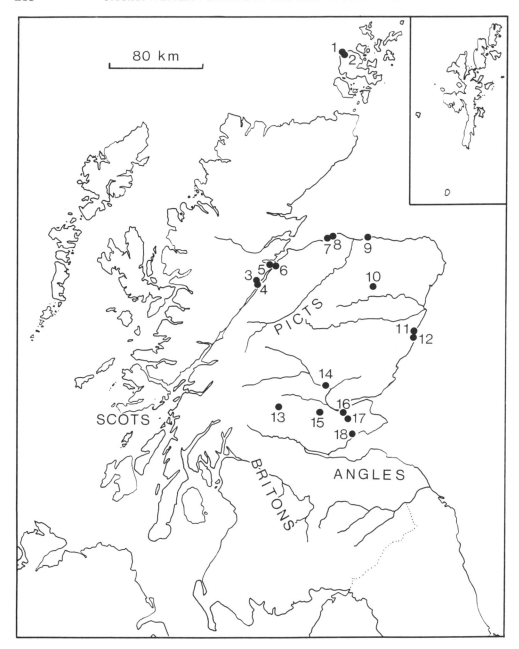

Figure 36. The location of Pictland and sites mentioned in the text: 1. Brough of Bursay;
2. Buckquoy; 3. Garbeg; 4. Urquhart; 5. Craig Phadrig; 6. Castle Hill, Inverness; 7.
Burghead; 8. Covesea; 9. Green Castle, Portknockie; 10. Rhynie; 11. Dunnicaer; 12.
Dunnottar; 13. Dundurn; 14. Inchtuthil; 15. Forteviot; 16. Clatchard Craig;
17. Collessie; 18. East Wemyss

seventh century Pictland is none the less rather difficult because there are severe limitations in our ability to recognise what is specifically seventh century or, more problematically, the activities of the fourth, fifth and sixth centuries from which it emerged.[2] Documentary references to the fourth to sixth centuries are few and little excavated material has yet been demonstrated to be of this date, a problem which in part relates to, and is exacerbated by, the relative absence of chronologically specific artifacts which belong to this period of time. But, in compensation, we can infer much of the processes of change which may have taken place through the more prevalent and readily recognisable activities of the eighth and ninth centuries.

The seventh century is part of the so-called Early Historic (EH) period (approximately late sixth to ninth centuries A.D.) and inevitably we must turn to the historical sources for any evidence of a general political background against which the archaeological sources might be reviewed and for evidence of peculiarly seventh century events which it is unlikely could be recognised on archaeological grounds alone (for critical use of such sources, see Barrett 1981 and Driscoll 1988b). It is probable that Pictish texts were never plentiful (Hughes 1970; 1980) and unfortunately the only extant native source is the so-called Pictish king-list. But references to the activities of Pictish kings and nobles are to be found in Irish sources which draw on Dalriadic material (between about 670 and 740 contemporary annals were probably compiled at Iona: Anderson 1987, 9). From these we have references both to specific sites (see below) and, more importantly, to a sequence of events which suggest that from the seventh century, if not earlier, this area of modern Scotland experienced an increasing centralisation of power which ultimately led to the formation of Pictland.[3]

The king-list suggests that stable political entities had emerged perhaps as early as the middle of the sixth century (Anderson 1980, 139–45) and by the end of the seventh century a Pictish political entity was certainly recognised by neighbouring countries (Smyth 1984, 133–4; Anderson 1987, 8). Writing in the eighth century, Bede makes a distinction between southern and northern Picts and Anderson (1987, 10) suggests that at this point we are seeing two provinces competing for a single Pictish overlordship, which was not hereditary.

---

2 See Garwood 1989 for an attempt to explain fifth and sixth century socio-political transformations in the Celtic world. He suggests that because many of the power relations elemental to social and political life were constituted *outside* the imperial domain, Celtic society reformed itself quickly and successfully after the Roman withdrawal from Britain. See also Smyth 1984.

3 Adomnan, writing at the end of the sixth century, records a tradition that the king of the Orcades (Orkney) was a *subregulus* of King Bridei, based at or near Inverness, who seems to have been the only Pictish 'overking' at the time (Henderson 1975, 8). Many of the groups probably have a particularly long history, for instance the fourth century Verturiones have been associated with the EH kingdom of Fortriu, centred on Strathearn).

Certainly the southern province was dominant by the late seventh century and both areas were subsumed into a single kingdom by the late eighth century (Davies 1984, 70).

Pictland has no parallel for the seventh century Dalriadic civil survey (the *Senchus Fer n'Alban*; Bannerman 1974) with its account of army and navy musters, but as in contemporary Ireland and Anglo-Saxon England (Charles-Edwards 1972; Wormald 1986, 167) the Picts may have been collecting tribute. By the eighth century there may have been a Pictish treasury (Anderson and Anderson 1961, 402–3) and there were *exactores* (Anderson 1973, 178). The role of *exactor* may have been similar if not identical to the *mormaer* of later times, a territorial magnate who acted as the king's deputy in an area and had the duty of collecting royal revenues and adminstering a district (Jackson 1972, 102–110). It can be suggested that the necessary prerequisites for the functioning of a proto-state (see Driscoll 1988a, 218–22) were therefore in place, modelled on 'relations of clientship which were, in turn, the outgrowth of kin dominated political structures' (Driscoll 1991, 109).

It is against this historical evidence for the growing concentration of ultimate power that the archaeological evidence for the development of seventh century Pictland has to be set.

Recognising the Seventh Century

The written sources conveniently also allude to military activities at sites which can often be identified. Upon this basis Alcock (1981) initiated a project of identifying those EH sites, largely hill-top fortifications, whose dates and identification could be inferred from the sources, of which seven are in Pictland; three of these (Dundurn, Dunnottar and Urquhart), after a successful campaign of trial trenching, can now be confirmed to have been occupied in the seventh century. Some non-fortified sites mentioned in the documentary sources have also been associated with recognisable field remains or crop-marks, such as the royal site at Forteviot.

The archaeological dating of these sites is dependent on absolute dating techniques, commonly radiocarbon (C-14) (with all its attendant problems in this period) and thermoluminescence dating, or relative dating of artifacts (Alcock 1981; Alcock, Alcock and Foster 1986; Foster, forthcoming). In the absence of a coin-using economy, precisely datable artifacts are few. It is commonly agreed that the main phase of importation of E-ware pottery was the seventh century but it is unfortunately still rare in Pictland. Some metalwork, specifically certain types of penannular brooch, stick pin and more unusual items such as hanging bowls or so-called Pictish chains have a currency in this period, although these too are beset with dating problems (Youngs (ed.) 1989, 20–23). Certain other artefacts such as bone pins and combs may also belong to this period (Stevenson 1955a; Foster 1990). Pictish Class I stones may be

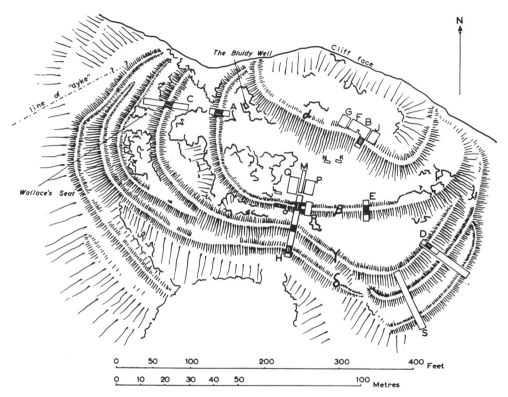

Figure 37. Plan of Clatchard Craig

seventh century (see below) and other objects decorated with Pictish symbols may also date to this period, but they are not themselves independently dated. Otherwise it is possible to suggest that some sites had a seventh century history on the basis of their distinctive morphology.

The Settlement Evidence

A wide range of settlement types are thought to be EH in date (Alcock 1984), although few have produced evidence for seventh century activity. *Fortified hill-tops*, characterised by the hierarchical organisation of space (Alcock, Alcock and Driscoll 1989), are the best known site-type, encompassing a range of sites previously referred to as nuclear forts (Stevenson 1949) or multi-phase citadels (Feachem 1955). They are peculiar to the north of Britain but have not yet been recognised N of Inverness. Many were thought to be Iron Age in date until investigated; some may have involved rebuilding earlier forts, but other excavated examples such as Dundurn (Alcock, Alcock and Driscoll 1989),

Clatchard Craig (Fig. 37; Close-Brooks 1986) and Urquhart (Alcock and Alcock forthcoming) have produced C-14 dates and artefactual evidence, commonly in the form of debris from fine metalworking, to suggest that they were built and occupied in the seventh century, if not slightly earlier. Some ramparts were timber-laced or used nails in their construction, and some of these are now vitrified as a result of subsequent burning (not in itself a chronological indicator: Sanderson et al 1985; 1988). On the basis of morphology, attempts have been made to identify other characteristic EH fort types, but with little success (Driscoll 1987). Alcock (in litt.) also considers the trivallate fort at Burghead in Morayshire (Fig. 38) with its timber-laced ramparts to be hierarchical because of its upper and lower enclosures. Almost certainly a Pictish naval base (Small 1969; Edwards and Ralston 1978; Ritchie 1989, 12–15), C-14 dates suggest that it was built between the fourth and sixth centuries A.D. with intermittent or continued activity for at least five centuries thereafter. The large assemblage of slabs incised with bulls may be seventh century in date, marking a possible refurbishment of the fort (Ritchie 1989, 14).

Some *coastal promontories* may be EH (Lamb 1973; 1980), for example Green Castle, Portknockie (Edwards and Ralston 1978; Ralston 1987) which enclosed a possible sub-rectangular building. Such sites offered some shelter for boats in their immediate vicinity. One coastal promontory, *Dun Fother* (to be associated with either Dunnottar Castle or Bowduns to the north: Alcock and Alcock forthcoming), mentioned twice in connection with late seventh century sieges, is particularly significant because of the proximity of the stack site Dunnicaer, which has produced a number of Class I symbol stones, and which may therefore have been an associated cult-focus.

Non-hierarchical single and multivallate forts which have been demonstrated to be EH in date are few. Forts such as Craig Phadrig (*D and E* 1972, 23) or Inchtuthil (RCAHMS forthcoming) are post-Roman in date. It is conceivable that the palisaded phase at Inchtuthil is also EH in date, and other small *palisaded sites* may be this late (Driscoll 1987, 221).

The royal or high status of many of these fortified sites, as suggested by the historical references, is supported by the type of artefactual assemblages which are recovered, often including evidence for high class metalworking, despite very small archaeological investigations. Their development coincides with the emergence of an increasingly powerful network of royalty and an associated, if not related, aristocratic class, which can be refered to as either nobles or potentates (Alcock 1987; Alcock 1988). For example, Alcock and Alcock (forthcoming) suggest that the site of king Bridei's *munitio*, visited by Saint Columba in the late sixth century, was on Castle Hill, Inverness, whilst the fort at Urquhart was an *urbs regis* related to this main centre, a noble estate which would have been visited by the king and court on their circuit (along Northumbrian lines) around their lands, physically reinforcing the relationships of control and clientship as they took hospitality and received tribute from their nobles and followers. On the basis of present evidence it also appears that

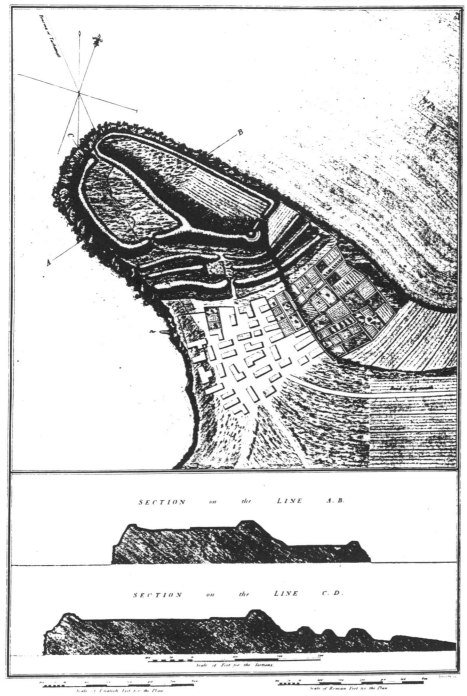

Figure 38. Plan of Burghead

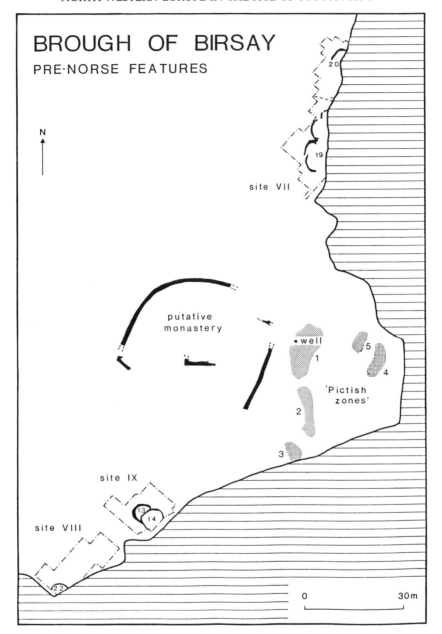

Figure 39. Plan of pre-Norse features at the Brough of Birsay. The features marked 'putative monastery' are likely to be Norse in date

most jewellery-making in EH Pictland is confined to these strongholds, perhaps because, as the result of the concentration of political power, social prestige and economic resources in the hands of a few, the powerful were able to concentrate high status activities under their immediate control (Alcock 1987,

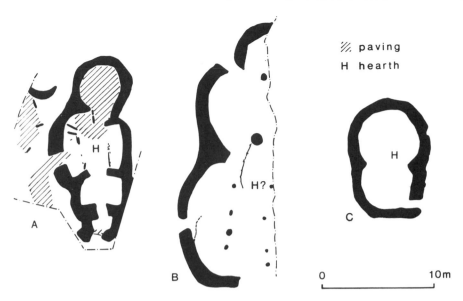

%. paving

H hearth

A

B

H

C

0   10m

Figure 40. Plans of polyventral structures at (A) Buckquoy; (B) Brough of Birsay; and (C) Red Craig

85). It can be suggested that this enabled them to emphasise their status in terms of personal appearance and to make the frequent gifts to their followers which were necessary to establish and maintain their relationships of power over increasingly long distances.

But not all royal or high status sites were necessarily enclosed, although it is likely that forts preceded *unenclosed high status sites* (Alcock 1987, 82). It has recently been suggested that the Brough of Birsay in Orkney (Fig. 39), situated on a tidal island, was the establishment of a territorial magnate (rather than a monastery) on the basis of the 'proto-urban' nature of its settlement (Hunter 1986), wealth of its metalworking debris (Curle 1982) and subsequent Norse importance. Likewise the royal palace site at Forteviot, known from documentary sources and identified from cropmarks (Driscoll 1991, pl. 5.4), which may have seventh or eighth century origins, was totally unenclosed (Alcock and Alcock forthcoming).

In the northern part of Pictland we see the *reuse of broch sites* (built in the Middle Iron Age, from about 400 B.C.–A.D.400) as the locus of seventh century and later open settlement (Foster 1989b; 1989c; 1990), some of which is associated with distinctive settlement forms described as 'polyventral', found also on non-broch sites (Fig. 40) such as Buckquoy (Ritchie 1977). *Farm or settlement mounds* found in the northern isles, sometimes with a cellular type of settlement, may also have their origins in the seventh century (Davidson et al. 1983, 52; Hunter 1990, 192).

Cave sites such as Covesea and East Weemys are known to have attracted

Figure 41. Distribution of presumed restangular timber buildings discovered by aerial reconnaissance

Pictish attention, on the basis of the carvings which they left there, although these may pre-date the seventh century (Shepherd 1983).

Round-houses are recognised all over the eastern lowlands of Pictland, particularly Tayside and Angus where they are generally found in clusters, sometimes with sunken floors (Driscoll 1991, pl. 5.3), often in conjunction with souterrains (e.g. Maxwell 1987, fig. 6). Assumed to date to the first millennium A.D. (and earlier: Maxwell 1987, 35–6; RCAHMS 1990; forthcoming), none of the souterrains have yet been found to date later than about the second or third century A.D. (Wainwright 1963; Watkins 1980a; 1980b; 1984; but see also Hingley forthcoming) although the open settlement associated with them may

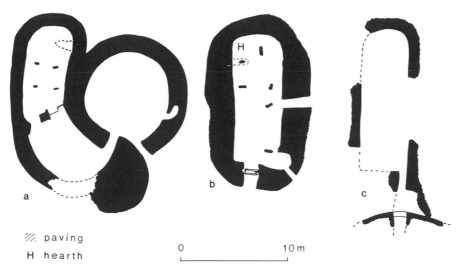

%%. paving

H hearth

0   10m

Figure 42. Plans of subrectangular buildings in northern Pictland at
(A) Langwell; (B) Wag of Forse; and (C) Burroughston

have a longer history. On the basis of dating elsewhere in Scotland and Ireland
some *crannogs* (Morrison 1985, Fig. 1.3) too might be expected to be Pictish, but
no crannogs in Pictland have yet been dated to this period. Seventh century
watermills have been found in Ireland (Baillie 1980) but await discovery in
Pictland.

Rectangular timber halls are an infrequent feature of the cropmark record, and
are confined largely to the 'Pictish heartland' (Fig. 41). Enclosed, but usually
occurring singly, some may be EH in date (Maxwell 1987). In the uplands of
Tayside the RCAHMS (1990; Stevenson 1991) has identified a distinctive, new
sub-rectangular house-type, the so-called 'Pitcarmick house' which may be
EH, although no example has yet been excavated. The subrectangular *wags* of
Caithness (Curle 1941; 1946; 1948) and similar buildings identified in Orkney
(Smith 1990) may in part also date to this period (Fig. 42).

Taking an overview of this range of settlement evidence there are some
suggestions that at around this period there was a shift in the nature and
distribution of settlement away from Iron Age settlement patterns (Alcock
1983; Shepherd 1983). Furthermore, it has long been recognised that the settle-
ment-record may contain intimations of the increasing centralisation of power
(Cottam and Small 1974; Watkins 1984, 78). More recently two studies, which
are in many respects complementary, have examined the settlement evidence
for the development of the Pictish state in areas of the so-called Pictish 'heartland' (Strathearn: Driscoll 1987; 1991) and 'periphery' (Orkney and Caithness:
Foster 1989a; 1989b; Barrett and Foster 1991). Both studies place equal emphasis on the evidence for social and economic arrangements which is to be
revealed in the patterns of landholding and agricultural exploitation. Evidence

for these derive from the archaeological evidence, place-names, literary sources and through the examination of contemporary evidence elsewhere in the British Isles, but the northernmost study, with its unrivalled settlement evidence, places a heavy emphasis on analysis of architecture and the use of social space. For the east of Scotland, Driscoll argues that as society grew more state-like, the importance of kin-based social relations diminished and relations of clientship became more important, thus extending both geographically and socially the limits within which relations of authority can operate. On the basis of profound changes in the architecture of Orkney and Caithness through the Iron Age to the EH (or Late Iron Age) period, it is suggested that there was a shift from a ranked society where local authority was locally based to more remote sources of central authority in the seventh, but more particuarly eighth century, reflecting precisely those changes identified in Strathearn, the ultimate source of this central authority. These changes can be related to changing agricultural practice, land tenure and, probably most significantly, the introduction of Christianity (Barrett and Foster 1991; see below). Local units became subsumed within new adminstrative arrangements as the southern leaders assumed more power (not without opposition, to judge from the historical accounts: cf. Ralston and Inglis 1984, 14) and regions were managed at the local level by a representative of the overall king (see above). Place-name evidence is particularly helpful because pett-names, now found largely in the so-called Pictish heartland and practically the only place-name element which can be exclusively limited to the Picts (Nicolaisen 1976) can be interpreted to suggest that the economy was based on a system of estates which formed the basis for large adminstrative units known as thanages (Barrow 1973; Jackson 1972; Bannerman 1974; Whittington 1975; Driscoll 1991). A similar arrangement may also have existed in Orkney where the Norse place-names suggest an adminstrative system quite unlike the divisions in their homeland, and which may therefore relate to a native arrangement which they took over. Driscoll (1991) thoroughly explores the archaeological and other place-name evidence for estates and thanages in Strathearn. It is suggested that the development of the Pictish kingdom is dependent on the maintenance and extension of these units, which were the basis for adminstration and the local sources of authority.

Other aspects of the archaeological record can be brought forward to support this general model, and it is to these that we now turn.

Symbol Stones, Burial and the Nature of Christianity

The Picts are best known for their symbol stones, but it is only the Class I stones (unshaped blocks of stone carved only with symbols; Fig. 43; plates 6–7) which are relevant here, because they are generally believed to have had a currency within the seventh century, although scholars dispute whether they

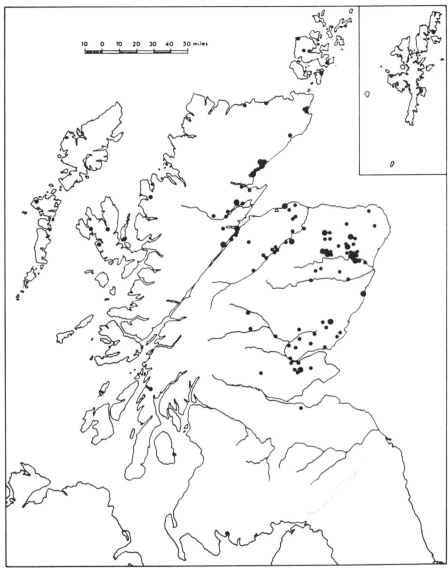

Distribution of stones incised with Pictish symbols

• Single incised stones
● Two or more stones

Figure 43. Distribution of Class I stones

originate in the fifth or late seventh century. An unusual example from Orkney has recently been associated with a sixth century C-14 date (Hunter 1990, 185–7, ill. 10.8). The carvings are diverse, ranging from abstract designs and naturalistic animal-symbols to unique depictions of what may be contemporary Picts; note the contrasting depictions of splendidly-robed warriors on the

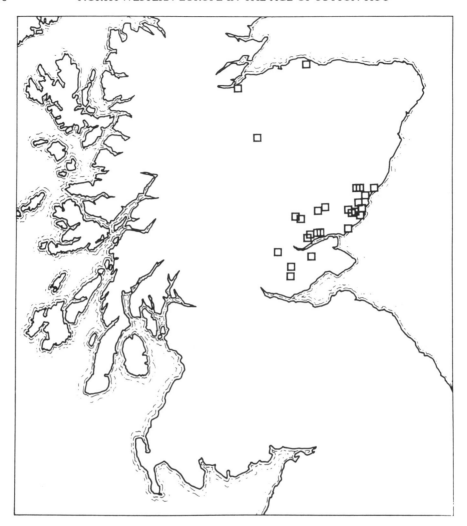

Figure 44. Distribution of square-barrow cemeteries discovered by aerial reconnaissance

stone from the Brough of Birsay, which Ritchie (1989, 52, 54) suggests may be late seventh century, and the single warrior from Collessie, Fife, which may be juxtaposed with a Pictish symbol (Plate 7; *D and E* 1989, 17). Class I stones occur singly, or in quite large assemblages. Whatever their meaning, the unity of much of their design (if not execution) suggests that they belong to a period when the Picts had attained political and in some measure cultural unity (Henderson 1975). In the absence of literacy it is feasible that the Picts used these symbol stones for their authoritative statements, and Driscoll (1988 a and b) sees a connection between the development of a royal administration and aristocracy with the invention and control of a standardized symbolic system. Some Class I stones seem to have been burial markers (see below), possibly erected by heirs who needed to emphasise their right to inheritance, hence acting as a form of property charter.[4]

The evidence for Pictish burial has been summarised elsewhere (Ashmore 1980; Close-Brooks 1984) and takes a variety of forms. Simple inhumations are known (Barclay 1983, 145–50), but the long cist, difficult to date in the absence of gravegoods, is the most typical and widepread type of EH burial, sometimes occurring in cemeteries (e.g. Henshall 1956). A recent development is the recognition that some long cists found under low stone circular or square kerbed barrows in the north of Scotland (Close-Brooks 1984, fig. 5.10) are also EH in date. A combination of C-14 dates, stratigraphy and analogy would suggest that they date between the fourth and eighth centuries A.D. (e.g. Close-Brooks 1980, 4; Morris 1989). Square platform graves (both cairns and barrows) also occur in cemeteries, sometimes sharing a common side and often found in association with circular ditches whether as cropmarks (Fig. 44; Close-Brooks 1984, fig. 5.2; RCAHMS forthcoming) or, more rarely, as upstanding field remains (Stevenson 1984; *D and E* 1989, 30). One particularly distinctive feature is that the corners of the ditches surrounding the square barrows may be interrupted. At Garbeg (Fig. 45) the barrows are arranged into at least three groups, arranged in roughly linear settings, which it has been suggested 'may be explained either chronologically or in social terms, with the linear setting possibly representing kinship groups' (Stevenson 1984, 147), a rare example of a type of evidence for social organisation not frequently available to students of the Picts. It yet remains to be investigated whether the people buried under the cairns and barrows were any more important than those simply buried in a long cist.

Class I stones have been found in association (although not necessarily primary) with a number of cairns and barrows (e.g. Wedderburn 1984; Gourlay 1984) and it can be suggested that this association contributes to 'positive evidence' of a non-literate society in the seventh century in which Christianity had little, if any, influence (Hughes 1970). In general there is little evidence that the early Columban church had any influence on Pictland (Hughes 1970; Thomas 1986; *contra* Ritchie 1989, 29), such evidence largely consisting of a

---

4   A catalogue of Pictish stones has been produced by RCAHMS (1985). Literature on the stones and the meaning of the symbols is diverse (Allen and Anderson 1903; Stevenson 1955b; Thomas 1963; Close-Brooks and Stevenson 1982; Ralston and Inglis 1984, 28–33; Jackson 1984; Inglis 1987; Driscoll 1988a; 1988b; E.A. Alcock 1989; Henderson 1990). A useful, well-illustrated popular survey has recently been published (Ritchie 1989). Whilst both the animal and abstract symbol designs belong sylistically with Irish and English metalwork, manuscript decoration and sculpture of the seventh and eighth centuries, it is uncertain which direction this influence went (Stevenson 1955b; Henderson 1967; G Henderson 1972). Ogam inscriptions are found on a small number of artifacts and symbol stones. Jackson (1955) dates most Pictish ogam to the eighth and ninth centuries, but some may be seventh century or earlier (Padel 1972; Ritchie 1987, 64).

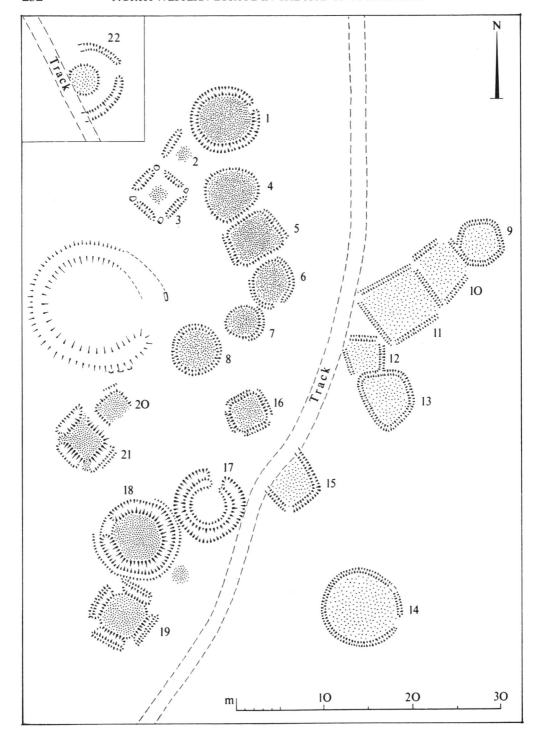

Figure 45. Plan of cemetery at Garbeg, Highland Region

number of bells (Bourke 1983), simple cross-incised slabs (Henderson 1987), and dedications to early saints, none of which are usually reliable or precise enough indicators for early foundations. Yet Adomnan does state that there were monasteries in Pictland by the seventh century (Hughes 1970, 12) and the inference must be that within about 50 years of Columba's death his followers may have been organising an infant church centred on the Moray Firth (Smyth 1984, 112). The role of other missionaries whose fame has been swallowed up by the Columban mission should not be forgotten (Ralston and Inglis 1984, 20). *Egles* place-names may also indicate early foundations, although not necesarily of Columban origin (Barrow 1983). So whilst there were obviously some Christians and Christian communities in seventh century Pictland (Henderson 1972, 167; Cowan and Easson 1976; Anderson 1980, 92–6) the first evidence that the church was exerting any influence on society comes with the activities of king Nechtan in the early eighth century when the Roman church, with its pastoral organisation, usurped the monastic-based Columban ecclesiastic order (cf. Lamb, forthcoming a and b). Prior to this the aristocracy did not give the church its full support.

This distinction between the seventh and eighth century nature of the church in Pictland is one which cannot be emphasised enough, because the church had a monopoly on the teaching and probably much of the production of the written word, thus virtually controlling an administrative tool which was essential to the aspiring secular authorities, (some of whom they had instructed in these skills) if they were to control far-flung areas. The church, state and secular nobility were therefore mutually dependent (a relationship demonstrated by the subjects of the Class II stones: Christian iconography juxtaposed with images of warriors and hunting secular patrons). One way in which the kings could extend their authority to peripheral areas was through granting land there to the Roman church, as Lamb (forthcoming) suggests was the case in Orkney and Shetland, in return for which clerics acted effectively as secular lords, their pastoral system being a means of establising an ideology which was pro-state (Barrett and Foster 1991). Such means were not available to the aristocracy of seventh century Pictland, and it was therefore not until the eighth century at the earliest that a Pictish proto-state could become fully established and operational. The process by which kings extended their authority must also have involved their assuming the rights over land which was not theirs, because this is the only means by which they could physically extend their territories, by granting it to both ecclesiastical and secular followers.

Seventh-Century Pictland

At the time of Sutton Hoo Pictland was not a state in the sense that we would undertand it, although ultimate authority may have rested at times in only one set of hands. But at the more local level there were aristocrats or potentates, living in fortified places, who had control over a wide-range of resources and people, but who may have been the agents of this higher authority. These potentates expressed their authority in a similar fashion to barbarian kings throughout northwestern Europe, through exhibiting a war-like lifestyle (Alcock, this volume), lavish self-adornment and through the regular giving of gifts, many of which share the same cultural repertoire as those from neighbouring kingdoms. Like the Anglo-Saxons, some seventh century Picts may have lived in timber halls and a number of them were buried under barrows or cairns. As the seventh century progressed an increasing number of Picts may have become Christian; certainly with the introduction of the Roman church in about A.D.715 the interests of the church and state were fully mutually dependent, and the precocious Pictish state can be said to have come into being. The final stages of this progression may have been revolutionary in the sense of the force and potential of the new technology – literacy – but there is every suggestion, both archaeological and historical, that the origins of the Pictish state, particularly the basis for its territorial divisions, can be found in the seventh century and earlier.

ACKNOWLEDGEMENTS

I must thank Professor Martin Carver for asking me to compile this summary of published evidence for seventh-century Pictland. Professor Leslie Alcock and Drs David Breeze, Richard Hingley and Lesley Macinnes kindly provided helpful and observant criticism of an earlier draft of this paper. Mr T.E. Gray was good enough to allow me to reproduce two of his photographs of Pictish stones, which give but a taste of this and other delights to be found in the National Monuments Record of Scotland. Dr Stephen Driscoll provided information about the work of the Scottish Field School.

16

Frankish Hegemony in England

IAN WOOD

At some point in the early 550s, a Merovingian king sent an embassy to Constantinople, asserting his authority over *Brittia* by which he seems to have meant some part of southern England. His claim depended on the settlement in his own kingdom of Angloi, who had previously been living in *Brittia* (Procopius, *Wars*, VIII, xx, 8–10). The episode is well-known, although not easily interpreted. It provides the clearest evidence for Merovingian claims to hegemony over parts of Britain, but it is not the only evidence. In the *Epistulae Austrasiacae* (20) King Theudebert I informs the emperor Justinian of this lordship over numerous dependent peoples, including the Eucii, who are probably the Jutes possibly of Kent or the Isle of Wight. The poet Venantius Fortunatus talks of Chilperic I's power over a whole host of peoples, including the Saxons, who are as likely to be insular as continental Saxons (*Carmina*, IX, 1, 11. 73–6). Finally, Gregory the Great assumed that Theuderic II and Theudebert II were in some way superior to Æthelbehrt of Kent (*Register*, VI 49). These claims and assumptions demonstrate beyond doubt that the Merovingians and some others on the continent, including Pope Gregory, thought that Anglian and Saxon groups in England were subordinate to the Franks. This does not mean that everyone agreed with them; merely that it was one way of interpreting the political structures on either side of the Channel in the sixth century (Wood 1983, 12–19).

For these claims neither the Franks nor anyone else evolved a specific vocabulary. In so far as notions of status and hegemony amongst the sub-Roman kingdoms were expressed in any specific terms, the terms were borrowed from the later Empire. Recognition from Constantinople had concerned the kings of the Visigoths, the Ostrogoths, the Franks and the Burgundians. They had vied for such offices as that of *magister militum*, which turned them into imperial agents in the West, and thus conferred status second only to that of the emperor, and superior to that of any other barbarian ruler. Equally, the emperor could grant the consulship, as a sign of special approval (McCormick, 1986, 266, 268, 335–7). Subsequently, kings both of the Visigoths and of the Lombards used the name Flavius, redolent with empire, to give themselves added, imperial dignity, which they further emphasised with regalia, thrones, and sometimes notable coin-issues (Paul the Deacon, III 16; Wolfram 1967, 56–76).

Also important was the avoidance of royal terminology in referring to contemporary rulers of lesser stature. The Merovingians did not use the term *rex* to described the leaders of such peripheral peoples as the Bretons, Frisians, continental Saxons, Thuringians, Alamans and Bavarians, and yet at various moments the rulers of these peoples did see themselves as kings. In the seventh and eighth centuries two figures, who are regarded as *reges* in non-Merovingian sources, Aldgisl and Radbod, emerged in Frisia, which may not have been independent previously (Stephanus, *Vita Wilfridi*, 26; Alcuin, *Vita Willibrordi*, 5, 9–11). In Thuringia, certainly part of the Merovingian kingdom, Radulf, a Frankish nobleman claimed to be king in the late 630s or shortly thereafter (Fredegar, IV 87). Even in Aquitaine, which had also been subject to the Franks since the early sixth century, one official, Lupus, made a bid for royal status after 657 (*Miracula Martialis*, 3). Further, some noblemen, in particular the Alaman *dux* Lantfred, and the Agilolfing rulers of Bavaria, issued law-codes, a practice usually thought of as a royal preserve (Wormald 1977, 108–9). These men must have thought of themselves as kings, or their equals. To the Merovingians they were rebellious *duces*. In eighth-century England, Offa's reign provides evidence of the same difficulties in perceiving power and status, and doubtless the problem was not new there (Stenton 1971, 206–7). The issue was a general one in the early Middle Ages, and is one aspect of the exceedingly slow emergence of a new, non-Roman, political order.

In the light of such observations the use of the word 'hegemony', to describe power structures in the early Middle Ages, can be no more than the exploitation of a single concept to cover a variety of untidy relationships, each of which might be seen in a number of ways. It is a shorthand which needs to be illustrated in concrete form; the two most obvious areas of illustration being tribute and marriage. Baptismal relationships could also be important, but they are little evidenced in the Merovingian record (Angenendt 1986, 755–78).

Tribute was usually the outcome of war. It could be an immediate pay-off after a single campaign, when it scarcely said anything about the relative status of the participants. It could be a much longer-term arrangement, whose eventual failure would in itself be significant. Thus, at the end of Clovis's war against the Burgundians Gundobad agreed to make an annual payment; he may also have offered military support against Clovis's enemies. The payment soon lapsed, and shortly after Clovis's death Gundobad was using the title of *magister militum* (Gregory of Tours, II 32–3; Avitus of Vienne, epp. 93–4). A hegemony established in 500 was well and truly over by 516. The continental Saxons provide more sustained evidence. The annual payment to which they agreed after a series of campaigns in the 550s was 500 cows (Gregory of Tours, IV 14; Fredegar, IV 74). At one stage they arranged for this to be exchanged for the obligation of defending the Frankish frontier. In addition they were among 'the peoples east of the Rhine' who were frequently called upon by the kings of the easternmost Merovingian kingdom of Metz or Austrasia in the Frankish civil wars. When they could they opted out of any or all of these obligations, and had to be drawn back into service by war (Wood 1983, 11–12).

Mightier than the Saxons were the Lombards, who offered an annual tribute of 12,000 solidi, as a result of their failures against the Franks in the 580s. They may even have ceded the towns of Susa and Aosta as well (Fredegar, IV 45). Relations with the Lombards, however, were further complicated by marriage. One Lombard queen, Chlodoswintha, wife of Alboin, had been a Merovingian princess (Gregory of Tours, IV 3). More important was the marriage of Theudelinda to Agilulf. Theudelinda was the daughter of Garivald, *dux* of Bavaria. She was to have been married to Childebert II, but he refused the match and instead she married the Lombard king Agilulf (Fredegar, IV 34; Paul the Deacon, III 30, 35). Nevertheless representatives of the Merovingian Theudebert II were present when her son, Adaloald, was elevated to the kingship during his father's lifetime (Paul the Deacon, IV 30). The Merovingians were also thought to have kept a sharp eye on Adaloald's sister, Gundeperga, insisting later on her reinstatement as queen (Fredegar, IV 51, 70–1). In the late sixth and early seventh centuries, therefore, the Lombards were tributary to the Franks, who also involved themselves in the Lombard royal succession.

The evidence for the exercise of Frankish power at the Lombard court is a clear reminder that Merovingian dominance could extend over very powerful peoples. At times it could even be a factor in Visigothic Spain although only in particular circumstances. Between Franks and Visigoths royal marriages took place on an equal footing, and the repudiation of wives could lead to war. Treasure, however, was paid on one occasion, when the Visigothic king Sisenand, who had been helped to the throne by Dagobert I, promised to give his benefactor a missorium which had once been the gift of the Roman general Aëtius to king Thorismund. His followers refused to let Sisenand hand over the salver, which had too many national and imperial connotations, and redeemed it with 200,000 gold solidi (Fredegar, IV 73). This was a one-off payment, and says little about long-term relationships between the Franks and the Visigoths. Nevertheless it is a reminder of the complicated shifts of status between even the greatest of the barbarian kingdoms.

The period in which Merovingian hegemony was most constant stretched from the late sixth through to the mid seventh century, and this despite rivalry between individual kings of the Franks. Thus, Chilperic I's hegemony, lauded by Venantius Fortunatus, was contemporary with the rule of Sigibert I, who exercised power over the peoples east of the Rhine. The elevation of Adaloald to the Lombard kingship in the presence of Frankish ambassadors in c.604 should be seen as reflecting only on Theudebert II, and not his two contemporary Merovingian kings. The event might be juxtaposed with his brother Theuderic II's search for a marriage alliance with the Visigoths about three years later (Fredegar, IV 30). The policies of these two brothers should be further contrasted with the confinement of their cousin Chlothar II to a kingdom limited to twelve cantons between the Seine and the sea in the years after 600 (Fredegar, IV 20). It is worth remembering that rivalry between Merovingian brothers and cousins could in itself be a spur to the creation of overlordships outside Francia. Looked at from this point of view hegemony was not just a matter of relations between the Franks and their neighbours, but also of competition for status within the Merovingian kingdom.

Civil war and accident brought the power first of Theudebert II and then of his brother to a sudden end, leaving Chlothar with the opportunity to create a more substantial hegemony than that of either, and one which was, arguably, only eclipsed by that of his son Dagobert I. Such reversals of fortune are a useful reminder of the transitory nature of Merovingian overlordship, and also of the difficulties of presenting any generalised picture of it. It is against such a fluid set of structures and concepts of power that the known relations between England and the continent need to be considered.

Observations on Merovingian power in Italy and east of the Rhine can be made in the light of a number of episodes which illustrate both the fullest extent of that power and also its fragile nature, allowing something of a nuanced picture, however great the gaps. When considering Merovingian influence in England, by contrast, the material is so fragmentary as to allow no insight into what was the full spectrum and what was the norm of relations with Francia. Unfortunately, no Merovingian source thought of the insular Angles or Saxons as being of more than passing interest, and there was no historian writing in sixth- or seventh-century Anglo-Saxon England.

Despite these caveats it is worth considering yet again the well-known anecdotes relating to the Franks and England in the light of what is known of Merovingian hegemony in general. First Procopius's account of the embassy claiming overlordship over the Angles must be read alongside Theudebert I's letter of a few years previous claiming a whole host of title indicating lordship over numerous peoples in Western Europe (Procopius, *Wars*, VIII, xx, 8–10; *Epistolae Austrasiacae* 20). Theudebert's assertion of hegemony was clearly made in part as a challenge to the emperor, and it is likely that the subsequent claim of Merovingian lordship over the Angles by one of Theudebert's uncles had similar implications. Nevertheless both sets of claims must also have had relevance to the competition for status between Merovingian kings: Theudebert I, Childebert I, Chlothar I were rivals.

Thus far we are dealing with high diplomacy, in which the realities of power in England may be of little relevance. Nevertheless, the curious tale of reverse migration from England to the continent, and the assertion that this gave the Merovingians their authority in the island suggests that something more was involved (Procopius, *Wars*, VIII, xx, 8–10). What this entailed can only be a matter of guesswork, but it is worth remembering that the Merovingians had long been interested in cross-Channel affairs, as can be seen in the clause of the *Pactus Legis Salicae* (39, 2) legislating for the return of slaves taken across the sea. The law may have some relation with fifth-century imperial legislation

(*Nov. Val.* 33, 1; compare also *Cod. Theod.* V, 6, 3). It is also, in some ways, a matter of the biter bit, for in the third and fourth centuries it had been the Franks who had posed the chief threat in the Channel, and only gradually, from the late fourth century onwards, did the Saxons emerge as a group of independent raiders (Wood 1990a, 94–5). Nor should Frankish sea-power be a matter of surprise; the Merovingians, after all, claimed descent from a sea-monster (Fredegar, III 9). In any event, the *Pactus* shows the Merovingians making arrangements for the enforcement of their power in courts outside Francia, and probably in England.

A second incident illustrative of Merovingian relations with England is the marriage of Bertha and Æthelbehrt (Wood 1983, 15–16). The fate of Meroving-ian princesses was a varied one. A very few married into the royal families of the Ostrogoths, Visigoths and Lombards. Such marriages were high level al-liances, involving the daughters of living kings. Bertha is unlikely to fit into this category. Chronologically, it is almost impossible that her father could have been alive at the time of her marriage. She is best compared with a host of secondary Merovingian women who were usually placed in nunneries, or with cast off brides who were married to such men as Garivald, *dux* of Bavaria. Alternatively, she might be compared with Emma, the wife of Eadbald, Æthelberht's son, who was the daughter, not of a Merovingian king, but of the *major domus*, Erchinoald (Werner 1985, 42). Neither Bertha nor Emma seem to have been ladies of the greatest importance in Frankish circles. In their cases, therefore, we are not dealing with marriage alliances between dynasties of equal status. If there were any other Frankish women who married into royal families of the English, as the use of Merovingian names, like Sigberct, in some Anglo-Saxon royal dynasties suggest, they too are likely to have fitted into this category (Wood 1991, 6–11).

The Merovingians kept their eye on the offspring of foreign liaisons. Athangild, the son of Ingund, and thus the grandson of Sigibert I and Brunhild, was at the centre of much diplomacy between the Franks, the Visi-goths and Byzantium (*Epistulae Austrasiacae*, 27–8, 43–5; Goubert 1956, 110–17, 139–41). Elsewhere the Merovingians took the fate of their relatives as an excuse to intervene in the politics of other kingdoms, as the histories of Theudelinda, Gundeperga and Adaloald in Lombard Italy demonstrate. The protection given by Dagobert to Bertha's daughter, Ethelberga, and her child-ren by Edwin can thus be paralleled with the concern shown to others who were of Merovingian blood (Bede, II 20). The exile of Sigberct of East Anglia, who also found a haven in Francia, may be another indication, to set alongside his name, that he was related to the Frankish royal family (Bede, II 15).

Known marriages between Franks and English fall into two clear groups; marriages where the male in the partnership was Anglo-Saxon, and those where he was Frankish. Thus there is Bertha and Æthelbald and Emma and Eadbald on the one hand, and Balthild and Clovis II, and perhaps Nanthild and Dagobert I on the other. The Merovingians themselves sometimes married princesses of neighbouring dynasties for reasons of dignity and diplomacy. There were also marriages with women of the Frankish aristocracy, but of these little is known. In addition the Merovingians took slaves as wives, indicating their own superiority to matters of social class. Whatever the original status of the Saxons Balthild and Nanthild before they were enslaved, they belong to the category of queens raised from nowhere (Wood 1983, 17). Their marriages were not the result of diplomatic links with the English: Saxon women brought no prestige to Merovingian men, but Merovingian women will have enhanced the status of Anglo-Saxon kings.

Overlapping with politics is the matter of religion. In the late sixth century the Merovingians failed to exploit the potential of religion as a means of enhancing Frankish authority. Gregory the Great had occasion to encourage Theuderic II and Theudebert II to back evangelisation of Kent (*Register*, VI 49). It appears that they had not responded to English appeals for missionary help – a point which shows that Æthelberht's acceptance of Augustine's Roman mission was in no sense an attempt to break away from Merovingian lordship. Theuderic and Theudebert had simply missed an open opportunity. Chlothar II may have done better. Justus of Rochester and Peter of Dover attended the council he summoned in Paris in 614, which dealt with matters both secular and ecclesiastical (de Clercq 1963, 282). Under Chlothar's son, Dagobert I, interest in the christianisation of England became stronger. The Burgundian Felix worked in East Anglia and the Frank Agilbert among the Gewissae (Bede, II 15, III 7, 18). Another Frank, Richarius, is also known to have been active in England (*Vita Richarii*, 7). Given the relative lack of missionary enterprises on the continent before the late sixth century this is remarkable, and suggests a deliberate policy. The recruitment of English nuns to Faremoutiers, Chelles and Les Andelys should perhaps be seen in the context of this Frankish concern to be involved in the christianisation of England (Wood 1991, 6–7).

Although this concern is nowhere attributed to Dagobert himself, it is likely to have been related to the authority achieved by him in Francia and also east of the Rhine, and to have been an aspect of the extension of Frankish hegemony during his reign. There may, however, have been another important figure in relations with England in the second quarter of the seventh century; Dagobert's relative Erchinoald, who was to become the Neustrian *maior domus*. A remarkable number of connections link Erchinoald with the kingdoms north of the Channel. The Saxon Balthild had been a slave in his household before she married Clovis II (*Vita Balthildis*, 2–3). His own daughter Emma married Eadbald, and her son Eorcenbert carried one element of his grandfather's name (Werner 1985, 42). One might wonder at the family connections of bishop Eorcenwald (i.e. Erchinoald) of London, who appears to have played a significant role in the development of the Anglo-Saxon charter, and whose foundation at Barking is markedly Frankish in character (Bede, IV 6; Bailey 1989, 103; Wormald 1984, 9–11; Wood 1990b, 14–15). In addition Erchinoald was Fursey's patron when he came to Francia, and was the first to back Foilan and Ultan. He thus had strong connections with Kent and East Anglia. Doubt-less, all these links enhanced Erchinoald's stature at court (*Vita Fursei* 9–10; *Additamentum Nivialense*).

Erchinoald's contacts cast light on relations between England and Francia at a non-royal level, in both religious and secular spheres. But they also reinforce the likelihood that Chlothar II and Dagobert I had significant influence north of the Channel. They mirror exactly the royal links with Kent forged through Bertha, and those with East Anglia which followed Sigberct's return from Francia. Such connections and the exercise of Merovingian influence through marriage, religion and law are a clue to political structures of southern England in the late sixth and early seventh centuries, and to those of Northumbria in the time of Ethelberga, Bertha's daughter. They are also a clue to the background to Mound One at Sutton Hoo and its coin collection (Wood 1991, 13–14). They belong, however, to a relatively shortlived period of time: to the century from Bertha's marriage to the death of Ebroin, when Merovingian Francia often played a dominant role in Western Europe. That the Franks should have shown an interest in English affairs is hardly surprising. The kingdoms of England were no larger or more powerful than the peripheral duchies of the Merovingian world, and could usefully be compared throughout the post-Roman period with such districts as Bavaria. That Merovingian hegemony involved vague and inconstant relationships, and that it depended on the internal politics of Francia as well as direct contacts with the outside world, should not detract from its importance. It is not without relevance to the formation of England.

17

Royal Burials among the Franks

EDWARD JAMES

The burial ritual observed in the ship burials at Sutton Hoo, together with items such as the helmet and shield, irresistibly make one examine Sutton Hoo in a Scandinavian, or specifically Swedish, context. But it has also to be recognised that East Anglia in the early seventh century was on the fringes of, or within, the cultural dominion of the Franks, the most powerful of all Germanic peoples at the time, who were living under the relatively stable rule of the Merovingian dynasty (c.481–751). Mound 1 contained objects which witnessed to the links with Frankish Gaul; the purse contained 37 Merovingian gold coins, and the gold-and-garnet jewellery may well have been made by a Frankish craftsman, who found his raw materials in the Frankish world (Arrhenius 1985). The Franks in the sixth century had claimed overlordship over southern England, and that overlordship may have been much more real than Bede was prepared to admit in his *Ecclesiastical History* (Wood 1983; James 1988a, 103; Wood, in this volume). Æthelberht of Kent's acceptance of Christianity from the Roman missionary Augustine rather than from his Frankish wife's bishop, the Frank Liudhard, for instance, may be seen as an attempt to assert his independence from the Franks. Rædwald of the East Anglians himself named his son Sigiberht, a name probably taken from the Frankish royal dynasty, and, when a quarrel arose between father and son, Sigiberht fled to Gaul, probably to the Merovingian court. When he returned to gain his throne, he was no doubt laden with gifts. Ian Wood has argued that those gifts may indeed have found their way into the ship-burial at Sutton Hoo, gifts such as the Byzantine silver-ware and the bronze bowl from the Eastern Mediterranean; 'if it is objected that Sigbert was a Christian and retired to a monastery', he writes, 'it should be remembered that this is not how the East Angles saw him. They summoned him from religious retreat to lead his people in battle and it was, doubtless, they who buried him. To them, nothing can have been more appropriate for him than a burial with his own Frankish treasure, together with ancestral goods from the treasury of the East Anglian kings' (Wood 1983, 14).

Whether the main ship-burial at Sutton Hoo belongs to Rædwald, or Sigiberht, or some other member of the Wuffinga dynasty, we can be sure that there were connections of some kind between the East Anglian court and Francia. To understand the full context of the culture which created the archaeological assemblage at Sutton Hoo we thus need to understand the Frankish context as well as the Scandinavian one.

That was the initial thought that led me to this paper (which was initially given as an Antiquary lecture at the University of Edinburgh, and subsequently partially published in James 1988a); whether my subsequent comments do in fact illuminate the problems of Sutton Hoo in any way is another matter. But the context of Frankish royal burials does at least provide a body of data, both archaeological and historical, which can be set against the sparse British data. The British Isles can only provide one early medieval burial which can be interpreted as royal; Francia can provide a number of graves which have been regarded as royal, and the historical evidence is also much fuller than it is for England, and may help us provide answers to some of the questions which Sutton Hoo raises. Is there in fact anything archaeologically distinctive about a royal grave? Is there thus anything to counter the arguments of those (such as Wallace-Hadrill 1960) who have seen Sutton Hoo as possibly the grave of an aristocratic but non-royal East Anglian? To what extent did choice rather than chance govern the burial-place of a king? Did the choice of burial-place have any political significance? Did, for instance, the burial-place of a king itself fulfil some political role for that king's descendants and successors? Were there early medieval equivalents of the great royal necropoloi fostered by the English and French kings from the mid-thirteenth century – Westminster Abbey and Saint-Denis – which served as royal cult-centres of some political importance?

For some Frankish kings some of the answers to this flurry of rhetorical questions may be in the affirmative. To take the obvious example: Charles the Great, the Frankish king who was crowned Emperor in Rome in 800, died at 9 o'clock in the morning on 28 January 814 in his own palace at Aachen. According to his biographer Einhard he had given no directions about where he should be buried, and there had to be some debate about this, presumably among his courtiers and advisers, for his son and heir Louis the Pious took some time to reach Aachen. The debate did not last long. All agreed that he should be buried in the cathedral of Aachen, the capella or chapel where the cappa or cape of St Martin was preserved. 'He was buried there on the day of his death', Einhard recorded, 'and a gilded arch with his statue and an inscription was raised above the tomb' (Einhard 31: Halphen 88–89). The Chronicle of Novalesa, written around thirty or forty years after the event, described the opening of this tomb by the Emperor Otto III in the millennial year of 1000. Count Otto of Lomello had been present, and described it to the chronicler.

> We entered where Charles was. For he did not lie, like the bodies of other dead men, but he sat on his throne as if he was alive. He was crowned with a golden crown, and held a sceptre in his hands, which were

covered with gloves through which his finger-nails had grown. Over him was a ceiling of limestone and marble. When we came to him we broke a hole in this ceiling. And when we entered into the chamber, we smelt a very strong smell. We immediately bent our knees and offered a prayer to him. Then Emperor Otto dressed him in white robes, trimmed his nails, and restored anything around him that was necessary. None of his limbs had been destroyed through putrefaction, but the tip of his nose had a little missing, which the Emperor replaced with some gold. He then took a tooth out of his mouth, replaced the ceiling of the chamber and went away (Beuman 1965, 10: my translation)

Thietmar of Merseberg, writing some twenty years earlier, also reported that Charles sat on his throne in the grave, and adds that Otto removed a gold cross that had hung around the corpse's neck before 'replacing the other things with great veneration' (Beuman 1965, 11). These passages are full of problems. If 'replacing' means 'relocating', then at least we are able to explain why later in the Middle Ages Charles's tomb was elsewhere in the church, and associated with an old Roman sarcophagus carved with the depiction of the Rape of Proserpina. But if we accept Thietmar as meaning that the body was translated elsewhere, then we have to reckon that Otto of Lomello's apparently eye-witness account is false. However we interpret it, there are few clear archaeo-logical parallels for the peculiar nature of Charlemagne's burial – 'not lying but sitting on his throne', as two of the sources say – unless, that is, we accept the suggestion raised and then discarded by Bruce-Mitford that the king in the Sutton Hoo ship-burial was buried in that fashion (Bruce-Mitford 1975, 520–521). But whether this tale is folk-lore or actual fact, the nature of the burial – Charles still sitting in his capital and holding his sceptre – had obvious politi-cal symbolism. It is also worth noting that Charlemagne was buried on the day of his death, which Donald Bullough has suggested was common in the early Middle Ages (Bullough 1983, 191): there was often very little time to elaborate a funeral ceremony.

It is the Merovingian predecessors of Charlemagne who are the topic of this paper, however. And it is hardly possible not to start with the most famous burial in early medieval archaeology, that discovered in Tournai in 1653, from which we may date the beginning of early medieval archaeology itself. It remains the only grave in the period which can fairly reliably be associated with a known personality whose date of death is known. The personality is Childeric, the royal father of Clovis, first Catholic king of the Franks, and the date is 481 or 482. Most of the huge treasure is no more; it was stolen from the Bibliothèque Nationale in 1831 and melted down, except for a few pieces: gold-and-garnet fittings from a scabbard, two gold bees, a plain gold buckle-loop, a crystal ball (Périn 1980, 5–8, gives the best account of the theft). But luckily Chifflet's publication of 1655, *The Resurrection of Childeric I*, included a large number of reasonably competent engravings, from which some at least of the contents of the grave can be reconstructed: these have been usefully reproduced recently by Kazanski and Périn (1988; see also Périn 1980). There were several hundred Roman and Byzantine gold coins; there was a considerable amount of gold-and-garnet jewellery, and a solid gold arm-ring such as has been associated with princely or royal status among the early Germans (Werner 1980); there was a gold cross-bow fibula, of the type worn by Roman officials in the late Roman period, mistaken by Chifflet for a very stylish stylus; there were weapons, such as the typically Frankish throwing-axe or francisca. And finally, and most important of all, there was the seal-ring with the inscription CHILDERICI REGIS. It too is now lost, but it was drawn by Chifflet and exists in a plaster impression. That it is a forgery, which has been suggested, seems unlikely; we can compare it with other contemporary or near-contemporary seal-rings, such as that of the Gothic king Alaric II, whom Childeric's son Clovis killed on the battlefield in 507 (if that seal is not a forgery: see Schramm 1954, 217–218 and plate 13). That it does not necessarily prove the grave to be that of Childeric is also true, although it may be argued that a royal seal-ring was a very personal object, unlikely to be passed on to others. The date of the coins found with the grave is consistent with the date of Childeric's death, c.482, and the ensemble is consistent with the grave of a very high- ranking Frankish warrior fighting on behalf of the Romans – Childeric, in short.

Childeric's grave was across the Scheldt from Tournai and very near the more modern church of St-Brice. Excavations in 1983 (revealed in various publications by R. Brulet 1981, 1986, 1988) seem to have shown that this church does not itself go back into the fifth century, the century of both St Bricius and Childeric. And they have also shown that Childeric's tomb was not within a late Roman cemetery, as had once been thought, but seems to have been one of the earliest graves in a Frankish cemetery which continued into the seventh century. The graves of Franks must have clustered around their king just as, in other cemeteries, they often cluster around the so-called 'founder-grave' of an aristocrat. One of the problems which is likely to remain unsolved is whether Childeric's grave was marked in any way on the surface, by a building or a monument. If so, it is quite remarkable that it was not robbed in antiquity, as so many thousand of early medieval graves were, including most of those at Sutton Hoo. Another insoluble problem, as with Sutton Hoo, is that of the religion of the king. If Chifflet can be believed, a richly caparisoned severed horse's head was found in the grave, which would appear to confirm the pagan character of the grave. But there is nothing in Chifflet's drawings which can be interpreted as the horse-harness which he claimed to have found, although some have argued that the bull's head and the thirty gold-and-garnet bees were once sewn onto horse-harness. Chifflet believed that they had been sewn onto a purple cloak (and Napoleon Bonaparte would presumably not have had replicas sewn onto his coronation robes in 1804 had he imagined that he was dressing up as Childeric's horse). We are of course entitled not to believe all that Chifflet wrote: he did arrive late on the scene, and was hence dependent upon eye-witness accounts (the original discoverer of the tomb was a deaf-mute); moreover the gravegoods, possibly from more than one grave, had been removed rapidly and indiscriminately, and some or many may have disappeared before Chifflet arrived. Even one of the more spectacular aspects of the recent excavations – the discovery of three pits containing the skeletons of horses, plausibly of late fifth- or early sixth-century, in the vicinity of the grave discovered in 1653 – is not conclusive proof of Childeric's paganism: even though it is certain that the sacrifice of horses at burials is a pagan custom, the exact topographical and chronological relationship between the horse-pits and Childeric's grave remains unclear. It is still important to note that Childeric's paganism must not be taken for granted, as it long has been: we have enough evidence from our other royal graves to know that extensive grave-goods do not imply paganism, and we know enough about Gregory of Tours's ignorance and prejudices not to take his claim that Childeric's son Clovis was the first Christian king as if it were Gospel. Nor must we assume, as many have, that just because Childeric was buried at Tournai then Tournai was in some sense his 'capital', or at the centre of his kingdom, and write the history of his career accordingly (see James 1988b). As we shall see, some kings did apparently choose where they were to be buried; others were buried where they died.

The next three significant 'royal' Frankish graves were not discovered for another three hundred years, and then, by a strange coincidence, were found within a matter of weeks of each other, in 1959: two under Cologne Cathedral and one under Saint-Denis. I shall not go into many details of these finds; they are well-known to the English archaeological community thanks to Werner's *Antiquity* article of 1964. But it is worth stressing some things. They were inserted below the floors of major Christian churches. The two Cologne graves date from the second quarter of the sixth century, and therefore from one or two generations after the conversion of King Clovis and many of the Franks: the choice of burial site and burial rite must have been made by Christians. The female grave, that of the 'princess', was within a coffin at one end of the stone chamber, and her body was laid out with her items of apparel, such as her gold-braid head-band and gold dress fasteners, her crystal ball and her amulet container. Outside the coffin lay the other objects: the vessels of pottery, glass, and bronze (including a vessel comparable to the Mediterranean bronze bowl from Sutton Hoo), containing, perhaps, as in many other contemporary graves, offerings of food and drink. This differential placing of personal adornment and vessels and other offerings may be significant, in the light of discussions among Anglo-Saxon archaeologists about the symbolism of funerary deposits (e.g. Pader 1982). It may be compared with other sixth-century graves, such as the chief's grave from Morken (Böhner 1958). It is the items placed outside the body area which were to disappear first from the Merovingian burial rite; the more personal items continued to be buried for another century before the body was to be placed in the grave with no more than a shroud to keep it company. But even if one is tempted to see anything specifi-cally religious or 'pagan' in the earlier custom, one must remember that it does not become common among the Franks until the beginning of the sixth cen-tury, the first generation after the conversion of Clovis to Christianity, and that it is to be found in church burials as well as rural burials. This fact is still not taken sufficiently into account by Anglo-Saxon archaeologists who attempt to distinguish 'pagan' from 'Christian' graves; the lessons of Young 1977 have not been fully assimilated.

The second 'royal' grave from Cologne is even more remarkable. The body of a six-year old boy was laid out upon a wooden bed, at the foot of which stood a chair: our only two surviving pieces of Frankish furniture. A child-sized helmet hung on the back of the chair; by the bed were laid adult-sized weapons, including a long-sword, a battle-axe, a bow (with arrows) and a shield. And by the boy's left side was placed a lathe-turned wooden stick or staff. That it was a sceptre has often been assumed, and that these two were buried within the cathedral of Cologne, a very great privilege, and with luxury grave-goods has, for some, been sufficient proof that the pair were royal. There is obviously plenty of room for doubt. Certainly these burials are richer than other known early sixth-century Frankish burials in churches, but we know enough about the wealth of sixth-century Frankish non-royal aristocrats to know that they could be very wealthy indeed – more so perhaps than many contemporary Anglo-Saxon kings. Nor is it clear who these royals could be, buried in Cologne rather than further west in Gaul like all the known descend-ants of Clovis. Perhaps they were relatives or descendants of the royal dynasty of Cologne whose last representative, Chloderic, had been killed by Clovis after Clovis had persuaded him to kill his own father Sigibert. But if so the significance of the wooden staff is even more important, and even more odd: if it represents royal power – if it is a Frankish equivalent of the whetstone (?) buried at Sutton Hoo – then it might suggest that the Cologne dynasty con-tinued to have some recognised status, which fits poorly with our (sketchy) idea of the development of the Frankish kingdom in the early sixth century gained from Gregory of Tours's *History*. But, if royal at all, perhaps they are unknown members of the family of Clovis's son Theuderic, who ruled that area after 511. Nothing, as yet, however, has emerged to resolve the question of whether these two were royal at all.

'Unproven' should also be the verdict on the third 'royal' burial found in 1959: the grave of Arnegundis from St-Denis. The lady herself is perhaps best known from the restoration painting in Talbot Rice 1965 (p. 201). It was a fascinating find. Sufficient fragments of clothing survived to enable a recon-struction of her clothing to be made, with the help of X-rays to reconstruct the gold-thread weave. Even traces of her hair and body tissue survived: frag-ments of lung were preserved by the embalming fluids that were forced down her throat after death. It was her ring – not a seal-ring, but nevertheless inscribed with a name – which identified her as Arnegund, and the monogram in the centre was almost immediately deciphered as REGINA, queen, allowing her to be identified as the third wife of King Chlothar I (511–561), Queen Aregund. Gregory of Tours tells us how Queen Ingund asked her husband Chlothar to find a suitable husband for her sister Aregund, and how, having met her, Chlothar chose himself. The date of this episode is unclear, but the bones were identified as those of a woman of around 45, and thus it was suggested that the date of burial could be no later than c.570. This, for archaeologists in the early 1960s, was of crucial significance, for it was the only historically datable Merovingian grave apart from that of Childeric, and it called for a revision of the chronology of late sixth and early seventh century material. The grave was seen as another example of that small category of royal graves, and one item – the belt with its great belt-buckle – was interpreted as an item of regalia: Fleury (Fleury and France-Lanord 1979, 30) argued that this must have been the late Chlothar I's sword-belt, placed in the grave with his former queen.

The only dissenting voice at this identification of the dead Arnegund with the royal Aregund at the time was Sir David Wilson who suggested commonsensically that the monogram read ARNEGUNDIS, not REGINA: all similar monograms are those of personal names, not titles (Wilson 1964). But increasingly during the seventies and eighties doubts were expressed at dating the grave as early as 565–570. The burial with personal adornments only and no grave-goods proper belongs more to the seventh century than to the sixth, and a number of the objects – the large buckle and plate, the smaller buckles and strap-ends, the pins and earrings, and the disc-brooches would all fit better at the very end of the sixth or at the beginning of the seventh century. Helmut Roth has argued that the developed Style II to be found on Arnegund's garter-buckles belongs to the seventh century, and not the sixth (Roth 1986). Patrick Périn, in an unpublished paper, has pointed out how one disc-brooch seems to be a maladroit copy of the other, and suggests that the woman may have been a south German, used to wearing one such brooch on her cloak, who had come to the Paris region, to find that current fashions there required two such brooches, one on each shoulder: this too casts doubt on the identification with Aregund. The title of the unpublished paper referred to 'Tomb 49, the so-called grave of Queen Aregund'. In the published version of the paper (Périn 1991), however, he seems to have cast most of these doubts aside: the tomb becomes that of Aregund, and he reconciles the traditional identification with Aregund and the chronological problems offered by the metalwork by arguing that the original aging of the skeletal material, which had been in poor condition, was wrong: the woman was not necessarily 45 at the age of her death, but could easily have been around 80, which is what would have been had she survived up to 590, which would seem be the very earliest possible date for the assemblage of jewellery. In the recent authoritative *Atlas des Monuments Paléochrétiens des la France*, Young and Périn (1991) seem to have abandoned any doubts about the royalty of the grave, and (p. 110) settle on the date of c.590 (giving

Aregund an age of around 80 at death: on which see Ewig's remarks cited in Périn 1991, 40). Ultimately this rests on the belief that the monogram in the centre of the ring reads REGINA; and, indeed, on the belief that a ring with a name on it which is *not* a seal-ring has to belong to the person named on it, rather than, for instance, indicating a relationship of kinship, friendship or subordination. At present it would still seem prudent to retain Périn's earlier phrase, the 'so-called grave of Aregund', and not to try to fit the archaeological material into the historical straitjacket. It must be remembered that, were it not for the ring, the grave would almost certainly be dated to the early seventh century, and perhaps even as late as c.625.

Our most famous royal burial from the period after Childeric may thus be illusory. But there may be one or two others. Burial no. 16 at St-Denis, robbed, but still with traces of a fine war-harness, rich embroidery, and three gold rings overlooked by the robber, including one ring with a sapphire, the only one known from a Frankish grave, has been interpreted by Édouard Salin (1958, 35–45), with grudging acceptance from Professor Wallace-Hadrill (1975, 44), as the possible burial of Chlothar III (d.673). It at least shows that wealthy people, buried in sarcophagi under the flags of a church were still deposited with all their finery. And it shows too that the sanctity of the site deterred the grave-robber no more effectively than the fierce penalties laid down in the law: Gregory of Tours indeed tells us of one aristocratic woman buried with her finery beneath a church near Metz whose grave was robbed only days after the funeral (*History* VIII.21; Thorpe 1974, 453).

Another possible royal burial was found in the same decade as Childeric I's tomb: that of Childeric II (see Périn 1980, 8–9). But it is surrounded by very much more uncertainty, since descriptions date only from 1724. It seems that in 1645 several tombs had been discovered under the floor of the church of St-Germain-des-Prés in Paris; they were re-opened, or others were discovered, in 1656, three years after the discovery of Childeric I had perhaps given an impetus to such investigations. One body had a head-band and clothes woven with gold thread, and belt- and shoe-buckles of silver: it appears to have been associated with a sarcophagus that had CHILDR REX inscribed on it. Nearby was a grave also with gold robes, which was identified as that of Belechildis, the young queen who had been assassinated in 675 together with Childeric II. But the description of the first grave, with its gold-thread head-band and shoe buckles, suggests the grave of another woman: such head-bands are known from quite a number of Frankish and Kentish women's graves (Crowfoot and Hawkes 1969). But there is a description of another grave, or even of the same grave (the accounts are very confused), which may be much more appropriate as that of a king. It had a large hazel-wood staff in it, as long as the tomb itself; a sword, gold belt-fittings and other metal objects. Only one of these apparently survived into the eighteenth-century to be illustrated: a small bronze plaque with a double-headed serpent, which Périn accepts to be from Childeric II's burial, and dated to 675 (see Périn 1980, pl. IIc). Montfaucon in

1724 wrote that a monk of St-Germain had confessed on his death-bed that he had sold everything else that had been found in the graves, and thereby raised 13000 livres for the building of a new organ. Rich graves they certainly were, but whether they were royal, let alone those of Childeric II and Belechildis (whom later traditions claim to have been buried in St-Ouen in Rouen and not St-Germain-des Prés at all) must remain very much an open question.

The archaeological evidence thus illuminates one aspect of the problem, even if it does raise rather more questions than it answers. We can see that extensive and wealthy grave depositions are not a formal sign of paganism, which should certainly lead us to question common assumptions about Sutton Hoo. We can see that symbols of authority may be placed in royal graves: the Latin-inscribed seal-ring of Childeric, who probably owed his power more to Roman subsidy than to Frankish tradition, and perhaps the more traditional Frankish symbols, wooden rods or staffs, found at Cologne and Paris. But, apart from Childeric I, Francia has no more examples of royal graves which can certainly be associated with historical personages than England does. What it does have, however, is much more historical data concerning royal burials.

The most detailed description of a royal burial in the Frankish sources is, typically, untypical: the burial of Queen Radegund, who died in 587 in the convent in Poitiers in which she had been a nun for over thirty years (for a discussion, see James 1980, 41–42). The funeral must have been at least two days after her death, for the nuns waited until Bishop Gregory could arrive from Tours to take the service; they did not see eye to eye with their own bishop, Maroveus. Gregory describes the funeral procession in detail, and the burial arrangements. Radegund was buried in the funerary basilica which she had had built for the nunnery, outside the walls of Poitiers; she had specified in a letter which Gregory of Tours preserves for us that she should be buried there. Perhaps she wanted to avoid the fate of Clovis's widow Clotild, who had lived as a nun for almost as long as Radegund, but whose body had been brought back from Tours to Paris so as to be buried by the side of Clovis in the chancel of the church she, or, according to other sources, they, had built, dedicated to the Apostles Peter and Paul.

The burial-place of a number of ruling Merovingian kings is known from historical sources (for a map see James 1988a, 158, redrawn from Müller-Wille 1982, 356; for full details see Krüger 1971). They are concentrated in the Paris area, and specifically in Paris itself, which had been chosen by Clovis as his 'capital'. The two major Parisian churches were the Holy Apostles, later St-Geneviève, and St Vincent's, later St-Germain-des-Prés. To the Holy Apostles, appropriately containing relics of the doorkeeper of heaven and the bulwark of orthodoxy, in imitation of the burial churches of Roman Emperors, was brought from a considerable distance not only the body of Clotild, to rest beside Clovis, but also that of their daughter, also called Chrotechildis or Clotild, who died on her way back home from a disastrous marriage in Spain.

But if Clovis had intended to found a dynastic mausoleum here, the division of the kingdom among his four sons after his death frustrated any such ambition. Of his sons only Childebert I was buried in Paris. Childebert had returned from an expedition to Spain in the early 530s with the cloak of St Vincent, and built a church in Paris to shelter the relic and to serve as his burial place. He died in Paris in 558 and was duly buried on St Vincent's. Later his nephew Chilperic seized Paris despite an agreement with his brother that none should enter it, and when he was assassinated in 584 at his estate in Chelles, the bishop of Senlis brought him to Paris for burial in St Vincent's. There too were buried his wife and three if not four of their children, including Chlothar II, the king who reunited the Frankish kingdom in 613. When Chilperic's childless brother Guntram had become the sole surviving Merovingian of his generation, and had become, according to Gregory of Tours, quite obsessed about the survival of the dynasty, he arranged for the bodies of two of Chilperic's sons whom Chilperic or his wife had had murdered to be brought to St Vincent's for burial. One of these bodies had been deliberately thrown into a river so that it might not receive honourable burial; it was caught in a fish-trap and recognised as royal by the long hair still adhering to the skull. And later still, as we have seen, Childeric II and his wife may have been brought there after their assassination in 675. Sadly none of these early graves were found in the excavations of 1807 (a contemporary illustration of which is reproduced in *Paris mérovingien* p. 19), when a number of late Merovingian sarcophagi were discovered: it is possible that the royal graves had all been disturbed in the explorations of 1644 and 1656.

Again, if it was an attempt to found a royal mausoleum, it was frustrated by political chance and the appeals of a rival church. Chlothar II's son Dagobert's favourite estate was Clichy, near the church containing the relics of the martyr St Denis. In addition to proximity, St Denis had an obvious claim to be a major patron saint of Francia and of the dynasty. Dagobert enlarged the church after he became king in Neustria in 629; Arnegund was apparently buried within his extension, which again argues against her identification with Aregund. But only two Merovingian kings were buried there: Dagobert himself, who fell ill near Épernay, and was brought to St Denis to die, and his son Clovis II. Clovis II's widow Balthild preferred burial in the monastery which she had founded at Chelles. Only much later, long after St-Denis had received the burials of a number of Carolingian rulers (including Charles Martel and Pippin I), did it become the almost undisputed burial place of the French kings.

In the Merovingian period itself, perhaps, the political geography was too changing and unstable for a dynastic mausoleum to emerge. There could be no equivalent to Canterbury, the burial place of Kentish kings for two centuries: the kingdom was too large, and too often divided among different branches of the dynasty. But it could also be argued that the Merovingian dynasty was so strong and unchallenged that it did not need the support of such a centre; it was in Kent, where new dynasties were constantly being created, that kings needed to celebrate their adherence to royal traditions. Even when Frankish kings seem deliberately to have built burial-churches for themselves, these churches served no more than one or two generations. St Medard's at Soissons, for instance, was built by Chlothar I, and his body was brought there from Compiègne in 561; 15 years later his son Sigibert I was brought there 100 kilometres from where he had been assassinated, and thereafter Soissons received no more royal burials. Guntram was buried in his own church of St Marcel at Chalon-sur-Saône, founded, he proclaimed, 'for the safety of the king and the salvation of his soul'; his wife and two sons, who all pre-deceased him, had already been buried there. *Laus perennis*, perpetual unceasing prayer for, above all, king and kingdom, was established there as, later, at St-Denis and St-Medard. But again St-Marcel was never used again for royal burials.

A survey like this can come to no resounding conclusions; there are far too many imponderables. The historical evidence suggests that it did matter to kings and queens where they were buried, and also suggests that particular kings (Childebert I, Guntram, Dagobert) may have tried to establish mausolea at least for their own immediate family. And kings do seem to have done what they could to build up the importance of their own burial-churches. It is surely significant that when the *Vita Balthildis* (c.9, p. 493) in the late seventh century names the six greatest churches of the kingdom, all but two – St Martin of Tours and St Anianus of Orleans – were royal burial-churches: St-Germain-des-Prés, St-Médard of Soissons, St-Denis and St Peter's – which may be either Paris or Sens). The inclusion of the churches of Germanus and Medard in the list, both dedicated to sixth-century bishops, suggests that it was the prestige of the *king's* bodies and not that of the bishops' bodies which made these churches important: neither of them would seem to be saints of exceptional importance in their own right. It is perhaps significant that with the exception of St Denis kings are *not* choosing to be buried near the holiest relics or in the most venerated churches.

Clearly the Merovingian kings, when it came to death and burial, were firmly within the cultural ambit of the Gallo-Roman church. From that point of view, their world was far removed from that of the kings of East Anglia. What would someone like Rædwald or Sigiberht have learnt from the Frankish kings who loomed so large on the political horizon and who served as obvious spurs to rivalry and imitation? That there was nothing barbaric or uncivilised or even unChristian in the deposition of treasure and offerings in the grave; that the siting of a grave could have political significance. They may have seen that the church was the most prestigious and safe of resting-places, but they will also have seen the newly Christianised Kentish aristocracy starting to adopt the habit of barrow burial, which might have seemed just as modern and prestigious to them (particularly in the absence of a tradition of building churches in stone). The contents of Sutton Hoo celebrate the dilemma which the men who buried the king found themselves in: they wanted to celebrate their king's connection with the powerful and civilised world of Byzantium and Francia, but they had to recognise the traditions of their people and their dynasty as well. Their problem was no different from that of any Frankish king: their burials too witnessed the tension between innovation and tradition.

18

The Undiscovered Grave of King Clovis I (+ 511)

PATRICK PÉRIN

I am a little embarrassed, I must confess, to help commemorate in this paper the fiftieth anniversary of the discovery of the most famous royal grave of the Dark Ages, that of Sutton Hoo, by discussing a regal tomb of the barbarian West that has never been found! But the subject of the burial of Clovis, King of the Franks, is well worth our time and attention. Indeed, I shall argue that there are parallels of interest between the two burials, although a century in time and the English Channel separate them. For they each mark a decisive stage in the evolution of royal graves, Anglo-Saxon on the one hand and Frankish on the other, at the moment when paganism was giving way to Christianity in the insular and the continental courts. If one can term the Sutton Hoo figure the 'last of the pagans', then Clovis, baptised between 496 and 499, deserves recognition among the Franks as 'the first of the Christians'! The first 'barbarian' king to be buried within a church, he began a funerary fashion which was rapidly successful. His successors adopted the practice, and it spread rapidly among the Gallo-Frankish aristocracy which served them. This new burial mode played a large role in the spread of Christianity into the countryside of Gaul through the construction of private funerary churches, many of which later evolved into parish churches (Werner 1976; Périn and Reynaud 1989). However, as we shall see, Clovis' own case was a particular one in Gaul, and did not serve as a specific model for his successors.

What we know about the grave of Clovis derives exclusively from written sources, in striking contrast to Sutton Hoo. In a few succinct passages, Gregory of Tours, the famous historian of the Franks, tells us that Clovis was buried in the *sacrarium* of the basilica of the Holy-Apostles which he and his wife Clotilde had caused to be built in Paris (Gregory of Tours II, 48, IV, 1). Gregory adds that several family members were buried beside the king: his daughter Clotilde, who had married the Visigothic king Amalaric, son of Euric; his grandchildren Theudoaldus and Gontarius (those unhappy boys murdered by their uncles Clotaire and Childebert after the death of their father Clodomir in

524); and of course his wife Clotilde, who died at the abbey of Saint-Martin in Tours in 544 (Gregory of Tours III, 10, 18).

The choice of the site of the royal mausoleum is highly significant. Clovis and Clotilde seem to have been deeply devoted to Saint Genevieve, the pious shepherd girl who became famous for stiffening the resolve of the Parisians and organising the town's defence during the great raid of Attila in 451 (Dubois and Beaumont-Maillet 1982; Heinzelman and Poulin, 1986). At that time she seems to have influenced Childeric, Clovis' father, and she may have even played a role in Clovis' own conversion to Christianity. In any event when she died, probably in 502, she was buried in one of the civil cemeteries of Late-Roman Paris, the one on the eastern slopes of the hill that has come to bear her name, the Montagne-Sainte-Genevieve, an area quite close to the surviving parts of the city on the Left Bank during the Late-Empire (Périn in Périn and Feffer 1984, 362–372).

According to the *Life of Saint Genevieve*, composed about 520, that is to say very soon after the death of the saint herself, the Parisians, in a spontaneous gesture, were moved to build a wooden *oratorium* over the grave (*Vita Genovefae* 55). Sometime soon after 507, the year that Clovis made Paris his capital, he and Clotilde replaced this early oratory by a new basilica, originally dedicated to the Holy Apostles, but later consecrated to Saint Genevieve.

There is more to this royal foundation than meets the eye. The newly-converted Frankish sovereigns intended not merely to honour the memory of a saint, employing a process that had become classic since the Peace of the Church, but also to entrust their own sepultures to her illustrious protection. The ultimate model was the example of Constantine the Great, who died in 337: he had his sarcophagus placed in the nave of the basilica of the Holy-Apostles in Constantinople, where it was surrounded by the cenotaphs of the twelve Apostles (Heisenberg 1908; Krautheimer 1965). Returning to Clovis, it seems to me that his decision to make the rather secondary town of Paris his capital – instead of choosing more prominent Gallic cities like Soissons, Reims or Tours – might have been linked to his desire to build his mausoleum beside the tomb of Saint Genevieve (Périn and Feffer 1987 I, 165–173; Périn et al. 1985, 149–154; Périn 1990a, 119–121).

Although there are no written sources posterior to Gregory of Tours which refer to the tomb of Clovis at all, the historians of the royal abbey of Saint-Genevieve which succeeded the Merovingian funerary basilica have never doubted where it was (Cabrol and Leclercq 1914 'Clovis (Baptême-sépulture)' 2038–2074). For them, it could only have been located in the crypt where the sarcophagus of the Protectress of the Parisians was housed (Pl. 8). When the church and crypt were rebuilt in eleventh century, it would have been transferred up into the nave of the new church where a *gisant* would had been placed over it at the beginning of the thirteenth century (Erlande-Brandenburg 1975, 133–134) (Pl. 9). According to another tradition, this *gisant* would have stayed much longer in the crypt, before being transferred into the upper church. Placed in the choir, like a cenotaph, its presence is attested from the beginning of the seventeenth century (du Breul 1639, 2–3) (Pl. 10). Today, it is conserved with the tombs of the kings of France in the basilica of Saint Denis. These traditions need to be verified in the light of the historical and archaeological sources available, which admittedly are meagre.

We have little precise knowledge of the crypt before the days of Abbot Stephen of Tournai (1176–1191), who continued the building campaigns begun back in the eleventh century, campaigns which saw the complete reconstruction of the chevet, of the crypt and of the first bays of the nave (Vieillard-Troïekouroff et al. 1960, 173–179). By this time, then, a new crypt had replaced the one dating to the earlier Middle Ages. There is general agreement as to the existence of such a crypt, at least from the second half of the eighth century, when it is thought to have been remodelled along the lines of the crypt under the basilica of Saint-Denis, where the celebrated bones of that Parisian saint were venerated and enjoyed royal favour (McKnight Crosby and Blum 1987). But of the original disposition of Genevieve's sepulture, as it was back in the early sixth century, we know nothing. By analogy with other contemporary cases when we do know something, we can imagine that the sarcophagus was either presented in the choir of the church itself, like that of Saint Martin in Tours (Vieillard-Troïekouroff 1976, 311–24), or had already been placed in an underground *memoria* (Bonnet 1977, 152–8). Her sarcophagus must have somehow been accessible to pilgrims, in keeping with the customs of the day: we know that about 630 the goldsmith Saint Eloi crafted gold decorations for this tomb (Saint Ouen I, Chap. 17, 688).

During the first Viking attack on Paris, in 845, Saint Genevieve's bones were removed from the tomb and enclosed in a reliquary for safekeeping (Cabrol and Leclercq 1914, 2072, Vieillard-Troïekouroff et al. 1960, 173; Krüger 1971, 48; Vieillard Troïekouroff 1976, 206–8). When the danger receded, the reliquary was displayed for veneration in the choir of the church. But the old stone sarcophagus, which remained in place throughout the successive transformations of the crypt, was itself considered to be a relic, and suffered more from the hands of generations of pilgrims than from the Vikings! The latter had no doubt removed the gold decorations, but the pilgrims chipped away at the stone itself, in order to carry off a sacred souvenir. Finally, in the seventeenth century, the surviving fragments were enclosed in a cenotaph. This is kept today, along with the bottom of the sarcophagus, in the church Saint-Etienne-du-Mont. This cenotaph has been there ever since the beginning of the nineteenth century, when the ruinous old church of Saint-Genevieve was demolished to allow the passage of a new street, which still exists there and is named, appropriately enough, 'rue Clovis'. The well-known neo-Classic architect Soufflot built a new church Saint-Genevieve nearby; today we know it as the Pantheon. Let us add, to make the record complete, that two other tombs originally part of the Gallo-Roman civil cemetery where Genevieve was first buried are said to have been transferred into the basilica of the Holy-Apostles when it was founded. They belonged to Prudentius, a Bishop of Paris at the end of fourth century, and to the female Saint Eusoz, of whom we know nothing more. The presence of these two tombs in the crypt is attested in the Middle Ages, and right down to the demolition of the church.

Although it is possible to follow the history of Genevieve's tomb and of the crypt throughout the Middle Ages, no mention is made of the graves of Clovis and his family. This silence is all the more striking because the other graves in the crypt of Saint Genevieve are mentioned, in medieval and post-medieval sources, although they were, of course, holy graves. It seems to me fair enough to suggest, then, that the royal graves themselves were not in the crypt, at least by the period when the written sources begin to describe it, that is, by the later Middle Ages.

I am led to a similar conclusion by a reinterpretation of the passage which Gregory of Tours devotes to Clovis' tomb. Gregory places the tomb 'in sacrario basilicae Sancti Petri'. Now the expression 'in sacrario' has generally been taken to mean the sanctuary itself (Erlande-Brandenburg 1975) or its choir (Vieillard-Troïekouroff et al. 1960, 170), and by extension the underlying crypt. But in fact, as Mrs Weidemann has perfectly established in her excellent study *Kulturgeschichte der Merowingerzeit nach den Werken Gregors von Tours* (Weidemann 1982), Gregory uses the term *sacrarium* in a rather precise sense: it designates the annex of a church, close to the choir and in general communicating with this. If we accept this interpretation of the term *sacrarium*, we must conclude that Clovis' tomb was not originally placed beside that of Saint Genevieve (whose grave, we are quite sure, was in the choir of the Holy Apostles basilica or under it); it was placed somewhere nearby, close to the choir but distinct from it. This topographical distinction does seem quite logical. It is hard to imagine that Clovis and Clotilde, intending to found a dynastic mausoleum, would have taken the liberty of occupying the small sacred area (necessarily quite limited) reserved for the cult of the saint, an area which remained open to public devotion and which already sheltered three sacred graves. The Church might well have been opposed to such topographic confusion of Genevieve's *memoria* with the royal mausoleum. Let us remember, by way of a parallel, that the sarcophagus of the Emperor Constantine was transferred into a funerary annex when the cenotaphs of the Twelve Apostles under the cupola of the sanctuary were replaced by the relics themselves, which were translated to Constantinople in 356–357 (Heisenberg 1908; Krautheimer 1965).

Let us argue, then, that Clovis and his family were buried in a funerary annex to the basilica of the Holy Apostles in Paris: what more can we learn about this burial? By placing himself within the context of Christian *ad sanctos* burial, Clovis was of course breaking decisively with the sumptuous funerary traditions of his father Childeric I (whom we can term the 'last of the pagan kings' among the Salian Franks) (Kazanski and Périn 1986), but, what is less obvious, his funerary choice differs from that of his successors as well (Krüger

1971, 30–37; Müller-Wille 1982). For, as a number of archaeological finds show – for example at Saint-Germain-des-Prés (Périn et al. 1985, 268–272) and Saint-Denis (Périn 1990b), the later Merovingians were not buried in annexes to churches but rather within the choir of the nave. The only striking exception – and it would bear discussion – is that of the two princely graves found in 1959 beneath Cologne cathedral (Doppelfeld and Weyres 1980). Both their sumptuous grave-goods and their privileged emplacement have been cited to argue that the woman and the boy buried there belonged to the royal family of the Franks of Cologne. The burial took place around 540 in a half-buried mausoleum which, according to Otto Dopplefeld, would have been built within the atrium of the early cathedral. Some archaeologists, like Charles Bonnet, have questioned this, but we cannot go into the discussion here. What seems clear is that the mode of burial Clovis chose remained unusual among the Merovingians and we must look elsewhere for points of comparison.

Gregory of Tours, who might have been drawing upon earlier sources lost to us, was the first to call Clovis the 'new Constantine' (Gregory of Tours II, 38) and to insist upon the parallels between the military victories and the spectacular conversions of the two sovereigns. Later historians did not hesitate to push the comparison even further whether in discussing the choice of a new capital city – Constantinople or Paris – or the construction of a dynastic mausoleum, in both cases dedicated to the Holy Apostles (Krüger 1971, 51–2). We shall never know if Clovis was at all conscious of a parallelism between his reign and that of Constantine, but the notion could have been suggested to him by his Roman and clerical entourage. What is clear, however, are the consequences of his victory over the Visigoths at Vouillé in 507. These included ceremonies which deliberately echoed the *imitatio imperii*. It is in this light I would argue, that we must interpret the 'ceremony of Tours' where Clovis received from envoys of the Emperor Anastasius the consular tablets, and, adorned with the chlamide and the diadem, rode through the streets of Saint Martin's city distributing largesse and hearing himself acclaimed 'consul' and 'Augustus', if we are to believe Gregory of Tours (II, 38). Thus it seems to me worthwhile to pursue the Constantinian parallel farther, and to ask whether the mausoleum of the Holy Apostles in Constantinople could have served as the model for the one built in Paris.

As I pointed out earlier, Constantine's sarcophagus was transferred in 356/7 into a mausoleum distinct from the Holy Apostles basilica. Although this monument was destroyed in 1469 and replaced by the mosque of the Conqueror, we know how it looked from descriptions (Downey 1959, 27–51). It was a circular construction that prolonged the sanctuary to the east (so we know the chevet was occidented). Niches were built into the inner wall to house the imperial sarcophagi, which were thus visible.

There is a monument in Rome which can offer us a rather concrete idea of what the Apostoleion of Constantiniope looked like before Justinian partly rebuilt it after 536 (but he did not alter Constantine's mausoleum). This monument is the Tor Pignattara, also called the Mausoleum of Helen (Guyon 1976) (Pl. 11). Constantine himself built it around 320 for his own tomb before he decided to move to Constantinople; the tradition is that his mother, Saint Helen, was buried there. Like the Apostoleion, the basilica of the Tor Pignattara had an occidented apse and was extended to the east by a circular mausoleum; it was also bordered by portico-lined courts to which secondary mausolea were added throughout the fourth century. It was in another mausoleum of this type, although in this instance not in apparent relation with a church, that King Theodoric the Great was buried in Ravenna, in 526 (Heidenreich and Johannes 1971). In his case the *imitatio imperii* seems certain: he had been brought up in Constantinople and his policy in Italy was to restore the grandeur of Rome. Nor does it seem remarkable that his chief rival in the West, Clovis, would also have opted for a mausoleum in the good antique manner a few years earlier. As the first Catholic king among the barbarian leaders who had taken charge in the West, Clovis could very well have considered that he was the heir of the old Imperial order.

Unfortunately, the available historical and archaeological sources do not confirm the existence of mausoleum of this type attached to the Holy-Apostles basilica in Paris. Apart from the *sacrarium* already discussed, the only available descriptions for the Merovingian period speak of a *secretarium* (sacristry), of a celing of carved wood over the nave, and of a portal decorated with painted scenes taken from the Bible and preceded by an *atrium* (*Miracula s. Genovefae*, 148). The only archaeological information is provided by excavations carried out in 1807 by the architects Rondelet and Bourla, on orders from the police prefect Frochot (Bourla; Lenoir 1807). The Emperor Napoleon himself had commanded that a search be made for the graves of Clovis and Clotilde before the old church of Saint-Genevieve was finally demolished. At that time a number of stone and plaster sarcophagi were discovered under the nave (Pl. 12). Five of these, situated near the western wall of the crypt, were quickly attributed to Clovis and his family (Pl. 13). But this claim was challenged fairly soon and recent research indicates that the type of sarcophagi found were not used before the second half of the sixth century (Delahaye 1985). We cannot regard them, then, as the tombs of Merovingian monarchs; they must have belonged to some important, but anonymous people who had obtained the right to be buried close to the saint. Indeed, from the days of Clovis the growing demand for *ad sanctos* burial space had led to the growth of a vast necropolis in this area, as numerous archaeological finds from the seventeenth century to our own day attest (Périn et al. 1985, 151–154) (Pl. 14).

A closer look at one of the water-colours done by young Bourla shows that the sarcophagi – which had remained *in situ* ever since the early Middle Ages – were enclosed within two parallel walls upon which the pillars of the nave of the thirteenth century church came to rest (Pl. 12). It seems likely, as is the case of Saint-Denis (McKnight Crosby and Blum 1987), that these walls, some 9 metres apart, were those of the exterior walls of the early basilica, reused as foundations by the medieval builders. Drawings made during the 1807 excavations, however, and later published by Albert Lenoir in his famous *Statistique monumentale de Paris* (1867) offer no supporting evidence of foundations which might have belonged to building campaigns earlier than the eleventh to thirteenth century church (Lenoir 1867, plates I and V; Pl.15).

This archaeological and historical documentation, unsatisfactory and incomplete as it is, does at least allow us to reject the hypothesis of a mausoleum which closely followed the Imperial model attached to Holy Apostles basilica in Paris. Since that basilica had its apse to the east, anchored by the relation between the saint's tomb and the choir, such a mausoleum would have had to have been placed at the western end of the nave. And that is where the *atrium* which preceded the porch of the sanctuary was located.

Another hypothesis for Clovis' mausoleum can now be considered, an hypothesis which returns us to the term *sacrarium* in the sense that Gregory of Tours uses it: an annexe to the choir of a church. Now let us remember that the tomb and the crypt of Saint Genevieve, under the altar, had always served to anchor the centre of the choir in the Holy Apostles basilica. The *sacrarium* must have been found around the periphery of the choir, that is where the deambulatory and the lateral chapels were later built. Since this area was not excavated in 1807, all we can study for the moment are the architectural plans made then and later published by Albert Lenoir. One interesting detail strikes the eye at once. The northern chapel has a singular look: compared to the other radiate chapels, it stands out by the manner by which it is joined to the apse, by its rectangular plan and by its massive walls as well (Pl. 15 and 16 at 'N'). Could it not in fact have conserved the plan of an earlier structure whose foundations, or even some of whose walls were reused? We note a reuse of this sort in the part of the nave excavated in 1807, and similar cases in medieval churches are very common. It would not be surprising, moreover, if medieval builders chose to retain the plan of the *sacrarium*, for it would have been a very solid construction. Instead of imagining the mausoleum of Clovis as a kind of rotunda situated at one end of the nave, we should picture a sort of underground or half-buried chamber connected to the choir of Holy Apostles. As we will see in conclusion, this hypothesis is still open to archaeological verification. But if we retain it as the most plausible, we must first raise the question of what happened to the royal graves over the centuries, since the written sources are so curiously silent about them.

Before we undertake this, a word about the Merovingian royal graves of the Saint-Vincent and Holy-Cross basilica in Paris (today Saint-Germain-des Prés) is in order (Périn et al. 1985, 272–278). King Childebert founded this as a funerary church in 558, and in the seventeenth century, when it was a royal abbey, the memory of the location of Merovingian dynastic graves are still alive. In 1645, in fact, during building work done in the choir, tombstones and medieval gisant-figures beneath the original sarcophagi were found (Bouillart 1724, 251–253).

Two intact burials were identified as King Childebert II and his wife Ultrogotha. Other sarcophagi were found in the same area during renewed building, in 1656. An inscription found within one of these attributes it to Childebert II who died in 674 (proving that the location of the same royal graves was approximate). From this grave were recovered remains of clothing, as well as a sword, a belt and gold ornament from a sword harness; the drawing of an applique with zoomorphic decoration has come down to us (Pl. 17). Other sarcophagi, opened in 1645 and intact, were uncovered again in 1656 and found to have been plundered. Many years later a monk confessed on his deathbed that he had secretly sold the precious objects for their gold. Dom Bernard de Montfaucon informs us that this grave-robbing monk still possessed 13,000 pounds from the sale (de Montfaucon 1729, 174); the money was put to use buying a new organ in 1664! This figure gives us some idea of the value of the objects found with these descendants of Clovis: they must have been essentially personal jewellery, the decoration of clothing accessories or of weapons, for such are about the only objects that can be fitted into a sarcophagus.

Whether or not these sarcophagi found in seventeenth century were in their original location – and there is no reason to think they were not – we are sure that they were carefully preserved over the following centuries, despite many major transformations of the church now known at Saint-Germain-des-Prés. The same respect would be expected at Saint-Genevieve for Clovis and Clotilde, as founders both of the church itself and of the first Catholic royal dynasty. However, unlike the case of the royal graves at Saint-Germain-des-Prés and at Saint-Denis, Clovis and Clotilde were not originally buried, in our hypothesis, directly under the church itself. This crucial difference may explain what happened to them and why no tradition about them survived at Saint-Genevieve. I shall argue that the Viking raids on Paris between 845 and 885 are the key to the enigma, and put forward the following hypotheses to explain their disappearance:

The first hypothesis is that, when the Viking attacks took place, the *sacrarium* was still as it always had been and probably had not been affected by building modifications in this church in the later eighth century. This is plausible enough: recent excavations at Saint-Germain-des-Prés have demonstrated, for example, that the walls of Childebert's sixth century basilica stood until the eleventh century, and were then partially reused (Fleury 1981). In this hypothesis, I shall assume that the royal graves were not removed to safety like Saint Genevieve's relics and were plundered. Even if the sarcophagi themselves were not destroyed, they need not have been deliberately preserved in later times, as there was nothing sacred about them. The mausoleum, then, would have lost its funerary function but continued to exist in some form: perhaps its walls, as I suggested above, would have been reused in the eleventh century.

The second hypothesis is that the old *sacrarium* had already been either destroyed or transformed before the Viking raids, that is during the eighth century remodelling referred to above. If this is so, let us entertain the following possibilities:

Either the *sacrarium* was a sunken-chamber, so its lower part was filled in; in this case the sarcophagi might have been buried; something of this sort happened in the case of the tombs of the young prince and princess of the cathedral of Cologne.

Or else the *sacrarium* was a ground-level construction, so that the royal tombs would have to have been transferred, and this would no doubt have been into the new crypt, or somewhere else under the nave of the church. I think the crypt unlikely, since in that case the sarcophagi would have survived the Viking raids, even in a damaged state, like the sarcophagi of Genevieve, Prudentius and Saint Eusoz which were there; in that case they too ought to have been mentioned in the sources and entered the abbey tradition. I like the second possibility better: it was more usual at that time to put royal graves in the earth under the floor of a church. In this case, the thirteenth century gisant could have been made to mark the site of the grave itself, which, as the Saint-Germain-des-Prés story reminds us (and there was a gisant there, too) could have remained known over the generations, even if a mention was not committed to writing. Why, then, did they not discover the king's sarcophagus in the seventeenth century when they moved the gisant into the choir to serve as a cenotaph? Perhaps the place where the gisant had been placed in the thirteenth century turned out to have been wrong, or perhaps an unrecorded and forgotten translation of the sarcophagus had taken place. In any event, as we have seen, the 1807 excavations in the nave failed to find Clovis' sarcophagus. However, these were not exhaustive; there are still unexplored areas accessible to new research, particularly the side-aisles of the nave and the parts of the apse outside the limits of the crypt.

Indeed, as I have been able to establish with the help of the Works Department of the City of Paris, the area under the rue Clovis has been little disturbed from the day it was built until the present. A new archaeological study is quite possible in theory; all that would be required would be to close off the street temporarily. A modern scientific study of the foundations of the former church and crypt of Saint-Genevieve and of the Holy-Apostles basilica would be reason enough to justify such an undertaking. It would then be possible to make a close look at the foundations of the northern chapel as well, and see if they could derive from the *sacrarium*. And they would allow us to excavate the Merovingian and later burials in the area which were not removed during the 1807 excavations.

This then is my proposal in the fiftieth year of Sutton Hoo. Let the competent authorities ensure the long term protection of the precious archaeological reserve under the rue Clovis, today protected by a recent resurfacing! (Pl. 18). Let the international scholarly community support a future project to reopen excavations which will take us back to the story of the Christian origins of

Paris, capital of the Franks! The scholarly merits of the case are strong. But since this is the era of public relations, perhaps we need a catchy slogan as well, something like 'The quest for Clovis' tomb'!

ACKNOWLEDGEMENTS

I wish to express my gratitude especially to my friends Bailey K. Young, Associate Professor at Assumption College (Worcester, USA), who translated into English the original version of this paper, Cathy Haith (British Museum), who helped me to condense this text for my lecture of 1 October 1989, and finally Joanna Sobczyk (then attached to Musée des Antiquités de la Seine-Maritime), who prepared with me the final version of this contribution.

My thanks also to M. Bauda, Ingénieur à la Divison des Plans de Voieries et Ouvrages d'Art de la Ville de Paris who authorised me to study the plans of the undergound street network.

19

Social Change around A.D.600: An Austrasian Perspective

GUY HALSALL

Introduction

In the past, there has been regretably little contact between the archaeologists and archaeologies of early Anglo-Saxon England and those of Merovingian Gaul. Merovingian archaeology may have lost most by this lack of communication; with notable exceptions, it remains out-dated at all but the most basic levels of analysis (Halsall 1990, ch. 2, sections 1 and 3, for a blunt critique of the situation in Lorraine). Nonetheless, Anglo-Saxon archaeologists interpretations might be more secure if continental evidence were more widely appreciated. As James (elsewhere in this volume, p. 248) says, if the work of Bailey Young (1975; 1977) on Christianity in Merovingian cemeteries were better known on this side of the Channel, Anglo-Saxon archaeologists might be less inclined to make the assumption that early Anglo-Saxon furnished inhumation is necessarily a 'pagan' custom (for example, implicitly, in Boddington 1990). Comparison with continental cemeteries might also weaken still further those 'Germanic' ethnic labels sometimes still applied to Anglo-Saxon grave-goods (James 1977:179–81; James 1979; Halsall 1992).

In this paper I should like to discuss evidence drawn from the region around Metz, the capital of Austrasia (fig. 46). This was an important part of the Frankish realms, and is fairly typical in the nature of its data-survival (Halsall 1990: ch.1). Important structural changes in Merovingian society in this part of Gaul can be shown to have taken place in the decades around A.D.600, and thus at about the same time as transformations in the nature of East Anglian society were producing such archaeologically visible results as the creation of the Ipswich trading centre and, of course, the Sutton Hoo barrow cemetery. An explanation of the Frankish changes might shed interesting light on East Anglian history around 600.

'A great many things keep happening.' So wrote Gregory of Tours some time after Easter 576 (Gregory of Tours, *L.H. praef.*; Halsall forthcoming [a]), fifty years before the usually-cited approximate date for Sutton Hoo mound 1

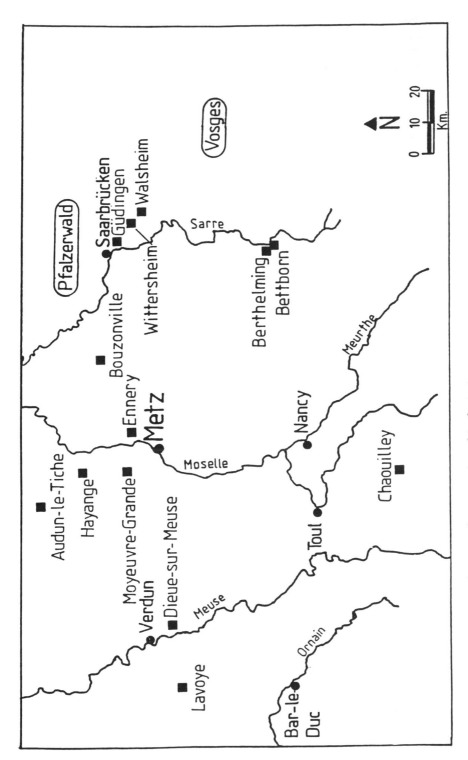

Figure 46. The area of Metz, showing places mentioned in the text.

(Carver 1989:150). He knew something was going on; it led him to begin his monumental history of his own times (Goffart 1988:ch. 3). Reading the last two books of Gregory's *Histories*, covering the years 586–91, leaves one in little doubt that by this time Gaul was in turmoil. Yet the massive changes in Gallic society in the decades around 600 have not generally been recognized. Goffart (1982:6) made it clear that vitally important developments in the nature of surplus extraction in the Frankish kingdoms can be dated to this period. He did not, however, fully explore or explain the implications of this, and they have thus gone unheeded. To Merovingian historians, the crucial changes come rather later, after the death of Dagobert I (638). Why, then, place major changes in Merovingian society a generation or so earlier? Let us consider the different aspects of the evidence in turn.

The Evidence for Change: Artefact Design

The fact that Merovingian artefacts underwent significant changes in their form and decoration around A.D.600 has long been recognized. Jules Pilloy and Eduard Brenner noted this in the 1890s, and it is still accepted. Wrangling over the end of Böhner's *Stufe* IV (from about 525 to about 600; see James, elsewhere this volume, p. 249) has not forced any major revision (Périn 1980; Périn & Feffer 1987:190) and Ament's chronology also sees the change from *Ältermerowingerzeit* to *Jüngermerowingerzeit* as taking place around 600 (Ament 1977).

The developments involve the introduction of large inlaid iron plaque-buckles, the abandonment of a number of brooch types and changes in the design of those which remain, the disappearance from the record of the *francisca*, a change in the design of the scramasax from the 'narrow sax' (*Schmalsax*) to the 'broad sax' (*Breitsax*), and so on. Furthermore, the important fields of decorative expression change from female artefacts such as brooches, to male ones such as plaque-buckles (hitherto generally undecorated; for the gender associations of artefacts, see Halsall 1990:chs 10–11; Halsall forthcoming [b]). These are important changes, of which we have been aware for almost a century, but changes which have never been explained except in the most vacuous terms of changing fashion.

Burial Custom

Camille Boulanger's drawings of typical Frankish burials from Picardie-Artois show that in 1902–5 he was aware of the differences between sixth-century graves and seventh-century burials (James 1988a:111–12). The difference was not simply that just mentioned, between artefact forms; the seventh-century deceased were buried with fewer, and less varied, objects.

Analysis of sites in modern Lorraine (Halsall 1990:chs 10–12) reveals these changes in more detail. Sixth-century grave-goods are numerous and varied. At the famous cemetery of Lavoye (Meuse; Joffroy 1974; Halsall 1990:307–27), there are no fewer than thirty-four general types of artefact, each found in two or more intact graves containing two or more such artefact-types. Seventh-century graves at Lavoye contain a range of only twenty-one artefact-types. These seventh-century grave-goods are also much more standardized than in the sixth century. The most common artefact-types at sixth-century Lavoye, the bronze buckle and the knife, were each found in about one third of intact burials. The plaque-buckle was found in over 56%, the grey-black vase in almost 45%, and the knife in 30% of intact seventh-century graves. The seventh-century site of Audun-le-Tiche (Moselle; Simmer 1988; Halsall 1990:334–47) shows a similar standardization, which is also indicated in analysis of the small sites of the diocese of Metz (Halsall 1990:282–98). At Dieue-sur-Meuse (Meuse; Guillaume 1974–5; Halsall 1990:327–34) there were similarly great differences between the sixth- and seventh-century phases.

Related to these points is the question of the grave-goods' associations. Analysis of the sixth-century sites of Ennery (Moselle; Delort 1947; Heuertz 1957; Clermont-Joly 1978; Halsall 1990:259–66) and Chaouilley (Meurthe-et-Moselle; Voinot 1904; Halsall 1990:301–5), and of the sixth-century phases of Lavoye and Dieue-sur-Meuse revealed that there were very clear associations between artefact-types and gender or position in the life-cycle (also summarized in Halsall, forthcoming [b]). In the seventh-century phases of Lavoye and Dieue-sur-Meuse, and on the small seventh-century sites of the diocese of Metz (Berthelming, Bettborn, Bouzonville, Hayange, Moyeuvre-Grande, Walsheim and Wittersheim; Halsall 1990:282–98) such associations were much less clear, and sometimes almost non-existant. Whether through greatly increased standardization or through apparently random distribution, the implication is clear: seventh-century grave-goods had less clear general meanings.

One can also distinguish, though less easily, the sixth-century methods used to show social differentiation other than that based upon age and gender: attempts to display class or rank. Such attempts are often subtle. As mentioned, the general rules governing the deposition of grave-goods highlight gender. Social distinction is shown by exaggeration of these community rules. When a young adult is supposed to be buried with masculine artefacts including weapons, social differentiation may be manifested by greatly increasing the numbers of such artefacts: he is not simply buried with weapons, he is buried with a lot of weapons. Analysing age-groups separately at sixth-century Lavoye, shows that among adult males a group of prestigious burials was really only marked out from its contemporaries by the number of gender-specific artefacts. The distribution of other object-types did not reveal as clear a 'pyramidal' structure. The site-plan showed these male 'prestige graves' often to be grouped within the cemetery. The clearly prestigious graves at

Chaouilley, Graves 19 and 20c, manifest the same feature of exaggeration and the same may be true at Güdingen (Saarland; Stein 1989; Halsall 1990:289–91), though this is far less clear.

At Ennery, however, the means of distinction were different. Graves 70 and 71, respectively of a 6–7 year-old boy and a man of over sixty, were both buried exclusively with masculine grave-goods, including two weapon types each. Study of the rest of the site showed very clearly that these age-groups were not generally associated with male-specific items, and especially not with weapons. Here were clear breaches of the community rules, combined with a slightly different grave orientation, positioning on the edge of the site, and similarity of rite between the burials, to show some form of social differentiation (Halsall 1990:279–80). Another group of burials in the south-west of the site was only distinguished by similarity of rite, positioning within the cemetery, and breach of an apparent rule governing where females should be buried. The group clustered around an interesting double-burial (Simmer 1983; Halsall 1990:276–7 & 280–2).

It is this breach, or inversion, of apparent rules which becomes the common means of displaying 'vertical' social differentiation in the seventh century – most clearly at Audun-le-Tiche, but also perhaps at Lavoye. It may be true, however, that by the seventh-century, the elites are being buried elsewhere; we will see shortly that this seems to be the time when churches are first founded in significant numbers. This leads us to discuss other methods of funerary status-display, other than those based around grave-goods. The shift from interment with a lavish display of grave-goods to burial in an expensively constructed above-ground chamber – a church – is reflected in the increased concern, very clear at Audun-le-Tiche, with permanent surface-level grave-markers: sarcophagus lids visible at ground-level, stone crosses, walls around graves or groups of graves, crude grave-stones (at Audun-le-Tiche reusing fragments of Roman sculpture). This suggests a change in audience. From a temporary display to local people (albeit probably drawn from a number of neighbouring communities) we perceive a shift to a concern with permanent monuments, possibly, as with the urban churches, aimed at a further-flung peer-group audience.

Probably related to the decrease in the significance of grave-goods and of temporary display to a local audience is a clear increase in the numbers of cemeteries. There are many more known seventh-century than sixth-century cemeteries, perhaps twice as many (Halsall 1990:diag. 4.5). Given that sixth-century sites are easier to notice in the fragmentary accounts of old chance discoveries, because of the existence of many more diagnostic sixth-century artefacts (*franciscas*, axes, *angones*, bird brooches, S-brooches, and so on), this has to be significant. From a large cemetery shared by a group of local settlements, we see a shift to a settlement to cemetery ratio nearer to 1:1. The temporary audience of the grave-goods display has shrunk; the message of the grave-goods is thus reduced; those who wish to display power do so by the construction of permanent above-ground markers, and, for the most powerful, by the removal of their dead from the community burial ground and their interment in a church.

Urbanism in Metz

A dramatic change in the fortunes of the settlement at Metz occurs in the late sixth century (Halsall, forthcoming [c]). In decline since the middle of the fourth century, the site probably ceased to be classifiable as urban from around 400, remaining an essentially ecclesiastical and administrative village. In the mid-sixth century, definitively by the 560s, Metz became the principal urban residence of the kings of Austrasia. From this date, we can detect a resurgence in the site's fortunes. Contrasting the evidence of the earlier sixth century with that from the later sixth century shows a clear increase in the number of cemeteries and churches in use. Comparing the late sixth-century with the seventh-century evidence, however, shows an even greater up-turn (Fig. 47; the dating of the churches is based upon that of Gauthier 1986:42–53). The important increase in churches is, for our purposes, particularly significant.

Economy

The changes in the form of artefacts, mentioned above, have important implications for the nature and control of manufacture. Sixth-century belt buckles, for example, are often of simple cast-bronze form – and often undecorated. Seventh-century buckles are of iron, inlaid with gold and silver wire, in often intricate forms. The large seventh-century disc brooches are often of similar complexity of design and manufacture. It does not seem unlikely that these changes represent greater craft specialization, and of course the ability to remove oneself from subsistence activities to engage in such specialization. The standardization of grave-goods is surely related to this, and representative of a change in the control of the distribution of socially important artefacts.

Other industrial changes can be seen in the period around 600. The stone sarcophagus industry reappears in the seventh century (Cuvelier and Guillaume 1988). This implies a supportive social context for the quarrying, decoration and transport over quite long distances, of heavy stone coffins. The revival of a stone-quarrying industry may have facilitated the up-turn in church building in Metz, though it is far from clear that such early churches were built of stone (James 1981:36–8). In any case, whatever the materials used, the upsurge in monumental building projects has clear implications for the existence and sponsorship of industrial activity. Perhaps most importantly, the early seventh century saw the revival of coinage in the region of Metz (Stahl 1982), as also in the neighbouring region of Trier (Gilles 1982), with all the changes in the nature and control of exchange which that implies.

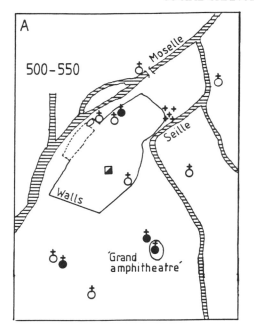

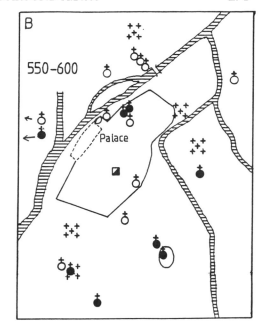

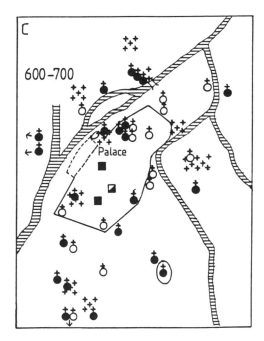

Urbanism in Metz, 500–700.

Church.
Possible Church.
Cemetery.
Occupation.
Partial or Summary Occupation.

Figure 47. The revival of urbanism in Metz

The Nature of the Aristocracy: Written Testimony

We come, finally, to a change in the nature of the social elite in northern Gaul, suggested by the documentary sources. There has been much debate upon the nature of the Frankish elite (Bergengruen 1958; Grahn-Hoek 1976; Irsigler 1979; James 1982:129–32) but differences between the sixth and seventh centuries have long been acknowledged.

As Grahn-Hoek (1976) persuasively argued, the sixth-century *Pactus Legis Salicae* (Murray 1983:ch. 5 for discussion of the dating) contains no recognition of an independent upper stratum of Frankish society. There is, for example, no hierarchical class within the free population which receives a higher *wergeld*, unlike the situation in late seventh-century Kent and Wessex, and unlike the situation even in sixth-century Burgundy (Burgundian Code II.2). Higher *wergelds* are assigned to women of child-bearing age, male children and individuals connected to, or owned by, the king. If an aristocracy is witnessed by the *Pactus*, it is a service aristocracy – a group of royal officials, the holders of titles bestowed by the king. Such titles – such social status – could be taken away by the king as easily as they were granted. There is, in sixth-century legal material, similarly little recognition of the existence of ties of dependence between freemen, such as we might later term lordship or vassalage. Apart from a vague distinction between 'the higher classes' and 'the lower classes' in an undated edict (*Pactus Legis Salicae* 102), there is no legally-acknowledged aristocracy, which derives its power independently of the king.

We have less seventh-century legal material from northern Gaul. Ripuarian Law, however, dates from the 620s, and applied in the region under discussion. Whilst in large part representing a reissue and fossilization of the *Pactus*, Ripuarian Law does show clear differences from its sixth-century precursor. Lords who held lands with immunity from royal exactions were recognized (ch. 68). Similarly, there is provision for free men with dependent followers (ch. 45.3; *homo cum satellitibus suis*), freemen in the service of others (ch. 35; *ingenuus in obsequio*) and for rent-paying tenants (ch. 65), all absent from the *Pactus*. These represent significant modifications of earlier law. Some of the same new features are to be found in Chlothar II's 614 Edict of Paris. This too recognizes legal immunities for some magnates, as well as the fact that certain aristocrats had acquired the power to appoint legal officials in the localities.

Gregory's *Histories* support the picture of the sixth-century Frankish aristocracy. The great men of Austrasia are (*pace* James 1982:130) entirely dependent upon royal favour and office to maintain their social position. Furthermore, Gregory's terminology is illuminating. With one possible exception (*L.H.* VIII.16), the only Franks he ever refers to as *nobiles* are the Merovingians themselves; yet Romans of the Past, sixth-century peoples living south of the Loire (Romano-Gauls and Burgundians) and even Goths could all be so described. If Gregory shared Isidore of Seville's definition of *nobilis* – one whose name and lineage are known (i.e. a rank acquired at birth; *Etymologies* 10.184) – this is significant. The same trend is manifested in the work of the first writer of the *Chronicon* of 'Fredegar', up to the 630s. Burgundians, Lombards and even Bavarians were recognized as having a caste of *nobiles*; but not the Franks. The word *nobilis* only comes to be used to describe Franks from 636 onwards ('Fredegar', *Chronicon* IV.78; Halsall 1990:229–31).

Other changes are detectable. The seventh century saw the creation of saints' lives in the Frankish regions of northern Gaul (eg. *Vita Arnulfi*). The very fact that such new literature was being written is, of itself, significant. Moreover, these new sources, in a way which is subtly different to both the sixth-century southern Gallic hagiography and later Saints' Lives, stress the *nobility* of the subject and his or her family (Sprandel 1961:57–58; Graus 1965:ch. 3; Prinz 1967:532). They dwell, also, on the time before the saint's conversion when he excelled in all areas of the secular life of an aristocrat. Irsigler (1979:121) claims that the *vita* of Arnulf of Metz is the earliest example of such hagiographic concerns: its subject lived between c.570/580 and c.640.

The concern to produce new literature extolling the virtues and nobility of Frankish saints and their families is linked to the explosion, again from around 600, of a new form of rural monasticism, associated with the Irish ascetic Columbanus. As Prinz (1981) argued, Columbanus was a catalyst. His brand of monasticism was eagerly seized upon by the northern, Frankish aristocracy as a means of expressing a newly acquired power and prestige. Goffart (1982), as mentioned, dated to the generation around 600 the Merovingian kings' loss of important royal rights to various forms of tax from aristocratic estates. From whatever perspective the problem is viewed, we cannot but perceive a massive difference between the sixth-century Frankish aristocracy – dependent upon the king, fluid in composition, lacking in legal or institutional recognition – and its seventh-century successor, with its growing sense of of group identity, its means of self-expression, its increasing institutional and legal privilege and social status, and its greater concentration upon birth – nobility – as a qualification for entry.

Conclusions (Fig. 48)

The foregoing all-too-cursory review demonstrates that throughout Frankish society and its material remains, important changes exist between the sixth and seventh centuries. In all of these areas the critical period appears to be that spanning the last quarter of the sixth century and the first quarter of the seventh. The explanation of these, at first sight, disparate changes has to be sought in a transformation of the ruling strata in Austrasia.

By the early fifth century, the rigid late Roman social hierarchy had collapsed in northern Gaul. The Imperial state's effective presence was withdrawn, probably rather earlier than we are accustomed to believe; wealthy

Sixth Century.	Seventh Century.
1. Archaeological Cemetery Evidence.	
Grave-goods are numerous and varied.	Grave-goods are reduced in numbers and type.
Variety in grave-assemblages.	Standardization of grave-assemblages.
Grave-goods appear to stress age and gender as the major structural principles of social organization.	Grave-goods do not have such strong connections with gender and age. They appear to be more related to wealth and rank.
Fewer, large, cemeteries.	More cemeteries, frequently quite small.
2. Economics.	
The economy appears to be localized, based primarily upon subsistence, with little evidence of industry, craft specialization or a monetary economy.	Changes in artefact types, styles and decoration.
	Increased evidence of craft-specialization.
	Stone sarcophagus industry revives.
	Non-royal coinage, lower denomination, gold emerges.
3. Urbanism in Metz.	
The town continues to stagnate for much of the century.	Metz recovers and begins to expand dramatically.
	Many churches founded in Metz.
4. The Leaders of Society.	
Aristocracy very much defined by de facto local prestige, and royal favour.	Creation of a nobility defined by family and birth, with legally recognized status and privilege.
Composition of the aristocracy fluid and ill-defined.	
Kings usually strong and retain complete control over their magnates.	The monarchy, after an early recovery, progressively slides into decline and loses control over the nobility.
	Politics dominated by rivalries between great families.
5. Law.	
An impression is given of free society as based upon gender and position in the life-cycle, with the only other forms of power based upon royal service.	Indications of more institutionalized social hierarchy and community leadership.
	Recognition of lords with retinues, rent-paying tenants and legal immunities.

Figure 48. Changes (in the region of Metz) c.600

landlords fled to the more stable areas of the south, and even further afield; Frankish and Alamannic settlers and conquerors sought to establish themselves in the area; villa-estates fragmented (Halsall 1990: ch. 4) local leaders, known to the central government as *bacaudae* (Van Dam 1985: ch. 3; Drinkwater 1989; 1992) struggled for power within communities. The social hierarchy became very unstable, and it is this instability which led to the rise of the furnished burial rite (Halsall 1990; 1992). When social standing and power was not easily transmitted from one generation to the next, acts of 'social theatre' such as the funerals, with attendant feasting, of family members and especially of family heads, became important as means of competitive display, and as occasions for the reaffirmation – and advancement – of social standing.

The early laws give the impression that, below the king, everyone in the free population was created equal. In the laws, as with the grave-goods, the image is given that age and gender are the major means of distinguishing between people. Yet closer inspection reveals real competition for authority, and, behind the ideology, real *de facto*, if not *de jure*, differences in power. As narrative sources and the laws show, royal favour and the ability to obtain official posts were important strategies in acquiring such power. But these titles and their attendant social status could be easily withdrawn. Thus we perceive a two-edged struggle for power in the sixth century. On the one hand, there was the conflict between the *de facto* powerful and their rivals at a local level, with royal favour often being used as a weapon. On the other was the higher-level struggle between this aristocracy and the monarchy, with the local power of the former often employed against the latter.

In the first side of this struggle, the strategy of acquiring royal or official support to establish local authority can be demonstrated at a slightly lower, regional level. Fig. 49 shows the distribution of graves with certain prestige items in the region of Metz. As can be seen, such burials do not become common until thirty or more kilometres from Metz. The 'exclusion zone' (very clear when just examining graves with shield-bosses, spurs or horse-harness) is best explained as showing the area within which local power struggles were resolved by appeal to the king, bishop, duke and other magnates, often resident in Metz. Beyond that the use of symbols of military power, or of access to military resources (shield-bosses, warhorses, prestige weapons), of the distribution of food and drink (bronze bowls and buckets) and of the control of exchange (balances), in funerals was a potent means of displaying local authority, where such power was open to competition.

The second side of the struggle, between monarchy and aristocracy, needs a little more attention. Merovingian kings needed their *de facto* powerful – their 'Franks' – to command their armies, to administer law and order, and so on. To this end, they had to acquiesce in the creation of local power, often by the leaders of armed bands. Hence the fairly lenient treatment of such bands in sixth-century Frankish law, where, however, they are described as bands of equals rather than as men with armed followings (*pace* Irsigler 1979:110).

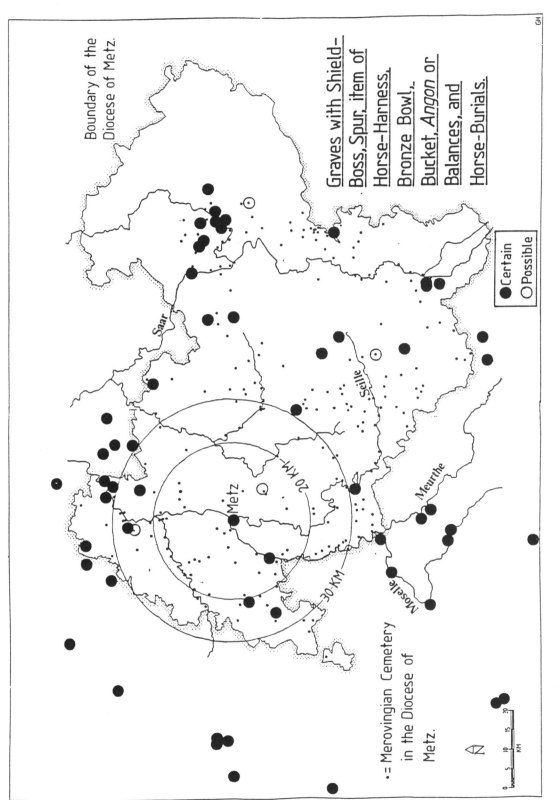

Figure 49. Lavish burials in the region of Metz

Nonetheless, in their attempts to secure control of the surplus directly from the free population through taxation (using such aristocrats as officials), the kings did not wish to create a permanent elite social rank – a nobility – between them and the remainder of this population. The aristocrats, on the other hand, wished to gain a more permanent control of surplus to enable them to maintain their social standing and pass it on to their heirs. Early Merovingian kings struggled to play aristocratic factions off against each other, to give power and take it away arbitrarily (*L.H.*VIII.36; IX.12), and to limit the extent to which estates could be inherited (cp. *L.H.* IX.35 & X.21). The aristocracy, on the other hand, fought for hereditary control of lands and men, and for the rights to extract royal dues from their own estates, and struggled to create group identity and self-consciousness. It is surely in this struggle that we see the real dynamic for social change in the post-Roman West, rather than in a 'class struggle' between slaves and masters, or between peasantry and nobility.

Some time between 575 and 625 the aristocracy won both of these struggles. As we have seen they acquired a clearer group identity as what we may term a nobility, with inheritable power and standing, and control over their estates. The lesson of Irsigler's (1979) lucid survey of the Merovingian aristocracy is, in spite of his attempts to prove the opposite, clearly that he could find no evidence of his defined characteristics of nobility before the early seventh century. With this more rigid social hierarchy there was less need for the essentially local and temporary display of grave-goods in a funeral: as stated, the arena for display shifted elsewhere. This new nobility also had the power to patronize and control trade, industry and manufacture, to sponsor monumental architecture, and to remove themselves from local struggles to spend time at higher-status settlements, all of this fostering the revival of urbanism.

Why had this change come about? The kings will always have had difficulties in preventing the creation of a landed self-conscious group of magnates. The tendency for large estates to become hereditary is often irresistable. With increasing contact and intermixture between the *de facto* Frankish *Oberschicht* and the *de jure* nobilities of southern Gaul (Gallo-Roman and Burgundian), this tendency will have been accentuated. The catalyst for important change was the series of royal minorities and wars, between the assassination of Sigibert I (575) and Chlothar II's conquest of Austrasia (613). During this period, Austrasia was ruled by minors between 575 and 585, and from 596 to 601 (and from 601–612 was ruled by the 'feeble-minded' Theodebert II; cp. 'Fredegar' *Chronicon* IV.35), Burgundy from 597–602, and Neustria from 584–99. During these years the Frankish aristocratic factions wielded power. The regents for Childebert II, Chlothar II, Theudebert II and Theuderic II often had to purchase support from these factions. The turmoil described in Gregory's last two books is at least partly the result of Childebert II's attempts to reassert royal power after coming of age (585). The Merovingian royal house revived its power, especially after Chlothar II unified Francia in 613, but henceforth the participants in the struggle were different. When the royal line was again smitten by a series of minorities in the mid-seventh century, it was a very different, and much more powerful aristocracy which seized control of the kingdoms. From this point on, in spite of the caution with which we must treat the traditional picture of late Merovingian weakness (see, e.g., Fouracre 1986; Wood 1992), this new nobility was not to be dislodged from its position of power.

These changes in north Gallic society, analagous to many taking place in Anglo-Saxon England, clearly have numerous implications for early Anglo-Saxon archaeology, but space permits only a brief examination. As has been argued before, above all by Ian Wood (1983; 1991; elsewhere in this volume), southern Anglo-Saxon England may be regarded as part of the fringe of the Frankish world. Is it not at least possible that the changes taking place in Francia would have had repercussions in Anglo-Saxon England? Let us look briefly to Kent, where the case for Frankish overlordship is strongest. Is it merely coincidence that Aethelberht, who was married to a minor Frankish princess, and who had had a Frankish bishop, Liudhard, foisted upon him, appealed directly to the Pope for a mission just as the powerful Childebert II died, plunging the Merovingian realms into more minorities and civil war? Could stress in Austrasia, which controlled the Rhineland and thus the supply of prestige-goods to eastern England, have prompted a similar East Anglian power display? The creation of a segregated cemetery at Sutton Hoo; the contents of Mound 1; the recently discovered horse-burial; the use of permanent above-ground monuments as part of the funerary display: all these are features which can be paralleled in the Frankish world, particularly on its fringes, around 600. It might not be unreasonable to conclude that in the critical decades around 600, whilst Frankish aristocrats became nobles, certain Anglo-Saxon aristocrats finally became kings.

ACKNOWLEDGEMENTS

For their help with the research for the doctoral thesis upon which this paper is based, I should like to record a debt of thanks, above all to my supervisor Dr Edward James (University of York), but also to Mr Steve Roskams (University of York), Prof. F. Stein (Universität des Saarlandes), Mme M. Clermont-Joly (Musées de Metz) and Mme C. Aptel (Musée Historique Lorrain).

20

Kingdoms, Ethnicity and Material Culture: Denmark in a European Perspective

LOTTE HEDEAGER   translated by John Hines

Introduction

During the Migration Period, when large areas of Europe move from Antiquity into the Early Middle Ages – to a historical period, with written sources, in other words – Scandinavia remains undocumented and thus 'prehistoric'. The history of Scandinavia in the fifth, sixth and seventh centuries has therefore been approached and dealt with on the basis of the archaeological evidence, with the result that a series of phenomena which are historical facts on the Continent, such as peoples and mass migrations, kings and kingdoms, have never properly found a place in the understanding of Scandinavian prehistory. To put it another way, a virtue has been made of what appears to be a methodological necessity, and Scandinavia has, on the whole, been denied a place in European history during those centuries for which archaeological data, legend and historical accounts allow one to imagine that there was far more contact and realization of a common history than today's culture-historians are inclined to accept. The aims of this article are firstly to clarify terms such as 'migration', 'people' and 'king', and secondly to interpret the archaeological material in the light of the written records. By way of introduction to this analysis, I shall sketch some of the basic features of Germanic social organization.[1]

---

[1] My thanks go to Anders Andrén, Morten Axboe, Aron Gurevich, Karen Høilund Nielsen, Stig Jensen, Kristian Kristiansen, Anne Kromann, Bjørn Myhre and Ian Wood for the use of as yet unpublished articles.

Comprehensive research has been carried out on the history of the Germanic tribes, with a combining of the historical sources, especially Caesar and Tacitus, with archaeological evidence. One of the major works is Wenskus 1961. In Steuer's largely archaeologically based *tour de force* through the early medieval period of central Europe (1982), social structure is interpreted on the basis of a historical model.

In contrast to Scandinavia, a steadily increasing amount of work has been done in

Germanic Warrior Ideology

The Germanic communities, whether they were on their own territory or on others', were warrior societies. At their heart lay an ideology which elevated religion and war into inseparable entities. The chief was first and foremost a war-leader (called *reiks* by the Goths); he was chosen as leader solely – or with a few qualifications – on the basis of his merits as a warrior. The sort of society in which the undisputed leader was the eldest of the tribe, or was a selected member of a particular clan (*thiudans* amongst the Goths), had gone for ever (James 1989, 42; for Tacitus' *dux* and *rex* cf. Wallace-Hadrill 1971, 1ff.).

The warrior elite, which came into existence apparently around the beginning of the first century A.D. and which was consolidated from around A.D.200, broke from the old kindred-based tribal society. The new aristocracy was constructed around a land-owning/land-controlling class whose members entered into personal relationships and alliances with one another. Loyalty and gift-giving were the core around which this society turned (Hedeager, in press).

It was, in other words, not sufficient for this new class to *possess* wealth; no leading man won influence for himself – or kept what he had – simply by sitting upon large areas of land or considerable treasure. On the contrary, his wealth had to circulate. Armed power required that a leading man should be able to harness warriors to himself through a tie of loyalty. And he could do this best by sharing out his wealth generously and thus committing those who accepted it to reciprocate – in the form either of gifts in return, military service, or in some other way.

The surplus which was essential in order to keep this flow of gifts going was not obtained solely through the products of the soil. War, plundering and theft were essential to keep the system intact. It is this warlord that we meet again and again in legend and saga literature; this is the lord of land, goods, horses, ships and gold, who determinedly hands out his wealth, and is lavish in the provision of hospitality.

The fundamental theme of the surviving legends and sagas, in those, that is, which are not affected by Christian attitudes, is an obsession above all else with the term *honour* (Gurevich, forthcoming). The message, or, if you like, the doctrine, is not to be missed: the purpose of life was to lose one's life with honour, and that was only possible in battle. In recompense, one was richly paid in this life.

Warrior societies such as these demand one thing in particular: war. Without the enriching contribution of raiding campaigns, the gift-system – and with

recent years on the Continental contacts and background of the Anglo-Saxon period in England (e.g. Wallace-Hadrill 1971, Hodges 1982, 1989b, Wood 1983, Hines 1984, James 1989). This book itself, *The Age of Sutton Hoo*, is a reflection of that same interest.

that the whole social network of ties and alliances – would fall apart; without battle, the warrior aristocracy's ideology would be empty, even meaningless. Its monopoly of power would then depend upon its capacity to maintain internal control instead of mobilization against some external enemy or towards external opportunities.

It is here indeed that we shall find the key to an understanding of the Germanic migrations; they have to be comprehended as an inevitable necessity for the maintenance of a newly-formed social order rather than as a chance solution to the problems of a failed harvest. They are not unique as a phenomena, but are unique in the strength of the effect they had in the emergence of Europe's first-ever nation-states.[2]

The Ideology of Migrations

The migrations created a new form of political community which was founded upon neither ethnic nor genetic connexions. The early-medieval nation was composed of groups that were brought together for political reasons and which thereby conclusively ruptured the old Germanic tribal groupings (Wenskus 1961).

The Franks, the Suebi, the Alamanni, the Vandals, the Goths, the Angles, the Saxons, the Heruli, the Jutes and the Burgundians did indeed migrate, but this should not be imagined to have taken the form of every single one of them uprooting themselves from their homeland and wandering at random around Europe. Some stayed put, others packed up and migrated; others joined in. What they shared was a common political destiny, and an ideology which turned them into Goths, Vandals, Burgundians, or whatever.

In this way, the powerful Ostrogoth kingdom – or tribal confederation – which was ruled by King Ermanaric at the end of the fourth century included not only the Goths themselves but also Finns, Slavs, Heruli, Alans, Antae, Huns and Sarmatians. The same polyethnic structure is found under King Theoderic in sixth-century Italy. Marching in his army were not only Ostrogoths, but also Rugii, Vandals, Alans, Heruli, Ascarii, Turcilingi, Suebians, Sarmatians, Taifali, Gepids and Alamanni, together with the not-to-be-forgotten Romans with 'Gothic hearts', not as foreign mercenaries but as

---

[2] Throughout prehistory, we see again and again 'archaeological horizons' which spread like wildfire over very large areas, only to disappear again just as rapidly as they came. Before the Germans it was the Celts who spread themselves across Europe. During an astonishingly short time they expanded out of a heartland that stretched from France to Bohemia so that in reality they covered the area that on the whole corresponds to that part of Europe which was neither, nor became, Germanic. Celtic warriors plundered Rome in 390 B.C. and the holy Greek city of Delphi in 279 B.C. Celtic society was constructed around a growing warrior aristocracy to a matching degree.

full members of the Gothic people (Wolfram 1990, 4). Even Clodevig's army comprised not only Franks but also Thuringians, Alamanni, Visigoths, Burgundians, Saxons and Germanic warriors 'from the islands and from Scandinavia' (Steuer 1987, 190).

The ethnic complexity of the Goths is known only because a greater part of their migration took place inside Roman territory. It may have comprised more different elements than those armies which did not turn up inside the Imperial borders. But it would not have been essentially different from the Alamanni, the Burgundians, the Franks and so on. What bound these all together was the assertion of tribal commonality: they belonged – ideologically at least – to the same *gens*, the same hereditary group. Although the Gothic army was as little Gothic as the Roman army was Roman, the difference was that the Roman army regarded itself as an army, the Gothic as a people.

According to the Goths' own national history they were then a *people*, with an equation of people and army being understood. A people thus did not comprise all the members of one genealogically linked family group but rather members of several different *gentes*. Etymologically, the words *gens*, *genus* – *genos*, *genealogia* and *natio* all contain some concept of genetic relationship (Wolfram 1990, 17). One people was ruled by one war-king; he belonged, really or ideologically, to a 'recognized' family, whose origins could be traced back to (for example) the Goths (in the case of Theoderic, for instance, to Amal). It was their *charisma* which formed the very heart of the tradition of the people; what linked them together was therefore the product of a common descent.[3] What connected the people to the war-king were the ties of loyalty and binding oaths, not real genealogical links and ties. The title of king was national, not territorial, and the origin of the kingdom has to be seen as the origin of the people (James 1989, 47). Their material culture, Germanic material culture, took on a new identity-forming function with this development. An independent germanic style became the symbol of the new communities of political federations or 'nations', but it was also, apparently, used to signal both the warrior aristocracy and the new kingships, in the same way as the set of warrior-equipment itself (Steuer 1987).

Kingship, Ethnicity and Material Culture in Scandinavia

Although the area was one with rich grave-finds and close Continental contact in the Roman Iron Age (the first to fourth centuries A.D.) (Hedeager 1978a, 1978b), the lack of finds in Denmark, not least the absence of graves, in the

3   Wolfram 1990. The common inheritance was attested to in the people's national history, for instance as written in the first place by Jordanes and Gregory of Tours in the sixth century, by Bede and Paul the Deacon in the eighth century, and so on in a series which ends around 1200 when Saxo Grammaticus composed his work on the history of the Danes (Goffart 1988).

period between 400 and 700 stands in sharp contrast to the rich graves of the period from the rest of Scandinavia and the Continent (Steuer 1987 Abb.9). Without doubt, the Migration Period in Denmark is a period of wealth in gold, but this gold was squirrelled away in hoards and poured out as votive deposits, in the form of ring gold and hackgold (Hedeager 1991). Not a lot besides isolated brooches – probably from disturbed graves – is known from the Merovingian Period. The gold of the Migration Period, however, has not altered the traditional view of a Denmark isolated from the world outside, a poor region in a state of crisis at a time when other parts of Europe – and not least the rest of Scandinavia – are demonstrating their wealth and their contacts on the Continent. The general consensus has been that it was not until the Viking Period, four hundred years later, that Denmark again took a place in the European community.

In recent years, however, this picture has begun to crack. To begin with, it stands in sharp contrast to the picture which settlement and agriculture now provide, in the form of large farmsteads, large villages and successful, intensive agriculture (Hedeager 1987, 133ff., Hedeager and Kristiansen 1988, Hedeager, in press). Secondly, it does not match with the picture of wide-ranging Continental contacts which the excavations of recent years at the trading and production site of Lundeborg and the central place at Gudme in south-western Fyn provide (Fig. 50) (Thrane 1987, Vang Petersen 1988, Thomsen 1989, Randsborg 1990). A re-assessment of Denmark's role in the fifth, sixth and seventh centuries is therefore called for (cf. Näsman and Lund, eds, 1988).

In an attempt to interpret the place of Denmark and Scandinavia in the European context, I shall start from the following two hypotheses:

— The political ideology of the early state societies was realized in material symbolism through which one signalled one's identity. This is to be expected to be strongest at the boundary between two political systems, or in periods of competition, such as in the course of political expansion (Hodder 1979, 1982).
— Symbols of power are used in funerary practice when new elites are being established (e.g. barrows/rich grave goods) but consolidated elites are more likely to deposit offerings to the gods in the form of hoards (Hedeager 1990, Hedeager, in press, Kristiansen in press, Fig. 2.5).

The marking of an emergent elite through investment in graves, often with weapons, while their consolidation is underpinned by votive deposits, is well-documented in the case of Denmark in a long-term perspective which covers the Iron Age from its inception around 500 B.C. up to the Viking Period. Both geographically and chronologically these two find-groups are in complementary distribution (Hedeager, in press).

If, by contrast, one sets the model in such a form that the chronological variations are converted into contemporary geographical variations in a large area, it could possibly explain some of the remarkable geographical variations

Figure 50. Places of production of imported goods of the Roman and Germanic Iron Ages (A.D.200–700) found in the Gudme region

and dislocations in material culture which are so striking in Europe during the three centuries of the Migration Period and the Merovingian Period. In order to understand this period, it is essential to assess it in a relatively broad chronological perspective. For this reason, the model starts in the Earlier Roman Iron Age and ends with the Viking Period – a period within which Denmark changes from traditional, kindred-based tribal societies to an emerging state society with its (historically known) kingdoms.

The Early Roman Iron Age (A.D.1–175/200)

The first two centuries after the birth of Christ represent the peak of the traditional tribal societies of the earlier Iron Age. Roman luxury wares – above all drinking sets of bronze, silver and glass – were distributed across free

Germania from the Roman Empire (Eggers 1951 Map 4). They were originally intended as diplomatic gifts to pro-Roman Germanic leaders (Hedeager and Kristiansen 1981) but were in due course taken over and used amongst the Germans themselves. These were goods which could not be bought and sold but which were purely expressions of personal relationships and ties. These goods – and their symbolic value – could not be transferred to others but followed the individual at death as an important part of the burial rituals, for use in the life hereafter. Through deposition in 'princely graves', they supported the common identity of the Germanic tribal aristocracy and its wide-ranging alliances in a Europe in which a global Roman Empire had become an obtrusive and magnetic political reality.[4]

The Later Roman Iron Age (A.D.175/200–375/400)

The decisive break with the traditional tribal societies takes place in this period, not only in Denmark but over the whole Germanic area. At this time the names of new political confederations such as, for example, the Franks, the Thuringians, the Alamanni, and so on, replaced a number of old tribal names. Population groups began to move: the Goths and the Gepids went towards the south-east from the Baltic coast, the Burgundians towards the south-west, and so on. The wars of the Marcomanni at the end of the second century show the result of these early migrations, when the Romans and the Germans clashed.

In Scandinavia too, national armies were on the move; this is directly reflected in the great war-booty sacrifices. Armies of many hundreds of men, whose equipment comes broadly from south-eastern Norway and the west coast of Sweden (Ilkjær 1991), were involved at various times in tremendous battles for eastern Jutland and Fyn. Of course, we do not know who these people were; we can only see that they were foreigners who were seeking to conquer a part of what now is Denmark.

Jordanes, in his History of the Goths, which contains occasional snippets about Scandinavia, writes that the Danes, who had 'grown from a Swedish root', 'had driven the Heruli from what had been their home'. According to information given by Procopius, the Danes were controlling parts of Jutland at least by the beginning of the sixth century.

Exceptionally rich grave finds, to begin with from eastern Sjælland and a few generations later from Fyn, do not clash with this view. If we put the

---

[4] Hedeager 1987, 127 ff. The existence of an aristocracy is indicated by the grave-type: compare Eggers' princely graves of the Lübsow type (Eggers 1949/50) and Steuer 1982 figure p. 211. In Denmark at least the exclusivity of these graves is emphasized by their geographical placing, as they always stand alone, occasionally together with a few more graves of the same character in small cemeteries, but never together with the more common graves in larger cemeteries.

archaeological and the historical data against one another we can draw the outlines of the course of events: an army, accompanied by a large following which, ideologically at least, belonged to the same *gens*, the same clan, whose shared denomination subsequently was as the Danes, came from the north and the east, occupied eastern Denmark and expelled parts of the original population, who, known as the Heruli, migrated southwards into Europe and thus rapidly wrote themselves into Roman history. They were unlikely to have been essentially different from the folk who occupied eastern Denmark and who took on an identity as the Danes. The difference was simply that the one group continued their migrations as troops of warriors within Europe down into the sixth century (Steuer 1982, 523) and the other stayed put in a given geographical location – southern Sweden and the Danish islands. It was the first representatives of this new people who used Roman luxury goods in great quantities to support their position with alliances and to betoken their power.

In this way, the Roman artifacts became a physical part of the language of power; the maintenance of a newly-won order of things was legitimized with symbols. But the new identity of the elite (which was, or became, *Danes*) encouraged the development of a more subtle language of power than one which only foreign exotica could express, and for the first time in the Iron Age 'regalia' were produced in the local context. This is found in the finger- and armrings of gold with dragon or serpents' heads as symbols (Beckmann 1969, Andersson 1986), in the simple, but heavy *Kolben*-armrings,[5] in drinking cups of silver and large silver- or gold-covered brooches (including 'monstrous brooches' – Werner 1988 Abb.5 and 6). The distribution of these in Scandinavia is an expression of the same alliances as those which lead to the distribution of Roman goods out of eastern Denmark into Sweden and Norway (Lund Hansen 1987, 223).

In this way, the outlines of a new royal identity and self-consciousness were drawn for the first time. A new Germanic symbolic language was in the course of development. At the same time, the Scandinavian writing-system, the runic script, was developed, most probably in Denmark, southern Sweden and to some extent southern Norway (Moltke 1976). The invention and function of the runic script must be seen as a integral part of the larger economic and political processes that took place in these centuries. The archaic nature of the runic language – it remains unchanged down to the eighth century –

---

[5] Werner 1980. These armrings, which are found as early as the third century in a grave on Sjælland (and in just one of the great bog-deposits) keep their symbolic character in European contexts from the Black Sea to the Atlantic (Werner 1980 Fig.2) down to the seventh century; they are found, *inter alia* in Childeric's grave (Werner 1980) and in the woman's grave in Cologne cathedral (Doppelfeld and Pirling 1966 p. 84). In the same period no less that twelve whole and four halved *Kolben*-armrings are known as loose finds/votive deposits from the Danish area.

emphasizes both its exclusivity and its political-ideological function (Hedeager, forthcoming).

Looked at in a broader, European perspective, eastern Denmark – along with Thuringia – has a special place in this period. In both areas, very rich graves with both Roman and Germanic regalia signalled the existence of a new elite: a land-controlling royal power with a warrior aristocracy which broke once and for all with the traditional Germanic family-based societies and which unlike other armed troops in these centuries stayed put in a given geographical area. In both places the new, land-owning upper class used the same type of new place-names to mark their rights – names which have survived to the present day (Fig. 51).[6]

The graves in Thuringia are dated to the fourth century and the beginning of the fifth (Schulz 1933, 1953). From the beginning of the fifth century at least we have to reckon with a Thuringian national community, and after the alliance with Attila in the middle of that century the kingdom is called Thoringi, the kings of which had close personal contacts with both the Franks and the Ostrogoths (Behm-Blancke 1973, 50). It is natural, therefore, to see the earlier, very rich graves in the light of the political development in which the Thuringians as a nation settled and took over land in the area between the River Werra and the Elbe, the territory which became the kingdom of Thoringi.

The graves of eastern Denmark, which began a few generations earlier, show so great a similarity with the graves in Thuringia that there must be a palpable case of personal connexions – of an alliance of equals between the newly-established kingdoms (= peoples) of the Thuringians and the Danes.

We can affirm, in summary, that both in eastern Denmark and in Thuringia a new Germanic symbolic language was employed in order to legitimize an ideological distancing from Roman culture and dominance. At the same time a Germanic written language was developed and settlements were named. All of this ideological repertoire reflected a new political consciousness, which we shall see developed in the centuries that follow.

The Migration Period (c.400–c.520/530)

Over large areas of Europe, the Migration Period was a turbulent time, which led finally to a number of 'peoples' obtaining more lasting territorial positions. From being exclusively politically defined kingdoms (the origin of the kingdom being the same as the origin of the people) these now became

---

6 In southern Scandinavia it is a personal name followed by -lev, in Thuringia by -leben, which in both areas means 'this person's property, received by inheritance': in other words land, which is owned and is heritable. These names are dated philologically in Denmark to the Migration Period – possibly even earlier (Søndergaard 1972, Jørgensen 1981); in respect of archaeology, both in Denmark and in Thuringia they are linked to grave-finds of the Later Roman Period (Mildenberger 1959/60, Nielsen 1979).

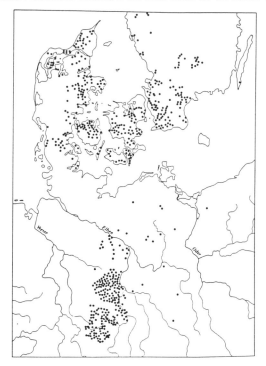

Figure 51. Distribution of place-names
ending in *-lev* (Scandinavian)/ *-leben*
(German)

territorially defined kingdoms, e.g. those of the Visigoths, the Burgundians, the Franks, the Vandals, and so on. The violent progress of the Huns and the conflicts which impermanent alliances with various Germanic peoples inevitably brought with them did nothing to lessen the chaos of affairs.

A number of the Germanic nations traced their origins back to Scandinavia – for instance the Goths, the Burgundians, the Langobards, the Heruli on the Continent, and the Jutes, the Angles and the Saxons in England. And this took place in a period in which the Franks established themselves as the dominant power in western Europe, rooted territorially in the old administrative system of the Romans. In other words, there was a ideological polarizing of the Germanic peoples between those who identified themselves with the Franks and those who regarded the origins of their nation as lying in Scandinavia.[7]

---

[7] Indirect support for the idea that the Heruli regarded themselves as Scandinavian is found in the most recent archaeological studies of the Swedish hoards from Sösdala, Fulltofta and Vennebo as belonging to mounted nomads, probably Hunnic – or Hunnic-inspired (Fabech 1989, 14). Fabech interprets them as Herulic on the strength of the consideration that they were found in southern Sweden, where the Heruli had returned at the beginning of the sixth century after having served, amongst other things, as highly valued mercenary soldiers with the Huns.

Scandinavia itself was less affected by mass migration, as 'migrations' here had already come to an end as far as the Danes were concerned, who had come from the north-east several centuries earlier, and perhaps for the Jutes too, who no later than the middle of the fifth century – and very possibly earlier – moved over to England. And if we were to put any trust in the various origin myths, the Continental peoples with Scandinavian roots would according to their histories have left Scandinavia at an earlier date.

All the same, the Danes, through dynastic alliances and trade, were part of Migration-period Europe. This is further revealed by the way that the violent events in European history in the fifth century lived on in the Scandinavian (and, in part, the Germanic) legends and saga tradition right down to the present day (for instance Sigurd's saga = Siegfried's saga = the Völsungs' saga = the Nibelungenlied; Lukman 1943). The legends are an expression of a collective memory which goes back to the three quarters of a century in which the Huns subjected the greater part of Europe to themselves and the Germanic warrior societies met their superiors for the first time (Hedeager 1990).

Archaeological, historical and literary sources agree with each other in describing an aristocratic life-style, the warrior ideology and the construction of the retinue – the *comitatus* – which characterized the Germanic kingdoms in Europe in the fifth, sixth and seventh centuries from Italy to Sweden (Steuer 1987, 225). In southern Scandinavia, the earliest traces of this ideology of social superiority are visible in the iconography of the gold bracteates, which clusters around the prince of the gods, Odin, and which in a number of cases can be interpreted in agreement with the Eddaic poems (Hauck, 1978, 1986, et al., Axboe, forthcoming, Axboe and Kromann, forthcoming). The establishment of a divine lord has to be looked at in the light of the worldly kings' attempts to underpin their power by transferring their own political ideals to the religious field and to deify their own lineage. This was what Theoderic the Great did with his dynasty, the Amals, and what Childeric and Clodevig did with the Merovingians; in due course a number of the English kings claimed to be descended from Woden (according to Bede) and a number of the Scandinavian kings to be descended from Odin (Axboe, forthcoming). And the unknown Danish kings would undoubtedly have done the same in the fifth century.

The bracteates formed a political medium, used in contexts where politics were in evidence, such as at the great feasts connected with religious ceremonies and the taking of the oath of loyalty (Andrén, forthcoming). The centre for these objects was south-eastern Fyn, around Gudme, their central distribution was in southern Scandinavia, but bracteates are found over the whole Continent from England to Hungary and the Ukraine (Fig. 52). Familiarity with them, and an understanding of their symbolic iconography, were sufficiently great for copies of them to be produced in several places in Europe where Scandinavian origins were an element in the aristocratic ideology as, for instance, amongst the Jutes in Kent and the Langobards in Pannonia (Hungary) (Andrén, forthcoming).

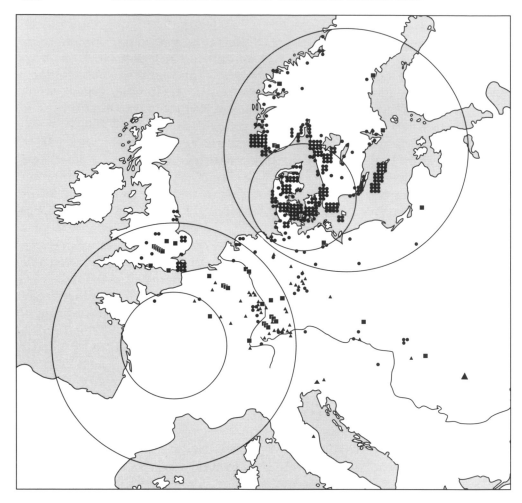

Figure 52. Distribution of: ● Bracteates ▲ Brooches of Scandinavian type on the Continent ■ Two-edged display swords (grave-finds) (the Snartemo-Fairford-Högom group) with Style I decoration (A.D.430/450–500)

The territory of the Danes, i.e. Denmark and southern Sweden, was the heartland of Scandinavia, in which royal power first consolidated its position by anchoring itself ideologically in a Scandinavian mythology. Earthly lords no longer sacrificed to themselves in their burials but to the king of the gods in heaven. This involved not only bracteates but also the great symbols of lordship – arm- and neckrings of solid gold (Hauck 1954, Vierck 1978, Abb.19, Hedeager 1991). The elite already had by this time a well-developed written language, the runic language, and they now developed a peculiar symbolic language, Scandinavian animal art, rooted in the pagan religious universe as a countertype to the Christian Roman/Frankish universe. This animal art undoubtedly contained recognizable and interpretable references to known pagan myths and deities, just as both the Gotlandic picture stones and the graves from Vendel and Valsgärde seem to (Andrén 1989). It appeared, 'suddenly, and without any precursor in Scandinavia' and evolved through the fifth century in a heartland of Jutland, the Danish islands, southern Sweden and the southern coast of Norway (Haseloff 1981, 706). It spread on to the Continent and to southern England, where the greatest concentrations of Scandinavian brooches are found in Thuringia and in the Frankish borderlands along the Rhine (Haseloff 1981, Abb. 359), and it was developed further by the Langobards in Pannonia and carried by them to Italy, where they arrived in 568 (Haseloff 1981, 708). Since a great proportion of the Scandinavian brooches were actually produced by Continental craftsmen (Haseloff 1981, 708), one must, as in the case of the bracteates, assume that the symbolic language was understood.

Politically, southern Scandinavia comprised a large number of minor kingdoms that were collected under a common ideological umbrella, the geographical centre of which was Gudme (god-home) in the south-east of Fyn, a *villa regalis* (Hauck 1987), with which the already mentioned trading and production site at Lundeborg (Fig. 50) was connected.

A matching development was under way in other parts of Scandinavia, albeit chronologically delayed in relation to southern Scandinavia where the royal dynasties were well-established. In central Sweden the political and ideological centre of the Svear appeared at a later date in Gamla Uppsala, where the royal barrows from the sixth century and the beginning of the seventh stand as the monumental symbols of the first kings, to which the trading and production site on Helgö is connected (Holmqvist 1976). A newly-established elite raised their huge symbolic mounds in other places too, such as at Högom in Medelpad in northern Sweden and at Bertnem, Nord-Trøndelag, northern Norway (Ramqvist and Müller-Wille 1988). And along the coast of southern and western Norway, the first substantial political units, petty chiefdoms or kingdoms, appeared in the fifth and sixth centuries, represented by very rich grave finds (Myhre 1987a, 1987b, forthcoming; for a synopsis see Magnus and Myhre 1976).

The long, two-edged display sword, the symbol of a dominant warrior ideology, is found in leading men's graves from northern Scandinavia to Francia (Fig. 52). These are situated in boundary areas, where new ideologies needed to be established – or to be preserved – as between the Franks and the Germanic peoples along the Rhine boundary and in southern England (cf. Wood 1983 and this vol.), and they are situated in the Scandinavian periphery, where new elites needed to find their foundations, not in areas, like southern Scandinavia, where that had already been done.

All in all, we can affirm that the consolidation of the Danish kings in the fifth century meant that rich graves disappeared and were replaced by ritual sacrifices – the gift-exchange and ritual dialogue between the kings and the gods. The ethos of the Danish elite and their ritual pre-eminence is made manifest through, amongst other things, the gold bracteates, while the Scandinavian self-consciousness and difference from the Roman-Catholic culture was reflected in the development of Scandinavian animal art. New aristocratic lineages mark themselves with rich burials around the periphery of the Danish kings – in Uppland and southern Norway – and in the Frankish borderlands.

The Merovingian Period (520/530–700)

The Franks established themselves beyond dispute as the strongest nation in western Europe in the sixth and seventh centuries. Their politics entailed the existence of various forms of Merovingian hegemony, not only over the Thuringians and the Saxons, but also over southern England, over the Continental North Sea littoral and over the northern German river systems around the Rhine, the Weser and the Elbe – in other words over the most important communication routes and channels of trade in western Europe (Wood 1983). Looked at in this light, Gregory of Tours' account of the Danish king Chochilaicus, who was killed in 515 during a maritime raid on the Frankish coast, probably the Lower Rhine region, is of especial significance. Many aspects of this short account are worthy of attention (after Wood 1983).

Looked at from a Danish angle, it is of interest that we here meet the earliest known named king of the Danes; we have to wait another two hundred years before we find the next one. Looked at in a broader European perspective it is quite crucial that the account in itself indicates the especial significance of the episode. In the first place, Gregory writes so very little about Scandinavia and the north-eastern regions, that this alone turns the account into something quite extraordinary. In the second place, he is very careful in his use of royal nomenclature. The Roman title *rex* is thus not used of kings over peripheral zones or over peoples dependent upon the Franks, such as the Bretons, the Frisians, the Continental Saxons, the Thuringians, the Alamanni or the Bavarians; for these, rather, the title *dux* is used. It must therefore be a conscious option when Gregory uses precisely this word *rex* in order to describe the leader of the Danish fleet. And it is finally worth battening on to the point that after 515 the Danes are not, on the whole, mentioned either in the annals of the kingdom or in Gregory (cf., however, Procopius and Jordanes). The death of Chochilaicus was presumably so serious a reverse that the raiding ceased – and possibly, too, an attempt to wrest control of the Frankish controlled Frisian areas. The popularity of the story in the Germanic narrative tradition helps to indicate the especial importance that was attached to the event (Wood 1983). Thus Frankish hegemony did not come to embrace the Danes; they were too far away for this. But after 515 what was wanted had clearly been achieved – that the Danes kept themselves away from the Frankish ruled coasts, and thus for a while yet would stand apart from European history.

In epic poetry, however, they found a place in the poem *Beowulf*. Without doubt, this poem is regarded as being later, and its historical value is much debated (synopsis in Skovgaard-Petersen 1977, Howe 1989), but the concrete descriptions of burial rites (cremation and boat burials) and artefact-forms (such as helmets, ring-swords, rings and standards) correspond closely with the archaeological material of the sixth and seventh centuries; probably too, the geography and the names. Various Scandinavian peoples are named in this poem, such as the Svear, the Geats, and not least the Danes, who formed a powerful nation that ruled over an extensive kingdom. A distinction is drawn, however, between North, South, East and West Danes, and the Scyldings are spoken of, the royal dynasty of the Danes. That this poem *Beowulf* was preserved in England is a reflection of the importance of southern Scandinavia in two ways. For one, it shows the presence of a Danish aristocratic mythology in England – i.e. political connexions emanating from the Danes – and for the other it shows the dynamism of southern Scandinavia. That *Beowulf* does not survive in Scandinavia in the later-recorded saga literature and royal chronicles is explained by new sovereign dynasties having emerged that had replaced the old myths with new ones. Only in the marginal areas, where contact with the Danes had perhaps ceased, did these legends find a local afterlife as an ideological legitimization of the southern Scandinavian origins of Anglo-Saxon kings.

The description of the Danes as the most powerful nation of Scandinavia, not only in *Beowulf* but also in many of the Icelandic sagas, such as *Ynglinga saga* (Sawyer 1988, 1), stands in sharp and direct contrast to the archaeological material, which produces no princely graves as in other parts of Scandinavia, in southern England or in the Frankish dominated areas along the Rhine. But the Scandinavian animal style, the Scandinavian symbol-language *par excellence*, shows a quite different picture: that is, that the central area of the animal style, now, as in the Migration Period – was southern Scandinavia, in other words Denmark and Skåne.[8] It is here and only here that continuity in production can be followed, and here that innovation takes place (Høilund Nielsen, forthcoming). Analyses show how political alliances and exchange brought exceptional pieces to Vendel and Valsgärde in the Mälar region, to Gotland and Öland, and how many of these pieces were locally copied.[9] The contacts and connexions leading from southern Scandinavia to the whole northern

---

8 Haseloff 1981. It is remarkable that Haseloff's researches point so uniformly to southern Scandinavia as the area of innovation in Scandinavian animal art even though grave-finds are virtually totally lacking. In this respect, this period does not differ from the Merovingian Period – nor do its products.

9 The area analysed by Høilund Nielsen is the Swedish *landskap* along the Baltic coast from Uppland southwards, the Baltic islands and Denmark. The relationships with Norway and the Swedish west coast have thus not been revealed. In consequence, the relationship with the 'North Sea zone' identified by Haseloff (1981) for the Migration Period, the areas of innovation for the early styles, has also not been considered.

European area seem to reach a peak in the seventh century, the century which more than any other is lacking in spectacular finds in Denmark. In other words, *de luxe* artifacts are lacking in the area of production, but amongst the finds from the gold-rich south-east of Fyn one comes across items such as massive gold rings for ring-swords, gold mouth pieces for sword scabbards with exceptional animal ornament and more, which belong to the sixth and seventh centuries. But a shift of dynastic power to Lejre, the mythic homestead of the Skjoldungs, probably took place at the beginning of the sixth century. Evidence for this is the new royal monumental barrows at Lejre, one of them constructed over a cremation patch, and robbed even in antiquity, although remains of gold brocade show as clearly as could be wished that what one had here was a princely burial, just as the central function of the place is preserved down to the end of the Viking Period and the assumption of power by the dynasty of Gorm.[10]

The political activity of the Danes was directed towards the north-east, towards central Sweden and the major Baltic islands in particular, perhaps also towards southern Norway, and however, in the end, we choose to interpret *Beowulf*, the poem is undeniably evidence for the existence of close cultural contacts between Scandinavia and the Anglo-Saxon realms. Only to the south-west, along the Frankish littoral, were contacts restricted.

The Danes remained the strong, well-established and expansive power in Scandinavia in the sixth and seventh centuries. Less certain was the state of political power elsewhere in Scandinavia. In the Mälar region, cemeteries such as Vendel and Valsgärde are expressions of an insecure leadership structure involving the Svea-kings right down to the middle of the eighth century (Arrhenius 1983); in Norway, rich cremation graves including helmets and ring-swords (Myhre, forthcoming) and not least the monumental barrows at Borre, which begin in the middle of the seventh century and continue down to the end of the ninth (Myhre, this vol.), are reflections of the establishment of an East Norwegian kingdom towards the end of the Merovingian Period.

The ring-sword and parade helmet were everywhere – on the Continent, in Scandinavia and in England – an expression of the same idea: the same political symbol of the warrior aristocracy that surrounded the king (Steuer 1987), not of the kings themselves. They are found in graves in the same marginal areas as the display swords of the Migration Period (Figs 53 and 54); in other words in areas where political power was not ideologically securely founded and which therefore needed special legitimizing rituals. Both Christianity and paganism were political tools, and these graves also belong therefore to areas in which the two religions were in conflict: the Frankish Rhineland and southern England. The Scandinavian graves are found first and foremost in Uppland and on Gotland, in the areas where the political base of the Svea-

---

[10] This burial-mound, Grydehøj, is carbon-14 dated to around A.D.550±100 (the age of the carbonized wood).

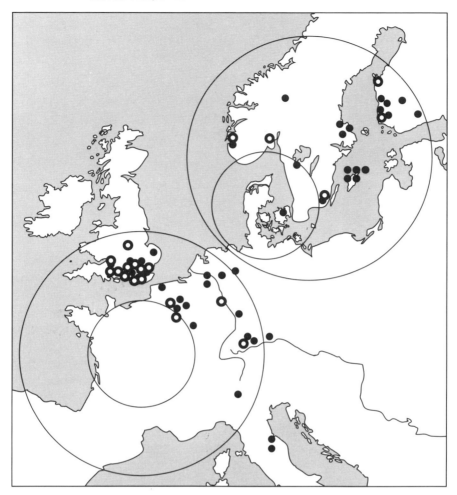

Figure 53. Distribution of ring-swords

kings could have been threatened by the Danes, when the latter turned their attention eastwards in the Merovingian Period, and such graves are found in southern Norway too, on the margins of Danish influence, in the areas where the great boat graves of the Viking Period, such as Oseberg and Gokstad, were later to be placed.

The Viking Period

When King Godfred of the Danes was murdered in the year 810 he was the overlord of Vestfold in southern Norway, Bohuslän, Halland and perhaps parts of Västergötland in western Sweden, and over the Frisians and Saxons to the south of Denmark, as is evidenced by the fact that he received dues from

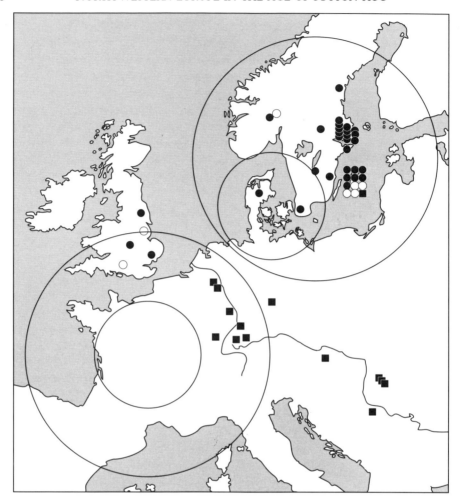

Figure 54. Distribution of: ■ Frankish crested helmets (graves)
● Scandinavian crested helmets (graves) ○ Scandinavian crested
helmets (uncertain contexts)

the merchants in Reric. Godfred's overlordship meant that these peoples owed tribute, and, perhaps most important of all, they were to provide military aid (Sawyer 1988, 4f.). This form of hegemony was a common feature of the early-medieval political system, and was most clearly expressed when the Franks established themselves as the greatest power in western Europe with control over the marginal regions of the North Sea littoral at the beginning of the sixth century, but it can also be recognized in the internal power relations of the early southern England kingdoms.

The power which was exercised by the Viking king Godfred was of the same kind and character, constructed in the same manner, as royal power elsewhere in Germanic Europe. He strengthened and protected the sphere of Danish interest, and he extended his power sufficiently far to the south that he prevented Charlemagne's conquest of land north of the Elbe: the king of the Danes and his allies obstructed none less than the undisputed great power of Europe.

The Danish kingdom was developed early, and from 800 at least – when the written sources begin – down to 1040 the Danes were also on the whole the dominant power in Scandinavia (Sawyer 1988, 1). What is meant by this is that the Danish kings of the Viking Period exercised hegemony with varying intensity over varying numbers of other Scandinavian kings, over greater or lesser parts of Scandinavia. The kings of the Svear thus owed tribute to the Danes for most of this time, until in the second half of the twelfth century they succeeded in transforming their unstable political system into an integrated kingdom around the archiepiscopal seat at Uppsala (Sawyer 1988, 40).

In the political turmoil and internal struggles for power after the murder of Godfred in the ninth century, the successive kings of the Danes were challenged by various pretenders who had been excluded from power and who had won wealth and glory as leaders of the Viking armies in western Europe. At the end of the ninth century the intensity of attacks meant that Danish overlordship collapsed. It was re-established in the middle of the tenth century by Harald Gormsson (Harold Bluetooth), who proclaimed on the Jellinge stone that he had won the whole of Denmark and Norway for himself and had christianized the Danes.

The number of dynastic conflicts and the confused political reality is reflected in the richly furnished chamber graves and the knightly graves from the area of Denmark (Hellmuth Andersen 1985) – last, but not least, by the monumental barrows at Jelling in central Jutland, where the founders of the dynasty of Gorm, Gorm and Thyra, are buried. In these we see, for the first time since the Migration Period (except perhaps at Lejre), how a new royal aristocracy marked and signalled its newly-won position in Denmark by raising monumental barrows, by richly furnished chamber graves, through the use of rune-stones, boat burials and weapons for the royal vassals (Randsborg 1980 Fig.34). The Denmark of the house of Gorm was a different political structure from the territory of the Danes under King Godfred, and by accepting Christianity Harald sought to strengthen the royal power by giving it a new ideological foundation in place of the pagan Scandinavian mythology. In this way a decisive step was taken which subsequently led to the assimilation of Scandinavia into the European Christian/feudal system.

The Scandinavian peoples, the Vikings, were amongst the last pagans of Europe; their society in the eighth, ninth and tenth centuries was at heart not so very different from Migration-period society, constructed as it was with wealth and gift-exchange as the bases for personal prestige and, thus, power.[11]

---

[11] These fundamental traits do not change even though from the beginning of the eighth century Denmark is integrated into an extensive economic network through the

Looked at in this light, the Viking expeditions appear as the close of an epoch in European history in which pagan warrior ethics were themselves the ideo- logical – *and* the economic – backbone of society.

But Europe had not stayed the same. It changed not least in those centuries in which Scandinavia became a serious player in the European arena and in which the old warrior ideology was now quite literally carried forward by a new technology – the light, swift, sailing warships of the Vikings, which allowed them to attack virtually every accessible coastal tract in Europe and to follow the rivers deep into the land. The ponderous European war machine had difficulty in coping with this form of attack; the defending armies were sluggish and very slow to mobilize, and best suited to big, pitched battles; defensive works were not designed for naval attacks; and monasteries, towns and cathedrals were unprotected – to begin with. As early as 800, Charlemagne organized the defence of the littoral between the Rhine and the Seine against pirates who were plundering the North Sea zone, and something similar was done in Kent.

King Godfred attacked the Frankish-controlled Friesland with a fleet of two hundred ships in 810. It was a strategic political attack: other Viking assaults were not on this scale. Down to about 830 the coastal defences functioned fairly well; the attacks were relatively few and far between, and were mostly directed against easily accessible Christian monastic communities on the coast or on small islands. After this they increased in strength and in range as the Frankish realm – for quite different reasons – grew weaker, and was divided, in 843, between Charlemagne's three grandsons. Down to 887–888 the state was plagued with endless strife, which was ended by the formation of three separate kingdoms in Germany, France and Italy.

The Vikings too came to play a part in these conflicts. They not only attacked the Frankish state, but they also let themselves be recruited to fight for the one Frankish king against the other. And they not only accepted being paid off not to attack towns and monasteries; they were also paid off to keep other Vikings away. They had just one goal: to win wealth and glory which could provide them with an attractive place in their Scandinavian communities, based as they were on alliances and gifts. Thus Vikings did not differ fundamentally from the Germanic war-kings and warrior aristocracy of either the Meroving- ian Period or the Migration Period. The only difference was that their activities were now recorded in writing.

The final flourish of animal ornament in the Viking Period can, in conse- quence, again be seen as a factor in the construction of an identity which unified the Scandinavian kings, armies and clans during their raiding expedi- tions and migrations over all of northern Europe. It was further used as a

founding of commercial trading and production sites such as Hedeby and Ribe (Ben- card, Bender Jørgensen and Brinch Madsen 1991, Jensen MS).

pagan symbol in what subsequently became internal religious conflicts. The end of the animal style as the ethnic and religious symbol-language of the elite therefore also marked the integration of Denmark into the Christian-fuedal household. Once more we see that the periphery holds on to the old traditions longest – in the substantial use of late rune-stones in the Mälar region, for instance, which is an example of how the discourse of power of the elite can be appropriated by lower social groupings.

Conclusion

The expansive force which the Viking expeditions reflect did not appear out of nothing in the eighth century. It was the culmination of the political, economic and social development of half a millennium in which the Danes established themselves as the strongest force in northern Europe under the leadership of a varying number of warrior-kings in shifting alliances, but with the common characteristic of having their ideological legitimization essentially founded in the mythology of Scandinavia. In other parts of Scandinavia this process was both chronologically retarded and more confused than in southern Scandinavia.

In sixth- and seventh-century Europe an ideological polarization took place between the Catholic-Christian Germanic Franks and the pagan or Arian-Christian Germanic peoples (Anglo-Saxon England with its Catholic mission is, however, an exception) whose mythical origins in many cases lay in Scandinavia. Scandinavia itself has to be seen as the contrasting pagan pole to Catholic Francia. While the Franks took over and reshaped the Roman culture of Gaul and accepted the Catholic faith, southern Scandinavia created its own ideological groundwork with the Scandinavian religion, with animal ornament as a developed symbolic language and with the runes as an advanced written language which despite the introduction of Christianity at the end of the Viking Period enjoyed a long late life down into the Middle Ages.

The Frankish chieftains along the Rhine border were buried according to a Germanic-pagan tradition in the same way as the first Merovingian king, Childeric, was buried in Tournai, and as burial was practised at Sutton Hoo, Vendel and Valsgärde. It was in the marginal areas of the cultural and political centres in Francia and southern Scandinavia respectively that the relations of power were unclear; it was, therefore, here too that the 'princely graves' were a politico-ideological instrument.[12] To make the Mälar region or southern Norway into the political centre of Scandinavia is, in other words, just as mistaken as to make the Rhine border the centre of the Frankish state as the archaeological finds invite one to. The difference is that the Frankish royal graves of the

---

[12] The burial monuments of Victorian England correspond to this (Parker Pearson 1982).

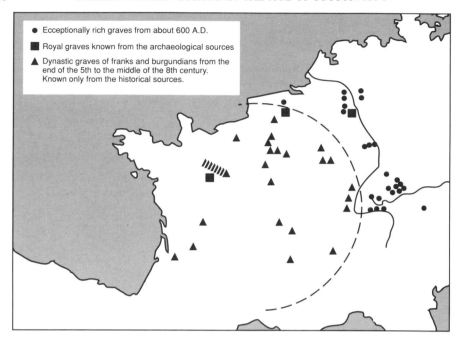

Figure 55. Distribution of historically and archaeologically known 'princely graves' and dynastic graves

sixth, seventh and eighth centuries are known; not on the basis of exceptional archaeological finds but solely thanks to historical documents[13] (Fig. 55). The royal graves of southern Scandinavia of these centuries lack this historical legitimization, and without written sources we would never have known that the Danish kings of the Viking Period such as Godfred and Harald Gormsson (Bluetooth) had existed.

The initial hypotheses proved themselves capable of explaining the relationship between archaeological and historical sources. As a result we can make two general observations concerning the relationship between power/identity and material culture in archaic state societies. Material culture is used by the political elite to mark a new social and religious identity (Christianity/paganism), and it is used to mark a politico-ethnic identity when two equally strong powers border on one another. Furthermore, the signalling of social status through burials is primarily found in areas under stress or where new elites are being established, often in areas marginal to established political centres.

[13] Out of fifteen historically documented graves of the Merovingian dynasty of the sixth century in the churches of St Geneviéve, St Germain des Pres, St. Cloud and St. Denis, only one, that of Arnegundis, is archaeologically known (Müller-Wille 1983; James and Périn, this vol.).

21

The Royal Cemetery
at Borre, Vestfold: A Norwegian centre
in a European periphery

BJØRN MYHRE

The Cemetery and the written Sources

Borre is a small village-like settlement on the western side of the Oslo fjord in the northern part of Vestfold. It is a rich agricultural area, and the prehistoric cemetery is situated on the eastern slope of a morenic ridge called the Ra, on the light sandy soils preferred by the Iron Age farmers. The site also has a strategic position at a particular narrow part of the fjord, where it must have been possible to control the sailing route into the heart of the east Norwegian lowlands (fig. 56).

At the top of the morenic ridge we find the twelfth-century stone church at Borre, and nearby the seventeenth century buildings of the vicarage on whose fields most of the large prehistoric grave-field is situated (fig. 57). The group of burial mounds at Borre is exceptional in Scandinavia. Today, seven large mounds and one cairn can be seen, but at least two other mounds and one cairn have been destroyed during recent centuries. Some of the monuments are more than 45 metres in diameter and 5–6 metres high, and they make an impressive sight among the old oaks in the Borre national park. There are also more than twenty-five smaller cairns, and the grave-field certainly was even larger before modern cultivation started.

Borre has a special name in Norway's early history. It is mentioned in the Sagas, and especially in the skaldic poem *Ynglingatal*, as the burial place of one or two kings of the royal dynasty of the *Ynglingas*, who the poem claims to have reigned in Vestfold during the seventh – ninth centuries A.D. *Ynglingatal*, first mentioned by Snorre Sturlason in 1230, but thought to be from the ninth century, was a tribute to king Ragnvald Heidumhár, a cousin of king Harald Fairhair, who united the Norwegian petty kingdoms during the last part of the ninth century. The poem explicitly mentions that Ragnvald's and Harald's great-grandfather, king Halvdan the Gentle (den Milde) was buried at Borre.

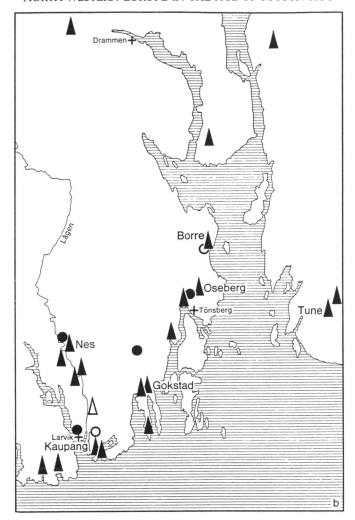

Figure 56. Important sites with boat- or ship burials from
the Viking Age on Oslo fjord, south-east Norway
(after Müller-Wille 1970)

According to one possible interpretation of the poem, so was his father king
Øystein Fret (Brøgger 1916, against this Løken 1977). Borre may also have been
the burial place of a dynasty of local kings ruling in Vestfold before the
Ynglinga dynasty, but such a conclusion is hypothetical, as it is only mentioned
by Snorre Sturlason, the saga-writer, not in the poem itself. King Øystein and
king Halvdan must probably have lived during the eighth century, so at least
the cemetery could be expected to be of this date.

Ynglingatal and Snorre Sturlason's *Heimskringla* connect the Vestfold
Ynglinga kings to the Svea *Ynglinga* dynasty of Uppsala in Sweden. Snorre tells
a story of how king Ragnvald's ancestors, seven generations back, gradually

conquered in battle, or won by marriage, the petty kingdoms of east Norway, from Hedmark in the north to Vestfold in the south. This Swedish connection has influenced Norwegian archaeologists when dealing with the archaeological sources from the Merovingian Period of the sixth to eighth century, and an influence from Uppland and the Mälar region of Sweden has always been looked for. So, when interpreting the Borre grave-field, we have found ourselves in a similar position as our English colleagues studying the Sutton Hoo find – we have tended to look to Sweden for parallels and influences.

The 1852 Investigation

Strangely enough only one of the large mounds at Borre has been investigated through excavation. In 1852 some local road-builders used mound No. 1 as a gravel pit, and as they dug into the central area, they came to destroy most of a richly equipped grave in a viking ship. Some decorated and gilt-bronze objects were collected and sent to Oslo. A young antiquary, Nicolay Nicolaysen, examined what was left of the mound and the ship the next year, and his written report is the only documentation of the find circumstances (1853).

He made no drawings, and it is obvious that he has misinterpreted some of his observations, but taking into consideration his lack of training and the early date of his excavation, the report gives us much useful information. His main conclusion is that a 15–20 metres long ship had been pulled ashore and set up in a shallow ditch. Because of the bad preservation conditions no wood was intact, so his interpretation was based on the distribution of boat-nails still in situ after the looting. Grave gifts, among them three horses with finely ornamented horse trappings and stirrups, sherds of a claw-beaker, iron cauldrons, some weapons and various tools, were found both within and beside the ship (Pl. 19, 20). Nicolaysen was quite clear in his interpretation that it had been a cremation burial, and that the burnt bones of the dead person had been buried in an iron cauldron in the ship. The burial mound had, according to Nicolaysen, been about 38–39 metres in diameter.

None of the preserved objects seem to have been burnt, however, and no cremated human bones have been curated in the museum. Therefore, later writers agree that Nicolaysen must have been wrong about the cremation (Brøgger 1916, 4), and the Borre find has always been presented as a Viking ship-burial of a similar kind as the well-preserved Oseberg and Gokstad graves.

Originally it must have been an extremely rich grave. A few weapons and three pairs of stirrups have been taken as an indication of a man's grave, while some archaeologists have questioned this conclusion mainly because of a spindle whorl and a rock crystal bead found by Nicolaysen (Brøgger 1916, 18, Blindheim 1954; Hougen 1968, 86, Braathen 1989, 50, Richardson 1989, 7–9). The date of the grave has for stylistic reasons been set to the late ninth or early tenth century, depending on the absolute chronology of the Borre style

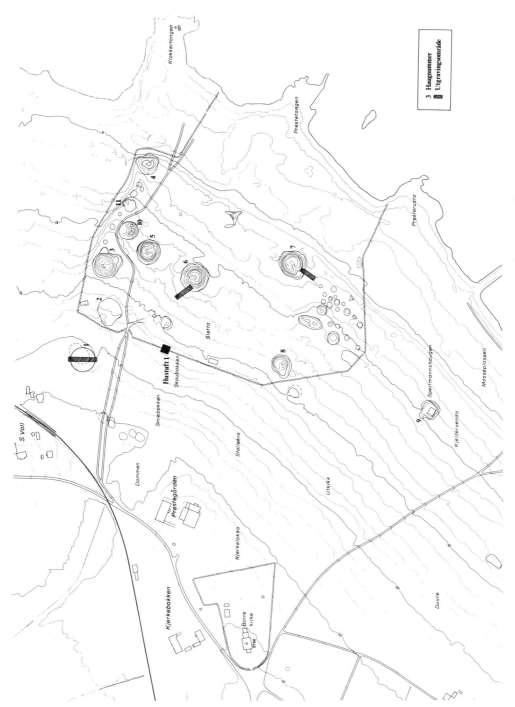

Figure 57. Borre cemetery, the Medieval church (Borre Kirke) and the vicarage (Prestegård) at Borre

(Hougen 1934, 92; Wilson & Klindt-Jensen 1980, 87; Janson 1985, 182). It has been more difficult to explain the sherds of a claw-beaker from the fifth to sixth century found by Nicolaysen at the site (Evison 1982a, 60, Näsman 1986, 68–71). Most writers have agreed that the glass vessel is a several hundred year old antiquity in a Viking grave (Pl. 20).

The Borre Project

None of the other large Borre mounds has been excavated. Some of the smaller cairns were investigated in 1925 and turned out to be simple cremation graves with no datable objects preserved. A few boat-nails indicate, however, a date in the Late Iron Age. During the last 50 years, the ship-burials at Gokstad and Oseberg and the excavation at the trading-centre at Kaupang have received most of the attention, and Borre's position in the early history of Norway has been little discussed since A.W. Brøgger's publication in 1916.

Since 1988, however, the University Museum of National Antiquites in Oslo has run the so-called Borre-project with the aim of studying the history of the Borre grave-field and its cultural and political background. We have tried to locate possible settlement sites, to study the contemporary agricultural landscape and to collect information about the chronology and the character of grave mounds. In addition to traditional archaeological field methods, different prospecting and sensing techniques were used, like georadar, magnetometer, phosphate analysis, pollen analysis, air photography and drillings (Myhre 1990, in press).

A large scale, well preserved system of ancient fields, has been located in the nearby forest, with still visible lynchets, terraces and clearance cairns. ^{14}C-dates are from the Viking and Early Medieval Periods, but the pollen analysis indicates an extended form of agriculture since the Early Roman Period, while a phase of intensive use starts in the sixth to seventh century (Bjørnstad 1989, Høeg 1990). The original field-system apparently has covered the whole neighbouring area of the grave-field, in fact at least two of the large mounds were built directly on soils of a ploughed field older than the late seventh century.

House sites have been identified in trial-trenches close to the western side of the mounds (fig. 58). Postholes, wall ditches and cultural layers were preserved under a 30–40 centimetre thick layer of modern ploughed soils. The calibrated ^{14}C-date is within the period 670–895 cal. A.D. (T-8845. Stuiver and Pearson 1986), so the settlement site has been used contemporary with the grave-field. As hearths and early structures were also found underneath the Viking-Period mound (No. 1), it is possible that the settlement area may be as large as 150 metres in length. A closer investigation of this area will be made during the 1991 season.

The proposed site of mound No. 1 was located by air photography as crop marks in a modern field. The use of georadar and magnetometer indicated that

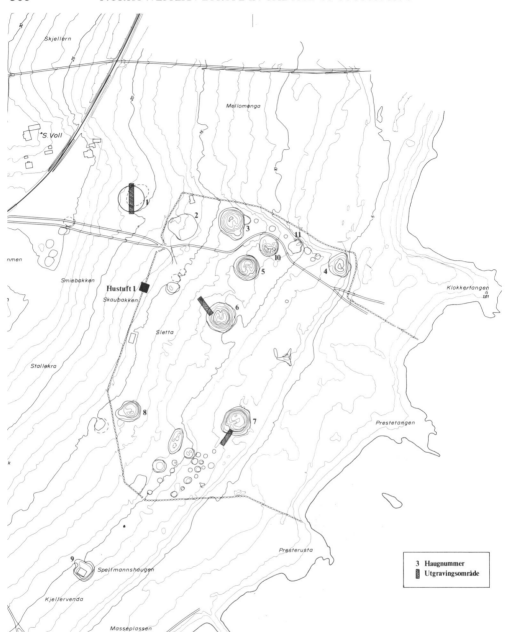

Figure 58. The large mounds at the Borre cemetery. Excavated areas are marked. A settlement area has been found between mound No. 1 and house site 1 (hustuft 1)

the bottom layer of the mound was still intact, and that metal objects might be found. A 10 metre broad and 60 metre long trench was therefore laid out across the central part of the mound, and the modern ploughed soil removed by machine.

It soon became clear that the mound had been completely levelled and destroyed. Only a 30 centimetre thick ploughed layer covered the original ground on which the mound had once been built. The ground, however, was nearly perforated by a large number of pits of different kinds and character. Some of them clearly were cooking pits, others were filled with stones and blackish soils, but their functions were difficult to interpret. Some of them must be older than the Viking grave in the mound, as the earliest ^{14}C-date is 665–775 cal. A.D. (T-8851. Stuiver & Pearson 1986) and may refer to previous activities on the site.

In the ploughed soils we also found several small pieces of glass of different colours and types, most of them probably from modern times. But at least two sherds of brownish glass come from claw-beakers. One of them has the same white trails as the original Borre beaker, while the other sherd comes from a long, narrow claw of a similar type as that found on the beakers in Valsgärde grave 5–8 and Vendel grave 1 from the seventh century (Arwidsson 1942, 1983; Arrhenius 1983, 44; Evison 1982b).

The find of a second claw-beaker and the indications of earlier activities on the site, mean that we have to consider the possibility of either an older grave in the mound, or a settlement before the mound was built. We may also consider the possibility that some of the objects collected by Nicolaysen in 1852 may not belong to the Viking Period grave, but to these earlier events. Especially the sherds of the Borre claw-beaker, maybe more than 400 years older than the grave, fit well into the date of this early use of the site. The spindle-whorl, in what is otherwise interpreted as a man's grave, may also have been mixed with the Viking grave-goods.

The ^{14}C-dated structures and the claw-beakers indicate activities on the site during the seventh to eighth centuries contemporary with the intensive agricultural phase and the earliest large mounds at the grave-field.

In the modern ploughed soils of the central part of mound No. 1 we also found a considerable number of boat-nails and some iron objects such as a knife, an arrow, a chisel and pieces of an iron cauldron. In an oval longish pit in the ground more than one hundred pieces of boat-nails were secondarily deposited, either by Nicolaysen during his excavation in 1852 or during the burial rituals around A.D.900. Also a large number of burnt bones were collected, some of them of human origin. Nicolaysen's observation of a large grave-ship has been confirmed. He may also have been right in his proposition about a cremation grave, but the evidence is scanty.

Trenches were also dug into the edges of mounds No. 6 and No. 7, and valuable information has been collected about their date and construction. Both mounds were found to have been built on ancient cultivated soils, and at least in mound No. 6, a cremation layer with scattered burnt bones was found directly upon the ancient field soil. The grave is dated to 600–675 cal. A.D. (T-8842. Stuiver & Pearson 1986). Mound No. 7 is dated to 555–670 and 595–675 cal. A.D. (T-10055–56) and Mound No. 3 to 675–885 and 770–895 cal. A.D. (Beta 51040–41).

At the moment it seems that the large mounds at the Borre cemetery cover a period of about 250 years, from the mid-seventh century to 900; broadly speaking one mound per generation. Some of the smaller barrows in the cemetery may be older, and it is possible that an ordinary Iron Age grave-field changed its character dramatically during the seventh century when the first large mounds were built.

Until now, very few archaeological finds from the Migration and Merovingian Periods have come to the museums from this area. This has led some archaeologists to suggest that the Borre cemetery was placed in a sparsely settled area. The investigations of the Borre project have revealed a different picture. The pollen analysis and the place-names indicate a continuous settlement since the Early Iron Age. From about A.D.600 the cultivation was intensified, large fields were taken into use, and the large mounds indicate that a strong political centre developed in this part of east Norway during the seventh century.

Borre as a Centre in East Norway

Traditionally we have connected Borre with the Viking Period, but now it is clear that we also have to consider its place in a Merovingian Period landscape. Generally speaking the sixth – eighth centuries seem to have been a period of settlement expansion and population growth in east Norway. For the first time it can be demonstrated that the mountain valleys were extensively settled, and the exploitation of mountain resources like iron became more intensive than before (Hougen 1947, Skjølsvold 1969, Martens 1988). A decrease in number of graves and prestigious objects during the seventh century has been taken as evidence of a period of general decline (Gudesen 1980, 124, 128, 138), but this conclusion is based mainly on the quantity and quality of the grave finds. The investigation at Borre clearly shows that this source material is not representative for the settlement and the social development, as the seventh century here seems to be the initial stage of a period of expansion, although very few archaeological objects and graves of such a date have been found in the area.

Also in Denmark few grave finds are known from these centuries, but new investigations have brought to light large settlements, market places and large defence works, and the interpretation that a strong kingdom with a powerful land-owning aristocracy was established in the seventh to eighth century, seems reasonable (Hedeager 1990, Sawyer 1988).

During the Migration and Merovingian Periods cremation graves dominate in east Norway, and usually the grave goods are so heavily burnt that only small fragments have been preserved. Occasionally such fragments may give us glimpses of the rich material culture that existed among the upper classes. Especially from the sixth and early seventh century some very rich finds have been found. The style II decorated objects from Åker in Hedmark are among the best examples (Pl. 21). Fragments of ring-swords come from Åker, Kjær-stad in Akershus and Nes in Vestfold, and from four graves fragments of helmets have been preserved, of a similar type as those from Vendel and Valsgärde in Sweden: By and Englaug in Hedmark, Stabu in Opland and Nes in Vestfold (Pl. 22). Ring-swords and helmets have recently been interpreted as special symbols for aristocratic members of the kings *hird*, an institution that can be traced back to, at least, the sixth – seventh centuries in Frankish written sources (Ganshof 1961, 3,12). Heiko Steüer suggests that ring-swords and hel-mets may be seen as an archaeological manifestation of a similar political organization and warrior ideology in most of the germanic kingdoms in north Europe (1987, 223 ff).

If the ring-swords and the helmets show us the graves of the aristocracy, where should we expect to find the seat of the kings? The most obvious answer would be to look for the most impressive monuments which have been preserved from this period; the large mounds.

I have earlier argued that petty kingdoms may have existed along the coast of south and west Norway during the fifth to sixth centuries. Their centres were strategically placed in rich agricultural areas with a dense population, where the large river valleys or the fiords meet the sea. To such centres various goods from varied ecological zones of the neighbouring territory could be transported, and from these strong-holds it was possible to exercise some control over the important communication route along the coast from North Norway (Myhre 1987b). Valuables and commodities collected through a redis-tributive economic system could be converted into chieftains' prestige and authority through gift exchange, feasts and administrated trade. Market places were later established near some of the centres by the king to control and to ease such an economic and political transaction (Christophersen 1991).

If we transfer this model to the Merovingian East Norway, we might expect to find the political centres at strategic places at the mouth of the largest river-system and along the Oslo fjord, as well as in central, densely populated inland regions, where valuables and commodities from the mountains and the forests could be collected.

Some of the largest mounds in East Norway have already been shown to be from the Migration and Early Merovingian Periods. Among them we find three mounds at Bjørntvet in Telemark and Jellhaugen in Østfold, where the Skien river-system and the large river Glomma meet the sea respectively (fig. 59). Two large mounds, not yet excavated, can be found at Huseby in Lier at the mouth of the Drammen river-system. Inland centres may be sought for near Norway's largest man-made mound, Raknehaugen in Akershus (dated to 542–672 and 554–674 cal. A.D. T-82,83,86) or near Sveinhaugen in Hedmark (dated to 670–780 cal. A.D. T.4133). Other large mounds that may be from the same centuries are found at Halvdanshaugen in Ringerike, close to Åker in Hedmark and at Hundorp in Gudbrandsdalen (fig. 59) (Brøgger 1937).

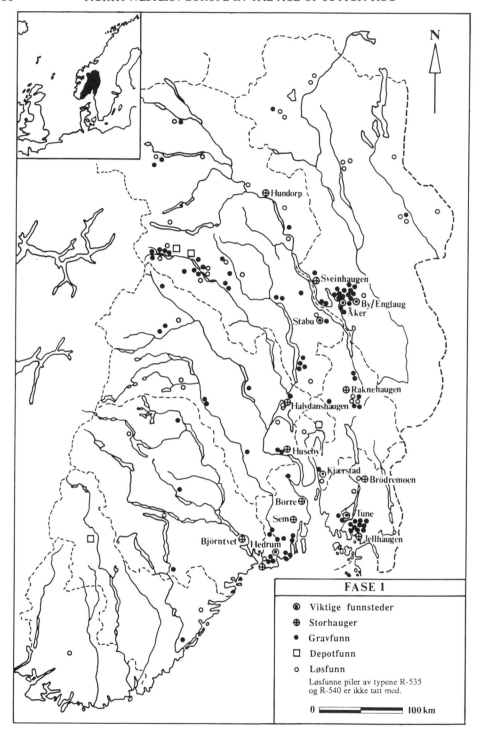

Figure 59. Large mounds and special grave-finds probably from the sixth to seventh centuries in east Norway

From the seventh century and onwards, the group of large mounds marks Borre as an exceptional place in East Norway, as we here can demonstrate a continuity of power found nowhere else. The hypothesis is that Borre kings at their strategic seat by the Oslo fiord, gradually managed to build up a political control over the other petty kingdoms of the region. The *Sagas* and the *Ynglingatal* describe the competition between east Norwegian kingdoms during the centuries before the Viking Period, as well as their unification under the leadership of the Vestfold kings of the *Ynglinga* dynasty in the ninth century. The mounds at Borre probably are the archaeological manifestation of the early phases of this economic and politic process towards a Norwegian State.

Borre in a North European Perspective

Three strong political centres in Mid-Scandinavia in the fifth to sixth centuries have been identified, each of them characterized by a group of three large mounds on a prehistoric grave-field: Høgom in Medelpad, Uppsala in the Mälar valley and Bertnem in Trøndelag. Each centre probably had a geographical sphere of interest, that met near the present border between Norway and Sweden, and from there resources and commodities probably were collected (Ramquist 1990, Ramquist & Müller-Wille 1988). The chieftains at Åker and By in Hedmark probably may also have had interests within parts of this Mid-Scandinavian territory, and during the seventh-eighth centuries also the kings at Borre (fig. 60).

On both sides of the English Channel the first emporia or market places were established already during the early seventh century. Luxury articles and prestige goods like glasses and jewellery were distributed between these centres, probably as part of a redistributive and administrated exchange system (Näsman 1986, 1990). Richard Hodges has named this 'phase 2' in a proposed step-wise development of exchange and trade on the southern North Sea coasts. 'Phase 3' starts, in his opinion, after 670 when Pepin of Herstal introduced a new coinage, the silver sceatta, and when not only prestigious goods were exchanged, but also commodities produced by craftsmen and specialists in the emporias, as well as resources from the surrounding regions (1989, 162). During this phase the market place at Ribe in south-west Jutland was established, probably by a strong Danish kingdom about 710, and from the very beginning lava-querns from the Rhine area and slate hones that may be of Scandinavian origin, were found in the cultural layers (Bencard and Jørgensen 1990, 145, Myrvoll 1991, Jensen 1990).

The first large mound at Borre was built at this important stage in the North European economic and political development when the trade got a new dimension, and demand for goods like iron, slate, furs and hides increased remarkably.

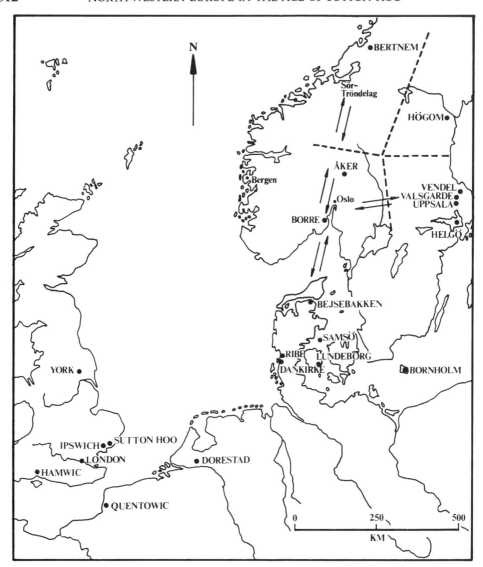

Figure 60. Important sites and market places in Northern Europe during the sixth to eighth centuries. Hypothetical link-lines are drawn between political centres in Trøndelag, Uppsala, Høgom and Borre, Vestfold. Høgom's position as a political centre was possibly reduced after the sixth century

The Oslo fjord is the gate to inner parts of East Norway and West Sweden, and along this route resources and commodities of great importance to the Danish, Merovingian and even the Anglo-Saxon kingdoms could be transported. A royal dynasty at Borre may have played an important role in the social and economic network of exchange and alliances reaching from the Norwegian mountains to the emporias at the English Channel, and from the

Svea kings at Uppsala to the courts of Kent and Anglia. Alliances between the ruling dynasties of the North European kingdoms led not only to the distribution of commodities, but also of ideas, styles and ideologies, and is the reason why the material culture found at these political centres have such a similar appearance.

The Svea kings at Uppsala enjoyed a high prestige in the Viking period, and the Vestfold kings in the ninth century preferred to link themselves genealogically to this *Ynglinga* dynasty. The Vendel and Valsgärde grave-finds have enjoyed a similar prestige among Scandinavian archaeologists, and most rich Merovingian Period finds and objects found in East Norway have been connected to Uppland in a similar way as the supposed Swedish connection of the Sutton Hoo grave (Blindheim 1984, Bruce-Mitford 1974, 47). David Wilson has recently tried to reduce this one-sided focusing on the Swedish finds when discussing traits found in north Germanic material culture during the seventh century (1983).

Some of the exclusive objects of the Merovingian Period found in Norway, may just as well have come from Jutland as from Sweden (Ørsnes 1966, 1970; Nielsen 1991). The claw-beakers from Borre, probably produced in Kent or Anglia, are objects that may indicate even a connection between south-east England and east Norway (Evison 1982a, Näsman 1986, Hines 1984; this vol.). They may have come to Borre as part of a gift system, as tributes, or as a manifestation of social contacts between kings and chieftains; the result of dynastic relations. From where they came to Borre is, of course, impossible to tell, depending not so much on where they were produced, as on what kind of alliances or gift exchange the glasses were part of.

I will suggest that when the first large mound was built at Borre in the seventh century, it was the centre of a complex society that was a part of a social network of alliances between royal courts in Scandinavia and on the southern shores of the North Sea. Gradually, the royal dynasty at Vestfold strengthened their position because they managed to take advantage of the strategic position Borre had at the Oslo fjord; the corridor to inland east Norway.

22

The Scandinavian Character of Anglian England: An Update

JOHN HINES

The title of my contribution to this collection refers to my doctoral thesis, *The Scandinavian Character of Anglian England in the pre-Viking Period*, which was published by BAR in 1984, presuming perhaps rather immodestly that it is worth updating. The heart of that thesis was the study of a series of artefact-types of the Migration Period, in the fifth and sixth centuries, within which particular Anglo-Scandinavian parallels had already been noticed. In fuller terms, the research effort was directed at the thorough examination of these long-distance parallels against both chronological and geographical parameters, in order to assess whether the Anglo-Scandinavian parallels were real or illusory and whether specific patterns of diffusion or influence might be identified. Naturally one hoped for an affirmative answer on the question of the reality of the Anglo-Scandinavian parallels, and happily this seems to have been obtained. A very varied set of spatial and temporal patterns of dispersal for the artefact-types concerned emerged, a picture made even more complex by attempts to identify the most probable forms of human behaviour which underlay these material traces. In different cases both *migration* and *fundamentally commercial links* were proposed as the best available explanations. Socially-motivated exchange – gift-giving – received little explicit consideration in the thesis but was for most cases, perhaps rather casually as far as presentation went, rejected.

A considerable amount of work of relevance to this whole topic has been done by myself and others since 1984, some of it published, some as yet not. I have prepared fuller publications of the most informative artefact-types involved, the clasps and the square-headed brooches.[1] Not surprisingly, a certain amount of new material has become available for study – and in one or two cases has simply been noticed – in the last few years. It is not my wish in this

---

[1] To appear as *Clasps: Hektespenner: Agraffen*, Kungliga Vitterhets, Historie och Antik-vitets Akademien, Stockholm, and *A New Corpus of Anglo-Saxon Great Square-Headed Brooches*, Society of Antiquaries of London, Research Report.

paper to go through the detailed additions and modifications that can be made to what was published before, especially as publication of this material is already in hand, but it is, I think, useful to report that the new data have served generally to support the essential points of the earlier conclusions rather than to raise significant doubts about them. A similarly unchanged state can be reported for the other artefact-types more or less extensively studied in the thesis – bracteates and scutiform pendants, annular and Anglian equal-armed brooches – with the important exception of the cruciform brooches. Comprehensive research on this brooch-type by Catherine Mortimer has shown that two of four features which had still appeared to me to define a distinct and consistent Anglo-Scandinavian 'area of common development' can now be attested in finds from Schmalstede, Kr. Rendsburg in Continental Anglian Schleswig-Holstein (Mortimer 1990). Clearly the relationship of this particular subset of data to the wider context must be re-assessed in due course.

The discovery on brooches in northern Germany of features that had pre-viously appeared to be especially Anglo-Scandinavian has a more significant impact than the recently published discovery of a solitary wrist-clasp, the first to be found in an indisputably Continental Anglian context, in grave 389 of the cremation cemetery at Süderbrarup (Bantelmann 1988, 41, 129 and Taf.50). One isolated intruder from the material culture of the neighbouring territory does not create a radically new impression of Continental Anglian material culture and how much it differs from the Scandinavian. With regard to the source of the Anglian English wrist-clasps, more significant than earlier densities of distribution is the variety of details of form which still point unmistakably towards a special connexion between southern and western Norway and east-ern England. It was perhaps foreseeable that stray wrist-clasps could appear in Angeln, and even more is it inferrable that wrist-clasps should have been in use in the hybrid fifth-century *Nordseeküstengruppe* culture north of the Elbe and in fifth-century Jutish Kent. The predictable forms of eventual finds in these areas are Class A and relatively simple varieties of form B1 clasps (as, in fact, the Süderbrarup clasp is). Finds of this nature would not weaken the case for a Norwegian-Anglian English link in the later fifth century.

There is, however, one argument concerning the interpretation of the evi-dence that I would like now to add, concerning in particular a counter-argument to the migration hypothesis that I consider to be the best explanation of the introduction of wrist-clasps in Anglian England. This counter-argument is that the migration hypothesis is weakened by the 'great abiding discrepan-cies' between western Norway and eastern England in the archaeological rec-ord, for instance in pottery-forms and the form of whole artefact-assemblages. The new argument in favour, coincidentally, harmonizes with the interest in problems of group or ethnic identity which has very recently come to the fore in cultural-historical thought. Via the study of other periods, and of other forms of evidence, especially language, I believe that a respectable case can be made that there was a relatively intense forging of new identities amongst the groups of folk of mixed origins settled in England from a very early date – from before the end of the fifth century. Such new identities did not necessarily involve sharp breaks with the past, but showed a hybridization and adaptation of traditions and heritage. Within the thesis the expansion and shift of the meaning of the ethnic label *Angle* between the fourth and eighth centuries was descriptively noted, but without any true consideration of the pertinent mechanisms by which this particular identity was maintained and adapted.

Bede clearly had a sense of common Englishness by the early eighth century, at the same time as having an acute sense of the difference of Angles and Saxons within England. I have argued elsewhere that a reduction of pre-settlement dialectal contrasts, converging on a focal set of Old English linguistic norms, is a probable philological correlate of this developing sense of identity – or rather of a hierarchy of identities (Hines 1990; cf. Richards 1987, 203–4).

One aspect of the distribution of wrist-clasps within England that has been noted is the apparently rapid extension of range from bridgeheads in Humberside and Norfolk into a larger area, with very clear boundaries to the south which can be identified with the boundaries of early Anglian England as given in historical records. It was never supposed that this represented the rate of Scandinavian colonization or of commercial activity. It was eventually suggested that a certain prestige may be attributed to the introducers of the clasp-costume, a prestige that encouraged the imitation of their dress. But the holding of prestige status alone perhaps overemphasizes just one side of the process of diffusion; it does not necessarily sufficiently cover the motives for exercising the option of imitation by those who adopted the new costume. I maintain that we still need a migration over the North Sea to introduce a Scandinavian dress-style into England, but that in addition an extensive communal consensus is needed for that style to be adopted as what is in effect a distinctive Anglian English 'national' costume. This costume, however, as was much more of the material culture of this group, was selectively put together from diverse inheritances. A creative and expressive form of selectivity such as this is, I believe, a very satisfactory explanation of the non-appearance of other distinctive Scandinavian artefact-forms.

The deliberate selection of material marks of identity is a topic to which I wish to return in due course, after shifting, chronologically, the focus of attention to the period with which this volume is primarily concerned, the 'Age of Sutton Hoo'. It has not escaped the notice of reviewers that this period was cursorily treated in the thesis (15 pages out of 300), and I particularly acknowledge the courteous criticism of Mogens Ørsnes, who in 1966 and 1970 had put forward a substantial art-historical argument for special links between England and southern Scandinavia in the later seventh and early eighth centuries (Ørsnes 1966, 1970 and 1985). The most substantial piece of updating I wish to do in this paper is to offer a re-assessment of Scandinavian parallels and connexions at Sutton Hoo and in this period, based on the one hand upon a review of Ørsnes's case and on the other upon a recent study by Ulf Näsman of Scandinavian glass imports in the period (Näsman 1986).

Ørsnes's art-historical arguments are complex and fine, and a short critical review is a graceless way to handle them. They represent a carefully constructed hypothesis in a field to master which one seems to need to be familiar with an artistic world which stretches from Coptic Egypt and the Byzantine Near East across the Continent to Scandinavia and the British Isles. Opinions on patterns of influence and development within this world vary greatly, and contradictory authorities can be cited on crucial points. In essence, Ørsnes argued that a number of parallels between southern Scandinavian Style C and D metalwork art and Hiberno-Saxon art principally represented in illuminated manuscripts – parallels in the form of relatively naturalistic zoomorphic ornament, extensive knotted interlace, and certain types of body sections (Figs. 61.1–2) – must represent Insular influence on Scandinavia because the forms concerned could only have arisen in Britain. Ørsnes followed the traditional attribution of knotwork interlace to Mediterranean sources, but argued that its introduction in northern Europe – which I take to mean north of the Alps – must be attributed to Irish monasticism and missionary activity. A key point in his argument is the proposition that the Durham gospel fragment (MS A II 10) is a product of England but dependent entirely on Celtic and Mediterranean artistic traditions; one can therefore only look west in the British Isles for its background.

But this analysis of the Durham fragment is open to dispute. The spiral rolls on the jaws of animal heads are better identified as a long-standing Germanic motif than as an Anglo-Irish one as Ørsnes proposes (Fig. 61.3a–d), and on these grounds I would argue (against Ørsnes) that even the animal heads in the *Cathach of St. Columba* look utterly Germanic (Fig. 61.3e). Turning to the knotwork interlace, it has been noted more than once that neither the quantity nor the character of appropriately dated Mediterranean interlace provides a very convincing source for the style in the British Isles (Adcock 1974; Cramp 1984, xxviii). Gwenda Adcock, in a thesis on the subject of interlace extensively used by Rosemary Cramp in the General Introduction to the British Academy *Corpus of Anglo-Saxon Stone Sculpture*, concluded that there was probably a local, Insular development of interlace, conceivably based upon textile craft.

Figures 61. Parallels between Insular Style II art and Scandinavian Style C motifs of forms cited by Ørsnes.
1a: from the Sutton Hoo great gold buckle; 1b: from Ørsnes 1966, Table 1 and 2; 2a: from the Book of Durrow, f. 192v; 2b: plate brooch from Bækkegård, Bornholm, grave 35; 3a, b: from MS Durham A II 10; c: from square-headed brooch, Hole, Grytten, Møre og Romsdal, Norway; d: from square-headed brooch, Morningthorpe, Norfolk, grave 371; e: from *The Cathach of St. Columba*; 4. Triple-stranded 'interlace' from late Anglian English square-headed brooches. a, b: Ruckington, Lincolnshire; c: Thornborough Pasture, North Yorkshire; d: Nettleton Top, Lincolnshire

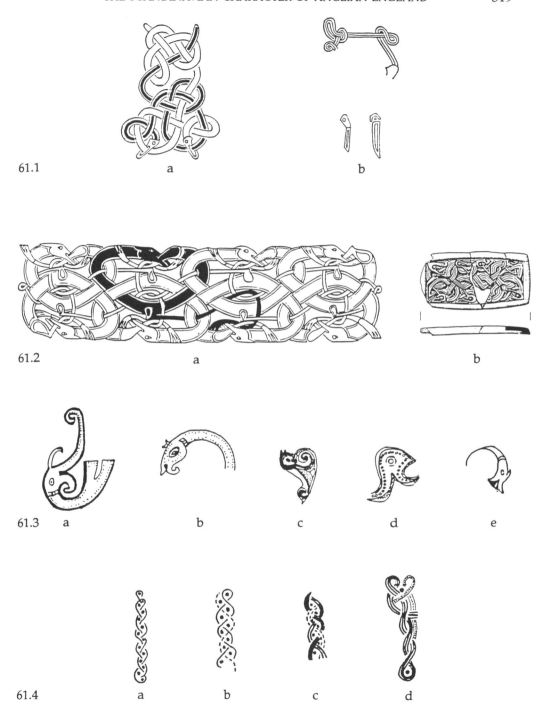

61.1   a   b

61.2   a   b

61.3   a   b   c   d   e

61.4   a   b   c   d

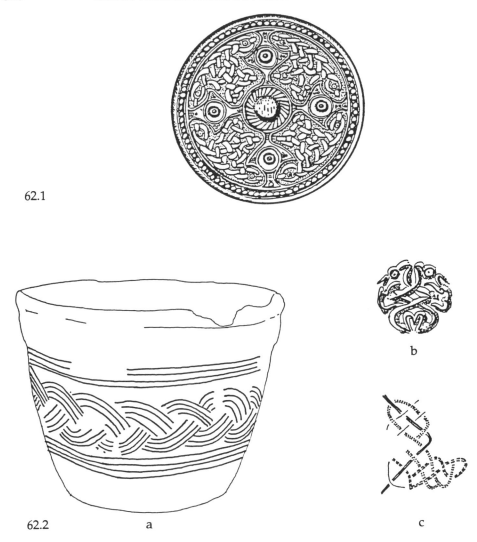

62.1

62.2   a   c

Figures 62. 1. Reconstruction of roundel from a mould found at the Mote of Mark, Kirkcudbright, Scotland; 2. 'Interlace' patterns on a: bucket-shaped pottery, Bjerkreim, Rogaland, Norway; b: D-bracteate, Holte, Strand, Rogaland, Norway; c: square-headed brooch, Jorenkjøl, Hå, Rogaland, Norway

I myself would draw attention to what may be a very early stage in the development of the interlace style on Anglian English metalwork, on three square-headed brooches of the very end of the Migration Period from Nettle-ton Top and Ruskington in Lincolnshire and Thornborough in North Yorkshire (Fig. 61.4).[2] On two of these brooches we can see what I would regard as the crucial step in the development of plaitwork to interlace: the turning of a

2 A fourth such brooch with three-stranded interlace (plaitwork) has recently appeared,

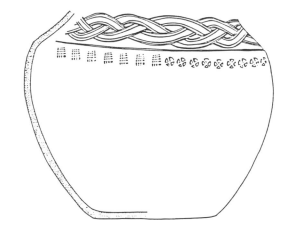

62.3

Figure 62. 3. 'Interlace' pattern on Anglo-Saxon cremation urn, Spong Hill, Norfolk urn 1797

strand back in upon itself. Note also the use of dots in the areas between strands. This I am sure provides an ample source for the zoomorphic interlace on a mould of what I believe to be the late sixth century from the Mote of Mark (Fig. 62.1). I further believe that the emergence of, or at least the attempt to produce, relatively complex patterns of plaitwork or interlace on the late Anglian English square-headed brooches is likely to be a matter of Scandinavian influence, for there is a longer and more consistent tradition of experimentation with such patterns to be found in Norway, from late fifth-century bucket-shaped pottery, through D-bracteates to late square-headed brooches (Fig. 62.2) (Magnus 1984). But even in England parallels can be found on cremation urns (Fig. 62.3).

Ørsnes, however, did not believe that the southern Scandinavian knotwork interlace of Styles C and D could be derived from Scandinavian tradition alone, and one may defer to his authority. Egil Bakka similarly saw no internal sources, but found it impossible to choose between seventh-century Continental art – where forms of knotwork are quite familiar – and Insular art as a source (Bakka 1983). Bakka too followed the traditional line in seeing the Mediterranean as the prior source of this feature of seventh-century artwork in the north.

My own working hypothesis would be that largely independent Scandinavian- and Mediterranean-derived styles converged to create such confusing similarities in art over an extensive range in the seventh century. In this situation it cannot be at all easy to identify specific instances and currents of inter-regional influence.

as a metal detector find. From Tothill, Lincolnshire; information, K. Leahy, Borough Museum, Scunthorpe.

63.1

63.2

Figures 63. 1. Rectangular plate brooch from Bækkegård,
Bornholm; 2. Gotland picture stone, dated c. 400–600 A.D.;
Havor II, Hablingbo, Gotland

Ørsnes extended his case with parallels in a variety of motif details, found in
Scandinavian Style D in particular. It is simply not practicable to try to evaluate these one by one here, but it may be useful, by way of example, to look
briefly at one of these parallels, the spiralled hips found on animals in southern Scandinavian Style D (Fig. 63.1). Spiral hips we know are a common

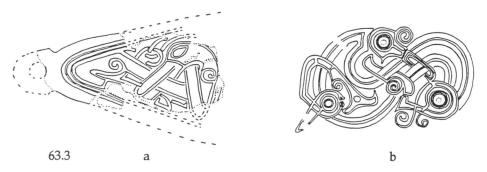

63.3   a   b

Figure 63. 3a. Zoomorphic ornament on pressed copper-alloy foil from Dunadd, Argyll, Scotland, scale 2:1; 3b. Zoomorphic ornament on cast rectangular plate brooch from Ulstrup, Rosnæs, Holbæk, Sjælland, Denmark

Insular art motif from about the time of the Book of Durrow onwards, and are alien to earlier Scandinavian zoomorphic art. But the spiral itself is not totally absent from Scandinavian art, as it occurs on earlier Gotlandic picture stones (Fig. 63.2) (Lamm and Nylén 1988, 25–39). Can one say that either parallel is more far-fetched a source than the other for the motifs in southern Scandinavian metalwork art? At least we are in a slightly better position now to produce parallels in Insular metalwork art to what appears on southern Scandinavian artefacts than Ørsnes was, he having to rely heavily and awkwardly on the evidence of Hiberno-Saxon manuscript art. Newly available finds, such as pressed foils from Northumberland (the 'Bamburgh beast': Bailey, forthcoming) and Dunadd, Argyll, Scotland (Fig. 63.3a, cf. Fig. 63.3b) (Lane and Campbell, forthcoming) at least offer similarities in the same medium, albeit still with different techniques.

The best evidence I had found for the sort of continuing Anglo-Scandinavian contacts in the seventh and eighth centuries which would allow such influence or interchange was historical rather than archaeological. But the archaeological case for such contacts is now much enhanced by Näsman's conclusions on the probably English origin of much glassware imported into Scandinavia – especially to Sweden – in this period. The major types which he adds to the long-known blue glass beakers of which a couple of examples have turned up in south-western Norway are claw beakers and reticella-decorated vessels. The latter type is the most interesting to comment upon in the present context. The evidence for reticella glass production in England is largely circumstantial: the union of an Irish reticella tradition – represented by sixth-century Irish beads – and English glass-vessel manufacture is sufficient to explain the production of these vessels, and equally good alternative sources in Europe have not been identified. Reticella glass vessels have been found on several sites in England; although recorded in the greatest quantities at Hamwih and Portchester in Hampshire, Näsman notes evidence, and the conclusions of others, that a major centre of production lay well to the north-east of here. A further, tiny clue drawing attention to Anglian England, to East Anglia or further north, is the apparently unique adoption in earlier seventh-century Anglo-Saxon craft of the previously Irish millefioré technique – closely related to the reticella technique – in the Sutton Hoo grave 1 treasures. Here, in the technical field, we have perhaps a stronger example of the sort of evidence of Anglo-Scandinavian contacts that Ørsnes argued for in the art-historical field: a distinctly Celtic element in material diffused across the North Sea from the British Isles via Anglian England.

Näsman builds upon the evidence of glass-vessel distribution to produce a model of trading relations between England and Scandinavia in the seventh and eighth centuries. Features he emphasizes are the prestigious or luxurious character of the items transported, and the hand-to-hand character of their transportation, through a series of ports intermediary between place of origin and the final destination, a system which seems eventually to give rise to special-function sites such as Ipswich, Quentovic, Dorestad and Ribe. In a comparison with the Viking Period, in which there is better evidence for the long-distance distribution of humbler raw materials and products such as stone and soapstone bowls, he describes the Vendel-period system as a less 'developed' stage. Looked at against the earlier period, the Migration Period, however, the Vendel-period system appears relatively sophisticated. In the earlier period the 'travelling-craftsmen' model for the diffusion of artefact-types such as square-headed brooches still seems to fit some of the relevant data very well, especially with respect to shorter distances. The continuing absence of true identity of form between corresponding features of separate brooches, however closely similar or related in design they may be, suggests that mechanical means of form-reproduction played a minor role in their production and dispersal and that by corollary human agencies – the skill and experience of craftsmen – should have played a major role. But over very long distances – for instance between Scandinavia and England – it seems impossible to explain how the products of such putative travelling craftsmen could be so thoroughly assimilated in overall appearance to the local style as they would appear to be. Should one rather suggest local imitation of imported models that were themselves too few to be represented in the small sample of the archaeological record? Of course, if this is an admissible argument, then so too is the argument that the products of incoming craftsmen were too few to be represented amongst, for instance, the 200 now known Anglo-Saxon great square-headed brooches! A general contrast one may tentatively propose between Migration-period and Vendel-period conditions is that in the earlier period, in many more cases, the movement of people – singly or communally – all the way from area A to area B is required to introduce material or influence from area A at area B. If in, or in the course of, the Vendel Period a reliable series of staging posts in between areas A and B emerges, this may well help us to understand why direct Anglo-Scandinavian interchange has proved so much harder to identify archaeologically in these centuries.

To draw such a contrast between Migration-period distribution and the Vendel-period system points up, I believe, an important difference between the periods, although it certainly does not provide a full description of trading conditions at those times. With regard to the principle theme of these proceedings, Sutton Hoo, the question finally to be addressed is not so much that of the nature of the lines of interchange in the northerly Germanic areas in this period, but rather why the ends of one productive line should lie where they appear to, for at least a time, in East Anglia and central Sweden.[3] Why should

---

3 One month before the deadline for submitting copy for this publication, Ulf Näsman gave a seminar in London, during questions after which he referred to research approaching completion, by Karen Høilund Nielsen, Moesgaard, which apparently reverses the long-supposed dependency of the area of Denmark upon central Sweden as the source of Vendel-period artefact-type models and developments in art-style. This would occasion a radical change in our understanding of long-distance relationships within Scandinavia, and, probably, between Scandinavia and the outside world too, at this time, although with details of this work not yet publicly available, and therefore no opportunity of seeing whether this reversal applies equally to all phases of the Vendel Period, it is impossible to revise the current paper in light of this information. It is possible, however,to identify some implications of what we seem to be promised from this research.
   This radically new development might provide a solution to the principal problem addressed in the second half of this paper, by demonstrating that problem to be based upon an incorrect perception of long-distance relationships in the Vendel Period. As is noted in this paper, Swedish pre-eminence in Scandinavia at the start of the Vendel Period is not easy to explain. If Denmark supersedes the *Svearike* as the heart of the Vendel-period Scandinavian developments in the forms of artefact-types and art-styles – and it is to be emphasized that as yet I have no information as to how consistently throughout the phases of the Vendel Period the traditional view of Swedish ascendancy and southern (and western) Scandinavian dependency is to be reversed – this problem disappears. It would then remain to be seen whether the supposed Swedish ascendancy over Norway at this time (see Vinsrygg 1979; Solberg 1981) can also be reattributed to Denmark. The question of the Scandinavian character of Sutton Hoo, especially boat grave 1, remains a problem, however. As far as artefact-types go, the possibility that some have canvassed for some time (e.g. Wilson 1983) that Sutton Hoo and the Uppland boat graves are related via some intermediary source remains no more than a possibility as long as close parallels to the Sutton Hoo and Swedish shields and helmets remain undiscovered in any such intermediary area. It is also possible that boat burial was introduced independently into eastern England and Sweden (Hines 1984: 287–288). If, however, we suppose that it was common circumstances in East Anglia and the Svearike rather than connexions between the two kingdoms that led to the extraordinary parallels in such conspicuous artefact-types and features that we find in these two areas, we seem to have come by another route to the same situation discussed towards the end of this paper: we end up postulating circumstances in which the exchange and imitation of material-cultural forms should be of mutual interest to these widely separated kingdoms.
   The publication of a paper on a topic concerning which one knows of the existence of, but not the details of, fundamentally relevant and innovative research findings, is

these areas be connected in any way? It must be stressed again that the prominence of Sutton Hoo in the study of Scandinavian connexions in seventh-century England may well be misleading. There are no grounds for denying that the Scandinavian connexions of seventh- and eighth-century Northumbria may have been equally strong, and indeed some of the art-historical evidence that has been considered in this paper may point this way. There is however a period in which East Anglia may be believed to have held some sort of pre-eminence amongst the English kingdoms, which justifies the concentration of attention, initially, there. This period is in the reign of Rædwald, identified by Bede as exercising *imperium* from about 615 to the later 620s, a period which appears too to be the date of Sutton Hoo grave 1, whether or not Rædwald himself was buried or commemorated there.

The evidence of the Migration Period suggests that a connexion between East Anglia and Scandinavia had been established well over a century before the reign of Rædwald, and had very probably remained active ever since. Need there be any further explanation of an East Anglian-Scandinavian connexion than the maintenance of an established line of communication and trade? I think in fact the answer is yes, for diachronic explanations of the existence of cultural phenomena are rarely of much relevance to the synchronic function of those phenomena if they are phenomena of any significance. One change that is apparent in the archaeological evidence for connexion from the late fifth century to the seventh century is the gradual shift to artefactual evidence of more and more exclusively prestigious status: uncommon and finely-crafted brooches, dress-accessories and military gear, and rare, presumably expensive, vessels. There is a seductive harmony between this observable shift and a mode of artefact dispersal in and between internally stratified polities, particularly at a relatively early stage of development, that dominates current theory; this theory has been especially clearly enunciated by Bjørn Myhre (albeit in Nynorsk, which I translate here):

> There will be good contact between the leading families within each political unit, either through peaceful exchange of goods and trade or through competition, dispute and war. Alliances between small states are usual, secured by marriages, fostering of children, gift-exchange or payment of tribute. New thoughts and ideas thus disperse rapidly, and social development will be uniform in all polities (1987a, 113).

This sort of two-part model, with the development of structures and then of

unsatisfactory to the author, and, no doubt, to the editor alike. Rather than withhold the paper, however, I prefer to let it go forward as evidence of a state of understanding in 1989, 50 years after the Sutton Hoo boat grave was discovered; as evidence of the problem that the apparent Sutton Hoo – Uppland connexions still then posed, and as a statement against which the significance of these new research results can be the more easily and rapidly assessed.

relationships between them, is the stage that was reached – albeit expressed with less clarity – in the thesis (Hines 1984).

The linkage between two so distant and apparently pre-eminent areas as East Anglia and central Sweden creates problems when one tries to apply this model. If they were linked by the sort of hand-to-hand trading line that Näsman describes, what sort of control by either or both centres is implied over intermediary centres, such as that represented by Dankirke/Ribe? Can one assess the relative probabilities of specifically economic or political superiority, or a general cultural superiority? And rather more interesting a problem – because, I believe, at least partially answerable – is that prestige goods, and diplomatic alliances, can be sought in various directions: why should such things be exchanged from perhaps the late sixth century onwards between East Anglia and *Sveariket*? What in actuality was achieved through this connexion was that Anglian-Scandinavian commonality – a heritable fact – was maintained and expressed down into the seventh century (at least). The expression of this appears particularly clearly in a series of subtle but significantly placed contrasts, such as differences in Style II and cloisonné art styles, between East Anglia and a contemporary Kent which would have been an obvious source for the 'new ideas' of Myhre's model. Kent was much more markedly falling into line with the Continent, and her material culture was arguably being aped to a greater degree by aspiring groups in the Upper Thames region than in East Anglia.

Reverting to the theme of the deliberate selection of marks of identity which was introduced with regard to the Migration Period, I would argue that the East Anglian-Swedish links in the age of Sutton Hoo were not simply the products of habit, or of the force of impersonal social and economic structural development, but much more significantly were the results of choice. The reasons for the choice of either side as a partner need not have been the same on both sides. For East Anglia, the Scandinavian connexion functioned as a source of sustenance, to maintain independence from an incipient Kentish cultural hegemony. Scandinavia would have been a convenient source because of the established connexion.

But why should the line of contact for East Anglia lead to the Mälardal? The leading place of central Sweden (in Scandinavia), especially in the earlier Vendel Period, is not easy to explain in simple terms of economic or social development. The area is archaeologically very rich at this time, and apparently influences much of the rest of Scandinavia in terms of artefact-forms and art style. Much importance has been attached to iron-production as lying at the economic heart of the kingdom, but in this and other exploitable economic resources central Sweden can be matched in several other parts of Scandinavia. Economic resources can of course be more effectively exploited by a more appropriately organized society, and evidence has been found for aristocratic control and exploitation of the resources of Vendel-period Sweden (Ambrosiani 1983). But from often very different evidence one can argue for very similar processes of stratification and 'state-formation' in many other areas of Norway, Denmark and southern Sweden - areas with similar resources to exploit (cf. Myhre 1987b; Särlvik 1982; Ringtved 1989; Hedeager in press). At best one could imagine a *Svearike* just stealing a lead over potential Scandinavian rivals in linked social and economic development around or just after the middle of the sixth century.

Nils Åberg, in 1953, tried three uncertainly associated explanations of the historical relationship between the Migration and Vendel Periods, by which he meant the establishment of Swedish pre-eminence: 1, the re-establishment of Sweden's 'natural' links with eastern Europe, restoring economic health to the area – which cannot be a long-term explanation now that the beginning of the Vendel Period is thought to pre-date the Avaric invasions and (especially) the occupation of Pannonia in 568; 2, the collapse of the North Sea 'block', as Kent turned her interest from Jutland to the Continent – which is simply indefensible as a theory now; and 3, simple force, the exercise of military might over neighbouring groups. Crude as it is, this latter may well be the most convincing proposition if more abstract and systemic explanations fail. It is not necessary to postulate that Sveariket was socially and economically more developed than her neighbours for the cutting of links with eastern Europe to stimulate the leaders within an organized polity to exploit, aggressively, westerly areas of Scandinavia and the North Sea, reaching to alternative sources of prestige models which included the British Isles.

It was not only East Anglia that could provide such models in the British Isles. The dynamism of late sixth- and early seventh-century Kent has been noted. It is interesting, however, to note that of six types of imported glass in Scandinavia noted by Näsman as of probably English origin (including two types of claw beaker) only one is described as 'probably made in Kent'. East Anglia would provide a ready partner on the other side of the North Sea. Kent's ties and preoccupations with the Continent were many and strong. The kingdom of Kent was a rival to East Anglia, and for about a quarter of a century, in the reign of Æthelberht, it seems to have held some form of pre-eminence, later noted by Bede by attributing *imperium* in southern England to Æthelberht. Sonia Hawkes has drawn a vivid and coherent picture of Kent's natural strength: the gateway to England, dominating, perhaps monopolizing cross-channel trade, with military might behind the commercial activities represented by the well-armed communities burying at Sarre and Dover (Hawkes 1982). But with just a slight shift of emphasis one could talk of the natural weakness of a small but strategically valuable kingdom rather than any inevitable superiority. Kent needed to be strong to survive, and political independence was lost in the course of the eighth century. Bede attributes Ceawlin of Wessex, *obit circa* 592, with superiority before Æthelberht, and for all Kent's material richness in the sixth century the area could still apparently be adopting an artefact-type – the scutiform pendant – from Anglian England at the end of the Migration Period. From the end of the Migration Period to the reign of Rædwald, East Anglia's material culture shows nothing very rich or spectacular that we can be sure of – though one may wonder about the date of some of the boat graves at Snape and Sutton Hoo – but there is absolutely no reason to suppose that East Anglia were particularly debilitated in this period. The extraordinarily sound common sense of Sir Frank Stenton's discussion of East Anglia in this period in association with Rædwald's *imperium* (he called it 'bretwaldaship') and the Sutton Hoo discoveries published in 1943 makes the point as solidly as is needed (Stenton 1943, 49–53). Whatever sort of pre-eminence Æthelberht had, Bede notes that he was already losing it to Rædwald before his death in 616. Kingly pre-eminence and power in England at this time seem to shift opportunistically as kings physically wax and wane. That has relatively little to do with deep cultural processes.

What I should now like to add to what was written in my thesis with regard to Sutton Hoo and its period is, then, the suggestion that at least in the earlier seventh century the Anglian-Scandinavian links that had been forged earlier were being deliberately and assertively maintained. The empirical archaeological data that we have to study are like a symphonic composition of different but harmonious strands. These strands include long-term processes in the development of centres of wealth and power, and the effects of relationships between particular centres of wealth and power. With regard to this particular case, however, many serious variations within the data, in terms of links and contrasts between several contiguous areas, are difficult if not impossible to explain as the predictable outcome of deep cultural processes, but may rather have depended upon the seizing of opportunities, and further upon the minds and ambitions of the people concerned.

23

Human Sacrifice in the Late Pagan Period in North Western Europe

HILDA ELLIS DAVIDSON

When using the term 'human sacrifice', so beloved of journalists, it is necessary to consider in what sense it may be applied to a given situation, and how precise the evidence really is. There has been much argument as to the nature and purpose of sacrifice since Robertson Smith's lectures on the religion of the Semites caused such excitement in 1894. Sacrifice has been explained in many ways: as gift or bribe, renewal of commitment to the totem animal of the tribe, act of homage, ritual linking human and divine worlds, re-enactment of primordial events, expression of communal anxiety and guilt, magical rite to gain power, giving back part of the gains from hunting or victory, or simply as an outlet for violent impulses in society. All these theories single out aspects of sacrificial rites, but none alone seems a wholly satisfactory explanation. Certainly sacrifice appears to satisfy a deeply-rooted human instinct, and has been part of religious practice from very early times to the present. It need not necessitate a living victim; there are firstling sacrifices consisting of part of the harvest, while food and drink may be offered, or part of the body such as a lock of hair or a finger; also both human beings and animals may be consecrated as a sacrifice and remain alive. In the *Encyclopedia of Religion* (1987) Professor Henninger defines sacrifice as the offering of a living creature or an inanimate object to a supernatural being, by a definite rite. He would not include under this heading expiation rites, whereby ill-luck or guilt may be transferred to a victim such as a scapegoat, or the slaying of a human or animal to provide companionship to the dead. Clearly nothing about sacrifice is straightforward and simple, and there can be endless debates about definitions and motivation.

The association with the dead is of especial interest in view of the claim that there are sacrificial victims buried at Sutton Hoo. 'Macabre evidence that the early Anglo-Saxons practised human sacrifice has been unearthed by archaeologists in Suffolk', began a reasonably serious article in the *Independent* in December 1986, and the writer, David Keys, was hopeful that 'Sutton Hoo could ultimately turn out to be Europe's most important sacrificial burial site'. In view of such claims, we need to consider the evidence leading to them, what is known of human sacrifice in Anglo-Saxon England, and what parallels are known to these particular burials.

The first group of graves, 18 in all, is a little to the east of the mound burials. They were mostly excavated between 1985 and 1987 (*Bulletin Sutton Hoo Research Committee* 5, 1988: 5–6; 7, 1990: 9). They were mainly unfurnished, with no consistent orientation, and in ten cases there were indications that these were not normal peaceful burials. Two were double graves, one holding two bodies side by side, face downwards, and the other with one supine body with a broken neck and a second crouched beneath it. In a third grave the arms of the dead were raised above the head, and in another the body was kneeling with the top of the head missing. Other cases consisted of a headless body, with its head reposing in another grave, and two which seem to have had wrists or ankles tied. The most puzzling was a large grave with a body in what has been described as a hurdling position, together with traces of a wooden object thought to be a primitive plough. Two of these graves have been radiocarbon dated to the seventh and late eighth century respectively. The second group of eleven graves was close to Mound 5, where traces of a cremation burial indicated a rich grave which had been robbed. Although irregularly placed, the graves appear to follow the outline of the mound on its south and east sides. There were eleven graves, one a double interment, and seven showed signs of violence. Three of the dead had their heads detached, in one case placed at the feet, and one of these, in the double interment, had a second body prone on top of it, with some additional limbs. One had the head wrenched, probably by hanging, with signs of what might be a rope round the neck, and in one grave there was one long bone only. This group of burials, if not exactly contemporary with Mound 5, is thought to have been made within a few years of it (*Bulletin Sutton Hoo Research Committee* 6, 1989: 7; 7, 1990: 7, 9).

Such signs of violent death might be the result of the execution of enemies or wrong-doers, or of a massacre. This would not necessarily rule out the possibility of a sacrificial death. Here we come up against problems raised by Karl von Amira, the German scholar whose monograph on Germanic death penalties was published in 1922. His theory, accepted for a considerable time, was that the cruel deaths imposed for various crimes in the later Middle Ages such as hanging, beheading, burning, drowning, breaking on the wheel, burying alive and stoning, were all based on earlier sacrificial rites among the Germanic peoples, the method of execution and the god to whom the sacrifice was offered depending on the nature of the crime. He based much of this on elaboration of brief statements in the *Germania* of Tacitus concerning death penalties for particularly shameful crimes, claiming that these were held to anger the gods. One critic of this theory was the Swedish scholar Folke Ström (1942). He felt that von Amira's interpretation of Tacitus was unjustifiable, since the gods were not held to deliver moral judgements, and there is no evidence for human sacrifice on such a scale; in fact the normal punishments for crime were fines and outlawry.

Rehfeld's work on death penalties, also published in 1942, makes further points. He argued that even when Christians committed acts of sacrilege, like the Englishman mentioned by Adam of Bremen who destroyed an image of Thor (II, 62: 97), they do not appear to have been put to death as deliberate sacrifices to the gods. In the incident in Sweden Adam refers to, the perpetrator was set upon by the crowd and killed, and his dead body mocked and mutilated and thrown into a swamp. Such victims were praised as martyrs, and a sacrificial death would surely have been remembered and emphasized.

The arguments have been largely concerned with bodies found in peat bogs in Denmark and north Germany, dating from the Iron Age, but they are clearly relevant in the case of burials in Anglo-Saxon cemeteries. Many of the bog bodies had sustained multiple injuries; a man from Datgen, for instance, had been stabbed in the region of the heart, probably the cause of his death, but also subjected to violent blows which broke his limbs, and finally beheaded, with the head left some distance from the body. Karl Struve (1967: 56 ff.) in discussing this find has made one of the most helpful conclusions to the debate. He felt that possible indications of deliberate sacrifice rather than death inflicted by execution, feud, murder or mutilation of the body for fear of the dead, would be the presence of animal bones or signs of burning near by. A sacrifice is likely to be accompanied by some rite, including the slaying of animal victims. Heinrich Beck (1970) pointed out that human sacrifice should not be viewed as an isolated phenomenon but as part of the general practice of killing living victims as religious offerings.

Cemeteries of the early Anglo-Saxon period have left little indication of the sacrifice of human beings at funerals. Nor is there much evidence for the slaying of animals, apart from horses, a few dogs, and joints of meat which could have been part of the funeral feast. There are some cases of a second body carelessly buried in or above a grave, as in an example from Sewerby in East Yorkshire excavated by Philip Rahtz in 1959 (Hirst 1985: 38 ff.). Here a woman had been laid in a deep grave with a bronze cauldron and some jewellery, and a second woman buried above her, with only a few inches of soil between them, apparently at the same time. This body lay face downwards with arms and feet raised, and a piece of a quern over the pelvis. Susan Hirst in her report on the cemetery gives several parallels, mostly from early excavations. Two were excavated in 1905 at Mitcham, Surrey; in one case a small woman lay face downwards between two males (Smith 1905:4). At Finglesham, Kent, a middle-aged man was laid out with gravegoods, while a second body, possibly a woman, lay across him (Chadwick 1958: 25, 113). Two more double burials with one of the pair without gravegoods were recorded from Bifrons in 1889 (Godfrey-Faussett 1876: 315; 1880: 553), while at recent excavations at Spong Hill, one young woman lay in a crouched position with several large flints over her body. Catherine Hills suggested that this and other burials found in the vicinity of a chamber grave might have been sacrificial victims put to death at the funeral (Hills 1984: 8, 41, 102). When so many Anglo-Saxon cemeteries have been inadequately recorded, other possible examples of sacrifice may have been missed, but on the other hand much of the evidence we have rests on conjecture only.

Anglo-Saxon written sources are similarly unrewarding concerning sacrifice at funerals. No such tradition seems to have lingered in the memory of heroic poets or indignant chroniclers. In *Beowulf* there is a fine description of the burning of warriors killed in battle (1110 ff.), so vivid that one feels that the poet himself must have witnessed such a scene or heard it described by an eye-witness. The account of the departure of the dead Scyld in his ship mentions weapons and treasures but no human or animal victims laid beside the king (32 ff.). Nor in the more prosaic sources is there anything equivalent to Pope Gregory's letter of 732 in reply to Boniface's query as to what should be done about Christians in Germany and Frisia who continued to sell slaves to the heathen for use as sacrifices (Talbot 1954: 86). Gregory was disapproving but not unduly shocked, replying that the penance should be the same as for culpable homicide. There is no reference to such problems however in Augustine's letters from Kent.

In Scandinavian graves at home and abroad, on the other hand, we find considerable evidence of sacrificial victims, borne out by written sources. A good example is the Viking grave at Ballateare on the Isle of Man, excavated by Gerald Bersu during the Second World War (Bersu and Wilson 1966: 45 ff.). Here a middle-aged man had been wrapped in a cloak and laid in a coffin or possibly a burial chamber with weapons. Higher up in the mound was a second skeleton near a layer of burnt bones, including those of horse, sheep or goat, and dog. This was a young woman with her skull broken by a blow and her arms raised above her head. The remains of an older woman, who had suffered from softening of the bones, was found at Orkney on top of a man's grave in 1968 (*Med. Arch.* 13, 1969: 242). In a mound at Donnybrook, Dublin, opened by Sir William Frazer in 1859, it was claimed by workmen that two smaller skeletons, assumed to be women, lay at the feet of a Viking warrior (Hall 1978: 68). In the Oseberg ship burial, there were the remains of two women, the older one generally assumed to be an attendant, although since the mound had been entered and only a small part of one skeleton remained, no firm conclusions can be drawn (Brøgger 1945: 3 ff.). Even though some of this evidence is early and incomplete, the case for human sacrifice is sufficiently strong for archaeologists to take further indications of it seriously.

There are several references in the literature to the killing of victims at funerals. We have a tale in *Landnámabók* (S 72; H 60) of Asmund Atlason, one of the early settlers in Iceland, being buried in his ship in a mound, with his thrall placed beside him. The thrall's body was said to be removed later, when a verse was spoken from the mound declaring that Asmund wanted to be alone in his ship, since room was better than ill company. His verse makes no direct reference to the thrall, and the tale may be invented to explain the rather osbcure little poem. There are also references in the legendary sagas to widowed queens who died of grief and were buried along with their husbands (Ellis 1943: 52). The ruthless Brynhild was said to prepare a funeral pyre so that she could be burned at the funeral of the hero Sigurd, whose death she had brought about because she could never be his wife. The Edda poem *Sigurdarkvida hin skamma* describes how she appeals to her women to die with her, promising to give them gold ornaments and rich garments, presumably for the funeral; but they are said to refuse. There are also references to five serving-women and eight well-born slaves being slain for the occasion, in the prose introduction to *Helreið Brynhildar*, while two dogs and two hawks were laid beside the hero. Another notorious queen, Sigrid the Proud, whose historical existence is suspect, was said to marry a Swedish king of the tenth century, but to depart hastily when he died, as she had no desire to be a sacrificial victim (*Flateyjarbók, Óláfs Saga Trygg.* I, 63). Such incidents may be assumed to be folklore or fiction, but at least they indicate that the idea of supplying human victims at a funeral was familiar in Scandinavia.

Of a different nature however is the celebrated travel diary of the Arab scholar and diplomat Ibn Fadlan, who in 920 set out on the long and difficult journey from Baghdad to Bulgar on the Middle Volga in order to instruct the king of the northern Bulgars in the Islamic faith (Smyser 1965). He has left a long account of a cremation ceremony when a chief of the Rus died at Bulgar; these are generally assumed to be Swedish merchant-adventurers coming to the market there to trade. Ibn Fadlan, who was intensely interested in strange customs, had heard that when one of their great men died, many things took place at the funeral, 'the least of which is cremation', and he was delighted to have the opportunity to be present. He was told that the dead man's slaves, both men and women, were usually asked if one of them would volunteer to die, but noted that only women were asked on this occasion. This may have been because the Scandinavians had only slave-girls with them, or possibly because a woman was needed to represent the dead man's wife. The girl who volunteered was feted and honoured during the nine days of feasting, while the dead man was temporarily buried, ale was brewed, and all made ready for the final ceremony. He was told that as much as a third of a man's possessions might be spent on ale for the funeral.

After nine days the dead man was taken from his grave, dressed in fine clothes and laid in a pavilion on his ship, which had been raised on to a kind of scaffold. Ibn Fadlan watched closely, and noticed that the body had no unpleasant odour when taken from the earth, but the face was very pale. A number of animals were then killed: two horses, first made to gallop and then cut to pieces, two cows, and later a dog and a cock; all were thrown into the ship. One of the last acts of the girl chosen to die was to cut off the head of a hen and throw this in also.

It may be noted from this unusually detailed account that the funerals of the

Rus were held to be elaborate and unusual, and also that the killing of animals and birds corresponds with the archaeological evidence from rich ship graves in Scandinavia from the seventh century onwards; remains of horses, dogs, sheep or goats, cattle, pigs and birds were found in graves at Vendel, Valsgärde, Oseberg, Gokstad and Ladby, to name the most important (Müller-Wille 1970: 65, 99). There were usually not more than one or two examples of each species, but a greater number of horses. Also the killing of the human victim was carried out according to an established ritual, and there were certain acts for her to perform and speeches to make. She was raised up to look through a frame representing a window or door, and according to the interpreter declared that she saw her dead kinsfolk and her master in the Otherworld awaiting her. When she drank her last cup of wine, she sang a song of farewell to her companions, like a bride before her wedding. Ibn Fadlan was told that some of the dead man's kinsmen had sexual intercourse with her before she died, but the two versions differ as to where this took place. He was told how she died after she was taken to the pavilion where the dead man lay; two men strangled her with a cord, while an old woman who conducted the sacrifice, known as the Angel of Death, stabbed her between the ribs with a dagger. Such a double form of death was traditionally associated in Scandinavia with the god Odin. The final rite was that of setting fire to the ship, which blazed up so fiercely that within an hour it was reduced to cinders and ashes. A mound was raised over the pyre, and a wooden marker set into it with the name of the dead man and the king of the Rus, suggesting that the chief was of royal lineage.

Scandinavians in eastern Europe may possibly have been influenced by Slavonic funeral customs; the slave-girls could well have been Slavs, and there is some indication that Slav wives were put to death when their husbands died (Ellis Davidson 1976; 308 ff.), while the old woman who managed the death ritual is unlikely to have come with the Rus traders from Scandinavia. Many features of the funeral however agree with the evidence from Scandinavian ship-graves, and the cremation as well as the burial of vessels was well established in Norway and Sweden. Although Ibn Fadlan may have been misled by what he heard at some points, he has the reputation of a reliable observer, being known as 'The Truthful', while he would not be tempted to give a biased account of what he saw. The chance survival of this description of a funeral by an eye-witness shows how much ritual and symbolism could form part of pre-Christian funeral ceremonies, and yet leave little or no evidence for the most scrupulous archaeologist to find. On the other hand, it would be foolish to assume that all dead of any standing were buried with fixed rites and dramatic ceremonial, or that there were numerous human sacrifices by the grave.

Much has been made of Adam of Bremen's account in the eleventh century of the great sacrifices held every nine years at Uppsala in Sweden, when a number of male animals and men are said to be killed; he was told by a

Christian informant that he had seen the corpses hanging from trees in the sacred grove by the temple, where 'dogs and horses hang with men' (IV, 27: 208). In one of the notes to the text, this is said to take place at the beginning of summer, the traditional time of sacrifice to Odin for victory. Adam states that all parts of the kingdom contributed, and the most convincing part of the account is his complaint that Swedish Christians could not obtain exemption. He knew also of incantations used at the ceremony, but refused to say more of these than that they were 'manifold and unseemly'. We cannot assume such an account to be accurate in every detail, since Adam can be both careless and credulous in his use of information. If his informant was a man of 72, as is stated, his memory may go back earlier than Adam's time. As for Thietmar of Merseburg's account of a similar sacrifice at Lejre in Denmark, he may simply be echoing Adam. We may assume however that various types of animal victims, and some human ones also, hung from trees at Uppsala when major sacrifices took place; the custom of hanging up sacrificed beasts, or at least their heads and hides after the feast, was recorded by Ibn Fadlan and also by Al-Tartushi, a Spanish Jew visiting Hedeby in Denmark in the tenth century (Birkeland 1954: 20, 103–4). Even while treating the evidence with caution, we can be reasonably certain that human as well as animal victims were sacrificed by Scandinavians at home and abroad in the Viking Age.

The majority of these sacrifices were probably associated with warfare, since there are many references to captives offered to the god to whom men turned for victory in battle. Roman historians refer to the Germans making vows which had to be fulfilled when the battle was won, and this was still taken seriously in the fifth century. Sidonius refers to Saxon pirates sacrificing one in ten of their captives after a successful voyage, and even sympathizes to some extent with their point of view, since they were bound by vows, and regarded the slaughter as a religious act (Dalton 1915: II, 149). There is plenty of archae-ological evidence for the killing of men and horses in this period, along with offerings of weapons and booty, in sacred places like Skedemosse on the Swedish island of Oland (Hagberg 1967: 57 ff.). A further reason for sacrifice in time of war was that the dying victims could be used for divination, to foretell what the outcome of a campaign would be. This was a practice also known to the Celts, and Strabo (VII, 2, 3) gives a particularly gruesome account of priestesses of the Cimbri, probably a Celtic tribe, hanging prisoners of war over bronze bowls to have their throats cut, the flow of blood revealing what the future held. Procopius (VI, 15, 24) tells us that the most important sacrifice was that of the first captive taken, while one of Odin's spells in the Edda poem *Hávamál* (157) is to use runes to compel a hanged victim to walk and talk with him. Both Celts and Germans placed great reliance on omens in warfare.

It was evidently felt that the gods themselves should select their desired victims. This would prevent individuals feeling responsibility for a killing and protect them from vengeance from kinsmen. A favourite method of choice was by casting lots, as described by Tacitus in *Germania* in the first century AD, and this was still taken seriously in the Viking Age, as can be seen from a number of instances in Rimbert's *Life of Anskar* written in the ninth century not long after the events described (Robinson 1921: 19: 68; 27:92; 30: 98). Julius Caesar in the first century has an instance of a young soldier escaping death at the hands of the Germans because the lots went against it (I, 53), and there is a similar incident in the *Life* of St. Willibrord, written in the seventh century (Talbot 1954: 10). After he had enraged the people of Helgoland by baptizing converts in a sacred spring and using sacred cattle for food, lots were cast three times a day for three days to decide whether he and his companions should be among the sacrificial victims, but Willibrord and all except one of the brothers escaped. Alternative methods were to take every tenth man, as the Saxons were said to do, or to call for volunteers, as was done on the Volga.

Undoubtedly human sacrifice must have been known to the Anglo-Saxons, even if it played no great part in their lives, possibly because there were no powerful religious centres to organize it. It would presumably be resorted to in times of crisis, such as plague, famine or enemy attack, and the victims would usually be people regarded as dispensable, such as slaves, prisoners of war or perhaps those guilty of some crime, particularly if like Willibrord they were foreigners. But our knowledge of the methods and symbolism of sacrifice is very limited. Increased evidence for violent death now coming to light in Anglo-Saxon cemeteries does not necessarily mean sacrifice; such deaths were no doubt frequent in turbulent Anglo-Saxon England.

When a case of sacrifice is suspected, we have to ask to what supernatural power the victims were likely to be offered. One possibility is the ancestors, whose importance is hinted at in Ibn Fadlan's account of the doomed girl summoned home by her kinsfolk. Another is the god presiding over battle, particularly if the occupant of an important grave has died in warfare. A possible example is the mound at Donnybrook, Dublin, where a Viking warrior was buried with two bodies at his feet (Hall 1978). In this mound there were three other levels of interments; some bodies were on ground level, where the warrior's grave was placed, and others were higher up and apparently at random. Many were young people, but all ages were represented and some bore signs of violence. Richard Hall suggested 'a cleaning-up operation after an indiscriminate massacre'. The burials seem all to have been made at the same time, and while it is possible that the warrior was inserted into a mass grave, another possibility is that a number of people had been killed in vengeance for his death, which was probably caused by a blow on the skull.

In discussing the double grave at Sewerby mentioned above, Susan Hirst gave a number of examples of possible burials of living persons, as at Camerton in Somerset (Horne 1934: 42). At Winnall II, near Winchester, several bodies were in semi-crouched or flexed positions; one girl had her arm bent in front of her face, another person was beheaded, a third had its head missing, and in two graves pieces of flint had been thrown on to the bodies (Meaney and Hawkes 1970, 29 ff.). Winnall is thought to have been a mainly Christian cemetery, possibly used at a transitional period when many Christians were buried nearer the church. In his study of Merovingian cemeteries, Bailey Young (1977) gives many parallels to the irregular disposal of bodies at Winnall. He also claims that in pre-Christian times there was no established rule about the disposal of the dead, which was governed by local and family traditions. Contrary beliefs might exist side by side, so that symbols of continued existence in the grave could be found along those in a journey to the Otherworld.

Thus we cannot make firm assumptions from the presence or absence of gravegoods or food offerings. Contact with the ancestors through feasting and sacrifice was important, and yet at the same time the concept of the dead informed with malignant energy against the living persisted; there might be attempts to immobilize the body by covering it with stones, cutting off the head, or putting a stake through the corpse. At first the Christian church gave no definite instructions about the disposal of the dead, apart from objecting to cremation or sacrifices, since the grave and funeral were under family control. Possibly some personal possessions, especially weapons and jewellery, were regarded as the rightful possessions of the dead, or might be put in the grave as status symbols. Fear of the malignant dead, and particularly of suspected sorcerers after death, continued long after the introduction of Christianity, so that there might be maltreatment of the corpse, as discussed by Simmer (1982) in relation to many headless bodies in Merovingian graves. Christians soon began to bury their dead close to a church or a saint's tomb for blessing and protection, and new fashions for laying out the body and orientating the grave were gradually established.

In the case of Sutton Hoo, one important question is the relationship of the unfurnished graves with the rich mound burials. There is some evidence for animal bones deposited in quarry pits used in building Mound 5, which were disturbed by some of the graves, and further signs of animal bones or burning which would strengthen the case for sacrifice may not have survived in the soil. If the interred were the servants of those in the mounds, one might expect them to be buried in the mounds themselves; but on the other hand one group of graves seems to be deliberately placed by Mound 5. This group might be compared with the skeletons with crossed legs arranged in a circle with heads outward found at Cuddeston, Oxfordshire in 1847 (Dickinson 1974). Unfortunately, it is not certain whether there was a grave in the centre, although rich objects were found in the vicinity. Tania Dickinson, in reviewing the evidence, noted that execution cemeteries usually have heaps of skeletons, often decapitated (Dickinson 1974, 23) and it may be significant that the Sutton Hoo burials were in single or double graves, dug with some care. The strongest suggestion of ritual sacrifice is afforded by the largest grave in the group to the east of the mounds, where a man's body lay in a strange running posture together with what may be a plough. Struve (1967: 57, 59) gives two examples of plough burial, one in Zealand, which is incomplete, together with pieces of wagons and bones of cattle, sheep and pigs, and the other with human skulls and animal bones near Burg in northern Germany.

He mentions in this connection the account by Tacitus of the cult of the goddess Nerthus in *Germania* 40. She was said to journey in her wagon through the countryside to bring good fortune and fertility, and afterwards the wagon was cleansed in a sacred lake by slaves, who were finally killed lest they revealed her secrets. For centuries, the plough was carried round at the time when spring ploughing began, and it is still sometimes paraded on Plough Monday, and brought into Church. Burial of plough and ploughman might form part of an annual ritual, or more probably be something resorted to in time of famine; the burial might be placed among the graves as an appeal to powerful ancestors in the mounds, as part of the rites of a goddess, or because the cemetery had been abandoned after the acceptance of Christianity.

But much of this is conjecture mainly, and we need much more information to read such riddles aright. We hope for more archaeological evidence, or possibly further clues from early laws, death penalties, treatment of the dead in early Christian times, concepts about the restless dead in popular tradition, or information from the early history of this region of East Anglia. We cannot rule out human sacrifices; the Anglo-Saxons were clearly capable of such practices, like other Germanic and Celtic peoples, especially after drinking deeply of the funeral ale for days on end, like the Rus on the Volga, or if they felt themselves threatened with extermination by forces beyond their control. But how far this formed part of an organized ritual, belonging to the pre-Christian religion in East Anglia, we are as yet unable to say. There are many possible reasons for signs of violence in the grave, such as accident, murder, revenge killing, attacks by bandits or invading parties, rough justice from neighbours, punishment by the family, or hatred or fear of the dead. Victims of a massacre might be buried by kinsmen in a cemetery no longer in use, or the dead might be people who for various reasons were isolated from other Christian burials. These discoveries give us the chance to consider the question and take the subject out of the realm of fantasy and wild conjecture which has bedeviled the case of Lindow Man. The longing to find cases of deliberate human sacrifice in the past shown by the general public, and indeed by some scholars, constitutes a fascinating problem in itself, but that is another story.

ACKNOWLEDGEMENTS

I am grateful to Susan Hirst for help and information on recent work on Anglo-Saxon cemeteries.

PART IV

POSTSCRIPT
The Site of Sutton Hoo
on the Completion of Fieldwork

24

The Anglo-Saxon Cemetery at Sutton Hoo: An Interim Report

MARTIN CARVER

Field-work at Sutton Hoo finished in April 1992. As this book went to press the excavations were being back-filled, and, in realisation of a cherished dream, Mound 2 was being rebuilt to its original seventh-century height – a great yellow-streaked hill similar in size and presence to Ottarshögen or one of the mounds at Gamla Uppsala. With the soil so freshly returned, and the compendius records so recently sorted and filed, readers will not be expecting a definitive account either of the curious burial practices of the Anglo-Saxons at this place, or of its role in history. Nevertheless, this is a special moment, that which immediately follows the closure of an archaeological site, – when the imagination is still feverish with discovery, and not yet sobered by analysis, mocked by lost records or dulled by delay. It is a time of excitement, optimism and speculation, when a *loi de carnaval* applies and we may still proffer the unprovable and think the unthinkable.

In this spirit, an interim report is given here, as a postscript to this valuable and unusual collection of essays, and as a foretaste of the monograph on the Anglo-Saxon cemetery to be published, after analysis of the finds, by the Society of Antiquaries and the British Museum. This interim report is dedicated to three matters only: briefly, a description of the recorded investigations at Sutton Hoo; secondly and more generously an account of what has been discovered there relating to the early middle ages, and thirdly and most sketchily, what these discoveries may be currently contrived to mean. The report is thus both a record and an agenda for research on Anglo-Saxon Sutton Hoo. Not discussed or hardly refered to are the two other research areas which comprised a major part of our efforts: the prehistoric (mainly late neolithic and early Bronze Age) settlement and the methodological developments, both of which are the subject of quite separate studies.

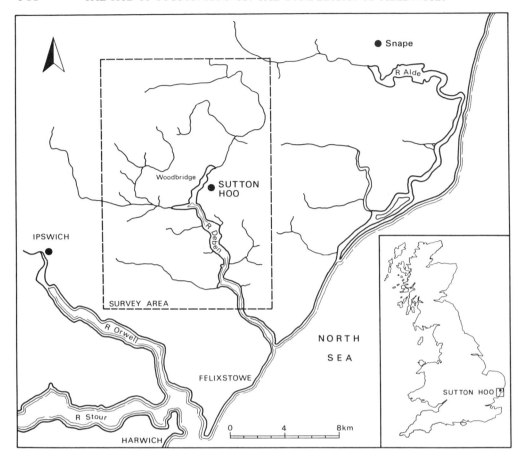

Figure 64. Sutton Hoo: Location

The Investigations and What they Encountered, before 1983

The earliest investigation of which we have any record occurs in the Ipswich Journal for 1860, and it is worth quoting in full if only because the excavations that are intimated were to become so closely entangled with our own:

ROMAN MOUNDS or BARROWS. – It is not known by many that not less than five Roman Barrows, lying close to each other, may be seen on a farm occupied by Mr Barritt, at Sutton, about 500 yards from the banks of the Deben, immediately opposite Woodbridge. One of these mounds was recently opened, when a considerable number (nearly two bushels) of iron screw bolts were found, all of which were sent to the blacksmith to be converted into horse shoes! It is hoped, when leave is granted to open the others, some more important antiquities may be discovered. These barrows were laid down in the Admiralty surveys by Captain

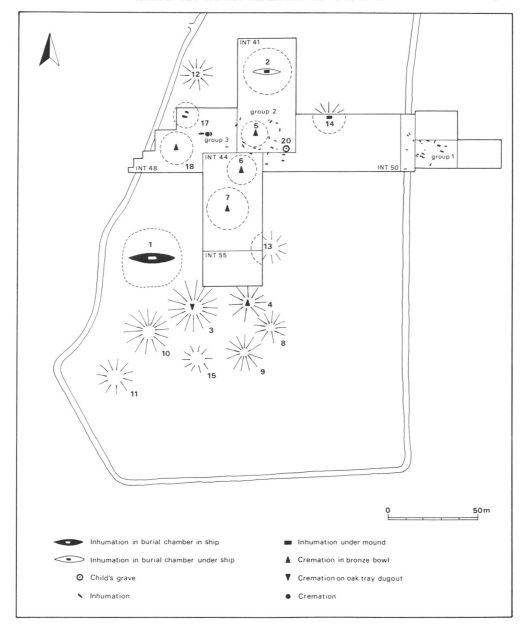

Figure 65. Sutton Hoo: Known and possible Anglo-Saxon burials and extent of Anglo-Saxon site

Stanley during the stay of the Blazer, when taking the soundings of the above-named river some years since. (*Ipswich Journal 24 Nov 1860*)

The mounds shown in the Admiralty survey are 1–4 and 6–8, so the victim should have been one of these (Hoppitt 1986), and from what we have since learnt the candidates can only be Mounds 2 or 8. Of these Mound 2 certainly contained ship-rivets, no doubt the 'iron screw bolts' of the journalist, and provided (on re-examination in 1986) a compatible setting for the barrow-opening of 1860. Leave, it seems, *was* subsequently granted to open at least some of the others, for the innocent-sounding announcement either heralds, or perhaps conceals, what was discovered on the ground to be a major nine-teenth-century excavation campaign, involving the opening of Mound 2 and at least six others. No records have been located and what became of the finds is quite unknown, although it may of course yet be discovered. The 1860 adventure at Sutton Hoo, unlike its sister excavation at Snape two years later (Bruce-Mitford 1974, 114–140), had at any rate been completely forgotten by 1938 when Mrs Pretty, the new landowner and Justice of the Peace, conceived (as landowners sometimes do) a curiosity about the humps and bumps of her barrow cemetery, by this time nearly flattened and covered in bracken. Assisted by Ipswich Museum and by the services of the free-lance self-taught Suffolk excavator Basil Brown, Mrs Pretty caused to be opened, by the traditional method of trenching, Mounds 2, 3 and 4. In each case the finds (Table 1) showed the burial to have been Anglo-Saxon, and in each case to have been previously disturbed. Mounds 3 and 4 had contained cremations, while Mound 2 had included iron rivets of a type used to fasten the planking of early medieval clinker-built ships.

Encouraged, or at least not discouraged, by these encounters, Mrs Pretty's team returned in 1939 to confront the then largest mound, Mound 1. Here the green fingers of Basil Brown, alerted by the early discovery of rivets, were able to trace the 27 metres long outline of a clinker-built rowing-boat buried in a trench below ground level (Fig. 66; Plate 24). In the centre of this ship, still the largest known from the early middle ages, was a dark rectangle '. . . the place where I expect the chief lies' as Basil Brown remarked in his diary for 3 July (Bruce-Mitford 1974, 166), which proved indeed to be the remains of a col-lapsed but otherwise undisturbed burial-chamber. In the sordid and profane history of British heritage management, such preservation from the hands of looters, treasure-hunters, and aquisitive royal agents must be counted a mira-culous deliverance, the true benefits of which were soon to be revealed.

Following the intervention of the British Museum (spurred by Christopher Hawkes) and the Ministry of Public Buildings and Works, a scratch team led by Charles Phillips and including in its illustrious contingent W.F. Grimes, Graham Clark, Peggy Guido and Stuart Piggott, dismantled the burial-deposit with its 263 finds in an astonishing ten days. This was one of the heroic episodes of British archaeology, the expeditious but measured, courageous but not cavalier retrieval of the richest burial-assemblage so far discovered in Britain, under pressure from heat, wind, unfamilarity, negligible resources, an inquisitive public and the approach of war. Given the circumstances of dis-covery, together with the immediate production of a report (Kendrick 1940) and the selfless gift of the entire treasure to the nation by Mrs Pretty, it is

MOUND 1

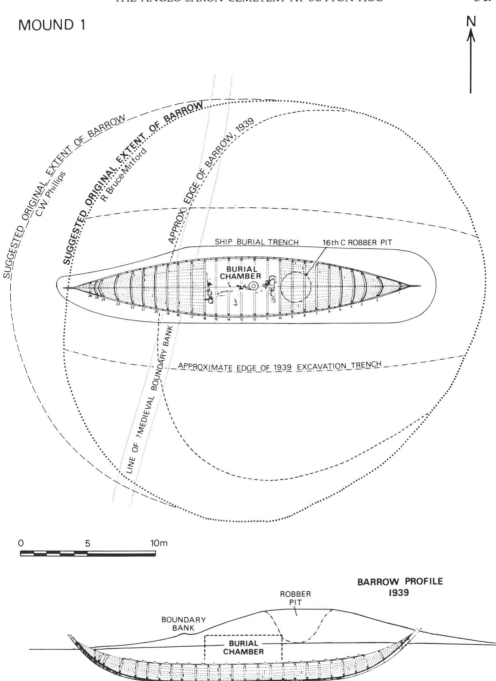

Figure 66. Mound 1: ship burial

scarcely surprising that this grave-group made the name of Sutton Hoo famous; it became and has remained an inspiration for the researches and speculations of archaeologists, art historians, historians, anthropologists, teachers and members of the general public alike.

Equally heroic, in its persistance and meticulous attention to detail, was the work of the British Museum team under Rupert Bruce-Mitford which conserved, reconstructed and studied the assemblage over the forty years which followed. The programme included a return to the field of battle from 1966 to 1971, in order to re-excavate the ship-burial, abandoned since 1939, test for the presence of 'Mound 5' and investigate the character of the prehistoric site first reported by Basil Brown. This succesful campaign enabled the inventory of the Mound 1 assemblage, and the account of the burial rite employed to be completed (Bruce-Mitford 1975, 1978, 1983), Mound 5 to be identified (1975, 11, 57) and the prehistoric site to be broadly defined: a settlement area exploited from the middle neolithic period to the Iron age (Longworth and Kinnes 1980). Two new types of burial were also encountered: flat graves containing sand-bodies and (less certainly Anglo-Saxon) two cremations (Bruce-Mitford 1975, 11; Longworth and Kinnes 1980; Table 1 nos 13, 14, 45, 50, 51 and 56). Bruce-Mitford's publication, a monument in its own right, provides not only a means for the world to share the treasure, but a point of departure for new interpretation, as understanding of the significance of the find and its context is altered by new discoveries, new students and above all by new archaeological theory.

Theory and Hypothesis

The Mound 1 burial will be reviewed in the context of the present campaign, the object of which is of course to publish the cemetery as a whole. In the final report, the Mound 1 burial will therefore reappear before the public, dressed as before but playing a new role. While hastening to relieve the reader of any anxiety that I might attempt such a reinterpretation here, it will be worth recounting how fundamentally perceptions of Mound 1 have changed since its discovery, so providing both the theoretical background and a prelude to the work of the recent campaign which is about to be reported. In 1939, and in spite of incompatible (and imprecise) archaeological dating, Chadwick identified Mound 1 as the burial of Raedwald, a documented king of East Anglia who died c.625 A.D. (Chadwick 1940). The arguments were simple and have been improved in presentation rather than substance in the hands of Bruce-Mitford: the wealth of the burial implies a king; that it now lies in East Anglia implies a king of East Anglia, and the date (early seventh century) implies an East Anglian king who died at about that time. The prime candidates are therefore Raedwald (died c.624), Eorpwald (died c.628), Sigeberht (died c.637), and Ecgric (died c.637). Each has had his champions, but Raedwald has carried the day with his successful capture of Chapter 10 in the definitive report (Bruce-Mitford 1975).

Behind such an attribution there are of course a number of assumptions, none of which need be wrong but none of which will enjoy many points of contact with a strictly archaeological inquiry. Archaeologists deal in material culture which is rarely specific or individual and has very little to say about who ruled which polity or where they were buried. Even if a personal attribution were plausible, it is hard to see that much has been thereby added to our knowledge of the ideas and practices of the Anglo-Saxons. Raedwald may indeed have been buried in Mound 1, (or indeed, as we shall see, in Mound 2), while Eorpwald may have ended as a handful of cremated bone in Mound 7 and Wuffa may be the blood-thirsty occupant of Mound 5. But attractive as they certainly are to public sentiment, these unprovable ascriptions have only passing relevance to the real business of archaeology: constructing the image of a people and their community in transition.

The change in archaeological interests from rather specific questions of cultural history to more general hypotheses about social process reached Anglo-Saxon archaeology during the 70s, and was an influential force at about the time that the new campaign began in 1983. The questions to be asked became not 'who was buried in these mounds?' or even 'was this a royal burial ground?' but 'what was the structure of Anglo-Saxon society in the seventh century and how did it change?'; 'what was a king?' and 'did the Anglo-Saxons have them?' And 'if so, when ?' and 'why then, why there?' As late as 1983 *Rescue News*, objecting to the new campaign, asserted that 'we know how the Anglo-Saxons buried their kings in the seventh century', a statement which illustrates in concentrated form the number of assumptions that Sutton Hoo had trailed after it into the 1980s. The new approach did not deny the likelihood of Sutton Hoo being a royal burial ground or one containing the mortal remains of Raedwald, it only suggested that there were more important questions to be asked, questions concerning the very fabric of early English society, and that Sutton Hoo was a site that could help answer them: how was that society structured ? How did its members think ? How did ideas, ideology and allegiance change during the seventh century? The questions were ambitious ones, and they were meant to be; the campaign was to generate a new page one for English history, otherwise there could be no justification for destroying the monument, however partially or systematically this might be done (Carver 1986a, *Bull.* 1986).

The research plans which were laid in 1983, therefore took it for granted that the bigger picture would require a bigger canvas. It would be assumed that the 'Anglo-Saxons' were a compound of indigenous with immigrant peoples from the coastal areas of north Germany and Denmark (following Bede) and from south-west Norway (following Hines 1984), and most probably from other areas also of the North Sea litoral (Carver 1990) in which early states or 'kingdoms' were already forming (Myrhe 1987b). The immigrant folk first took root in fifth-century East Anglia (following Böhme 1986) and their subsequent so-cial evolution can be followed through material culture (Carver 1989). The early *settlements* were small and dispersed (West Stow providing the para-digm), but by the late sixth century were augmented or replaced by nucleated proto-manors (such as Brandon or Wicken Bonhunt) or emporia (Ipswich). The early *cemeteries* were large and already hierarchical (Spong Hill) but by the late sixth century had became more demonstratively extravagant for an aristocratic minority. This extravagance included wealthy barrow-burial, which, together with the new types of settlement can be read as indicating the onset of that particular social strategy known as kingship (Carver 1989, passim).

It was with the testing of this model that the Sutton Hoo project was to be mainly concerned. Accordingly, there were to be three concentric research zones: a north sea zone where comparative studies would be made of the formation processes of contemporary and near contempory states, a regional zone where the settlement pattern and burial repetoire would be surveyed and sampled in the search for social and economic change, and a little patch of hectares around the Sutton Hoo burial ground itself. Of these, the *comparative studies* were to flourish through seminars organised at Ipswich, Cambridge, Oxford and York – this volume being the proceedings of that last inspiring occasion. The *regional studies* developed in the systematic hands of East Anglia's archaeological units and Suffolk's John Newman in particular (this vol. ch. 2). The *site* itself was the nodal point of the campaign: not only would it be asked the hardest questions, but would be obliged to bear the publicity and the irreversible loss of destruction by excavation (Plate 23; *Bull.* 1983).

Even when the die was cast and the long itinerary from data aquisition to analysis had begun, theory would not lie down, and hypothesis would not sleep. During our 8 years cultivating data in the field, the kitchen of British archaeology changed its cuisine, from processual to structuralist flavours, just as it had changed from a cultural-history to processual viewpoint ten years earlier. And just as before, the adrenalin provided by the theoretical debate was entirely beneficial to the Anglo-Saxon archaeology of Sutton Hoo. Without invalidating our quest for evidence for the formation of an early English king-dom, we were able to add to our agenda the subtle levels of interpretation allowable by the new post-processual thinking and so appropriate to burials. Mound 1 was not to be construed as some mindless custom, the helpless betrayal of a fossilised social system, but the artificial contrivance of a creative mind; not so much an assemblage of finds, as a statement or text, composed of carefully selected symbols. Far from being hard evidence for the reality of the heroic world of *Beowulf*, the Mound 1 ship-burial was itself a poem, a heroic dirge declaimed in a theatre of death, which (assuming we can read it) carries all the aspirations and agonies of the Anglo-Saxon political soul in transition. In short, the *historicity* of each burial mound came back into fashion, at the time we were finding on the ground that the Anglo-Saxons had indeed concentrated their ideological investment upon them. Henceforward, our interpretative statements could claim each mound as a signal of political dogma and allegiance; our excavations were not chronicling changes in social and economic strategy but changes in Anglo-Saxon attitudes (Carver, in press). Therefore, just as the beginning of the Sutton Hoo campaign coincided with the optimism of processual archaeology and its assumed ability to sample social systems in the field, so its conclusion coincides with the optimism of structural and contextual archaeology, with its assumed ability to see deep into the minds of long dead Anglo-Saxon aristocrats. Finding myself thus a member of an anti-empirical community, hungry for meaning and stories, is a piece of good fortune I have no intention of ignoring.

Evaluation and Strategy

Fieldwork began in 1983, but it was to be three years before any burial mound was newly broached. It was not enough to have a rigorous research programme; there had to be some confidence that the Sutton Hoo site could actually still answer the questions to be posed. There was also an ethical principle to include in the reckoning: I did not and do not feel that any of us is justified in excavating the *whole* of any site, however defined. The 1980s passion for so-called total excavation struck me then, as it strikes me now, not only as immoral but unscientific. If we had no questions to ask, then no digging at all was justified. If we had questions, but the destruction of the whole site was required to answer them, then they were the wrong questions and we should think again. Accordingly an intensive period of non-destructive investigation was required to establish the extent and quality of the archaeological deposits still present at Sutton Hoo. This was the three year 'evaluation' (*Bull.* 1986), requested from and granted by the imaginative, intelligent and patient Sutton Hoo Research Trust which governed the project.

The predictions of the evaluation were reasonably straightforward, and as we can now see with hindsight, not too wide of the mark. A prehistoric settlement of about 12 hectares in extent comprised boundary-ditches and buildings as well as a few cremations, and flourished between the middle neolithic and the Iron Age, peaking in the Beaker period (c.2000 B.C.). Whether the prehistoric settlement remained recognisable by the Anglo-Saxons – at least as an element of the vocabulary of landscape – has yet to be determined. But it was after two millennia of no great activity on the same modest promontary overlooking the River Deben that the Anglo-Saxons initiated their prestigious cemetery, extending to 4.5 hectares and expected to contain cremations and flat-graves in large numbers as well as barrow-burials. Fairly intensive looting of most but not all the mounds was surmised, and it was plain that there had been many holes dug between and around the mounds as well as in them, for reasons that were not likely to have been scientific. It was supposed (and afterwards demonstrated) that the barrow cemetery had been rubbed nearly flat through cultivation; so that, ploughed by farmers, looted by treasure-seekers, tunnelled by rabbits, scrambled by bracken and shot at by the army (which trained there in the war), the site had been sadly impoverished by time and neglect. The terrain – an acid porous sand and light gravel – had also played its part in the reduction of the archaeological assets. The bodies of the Anglo-Saxons left very little skeletal material, but were recognisable as sandy lumps carrying the shape of the flesh – the anthropomorphs or 'sandmen' so beloved of the media. Ageing, sexing and dating our population would therefore be a problem.

In spite of these obvious deficiencies, burial rite was still generally readable, even in previously excavated chambers, as Basil Brown had already demonstrated in 1938, and a strategy for excavation could be proposed within a more general data-aquisition package (*Bull.* 1986; and for the principles Carver 1990c), which was feasible and important enough to justify the destruction of part of the site. Our objectives were clear: to explore a changing early English community and its ideology by chronicalling its changing burial rites. A sample of these burial rites would be obtained by excavating a transect 32 metres wide from the western edge to the eastern edge of the burial ground. If I believed that I knew where the western edge was, (on the undulating crest of the promontory where the ground fell rapidly away to the flood plain of the river Deben), the eastern (inland) edge was unlocated and we would have to dig for it. The 150-metre long transect was therefore extended eastwards for some 50 metres beyond the most easterly burial, an operation tedious but conclusive. The width of the transect was suggested by the geography of the seventh-century palace site at Yeavering (Hope-Taylor 1977); if there were buildings they should not be able to escape us.

The rationale behind this transect was that the Sutton Hoo community would begin burying on the crest and continue eastwards, that is inland, until overtaken by history. This assumption bore heavily on an (unproven) Anglo-Saxon sense of logic. No such 'axis of growth' may have been intended or adopted by them. The buried population might grow organically from several nodes, or wander northwards or southwards along the crest or enter their final resting places in a manner which for us was entirely random. Accordingly a north-south transect, 138m long, was planned at right-angles to the first, so that any geographical or chronological trends might be captured. The cruciform transect so formed offered a sample almost exactly 1 hectare in extent: an expenditure of the resource of slightly over 20% (*Bull.* 1988,4; Fig. 65; plate 25). This area was declared the largest that we could be justified in taking and the smallest that would make sense. It was sited at the northern end where the majority of the recorded excavations had taken place, and the mounds were among the most damaged. The sectors reserved for the future should be both the biggest and the best. And in 1986, with the agreement of the authorities, the grudging concord of the professional fraternity and the tireless support of the Sutton Hoo Research Trust, excavation began.

What has been Found

The areas examined were dug in large pieces known as 'interventions', begining in the extreme east 'INT 32, 39' then north 'INT 41', then south 'INT 44, 55' then east again 'INT 50, 52' and then west 'INT 48' (Fig. 65). I now propose to take readers on a site-tour showing them, and briefly describing to them, the Anglo-Saxon burials discovered in approximately the order of their discovery. The inventory of all burials so far known at Sutton Hoo and identified as Anglo-Saxon is contained in Table 1.

Eastern cemetery

Accordingly we must begin, as we did in 1986, out in the fields, in our extreme eastern sector. Here the original purpose was to determine the limits of the cemetery (see above), but the peripheral group of burials that were defined there did little to establish a 'norm' against which to set the extravagance of the barrows. These 23 graves (Fig. 67) were in general without grave-goods or constructional features, although there were two well-defined coffins, a box or chest, signs of a cairn, a joint of meat and an ard (Table 1; Burials 20,27,34). The principal attributes of each grave were therefore the orientation and posture of the body, and here there was great variety: some were supine, some were prone, some were kneeling, some were flexed and some extended. What characterised the group, other than their variety, was the recurrent stress implicit in the body position. In four cases, the juxtaposition of limbs implied that wrists or ankles had been tied. In three others the head had been removed or the neck broken (Plate 26). Early attempts to rationalise these burials as the work of a 'shoddy undertaker', who dumped corpses in graves that were too small, were soon confounded: one grave had been dug much longer and another much broader than was necessary (Burials 29,27). The additional investment, the trauma or post-mortem abuse, and the curious if exiguous furnishing were most easily explained as having ritual meaning. The dating so far is seventh to eighth century, broadly contemporary with the mound-burials further west (Table 1). Were these people the victims of battle, execution or sacrifice? There are no military honours here, and the trauma for which we have evidence (hanging and beheading) hardly implies them. Execution and sacrifice are hard to distinguish archaeologically – and no easier, it might be argued for an eye-witness. How should a spectator at a public hanging in the nineteenth century distinguish the moral from the ritual in the ideology of the state? Further support for a ritual interpretation comes from the plan. Far from heralding contact with a densely packed burial ground extending to the west, the group appeared to be arranged in an isolated circle, continuing neither to north, east south or west (Figs 65, 67). In the centre of of this circle was an unexceptional pit, containing nothing that would suggest it was itself a burial or a structure, merely the undated natural deposits attributed elsewhere to a

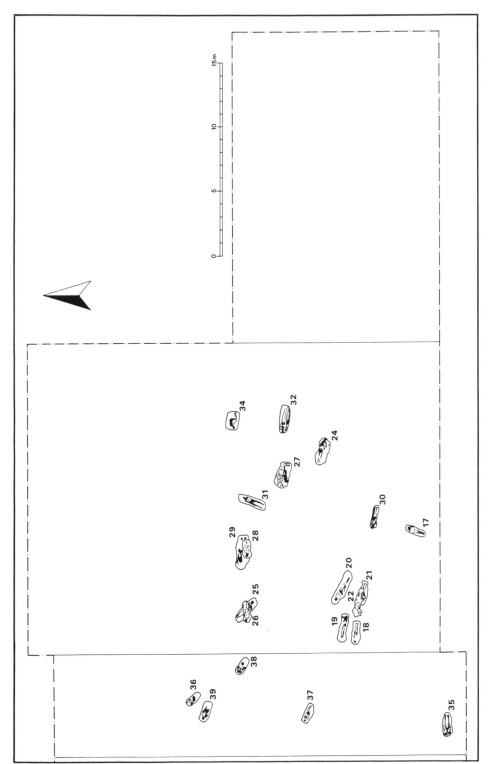

Figure 67. Eastern sacrificial group

rotted root-mantle: it was a tree. At this moment therefore and in anticipation of the analytical and dating exercises that are still to be carried out, I feel obliged to suggest that the eastern group of graves is destined to be interpreted as a ritual area, contemporary with the mounds and involving human sacrifices around a tree.

North sector

With some relief, we may now travel to the sector which represents the northern arm of the excavation sample and contains Mounds 2 and 5 (Plate 28). Mound 2 was one of those explored by Basil Brown in 1938, and his excavation trench was re-used during the evaluation phase of the present campaign in order to study the problems of mound excavation. Mound 2 and the quarry ditch that appeared around it were subsequently completely dissected, and provided our most credible evidence for the way that mounds were built. Inside the mound was a veritable chinese puzzle of earlier cuts and intrusions, which resolved into three principal episodes: a chamber-grave, a robbing operation probably of the nineteenth century, and the east-west trench cut by Basil Brown, who unwittingly spent the greater part of his excavation inside the trench cut by his predecessor (Plate 27; frontispiece). To the finds collected by Basil Brown (Bruce-Mitford 1975, 115–123), were added a further 140 scraps of gold, silver, bronze and other materials, as well as nearly 500 ship-rivets, from the robber-trench or its spoil-heaps. On the floor of the chamber itself, traces of rusty soil and other anomalies enhanced by chemical mapping indicated the original positions of large objects of iron and copper-alloy, and indeed that of the body itself (*Bull.* 6, 1989, 7–13; 21–23).

In spite of the trail of confusion left in the centre of this much-visited monument, the original ritual could be plausibly modelled. A chamber 3.8 by 1.5 metres had first been dug more than 2 metres deep, through topsoil and sand and gravel subsoil, to provide a rectangular room revetted with vertical timber planking. The body of a man laid at the west end (and therefore feet most probably to the east) had been accompanied by a sword, shield, drinking horns, silver-mounted cup, 5 knives in their sheaths, a blue glass jar, an iron-bound bucket and a cauldron, to list only those items whose original presence is reasonably certain. Basil Brown had not been wrong in supposing that Mound 2 contained a ship, only in that the ship had been underground. The distribution of the ship-rivets makes it plain that early excavators had encountered a ship all along the length of their trench, which had followed the yet intact old ground surface (Fig. 68). The types of rivets present indicate that while there is a full complement (155) of rivets with angled roves – from the two ends – the majority from the centre are missing. These indications suggest that the ship originally lay at ground level on top of the chamber, as in the much later example found at Haithabu (Müller-Wille 1976). Such a vessel would have eventually collapsed amidships under the weight of the mound, depositing within the chamber a mass of rivets – some still attached to the

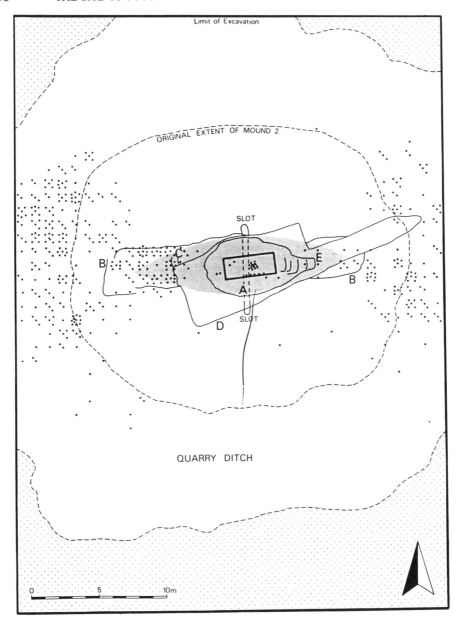

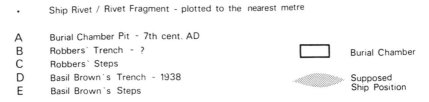

•   Ship Rivet / Rivet Fragment - plotted to the nearest metre

A   Burial Chamber Pit - 7th cent. AD
B   Robbers' Trench - ?
C   Robbers' Steps
D   Basil Brown's Trench - 1938
E   Basil Brown's Steps

☐   Burial Chamber

⬮   Supposed Ship Position

Figure 68. Mound 2: ship burial

planking. This eventuality offers a context for the disingenuous announcement in the Ipswich Journal already cited, and an explanation for the rivet patterns which understandably misled Brown. The ship buried in Mound 2 would have been in the order of 20 metres (60 feet) long, and the burial which lay beneath must have scored highly on the scale of contemporary wealth. Mound 1 and Mound 2, both rich ship-burials, show no great differences from each other in either rank or date, and only a thematic variation, if an intriguing one, in the burial rite employed.

The curious ritual composition was covered by a mound, which, from the geometry of the quarry ditch can be shown to have risen over 4 metres from its contemporary ground surface – a giant of a barrow and one unlikely to have been easily robbed before its reduction by those hungry for topsoil. Such a reduction had already rendered Mound 5 almost invisible, but it was in its day a monument no less significant than Mounds 1 or 2 – although for a very different reason. The original burial here, subsequently robbed at least twice, had been a cremation wrapped in cloth and placed in bronze bowl accompained by a comb, shears, and gaming pieces among other less identifiable objects. The head of the cremated person had been cloven, probably by a sword. Over this burial, Mound 5 was erected, but the spoil here was gained not from a quarry ditch but a series of pits, originally linked at ground level. The altitude of the ground surface under Mound 5, and the rather hesitant technique of construction suggest it to have been among the earliest. But it was not in that that the primary interest lay. The three bodies discovered and excavated by the British Museum team in the 1960s proved to belong to a set of 16 disposed in a gentle arc around the putative periphery of the original Mound 5 (Fig. 69). They shared some of the gruesome attributes of the eastern group: evidence for binding, hanging and beheading (Table 1; Plate 26). They should certainly be closely associated with Mound 5 – not only thanks to their position in plan, but because in six cases graves had been cut into the base of quarry pits which had partially silted up. These burials ('Group 2') were named by us 'satellite burials' after their relationship in space to the mound. Like the examples in the eastern field ('Group 1') they may be seen as sacrifices – in this case added to the Mound 5 obsequies immediately after its construction and thereafter at intervals for an indefinite but not extended period; the observation of silting patterns in open ditches during our own fieldwork suggests a total span of years rather than decades.

The fashion of cremation was found to continue in the *southern* sector: Mounds 6 and 7 were both cremations in origin, although both had been hideously transformed by earlier excavators. The methodology of the early diggers here resembled those who had entered Mound 2 and the morphology of their work-pattern was still clearer (Fig. 71). The excavators' trench of the time was characteristically 'bull-nosed' and 'fish-tailed' and ran west to east. The trench was driven in to the mound at one side, following the brown soil of the old ground surface until it was interrupted by the bright sand of a back-

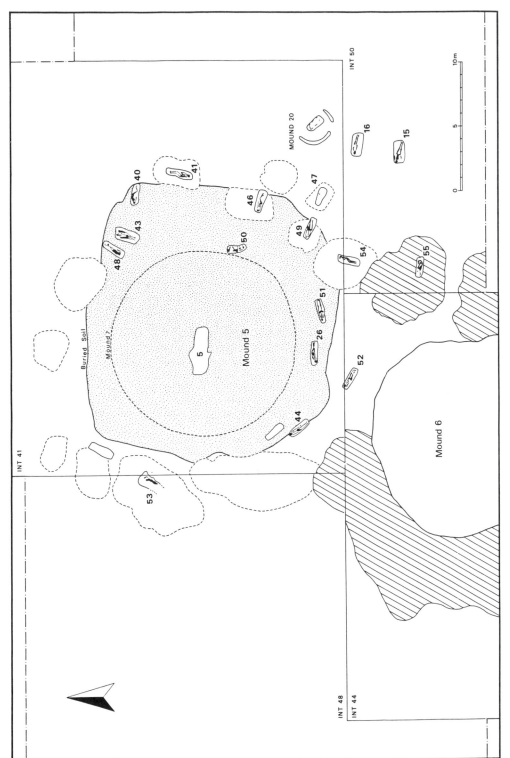

Figure 69. Mound 5 and satellite burials

filled burial-pit. At the bull-nosed end, steps were cut down into the burial chamber – and it was here on a ledge that the gentlemen antiquary could stand, in tail coat and top-hat no doubt, stooping only to receive the good things which the earth had to offer. At the other end, splayed towards the spoil heaps, were the barrow-runs of the honest rustics, earning a supplementary shilling by removing, and in the case of Mounds 6 and 7, sieving, four or five hundred tons of sandy soil. What little survived from these exceptionally dilligent exertions, allows Mound 6 to be stated as containing a cremation wrapped in cloth and placed in a bronze bowl accompanied by a bronze sword-pyramid and bone comb; and Mound 7 to have been a cremation, also most probably in a bronze bowl, and accompanied (at the least) by a playing piece and a reticella bead.

The southern sector was eventually extended to join hands with Mounds 3 and 4, which like Mound 13 (sectioned in 1991), had been involved in the nineteenth century campaign. The excavators may have continued on to Mound 10, which is scarred by the axial dent characteristic of all mounds found to have been robbed. Our jolly diggers therefore denied themselves a rather particular treat: Mound 1. Why did they stop? It would have been more human to lay their trench across it, as across all the others – but perhaps they tried. It was after all very much deeper and the burial rite meant that the usual tell-tale guide to the location of the burial chamber (an interruption to the buried soil) was lacking. At any rate they turned away – and the early history of England was richer as a result.

Eastern arm

The eastern arm (INT 50) was the large open area, crossed by a medieval hollow way, which connects the group of peripheral burials named as group 1 (above) with the world of the burial mounds, 5, 6 and 7. Any expectations that this sector would be densely packed with flat graves on the one hand or reserved for hall-buildings or a church on the other were speedily disappointed. The sector was nearly, but not quite, empty of Anglo-Saxon features. Near the barrows lay a row of three graves, each of them furnished. The more northerly ('Mound 20') was the burial of a child of less than four years old in a coffin, accompanied by a tiny spear and tiny buckle. Equally diminutive was the mound that had once covered it, betrayed by a circular truncated ditch; the mound could hardly have been 2 metres in diameter. The companions of this grave, which were parallel to it to the south, were probably also young, adolescents or young adults. They too were in coffins and modestly furnished with bronze and ironwork (Table 1), but with no evidence for mounds. Some metres to the east lay the unobtrusive profile of Mound 14, which the sector was designed to cut in half, exposing the residual mound and its buried soil in section and any central burial in plan (Fig. 70, Plate 29). The quarry ditch was of the 'Mound 2' type, ragged but continuous except for interruptions at the east and west, and in the middle lay the lozenge-shaped depression of a robbed chamber-grave. The chamber was a delicate affair, built with thin

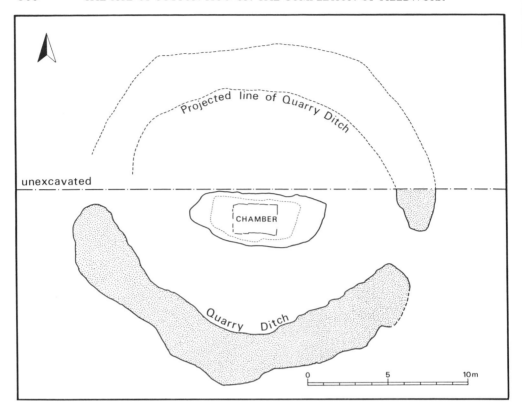

Figure 70. Mound 14

planks set vertically in a technique which also echoed that of Mound 2. By good fortune the pillaging of Mound 14 had been interupted by an East Anglian squall:- fans of rain-washed silt were defined above the natural subsoil to the east, while the west had turned into an extensive mush. At a given moment the looters of Mound 14 must have decided to call it a day, since they departed, abandoning within the 'mush' of their sodden tread more than one hundred finds. Enticing things have since been glimpsed in this assemblage, as it lies in the intensive care of the British Museum: a small silver buckle, a silver chain, a chatelaine – enough to promise an important statement from a grave which is set fair to be the first burial at Sutton Hoo which is incontravertibly the inhumation of a female.

The west
The last sector to be explored, reaching over the crest into Top Hat Wood with the river beyond, should have been the first to be exploited – and this may well prove to be the case. The British Museum excavations of the 60s had located here two putative cremations (neither wholly convincing as Anglo-Saxon) and a grave containing only a skull (Table 1, no. 56; Longworth and Kinnes 1980).

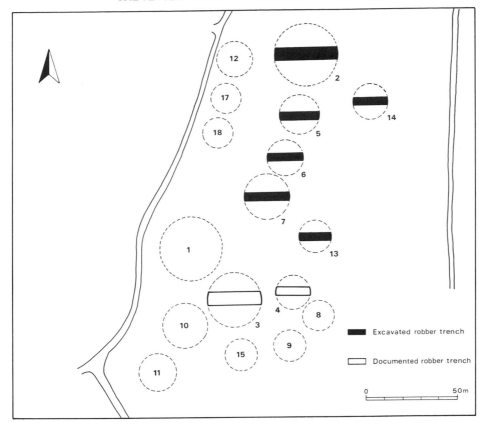

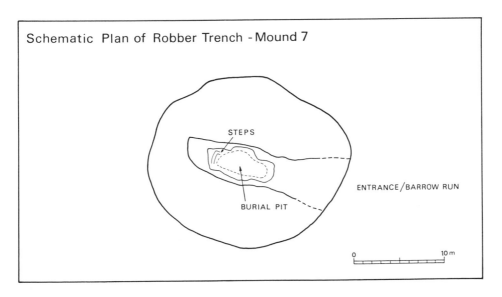

Figure 71. The nineteenth-century excavation campaign, with (below) diagram of the excavators' methodology at Mound 7

To these we would add two burial mounds (nos 17 and 18). The damage suffered by the western end of the site, owed most likely to ploughing and erosion, had reduced the earthworks to shadows. Mound 18 was ploughed to pieces, only a scatter of burnt bone and bronze fragments, and a comb-tooth, radiating from a square depression a few millimetres deep survived to signal the former emplacement of an Anglo-Saxon cremation. Mound 17, to the north, was quite a different experience, for here fortune had decreed that we should encounter the second intact wealthy burial to be found at Sutton Hoo in modern times. Although no ship-burial, it was not lacking in interest, either as a mortuary ritual of a special kind or as a key episode in the development of the cemetery.

Two grave-pits lay west-east, parallel and side by side (Plate 30, Fig. 65). In the northernmost of the two was a fully-articulated remains of a horse or pony, surviving both as sand-stain (mainly the belly and neck) and as bone (Plate 32). There were no grave-goods, but some kind of organic furnishing was implied by traces of as yet unidentified detritus. The more southerly grave was that of a young person of high status – the so-called 'Sutton Hoo prince' (Plate 31). The body of a young man lay in a coffin that was originally cylindrical in shape, recalling a tree-trunk, and held together with curved iron clamps. Beside him lay a sword with bronze buckle inlaid with garnets and two sword pyramids. By his ear was a strike-a-light purse. Outside the coffin to the north was a comb set on end, an iron-bound bucket, a cauldron with a pottery vessel inside, and at the east end a bronze drinking bowl over four animal ribs – lamb or pork chops. The persistant staining observed around this latter area may have been due to the decay products of the meat, or to some cloth or leather container – such as a haversack. At the west end, a complex of metal objects and traces of leather was lifted in a block and is being dissected in the British Museum; enough has now been seen to identify the complex as belonging to a bridle or bridles or caparison. We should eventually be able see this or-namented harness reconstructed; it has an iron snaffle bit and gilt-bronze axe-shaped pendants, circular gilt-bronze strap-distributors and many small copper alloy pendants which seem to have hung from breast-straps or brow-bands. Above the bridle was the stain of a circular wooden tub, and beneath the coffin lay two spears and a shield.

The excavation of this grave was greatly enhanced by the expertise of col-leagues from the British Museum Conservation Laboratory, whose job was to save the finds from deterioration by getting them out, at the same time as mine was to resolve the stratigraphic sequence by keeping them in. It can be con-fidently reported that both objectives succeeded. The finds arrived intact in the Museum, and the ritual and sequence of the burial can be written with some precision. A rectangular pit 3.4 by 1.7 metres and some 1.36 metres deep, was abandoned for a few hours under rain. The pit was then furnished. After the spears, the shield was placed flat with the boss uppermost. On the rim of the shield, was put the iron-bound bucket, next to it the cauldron, and next to that the haversack. At the west end, the bridle was deposited. Only then did the coffin arrive. Presumably destined for the empty south side, it ended up, no doubt due to the cumbersome mechanics of its installation, in the centre, where it settled canted up on top of the shield boss. In the tilted coffin, the body rolled southwards on top of the sword. The coffin was now in place, but the assemblage was not complete. The comb, disturbed from the coffin roof by backfilling, or thrown by a mourner, must have slipped down the north side of the curved coffin until it assumed the vertical postion in which it was found. The backfilling then proceeded. After some 30 centimetres of earth had already filled the grave, a wooden tub was placed at the west end. If such a tub can be associated with feeding a horse, then it may have been at this moment that the horse was dispatched to join his master. About the mound that was thrown over the two burials we know little, but that it was modest; there were no quarry ditch or quarry pits. The scraping of topsoil had been reduced on discovery to a barely detectable swelling some 14 metres in diameter.

A Provisional Model

Although there had been some trimming and a great deal of discussion, the area completed in 1992 was essentially that proposed in 1986. It is important to realise that the sample proposed was that deemed necessary to answer the question; we stopped because the work had been finished, not because we had run out of money or interest. Sutton Hoo is not merely the first British excavation to follow a published research design, but one of the few to stop because it was completed. That is not to say that knowledge of the Sutton Hoo cemetery is complete or ever will be, or even that it is yet possible to appreciate the full significance of what has been found. The analysis on which the post-excavation teams at the British Museum and the University of York are now embarked would certainly be pointless if the full story could already be told. The prudent interim therefore halts here. But it is no more than human to wish to inspect the summary plan of the burial ground assembled in Fig. 65, to wonder what the story may turn out to be, and whether the research procedure so publicised and so exposed in so many media, will turn out to have been valid.

Two assertions on behalf of the excavation sample might be made with reasonable security. First that the cemetery is generally late – late sixth to eighth century – and of uniformly high status. There are no convincing burials, whether cremation or inhumation, of conventional fifth-sixth century type. This is no 'folk cemetery' which developed extravagant burial styles in its later phases, but a 'separated' cemetery, reserved for the elite, where to gain entry you must either belong to the aristocracy or be co-opted into their ideological drama. At a superficial level, the evidence offers endorsement to the suggestion that Sutton Hoo was the burial ground of 'kings', who can now be shown

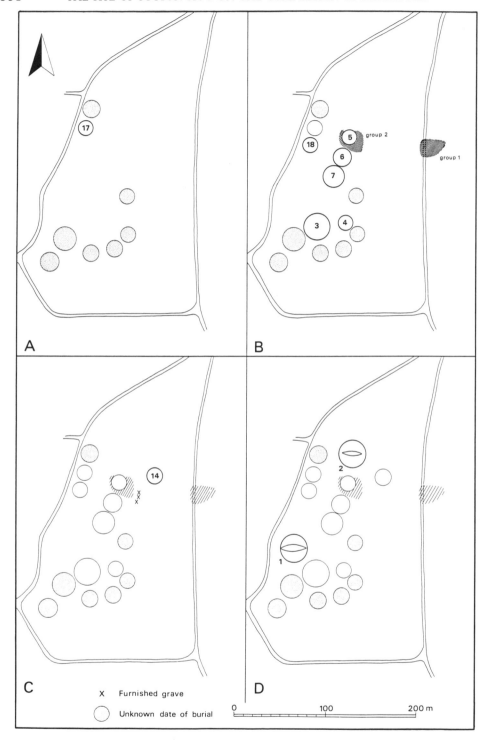

Figure 72. The development of the Anglo-Saxon burial ground: a preliminary model

to have been dynastic (honouring children), militantly pagan and claiming the right over life and death. It will I believe be accepted that cremation under mound, ship burial and human sacrifice which are all new to the ritual repertoire of East Anglia, are intended to convey pagan rather than Christian ideological signals. The burial rites, moreover find their parallels in Scandinavia (we need say nothing of the finds whose implications are far less specific). So, if we believe (in line with modern theories of material culture) that burial, and perhaps most particularly burial at this level of status, is a deliberate statement made by intelligent humans at a moment of crisis, then the signals which emanate from Sutton Hoo are specific, the cry of a people at once pagan, autonomous, maritime and concerned to conserve an ancestral allegiance with the Scandinavian heartlands and their politics, across the North sea. In this interpretation, the context in which such signals become necessary can only be where the protagonists are threatened by their converse: Christianity, the adoption of which reaches beyond the tonsure and the church to fealty to the Franks and their imperial echoes. Sutton Hoo is therefore a theatre in which the longest running theme is the defiant pagan politics of an arriviste monarchy (Carver in press).

Very much more difficult will be the task of ordering the burials encountered into a coherent sequence of events, to chronicle the history of how such rituals and attitudes became adopted, when and why. It must be said at once that the evidence for the sequence in which the burials were celebrated is very poor and unlikely to improve greatly. We have a stratigraphic hint that Mound 6 was constructed after Mound 5. We may expect a sequence of radio-carbon dates from the British Museum's laboratory which may distinguish episodes more than 50 years apart. And it can be hazarded, although with more than usual rashness, that Mound 17 will turn out to be datable from its metalwork to the mid or late sixth century. Such fragile and equivocal data, even when we have them, will hardly support a historical sequence; but a sequence there obviously was. A most tentative, almost recreational attempt follows here – the final part of my model (Fig. 72).

Mound 17 was a rich burial, but not especially so, and might not be out of place at the high status end of those 'folk cemeteries' that abound in East Anglia, such as at Spong Hill, or at nieghbouring Snape (this vol., Ch. 3). Its position on the crest of the riverward slope adds to the impression that it might be among the earliest graves, a young member of an aristocratic family whose new separate cemetery this was to be. In a second phase, and in a severe change of mood, Mound 5 was erected on the highest part of the promontory. The honoured person was cremated and his memory exacted, and subsequently continued to exact, the right of human tribute. These are signs which may be connectable with the assumption of kingship, and kingship in a pagan context. Similar sacrificial rituals were practised around a tree on the eastern periphery. Cremation was adopted in subsequent high-ranking burials all along the spine of the cemetery, Mounds 6, 7, 3 and 4, each one on this interpretation endorsing, or at least not contradicting, the pagan and probably Scandinavian manifesto initiated by Mound 5.

In a third phase, two new burial rites are introduced: coffin burial in rather plain graves for children or adolescents, and a chamber-grave under a mound for a woman. These, like Mound 17 in the putative 'phase 1', have nothing specifically Scandinavian about them, and they are being said to sit in the sequence where they do simply by virtue of their position in the cemetery. In a fourth and final phase, with the most extravagant and defiant non-Christian gesture of all, two ship-burials are added : that to the north (Mound 2) has a chamber grave beneath the ship under the mound; while that to the west (Mound 1) has a chamber constructed within a ship in a trench under a mound.

As a final and illicit indulgence, (and because if I do not, then others will) it would be highly diverting, if wholly unscientific, to place this sequence in a framework of early English history and even furnish it with some of the characters involved. We could surmise how the family which chose the site were, or became, the Wuffingas, succesful landowners who claimed kingship under Wuffa and began to contrive the ideological apparatus to secure its continuance without the assistance of the font, the Bishops or the Franks. While Wuffa lay implacably beneath Mound 5, the men of Kent succumbed to both Christianity and the domination of Frankia. Wuffa's successors were cremated, giving a nod to their political mentors across the North sea. Other members of the family, such as the children and at least one woman, were honoured, but not used to signal the exotic political affinities of the kingdom. In a final lurid twilight, Raedwald or Sigeberht, Eorpwald or Ecgric, the last champions of an independant East Anglia, set out in ships laden with newly-contrived regalia, to bring the bad news to the gods. In an episode lasting less than a century, perhaps much less, a peculiar political experiment had flared and failed.

Sutton Hoo is an intriguing site and has not become less so after the intensive scientific scrutiny of the last nine years. It remains a constant temptation to the story teller and I am aware of succumbing. This sequence of events is the weakest of my offerings and the most vulnerable to the rigours of future analysis. At present the story is little more than the stuff of dreams, which I share with the reader, more out of camaraderie than conviction. But the readers of this book will be dreamers too, otherwise they would never have picked it up.

ACKNOWLEDGEMENTS

The Sutton Hoo Research project has benefited greatly from the friendship and advice of the Sutton Hoo Research Committee, and from the supportive management of the Sutton Hoo Research Trust (at various times Christopher Brooke, John Evans, Micheal Robbins, Paul Ashbee, David Attenborough,

Martin Biddle, Rupert Bruce-Mitford, Barry Cunliffe, Catherine Hills, John Hurst, Ian Longworth, Henry Loyn, David Phillipson, Robert Pretty, David Pretty, Phillip Rahtz, Micheal Tite, Keith Wade, Leslie Webster, Martin Welch, Stanley West, David Wilson, Ted Wright). To these must be added Angela Evans, who was seconded from the British Museum for successive seasons and who has the reponsibility for the curation of the early medieval finds, all of which (thanks to the Pretty family) are destined for the national collection. John Knight steered us through the legal thickets which beset us. The local landowners (Anne Tranmer, John Miller and Peter Waring) gave the project their support. Our principal sponsors were the Society of Antiquaries of London, the British Museum and the British Broadcasting Corporation. The project team numbered many hundreds of students, volunteers, professionals and volunteer-professionals from Universities and Units in many countries, but the nucleus was provided by Madeleine Hummler, Andrew Copp, Jenny Glazebrook, Cathy Royle and Linda Peacock of the University of York, and Annette Roe, Justin Garner-Lahire and Gigi Signorelli of the Società Lombarda d'Archeologia. Post-excavation work is being carried out at the Department of Archaeology, University of York, Micklegate House, York, UK, to which any correspondence should be addressed.

TABLE 1

Sutton Hoo: Inventory of Anglo-Saxon Burials, 1992

Mounds, Unexcavated and Conserved for Future Study

MOUNDS 8, 9, 10 [possibly robbed], 11 [attempted robbing 1982: INT 17], 12, 15, 16.

Mounds, or Former Mounds, Excavated to Date

MOUND 1: [*Burial 1*] INHUMATION W-E in chamber in ship in trench; with sword, shield, helmet, regalia, silverware, lyre, drinking horns, clothing, buckets, cauldron etc.

INTACT. Excavated 1939, 1965–71 (INT 5–10); published Bruce-Mitford 1975, 1978, 1983.

DATED: c.625 A.D. (grave-goods)

MOUND 2: [*Burial 2*] INHUMATION W-E in chamber under ship; originally with sword, shield, belt-buckle(?), silver buckle, drinking-horns, tub(?), iron-bound bucket, cauldron(?), bronze bowl, blue glass jar, silver-mounted box, silver-mounted cup, 5 knives in sheaths, textiles.

ROBBED or EXCAVATED without record, possibly in 1860 (INT 1). Excavated 1938 (INT 3; Bruce-Mitford 1975). Excavated 1986–9 (INT 26, 41).

DATED: late sixth/early seventh century (grave-goods)

MOUND 3: [*Burial 3*] CREMATION on oak tray or dug-out boat; with limestone plaque, bone-facings (for box?), bronze ewer-lid, francisca, comb, textile, pottery sherds (?), horse (cremated).

ROBBED or EXCAVATED without record (nineteenth century?). Excavated 1938 (INT 2; Bruce-Mitford 1975).

DATED: late sixth/early seventh century (grave-goods)

MOUND 4: [*Burial 4*] CREMATION in bronze bowl (fragments), with playing piece, textile, horse (cremated).

ROBBED or EXCAVATED without record (nineteenth century?). Excavated 1938 (INT 4; Bruce-Mitford 1975).

DATED: late sixth/early seventh century (grave-goods)

MOUND 5: [*Burial 5*] CREMATION in bronze bowl (fragments), with composite playing pieces, iron shears, silver-mounted cup, comb, knife in sheath, ivory fragment, glass fragments, textiles, animal bone – possibly dog (cremated).

ROBBED or EXCAVATED without record (twice). Excavated 1970 (INT 12; Longworth and Kinnes 1980), 1988 (INT 41).

SURROUNDED by 'satellite burials' of Group 2 (see below).

DATED: late sixth/early seventh century (grave-goods)

MOUND 6: [*Burial 6*] CREMATION in bronze bowl (fragments), with copper-alloy sword-pyramid, bone comb (fragments), textiles.

ROBBED or EXCAVATED without record (nineteenth century?). Excavated 1989–91 (INT 44).

DATED: late sixth/early seventh century (grave-goods); stratigraphically later than mound 5.

MOUND 7: [*Burial 7*] CREMATION in bronze bowl (fragments), with reticella bead, bone gaming-counters, silver-gilt fragment, iron knife, textiles, animal bone.

ROBBED or EXCAVATED without record (nineteenth century?). Excavated 1990–1 (INT 44).

DATED: late sixth/early seventh century (grave-goods)

MOUND 13: Unidentified burial rite.

ROBBED or EXCAVATED without record (nineteenth century?). Mound sectioned 1991–2. Burial unidentified (INT 55).

UNDATED

MOUND 14: [*Burial 8*] INHUMATION (possible female) in chamber, with silver-mounted cup (?), silver buckle, silver chain, bronze fittings for box (?), bronze pins, bronze chateleine, bronze girdle hangers, bronze bowl (?), textiles.

ROBBED or EXCAVATED without record (nineteenth century?). Excavated 1991 (INT 50).

DATED: late sixth/early seventh century (grave-goods)

MOUND 17: [*Burial 9*] INHUMATION W-E in iron-clamped wooden coffin, with (in coffin) sword, bronze buckle inlaid with garnets, two silver(?) sword pyramids, bronze-fitting, iron dagger, strike-a-light purse (containing garnet and millefiori fragments and buckle); (outside coffin, within grave pit) two spears, shield, bucket, cauldron, pottery vessel, 'haversack'(?) containing animal ribs and flanged bronze bowl; comb, harness for horse (including gilt-bronze discs, axe-shaped pendants with animal ornament, an iron snaffle bit, leather straps), wooden tub.

Associated with: [*Burial 10*] INHUMATION of HORSE, adjacent and parallel. Unfurnished.
    INTACT. Excavated 1991 (INT 48).
    DATED: sixth/seventh century (grave-goods)

MOUND 18: [*Burial 11*] CREMATION in bronze bowl (fragments), with textiles and bone comb (teeth only).
    PLOUGHED AWAY. Excavated 1966, 1989 (INT 11, 48)
    DATED: Anglo-Saxon (comb)

[MOUND 19 – shown not to have existed during excavation in 1991 (INT 55).]

MOUND 20: [*Burial 12*] INHUMATION NW-SE in wooden coffin of child, with iron spear-head, bronze buckle and bronze pin.
    INTACT. Excavated 1987 (INT 41).
    DATED: Anglo-Saxon (grave-goods)

Burials without Evidence for Mounds

CREMATIONS

Burial 13 [INT 11, Aiii]: Unurned cremation.   Undated
Burial 14 [INT 11, Aiv] : Cremation in pottery vessel. Sixth–seventh century(?)

FURNISHED INHUMATIONS

Burial 15 [INT 50, F54]: W-E, extended on back, in coffin, with two bronze buckles and dagger/knife in sheath.

Burial 16 [INT 50, F58]: W-E, extended on back, in coffin with bronze needle-case(?) having leather stopper, bronze ring-headed pin and glass ring-beads, and iron rod, chain or coffin-fitting.

SATELLITE BURIALS

    GROUP 1:   On Eastern Periphery

INT 32

Burial 17 [F9(254)]: N-S, flexed, on back.   DATED: 540–700 A.D. (C 14)
Burial 18 [F39(101,245,246): W-E, extended, on back, in coffin.
Burial 19 [F40(102,247)]: E-W, extended, prone, with hands tied behind back (?)
Burial 20 [F106(248,249)]: NW-SE, extended, on back, in coffin/tree-trunk, with animal joint(?). Under cairn.
Burial 21 [F108(251)]: W-E, extended, on back, without head.
Burial 22 [F109(252)]: W-E, extended, on back; above *Burial 21* and with head of F251 in lap.   DATED: 680–820 A.D. (C 14-accelerator)
Burial 23 [F137/1]: E-W, MALE, extended, on back, with broken neck.
Burial 24 [F137/2]: Prob. MALE, crouching; beneath *Burial 23*.
Burial 25 [F146(258)]: SE-NW, prob. MALE, extended, prone, with wrists and ankles 'tied'.

Burial 26 [F154(259)]: W-E, extended, on back, above *Burial 25*.

Burial 27 [F161(260,261)]: W-E, on side, in 'ploughing position', with ard and rod. Prob. MALE.

Burial 28 [F163(262)]: W-E, kneeling, top of head missing.

Burial 29 [F166(263)]: W-E, extended, on back, hands 'tied' and stretched above the head.

Burial 30 [F173(264)]: W-E, MALE, extended, on back, wrist over wrist.

Burial 31 [F231(237)]: N-S, extended.

Burial 32 [F227/1(238)]: W-E, extended, prone.

Burial 33 [F227/2(239)]: W-E, extended, prone, lying with *Burial 32*.

Burial 34 [F235(240)]: W-E, flexed, in square coffin, chest or barrel.

INT 52

Burial 35 [F4(34)]: W-E, extended, on back, head detached and placed looking north on right arm.

Burial 36 [F37(71)]: NW-SE, tightly crouched, lying on right side, head facing north.

Burial 37 [F25(72)]: NW-SE, flexed at knees, lying on back.

Burial 38 [F35(75)]: NW-SE, lying on back, knees bent back to shoulders.

Burial 39 [F36(74)]: NW-SE, kneeling, face down, left arm behind back.

GROUP 2:   Associated with Mound 5

INT 41

Burial 40 [F81(152)]: W-E, prob. MALE, flexed, on side in 'sleeping' position, with head detached and rotated.

Burial 41 [F82(507,509,510)]: S-N, flexed, on side; with organic stains (=additional human limbs?). Cuts quarry pit F508.

Burial 42 [F86/1(148)]: N-S, MALE, extended, on back, with head detached and lying with neck uppermost.

Burial 43 [F86/2(149)]: N-S, prob. FEMALE, extended, prone on top of *Burial 42* with human limbs/jaw.

Burial 44 [F124(542)]: NW-SE, extended, on back.

Burial 45 [F154(55) = INT 12, grave 3]; W-E, prob. MALE, prone.

Burial 46 [F424(499)]: NW-SE, flexed, on side. Cuts quarry pit F130.

Burial 47 [F435]: Body piece, possibly part of a long-bone. Grave cuts quarry pit F133.

Burial 48 [F486(555)]: S-N, slightly flexed, on side, head detached and placed below knee.

Burial 49 [F517(524,525)]: NW-SE, extended, on back, head wrenched out of alignment, with organic 'scarf' around neck. Cuts quarry pit F129, which contained bone fragments of large mammal.

Burial 50 [F588=INT 12, grave 1]: S-N, flexed, on side.

Burial 51 [F590=INT 12, grave 2]: W-E, extended, on back.

INT 44

Burial 52 [F215(216)]: NW-SE, extended, on back, lower left leg broken, head detached and turned through 180 degrees.

INT 48

Burial 53 [F349(351)]: N-S, extended, prone, under plank, right arm extended above head; with organic stains; within quarry pit F287.

INT 50

Burial 54 [F141(162)]: S-N, flexed, on side, in 'sleeping' position, without head. Cuts quarry pit F30.

Burial 55 [F341(379)]: E-W, bent over backwards, or truncated. Cut by later cow-burial F342).

GROUP 3: Isolated Grave near Mound 17

Burial 56 [INT 11, pit 1]: E-W, skull only, detached and facing foot end, with glass bead and bronze fitting. (Longworth and Kinnes 1980).
    DATED: 670–830 A.D. (C 14)

BIBLIOGRAPHY

Åberg, N. 1953: *Den historiska relationen mellan folkvandringstid och Vendeltid*, KVHAA handlingar, Antikvariska serien 5, Stockholm.

Adam of Bremen: *History of the Archbishops of Hamburg-Bremen*. Trans. F.J. Tschan. (Columbia UP. 1959).

Adcock, G. 1974: *A study of the types of interlace on Northumbrian sculpture* (unpub. M.Phil. thesis, University of Durham).

Additamentum Nivialense de Fuilano, ed. B. Krusch, Monumenta Germaniae Historica, Scriptores Rerum Merovingiarum IV (Hannover, 1902).

Åkerland, W. 1939: *Studier över Ynglingatal* (Lund).

Alcock, E.A. 1989: 'Pictish stones Class I: where and why', *Glasgow Archaeol. J.*, 15 (1988–9), 1–21.

Alcock, L. 1981: 'Early Historic fortifications in Scotland', in G. Guilbert (ed.), *Hillfort Studies* (Leicester), 150–81.

Alcock, L. 1983: 'The archaeology of Celtic Britain, fifth to twelfth centuries AD', in D.A. Hinton (ed.), *25 Years of Medieval Archaeology* (Sheffield), 48–66.

Alcock, L. 1984: 'A survey of Pictish settlement archaeology', in J.G.P. Friell and W.G. Watson (eds), 7–41.

Alcock, L. 1987: 'Pictish studies: present and future', in A. Small (ed.), 80–92.

Alcock, L. 1988: 'The activities of potentates in Celtic Britain, 500–800 AD: a positivist approach', in S.T. Driscoll and M. Nieke (eds), 22–46.

Alcock, L. and Alcock, E.A. forthcoming: 'Reconnaissance excavations in Early Historic fortifications and other royal sites in Scotland, 1974–1984. 5, A, Excavations and other fieldwork at Forteviot, 1981; B, Excavations at Urquhart, 1983; C, Excavations at Dunnottar, 1984', *Proc. Soc. Antiq. Scot.*

Alcock, L., Alcock, E.A. and Driscoll, S.T. 1989: 'Reconnaissance excavations on Early Historic fortifications and other royal sites in Scotland, 1974–84: 3 Excavations at Dundurn, Strathearn, Perthshire, 1976–77', *Proc. Soc. Antiq. Scot.*, 119, 189–226.

Alcock, L., Alcock, E.A. and Foster, S.M. 1986: 'Reconnaissance excavations on Early Historic fortifications and other royal sites in Scotland, 1974–1984: 1, Excavations near St Abb's Head, Berwickshire, 1980', *Proc. Soc. Antiq. Scot.*, 116, 255–79.

Alcuin, *Vita Willibrordi*, ed. and trans. H.-J. Reischmann, *Willibrord, Apostel der Friesen* (Darmstadt, 1989).

Allen, J.R. 1900: 'Bronze bowl found at Needham Market, Suffolk', *The Reliquary and Illustrated Archaeologist*, 6:242–50.

Allen, J. R. and Anderson, J. 1903: *The Early Christian Monuments of Scotland* (Edinburgh).

Allison, J. 1955: 'The Lost Villages of Norfolk', *Norfolk Archaeology*, 31, pp. 116–162.

Ambrosiani, B. 1983: 'Background to the boat-graves of the Mälaren valley', in J.P. Lamm and H.A. Nordström (eds), *Vendel Period Studies* (Stockholm 17–22).

Ament, H. 1977: 'Zur archäologischen Periodisierung der Merowingerzeit', *Germania* 55, pp. 133–40.

Amira, K. von, 1922: *Die germanischen Todestrafen* (Abhandl. Bayer. Akad. Wiss. Phil. Philol. Hist. Kl. 31 (3). Munich).

Anderson, A.O. and Anderson, M.O. (eds) 1961: *Adomnan's Life of Saint Columba* (Edinburgh).

Andersson, K. 1986: 'Nytt ljus över ett gammalt fynd', *Fjölnir* 5:3 (Uppsala).

Anderson, M.O. 1973: *Kings and Kingship in Early Scotland* (Edinburgh).

Anderson, M.O. 1987: Picts – the name and the people', in A. Small (ed.), 7–14.

Andrén, A. 1989: Dörrar till förgångna myter – en tolkning av de gotländske bildster-narna. A. Andrén (ed.): *Medeltidens Födelse* (Lund).

Andrén, A. (forthcoming): Guld och makt – en tolkning av de skandinavisk guldbrak-teaternas funktion. Kommer i: *Samfundsorganisation og Regional Variation*. C. Fabech & J. Ringtved (eds) (Jysk arkæologisk Selskab. Århus).

Angenendt, A. 1986: 'The conversion of the Anglo-Saxons considered against the back-ground of the early medieval mission', *Angli e Sassoni al di qua e al di là del mare*, Settimane di Studio del centro italiano di studi sull'alto medioevo 32 (Spoleto), 747–81.

Anon 1987: 'Garton Station', *Current Archaeology*, 103:234–7.

Archibald, M. 1985: 'The coinage of Beonna in the light of the Middle Harling hoard', *The British Numismatic Journal*, 55, 10–54.

Armit, I. (ed.) 1990: *Beyond the Brochs. Changing Perspectives on the Atlantic Scottish Iron Age* (Edinburgh).

Arndt, W. and Krusch, B. (eds), 1885: *Gregorius Turonensis Opera*.

Arne, T.J. 1919: 'Graver fran 'Vendeltid' vid Lagerlunda i Kärna socken, Östergötland', *Fornvännen*, 14, 1–20

Arne, T. and Stolpe, H. 1927: *La Nécropole de Vendel* (Stockholm).

Arnold, C.J. 1980: 'Wealth and social structure: a matter of life and death', in P. Rahtz, T. Dickinson and L. Watts (eds), *Anglo-Saxon cemeteries 1979. The Fourth Anglo-Saxon Symposium at Oxford*. Oxford (B.A.R. 82), 81–142.

Arnold, C.J. 1982a: 'Stress as a stimulus to socio-economic change: England in the seventh century', in C. Renfrew and S. Shennan (eds), *Ranking, resource and exchange*. Cambridge University Press (New Directions in Archaeology), 124–131.

Arnold, C.J. 1982b: *The Anglo-Saxon cemeteries of the Isle of Wight* (London: British Museum Publications).

Arnold, C.J. 1984: *Roman Britain to Saxon England* (London: Croom Helm).

Arnold, C.J. 1988: *An archaeology of the early Anglo-Saxon kingdoms* (London: Croom Helm).

Arnold, T. 1898: *Notes on* Beowulf (London).

Arnott, W.G. (ed.) 1946: *The place-names of the Deben valley parishes* (Ipswich).

Arnott, W. 1955: *Suffolk Estuary: the story of the river Deben* 2nd ed. (Ipswich).

Arrhenius, Birgit. 1983: The chronology of the Vendel graves. *Vendel Period Studies* 2. J.P. Lamm and H.-Å. Nordström (eds.) (Stockholm).

Arrhenius, Birgit. 1985: *Merovingian Garnet Jewellery: Emergence and Social Implications* (Stockholm).

Arwidsson, G. 1942: *Die Gräberfunde von Valsgärde I: Valsgärde 6* (Uppsala).

Arwidsson, G. 1977: *Die Gräberfunde von Valsgärde III: Valsgärde 7* (Uppsala).

Arwidsson, G. 1983: 'Valsgärde' in *Vendel Period Studies*, ed. Lamm, J.P. & H.-Å. Nordström 71–82.

Ashmore, P. J. 1980: 'Low cairns, long cists and symbol stones', *Proc. Soc. Antiq. Scot.*, 110, 346–55.

Atkin, M. 1985: 'The Anglo-Saxon urban landscape in East Anglia', *Landscape History 7*, 27–40.

Austin, D. 1990: 'The "proper study" of medieval archaeology', in L. Alcock and D. Austin (eds), *From the Baltic to the Black Sea: studies in medieval archaeology*, 9–42. (London: Unwin Hyman).

Avent, R. 1975: *Anglo-Saxon Disc and Composite Brooches* (British Archaeol. Rep. 11, Oxford).

Avitus of Vienne, ed. R. Peiper, *Monumenta Germaniae Historica, Auctores Antiquissimi* VI ii (Berlin, 1883).

Aalbjarnason, Bjarni (ed.), 1941: *Heimskringla*, Íslenzk Fornrit, 26 (Reykjavík).

Axboe, M. forthcoming: Guld og guder i folkevandringstiden. Brakteaterne som kilde til politisk/religiøse forhold. *Samfundsorganisation og Regional Variation*. C. Fabech & J. Ringtved (red.) (Symposieberetning fra Sandbjerg Slot 11.–15. april 1989. Jysk Arkæologisk Selskabs Skrifter).

Axboe, M. and Fromann, A. (forthcoming): D.N. Odinn P. F. AUC? Germanic 'imperial portraits' on Scandinavian Gold Bracteates. *Acta Hyperbora. Danish Studies in Classical Archaeology* vol. 4 (Udkommer, 1992).

Bailey, R. forthcoming: Sutton Hoo and Seventh-century Art in R. Farrell and C. Neuman de Vegvar, ed., *Sutton Hoo: Fifty Years After* (Western Michigan University Press, Kalamazoo).

Bailey, K. 1989: 'The Middle Saxons', in S. Bassett, *The Origins* of Anglo-Saxon Kingdoms (Leicester), 108–22.

Baillie, M. 1980: 'Dendrochronology – the Irish view', *Current Archaeology*, 73, 61–3.

Bakka, E. 1983: Westeuropäische und nordische Tierornamentik des achten Jahrhunderts in Überregionalem Stil III, *Studien zur Sachsenforschung*, 4, 1–56.

Bantelmann, N. 1988: *Süderbrarup. Ein Gräberfeld der römischen Kaiserzeit und Völkerwanderungszeit in Angeln. I: Archäologische Untersuchungen*, Offa-Bücher 63.

Bannerman, J. 1974: *Studies in the History of Dalriada* (Edinburgh).

Baratte, F. 1981: *Le Trésor d'Argenterie Gallo-Romaine de Notre-Dame-d'Allençon (Maine-et-Loire)* (Gallia Supplément 40, Paris).

Baratte, F. and Painter, K. (eds), 1989: *Trésors d'Orfèvrerie Gallo-Romains* (Éditions de la Réunion des Musées Nationaux, Paris).

Barclay, G. 1983: 'Sites of the third millenniun bc to the first millennium ad at North Mains, Strathallan, Perthshire', *Proc. Soc. Antiq. Scot.*, 113, 122–281.

Barley, N. 1974: *Anthropological aspects of Anglo-Saxon symbolism* (unpub D.Phil. thesis, University of Oxford).

Barrett, J.C. 1981: 'Aspects of the Iron Age in Atlantic Scotland. A case study in the problems of archaeological interpretations', *Proc. Soc. Antiq. Scot.*, 111, 205–19.

Barrett, J.C. and Foster, S.M. 1991: 'Passing the time in Iron Age Scotland', in W.S. Hanson and E.A. Slater (eds), 44–56.

Barrow, G.W.S. 1973: *The Kingdom of the Scots. Government, Church and Society from the eleventh to the fourteenth century* (London).

Barrow, G.W.S. 1983: 'The childhood of Scottish Christianity: a note on some place-name evidence', *Scottish Studies*, 27, 1–15.

Bassett, S. 1989: 'In search of the origins of Anglo-Saxon kingdoms', in S. Bassett (ed.) *The origins of Anglo-Saxon kingdoms*, 3–27 (Leicester: University Press).

Bassett, S. (ed.), 1989: *The Origins of Anglo-Saxon Kingdoms* (Leicester University Press)

Bateman, T. 1861: *Ten Years' Diggings in the Celtic and Saxon Grave Hills, in the Counties of Derby, Stafford and York, from 1848 to 1858* (London).

Beck, H. 1970: 'Germanische Menschenopfer in der literarischen Überlieferung', *Vorgeschichtliche Heiligtümer und Opferplätze in Mittel – und Nordeuropa*, ed. H. Jankuhn. AAWGPH (3) 74: 240–58.

Beckmann, C. 1969: Metallfingerringe der römischen Kaiserzeit im freien Germanien. *Saalburg. Jahrbuch* Bd. 26.

Bede, *Historia Ecclesiastica*, ed. C. Plummer (Oxford, 1896).

Bede, *Historia Ecclesiastica*, ed. B. Colgrave and R.A.B. Mynors (eds), 1969: *Bede's ecclesiastical history of the English people* (Oxford: University Press).

Behm-Blancke, G. 1973: *Gesellschaft und Kunst der Germanen. Die Thrüringer und ihre Welt* (Dresden).

Bell, M. 1978: 'Saxon settlements and buildings in Sussex', in P. Brandon (ed.) *The South Saxons* (Chichester), 36–53.

Bencard, M. and Jørgenson L.B. 1990 (eds): Excavation and Stratigraphy. *Ribe Excavations 1970–1976*, vol. 4 (Sydjysk forlag, Esbjerg).

Bencard, M., Bender Jørgenson, L., & Brinch Madsen, H. (eds), 1990: *Ribe Excavations 1970–76*, vol. 4 (Sydjysk Universitetsforlag, Esbjerg).

Benediktsson, Jakob (ed.), 1950–57: *Arngrimi Jonae: Opera Latine Conscripta* Bibliotheca Arnamagnæana, vols 9–12 (Copenhagen, 1950–1957).

Benediktsson, Jakob (ed.), 1957–1959: 'Icelandic Traditions of the Scyldings', *Saga Book*, 15, pp. 48–66.

Beowulf, 1936: *Beowulf and the Fight at Finnsberg*, ed. F. Klaeber, 3rd ed. (Boston and London).

Bergengruen, A. 1958: *Adel und Grundherrschaft im Merowingerreich* (Wiesbaden).

Bersu, G. and Wilson, D.M. 1966: *Three Viking Graves in the Isle of Man* (Med. Arch. Monograph Series 1).

Beuman, Helmut 1965: 'Grab und Thron Karls des Grossen zu Aachen', in Beumann, ed. *Karl der Grosse* I (Düsseldorf), 9–25.

Bird, J. 1986: 'The silver bowl', in J.M.C. Toynbee, *The Roman Art Treasures from the Temple of Mithras* (London and Middlesex Archaeol. Soc. Special Paper, 7).

Birkeland, H. 1954: *Nordenshistorie i middelalderen etter arabiske kilder* (Norske Vid-Akad i Oslo, histfilos K1–2).

Bjørnstad, G. 1989: Innberetning om registrering og kartlegging av fossile dyrkingsspor 13/6–15/9 1989. *Rapport fra Borre-prosjektet 1990* (Univ. Olds., Oslo).

Blair, J. 1988: 'Minster churches in the landscape', in D. Hooke (ed.) *Anglo-Saxon Settlement* (Oxford: Blackwell), 35–58.

Blair, W.J. 1989: 'Frithuwold's kingdom and the origins of Surrey', in S. Bassett (ed.), *The origins of Anglo-Saxon kingdoms*, 97–107 (Leicester: University Press).

Blake, E.O. (ed.), 1962: *Liber Eliensis* (London: Camden Society).

Blindheim, Ch. 1954: Borre i lys av Borrefunnet og Nasjonalparken. *Borre bygdebok*, 1–26 (Borre Kommune, Horten).

Blindheim, Ch. 1984: From Uppland in Sweden to the Uplands of Eastern Norway? Some reflections concerning a new Merovingian find. *Univ. Olds. Skrifter 5*, 43–56.

Boas, F. 1955: *Primitive Art* (New York).

Boddington, A. 1990: 'Models of burial, settlement and worship: the final phase reviewed.' in E. Southworth (ed.) *Anglo-Saxon Cemeteries. A Reappraisal* (London, 177–99).

Böhme, H.W. 1974: *Germanische Grabfunde des 4. bis 5. Jahrhunderts zwischen unterer Elbe und Loire* (Munich: C.H. Beck'sche).

Böhme, H.W. 1986: 'Das Ende der Römerherrschaft in Britannien und die angelsächsische Besiedlung Englands im 5. Jahrhundert' *Jahrbuch des Römisch-Germanischen Zentralmuseums Mainz* 33, 469–574.

Böhner, Kurt 1958: 'Das Grab eines frankischen Herren aus Morken im Rheinland', *Neue Ausgrabungen in Deutschland* (Berlin), 452–468.

Bonnet, C. 1977: *Les premiers édifices chrétiens de la Madeleine à Genève* (Genève).

Bosworth, J. and Toller, T.N. (eds) 1898: *An Anglo-Saxon Dictionary* (London).

Bouillart, Dom Jacques 1724: *Histoire de l'abbaye royale de Saint-Germain des Prez* (Paris).

Bourdieu, P. 1979: 'Symbolic power' *Critique of Anthropology* 13–4: 77–85.

Bourke, C. 1983: 'The hand-bells of the early Scottish church', *Proc. Soc. Antiq. Scot.*, 113, 464–68.

Bourla Alexandre (dit Bourla fils) 1807: 'Documents archeologiques pour ecrire l'histoire de l'ancienne abbaye Sainte-Genevieve de Paris, dont l'eglise a ete fouille en 1807 par mon pere pour trouver les tombes des rois Clovis ier . . . Clothilde . . . et autres' *Bibl. Historique de la Ville de Paris, ancien manuscrit 16.563 fol.*

Bowen, E.G. 1977: *Saints, Seaways and Settlements.*

Braathen, H. 1989: Ryttergraver. Politiske strukturer i eldre rikssamlingstid. *Varia 19* (Univ. Olds., Oslo).

Bradley, R. 1987: 'Time regained – the creation of continuity' *Journal of the British Archaeological Association* 140, 1–17.

Bradley, R. and Gorden, K. 1988: 'Human skulls from the Thames, their dating and significance', *Antiquity* 62: 503–509.

Bradley, S.A.J. 1982: *Anglo-Saxon Poetry* (Everyman: London, Melbourne and Toronto).

Braithwaite, M. 1982: 'Decoration as ritual symbol: a theoretical proposal and an ethnographic study in southern Sudan' in I. Hodder (ed.), *Symbolic and Structural Archaeology* (Cambridge), 80–88.

du Breul, Dom Jacques. 1639: *Le théâtre des antiquitez de Paris* (Paris).

Briscoe, T. 1985: 'The use of brooches and other jewellery as dies on pagan Anglo-Saxon pottery' *Medieval Archaeology*, 30: 137–42.

Brøgger, A.W. 1916: Borrefundet og Vestfoldkongenes graver. *Vid. Sel. Skrifter. Hist. - fil.klasse 1916, no. 1*, 1–67 (Oslo).

Brøgger, A.W. 1937: Gullalder. *Viking I*, 137–196.

Brøgger, A.W. 1945: 'Oseberggraven-Haugbrottet', *Vik* 9: 1–44.

Broholm, H.C. 1960: *Kulturforbindelser mellem Danmark og Syden i aeldre Jaernalder* (Copenhagen).

Brooks, N. 1984: *The Early History of the Church of Canterbury: Christ Church from 597 to 1066.*

Brooks, N. 1989: 'The creation and early structure of the Kingdom of Kent'. In S. Bassett (ed.) *The Origins of Anglo-Saxon kingdoms*, 55–74 (Leicester: University Press).

Brown, D. 1990: 'Dice, a games-board, and playing pieces', in M. Biddle, *Object and Economy in Medieval Winchester*, Winchester Studies 7.ii (Oxford), 692–706.

Brown, R. 1969: 'The external relations of the Ndebele kingdom in the pre-partition era'. In L. Thompson (ed.), *African societies in southern Africa*, 259–81 (London: Heineman).

Bruce-Mitford, R.L.S. 1948: 'Saxon Rendlesham' *Proc. Suffolk Inst. Archaeol.* 24, 228–251.

Bruce-Mitford, R.L.S. 1969: 'The art of the *Codex Amiatinus*' *J.Brit. Archaeol. Ass.* 3S 32: 1–25.

Bruce-Mitford, R.L.S. 1974: *Aspects of Anglo-Saxon archaeology. Sutton Hoo and other Discoveries* (London: Gollancz).

Bruce-Mitford, R.L.S. 1975: *The Sutton Hoo ship burial* (vol. 1) (London: British Museum Publications).

Bruce-Mitford, R.L.S. 1978: *The Sutton Hoo ship burial* (vol. 2) (London: British Museum Publications).

Bruce-Mitford, R.L.S. 1983: *The Sutton Hoo ship burial* (vol. 3) (London British Museum Publications).

Brulet, Raymond 1981: 'Tournai, fouille d'une nécropole du Bas-Empire', *Archéologia* 145 (August 1981), 55–59.

Brulet, Raymond et al. 1986: *Archéologie du Quartier Saint-Brice à Tournai* (Tournai).

Brulet, Raymond et al. 1988: 'Nouvelles recherches à Tournai autour de la sépulture de Childéric', *Revue Archéologique de Picardie* 1988 (3–4) (= *Actes des VIIIe Journées internationales d'archéologie mérovingienne de Soissons (19–22 juin 1986)*), 39–43.

Bull.: *Bulletin of the Sutton Hoo Research Committee* (1–8, 1983–1992).

Bullough, D.A. 1983: 'Burial, community and belief in the early medieval West', in P. Wormald, D. Bullough and R. Collins, eds, *Ideal and Reality in Frankish and Anglo-Saxon Society: Studies Presented to J.M. Wallace-Hadrill* (Oxford), 177–201.

Bryan, W.F. 1929: 'Epithetic Compound Names in *Beowulf*. *Studies in English Philology: a Miscellany in Honour of Frederick Klaeber*, eds K. Malone and M.B. Ruud (Minneapolis), pp. 120–134.

Cabrol, Dom F., and Leclercq, Dom Henri, 1914: *Dictionnaire d'archéologie chrétienne et de liturgie*, tome III, 2 (Paris).

Cameron, K.H. (ed.), 1959: *The Place-Names of Derbyshire*, 3 vols (Cambridge).

Cameron, K.H. 1968: *Eccles* in English Placenames, in *Christianity in Britain*, eds M.W. Barley & R.P.C. Hanson, 87–92.

Campbell, A. 1972: *An Anglo-Saxon Dictionary: enlarged addenda and corrigenda* (Oxford).

Campbell, J. 1971: The first century of Christianity in Anglo-Saxon England, *Ampleforth Journal* 76, 12–29.

Campbell, J. 1979: 'Bede's *Reges* and *Principes*'. Jarrow Lecture.

Campbell, J. 1982: *The Anglo-Saxons* (London: Phaidon).

Capelle T. 1987: 'Animal stamps and animal figures on Anglo-Saxon and Anglian pottery' *Medieval Archaeology*, 31: 94–96.

Carnegie, S. and Filmer-Sankey, W. forthcoming: 'A Saxon Cremation Pyre from the Snape Anglo-Saxon cemetery, Suffolk'.

Carneiro, R.L. 1970: 'A Theory of the origins of the state'. *Science*, 169, 733–38.

Carneiro, R.L. 1978: 'Political expansion as an expression of the principle of competitive exclusion', in R. Cohen and E.R. Service (eds), *Origins of the state*, 205–223. Philadelphia: Institute for the Study of Human Issues.

Carr, R.D., Tester, A., and Murphy, P. 1988: 'The Middle Saxon settlement at Staunch Meadow, Brandon'. *Antiquity*, 62, 371–77.

Carver, M.O.H. 1986a: 'Research design', *Bulletin of the Sutton Hoo Research Committee*, 4.

Carver, M.O.H. 1986b: 'Sutton Hoo in context', *Settimane di Studio del Centro Italiano di studi sull'alto medioevo* 32 (Spoleto), 77–123.

Carver, M.O.H. 1986c: 'Anglo-Saxon objectives at Sutton Hoo 1985', *Anglo-Saxon England* 15: 139–52.

Carver, M.O.H. 1988: 'Anglo-Saxon discoveries at Sutton Hoo, 1987–8', *Bulletin of the Sutton Hoo Research Committee*, 6: 5–7.

Carver, M.O.H. 1989: 'Kingship and material culture in early Anglo-Saxon East Anglia'. In S. Bassett (ed.), *The origins of Anglo-Saxon kingdoms*, 141–58 (Leicester: University Press).

Carver, M.O.H. 1990a: 'Interim conclusions for the Anglo-Saxon period', *Bulletin Sutton Hoo Research Committee*, 7, 9 Table 2 and 17–19.

Carver, M.O.H. 1990b: 'Pre-Viking traffic in the North Sea', in McGrail, S. (ed.) *Maritime Celts, Frisians and Saxons* (CBA), 117–25.

Carver, M.O.H. 1990c: 'Digging for data: archaeological approaches to data definition, aquisition and analysis' in R. Francovich and D. Manacorda (eds), *Lo Scavo Archeologico: dalla diagnosi all'edizione* (Florence): 45–120.

Carver, M.O.H. in press: 'Ideology and Allegiance in Early East Anglia', in R. Farrell and C. Neuman de Vegvar (eds) *Sutton Hoo: Fifty years after* (Proceedings of the International Congress of Medieval Studies at Kalamazoo, 1989).

Carver, M.O.H. and Evans, A. 1989: 'Mound 2: the ship' *Bulletin of the Sutton Hoo Research Committee*, 6, 7–11.

Chadwick, H.M. 1907: *The Origin of the English Nation* (Cambridge).

Chadwick, S.E. 1958: 'The Anglo-Saxon Cemetery at Finglesham, Kent' *Med. Arch.*, 2: 1–71.

Chambers, R.A. 1976: 'Excavations in the Witney area', *Oxoniensia*, 41.

Chaney, W.A. 1962: 'Grendel and the *gifstol*: a legal view of monsters', PMLA 77, 513–20.

Charles-Edwards, T.M. 1972: 'Kinship, status and the origins of the hide', *Past and Present* 56, 3–33.

Charles-Edwards, T.M. 1976: 'The distinction between land and moveable wealth in Anglo-Saxon England', in *Mediaeval settlement: continuity and change*, ed. P.H. Sawyer (London), 180–7.

du Châtelier, P. 1889: 'Le Trésor de Saint-Pabu', *Revue Archéologique*, 3rd ser., 14, 188–93.

Cherry, J. 1978: 'Generalization and the archaeology of the state', in D. Green, C. Haselgrove and M. Spriggs (eds), *Social organisation and settlement: contributions from archaeology, anthropology and geography*, 411–37 (Oxford:B.A.R. S47).

Chlothar II, 614 Edict of Paris. Ed. C. de Clercq, *Corpus Christianorum* Vol.148a. *Concilia Galliae* (Turnhout 1963), 283–5.

Chomsky, N. 1957: *Syntactic Structures* (The Hague).

Christlein, R. 1973: 'Besitzabstufung zur Merowingerzeit im Spiegel reicher Grabfunde aus West- und Südwestdeutschland' *Jahrbuch des Römisch-Germanischen Zentralmuseums Mainz*, 20, 147–80.

Christophersen, A. 1989: Kjøpe, selge, bytte, gi. Vareutveksling og byoppkomst i Norge ca.800–1100: en modell. *Medeltidens föelse*. Gyllentiernska Krapperupsstiftelsen (Lund), 109–145.

Christophersen, A. 1991: 'Port and trade in Norway during the transition to historical times', *Aspects of Maritime Scandinavia AD 200–1200* (Roskilde).

Claessen, H.J. 1978: 'The early state: a structural approach', in H.J. Claessen and P. Skalník (eds), *The early state*, 533–96 (The Hague: Mouton).

Claessen H.J. and Skalník P. 1978: 'Introduction'. In R. Cohen and E.R. Service (eds), *Origins of the state*, 1–20 (Philadelphia Institute for the Study of Human Issues).

Clark Hall, J.R. 1960: *A concise Anglo-Saxon Dictionary* (4th edn with supplement by H.D. Meritt: Cambridge).

Clarke, H.B. and Brennan, M. (eds) 1981. *Columbanus and Merovingian Monasticism*. Oxford (British Archaeological Reports Supplementary Series 113).

Clarke, R. R., 1960: *East Anglia* (London).

de Clercq, C. 1963: *Concilia Galliae A.511–A.695, Corpus Christianorum Series Latinae* 148A (Turnhout).

Clermont-Joly, M. 1978: *L'Epoque Mérovingienne (Catalogues des Musées de Metz 1)* (Metz).

Close-Brooks, J. 1984: 'Pictish and other burials', in J. Friell and G. Watson (eds), 87–114.

Close-Brooks, J. 1986: 'Excavations at Clatchard Craig, Fife', *Proc. Soc. Antiq. Scot.*, 116, 117–84.

Close-Brooks, J. and Stevenson, R.B.K. 1982: *Dark Age Sculpture: a Selection from the Collections of the National Museum of Antiquities* (Edinburgh).

Clutton-Brock, J. 1976: 'The animal resources', in D.M. Wilson (ed.) *The Archaeology of Anglo-Saxon England* (London), 373–92.

Codex Theodosianus, ed. T. Mommsen and P.M. Meyer (Berlin, 1904–5).

Cohen, A. 1974: *Two-Dimensional Man* (London).

Cohen, R. 1978: 'Introduction'. In R. Cohen and E.R. Service (eds), *Origins of the state*, 1–20 (Philadelphia: Institute for the Study of Human Issues).

Colgrave, B. (ed.), 1956: *Felix's Life of Saint Guthlac* (Cambridge).

Colgrave, B, and Mynors, R.A.B. (eds), 1969: *Bede's Ecclesiastical History of the English People* (Oxford).

Copley, G.J., 1988: *Early Place-Names of the Anglian Region of England* (Oxford, British Archaeological Reports 185).

Cosack, E. 1982: *Das sächsische Gräberfeld bei Liebenau, Kr. Nienburg (Weser)*, G.D.V. A.15 (Berlin).

Cottam, M.B. and Small, A. 1974: 'The distribution of settlement in southern Pictland', *Medieval Archaeol.*, 18, 43–65.

Courtney, P. 1981: 'The early Saxon fenland: a reconsideration', *Anglo-Saxon Studies in Archaeology and History*, 2, 91–99.

Cowan, I.B. and Easson, D.E. 1976: *Medieval Religious Houses, Scotland* (London).

Cox, B. 1973: 'The significance of the distribution of English place-names in *ham* in the Midlands and East Anglia', *Journal of the English Place-Name Society*, 5, 15–73.

Cox, B. 1976: 'The place-names of the earliest English records', *ibid.*, 8, 12–66.

Crabtree, P.J. 1989: *West Stow: Early Anglo-Saxon Animal Husbandry* (East Anglian Archaeology 47).

Cramp, R.J. 1957: '*Beowulf* and archaeology', *Medieval Archaeology*, 1:57–77.

Cramp, R. 1984: General Introduction, *The British Academy Corpus of Anglo-Saxon Stone Sculpture. Volume I: County Durham and Northumberland* (Oxford University Press).

Crowfoot, Elizabeth and Hawkes, Sonia C. 1969: 'Early Anglo-Saxon gold braids', *Medieval Archaeology*, 11: 42–86.

Cunliffe, B.W. 1976: *Excavations at Portchester Castle Vol II: Saxon* (London: Society of Antiquaries Res. Rep. 33).

Curle, A.O. 1912: 'Excavation of a galleried structure at Langwell, Caithness', *Proc. Soc. Antiq. Scot.*, 46, 77–89.

Curle, A.O. 1941: 'An account of the partial excavation of a "wag" or galleried building at Forse, in the parish of Latheron, Caithness', *Proc. Soc. Antiq. Scot.*, 75, 23–39.

Curle, A.O. 1946: 'The excavations of the "wag" or prehistoric cattle-fold at Forse, Caithness, and the relation of "wags" to brochs, and implications arising therefrom', *Proc. Soc. Antiq. Scot.*, 80, 11–24.

Curle, A.O. 1948: 'The "wag" of Forse, Caithness. Report of further excavation made in 1947 and 48', *Proc. Soc. Antiq. Scot.*, 82, 275–85.

Curle, C.L. 1982: *Pictish and Norse finds from the Brough of Birsay 1937–74* (Edinburgh, Society of Antiquaries of Scotland Monograph Series 1).

Cuvelier, J. and Guillaume, J. 1988: 'Inventaire et Typologie des sarcophages en Lorraine.' Résumé circulated at Xe Journées Internationales de l'Association Française d'Archéologie Mérovingienne, Metz.

D and E: *Discovery and Excavation in Scotland* (Council for Scottish Archaeology).

Dalton, O.M. 1915: *Letters of Sidonius Apollinaris* (Oxford).

Darby, H.C. 1934: 'The fenland frontier in Anglo-Saxon England', *Antiquity*, 8, 185–201.

Darby, H.C. 1952: *The Domesday Geography of Eastern England* (Cambridge).

Daunt, M. 1966: 'Some modes of Anglo-Saxon meaning', in *In memory of J.R. Firth*, ed. C.E. Bazell *et al.* (London), 66–78.

David, N., Sterner, J. and Gavua, K. 1988: 'Why pots are decorated', *Current Anthropology* 29: 365–89.

Davidson, D.A., Lamb, R. and Simpson, I. 1983: 'Farm Mounds in north Orkney: a preliminary report', *Norw. Archaeol. Rev.*, 16, 39–44.

Davidson, S. 1863: in *Proceedings of the Society of Antiquaries*, 2nd. Series 2, 177–82.

Davies, W. 1977: 'Annals and the origins of Mercia', in A. Dornier (ed.), *Mercian Studies*, 17–29 (Leicester: University Press).

Davies, W. 1984: 'Picts, Scots and Britons', in L.M. Smith (ed.), *The Making of Britain. The Dark Ages* (Basingstoke), 63–76.

Davies, W. and Vierck, H. 1974: 'The contexts of Tribal Hidage: social aggregates and settlement patterns', *Frühmittelalterliche Studien*, 8, 223–93.

Davis, R.H.C. 1955: 'East Anglia and the Danelaw', *Transactions of the Royal Historical Society*, 5th series 5, 23–39.

Deetz, J. 1967: *Invitation to Archaeology* (New York).

Delahaye, G-R. 1985: 'Les sarcophages mérovingiens de pierre découverts à Paris', in *Collections mérovingiennes du Musée Carnavalet* (Paris), 689–699.

Delort, E., 1947: 'Le cimetière franc d'Ennery.' *Gallia* 5, pp. 351–403.

Dewing, H.B. (ed. & trans.), 1923: Procopius, *History of the Wars* Books VII and VIII.

Dickinson, T.M. 1974: *Cuddesdon and Dorchester-on-Thames, Oxfordshire: two early Saxon 'princely' sites in Wessex* (British Archaeol. Rep. 1, Oxford).

Dickinson, T.M. 1976: 'The Anglo-Saxon Burial Sites of the Upper Thames Region and their Bearing on the History of Wessex, circa A.D. 400–700' (unpub. D.Phil. thesis, University of Oxford).

Dodgson, J.M. 1966: 'The significance of the distribution of English place-names in -ingas, -inga- in south-east England', *Medieval Archaeology*, 10, 1–29.

Doppelfeld, O. and Pirling, R. 1966: *Fränkische Fürsten im Rheinland* (Düsseldorf).

Doppelfeld, O. and Weyres, W., *Die Ausgrabungen im Dom zu Köln* (Mayence).

Douglas, J. 1793: *Nenia Britannica: or, a sepulchral history of Great Britain* (London).

Douglas, M. 1973: *Natural Symbols: explorations in cosmology* (Harmondsworth).

Down, A. and Welch, M. 1990: *Chichester Excavations VII: Apple Down and The Mardens* (Chichester).

Downey, G. 1959: 'The tombs of the byzantine emperors at the church of the Holy-Apostles in Constantinople', in *The Journal of Hellenic Studies*, 79, 27–51.

Drewett, P. et al., 1988: *The South East to A.D. 1000*.

Drinkwater, J.F. 1989. 'Patronage in Roman Gaul and the problem of the Bagaudae.' in A. Wallace-Hadrill (ed.) *Patronage in Ancient Society* (London), pp. 189–203.

Drinkwater, J.F. 1992. 'The Bacaudae of fifth-century Gaul', in Drinkwater & Elton (eds), pp. 208–17.

Drinkwater, J.F. and Elton, H. (eds), 1992. *Fifth-Century Gaul: A Crisis of Identity?* (Cambridge).

Driscoll, S.T. 1987: *The Early Historic Landscape of Strathearn: the Archaeology of a Pictish Kingdom* (unpub. Ph.D. submitted to Glasgow University).

Driscoll, S.T. 1988a: 'Power and authority in Early Historic Scotland: Pictish symbol stones and other documents', in J. Gledhill, B. Bender and M. Larsen (eds), *State and Society. The Emergence and Development of Social Hierarchy and Political Centralisation* (London), 215–36.

Driscoll, S.T. 1988b: 'The relationship between history and archaeology: artefacts, documents and power', in S.T. Driscoll and M.R. Nieke (eds), 162–87.

Driscoll, S.T. 1991: 'The archaeology of state formation in Scotland', in W.S. Hanson and E.A. Slater (eds), 81–111.

Driscoll, S.T. and Nieke, M.R. (eds) 1987: *Power and Politics in early medieval Britain and Ireland* (Edinburgh).

Dubois, Dom Jacques, and Beaumont-Maillet, L. 1982: *Sainte Geneviève de Paris. La vie, le culte, l'art* (Paris).

Dumville, D.N. 1973: 'A New Chronicle-Fragment of Early British History', *English Historical Review*, 88, 312–314.

Dumville, D. 1976: 'The Anglian collection of royal genealogies and regnal lists', *Anglo-Saxon England*, 5, 23–50.

Dumville, D.N. 1977: 'Kingship, Genealogies and Regnal Lists', *Early Medieval Kingship*, ed. P. Sawyer and I. Wood (Leeds), pp. 72–104.

Dumville, D.N. 1988: '*Beowulf* come lately: some Notes on the Palaeography of the Nowell Codex'. *Archiv für das Studium der neueren Sprachen und Literaturen*, 225, 49–63.

Dumville, D.N. 1989a: 'Essex, Middle Anglia and the expansion of Mercia in the south-east Midlands', in S. Bassett (ed.) *The origins of Anglo-Saxon kingdoms*, 123–140 (Leicester: University Press).

Dumville, D.N. 1989b: The Tribal Hidage: an introduction to its texts and their history, in *The Origins of Anglo-Saxon Kingdoms*, ed. S. Bassett, 225–30.

Durkheim, E. 1915: *The elementary forms of the religious life* (London).

Duval, Yves and Picard, Jean-Charles (ed.) 1986: *L'Inhumation privilégiée du IVe au VIIIe siècles en Occident*. Actes du colloque tenu à Creteil les 16–18 mars 1984 (Paris).

Dymond, D.P. 1968: 'The Suffolk landscape'. In L.M. Munby (ed.), *East Anglian Studies*, 17–47 (Cambridge: Heffer).

Edwards, J.H. 1948: 'The Anglo-Saxon pagan cemetery at Baginton', *Proc. Coventry Natural Hist. and Sci. Soc.*, 2, 48–53.

Edwards, K. and Ralston, I. 1978: 'New dating and environmental evidence from Burghead Fort, Moray', *Proc Soc. Ant. Scot.*, 109: 202–11.

Eggers, H.J. 1949/50: Lübsow, ein germanischer Fürstensitz der älteren Kaiserzeit. *Prähistorische Zeitschrift*, Bd. 34/35.

Eggers, H.J. 1951: *Der römische Import im freien Germanien* (Hamburg).

Ekholm, G. 1931: 'Gravhogen vid Staby Uppsala', *Upplands Fornminnesforenings Tidskrift*, 43: 65–9.

Ekwall, E. 1960: *The Concise Oxford Dictionary of English Place-Names*, 4th ed.

Elene: Elene in *The Vercelli Book*, ed. G.P. Krapp, The Anglo-Saxon Poetic Records 2 (London and New York, 1932), 66–102.

Ellis, H.R. 1943: *The Road to Hel* (Cambridge UP).

Ellis Davidson, H.R. 1967: *Pagan Scandinavia* (London).

Ellis Davidson, H.R. 1972: *The Battle God of the Vikings* (University of York Medieval Monograph 1).

Ellis Davidson, H.R. 1976: *The Viking Road to Byzantium* (London).

Ellis Davidson, H.R. 1988: *Myths and symbols in pagan Europe* (Manchester).

Ellis Davidson, H.R. and Webster, L. 1967: 'The Anglo-Saxon burial at Coombe (Woodnesborough), Kent', *Medieval Archaeol.*, 11, 1–41.

Enright, M.J. 1988: 'Lady with a mead-cup. Ritual, group cohesion and hierarchy in the Germanic warband', *FS* 22, 170–203.

Epistulae Austrasiacae, ed. W. Gundlach, *Monumenta Germaniae Historica, Epistulae* III (Berlin, 1892).

Erlande-Brandenburg, A. 1975: *Le roi est mort. Etude sur les funérailles, les sépultures et les tombeaux des rois de France jusqu'à la fin du XIIIe siècle* (Paris).

Van Es, W.A. and Ypey. J. 1977: 'Das Grab der »Prinzessin« von Zweelo und seine Bedeutung im Rahmen des Gräberfeldes', *Studien zur Sachsenforschung* 1, 97–126.

Esmonde-Cleary, S. 1989: *The ending of Roman Britain* (London: Batsford).

Evans, A.C. 1986: *The Sutton Hoo Ship Burial* (London: British Museum).

Evans, A.C. 1989: 'Finds from mound 2 and mound 5', *Bulletin Sutton Hoo Research Committee*, 6, 11–15.

Evison V.I. 1956: 'An Anglo-Saxon cemetery at Holborough, Kent' *Archaeologia Cantiana* 70: 84–118.

Evison, V.I. 1974: 'The Asthall type of bottle', in V.I. Evison, H. Hodges and J.G. Hurst (eds), *Medieval Pottery from Excavations: Studies Presented to G.C. Dunning* (London), 77–94.

Evison, V.I. 1976: 'Sword rings and beads', *Archaeologia*, 105, 303–315.

Evison, V.I. 1977: 'Supporting-arm brooches and equal-arm brooches in England', *Studien zur Sachsenforschung*, 1, 127–48.

Evison, V.I. 1979: *Wheel-thrown Pottery in Anglo-Saxon Graves* (London).

Evison, V.I. 1981: 'Distribution maps and England in the first two phases of settlement'. In V.I. Evison (ed.), *Angles, Saxons and Jutes: essays presented to J.N.L. Myers*, 126–67 (Oxford: University Press).

Evison, V.I. 1982a: 'Anglo-Saxon glass claw-beakers', *Archaeologia*, 107, 43–76.

Evison, V.I. 1982b: Bichrome glass vessels of the 7th and 8th centuries. *Studien zur Sachsenforschung*, 3, 7–21.

Evison, V.I. 1987: *Dover: The Buckland Anglo-Saxon cemetery* (English Heritage Archaeology Report 3, London).

Exodus: Exodus in *The Junius Manuscript*, ed. G.P. Krapp, The Anglo-Saxon Poetic Records 1 (London and New York, 1931), 91–107.

Fabech, C. 1989: Sydskandinaviske offerfund som kilde til jernalderens religion og ideologi. *Arkeologi och Religion* (University of Lund. Institute of Archaeology Report Series No. 34).

Fabech, C. 1991: 'Booty sacrifices in southern Scandinavia: a re-assessment', in P. Garwood, D. Jennings, R. Skeates and J. Toms (eds) *Sacred and Profane: proceedings of a conference on archaeology, ritual and religion* (Oxford: OUCA Monograph 32), 88–99.

Farrell, R.T. 1972: *Beowulf, Swedes and Geats* (London).

Faulkes, A. 1978–1979: 'Descent from the Gods', *Medieval Scandinavia*, II, 92–125.

Feachem, R. 1955: 'Fortifications', in F. T. Wainwright (ed.), 66–86.

Fennell, K.R. 1957: 'Excavation of an Anglo-Saxon cemetery at Hough-on-the-Hill, Lincolnshire', *J. of the R.A.F. Cranwell*, 4, 127–8.

Fennell, K.R. 1960: 'Hanging bowls with pierced ecutcheons' *Medieval Archaeology*, 4: 127–8.

Fennell, K.R. 1964: 'The Anglo-Saxon cemetery at Loveden Hill (Hough-on-the-Hill) Lincolnshire, and its significance in relation to the Dark Age settlement of the East Midlands' (unpub. Ph.D. Thesis, University of Nottingham).

Fennell, K.R. 1969: 'The Loveden Man' *Frühmittelalterliche Studien*, 3: 211–15.

Fenwick, V. 1984: 'Insula de Burgh: Excavations at Burrow Hill, Butley, Suffolk 1978–1981', in Hawkes, S.C., Campbell, J. and Brown, D. (eds), *Anglo-Saxon Studies in Archaeology and History*, 3, 35–54.

Filmer-Sankey, W. 1984: 'The Snape Anglo-Saxon Cemetery and Ship Burial: the current state of knowledge', *Bulletin of the Sutton Hoo Research Committee*, 2, 13–15.

Filmer-Sankey, W. 1988: Excavations at Snape, 1986', *Bulletin of the Sutton Hoo Research Committee*, 5, 13–17.

Filmer-Sankey, W. 1990a: 'A New Boat Burial from the Snape Anglo-Saxon Cemetery, Suffolk', in McGrail, S. (ed.) *Maritime Celts, Frisians and Saxons* (CBA), 126–34.

Filmer-Sankey, W. 1990b: *On the function and status of finger-rings in the early Medieval Germanic World, c. 450–700* (unpub. D.Phil. Thesis submitted to the University of Oxford).

Fisher, G. 1988: 'Style and socio-political organization: a preliminary study from early Anglo-Saxon England', in Driscoll, S. and Nieke, M. (eds) *Power and Politics in Early Medieval Britain and Ireland* (Edinburgh), 128–44.

Fleury, M. 1981: 'Les fouilles récentes de la chapelle Saint-Symphorien (Cour des Catéchismes) de l'église Saint-Germain des Prés', in *Cahiers de la Rotonde*, N° 4: 17–32.

Fleury, M. and France-Lanord, A. 1979: *Bijoux et parures mérovingiennes de la Reine Arégonde, belle-fille de Clovis, découverts à Saint-Denis* (= Dossiers de l'Archéologie 32 (Janvier-Février 1979).

Ford, S. 1987: *East Berkshire Archaeological Survey* (Berkshire County Council, Occasional Paper No.1).

Foster, S.M. 1989a: 'Analysis of spatial patterns in buildings (gamma analysis) as an insight into social structure: examples from the Scottish Atlantic Iron Age', *Antiquity*, 63, 40–50.

Foster, S.M. 1989b: 'Transformations in social space: Iron Age Orkney and Caithness', *Scot. Archaeol. Rev.*, 6, 34–55.

Foster, S.M. 1989c: *Aspects of the Late Atlantic Iron Age* (unpub. Ph.D. submitted to Glasgow University).

Foster, S.M. 1990: 'Pins, combs and the chronology of later Atlantic Iron Age settlement', in I. Armit (ed.), 143–74.

Foster, S.M. forthcoming: 'Dating and the developments of the Atlantic Iron Age: the impact of radiocarbon calibration on dating change in later prehistory'.

Fouracre, P. 1986: '*Placita* and the settlement of disputes in later Merovingian Francia', in W. Davies and P. Fouracre (eds) *The Settlement of Disputes in Early Medieval Europe* (Cambridge), 23–43.

Fowler, E. 1968: 'Hanging bowls', in J.M. Coles and D.D.A. Simpson (eds), *Studies in Ancient Europe* (Leicester), 287–310.

Fox, C. 1923: *The archaeology of the Cambridge region* (Cambridge: University Press).

Francis, F. 1863a: in *The Field, the Country Gentleman's Magazine*, January & March, 61–2 & 74–5.

Francis, F. 1863b. in *Archaeological Journal*, 20, 373–4.

Frank, R. 1981: 'Skaldic Verse and the Date of *Beowulf*', *The Dating of Beowulf*, ed. C. Chase (Toronto), 123–139.

Fredegar, *Chronicle*, ed. and trans. H. Wolfram and A. Kusternig, *Quellen zur Geschichte des 7. und 8. Jahrhunderts* (Darmstadt 1982).

'Fredegar's' *Chronicon*. Ed. B. Krusch, *Monumenta Germaniae Historica. Scriptores Rerum Merovingiarum*. Vol. 2, Hanover 1888, pp. 1–193; ed. & trans. J.M. Wallace-Hadrill, *The Fourth Book of the Chronicle of Fredegar with its Continuation* (London 1960).

Frend, W.H.C. 1979: 'Ecclesia Britannica: prelude or dead end?', *Journal of Ecclesiastical History*, 30, 129–44.

Friell, J.G.P. and Watson, W.G. (eds), 1984: *Pictish Studies. Settlement, Burial and Art in Dark Age Northern Britain* (Oxford: Brit. Archaeol. Rep., Brit. Ser. 125).

Fulk, R.D. 1982: 'Dating *Beowulf* to the Viking Age', *Philological Quarterly*, 61, pp. 341–359.

Gaimster, D.R.M., Margeson, S. and Barry, T. 1989: 'Medieval Britain and Ireland in 1988', in *Med. Arch.* 33, 161–241.

Ganshof, F.L. 1961: *Feudalism* (Harper torchbook, New York).

Garmonsway, G.N. and Simpson, J. (eds), 1960: *Beowulf and Its Analogues* (London).

Garwood, P. 1989: 'Social transformation and relations of power in Britain in the late fourth to the sixth centuries AD', *Scot. Archaeol. Rev.*, 6, 90–106.

Gauert, Adolf 1972: 'Der Ring der Königin Arnegundis aus Saint-Denis', *Festschrift für Heinrich Heimpel* 3 (Göttingen 1972), 328–347.

Gauthier, N. 1986: *Topographie Chrétienne des Cités de la Gaule des Origines au Milieu du VIIIe Siècle. 1. Province Ecclésiastique de Trèves (Belgica Prima)* (Paris).

Geary, P.J. 1988: *Before France and Germany: the Creation and Transformation of the Meovingian world* (New York and Oxford).

Gelling, M. 1961: 'Place-names and Anglo-Saxon paganism', *University of Birmingham Historical Journal*, 8(i), pp. 7–25.

Gelling, M. 1967: 'English place-names derived from the compound *wicham*', *Medieval Archaeology*, 11, pp. 87–104.

Gelling, M. 1977: 'Latin loan-words in Old English place-names', *Anglo-Saxon England* 6, pp. 1–13.

Gelling, M. 1978: *Signposts to the Past; Place-Names and the History of England* (London).

Gelling, M. 1984: *Place-Names in the Landscape* (London).

Gelling, M, 1988: *Signposts to the Past: Placenames and the History of England* (2nd edn. Chichester).

Genrich, A. 1981: *Die Altsachsen* (Hildesheim).

Gilles, K.-J. 1982: *Die Trierer Münzprägung im frühen Mittelalter* (Koblenz).

Gjessing, G. 1934: Studier i norsk merovingertid. *Vid. Sel. Skrifter. Hist. -fil.klasse no.1* (Oslo).

Godfrey-Faussett, T.G. 1876: 'The Saxon Cemetery at Bifrons', *Arch. Cant.*, 10: 298–315. 1880: *Ibid.* 13: 552–56.

Goffart, W. 1982: 'Old and new in Merovingian taxation.' *Past and Present*, 96, August 1982, pp. 3–21.

Goffart, W. 1988: *The Narrators of Barbarian History (a.d. 550–800). Jordanes, Gregory of Tours, Bede, Paul the Deacon* (Princeton).

Gordon, E.V. 1935: 'Wealhþeow and Related Names', *Medium Ævum*, 4, 169–175.

Gordon, I.L. (ed.) 1960: *The Seafarer* (London).

Goubert, P. 1956: *Byzance avant L'Islam* II i, *Byzance et les Francs* (Paris).

Gould, S.J. 1989: *Wonderful Life: the Burgess Shale and the nature of History* (London: Hutchinson).

Gourlay, R. 1984: 'A symbol stone and cairn at Watenan, Caithness', in J. Friell and G. Watson (eds), 131–33.

Grahn-Hoek, H. 1976: *Die frankische Oberschicht im 6 Jahrhundert. Studien zu ihrer rechtlichen und politische Stellung* (Sigmaringen).

Grattan, J.H.G. and Singer, C. (eds and trans.), 1952: *Anglo-Saxon Magic and Medicine.*

Graus, F. 1965: *Volk, Herrscher und Heiliger im Reich der Merowinger* (Prague).

Green, B., Milligan, W.F., and West, S.E. 1981: 'The Illington/Lackford workshop', in V.I. Evison (ed.), *Angles, Saxons and Jutes: essays presented to J.N.L. Myres*, 187–226 (Oxford: University Press).

Green, B., Rogerson, A. and White, S.G. 1987: *The Anglo-Saxon cemetery at Morning Thorpe, Norfolk* (Gressenhall, East Anglian Archaeology 36).

Gregory I, *Register*, P. Ewald and L.M. Hartmann, *Monumenta Germaniae Historica, Epistulae* I–II (Berlin 1887–99).

Gregory of Tours, *Libri Historiarum* [*L.H.*; The *Histories*] ed. B. Krusch and W. Levison, *Monumenta Germaniae Historica. Scriptores Rerum Merovingiarum* vol.1, part 1 (2nd edition) Hanover 1951; Trans. L. Thorpe, Gregory of Tours. The History of the Franks (Harmondsworth 1974).

Gregory, T. 1982: 'Romano-British settlement in west Norfolk and on the Norfolk fen edge', in D. Miles (ed.), *The Romano-British countryside: studies in rural settlement and economy*, 352–76 (Oxford: B.A.R. 103).

Gregory, T. 1986: 'An enclosure at Wighton', in T. Gregory and D. Gurney, *Excavations at Thornham, Warham, Wighton and Caistor, Norfolk*, 27–31 (East Anglian Archaeology 30).

Gudesen, G. 1980: Merovingertiden i Øst-Norge. *Varia* 2 (Univ. Olds., Oslo).

Guillaume, J. 1974–5: 'Les nécropoles mérovingiennes de Dieue/Meuse (France).' *Acta Praehistorica et Archaeologica*, 5–6, 211–349.

Gurevich, A. (forthcoming): Odal and the World Picture. *Past and Present.*

Gurney, D. 1986: *Settlement, religion and industry on the fen edge: three Roman sites in Norfolk* (East Anglian Archaeology 31).

Guþnasson, Bjarni. 1963: *Um Skjöldungasögu* (Reykjavík).

Guyon, J. 1976: 'La catacombe aux deux lauriers', in *Les dossiers de l'archéologie, Débuts de l'art chrétien: Rome*, n° 18, Septembre-Octobre 1976, 66–85.

Hagberg, U.E. 1967: *The Archaeology of Skedemosse* II, KVHAAH (Stockholm).

Hall, E.T. 1959: *The Silent Language* (New York).

Hall, R.A. 1978: 'A Viking-Age Grave at Donnybrook, Co. Dublin, *Med. Arch.*, 22: 64–73.

Halphen, Louis (ed.) 1967: *Éginhard: Vie de Charlemagne* (4th ed. Paris).

Halsall, G. 1988: La 'civitas' mérovingienne de Metz: quelques idées pour la recherche archéologique. *Association Française d'Archéologie Mérovingienne, Bulletin de Liaison* 12. 50–52.

Halsall, G. 1990: '*Civitas Mediomatricorum*; Settlement and social organisation in the Merovingian region of Metz, c.450–c.750' (D.Phil. thesis, Department of History, University of York).

Halsall, G. 1992: 'The origins of the *Reihengräberzivilisation* Forty years on.' in Drinkwater and Elton (eds), pp. 196–207.

Halsall, G. forthcoming [a]: 'The preface to Book V of Gregory of Tours', *Libri Historiarum*; Its form, context and significance.'

Halsall, G. forthcoming [b]: 'Female status and power in Merovingian central Austrasia.'

Halsall, G. forthcoming [c]: 'Towns in pre-feudal social formations: the example of Merovingian Metz.'

Hanson, W.S. and Slater, E.A. (eds), 1991: *Scottish Archaeology: New Perceptions* (Aberdeen).

Harden, D.B. 1983: 'The glass hoard', in S. Johnson, *Burgh Castle, excavations by Charles Green 1958–61*, 81–88 (East Anglian Archaeology 20).

Härke, H. 1989a: 'Early Saxon weapon burials: frequencies, distributions and weapon combinations', in S.C. Hawkes (ed.), *Weapons and Warfare in Anglo-Saxon England*, Oxford (Oxford University Committee for Archaeology, Monograph No. 21) 49–61.

Härke, H. 1989b: Knives in Early Saxon burials: blade length and age at death. *Medieval Archaeology*, 33, 1989. 144–148.

Härke, H. 1990: ' "Warrior Graves"? The background of the Anglo-Saxon weapon burial rite', *Past and Present*, 126, 22–43.

Härke, H. (forthcoming, 1992): *Angelsächsische Waffengräber des 5.–7. Jahrhunderts*. Cologne and Bonn: Rheinland-Verlag. (Beihefte der Zeitschrift für die Archäologie des Mittelalters).

Harman, M., Molleson, T.J. and Price, J.L. 1981: Burials, bodies and beheadings in Romano-British and Anglo-Saxon cemeteries. *Bulletin of the British Museum: Natural History (Geology)* 35 no. 3. 145–188.

Hart, C. 1966: *The early charters of eastern England*. Leicester: University Press.

Hart, C.R. 1971: 'The Tribal Hidage', *Transactions of the Royal Historical Society*, 5th series 21, 133–58.

Haselgrove, S. 1979: 'Romano-Saxon attitudes', in P.J. Casey (ed.), *The End of Roman Britain*, 4–13. Oxford: B.A.R. 71.

Haseloff, G. 1981: *Die germanische Tierornamentik der Völkerwanderungszeit. Studien zu Salin's Stil I*. Bd. I–II (Berlin – New York).

Hassall, M.W.C. and Tomlin, R.S.O. 1981, Roman Britain in 1980: Inscriptions, 1981 *Britannia* 12 (1981), 369–96.

Hauck, K. 1954: Halsring und Ahnenstab als herrscherliche Würdezeichen. *Herrschaftszeichen und Staatssymbolik*. P.E. Schramm (ed.) (Schriften der Monumenta Germaniae historica 13. Stuttgart).

Hauck, K. 1978: Götterglaube im Spiegel der goldenen Brakteaten. *Sachsen und Angelsachsen* (Veröffentlichungen des Helms-Museums Nr. 32. Hamburg).

Hauck, K. 1986: Die Wiedergabe von Göttersymbolen und Sinnzeichen der A-, B- and

C-Brakteaten auf D- und F-Brakteaten exemplarisch erhellt mit Speer und Kreuz. *Frühmittelalterliche Studien* 20.

Hauck, K. 1987: Gudme in der Sicht der Brakteaten-Forschung. *Frühmittelalterliche Studien* BD. 21.

Hawkes, S.C. 1982: 'Anglo-Saxon Kent c.425–725', in P.E. Leach (ed.), *Archaeology in Kent to A.D.1500* (London: CBA Research Report no. 48), 64–78.

Hawkes, S.C. 1986: 'The early Saxon period', in G. Briggs et al., *The Archaeology of the Oxford Region*, 64–108, esp. at 91.

Hawkes, S.C. and Dunning G. 1961: 'Soldiers and settlers in Britain, fourth to fifth century', *Medieval Archaeology*, 5, 1–70.

Hawkes, S.C. 1973: 'The dating and social significance of the burials in the Polhill cemetery' in B. Philp (ed.) *Excavations in West Kent 1960–1970* (Kent Archaeological Rescue Unit, Dover), 186–201.

Hawkes, S.C. and Pollard, M. 1981: 'The gold bracteates from sixth-century Anglo-Saxon graves in Kent in the light of a new find from Finglesham', *Frühmittelalterliche Studien*, 15, 316–70.

Hawkes S.C. 1990: 'Bryan Fausset and the Fausset collection: an assessment', in E. Southworth (ed.) *Anglo-Saxon Cemeteries: a reappraisal* (Stroud: Alan Sutton), 1–24.

Häßler, H-J, 1990: *Das sächsische Gräberfeld bei Liebenau, Kr. Nienburg (Weser) Teil 4* (Hildesheim).

Hedeager, L. 1978a: 'A quantitative analysis of Roman imports in Europe north of the *Limes* (0–400 A.D.) and the question of Roman-German exchange', in K. Kristiansen and C. Paludan-Müller (eds), *New directions in Scandinavian archaeology*, 191–216 (Copenhagen: National Museum of Denmark).

Hedeager, L. 1978b: 'Processes towards state formation in early Iron Age Denmark', in K. Kristiansen and C. Paludan-Müller (eds), *New directions in Scandinavian archaeology*, 217–223 (Copenhagen: National Museum of Denmark).

Hedeager, L. 1980: 'Besiedlung, soziale Struktur und politische Organisation in der älteren und jüngeren Kaiserzeit Ostdänemarks', *Prähistorische Zeitschrift*, 55, 38–109.

Hedeager, L. 1987: 'Empire, frontier and the barbarian hinterland: Roman and northern Europe from A.D.1–400'. In M. Rowlands, M. Larsen and K. Kristiansen (eds), *Centre and periphery in the ancient world*, 125–40 (Cambridge: University Press).

Hedeager, L. 1988: 'Money economy and prestige economy in the Roman Iron Age', in B. Hårdh et al. (eds), *Trade and Exchange in Prehistory, Studies in Honour of Berta Stjernquist* (Lund), 147–53.

Hedeager, L. 1990: *Danmarks Jernalder. Mellem Stamme og Stat* (Århus Universitetforlag).

Hedeager, L. 1991: Die Golddepots der Völkerwanderungszeit Dänemarks. Versuch einer Deutung. *Frühmittelalterliche Studien* Bd. 25.

Hedeager, L. (in press): *Iron Age Societies: From Tribe to State in Northern Europe 500 B.C. to 700 A.D.* (Oxford: Basil Blackwell).

Hedeager, L. (forthcoming): Germanic society in the time of the first runic inscriptions. *Literacy and Society in North-West Europe 400–1200*. G. Caie (ed.) (Copenhagen, Center for European Medieval Studies).

Hedeager, L. and Kristiansen, K. 1981: Bendstrup- a princely grave from the Early Roman Iron Age: Its social and historical Context. *Kuml* (Århus).

Hedeager, L. and Kristiansen, K. 1988: Oldtidens landbrug. *Det Danske Landbrugs Historie* Bd. 1. C. Bjørn (ed.) (Odense).

Hedges, R., Housely, R.A., Bronk, C.R., and van Klnken, G.J. 1991: 'Radiocarbon dates from the Oxford AMS system: *Archaeometry* date-list 13', *Archaeometry*, 33: 279–96.

Heidenreich, R., and Johannes, H. 1971: *Das Grabmal Theodorichs zu Ravenna* (Wiesbaden).

Heinzelman, M. and Poulin, J-C. 1986: *Les vies anciennes de sainte Geneviève de Paris. Etudes critiques* (Paris).

Heisenberg, A. 1908: *Grabeskirche und Apostelkirche* (Leipzig) II.

Hele, N. 1870: *Notes or Jottings about Aldeburgh* (London).

Hellmuth Anderson, H. 1985: Graves of pre-Christian Danish monarchs and their historical background. *Kuml.*

Henderson, G. 1972: *Style and Civilisation: Early Medieval* (Harmondsworth).

Henderson, I. 1967: *The Picts* (London).

Henderson, I. 1972: 'The Picts of Aberdeenshire and their monuments', *Archaeol. J.*, 129, 166–74.

Henderson, I. 1975: 'Pictish territorial divisions', in P. McNeill and J. Nicholson (eds), 8–9.

Henderson, I. 1987: 'Early Christian monuments of Scotland displaying crosses but no other ornament', in A. Small (ed.), 45–58.

Henderson, I. 1990: *The Art and Function of Rosemarkie's Pictish Monuments* (Inverness).

Henige, D.P. 1971: 'Oral Tradition and Chronology', *Journal of African History*, 12, 371–389.

Henry, F. 1936: 'Hanging bowls', *J.Royal Soc. Ant. Ireland*, 66: 209–46.

Henshall, A. 1956: 'The long cist cemetery at Lasswade, Midlothian', *Proc. Soc. Antiq. Scot.*, 89, 252–83.

Heuertz, M. 1957. 'Etudes des squelettes du cimetière franc d'Ennery.' *Bulletin et Mémoire de la Société d'Anthropologie de Paris* 8, pp. 81–147.

Hicks, C. 1986: 'The birds on the Sutton Hoo purse', *Anglo-Saxon England*, 15, 153–65

Higham, N. 1986: *The Northern Counties to 1000* (London: Longman).

Hill, J.M. 1982: 'Beowulf and the Danish succession: gift-giving as an occasion for complex gesture', *Medievalia et Humanistica* ns 11, 177–97.

Hills, C. 1974: 'A runic pot from Spong Hill, North Elmham, Norfolk', *Antiq. J.*, 54, 87–91.

Hills, C.M. 1979: 'The archaeology of Anglo-Saxon England in the pagan period: a review', *Anglo-Saxon England*, 8, 297–329.

Hills, C.M., and Penn, K., 1981: *The Anglo-Saxon Cemetery at Spong Hill, North Elmham, Part II* (East Anglian Archaeology Report No. 11).

Hills, C.M. 1983: 'Animal stamps on Anglo-Saxon pottery in East Anglia' *Studien zur Sachsenforschung*, 4: 93–110.

Hills, C., Penn, K. and Rickett, R. 1984: The Anglo-Saxon cemetery at Spong Hill, North Elmham. Part III: *catalogue of the inhumations* (East Anglian Archaeology 21).

Hills, C.M., Penn, K. and Rickett, R. 1984a: *The Anglo-Saxon cemetery at Spong Hill, North Elmham, Part IV: catalogue of cremations* (East Anglian Archaeology 34).

Hines, J. 1984: *The Scandinavian character of Anglian England in pre-Viking period* (Oxford: British Archaeological Reports 124).

Hines, J. 1989: 'The military context of the *adventus Saxonum*: some continental evidence'. In S.C. Hawkes (ed.), *Weapons and warfare in Anglo-Saxon England*, 25–48 (Oxford: O.U.C.A.).

Hines, J. 1990: 'Philology, archaeology and the *adventus Saxonum vel Anglorum*'. In A. Bammesberger and A. Wollmann (eds), *Britain 400–600; Language and History*, 17–36 (Heidelberg: Carl Winter).

Hingley, R. forthcoming: 'Society in Scotland from 700BC to AD 200', *Proc. Soc. Antiq. Scot.*

Hirst, S.M. 1985: *An Anglo-Saxon Inhumation Cemetery at Sewerby, East Yorkshire* (York Univ. Archaeol. Publ. 4).

Hoare, F.R. 1954: (trans.), *The Western Fathers.*

Hodder, I. 1979: Social and economic stress and material culture patterning. *American Antiquity*, 44.

Hodder, I. 1980: 'Social structure and cemeteries: a critical appraisal' in Rahtz et al. (eds) *Anglo-Saxon Cemeteries 1979*, 161–9.

Hodder, I. 1982: *Symbols in Action* (Cambridge).

Hodder, I. 1989: 'Post-modernism, post-structuralism and post-processual archaeology' in I. Hodder (ed.) *The Meanings of Things* (London: One World Archaeology 6), 64–78.

Hodges, R. 1978: 'State formation and the role of trade in Middle Saxon England'. In D. Green, C. Haselgrove and M. Spriggs (eds), *Social organisation and settlement: contributions from archaeology, anthropology and geography*, 439–54 (Oxford: B.A.R. S47).

Hodges, R. 1982: *Dark Age Economics. The origins of towns and trade A.D.600–1000* (Duckworth).

Hodges, R. 1982a: 'Method and theory in medieval archaeology', *Archaeologia Medievale*, 1, 7–37.

Hodges, R. 1982b: 'The evolution of gateway communities: their socio-economic implications', in C. Renfrew and S. Shennan (eds), *Ranking, resource and exchange*, 117–23 (Cambridge: University Press).

Hodges, R. 1986: 'Peer-polity interaction and socio-political change in Anglo-Saxon England'. In C. Renfrew and J.Cherry (eds), *Peer-polity interaction and socio-political change*, 69–78 (Cambridge: University Press).

Hodges, R. 1989a: Charlemagne's elephant and the beginnings of commodisation in Europe. *Acta Archaeologica*, 59, 155–168.

Hodges, R. 1989b: *The Anglo-Saxon achievement* (London: Duckworth).

Hodges, R. and Moreland, J. 1988: 'Power and exchange in Middle Saxon England', in S.T. Driscoll and M.R. Nieke (eds), *Power and Politics in early medieval Britain and Ireland*, 79–95 (Edinburgh: University Press).

Høeg, H.I. 1990: En pollenanalyse i Borre, Vestfold. *Rapport fra Borre-prosjektet 1990* (Manuskript. Univ. Olds., Oslo).

Hogarth, A.C. 1973: 'Structural features in Anglo-Saxon graves' *Archaeological J.*, 130: 104–119.

Høilund Nielson, K. (in press): Centrum og periferi i 6.–8. årh. Territoriale studier af dyretsil og kvindesmykker i yngre germansk jernalder i Syd- og Østskandinavien. *Jernalderens Stammesamfund.* C. Fabeck and J. Ringtved (eds) (Moesgård, Århus).

Holmqvist, W. 1976: Die Ergebnisse der Grabungen auf Helgö (1954–1974). *Prähistorische Zeitschrift*, Bd. 51.

Hooke, D. 1985: *The Anglo-Saxon Landscape, The Kingdom of the Hwicce* (Manchester).

Hope-Taylor, B. 1976: 'The Devil's Dyke investigations, 1973'. *Proceedings of the Cambridge Antiquarian Society*, 66, 123–5.

Hope-Taylor, B. 1977: *Yeavering: an Anglo-British centre of early Northumbria* (London: DoE Archaeological Report 7).

Hoppit, R. 1985: 'Sutton Hoo 1860' *Proceedings of the Suffolk Institute of Archaeology* 36(1), 41–2.

Horne, Prior 1934: 'Anglo-Saxon Cemetery at Camerton, Somerset', *Proc. Somerset Arch. Nat. Hist.*, 79: 39: 63.

Hougen, B. 1934: Studier i Gokstadfunnet. *Univ. Olds. Årbok 1931–32*, 74–112.

Hougen, B. 1947: *Fra seter til gård* (Univ. Olds., Oslo).

Howe, N. 1989: *Migration and Mythmaking in Anglo-Saxon England* (Yale University).

Huber, H.M. 1967: *Anthropologische Untersuchungen an Skeletten aus dem alamannischen Reihengräberfeld von Weingarten, Kr. Ravensburg.* Stuttgart: Müller & Gräff (Naturwissenschaftliche Untersuchungen zur Vor- and Frühgeschichte in Württemberg und Hohenzollern 3).

Huggett, J.W. 1988: 'Imported grave goods and the Early Anglo-Saxon economy', *Medieval Archaeol.*, 32, 63–96.

Huggins, P.J. 1978: 'Excavation of a Belgic and Romano-British farm with middle Saxon cemetery and churches at Nazeingbury, Essex' *Essex Archaeology and History*, 10: 29–117.

Hughes, K. 1970: *Early Christianity in Pictland* (Newcastle, Jarrow Lecture).

Hughes, K. 1980: 'Where are the writings of early Scotland?', in D. Dumville (ed.), *Celtic Britain in the Early Middle Ages, Studies in Scottish and Welsh Sources by the late Kathleen Hughes* (Woodbridge).

Hunter, J.R. 1986: *Rescue Excavations on the Brough of Birsay 1974–82* (Edinburgh: Society of Antiquaries of Scotland Monograph 4).

Hunter, J.R. 1990: 'Pool, Sanday: a case study for the Late Iron Age and Viking periods', in I. Armit (ed.), 175–93.

Hymes, D. 1970: 'Linguistic models in archaeology', in J-C. Gardin (ed.), *Archeologie et Calculateur* (Paris).

Hyslop, M. 1963: Two Anglo-Saxon cemeteries at Chamberlains Barn, Leighton Buzzard, Bedfordshire. *Archaeological Journal*, 120, 161–200.

Ilkjær, J. 1991: *Illerup Ådal. Die lanzen und Speere I–II*. Jysk arkæologisk selskab (Århus).

Ilkjaer, J. and Lønstrup, J. 1982: 'Interpretation of the great votive deposits of Iron Age weapons', *Journal of Danish Archaeology*, 1, 95–103.

Inglis, J. 1987: 'Patterns in stone, patterns in population: symbol stones seen from beyond the Mounth', in A. Small (ed.), 73–9.

Ingram, J. 1989: *Animal Form and symbolism in early Medieval England and Ireland* (unpub. MA thesis, University of York).

Irsigler, F. 1979: 'On the aristocratic character of early Frankish society.' in T. Reuter (ed. & trans.) *The Medieval Nobility*. Amsterdam, pp. 105–36.

Isidore of Seville, *Etymologies*. Ed. W.M. Lindsay, *Isidori Hispanensis Episcopis Etymologiarum sive Originum Libri XX*. 2 vols (Oxford 1911).

Jackson, A. 1984: *The Symbol Stones of Scotland. A Social Anthropological Resolution of the Problem of the Picts* (Kirkwall).

Jackson, K.H. 1955: 'The Pictish language', in F.T. Wainwright (ed.), 129–66.

Jackson, K.H. 1972: *The Gaelic Notes in the Book of Deer* (Cambridge).

James, Edward 1977: *The Merovingian Archaeology of South-West Gaul*. Oxford (British Archaeological Reports, Supplementary Series 25).

James, Edward 1979: 'Cemeteries and the Problem of Frankish Settlement in Gaul', in P.H. Sawyer (ed.) *Names, Words and Graves* (Leeds), pp. 55–89.

James, Edward 1980: 'Merovingian cemetery studies and some implications for Anglo-Saxon England', in P. Rahtz, T. Dickinson and L. Watts (eds), *Anglo-Saxon Cemeteries 1979: The Fourth Anglo-Saxon Symposium at Oxford* (British Archaeological Reports British Series 82: Oxford), 35–55.

James, Edward 1981: 'Archaeology and the Merovingian monastery', in Clarke and Brennan (eds), pp. 33–55.

James, Edward 1982: *The Origins of France. From Clovis to the Capetians, 500–1000* (London).

James, Edward 1988a: *The Franks* (Oxford).

James, Edward 1988b: 'Childéric, Syagrius et la disparition du royaume de Soissons', *Revue Archéologique de Picardie* 1988 (3–4) (= *Actes des VIIIe Journées internationales d'archéologie mérovingienne de Soissons (19–22 juin 1986)*), 9–12.

James, Edward 1989: 'Burial and status in the Early Medieval West', *Trans. Royal Historical Soc.*, 5th ser., 39, 23–40.

James, E. 1989: The origins of barbarian kingdoms: The continental evidence. *The Origin of Anglo-Saxon Kingdoms*, S. Bassett (ed.) (Leicester University Press).

James, M.R. (ed.), 1917: 'Two Lives of St. Ethelbert, King and Martyr', *English Historical Review*, 32, pp. 214–244.

Jansson, I. 1985: Ovala spännbucklor. *Aun 7* (Uppsala).

Jarman, A.O.H. 1988: (trans. and commentary) *Aneirin: Y Gododdin* (Llandysul).

Jensen, S. 1990: Handel med dagligvarer i vikingetiden. *Hikuin 16*, 119–138.

Jensen, S. (in press): Dankirke-Ribe. Fra handlsgård til handelsplads. Kommer I. *Fra Stamme til Stat II–III*. P. Mortensen and B. Rasmussen (eds) (Jysk arkæologisk Selskab. Århus).

Joffroy, R. 1974: *Le Cimetière de Lavoye (Meuse)* (Paris).

John, E. 1960: *Land Tenure in early England* (Leicester: Univ Press).

John, E. 1973–4: 'Beowulf and the margins of literacy', *Bulletin of the John Rylands Library*, 56, 388–422.

Johnson, S. 1983: *Burgh Castle: Excavations by Charles Green* 1958–61 (East Anglian Archaeology 20).

Jones, G. 1968: *A History of the Vikings*.

Jørgensen, B. 1981: *Dansk Stednavne Leksikon* (København).

Jörgensen, L. 1990: *Bækkegård and Glasergård. Two Cemeteries from the Late Iron Age on Bornholm* (Arkæologiske Studier VIII, Universitetsforlaget, Copenhagen).

Kazanksi, Michel and Périn, Patrick 1988: 'Le mobilier funéraire de la tombe de Childéric Ier; état de la question et perspectives', *Revue Archéologique de Picardie* 1988 (3–4) (= *Actes des VIIIe Journées internationales d'archéologie mérovingienne de Soissons (19–22 juin 1986))*, 13–38.

Kendrick, T.D. 1932: 'British hanging-bowls' *Antiquity* 6: 161–84.

Kennett, D.H. 1971: 'Graves with swords at Little Wilbraham and Linton Heath', *Proc. Cambridge Antiq. Soc.*, 63, 9–26.

Klaeber, F. (ed.) 1950: *Beowulf and the Fight at Finnsburg* (3rd edition, with first and second supplements, Lexington, Mass.).

Koch, R. 1967: *Bodenfunde der Völkerwanderungszeit aus dem Main-Tauber-Gebiet* (G.D.V. A.8, Berlin).

Koch, U. 1977: *Das Reihengräberfeld bei Schretzheim*, Berlin (Germanische Denkmäler der Völkerwanderungszeit, A 13).

Krag, C. 1991: *Ynglingatal og Ynglingesaga: En Studie i Historiske Kilder*, Studia Humaniora s (Oslo).

Krautheimer, R. 1965: *Early christian and byzantine architecture* (The Pelican History of Art).

Kristiansen, K. (in press): Chiefdoms, states, and systems of social evolution. *Chiefdoms – Economy, Power and Ideology*. T. Earle (ed.) (Cambridge).

Krüger, K.H. 1971: *Königsgrabkirchen der Franken, Angelsachsen und Langobarden bis zur Mitte des 8. Jahrhunderts. Ein historischer Katalog* (Münstersche Mittelalter Schriften 4) (Munich).

Krusch, B. (ed.), 1902: *Passiones Vitaeque Sanctorum Aeui Merouingici IV*.

Krusch, B. and Levison, W. (eds), 1920: *Passiones Vitaeque Sanctorum Aeui Merouingici VII*.

Laing, L. 1975: The Mote of Mark and the origins of Celtic interlace, *Antiquity*, 49, 98–108.

Lamb, R.G. 1973: 'Coastal settlements of the North', *Scot. Archaeol. Forum*, 5, 76–98.

Lamb, R.G. 1980: *Iron Age Promontory Forts in the Northern Isles* (Oxford: Brit. Archaeol. Rep., Brit. Ser. 79).

Lamb, R.G. forthcoming a: 'The Papar of Papil', in B. Smith and V. Turner (eds), *Shetland Settlement: Past and Present*.

Lamb, R.G. forthcoming b: 'Carolingian Orkney and its transformation', in C. Batey and J. Jesch (eds), *Proceedings of the Eleventh Viking Congress*.

Lamm, J.-P. 1962: 'Ett vendeltida gravfynd fran Spelvik', *Forvannen* 57: 277–99.

Lamm, J.O. and Nordström H.-Å. (eds) 1983: *Vendel Period Studies. Statens Historiska Museum. Studies 2*. Sth.

Lamm, J. P. and Nylén, E. 1988: *Stones, Ships and Symbols. The Picture Stones of Gotland from the Viking Age and Before* (Gidlunds, Stockholm).

Lane, A. and Campbell, E., forthcoming: Celtic and Germanic Interaction in Dalriada – the seventh-century metalworking site at Dunadd, in J. Higgitt and M. Spearman (eds), *The Age of Migrating Ideas: Early Medieval Art in Britain and Ireland*, (Proceedings of the Second International Conference on Insular Art, National Museums of Scotland).

Lawson, A. (ed.), 1983: *The Archaeology of Witton, near North Walsham* (East Anglian Archaeology, 18).

Leach, E. 1958: 'Magical hair' *J.Roy. Anthrop. Inst.*, 88: 147–64.

Leach, E. 1976: *Culture and communication: the logic by which symbols are connected* (London).

Leeds, E.T. 1924: 'An Anglo-Saxon cremation-burial of the seventh century in Asthall Barrow, Oxfordshire'. *Antiq. J.*, 4, 113–26.

Leeds, E.T. 1936: *Early Anglo-Saxon Art and Archaeology* (Oxford).

Leeds, E.T. 1939a: 'Early man III: Bronze Age', in L.F. Salzmann (ed.) *The Victoria County History of the County of Oxford* (London), 241–51.

Leeds, E.T. 1939b: 'Anglo-Saxon remains', in L.F. Salzmann (ed.), *The Victoria History of the County of Oxford*, I, 346–72.

Leigh, D. 1984: ' Ambiguity in Anglo-Saxon *style 1* art' *Ant. J.*, 63: 34–42.

Leisi, E. 1952–3: 'Gold und Manneswert im *Beowulf*', *Anglia*, 71, 259–73.

Lenoir, A. 1867: *Statistique monumentale de Paris*, Paris, 1867, 2 vol. in-fol. (Atlas) and 1 vol. in-4º (*Explication des planches*), pl. I et V.

Lethbridge, T.C. 1931: *Recent excavations in Anglo-Saxon cemeteries in Cambridgeshire and Suffolk*. Cambridge (Cambr. Ant. Soc. Quarto Publ., New Ser., III).

Lethbridge, T.C. 1936: *A cemetery at Shudy Camps,Cambridgeshire*. Cambridge (Cambr. Ant. Soc. Quarto Publ., New Ser., V).

Levi-Strauss, C. 1964: *Totemism* (London).

Levi-Strauss, C. 1977: *Structural Anthropology* (London).

Liebermann, F. 1903 *Die Gesetze der Angelsachsen* Vol.1 (Halle).

Lindqvist, S. 1936: *Uppsala Högar och Ottarshögen* (Stockholm).

Løken, T. 1977: Mølen – et arkeologisk dateringsproblem og en historisk identifikasjonsmulighet. *Univ. Olds. Årbok 1975–1976*, 67–86.

Loyn, H. 1953: 'The term *ealdorman* in the translations prepared at the time of King Alfred' *English Historical Review*, 68: 513–25.

Loyn, H. 1955: 'Gesiths and Thegns in England from the seventh to the tenth centuries' *English Historical Review*, 70: 529–49.

Lukman, N. 1943: Skjoldunge und Skilfinge. Hunnen- und Herulerkönige in ostnordischer Überlieferung. *Classica et Mediaevalia. Dissertationes III*.

Lundborg, L. 1961: 'Ett gravfält och ett Boplastsomrade fran yngre Järnaldern vid Sund, Saffle. En översikt', *Fornvannen*, 56, 161–76.

Lund Hansen, U. 1987: *Römischer Import im Norden* (Nordiske Fortidsminder Ser. B, Bd. 10. København).

Magnus, B. 1984: The interlace motif on the bucket-shaped pottery of the Migration period, *Universitets Oldsaksamlings Skrifter* nr.5 (Oslo), 139–157.

Magnus, B. and Myhre, B. 1976: *Norges Historie bd. 1. Fra jegergrupper til høvdingesamfunn*. K. Mykland (ed.) (Oslo).

Magoun, F.P. Jr. 1953: 'The Geography of Hygelac's Raid on the Lands of the West Frisians and the Hætt-ware, ca 530 A.D.', *English Studies*, 34, 160–163.

Magoun, F.P. 1954: 'Beowulf and King Hygelac in the Netherlands', *English Studies*, 35, 193–204.

Malone, K. 1927: 'Hrethric', *Publications of the Modern Language Association*, 42, 268–313.

Malone, K. 1931: Untitled review, *Speculum*, 6, pp. 149–150.

Malone, K. 1940: 'Ecgþeow', *Modern Language Quarterly*, I, pp. 37–44.

Malone, K. 1959: 'The Daughter of Healfdene', *Studies in Heroic Legend and in Current Speech*, ed. S. Einarsson and N.E. Eliason (Copenhagen).

Malone, K. (ed.), 1962: *Widsith*, second edition (Copenhagen).

Mango, M.M., Mango, C., Evans, A.C. and Hughes, M. 1989: 'A 6th-century mediterranean bucket from Bromeswell parish, Suffolk' *Antiquity* 63, 295–311.

Martens, I. 1988: Jernvinna på Møsstrand i Telemark. En studie i teknikk, bosetning og økonomi. *Norske Oldfunn XIII* (Univ. Olds. Oslo).

Martin, E. 1976: 'The *Iclingas*', *East Anglian Archaeology*, 3, pp. 132–134.

Martin, E. 1988. *Burgh: the Iron Age and Roman Enclosure* (East Anglian Archaeology 40).

Martin, E., Plouviez, J. and Feldman, H. 1983: 'Archaeology in Suffolk, 1982', in *Proc. Suffolk Inst. Archaeol.*, 35, 235.

Martin, E., Plouviez, J. and Feldman, H. 1986: 'Archaeology in Suffolk 1985' *Proceedings of the Suffolk Institute of Archaeology*, 36(2), 139–56.

Martin, E.A., Plouviez, J. and Ross, H.A. 1983: 'Archaeology in Suffolk in 1982', *Proceedings of the Suffolk Institute of Archaeology and History*, 35/3, 229–36.

Matthews, C.L. 1962: 'The Anglo-Saxon cemetery at Marina Drive, Dunstable', *Bedfordshire Archaeol. J.*, 1, 25–47.

Mattingley, H. and Pearce, J.W.E. 1937: 'The Coleraine hoard' *Antiquity*, 11, 39–45.

Mayr-Harting, H. 1972: *The Coming of Christianity to Anglo-Saxon England* (London).

Maxims I: Maxims I in *The Exeter Book*, ed. G.P. Krapp and E. van K. Dobbie, The Anglo-Saxon Poetic Records 3 (London and New York, 1936), 156–63.

Maxims II: Maxims II in *The Anglo-Saxon Minor Poems*, ed. E. van K. Dobbie, The Anglo-Saxon Poetic Records 6 (London and New York, 1942), 55–7.

Maxwell, G.S. 1987: 'Settlement in southern Pictland: a new overview', in A. Small (ed.), 31–44.

McCormick, M. 1986: *Eternal Victory* (Cambridge).

McGrail, S. 1987: *Ancient Boats in N.W. Europe* (London).

McKinley, J. 1989: 'Spong Hill Anglo-Saxon cremation cemetery', in C.A. Roberts, F. Lee, and J. Bintliff (eds) *Burial Archaeology: current research methods and developments* (Oxford: Brit. Archaeol. Rep. 211), 241–48.

McKnight Crosby, S. and Blum, P.Z. 1987: *The royal abbey of Saint-Denis from its beginnings to the death of Suger (475–1151)* (Yale).

McNeill, J.T. and Gamer, H. (trans.) 1938: *Medieval Handbooks of Penance.*

McNeill, P. and Nicholson, J.W. (eds), 1975: *Historical Atlas of Scotland c.400–c.1600* (St Andrews).

Meaney, A.L.S. 1964: *A Gazetteer of Early Anglo-Saxon Burial Sites* (London).

Meaney, A.L. and Hawkes, S.C. 1970: *Two Anglo-Saxon cemeteries at Winnall, Winchester, Hampshire.* London (Soc. for Med. Arch., Monogr. Ser., 4).

Meaney, A.L.S. 1981: *Anglo-Saxon Amulets and Curing Stones* (Oxford: British Archaeol. Rep. 96).

Merewether, J. 1851: 'Diary of the examination of barrows and other earthworks in the neighbourhood of Silbury Hill and Avebury, Wilts, in July and August 1849', in The Archaeological Institute of Great Britain and Ireland, *Memoirs Illustrative of the History and Antiquities of Wiltshire and the City of Salisbury* (London), 82–112.

Mildenberger, G. 1959/60: Archäologische Betrachtungen zu den Ortsnamen auf –leben. *Archäologica Geographica* Bd. 8/9 (Hamburg).

Miller, D. 1985: *Artifacts as categories: a study of ceramic variability in Central India* (London).

Miller, D. and Tilley, C. (eds) 1984: *Ideology, Power and Prehistory* (London).

Miller, T. (ed.) 1890–91: *The Old-English version of Bede's Ecclesiastical History* (Early English Text Society, 95, 96).

Millet, M. 1975: 'Bede's use of Gildas', *English Historical Review*, 90, 241–61.

Millet, M. with James, S. 1983: 'Excavations at Cowdery's Down, Basingstoke, Hampshire 1978–81', *Archaeol. J.* 140: 151–279.

Miracula S. Genovefae post portem, in AA.SS., January, V, 12.

Miracula Martialis, ed. G. Waitz, *Monumenta Germaniae Historica, Scriptores* XV (Hannover 1887).

Moisl, H. 1981: 'Anglo-Saxon Royal Genealogies and Germanic Oral Tradition', *Journal of Medieval History*, 7, pp. 215–248.

Molte, E. 1976: *Runerne i Danmark og deres Oprindelse* (København).

de Montfaucon, Dom Bernard, 1729: *Les monuments de la monarchie françoise* (Paris), 1729, I.

Moore, I.E. with Plouviez, J. and West, S. 1988: *The Archaeology of Roman Suffolk* (Suffolk County Council).

Morphy, H. 1989: 'Introduction' in Morphy H. (ed.) *Animals into Art* (London: One World Archaeology 7), 1–17.

Morris, C.D. 1989: *The Birsay Bay Project*. Volume I. Coastal Sites beside the Brough Road, Birsay, Orkney. Excavations 1976–1982 (Durham, University of Durham, Department of Archaeology Monograph Series 1).

Morris, C.D. 1991: 'The Viking and Early Settlement Archaeological Research Project', *Current Archaeol.*, 127, 298–302.

Morris, R.K. 1983: *The church in British archaeology* (CBA Res. Rep. 47, London).

Morris, R.K. 1989: *Churches in the landscape* (London: Dent).

Morrison, I. 1985: *Landscape with Lake Dwellings: the Crannogs of Scotland* (Edinburgh).

Mortimer, C. 1990: *Some Aspects of Early Medieval Copper-alloy Technology, as illustrated by the Anglian Cruciform Brooch*, (Oxford University unpub. D.Phil. thesis).

Müller-Wille, M. 1970: Bestattung im Boot. Studien zu einer nordeuropäischen Grabsitte. *Offa 1968–1969, bd. 25/26* (Neumünster).

Müller-Wille, M. 1970–71: 'Pferdegrab und Pferdeopfer in frühen Mittelalter', *Berichten v.d. Rijksdienst v.h. Oudheidkundig Bodemonderzoek*, 20–21, 119–248.

Müller-Wille, M. 1976: *Das Bootkammergrab von Haithabu* (Berichte über die Ausgrabungen in Haithabu 8).

Müller-Wille, M. 1982: 'Königsgrab und Königsgrabkirche: Funde und Befunde im frühmittelalterlichen und mittelalterlichen Nordeuropa', in *Bericht der Römisch-Germanischen Kommission* 63: 350–411.

Müller-Wille, M. 1983: Royal and aristocratic graves in central and western Europe in the Merovingian period. *Vendel Period Studies*, J.P. Lamm and H.-Å. Nordström (eds) (Stockholm).

Müller-Wille, M. 1986: Bild und Bildträger. Beispiele im Borre- und Jellingstil. P.153–174 in H. Roth (ed.), *Zum Problem der Deutung frühmittelalterlicher Bildinhalte* (J. Thorbecke Verlage, Sigmaringen).

Munn, N. 1973: *Walibiri Iconography* (Ithaca).

Mundell Mango, M. 1986: *Silver from Early Byzantium, The Kaper Koraon and Related Treasures* (Baltimore).

Mundell Mango, M. 1990: 'The Sevso Treasure hunting plate', *Apollo* (July 1990), 2–13, 65–67.

Mundell Mango, M., Mango C., Evans, A.C. and Hughes, M. 1989: 'A 6th-century Mediterranean bucket from Bromeswell parish, Suffolk', *Antiquity*, 63, 295–311.

Murray, A.C. 1983: *Germanic Kinship Structure: Studies in Law and Society in Antiquity and the Early Middle Ages* (Toronto).

Myhre, B. 1987a: Fra smårike til stat. *Hafrsfjord* (Stravanger).

Myhre, B. 1987b: 'Chieftain's graves and chiefdom territories in south Norway in the migration period', *Studien zur Sachsenforschung*, 6, 169–87.

Myhre, B. 1990: En samlet oversikt over undersøkelser av gravfeltet 1989–1990. *Rapport fra Borre-prosjektet 1990* (Univ. Olds., Oslo).

Myhre, B. (in press): Borre – et merovingertidssenter i Øst-Norge. *Univ. Olds. Skrifter*, 13, 1992.

Myres, J.N.L. 1956: 'Romano-Saxon pottery', in D.B. Harden (ed.), *Dark age Britain: studies presented to E.T. Leeds*, 16–39 (London: Methuen).

Myres, J.N.L. 1969: *Anglo-Saxon pottery and the settlement of England* (Oxford: University Press).

Myres, J.N.L. 1972: 'The Angles, the Saxons and the Jutes', *Proceedings of the British Academy* 56, 145–74.

Myres, J.N.L. 1977: *A Corpus of Anglo-Saxon Pottery of the Pagan Period* (Cambridge).

Myres, J.N.L. 1986: *The English Settlements* 2nd edn (Oxford).

Myres, J.N.L. and Green, B. 1973: *The Anglo-Saxon cemeteries of Caistor by Norwich and Marskshall, Norfolk* (London: Society of Antiquaries).

Myrvoll, S. 1991: Hones found in Ribe 1970–1976. *Ribe Excavations 1970–1976, vol. 3* (Sydjysk Universitetsforlag, Esbjerg).

Mytum, H.C. 1992: *The Origins of Early Christian Ireland* (London and New York: Routledge).

Näsman, U. 1986: Vendel Period glass from Eketorp II, Öland, Sweden. *Acta Archaeologica* 55, 66–116.

Näsman, U. 1990: Om fjärrhandel i Sydskandinaviens yngre jernålder. *Hikuin 16*, 89–118.

Näsman, U. and Lund, J. (eds) 1988: *Folkevandringstiden i Norden. En krisetid mellem ældre og yngre jernalder* (Århus Universitetsforlag).

Neuffer-Müller, C. 1983: *Der alamannische Adelsbestattungplatz und die Reihengraberfriedhöfe von Kircheim-am-Ries* (Stuttgart).

Neville, R.C. 1852: *Saxon obsequies* (London).

Newman, J. 1988: 'The East Anglian kingdom survey', *Bulletin of the Sutton Hoo Research Committee*, 5, 10–12.

Newman, J. 1989: 'East Anglian Kingdom Survey – Final Interim Report on the South East Suffolk Pilot Field Survey', in M.O.H. Carver (ed.), *Bulletin of the Sutton Hoo Research Committee*, 6, 17–20.

Newman, J. 1991: 'The Boss Hall Anglo-Saxon Cemetery', in M.O.H. Carver (ed.), *Bulletin of the Sutton Hoo Research Committee*, 8 (forthcoming).

Newman, J. (forthcoming): 'Barham, Suffolk – Middle Saxon market or meeting place?', in Metcalf, D.M. and Blackburn, M. (eds), *Productive Sites of the Middle Saxon Period*: Proceedings of the 12th Oxford Coin Symposium.

Newton, Sam forthcoming: *The Origins of Beowulf and the pre-Viking Kingdom of East Anglia* (Woodbridge).

Nicolaisen, W.F.H. 1976: *Scottish Place-Names* (London).

Nicolaysen, N. 1853: Om Borrefundet i 1852. *Aarsb. 1853*. s. 25–32.

Nielsen, H. 1979: Jernalderfund og stednavnetyper – en sammenligning af fynske og sjællandske forhold. *Fra Jernalder til Middelalder*, H. Thrane (ed.). Skrifter fra Historisk Institut. odense Universitet.

Nielsen, K.H. 1991: Centrum og periferi i 6.–8. årh. Territoriale studier af dyrestil og kvindesmykker i yngre germansk jernalder i Syd- og Østskandinavien. *Fra Stamme til Stat bd. 2* (Århus).

Novellae Valentiniani, ed. T. Mommsen and P.M. Meyer, *Codex Theodosianus* (Berlin 1904–5).

O'Loughlin, J.N.L. 1964: 'Sutton Hoo: the evidence of the documents', *Medieval Archaeology*, 8, 1–19.

O'Brien, M.A. 1983: Old Irish personal names (ed. R Baumgarten), *Celtica*, 10, 211–36.

Olrik, J. and Raeder, H. (eds) 1931: *Saxonis Gesta Danorum* (Copenhagen).

Ørsnes, M. 1966: *Form og Stil*, Nationalmuseets Skrifter (Copenhagen), Arkæologisk-historisk række XI.

Ørsnes, M. 1970: Südskandinavische Ornamentik in der jüngeren germanischen Eisenzeit. *Acta Archaeologica*, 40, 1–121.

Ørsnes, M. 1985: Review of J. Hines, *The Scandinavian Character of Anglian England in the pre-Viking Period, Journal of Danish Archaeology*, 4, 211–212.

Owen, G.R. 1981: *Rites and Religions of the Anglo-Saxons* (London).

Owen-Cooper, J.D. 1966: *The Zulu aftermath: a nineteenth century revolution in Bantu Africa* (London: Longman).

Owen-Cooper, J.D. 1969: 'Aspects of political change in the nineteenth-century Mfecane', in L. Thompson (ed.), *African societies in southern Africa*, 207–29 (London: Heineman).

Owen-Crocker, G.R. 1986: *Dress in Anglo-Saxon England* (Manchester University Press).

Owles, E. 1970: 'Archaeology in Suffolk' *Proceedings of the Suffolk Institute of Archaeology*, 32, 92–107.

Ozanne, A. 1962–3: 'The Peak dwellers', *Medieval Archaeol.*, 6–7, 15–52.

Pactus Legis Salicae. K.-A. Eckhardt (ed.) *Monumenta Germaniae Historica. Legum. Sect. I*, Vol. 4, Part i. *Pactus Legis Salicae* (Hanover 1962); Trans. T.J. Rivers, *The Laws of the Salian and Ripuarian Franks* (New York 1987); Trans. K. Fischer Drew, *The Laws of the Salian Franks* (Philadelphia 1991).

Padel, O.J. 1972: *Inscriptions of Pictland* (unpub. M.Litt. thesis submitted to Edinburgh University).

Pader, Ellen-Jane 1982: *Symbolism, social relations and the interpretation of mortuary remains* (British Archaeological Reports, British Series 130: Oxford).

Page, W. (ed.) 1911: A History of Suffolk, Vol. 1 Victoria County History (reprinted 1975).

Painter, K. 1977: *The Water Newton Early Christian Silver* (London).

Painter, K. 1990: 'The Seuso Treasure', *Minerva*, 1(4), 4–11.

Paris mérovingien, guide to the exhibition in the Musée Carnavalet, 1981/82 (*Bulletin du Musée Carnavalet*, 33 nos. 1 and 2).

Parker Pearson, M. 1982: Mortuary practices, society and ideology: an ethnoarchaeological study. *Symbolic and Structural Archaeology*. I. Hodder (ed.) (New Directions in Archaeology, Cambridge).

Parker Pearson, M. 1984: 'Economic and ideological change: cyclical growth in the pre-state societies of Jutland'. In D. Miller and C. Tilley (eds), *Ideology, power and prehistory*, 69–92 (Cambridge: University Press).

Paul the Deacon, *Historia Langobardorum*, ed. G. Waitz, *Monumenta Germaniae Historica, Scriptores Rerum Germaniarum in usum scholarum separatim editi* (Hannover 1878).

Périn, Patrick 1980: *La Datation des Tombes Mérovingiennes: Historique – Méthodes – Applications* (Geneva 1980).

Périn, Patrick 1990a: *Clovis et la naissance de la France* (Paris).

Périn, Patrick 1990b: 'Quelques considérations sur la basilique de Saint-Denis et sa nécropole à l'époque mérovingienne', to be published in *Mélanges Georges Despy. Villes et campagnes dans l'Occident médiéval* (Liège).

Périn, Patrick 1991: 'Pour une révision de la datation de la tombe d'Arégonde, épouse de Clotaire Ier, découverte en 1959 dans la basilique de Saint-Denis', *Archéologie Médiévale*, 21: 21–50.

Périn, P. and Feffer, L-C. 1984: *Lutèce. Paris de César à Clovis* (Paris) (cat. of the exhibition in Musée Carnavalet).

Périn, P. and Feffer, J-F. 1987: *Les Francs. I. A la conquête de la Gaule. II. A l'origine de la France* (Paris).

Périn, P. and Reynaud, J.F. 1989: 'Les premières églises et les origines de la paroisse dans les campagnes', in *Archéologie de la France, 30 ans de découvertes* (Paris), 125–131 (cat. of the exhibition of Grand Palais).

Périn, P., Velay, P.L. and Renou, L. 1985: *Collections mérovingiennes du Musée Carnavalet, Paris (Catalogues d'Art et d'Histoire du Musée Carnavalet, II)*.

Phillips, C.W. (ed.) 1970: *The fenland in Roman times* (London: Royal Geographical Society).

Philp, B. 1973: *Excavations in West Kent 1960–1970* (Dover. Kent Series, Res. Rep. 2).

Pirling, R. 1974: *Das römisch-frankische Gräberfeld von Krefeld-Gellep 1960–63, Serie B, Band 8* (Berlin).

Potts, W. 1907: 'Ancient earthworks', in W. Page (ed.), *The Victoria County History of the County of Oxford, vol. II* (London), 303–49.

Prinz, F. 1967: 'Heiligenkult und Adelsherrschaft im Spiegel merowingischer Hagiographie.' *Historische Zeitschrift*, 204: 529–44.

Prinz, F. 1981: 'Columbanus, the Frankish nobility and the territories east of the Rhine', in Clarke and Brennan (eds), 73–87.

Procopius, *Wars*, ed. and trans. H.B. Dewing (London, 1914–40).

Rahtz, P.A. 1977: 'Late Roman Cemeteries and beyond', in R. Reece (ed.) *Burial in the Roman world* (CBA Res. Rep. 22, London), 53–64.

Rahtz, P.A., Dickinson T.M. and Watts L. (eds) 1980: *Anglo Saxon Cemeteries 1979* (Brit. Archaeol. Reps 82, Oxford).

Rahtz, P. 1980: 'Sutton Hoo Opinions – Forty Years After', in Rahtz, P. Dickinson, T. and Watts, L. (eds), *Anglo-Saxon Cemeteries* (BAR British Series 82).

Ralston, I. 1987: 'Portknockie: promontory forts and Pictish settlement in the north-east', in A. Small (ed.), 15–26.

Ralston, I. and Inglis, J. 1984: *Foul Hordes: the Picts in the north-east and their background* (Aberdeen).

Ramquist, P. 1990: Helgö – unikt handelscentrum eller vanlig bondgård? *Fornavännen 1990*, no. 1, 57–67.

Ramqvist, P. and Müller-Wille, M. 1988: Regionale und überregionale Bedeutung des völkerwanderungszeitlichen Gräberfeldes von Högom, Medelpad, Nordschweden. *Germania*, Bd. 66.

Randsborg, K. 1980: *The Viking Age in Denmark*, London.

Randsborg, K. 1981: 'Burial, succession and early state formation in Denmark', in R. Chapman, I. Kinnes and K. Randsborg (eds), *The Archaeology of Death* (Cambridge: Univ. Press), 105–21.

Randsborg, K. 1990: Beyond the Roman Empire: archaeological discoveries in Gudme on Funen, Denmark. *Oxford Journal of Archaeology*, vol. 9 no. 3.

Read, C.H. 1894: 'Account of the exploration of a Saxon grave at Broomfield, Essex'. *Proc. Soc. Antiq. London*, 15, 250–5.

Redin, M. 1919: *Studies in Uncompounded Personal Names in Old English* (Uppsala).

Rehfeld, B. 1942: *Todestrafen und Bekehrungsgeschichte* (Berlin).

Reid Moir, J. 1921: 'The excavation of two tumuli on Brightwell Heath, Suffolk', *J. Ipswich and District Field Club*, 6, 1–14.

Renfrew, C. 1974: 'Space, time and polity', in M. Rowlands and J. Friedman (eds), *The evolution of social systems*, 89–114 (London: Duckworth).

Renfrew, C. 1975: 'Trade as action at a distance', in J.A. Sabloff and C.C. Lamberg-Karlovsky (eds), *Ancient civilisation and trade*, 3–59 (Albuquerque: University of New Mexico Press).

Renfrew, C. 1982: 'Post-collapse resurgence: culture process in the Dark Ages', in C. Renfrew and S. Shennan (eds), *Ranking, resource and exchange*, 113–116 (Cambridge: University Press).

Renfrew, C. 1986: 'Introduction: peer-polity interaction and socio-political change', in C. Renfrew and J. Cherry (eds), *Peer Polity Interaction and Socio-Political change* (Cambridge: UP), 1–18.

Renfrew, C. 1987: *Archaeology and language: the puzzle of Indo-European origins* (London: Jonathan Cape).

Reynolds, N. 1980: 'The King's whetstone: a footnote' *Antiquity*, 54: 232–7.

Rice, David Talbot 1965: *The Dark Ages* (London).

Richards, J.D. 1987: *The significance of form and function of Anglo-Saxon cremation urns* (Oxford: British Archaeological Reports 166).

Richards, J.D. 1987: 'Style and symbol: explaining variability in Anglo-Saxon cremation burials', in S. Driscoll and M. Nieke (eds) *Power and Politics in early Medieval Britain and Ireland* (Edinburgh), 145–161.

Richards, P. 1980: *Byzantine Bronze Vessels in England and Europe* (unpub. Ph.D. thesis, University of Cambridge).

Richardson, L., Arkell, W.J. and Dines, H.G. 1963: *Geology of the Country around Witney* (HMSO, London).

Richardsson, C. 1989 (manuscript): *The Borre find – A brief discussion*.

Riek, F. and Crumlin-Pedersen, O. 1988: *Både fra Danmarks Oldtid* (Copenhagen).

Rigold, S.E. 1975: 'The Sutton Hoo coins in the light of the contemporary background of coinage in England. In R.L.S. Bruce-Mitford, *The Sutton Hoo ship burial* (vol. 1), 653–77 (London: British Museum Publications).

Ringtved, J. 1989: Jyske gravfund fra yngre romertid og ældre germanertid, *Kuml* 1986, 95–231.

Ripuarian Law. Ed. F. Beyerle and R. Buchner. *Monumenta Germaniae Historica. Legum* Sect.1, Vol.3, *Lex Ribvaria*. Hanover, 1951; Trans. T.J. Rivers, *The Laws of the Salian and Ripuarian Franks* (New York 1987).

Ritchie, A. 1977: 'Excavation of Pictish and Viking-age farmsteads at Buckquoy, Orkney'. *Proc. Soc. Antiq. Scot.*, 108, 174–227.

Ritchie, A. 1987: 'The Picto-Scottish interface in material culture', in A. Small (ed.), 59–67.

Ritchie, A. 1989: *Picts. An Introduction to the Life of the Picts and the Carved Stones in the care of the Secretary of State* (Edinburgh).

Ritter, E.A. 1955: *Shaka Zulu: the rise of the Zulu empire* (London: Longmans).

Roberts, J. 1978: 'Towards an Old English Thesaurus', *Poetica* 9:56–72.

Roberts, J. (ed.) 1979: *The Guthlac poems of the Exeter Book* (Oxford: Clarendon Press).

Roberts, J. 1985: 'Some problems of a thesaurus-maker', *Problems of Old English Lexicography: Studies in memory of Angus Cameron* (Eichstatte Beitrage 15): 229–43.

Robinson, C.H. 1921: *Anskar, the Apostle of the North* (SPG. London).

Roesdahl, E. 1982: *Viking Age Denmark* (London: Brit. Museum).

Rollason, D. 1989: *Saints and Relics in Anglo-Saxon England* (Oxford).

Roth, Helmut 1986: 'Zweifel an Aregunde', *Marburger Studien zur Vor- und Frühgeschichte*, 7, 267–276.

Roth, H. and Wamers, E. (eds), 1984: *Hessen im Frühmittelalter: Archäologie und Kunst* (Sigmaringen).

RCAHMS *Royal Commission on the Ancient and Historical Monuments of Scotland.*

RCAHMS 1946: *Twelfth Report with an Inventory of the Ancient Monuments of Orkney and Shetland* (Edinburgh).

RCAHMS 1985: *Pictish Symbol Stones, a handlist* (Edinburgh).

RCAHMS 1990: *North-east Perth, an archaeological landscape* (Edinburgh).

RCAHMS forthcoming: *South-east Perth.*

Roy, W. 1793: *The Military Antiquities of the Romans in Britain.*

Rumble, A. 1977: '*Hrepingas* Reconsidered', *Mercian Studies*, ed. A. Dornier (Leicester), pp. 169–172.

Russel, A.D. 1983: *Early Anglo-Saxon ceramics from East Anglia: a microprovenience study* (unpub. Ph.D. thesis, University of Southampton).

Saint Ouen, 1888: Saint Ouen, *Vita Eligii*, éd. Krusch, Hanovre 1888 (M.G.H., S.R.M., IV, 634–771).

Sales, W. 1991: *Early Anglo-Saxon Cremation Burials: towards establishing a basic framework* (unpub. BA dissertation, Department of Archaeology, University of York).

Salin, Édouard 1958: *Les Tombes Gallo-Romaines et Mérovingiennes de la Basilique de Saint-Denis (Fouilles de Janvier-Février 1957)*, extracted from *Mémoires de l'Académie des Inscriptions et Belles-Lettres*, 44 1958.

Salway, P. 1981: *Roman Britain.*

Sanderson, D.C.W., Placido, F. and Tate, J.O. 1985: 'Scottish vitrified forts: background and potential for TL dating' *Nucl. Tracks Radiat. Meas.*, 10, 799–809.

Sanderson, D.C.W., Placido, F. and Tate, J.O. 1988: 'Scottish vitrified forts: TL results from six study sites' *Nucl. Tracks Radiat. Meas.*, 14, 307–16.

Sandred, K.I. 1963: *English Place-Names in -stead* (Uppsala).

Särlvik, I. 1982: *Paths towards a Stratified Society* (Stockholm Studies in Archaeology 3).

Sarrazin, G. 1807: 'Neue *Beowulf*-Studien', *Englishche Studien*, 23, pp. 221–267.

Saussure, F. de 1959: *A course in general linguistics* (New York).

Sawyer, P.H. 1978: *From Roman Britain to Norman England* (London: Methuen).

Sawyer, P. 1988: *The Making of Sweden.* Occasional Papers on Medieval Topics nr. 3 Viktoria Bokforlag, Allingsås, in co-operation with The Department of History, Gotenburg University, Sweden.

Sawyer, P. 1988: Da Danmark blio Danmark, Fra är 700 til 1050 *Gyldendslog Politikkens Danmarkshistorie 3* (Copenhagen).

Schmid, P. 1978: 'New archaeological results of settlement structure (Roman Iron Age) in the north-west German coastal area'. In B. Cunliffe and T. Rowley (eds), *Lowland Iron Age communities in Europe*, 123–145 (Oxford: B.A.R. S48).

Schramm, P.E. 1954: *Herrschaftszeichen und Staatssymbolik* I (Schriften der Monumenta Germaniae Historica XIII/1) (Stuttgart 1954).

Schulz, W. 1933: *Das Fürstengrab und das Grabfeld bei Haleben.* Römish-germanische Forschungen 7 (Berlin – Leipzig).

Schulz, W. 1953: *Leuna, Ein germanischer Bestattlungsplatz der spätrömischen Kaiserzeit* (Berlin).

Scull, C.J. 1985: 'Further evidence from East Anglia for enamelling on early Anglo-Saxon metal work', *Anglo-Saxon Studies in Archaeology and History*, 4, 117–24.

Scull, C.J. 1990: 'Scales and weights in early Anglo-Saxon England', *Archaeological Journal*, 147, 183–215.

Selkirk, A. 1975: 'Mucking: the Saxon cemeteries' *Current Archaeology*, 50, 73–80.

Service, E.R. 1971: *Primitive social organisation: an evolutionary perspective*, 2nd. edn. (New York: Random House).

Service, E.R. 1975: *Origins of the state and civilisation* (New York: Norton).

Shanks, M. and Tilley C. 1987: *Social Theory and Archaeology* (Cambridge).

Shepherd, I.A.G. 1983: 'Pictish settlement problems in N.E. Scotland', in J.C. Chapman and H.C. Mytum (eds), *Settlement in North Britain 1000 BC–AD 1000* (Oxford: Brit. Archaeol. Rep., Brit. Ser. 118), 327–356.

Shephard, J. 1979a: 'The social identity of the individual in isolated barrows and barrow cemeteries in Anglo-Saxon England', in B.C. Burnham and J. Kingsbury (eds), *Space, Hierarchy and Society, Interdisciplinary Studies in Social Area Analysis* (British Archaeol. Rep. Internat. Ser. 59 Oxford), 47–79.

Shephard, J. 1979b: *Anglo-Saxon Barrows of the Later Sixth and Seventh Centuries A.D.* (unpub. Ph.D. thesis, University of Cambridge).

Shoesmith, R. 1980: *Excavations at Castle Green, Hereford* (London: CBA Res. Rep. 36).

Simmer, A. 1982: 'Le prélèvement des crânes dans l'est de la France à l'époque mérovingienne', *Archéol. Med.*, 12: 35–49.

Simmer, A. 1983: 'Les tombes doubles à l'epoque Mérovingienne: l'exemple d'Audun-le-Tiche (Moselle).' *Revue Archéologique de l'Est et de Centre-Est*, 34, pp. 170–72.

Simmer, A. 1988: *Le Cimetière Mérovingien d'Audun-le-Tiche. Archéologie d'Aujourd'hui No.1 (Mémoire de l'Association Française d'Archéologie Mérovingienne no. 2)* (Paris).

Simonett, C. 1946: 'Der römische Silberschatz aus Wettingen', *Zeitschrift f. Schweizerische Archäologie und Kunstgeschichte*, 8, 1–15.

Sims-Williams, P. 1983: 'The Settlement of England in Bede and the "Chronicle" ', *Anglo-Saxon England*, 12, pp. 1–41.

Sims-Williams, P. 1990: *Religion and Literature in western England, 600–800* (Cambridge).

Sisam, K. 1953: 'Anglo-Saxon Royal Genealogies', *Proceedings of the British Academy*, 39, pp. 287–348.

Sjösvärd, L., Vretemark, M. and Gustavson, H. 1983: 'A Vendel warrior from Vallentuna', in J-P. Lamm and H-A. Nordström (eds), *Vendel Period Studies* (Stockholm), 133–50.

Skeat, W.W. (ed.) 1881–1900: *Aelfric's Lives of the Saints* (Early English Text Society, 76, 82, 94, 114).

Skjølsvold, A. 1969: En fangstmanns grav i Trysilfjellene. *Viking XXXIII*, 139–200.

Sklute, L.M. 1971: '*Freoþuwebbe* in Old English Poetry', *Neuphilologische Mitteilungen*, 71, pp. 534–541.

Skovgaard-Petersen, I. 1977: Oldted og vikingetid. *Danmarks Historie be. 1. Tiden indtil 1340.* A.E. Christensen, H.P. Clausen, S. Ellehøj and S. Mørch (eds) (Kōbenhavn).

Slay, D. (ed.), 1960: *Hrólfs saga Kraka* (Copenhagen).

Small, A. 1969: 'Burghead', *Scot. Archaeol. Forum*, 1, 61–8.

Small, A. (ed.), 1987: *The Picts. A New Look at Old Problems* (Dundee).

Smith, A.H. (ed.), 1961–63: *The Place-Names of the West Riding of Yorkshire*, 8 vols (Cambridge).

Smith, B. 1990: 'New insights into later Iron Age settlement in the north: Howe', in I. Armit (ed.), 32–40.

Smith, R. 1905: 'The Anglo-Saxon Cemetery at Mitcham, Surrey'. *Surrey Archaeol. Coll.* 56; *Proc. Soc. Antiq.*, 21: 4.

Smith, W.R. 1894: *Lectures on the Religion of the Semites* (London).

Smithers, G. 1971: 'The Geats of Beowulf' *Durham University Journal*, 63: 87–103.

Smyser, H.M. 1965: 'Ibn Fadlan's Account of the Rus'. *Medieval and Linquistic Studies in honour of Francis Peabody Magoun Jr.* Ed. J.B. Bessinger and R.P. Creed (London), 95–119.

Smyth, A.P. 1984: *Warlords and Holymen: Scotland A.D.80–1000* (London).

Solberg, B. 1981: Spearheads in the transition period between the early and the late Iron Age in Norway, *Acta Archaeologica*, 51, 153–172.

Solomon: Solomon and Saturn in *The Anglo-Saxon Minor Poems*, ed. E. van K. Dobbie, The Anglo-Saxon Poetic Records 6 (London and New York, 1942), 31–48.

Søndergaard, B. 1972: *Indledende Studier over den Nordiske Stednavnetype -lev (löv)* (København).

Speake, G. 1980: *Anglo-Saxon Animal Art and its Germanic Background* (Oxford).

Speake, G. 1989. *A Saxon Bed Burial on Swallowcliffe Down* (London).

Sprandel, R. 1961: 'Struktur und Geschichte des merovingischen Adels.' *Historische Zeitschrift*, 193, pp. 33–71.

Stahl, A. 1982: *The Merovingian Coinage of the Region of Metz* (Louvain-la-Neuve).

Stanford, S.C. 1980: *The Archaeology of the Welsh Marches* (London: Collins).

Stanley, E.G. 1981: 'The dating of Beowulf: some doubts and no conclusions' *The Dating of Beowulf* ed. C. Chase (Toronto), 197–211.

Stein, F. 1967: *Adelsgräber des achten Jahrhunderts in Deutschland*. Berlin (Germanische Denkmäler der Völkerwanderungszeit A 9).

Stein, F. 1989: 'Les tombes d'un chef franc et sa famille a Gudingen: considérations sur le rôle de l'aristocratie dans l'implantation franque entre la Meuse et la Sarre.' *Actes des Xe Journées Internationales d'Archéologie Mérovingienne. Metz 20–23 Octobre 1988* (Sarreguemines), 153–69.

Sten, S. and Vretemark, M. 1988: 'Storgravsprojektet – osteologiska analyser av yngre jarnalderns benrika brandgravar' *Fornvannen*, 83: 145–56.

Stenberger, M. 1961: 'Das Gräberfeld bei Ihre im Kirchspiel Hellvi auf Gotland', *Acta Archaeologica*, 32, 1–134.

Stenton, F.M. 1943: *Anglo-Saxon England*, The Oxford History of England II, 1st. edition (Oxford University Press).

Stenton, F.M. 1959: 'The East Anglian kings of the seventh century'. In P. Clemoes (ed.), *The Anglo-Saxons. Studies in some aspects of their history and culture presented to Bruce Dickens*, 43–52 (London: Bowes and Bowes).

Stenton, F.M. 1971: *Anglo-Saxon England*, 3rd. edn (Oxford: University Press).

Stephanus, *Vita Wilfridi*, ed. and trans. B. Colgrave, *The Life of Bishop Wilfrid by Eddius Stephanus* (Cambridge 1927).

Sterner, J. 1989: 'Who is signalling whom? Ceramic style, ethnicity and taphonomy among the Sirak Bulahay' *Antiquity*, 63: 451–9.

Steuer, H. 1982: *Frühgeschichtliche Sozialstrukturen in Mitteleuropa*. Abhandlung der Akademie der Wissenschaften in Göttingen Nr. 128 (Göttingen).

Steuer, H. 1987: Helm und Ringschwert: Prunkbewaffnung und Rangabzeichen germanischer Krieger. Eine Übersicht. *Studien zur Sachsenforschung*, 6, 189–236.

Stevenson, J.B. 1984: 'Garbeg and Whitebridge: two square-barrow cemeteries in Inverness-shire', in J. Friell and G. Watson (eds), 145–50.

Stevenson, J.B. 1991: 'Pitcarmicks and Fermtouns', in *Current Archaeol.*, 127, 288–91.

Stevenson, R.B.K. 1949: 'The nuclear fort of Dalmahoy, Midlothian, and other Dark Age capitals', *Proc. Soc. Antiq. Scot.*, 88, 186–98.

Stevenson, R.B.K. 1955a: 'Pins and the Chronology of Brochs', *Proc. Prehist. Soc.*, 21, 282–94.

Stevenson, R.B.K. 1955b: 'Pictish art' in F. T. Wainwright (ed.), 97–128.

Stjerna, K. 1912: *Essays on questions connected with the Old English poem of 'Beowulf'* (Viking Club Extra Series, 3).

Storms, G. 1957: *Compounded Names of Peoples in Beowulf* (Utrecht and Nijmegen).

Storms, G. 1970: 'The significance of Hygelac's raid' *Nottingham Medieval Studies*, 14: 3–26.

Storms, G. 1978: 'The Sutton Hoo Ship Burial: an interpretation', *Berichten van de Rijksdienst voor het Oudenheidkundig Bodemonderzoek*, 28: 309–44.

Straub, R. 1956: Zur Kontinuität der voralamannischen Bevölkerung. *Badische Fundberichte*, 20. 127–137.

Ström, H. 1939: *Old English Personal Names in Bede's History* (Lund).

Ströme, F. 1942: *On the Sacral Origin of the Germanic Death Penalties*. KVHAAH 52 (Stockholm).

Strong, D.E. 1966: *Greek and Roman Gold and Silver Plate* (London).

Struve, K.W. 1967: 'Die Moorleiche von Dätgen', *Offa*, 24: 33–76 (Kiel).

Stuiver, M. and Pearson, G.W. 1986: High-precision calibration of the radio-carbon time scale A.D.1950–500 B.C. *Radiocarbon 28, No. 2B*.

Swanton, M.J. 1973: *The Spearheads of the Anglo-Saxon Settlements* (London).

Talbot, C.H. 1954: *The Anglo-Saxon Missionaries in Germany* (London).

Tangl, M. (ed.), 1916: *Die Briefe des heiligen Bonifatius und Lullus*.

Tapper, R. 1988: 'Animality, humanity, morality, society' in T. Ingold (ed.) *What is an animal?* (London: One World Archaeology 1), 47–62.

Taylor, C. 1989: *The symbolism of material culture: a case study of the Anglo-Saxon combs of East Anglia* (unpub. MA thesis, Unversity of York).

Taylor, H.M. and Taylor, J. 1965: *Anglo-Saxon Architecture* (Cambridge: Univ Press).

Thackray, D.W.R. 1980: *The defensive linear earthworks of East Anglia, with particular reference to Anglo-Saxon settlement* (unpub. Ph.D. thesis, University of Cambridge).

Thomas, C. 1963: 'The interpretations of the Pictish symbols', *Archaeol J.*, 120, 31–98.

Thomas, C. 1986: *Celtic Britain* (London).

Thompson, L. 1975: *Survival in two worlds: Moshoeshoe of Lesotho, 1786–1870* (Oxford: University Press).

Thomsen, P.O. 1989: Lundeborg. *Årbog for Svendborg og Omegns Museum* (Svendborg).

Thorpe, Lewis, transl. 1974: *Gregory of Tours: History of the Franks* (Harmondsworth).

Thrane, H. 1987: Das Gudme-Problem und die Gudme-Untersuchung. *Frühmittelalterliche Studien*, Bd. 21.

Toller, T.N. 1921: *An Anglo-Saxon Dictionary: supplement* (London).

Tomlin, R.S.O. 1982: Roman Britain in 1981: Inscriptions, *Britannia*, 13, 398.

Tomlin, R.S.O. 1987: Was ancient British Celtic ever a written language? Two texts from Roman Bath, *Bulletin of the Board of Celtic Studies*, 34, 18–25.

Toynbee, J.C.M. 1968: Pagan motifs and practices in Christian art and ritual in Roman Britain, in *Christianity in Britain*, eds M.W. Barley & R.P.C. Hanson, 177–92.

Turner, V. 1967: *Forest of Symbols: aspects of Ndembu Ritual* (New York).

Turville-Petre, J.E. 1958: 'Hengest and Horsa', *Saga Book*, 14, 273–290.

Turville-Petre, J.E. 1978–1979: 'On *Ynglingatal*', *Medieval Scandinavia*, II, 47–67.

Van Dam, R. 1985: *Leadership and Community in Late Antique Gaul* (Berkeley).

Vang Petersen, P. 1988: Gudme II, en guldskat i hus. *Årbog for Svendborg & Omegns Museum*.

Veeck, W. 1931: *Die Alamannen in Württemburg* (Berlin/Leipzig).

Venantius Fortunatus, *Carmina*, ed. F. Leo, *Monumenta Germaniae Historica, Auctores Antiquissimi*, IV i (Berlin 1881).

Vendel Period Studies: Statens Historiska Museum, *Studies* 2: Vendel Period, ed. J.P. Lamm and H-A. Nordstrom (Stockholm 1983).

Vieillard-Tröiekouroff, May, Fossard, Denise, Chatel, Elisabeth and Lamy-Lassalle, Colette, 1960: 'Les anciennes églises suburbaines de Paris (IVe–Xe siècles)', in *Paris et Ile-de-France, Mémoires de la Fédération des Sociétés historiques et archéologiques de Paris et de l'Ile-de-France*, t.XI.

Vieillard-Troïekouroff, M. 1976: *Les monuments religieux de la Gaule d'après les oeuvres de Grégoire de Tours* (Paris).

Vierck, H. 1970: 'Zum Fernverkehr über See im 6. Jahrhundert angesichts angelsächsischer Fibelsätze in Thüringen', in K. Hauck (ed.), *Goldbrakteaten aus Sievern* (Munich: Wilhelm Fink).

Vierck, H. 1970–1: 'Pferdegräber im Angelsächsischen England', in Müller-Wille 1970–71, 189–99, 218–220.

Vierck, H. 1972: 'Redwalds Asche. Zum Grabbrauch in Sutton Hoo, Suffolk', *Offa*, 29, 20–49.

Vierck, H. 1978: 'Von der Trachtprovinz zur bevölkerungs-geschichtlichen Aussage', in C. Ahrens (ed.), *Sachsen und Angelsachsen* (Hamburg), 285–91.

Vierch, H. 1978: Religion, Rang und Herrschaft im Spiegel der Tracht. *Sachsen und Angelsachsen* (Veröffentlichungen des Helms-Museums Nr. 32. Hamburg).

Vierck, H. 1980: 'Sutton Hoo Comment' in Rahtz, P., Dickinson, T. and Watts, L. (eds), *Anglo-Saxon Cemeteries* 1979 (BAR British Series 82).

Vigfússon, G. and Powell, F.Y. (eds), 1888: *Corpus Poeticum Boreale*, 2 vols (New York).

Vinsrygg, S. 1979: Merovingartid i Nord-Noreg (Historisk Museum, Bergen, Arkeologiske avhandlinger 2).

Vita Arnulfi, ed. B. Krusch, *Monumenta Germaniae Historica. Scriptores Rerum Merovingiarum*. II (Hannover 1888), pp. 426–46.

Vita Balthildis, ed. B. Krusch, *Monumenta Germaniae Historica , Scriptores Rerum Merovingiarum* V (Hannover 1888), 475–508.

Vita Genovefae virginis Parisiensis, ed. B. Krusch, *Monumenta Germaniae Historica , Scriptores Rerum Merovingicarum*, III (Hannover 1988), 204–238.

Vita Richarii, ed. B. Krusch, *Monumenta Germaniae Historica, Scriptores Rerum Merovingiarum* VII (Hannover, 1920).

Voinot, J. 1904: 'Les fouilles de Chaouilley. Cimetière mérovingien.' *Mémoires de la Société Archéologique de la Lorraine*, 54, pp. 5–80.

de Vries, J. (ed.), 1962: *Altnordisches Etymologisches Wörterbuch* (Leiden).

Wade, K. 1986: 'Proposals for a Regional Survey' *Bulletin of the Sutton Hoo Research Committee*, 4: 60–62.

Wade, K. 1988: 'Ipswich'. In R. Hodges and B. Hobley (eds), *The rebirth of towns in the west A.D.700–1050* (London: CBA).

Wade, K. and West, S. 1983: 'The Origin and Development of the Kingdom of East Anglia Project', in M.O.H. Carver (ed.), *Bulletin of the Sutton Hoo Research Committee*, 1, 18.

Wade-Martins, P. 1974: 'The linear earthworks of west Norfolk', *Norfolk Archaeology*, 36, 23–38.

Wade-Martins, P. 1980: *Excavations in North Elmham Park 1967–72* (East Anglian Archaeology 9).

Wainwright, F.T. 1963: *The souterrains of Southern Pictland* (Edinburgh).

Wainwright, F.T. (ed.), 1955: *The Problem of the Picts* (Edinburgh).

Wallace-Hadrill, J.M. 1960: 'The graves of kings: an historical note on some archaeological evidence', *Studi Medievali*, 3rd ser. 1, 177–194, and reprinted in Wallace-Hadrill, *Early Medieval History* (Oxford 1975), 39–59.

Wallace-Hadrill, J. 1962: *The long-haired Kings* (University of Toronto).

Wallace-Hadrill, J.M. 1971: *Early Germanic Kingship in England and on the Continent* (Oxford: Clarendon Press).

Wallace-Hadrill, J.M. 1975: 'The graves of kings: an historical note on some archaeological evidence'. In J.M. Wallace-Hadrill, *Early medieval history*, 39–59 (Oxford: Basil Blackwell).

Warner, P. 1984, 1985: 'Documentary Sources', *Bulletin of the Sutton Hoo Research Committee*, No. 2, 7–8; 'Documentary survey', *ibid.* no. 3, 17–21.

Warner, P. 1987: *Greens, commons and clayland colonisation: the origins and development of green-side settlement in east Suffolk* (Leicester: University Press).

Watkins, T. 1980a: 'Excavation of an Iron Age open settlement at Dalladies, Kincardine-shire', *Proc. Soc. Antiq. Scot.*, 110, 122–64.

Watkins, T. 1980b: 'Excavation of a settlement and souterrain at Newmill, near Bankfoot, Perthshire', *Proc. Soc. Antiq. Scot.*, 110, 165–208.

Watkins, T. 1984: 'Where were the Picts? An essay in settlement archaeology', in J. Friell and G. Watson (eds), 63–86.

Webster, L. 1980: 'Copper alloy object' in Longworth, I.H. and Kinnes, I.A., *Sutton Hoo Excavations 1966, 1968–70* (British Museum Occasional Paper 23).

Webster, L. and Backhouse, J. 1991: *The Making of England: Anglo-Saxon Art and Culture A.D.600–900* (The British Museum and The British Library).

Webster, L. and Cherry, J. 1977: 'Medieval Britain in 1976', *Medieval Archaeol.*, 21, 204–62.

Wedderburn, L.M.M. and Grime, D.M. 1984: 'The cairn cemetery at Garbeg, Drumnadro-chit', in J. Friell and G. Watson (eds), 151–67.

Weidemann, M. 1982: *Kulturgeschichte der Merowingerzeit nach den Werken Gregors von Tours* (Mayence) 2 vols.

Welch, M.G. 1971: 'Late Romans and Saxons in Sussex', *Britannia*, 2, 232–7.

Welch, M.G. 1983: *Early Anglo-Saxon Sussex* (British Archaeol. Rep. British Ser. 112 Oxford).

Welch, M.G. 1991: 'Contacts across the channel between the fifth and seventh centuries: a review of the archaeological evidence'. *Studien zur Sachsenforschung*, 7, 261–69.

Wells, L.H. 1969: Stature in earlier races of mankind. In D. Brothwell and E. Higgs (eds), *Science in archaeology*, 2nd edn (London: Thames & Hudson), 453–467.

Wenskus, R. 1961: *Stammesbildung und Verfassung* (Köln).

Werner, J. 1957: 'Zwei gegossene koptische Bronzeflaschen aus Salona', *Vjesnik za arheo-logija i historiju dalmatinsku*, 56–59 (for 1954–57; =Antidoron Michael Abramic I), Split, 115–28.

Werner, J. 1964: 'Frankish royal tombs in the cathedrals of Cologne and St Denis', *Antiquity*, 38, 201–216.

Werner, J. 1980: 'Der goldene Armring des Frankenkönigs Childerich und die germani-schen Handgelenkringe der jüngeren Kaiserzeit', *Frühmittelalterliche Studien*, 14, 1–49.

Werner, J. 1988: Danceny und Brangstrup. *Bonner Jahrbücher*, Bd. 188.

Werner, K-F. 1976: 'Le rôle de l'aristocratie dans la christianisation du nord-est de la Gaule', *Revue d'Histoire de l'Eglise de France*, 62, 45–73.

Werner, K-F. 1985: 'Les rouages de l'administration', in P. Périn and L.-C. Feffer, *La Neustrie* (Créteil), 41–6.

West, S.E. 1978: 'Die Siedlung West Stow in Suffolk'. In K. Ahrens (ed.), *Sachsen und Angelsachsen*, 395–412 (Hamburg-Harburg: Helms Museum).

West, S.E. 1985: *West Stow, the Anglo-Saxon Village* (East Anglian Archaeology 24).

West, S.E. 1988: *The Anglo-Saxon cemetery at Westgarth Gardens, Bury St. Edmunds, Suffolk: Catalogue* (East Anglian Archaeology 38).

West, S.E. and Owles, E. 1973: 'Anglo-Saxon Cremation Burials from Snape' *Proceedings of the Suffolk Institute of Archaeology*, 33 (for 1973), 47–57.

West, S.E., Scarfe, N. and Cramp, R. 1984: 'Iken, St. Botolph, and the coming of East Anglian Christianity', *Proceedings of the Suffolk Institute of Archaeology*, 35(4), 279–301.

White, R.H. 1988: *Roman and Celtic Objects from Anglo-Saxon Graves* (British Archaeol. Rep. British Ser. 191, Oxford).

Whitelock, D. (ed.), 1955: *English Historical Documents I.*

Whitelock, D. 1972: 'The pre-Viking church in East Anglia', *Anglo-Saxon England*, 1, 1–22.

Whittington, G. 1975: 'Place-names and the settlement pattern of Dark Age Scotland', *Proc. Soc. Antiq. Scot.*, 106, 99–110.

Widsith: Widsith in *The Exeter Book*, ed. G.P. Krapp and E. van K. Dobbie, The Anglo-Saxon Poetic Records 3 (London and New York, 1936), 149–53.

Williamson, T. 1984: 'The Roman countryside settlement and agriculture in N.W. Essex', *Britannia*, 15, 225–30.

Williamson, T. 1987: 'Early co-axial field systems on the East Anglian boulder clays', *Proceedings of the Prehistoric Society*, 53, 419–431.

Wilson, D. 1985: A note on OE *hearg* and *weoh* as placename elements representing different types of pagan Saxon worship sites, *Anglo-Saxon Studies in Archaeology and History*, 4, 179–83.

Wilson, D.M. and Hurst, J.G. 1959: 'Medieval Britain in 1958' *Medieval Archaeology*, 3: 295–326.

Wilson, D.M. 1964: 'A ring of Queen Arnegunde', *Germania*, 42, 265–268.

Wilson, D.M. 1976: Introduction to Wilson, D.M. (ed.) *The Archaeology of Anglo-Saxon England* (London: Methuen).

Wilson, D.M. 1983: 'Sweden-England', in J.P. Lamm and H.-Å. Nordstrum (eds), *Vendel period studies*, 163–66.

Wilson, D.M. and Hurst, J.G. 1957: 'Medieval Britain in 1956', *Medieval Archaeol.*, 1, 147–71.

Wilson, D.M. and Hurst, J.G. 1958: 'Medieval Britain in 1957', *Medieval Archaeol.*, 2, 183–213.

Wilson, D.M. and Klindt-Jensen, O. 1980: *Viking Art* (2nd ed.) (Allen and Unwin, London).

Winterbottom, M. (ed. and Gildas, trans.), 1978: *The Ruin of Britain and Other Works.*

Wolfram, H. 1967: *Intitulatio I, lateinische Königs- und Fürstentitel bis zum Ende des 8. Jahrhunderts* (Vienna).

Wolfram, H. 1990: *Die Goten* (München).

Wood, I.N. 1977: Kings, kingdoms and consent. *Early Medieval Kingship.* P.H. Sawyer and I.N. Wood (eds) (University of Leeds).

Wood, I.N. 1983: *The Merovingian North Sea. Occasional Papers on Medieval Topics nr. 1 Viktoria Bokforlag* (Alingsås).

Wood, I.N. 1990a: 'The Channel from the 4th to the 7th centuries A.D.', in S. McGrail, *Maritime Celts, Frisians and Saxons*, CBA Research Report 71 (London), 93–97.

Wood, I.N. 1990b: 'Ripon, Francia and the Franks Casket', *Northern History*, 26, 1–19.

Wood, I.N. 1991: 'The Franks and Sutton Hoo', in I.N. Wood and N. Lund (eds), *People and places in Northern Europe 500–1600: Essays in Honour of Peter Hayes Sawyer*, 1–14 (Woodbridge: Boydell).

Wood, I.N. 1992: 'The Merovingian Kingdoms, 481–751', *Medieval History* vol. 2, no. 1, 14–27.

Wormald, P. 1977: '*Lex Scripta and Verbum Regis:* Legislation and Germanic Kingship from Euric to Cnut', in P.H. Sawyer and I.N. Wood, *Early Medieval Kingship* (Leeds), 105–38.

Wormald, P. 1983: 'Bede, the *Bretwaldas* and the origins of the *gens anglorum*' in P. Wormald (ed.) *Ideal and Reality in Frankish and Anglo-Saxon society* (Oxford: Blackwell), 99–129.

Wormald, P. 1984: *Bede and the Conversion of England: the charter evidence*, Jarrow Lecture.

Wormald, P. 1986: 'Celtic and Anglo-Saxon kingship: some further thoughts', in P.E. Szarmach (ed.), *Sources of Anglo-Saxon Culture* (Kalamazoo), 151–83.

Wright, D.H. and Campbell, A. (eds) 1967: *The Vespasian Psalter* (Early English Manuscripts in Facsimile 14: Copenhagen).

Wright, H.T. 1978: 'Towards an explanation of the origin of the state', in R. Cohen and E.R. Service (eds), *Origins of the state*, 46–68 (Philadelphia: Institute for the Study of Human Issues).

Yorke, B. 1990: *Kings and kingdoms of early Anglo-Saxon England* (London: Seaby).

Young, Bailey K. 1975: *Merovingian funeral rites and the evolution of Christianity: A study in the historical interpretation of archaeological material* (Ph.D. thesis, University of Pennsylvania).

Young, Bailey K. 1977: 'Paganisme, christianisation et rites funéraires mérovingiens', *Archéologie Médiévale*, 7, 5–81.

Young, Bailey K. and Périn, Patrick 1991: 'Les nécropoles (IIIe–VIIIe siècle)', in N. Duval et al. (eds), *Naissance des Arts Chrétiens. Atlas des Monuments Paléochrétiens de la France* (Paris), pp. 94–121.

Youngs, S. (ed.), 1989: *'The Work of Angels'. Masterpieces of Celtic Metalwork, 6th–9th centuries A.D.* (London).

Youngs, S.M., Clark, J. and Barry, T.B. 1984: 'Medieval Britain and Ireland in 1983' in *Med., Arch.*, 28, 203–265.

Zimmerman, W.H. 1974: 'A Roman Iron Age and early migration settlement at Flögeln'. In T. Rowley (ed.), *Anglo-Saxon settlement and landscape*, 56–73 (Oxford: B.A.R. 6).

Zimmerman, W.H. 1978: 'Economy of the Roman Iron Age settlement at Flögeln', in B. Cunliffe and T. Rowley (eds), *Lowland Iron Age communities in Europe*, 147–65. (Oxford: B.A.R. S48).

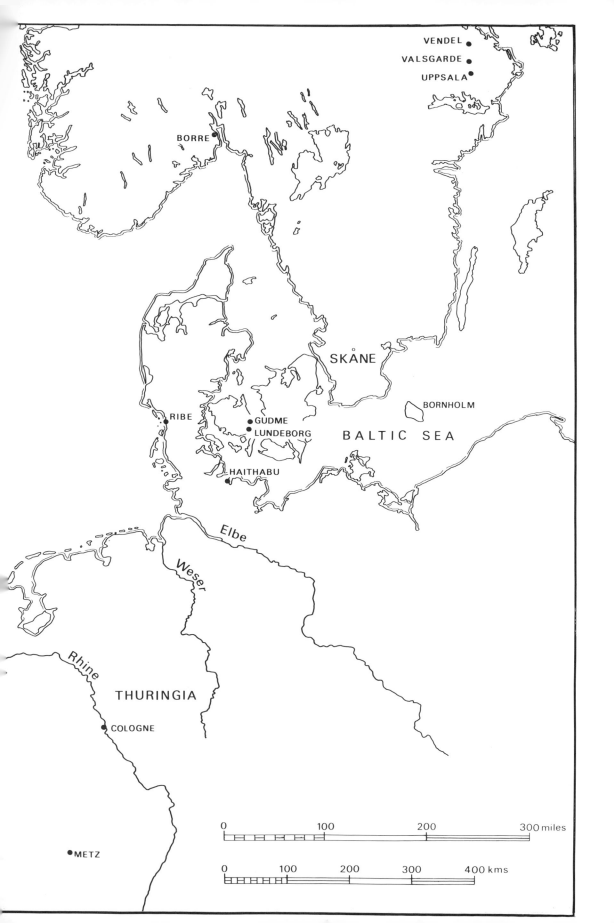

VENDEL
VALSGARDE
UPPSALA

BORRE

SKÅNE

BORNHOLM

RIBE
GUDME
LUNDEBORG
BALTIC SEA

HAITHABU

Elbe

Weser

Rhine

THURINGIA

COLOGNE

METZ

0   100   200   300 miles

0   100   200   300   400 kms